THE BIG BASICS BOOK OF
WINDOWS 98

by Joe Kraynak

A Division of Macmillan Computer Publishing
201 West 103rd Street, Indianapolis, Indiana 46290 USA

International Standard Book Number: 0-7897-1513-9

Library of Congress Catalog Card Number: 97-075464

Printed in the United States of America

00   99   98   4   3   2   1

Executive Editor
  Christopher Will

Development Editor
  Robin Drake

Managing Editor
  Sarah Kearns

Project Editor
  Christopher Morris

Copy Editor
  Audra McFarland

Indexer
  Kevin Fulcher

Technical Editor
  Brad Lindass

Production
  Terri Edwards
  Brad Lenser
  Donna Martin

Contents at a Glance

Contents

Part 1   How To...

Use the Windows 98 Accessories   **169**

Use Windows 98 on the World Wide Web   **217**

Part 2   Do It Yourself...

Use the Internet Tools   467

Optimize Your System   493

Part 3   Quick Fixes

101 Quick Fixes   513

Part 4   Handy References

Handy References   567

About the Author

Joe Kraynak has been writing and editing training manuals and computer books for over ten years. His long list of computer books includes *The Complete Idiot's Guide to PCs*, *The Big Basics Book of Microsoft Office*, *Microsoft Internet Explorer 3 Unleashed*, and *Windows 95 Cheat Sheet*. Joe has a master's degree in English and a bachelor's degree in philosophy and creative writing from Purdue University.

Dedication

To Debbie and Scott Weddle, of Speedway, Indiana, whose dedication to family and community is a constant inspiration.

Introduction

Windows ushered in the era of simplified computing, providing a graphical user interface that allowed people to click icons and select commands from menus. With the increased popularity of the Internet, Windows 98 is focused on helping people communicate more efficiently and tap the resources available on computers worldwide. In addition, Windows 98 includes several usability enhancements to make your day-to-day computing even easier.

Although Windows has simplified the tasks of navigating your PC, your company's network, and the Internet, it is not completely intuitive. You need instructions that tell you where to find the newest features and how to fully exploit them. And you need this information in a format that is easy to understand. Welcome to *The Big Basics Book of Windows 98*.

Why This Book?

When you start using a computer or a new operating system, such as Windows 98, you can learn by trial and error or by reading through the documentation that was included with your PC or software. However, "trial and error" usually translates into "hit or miss," and manuals typically *tell* you what to do instead of *showing* you.

The Big Basics Book of Windows 98 lets you take a different approach. It is designed to act as a visual guide to Windows 98, providing step-by-step, illustrated instructions on how to perform the most common tasks in Windows 98. This approach allows you to avoid the problems you encounter with trial and error, and it shows what you are about to get yourself into *before* you get there.

Where's the Information I Need?

Unlike most manuals that expect you to read the book from cover to cover, *The Big Basics Book of Windows 98* is structured in such a way that it allows you to decide how you want to use it. You can use the book as a tutorial, performing the tasks from cover to cover. You can use it as a quick reference guide by looking up specific topics in the table of contents or the index. Or, you can flip through the book and use the running heads at the top of each page to scan for topics of interest.

In addition, the book is divided into four parts to make it easier for you to find the instructions you need:

- *Part 1: How To...* covers the Windows 98 basics. Here, you will learn how to start and exit Windows; run and use Windows programs; manage your disks, folders, and files; use Windows to explore the World Wide Web, access email, and read messages posted on the Internet; and much more. Not all the tasks in this part are easy, but they introduce you to the core features that make Windows 98 so powerful.

- *Part 2: Do It Yourself...* teaches you how to put the basic skills you learned in Part 1 to practical use. In this part, you will learn how to create and send faxes, design an attractive résumé, dial the phone with your modem, find a job on the Internet, optimize Windows, use Windows on a notebook computer, and much much more.

- *Part 3: Quick Fixes* provides a list of common problems and solutions. If your display goes fuzzy, your mouse gets jumpy, an error message pops up on your screen, or you run into some other problem, flip to the Quick Fixes to find the answer you need. The Quick Finder tables help you zero in on the cause of the problem and find the appropriate solution.

- *Part 4: Handy References* provides tables full of keyboard shortcuts and DOS commands to help you streamline your encounters with Windows and with your old DOS applications. When you are ready to shed your mouse and bypass the menu system, turn to Part 4.

Conventions Used in This Book

This book is designed to be easy to use. Each task has a descriptive title that tells you what you'll be doing, followed by a brief description that introduces you to the task and provides additional background material. Immediately following the introduction is a *Guided Tour*, which shows you step by step how to perform the task. The following figure shows how a typical task is laid out.

Running heads help you find topics of interest.

Background information prepares you for the task.

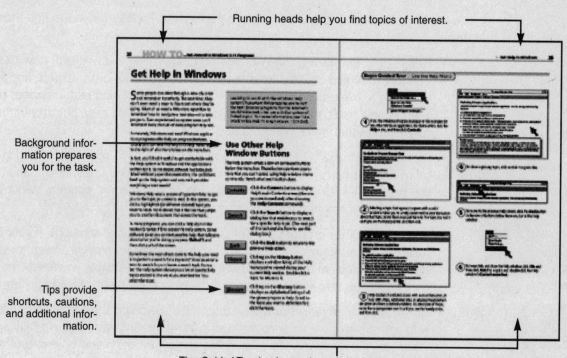

Tips provide shortcuts, cautions, and additional information.

The *Guided Tour* leads you through each task with illustrated steps.

To make it easier to scan steps and follow their instructions, this book uses the following conventions:

Text you are supposed to type appears **bold**. For example, if the step tells you to type **win** and press **Enter**, type the command "win" and press the Enter key. Note that keys, such as Enter, appear bold as well.

Key+Key combinations are used when you must press two or more keys to enter a command. Hold down the first key and then press the second key. Then release both keys.

Menu names and **commands** you need to choose are also bold. When you are told to select a command from a menu or click an option in a dialog box, rest the mouse pointer on it and click.

Look to these sidebars for tips, cautions, shortcuts, and additional background information.

Trademarks

Terms suspected of being trademarks or service marks have been appropriately capitalized. Que Corporation cannot attest to the accuracy of this information. Use of a term in this book should not be regarded as affecting the validity of any trademark or service mark.

PART 1

How To...

Whether you need to run a program, copy files, create and print a document, use the Windows accessories, explore the Internet, or send and receive email messages, you must be able to access and use the most basic Windows features. This part covers the major features of Windows 98, leading you step-by-illustrated-step through the process of completing hundreds of tasks.

Here, you will learn everything you need to know to successfully perform tasks ranging from the most simple, such as running programs, to the most complicated, including setting up new hardware devices and maintaining your computer.

To learn how to perform the most common Windows tasks, flip to the desired topic and follow the Guided Tour.

What You Will Find in This Part

HOW TO...

Master Windows 98 Basics

To become a Windows master, you first need to acquire the basic skills covered in this section. Here, you will learn everything you need to know to navigate the Windows 98 desktop, use the new Active Desktop, open and close windows, enter commands, respond to dialog boxes, get online help, and much more. This section shows you how to perform the fundamental Windows tasks that you need to know to move around not only in Windows but also in any program designed for Windows.

What You Will Find in This Section

Find Out What's New with Windows 98

What you will consider to be "new" features in Windows 98 depends on which operating system you are moving up from. If you are one of those people who decided to stick it out with Windows 3.1 until Microsoft perfected its new product, you will find that Windows 98 contains some dramatic changes, both in appearance and functionality.

However, if you are upgrading from Windows 95, the enhancements will appear to be a little more subtle. Microsoft has not completely overhauled the Windows desktop (the screen that greets you on startup), and you still use the Start button to run your programs. At first glance, you may not even realize that you have a new version of Windows on your system.

The following sections show you the changes you can expect, depending on whether you are upgrading from Windows 3.1 or Windows 95.

Move Up from Windows 3.1

If you are moving from Windows 3.1 to Windows 98, you will notice that just about everything in Windows 98 is new. You no longer see stacks of program windows on your desktop, and a new gray bar (the *taskbar*) appears at the bottom of your screen. You will also find that the Windows File Manager has been replaced with two improved file management tools: My Computer and Windows Explorer.

The following list summarizes the major differences between Windows 3.1 and Windows 98:

- The Windows screen has been completely revamped. *Shortcut icons* on the Windows *desktop* (your onscreen work surface) provide quick access to your programs, folders, and documents. ▶See "Work on the Windows Desktop" on page 13 for details.◀

- The Start button takes the place of Windows 3.1 program groups (which contained icons for running programs). To run a program, you click the Start button, point to Programs, and select the program from the Programs menu or one of its submenus.

- The taskbar at the bottom of the screen allows you to quickly switch from one active program to another. You no longer have to call up the Task List or press key combinations (although those still work) to select the desired program. ▶See "Switch Between Active Programs" on page 46 for details.◀

- Windows Explorer has replaced File Manager. Windows Explorer provides a two-paned window, like the File Manager window, which allows you to quickly copy and move files from one folder to another. Windows 98 also features My Computer, a single-framed window that provides quick access to folders, files, and other resources on your computer. ▶See "Manage Disks, Folders, and Files," starting on page 79.◀

- The Start, Documents submenu contains a list of recently opened documents, allowing you to quickly open a document you have just created or edited.

- You can use longer filenames in Windows 98 (up to 255 characters, including spaces). Windows 3.1 limited filenames to a mere eight characters with a three-character extension.

- Windows has enhanced support for the right mouse button. In Windows 98 and in most Windows applications, you can right-click areas of the screen or selected text or objects to display a *context menu*, which offers commands and options only for the selection.

- Print Manager, Control Panel, Write (now WordPad), and Paintbrush (now Paint) have been tweaked to improve performance and usability.

- Windows now has a Recycle Bin that stores the files you choose to delete. If you delete a file by mistake, you can quickly restore it from the Recycle Bin. ▶See "Delete and Undelete Using the Recycle Bin" on page 117.◀

- Windows 98 supports Plug and Play technology, which makes it easier to upgrade your computer, assuming that both the computer and the device you are adding support Plug and Play. ▶See "Install Hardware," starting on page 363.◀

This list describes only a few obvious changes you will notice when you move from Windows 3.1 to Windows 98. The following section explains additional enhancements that Microsoft made when moving up from Windows 95 to Windows 98.

Move Up from Windows 95

If you are a seasoned Windows 95 user, you may notice that not much has changed in Windows 98. You are accustomed to the Start button, the taskbar, shortcut icons, My Computer, and the Recycle Bin. However, Windows 98 has several subtle enhancements and some not-so-subtle enhancements that you can uncover by poking around a little:

- Windows 98 features the Active Desktop, which provides single-click access to programs and documents on your computer. ▶You learn how to turn the Active Desktop on or off in "Use the Active Desktop" on page 16.◄

- The taskbar includes a new toolbar called *Quick Launch*, which allows you to quickly run programs for accessing the Internet. You can turn on additional toolbars and drag icons to the Quick Launch toolbar to configure it. ▶See "Use the New Taskbar Toolbars" on page 308.◄

- The Start, Find submenu (which you may have used to search for files on your computer) now helps you search for people and resources on the Internet. ▶See "Find Files and Folders" on page 111.◄

- Windows 98 comes with the Internet Explorer Suite, a set of programs for accessing the Internet. The Suite includes Internet Explorer (for viewing Web pages), Outlook Express (for email and newsgroups), NetMeeting (for placing phone calls across the Internet), FrontPad (for creating your own Web pages), and a few additional Internet tools. ▶See "Use Windows 98 on the World Wide Web" on page 217 and "Use Outlook Express for Email and Newsgroups" on page 321.◄

- The Start, Favorites submenu allows you to quickly access Web pages and other objects that you have marked as favorites. ▶See "Create a List of Your Favorite Sites" on page 246.◄

- Windows 98 supports FAT32 for enhanced data storage. The Drive Converter lets you divide a large hard drive into smaller sectors, so small files don't take up so much space. This can increase your hard drive capacity by 50 percent or more. ▶See "Increase Disk Space" on page 498.◄

- Automatic updates allow you to upgrade to the latest release of Windows by downloading updates from Microsoft's Web site (on the Internet). This ensures that you are working with the latest release. ▶See "Update Windows" on page 420.◄

- OnNow Technology allows you to quickly turn on your PC without having to boot it. ▶See "Start and Shut Down Windows" on page 10.◄

- The Windows 98Maintenance Wizard optimizes your system for you to increase performance. ▶See "Use the Windows Maintenance Wizard" on page 494.◄

- A new Effects tab in theDisplay Properties dialog box provides additional control over the appearance of desktop icons.

- The new Backup applet supports additional backup devices, making it less likely that you will need a special backup program. ▶See "Back Up Files" on page 432.◄

- Task Scheduler allows you to automate your computer by having Windows run programs or open documents at a scheduled time or when a particular event occurs (such as when you start your computer). ▶See "Run Programs Automatically with Task Scheduler" on page 65.◄

The most significant improvements in Windows 98 center on the Internet, a worldwide network of computers, which you can connect to by using a network connection or modem. The World Wide Web (Web, for short) is a feature of the Internet that allows you to navigate multimedia Web pages by clicking *links* (highlighted words, icons, or graphics that point to different pages). The Web is sort of like TV for your PC. ▶To learn more about the Internet and the Web, see "Use Windows 98 on the World Wide Web," starting on page 217.◄

The *Guided Tour* introduces you to the most prominent new features in Windows 98.

Guided Tour   Explore Windows 98 New Features

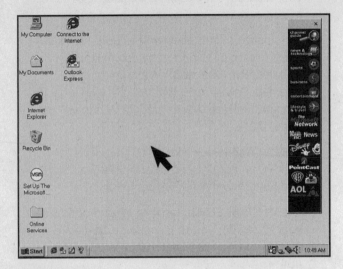

1 When you turn on your computer, Windows 98 starts automatically and displays the Windows desktop.

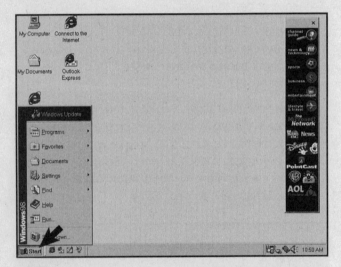

2 Click the **Start** button to display the menu that contains program groups and icons. Near the top of the menu is the Windows Update icon, which allows you to download Windows updates from the Internet.

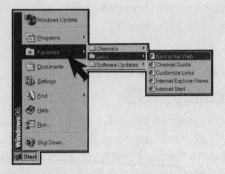

3 Point to **Favorites**. The Favorites submenu contains submenus for accessing premium Web sites on the Internet. You can add your own favorite sites to the menu.

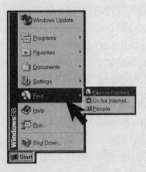

4 Point to **Find**. The Find submenu contains additional options for searching the Internet for Web pages or people. Click a blank area of the Windows desktop to close the Start menu.

5 The taskbar at the bottom of the screen displays an additional toolbar called *Quick Launch* (located just to the right of the Start button). You can drag icons for programs or documents to the Quick Launch toolbar to make them easily accessible.

> **Guided Tour**   Explore Windows 98 New Features

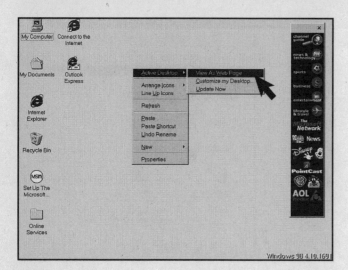

6 Right-click a blank area of the desktop, point to **Active Desktop**, and make sure there is a check mark next to **View as Web Page**. If **View as Web Page** is not checked, click it; otherwise, click outside of the menu to close it. This turns on the Active Desktop.

> View as Web Page is a check mark option. A check mark next to the option indicates that it is on. Selecting the option again turns it off, removes the check mark, and closes the menu.

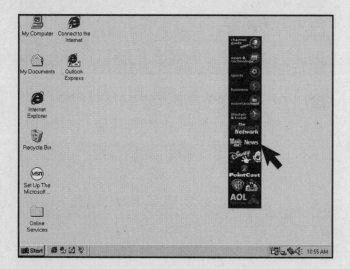

7 The Active Desktop is a Web page on which you can place desktop components, such as the Channel Bar shown above.

> The Channel Bar allows you to tune in to Web sites that offer premium content simply by clicking a button. It acts as a channel changer for the Web. ▶See "Tune In to the Web with Channels" on page 258.◀

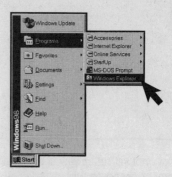

8 Choose **Start**, **Programs**, **Windows Explorer** to display the Windows Explorer window. (To close the window, click the Close button—the button with the X on it in the upper-right corner of the window.)

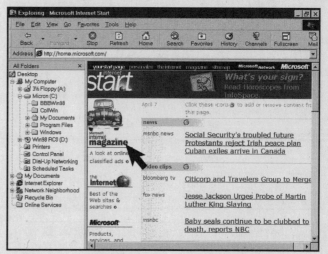

9 You can also navigate the Web from Windows Explorer, as shown above. The right pane displays the currently open Web page. (You must be connected to the Internet to open Web pages in Windows Explorer.)

(continues)

Guided Tour   Explore Windows 98 New Features   *(continued)*

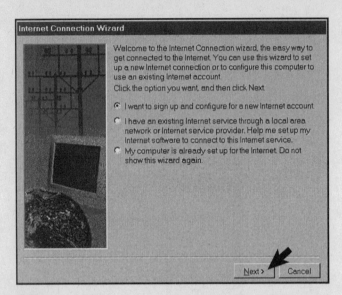

10 If you have not yet set up your connection to the Internet, the Internet Connection Wizard walks you through the process of setting up your Internet connection.

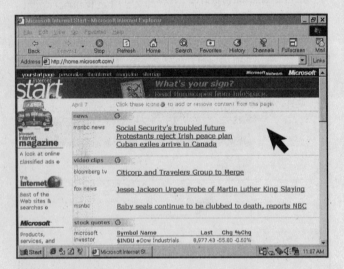

11 The Internet Explorer Suite, included in Windows 98, contains a Web browser, email program, newsreader, and additional Internet tools. The Internet Explorer Web browser is shown here.

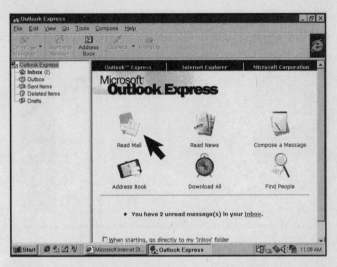

12 You can use Outlook Express to send and receive email messages and to read and post messages in Internet newsgroups.

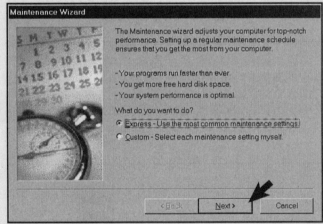

13 The Windows Maintenance Wizard can automatically optimize your computer.

Guided Tour Explore Windows 98 New Features

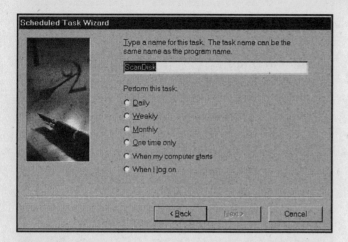

14 You can use the Task Scheduler to run programs at scheduled times or only when a particular event occurs (at startup, for example).

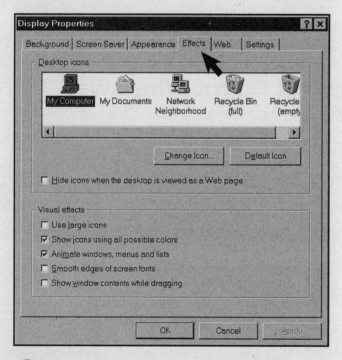

15 Right-click a blank area of the desktop and select **Properties** to view the Display Properties dialog box shown here. Take note of the new Effects tab for controlling the appearance of desktop icons and the Web tab for adding Web components to the desktop.

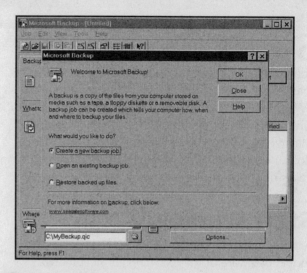

16 Microsoft has redesigned the Backup applet to make it easier to back up your system and has added support for a wider range of backup devices.

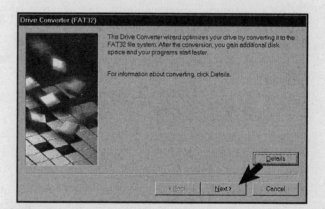

17 The new Drive Converter (FAT32) can optimize your hard disks to store files more efficiently and increase your hard disk's storage capacity.

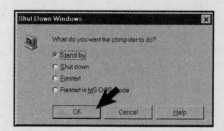

18 When you choose **Start**, **Shut Down** (don't actually do this right now), Windows displays the Shut Down Windows dialog box, which now offers the additional option of going into Stand By mode (only on computers that support this feature). This powers down your computer without turning it completely off. To restart it, simply press any key.

Start and Shut Down Windows

Starting Windows is easy. You don't have to enter any commands or press any special keys. You turn on your monitor and computer, and Windows starts automatically. The first time you run Windows, a multimedia "Welcome To Windows 98" presentation starts to play, which provides access to the Registration Wizard, the Maintenance Wizard, and documentation. You can close the window by clicking the **Close** button (X) in the upper-right corner of the window.

Start Windows

Although starting Windows requires little effort, you should be aware of the following considerations:

- If your screen is blank on startup, you probably forgot to turn on your monitor.

- If you are connected to a network or you chose to use a password during the installation, you may be prompted to enter your username or logon name and password. Check with your network administrator for details on how to log on to your network.

- Your Windows desktop may differ from the desktop shown in the figures in this book. The icons will vary depending on which Windows components you installed and on whether you upgraded from a previous version of Windows or had Windows 98 preinstalled on your computer. In addition, for the figures in this book, we lightened the Windows background and menus to improve their appearance in print.

- If you encounter problems on startup, ▶see "Installation and Startup Issues," on page 528.◀

- You can use Task Scheduler to run programs automatically on startup. ▶See "Run Programs Automatically on Startup" on page 460.◀

If you did not exit Windows properly the last time you shut down, or if Windows crashed (locked up your computer), Windows may prompt you to run ScanDisk before starting. ScanDisk automatically checks your hard drive for corrupted files, and it fixes any problems that might cause Windows and your programs to run erratically.

If you did not make an emergency startup disk when you installed Windows 98, you should make a startup disk now. If your system ever locks up and you cannot restart Windows, the emergency disk can help you start your computer and recover your system. ▶Skip to "Create and Use an Emergency Disk" on page 442.◀

Shut Down Windows

You are probably aware that you do not simply turn off your computer when you are done working. Windows and your programs store data electronically in memory while you work, and you must follow the proper shut down procedure to ensure that anything you have been working on is saved to your hard disk. Using the Windows Shut Down command ensures that your work is saved before you exit. The *Guided Tour* shows you how to properly shut down your computer.

When shutting down, you should be aware of the following options:

- When you choose Start, Shut Down, a dialog box appears, allowing you to restart your computer. This is useful if you make changes to Windows or install a new program that requires you to restart.

- The Shut Down Windows dialog box also allows you to restart in MS-DOS mode, in which you can enter commands at the DOS prompt.

- Your Shut Down Windows dialog box may offer Stand By and Hibernation modes, which allow you to keep the computer on and conserve energy. In Stand By mode, your work is not saved to disk, so if the power goes out, you could lose your work. In Hibernation mode, Windows saves your work to disk before powering down.

For more details about the power conservation utility in Windows, ▶see "Save Energy" on page 400.◀

Before you select the Start, Shut Down command, be sure to save any files you have been working on and to exit any running programs. Although Windows will prompt you to save your work before shutting down, saving and exiting the programs individually is safer.

Guided Tour   Start Windows

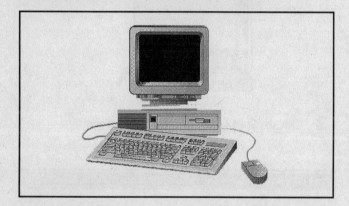

1 Turn on your monitor first, so you can see any startup messages that might appear. If you are using a notebook computer, you can skip this step. (If you have an external modem, turn it on.)

2 Turn on your system unit. Your system performs its internal checks and loads any startup commands it is set up to use.

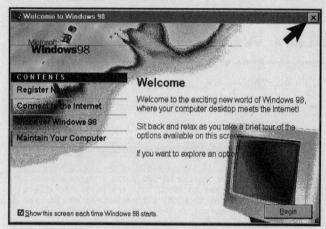

3 Windows proceeds through its startup routine and then displays the Windows desktop. If this is the first time you are running Windows, the Welcome to Windows 98 window appears. You can click the **Begin** button to register and take a tour of Windows 98. When you are done, click the **Close** (X) button in the upper-right corner of the window.

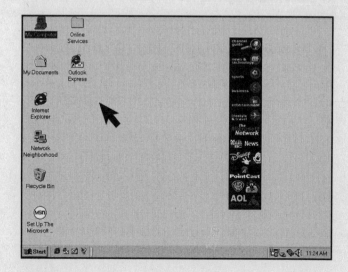

4 The Windows desktop appears, displaying several icons and the taskbar. Your desktop may differ depending on the options you selected during installation.

Guided Tour Shut Down Windows

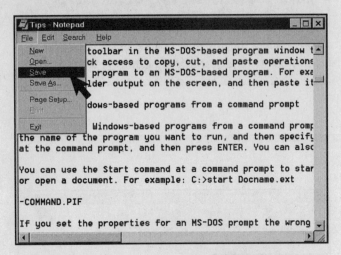

1 Save any files you are working on using the program's **File**, **Save** command.

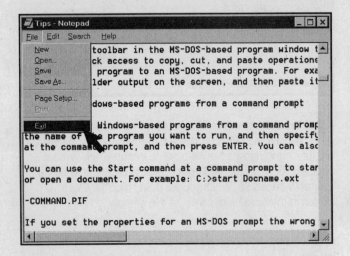

2 Exit any running program by opening its **File** menu and selecting the **Exit** command. If you're prompted to save your work, confirm that you want to save.

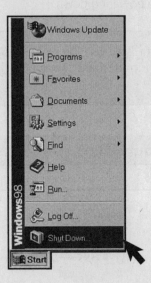

3 Click the **Start** button and select **Shut Down**.

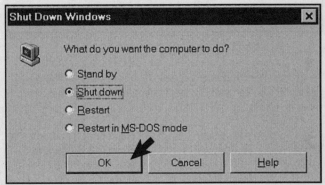

4 The Shut Down Windows dialog box appears, displaying the shut down options. You can shut down Windows completely, restart it, restart it in MS-DOS mode, power down to Stand By mode (on some computers), or possibly perform some other option, depending on your setup. Select the desired option and click **OK**.

5 Windows shuts down, and then displays a message indicating when it is safe to turn off your computer. When you see such a message, turn off your system unit and monitor. (If you have a notebook computer or a desktop computer that includes an auto shut down feature, it may shut down the power automatically.)

Work on the Windows Desktop

The Windows desktop is modeled after a physical desktop. It is a work area that contains the tools required to perform your computing tasks, and it allows you to spread out any documents you are creating or editing.

The Start button gives you access to programs on your system. The taskbar acts as a navigational tool for switching from one open program to another. The *shortcut icons* (usually located on the left side of the desktop) allow you to quickly run programs, delete and restore files, explore your system resources, access the Internet, and more. Following is a list of the shortcut icons you might see on your desktop:

My Computer displays a window that allows you to view the contents of your disks and folders, set up printers, configure Windows (via the Control Panel), set up Internet connections, and schedule programs to run automatically. ▶See "Navigate My Computer" on page 85.◀

My Documents is a folder on your hard disk you can use for storing any files you create. (You can also use other folders for storing your files.)

Internet Explorer runs Internet Explorer, the Web browser that is included with Windows 98. The first time you select this icon, the Internet Connection Wizard appears, prompting you to select a service provider. ▶See "Set Up Your Internet Connection" on page 220.◀

Network Neighborhood appears only if you installed network support for Windows. This icon opens a window that allows you to access other computers and resources on your company's network (assuming your computer is connected to a network).

Outlook Express runs the Windows email program, which allows you to send and receive typed messages over the Internet.

Recycle Bin is a safety net for files that you choose to delete. When you delete a file, it is placed in the Recycle Bin and remains there until you choose to empty the Recycle Bin. You can restore deleted files by pulling them out of the Recycle Bin. ▶See "Delete and Undelete Using the Recycle Bin" on page 117.◀

My Briefcase appears only if you chose to install the Windows notebook tools during the Windows installation. You can use the Briefcase to quickly transfer data from your desktop computer to your notebook or vice versa. ▶See "Synchronize Your Notebook and Desktop with Briefcase" on page 389.◀

Online Services provides tools for subscribing to most of the major commercial online services, including America Online, Prodigy, CompuServe, and The Microsoft Network. ▶See "Access Commercial Online Services" on page 218.◀

Set Up the Microsoft... is a shortcut for subscribing to The Microsoft Network. This is the same icon you find in the Online Services folder.

Guided Tour Use the Windows Desktop

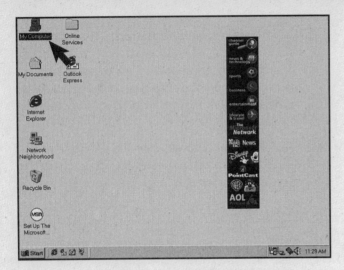

1 Double-click **My Computer** to display the My Computer window.

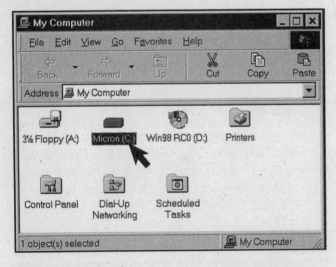

2 My Computer displays icons for all your disk drives and for common Windows utilities, including Control Panel. Double-click a disk icon to view the contents of the disk. (To close My Computer, click the **X** button in the upper-right corner of the window.)

3 Click the **Start** button and point to **Programs** to display a menu of the programs installed in Windows. The Accessories menu contains several programs you can use to create documents, perform calculations, and maintain your system.

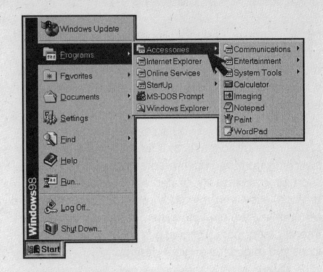

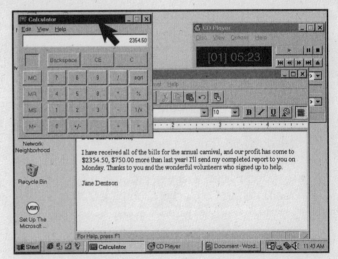

4 When you run programs, each program appears in its own window. As you can see, your Windows desktop—like any desktop—can become cluttered.

5 To switch between programs that are currently running, you can click the name of the desired program in the taskbar.

Guided Tour Use the Windows Desktop

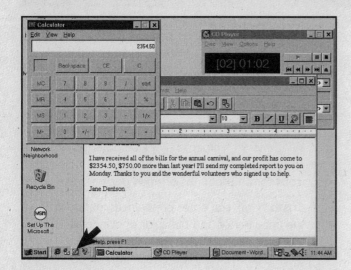

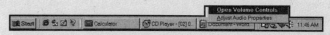

7 On the right end of the taskbar is the *system tray*, which displays the time and might display some icons, such as the Volume icon. Right-click an icon to display a context menu for that icon. Select the desired options. (You can point to an icon to view its name.)

6 To quickly return to the Windows desktop, click the **Show Desktop** button in the Quick Launch toolbar.

Use the Active Desktop

One of the greatest improvements to Windows is the Active Desktop, a feature that transforms your Windows desktop into an automated information center. With the Active Desktop and an Internet connection, you can place objects such as stock tickers and weather maps right on your Windows desktop and have them automatically updated via the Internet. ▶You will learn how to do all this in "Master the Active Desktop," starting on page 301.◀

The Active Desktop also offers a new, improved interface for accessing your programs and documents (even if you don't connect to the Internet). With the Active Desktop turned on, the Windows desktop functions as a Web page, allowing you to run programs and open documents with a single click of the mouse.

The new desktop allows you to choose which of the following three modes you want to work in:

- **Web Style** treats the Windows desktop and My Computer as Web pages, providing single-click access to files and programs. Because this book assumes that you are using Web Style, make sure it is on, as explained in the *Guided Tour*.

- **Classic Style** makes Windows 98 act like Windows 95. Folders in My Computer do not appear as Web pages, and you must double-click icons to run programs or open documents.

- **Custom** lets you enter preferences that control the appearance and behavior of Windows. For example, you can keep the Web page backgrounds for My Computer but turn on double-click access.

The *Guided Tour* shows you how to change modes for the Active Desktop and illustrates the basics of working on the Active Desktop in Web Style mode.

Guided Tour Select Web or Classic Style

1 Click or double-click **My Computer** on the Windows desktop. If My Computer runs with a single click, Web Style is turned on.

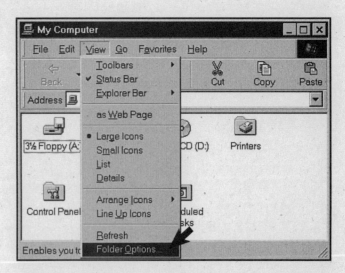

2 The My Computer window appears. Open the **View** menu and select **Folder Options**.

Guided Tour Select Web or Classic Style

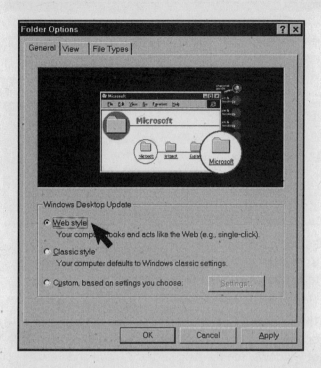

3 The Folder Options dialog box appears, displaying the General tab. For single-click access to files and programs, make sure **Web Style** is selected. To make Windows 98 look and act like Windows 95, select **Classic Style**.

4 Click **OK** to save the selected setting. If you are prompted to confirm that you want single-click access to files and folders, choose **Yes** and click **OK**. ➤See "Work in Web View" on page 83 for instructions on how to use My Computer with Web Style.◄

Guided Tour View Your Desktop as a Web Page

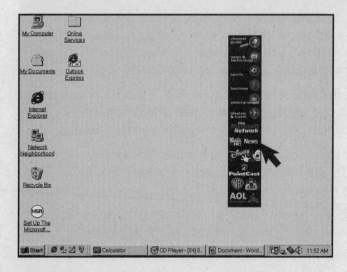

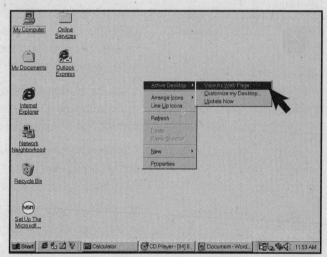

1 If the Channel Bar is displayed on the desktop, the Active Desktop is already set up to display the desktop as a Web page.

2 If the Channel Bar is not displayed, right-click a blank area of the desktop, point to **Active Desktop**, and click **View as Web Page**.

Open and Close Windows

In order to master Windows 98 (or any other version of Windows), you need to know how to work with windows—the boxes that appear on the desktop whenever you run programs or open files. As you perform tasks in Windows, you will work with two types of windows: program windows and document windows.

When you run a program, it opens its own *program window* (like the My Computer window you encountered earlier). The program window contains menus, buttons, and other commands that allow you to work with documents created in that program.

When you create or open a file in a program, the program displays the file in a *document window*. If you open several documents in a program, the program displays each document in its own document window. All document windows appear inside the program window.

While it may be mind-boggling to think of so many windows (windows inside windows inside Windows), keep in mind that all windows work the same way. After you

learn how to open, close, minimize, maximize, and resize windows in this *Guided Tour* and the next, you will know how to perform these tasks on all windows.

> All programs and documents use a portion of your computer's memory; so as you open more windows, you use more memory. If your system seems sluggish or you receive an "Insufficient Memory" error message, close some windows.

Before you move on to the *Guided Tour*, open the My Computer window (a program window) and, using the following table, identify the standard window controls in the My Computer window.

The following *Guided Tour* shows you the basics of opening and closing windows. For more precise control of windows, see the next section "Move and Resize Windows."

Icon	Name	Description
	Control Menu	Click this icon in the upper-left corner of the window to display a menu of commands for controlling the window's size and location. The appearance of this icon varies depending on the program; it may appear as the program's logo.
	Minimize	Click this button to make the window as small as possible. If you minimize a program window, it retreats to the taskbar. If you minimize a document window, you can reopen the window by selecting it from the program's Window menu.
	Maximize	Click this button to make the window as large as possible. The window takes up the entire screen, except for the area with the taskbar. After you click it, the Maximize button changes into the Restore button.
	Restore	When a window is maximized, use this button to restore it to its previous size. After you click the Restore button, it changes into the Maximize button.
	Close	Click this button to close the window completely. If you close a window before saving changes to a document, the program prompts you to save your changes before closing the window.

Guided Tour Open a Window

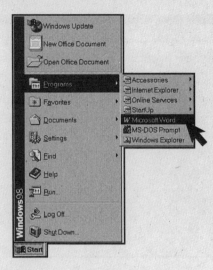

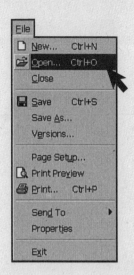

1 To open a program window, click the shortcut icon for the program you want to run, or select the program from the **Start**, **Programs** menu or one of its submenus.

3 To open a document you've already created, use the program's **File**, **Open** command; to open a brand new document, use the **File**, **New** command.

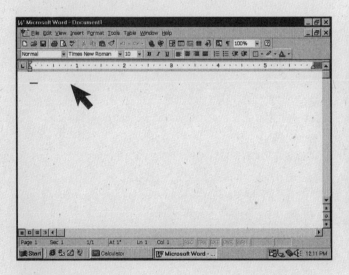

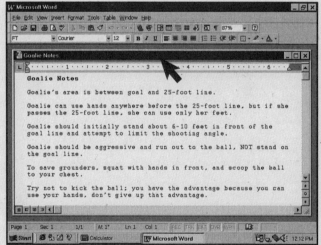

2 The program opens its own window on the desktop. The figure above shows Word for Windows, which is not included as part of Windows 98.

4 A document window appears inside the program window. You can now create or edit the document.

Guided Tour Close a Window

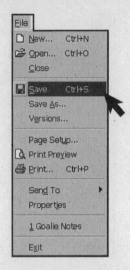

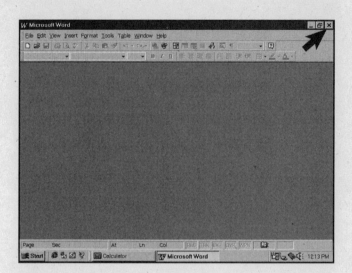

1 Before closing a document or program window, save any open documents using the program's **File**, **Save** command. ▶See "Save a Document" on page 139 for instructions on how to use My Computer with Web Style.◀

3 The program closes the document window but keeps its program window open. To close the program window, click its **Close** (X) button.

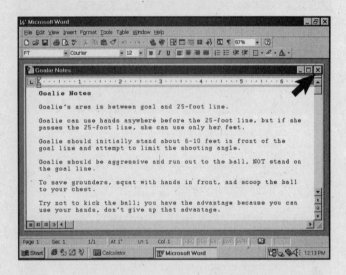

2 To close a document window, click its **Close** (X) button. A document window's Close button may appear directly below the program window's Close button if the document window is maximized.

4 Windows closes the program window. Note that the taskbar no longer displays a button for the program.

Move and Resize Windows

It's common practice to have several items on the desktop at the same time. You may be writing a letter to your insurance company in the WordPad window, using the Windows Calculator in another window, and playing a game of Solitaire in still another window. As you open more windows, your desktop can become quite cluttered, making it difficult to access programs or copy data from one program to another.

The solution is to move and resize your windows to arrange them in convenient areas on the desktop. Windows offers several options for resizing and arranging windows on the desktop, as you can see in the *Guided Tour*.

Guided Tour   Resize a Window

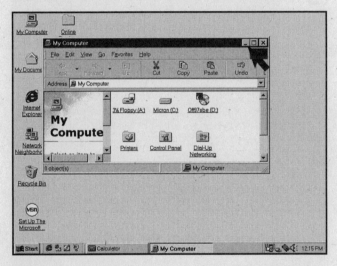

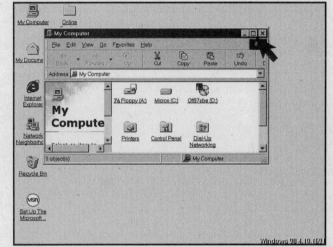

1 Click the **Minimize** button to quickly clear a window from the desktop.

3 To make a window appear full-screen, click its **Maximize** button. The Maximize button is then replaced by the Restore button.

(continues)

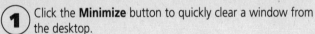

2 The window retreats from the desktop. To bring it back into view, click its button in the taskbar.

Guided Tour Resize a Window *(continued)*

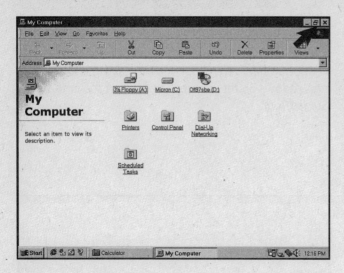

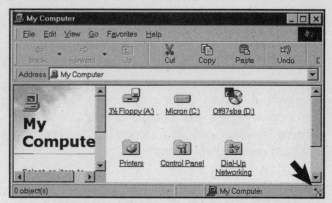

4 To return a maximized window to its previous size, click the **Restore** button.

5 If a window is neither maximized nor minimized, you can resize it by dragging one of its borders or a corner of the window.

To quickly maximize or restore a window, double-click its title bar (the blue bar at the top of the window). You can right-click a button in the taskbar to view options for controlling a minimized window (such as closing the window). In addition, you can quickly minimize or restore a program window by clicking its button in the taskbar.

Guided Tour Move a Window

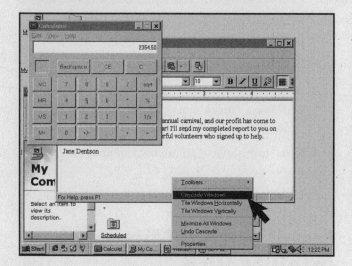

1 Windows can automatically arrange your program windows on the desktop. Right-click a blank area of the taskbar and select the desired arrangement: **Cascade Windows** (overlapping windows), **Tile Windows Horizontally** (side-by-side), **Tile Windows Vertically** (stacked), or **Minimize All Windows**.

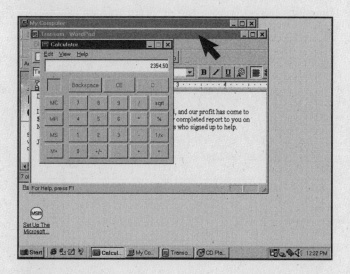

2 With cascading windows, the title bar of each window is visible. Click any exposed portion of the desired window to bring it to the front.

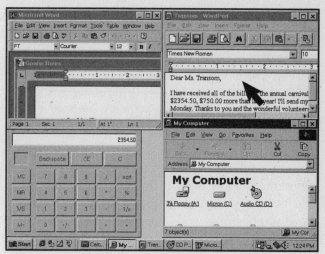

3 Tiled windows are useful for copying data from one program to another or for referring to one program while working in another. However, the windows are a usually very small.

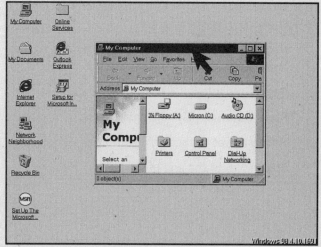

4 You can move a window yourself if it is not maximized. Position the mouse pointer in the window's title bar, and then drag the window to the desired location—left, right, up, down, or on an angle.

Use Scroll Bars

Program and document windows are like windows in your house or car. If you peer through a window, you see only a portion of the landscape. Program and document windows limit your view in a similar way. If the window contains more data than it can display, some of the data will be outside of your viewing area.

To overcome this limitation, windows offer scroll bars. If the contents of a window exceed the window's height or width, scroll bars appear along the right side or bottom of the window. You can use the scroll bars to bring data into the window's display area. The *Guided Tour* shows you how.

Scroll with Your Keyboard

When you are working on a document, your fingers often spend more time on the keyboard than on the mouse. You might find it more convenient to use your keyboard to scroll. Use the following keystrokes to scroll in most windows containing text:

Arrow keys move up, down, left, or right in small increments.

Page Up displays the previous screen.

Page Down displays the next screen.

Home moves to the beginning of the current line.

End moves to the end of the current line.

Ctrl+*arrow key* moves one word to the left or right or one paragraph up or down.

Ctrl+Page Up moves to the top of the previous page.

Ctrl+Page Down moves to the top of the next page.

Ctrl+Home moves to the beginning of the document.

Ctrl+End moves to the end of the document.

Scroll with a Microsoft IntelliMouse

Microsoft recently developed a new mouse, called the IntelliMouse, which has a wheel between the left and right mouse buttons. You can quickly scroll with the IntelliMouse by rotating the wheel. Spin the wheel toward you to scroll downward, or spin the wheel away from you to scroll upward. The wheel performs different functions depending on the program you are using it with.

Although the Microsoft IntelliMouse buttons are compatible with most programs, the wheel may not be supported in some programs. The IntelliMouse is supported in all of the Windows 98 accessories, including Internet Explorer.

Guided Tour Scroll Inside a Window

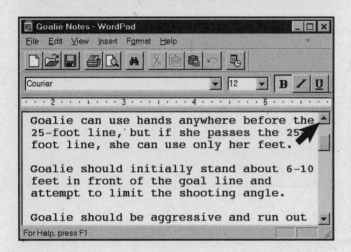

1 If a window's contents are longer or wider than the window, scroll bars appear at the bottom and/or right side of the window. Click the up or down scroll arrow to scroll one line at a time.

> To scroll continuously, point to a scroll arrow and hold down the left mouse button.

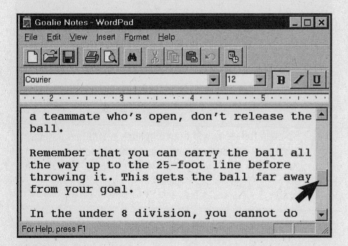

2 To scroll faster, drag the scroll box that is inside the scroll bar. In some programs, such as Microsoft Word, a little indicator box or balloon appears next to the scroll bar to indicate the new position in the document.

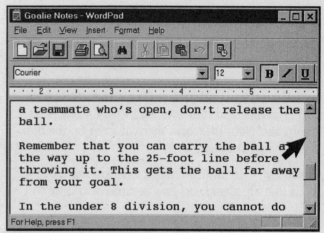

3 To scroll one screenful up, down, left, or right, click inside the scroll bar to the appropriate side of the scroll box.

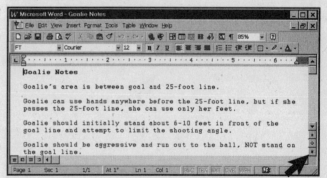

4 Some programs, such as Microsoft Word, have additional scroll controls. You can click the Next Page or Previous Page button (the double arrow buttons) to scroll one page at a time. In addition, the button between the up and down buttons allows you to enter preferences for the controls. (For example, you can set the up and down buttons to take you to the next or previous graphic.)

Arrange Shortcut Icons

Windows places several shortcut icons on the desktop to provide quick access to the most useful Windows tools and features, such as My Computer. You can add icons for programs and documents you frequently use, ▶as explained in "Create Shortcuts to Disks, Folders, and Files" on page 114.◀ Many programs also place their own shortcut icons on the desktop during installation.

In addition to adding shortcut icons, you can move the icons that are already on your desktop or choose to

have Windows rearrange the icons for you. The *Guided Tour* shows you what to do.

> If you try to move a shortcut icon and it shoots back to its original location, the Auto Arrange feature is turned on. To turn it off, right-click the desktop, point to **Arrange Icons**, and click **Auto Arrange** to remove the check mark.

Guided Tour Move Shortcut Icons

1 Point to the shortcut icon you want to move, and then hold down the mouse button and drag the icon to the desired location.

2 The icon appears translucent as you drag it. Release the mouse button to finalize the move.

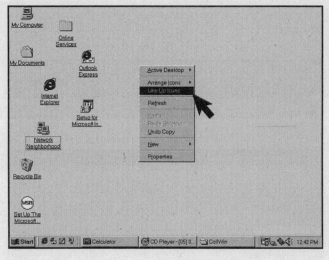

3 To align the icons without completely rearranging them, right-click the desktop and select **Line Up Icons**.

> If the Active Desktop is on (shortcut names appear underlined), be careful about clicking and dragging. If you click a shortcut icon, you run the associated program or open the folder or file that the icon points to. So make sure you keep holding down the mouse button after you press it, and then move the mouse to drag.

Guided Tour Move Shortcut Icons

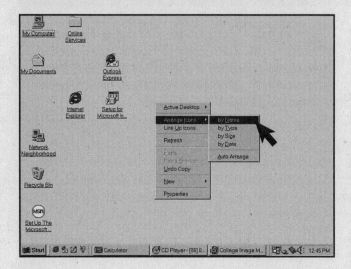

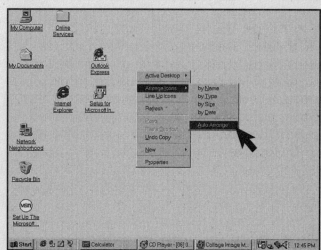

4 Windows can arrange the icons for you. Right-click the desktop and point to **Arrange Icons**. Then select the desired arrangement: **By Name**, **By Type**, **By Size**, or **By Date**.

5 To have Windows automatically align icons when you move them, right-click the desktop and select **Arrange Icons**, **Auto Arrange**.

Enter Commands

Windows provides several ways to enter commands. The most common method is to click a menu's name to open it and then select the desired option from the menu. You can also click shortcut, program, or document icons to run programs or open documents. To save you some time, Windows offers keyboard shortcuts that allow you to bypass the menu system for common commands, such as saving and printing documents. For example, you can press Ctrl+S in most programs instead of opening the File menu and selecting Save. The following sections explain the procedures for entering commands in Windows. The *Guided Tour* shows you how to enter commands.

Enter Menu Commands

The easiest way to enter commands in Windows and Windows programs is to select commands from menus. You have already selected commands from the Start menu at the bottom of the Windows desktop. Most programs contain a menu bar near the top of the program window that provides several menus. You open a menu by clicking its name or by holding down the Alt key and pressing the underlined letter in the menu's name (for instance, you press Alt+F to open the File menu).

As you work with menus, you will notice that menu commands may not all look the same. The appearance of each command provides a clue as to what will happen if you select the command:

- A standard command with no arrow or ellipsis (...) executes immediately when you select it. For instance, if you select Edit, Paste, the program immediately pastes the object you just copied into your document at the insertion point—no questions asked.

- A command followed by an ellipsis (...) displays a dialog box that prompts you to enter additional preferences or give your confirmation. You must respond to the dialog box and click a button or press a key to complete the command. ▶See "Respond to Dialog Boxes" on page 32.◀

- A command followed by an arrow (▶) opens a submenu that provides a list of additional

commands. For example, if you click the Windows Start button and point to Programs, a submenu appears, displaying a list of installed programs you can select. Simply rest the mouse pointer on the option to open the submenu.

- A checked option allows you to turn the option on or off. If the option has a check mark next to it, the option is on. You select the option to turn it off (removing the check mark). For example, a program may have several toolbars you can turn on or off.

- A grayed or dimmed command is disabled; you cannot select it. For example, if you run My Computer and open the Go menu, the Back option appears gray because you haven't moved forward yet.

Run Quick Commands with Toolbars

Many Windows programs display a toolbar near the top of the window (typically just below the menu bar) that allows you to bypass the menu system and quickly enter commands. To enter a command, you click the appropriate button on the toolbar.

> In many programs, when you rest the mouse pointer on a toolbar button, a box or balloon pops up displaying the name or function of the selected button. In Microsoft programs, these are called *ToolTips* or *ScreenTips*.

Right-Click for Context Menus

Before Windows, your right mouse button was fairly useless. However, now in Windows, you can use the right mouse button to display *context menus*. For instance, if you right-click the Windows desktop, a context menu pops up, offering commands for controlling the Windows desktop. Context menus are useful because they display the most common commands for the selected object.

Bypass Menus with Shortcut Keys

Although menus are the most intuitive tools for entering commands, they are also one of the slowest. To streamline the process, Windows and most Windows programs allow you to press key combinations to bypass the menu system. For example, you can press F1 to get help or press Alt+F4 to exit a program. The following table lists the most common keyboard shortcuts for Windows. Check the documentation that came with your other programs for additional keyboard shortcuts.

> Although these shortcut keys may not be of much use to you when you're first learning Windows, they can come in handy later. Mark this page with a Post-It note, so you can quickly return to it.

Windows Keyboard Shortcuts

Press	To
F1	Display general help screens or context-sensitive help for the current dialog box.
Alt+F4	Exit a program or shut down Windows (if no program is active).
Shift+F10	Display the context menu for the selected object.
Ctrl+Esc	Activate the taskbar and open the Start menu.
Alt+Tab	Switch to the program window that was previously active.
Ctrl+X	Cut the selected object.
Ctrl+C	Copy the selected object.
Ctrl+V	Insert the cut or copied object.
Ctrl+Z	Undo the previous action.
Delete	Delete the selected object or the character to the right of the insertion point.
Ctrl+A	Select all objects (in My Computer or Windows Explorer).
F5	Refresh the My Computer or Windows Explorer window.
Backspace	View the folder one level up from the current folder. Backspace also deletes the character to the left of the insertion point when you are using the key to edit an object's name (as it would within a document).
F2	Rename the selected icon.
F3	Find a folder or file.
Alt+Enter	Delete the selected file(s) or folder(s) without using the Recycle Bin.
Shift (CD Player)	Disable AutoPlay for the CD-ROM you are inserting.

Guided Tour Enter Menu Commands

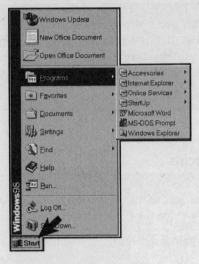

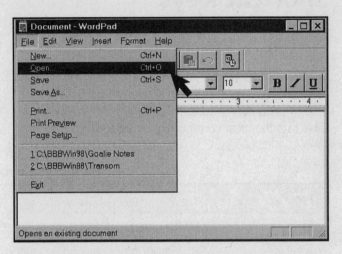

1 Click the **Start** button to open the Start menu. A list of commands and submenus appears.

2 Point to a submenu's name to open it. When a menu option is followed by an arrow, it opens a submenu that contains additional options.

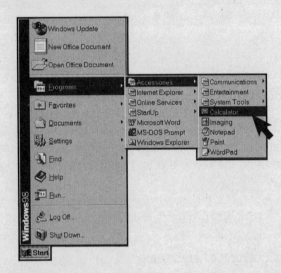

3 Click the desired command to execute it. Commands listed on the Start, Programs menu or one of its submenus run programs.

4 Most programs have a menu bar directly below the program window's title bar. To open a menu, click its name.

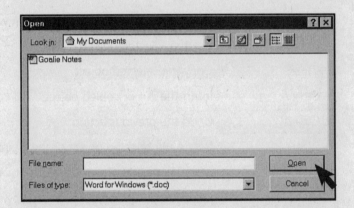

5 Selecting an option that is followed by an ellipsis (...) displays a dialog box like the one shown here. Enter your preferences, and then click a command button to execute the command. ▶For more information on how to use the controls you see here, see "Respond to Dialog Boxes" on page 32.◀

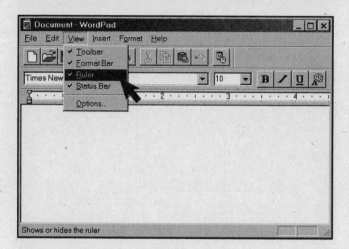

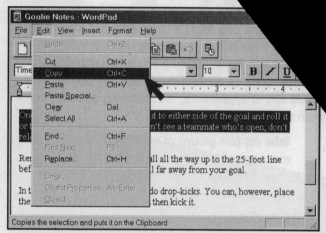

6 Check mark options allow you to turn a feature on or off. The picture above shows check mark options for turning features on or off in WordPad.

8 Most programs, including Windows, offer keyboard shortcuts for common commands. The keyboard alternative is typically specified next to the equivalent menu option to help you learn the shortcuts.

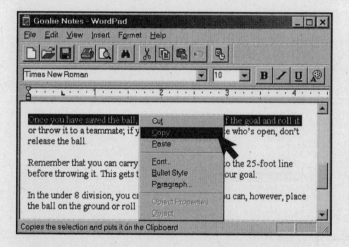

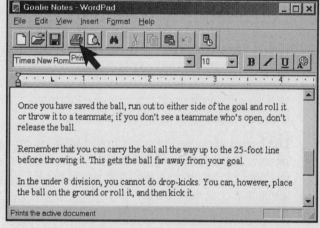

7 Right-click an area of the screen, selected text, or any other object to display a context menu that displays options only for that area or object. Then click the desired command.

9 Most programs have a toolbar that displays buttons for common commands. To view a description of the button, rest the mouse pointer on it.

10 To enter a command using the toolbar, click the desired button.

> Right-click a shortcut, program, or file icon and select **Properties** to view information about the icon or file. ▶See "View Disk, Folder, and File Properties" on page 121.◀

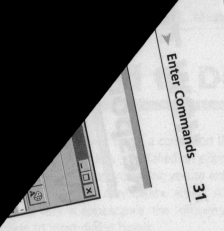

alog Boxes

...followed
...indows dis-
...ditional
...n dialog
...are com-

...or related options. To switch
...page of options, click the tab for that page.
(Press **Ctrl+Tab** to cycle through the tabs with
your keyboard.)

Text boxes allow you to fill in the blanks. You
click in a text box and type the desired setting or
information. In most text boxes, you can double-
click to highlight the selected entry and then start
typing to replace it.

Option buttons allow you to select only one
option in a group of options. When you select a
different option, the currently selected option is
automatically turned off.

Check boxes allow you to select any of several
options in a group. Unlike option buttons, you can
select as many check box options as you want. To
turn an option on or off, click its check box. A
check mark indicates that the option is on.

List boxes allow you to select from two or more
options. If the list is long, a scroll bar appears to
the right of the list. Use the scroll bar to bring
additional options into view.

Drop-down lists are similar to list boxes, but the
list initially displays only the currently selected
option. To open the list, click the down arrow to
the right of the list. You can then select the
desired option.

Spin boxes typically double as text boxes. You
can click in the text box and type the desired setting, or you can click the up and down arrows to
the right of the list to change the setting incrementally.

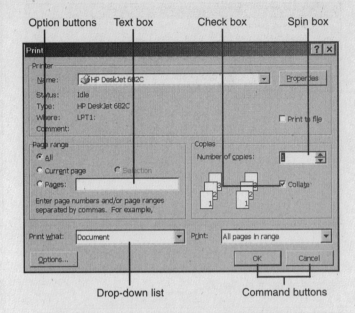

Option buttons   Text box   Check box   Spin box

Drop-down list   Command buttons

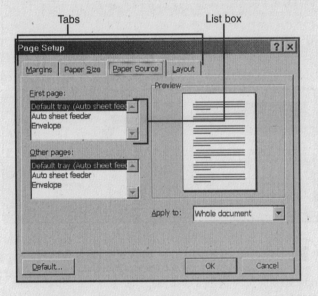

Tabs   List box

Command buttons allow you to execute or cancel the command. Most dialog boxes have three
command buttons: OK or Yes (to execute the
command), Cancel (to abort), and Help (to display
additional information about the listed options).

You can use your mouse or keyboard to navigate dialog boxes, as shown in the *Guided Tour.* To use the mouse, click the desired option or command button. To use the keyboard, press **Tab** to move to the desired option. You can then press the Spacebar to select the option button or check box, press the arrow keys to select an item from a list box or drop-down list, or press **Enter** to "press" the selected command button.

Many dialog boxes have their own built-in help systems. If a question mark button appears in the upper-right corner of the dialog box, you can click it and then click the specific option for which you need help. In some cases, you can right-click the option and select **What's This** to display context-sensitive help.

Guided Tour Navigate Dialog Boxes

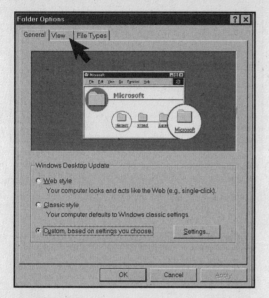

1 Dialog boxes that contain many options group related options on pages. Click a tab to bring that page to the front.

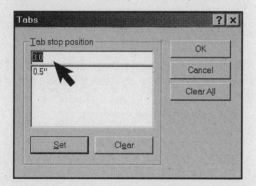

2 To change a text box entry, double-click the current entry and type the desired text or setting. Or, instead of replacing the entry, you can click in the text where you want to make a change and then edit the existing entry.

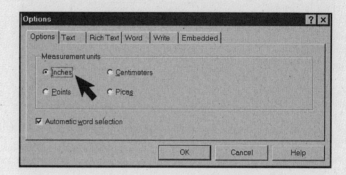

3 Option buttons allow you to select only one option in a group of options. Click the desired option to activate it and to deactivate the currently selected option.

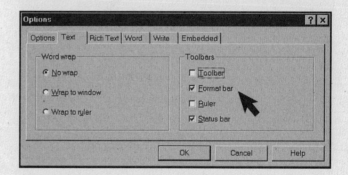

4 In a group of check box options, you can select none, all, or some of the options in the group. Click a check box to add a check mark (turn on the option) or to remove an existing check mark (turn off the option).

(continues)

Guided Tour Navigate Dialog Boxes *(continued)*

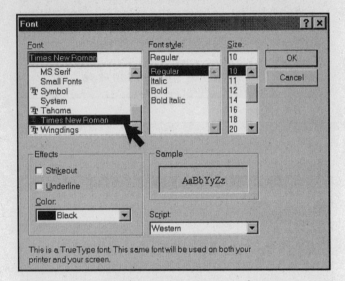

5 List boxes display two or more options. To select an option, click its name.

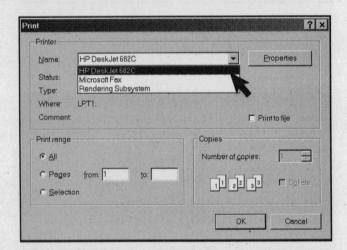

6 A drop-down list displays only the currently selected option. To open the list, click the arrow to the right of the box. You can then click the desired option to select it.

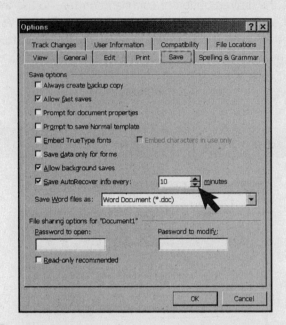

7 You can double-click an entry in a spin box and type the desired setting, or you can use the up and down arrow buttons to change the setting incrementally.

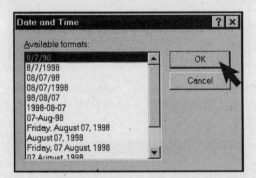

8 After entering the desired settings, click a command button to save your settings and close the dialog box or to cancel the command.

Access Windows Help

Windows contains its own online Help system that can answer most of your Windows questions and provide additional background information about Windows features. It offers a table of contents and an index to help you find specific information.

When you select the Start, Help command, Windows displays the Windows Help window, which offers the following three kinds of help:

- **Contents** works like an online user's manual. You click a book icon or name to view a list of related topics, and then you click the desired topic to display detailed information in the right pane.

- **Index** displays a comprehensive list of topics. You type the desired topic in the text box above the index, and Windows scrolls down to display a list of topics that match your entry. You then click the

desired topic to display detailed information in the right pane.

- **Search** provides a tool that searches through the entire contents of the Help system to find references to the word or phrase you specify. (Although this feature can help you track down less common help topics, it usually provides a list of topics that's too long to be of much use. Stick with the Contents and Index tabs for now.)

The *Guided Tour* shows you how to access and navigate the Help system.

> When you click some topics, Windows may display a dialog box showing additional subtopics. Click the desired subtopic.

Guided Tour Use the Windows Help System

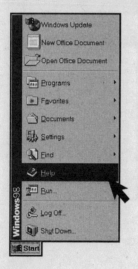

1 To use the Windows Help system, click **Start**, **Help**.

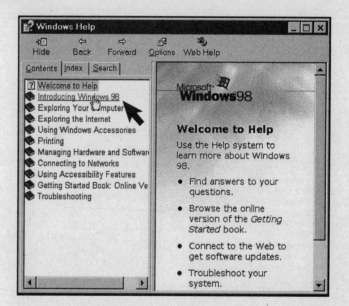

2 The Help window appears, displaying the Contents tab in front. The table of contents is the best place to find general information about Windows. Click a book icon for the desired Windows topic.

(continues)

Guided Tour Use the Windows Help System *(continued)*

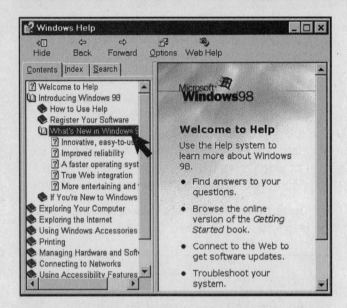

3 A list of subtopics appears. Click the desired subtopic and then click a topic with a question mark next to it. (You can collapse (hide) the list of subtopics by clicking the book icon again.) Click the desired subtopic.

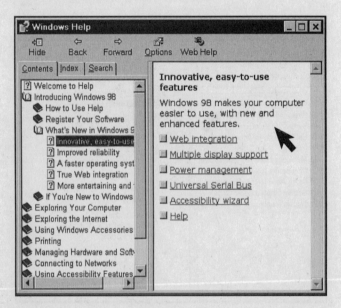

4 The contents of the selected subtopic appear in the pane on the right. Read or use the information as necessary.

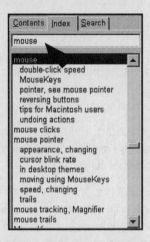

5 If you know you're looking for a specific topic, click the **Index** tab. A list of indexed topics appears.

6 Click in the text box above the index and type one or more words that describe the desired topic. For example, you might type **mouse**. As you type, Windows highlights the first topic in the index that matches your entry.

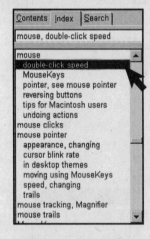

7 Scroll down the list, and double-click the desired topic to displays its contents in the right pane.

Guided Tour   Use the Windows Help System

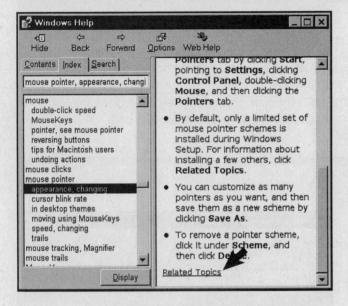

8 Many help topics contain *jumps* that point to related topics. Jumps are displayed in a different color and have a solid underline. Click a jump to display additional information.

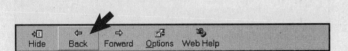

9 You can back up in the Help system by clicking the **Back** button.

10 To print the contents of the selected topic for future reference, click **Options** and then **Print**.

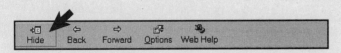

11 Click the **Hide** button to close the left panel and display only the contents of the selected topic. This opens up

more room in the window for the help contents. (When you click the Hide button, it is replaced by the Show button, which you can then click to redisplay the left pane.)

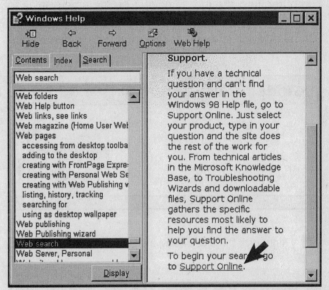

12 To access help at Microsoft's Web site, click the **Web Help** button, and then scroll down in the right panel and click the **Support Online** link to connect to Microsoft technical support on the Web.

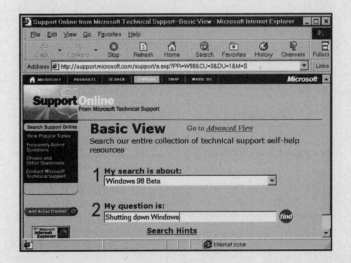

13 Windows runs Internet Explorer, establishes your Internet connection, connects you to Microsoft's Web site, and displays the Windows 98 Help page. ▶See "Use Windows 98 on the World Wide Web" on page 217.◀

Change the System Date and Time

Before completing this section, take a look at the right end of the taskbar. In the system tray, Windows displays the current time according to your computer. Rest the mouse pointer on the time display to view the date. If the date and time are incorrect, you can quickly adjust them, as shown in the *Guided Tour*.

If you just purchased your computer, it may display the current time of the manufacturer's geographical location. If you have an older computer that keeps losing time, you should have the computer checked by a qualified technician. You might need to replace the battery that supplies power to the internal clock.

Guided Tour Set the Date and Time

1 Right-click the time display and select **Adjust Date/Time**.

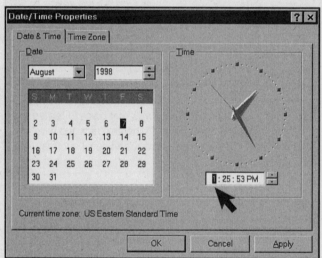

3 To set the time, click the hour, minute, or second, and click the up or down arrow to the right of the time display to set the correct hour, minute, or second. Repeat this step as needed until the correct time is shown.

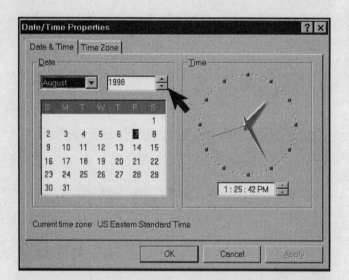

2 The Date/Time Properties dialog box appears. Click the up or down arrow to the right of the year spin box to set the current year. Open the month drop-down list and select the current month. Then click the current date in the calendar.

Guided Tour Set the Date and Time

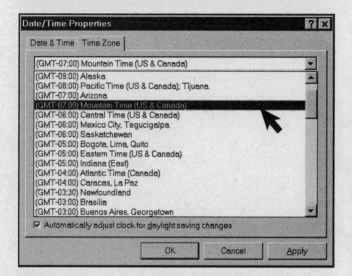

4 To have Windows automatically adjust the time for daylight savings changes, click the **Time Zone** tab. Open the drop-down list and select the time zone in which you live.

5 Make sure **Automatically Adjust Clock for Daylight Saving Changes** has a check mark next to it. Then click **OK**. The correct time should now appear in the taskbar.

HOW TO...

Install and Run Programs

Windows comes with several programs and utilities, including WordPad for creating documents, Paint for drawing pictures, and Microsoft Backup for protecting the files on your hard drive. You need to know how to run these programs in Windows and how to install and run any additional programs that may have come with your computer or that you have purchased. In this section, you will learn everything you need to know to install and run programs in Windows.

What You Will Find in This Section

Start and Exit Programs

Whenever you install a program, the installation utility places the program on the Start, Programs menu or one of its submenus. To run the program, you select it from the menu. In addition, the installation utility might place a shortcut icon on the Windows desktop to make the program easier to access. You can then run the program by clicking its shortcut icon.

Even if you have not installed any new programs in Windows, the Start, Programs menu is loaded with several Windows programs you can run, including WordPad, Paint, CD Player, Calculator, and Internet Explorer. The *Guided Tour* shows you the basics of running these and other programs.

> The contents of the Start, Programs menu are stored in the \Windows\Start Menu\Programs folder (or, if you enter your username on startup, in the \Windows\Profiles*yourname*\Start Menu\Programs folder). You can display the contents of this folder in My Computer or Windows Explorer and delete, copy, and move subfolders and icons just as you do with other folders and files on your computer. ▶See "Manage Disks, Folders, and Files," on page 79.◀

Use the Start Menu

The Start menu gives you access to all the programs that come with Windows, any Windows programs you install, and additional utilities that come with Windows. Click the Start button, and you will see the following icons:

Windows Update downloads and installs files from Microsoft's Internet site to upgrade your copy of Windows 98.

Programs contains a list of programs installed on your computer. The Programs menu contains additional submenus, such as Accessories, to group related programs.

Favorites displays a list of Web sites and other resources that you have chosen to add to the Favorites list or that Windows has added for you.

Documents contains a list of the 15 most recently opened documents. When you select a document from this list, Windows runs the associated program, which then opens the selected document.

Settings lists tools you can use to customize Windows 98 for your system. Control Panel provides tools for adding and removing programs, setting up hardware, setting the system date and time, and entering preferences for your modem, mouse, and keyboard. Printers lets you install and configure your printer. Taskbar & Start Menu provides options for configuring the Windows taskbar and Start menu. Folder Options lets you control the way My Computer and Windows Explorer display the contents of your disks and folders. Active Desktop presents options for the Windows desktop, ▶as explained in "Work in Web View," on page 83.◀ Windows Update allows you to download Windows updates from the Internet, ▶as explained in "Update Windows," on page 420.◀

Find displays a submenu, which allows you to search for files and folders on your computer or network, for pages and other resources on the Internet, and for people. The People option connects you to a white pages directory, in which you can enter a person's name and search for the person's email address, mailing address, or phone number.

Help displays the Windows Help window, where you can find answers to your Windows 98 questions.

Run displays a dialog box you can use to run programs. This is especially helpful if you need to run older DOS programs.

Log Off disconnects you from the network without shutting down Windows, or it allows another user to log on if Windows is set up for multiple users.

Shut Down displays the Shut Down Windows dialog box, which allows you to completely shut down Windows, restart it, or shut down in Stand By mode to conserve power and quickly restart. On some notebook computers, Windows also offers a Hibernation mode option, which places your computer in Stand By mode when you press the power button or close the lid.

Exit a Program

Before you exit a program, you should use the program's File, Save command to save any work you have done. As you work on a document, your changes are stored in RAM (random access memory), which is erased when you shut down Windows. When you save your document, Windows stores it as a file on your hard disk, so you can open the file the next time you start your computer.

You can exit Windows programs using any of several methods. The *Guided Tour* shows you how to exit using

the File, Exit command. You can also close a program window by double-clicking the **Control-menu** icon in the upper-left corner of the window, by clicking the **Close** (X) button in the upper-right corner, or by pressing **Alt+F4**. Or, you can use the Windows taskbar: Right-click the program's button and select **Close**.

Although Windows 98 will prompt you to save changes to any open documents before allowing you to shut down, you should save your documents and individual programs before you shut down Windows. ▶See "Save a Document," on page 139.◀ By following this safeguard, you prevent losing data if Windows locks up your computer during shut down.

Guided Tour Start A Program

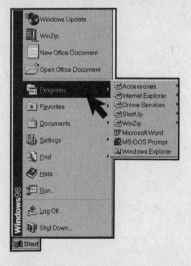

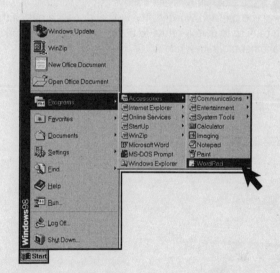

1 Click the **Start** button and point to **Programs**. The Start, Programs menu contains a list of Windows programs.

2 The Programs menu contains additional submenus for some programs. If the program is on a submenu, point to the name of the desired submenu. (You may need to point to multiple additional submenus.)

3 When you see the icon or name of the program you want to run, click it. In the picture above, WordPad is selected.

(continues)

Guided Tour Start a Program

(continued)

Taskbar button for the
open WordPad program

4 The program runs and displays its own window, in which you can start working. The taskbar displays a button that you can use to quickly return to the program if you are working in another program window.

6 When you install some programs, an icon for the program is added to the top of the Start menu, providing quick access to the program.

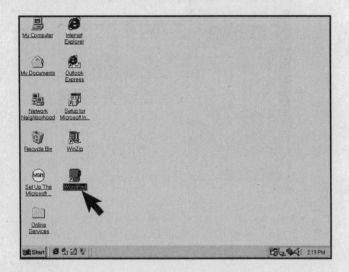

5 If the desktop contains a shortcut icon for running the program, you can click that icon to run the program. This allows you to bypass the Start, Programs menu.

Guided Tour Quit a Program

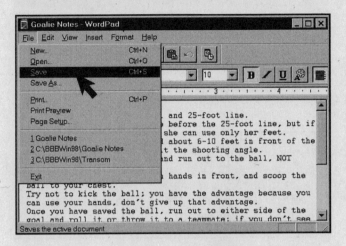

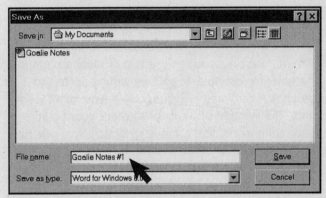

1 Before you exit a program, save any documents you have created or edited. To do so, select **File**, **Save**.

2 If you have not yet named and saved the document, the Save As dialog box prompts you to enter a name and select a folder in which to save the file. Enter the desired file-name in the **File Name** text box.

3 Choose the disk and folder in which you want the file saved, and then click the **Save** or **OK** button. ▶See "Save a Document" on page 139.◀

4 After saving all open documents, select **File**, **Exit**. Windows closes the program window.

Switch Between Active Programs

In addition to providing a graphical interface that simplifies computing, Windows enables *multitasking*. With multitasking, you can use two or more programs at a time; for example, as you are writing a letter to a company regarding a bill you received, you might want to use the Windows Calculator to check your figures. With multitasking, you can quickly switch from one running program to another, and you can even command one program to perform tasks (such as printing) in the background while you work in other programs.

To successfully multitask in Windows 98, you need to know how to switch from one program to another. The

easiest way to switch to a program is to click its button in the Windows taskbar. Windows moves the selected program window to the front. The *Guided Tour* shows you how to activate a program window using the taskbar and other methods.

If any portion of the desired program window is visible, you can quickly switch to it by clicking any part of the window. Switching programs is as easy as shuffling through folders and stacks of papers on your desk.

Guided Tour Switch from One Program to Another

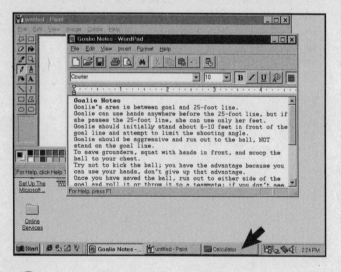

1 When you run a program, Windows adds a button for it to the Windows taskbar. Click the button for the desired program.

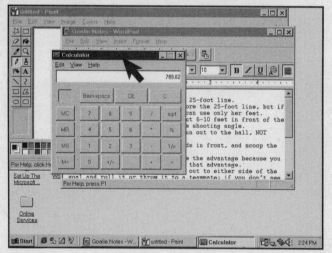

2 Windows moves the selected program window to the front, and you can start using the program.

Guided Tour Switch from One Program to Another

Solitaire

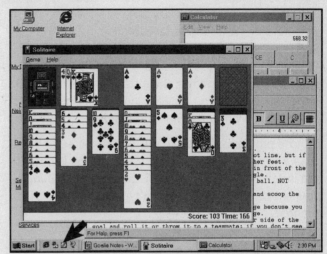

3 You can switch to a program by using the Alt+Tab key-stroke. Hold down the **Alt** key and press **Tab** to display the dialog box shown here. Keep holding down the **Alt** key and press the **Tab** key repeatedly to cycle through the programs. When the desired program is selected, release both keys.

4 You can minimize all program windows and return to the Windows desktop by clicking the **Show Desktop** icon in the Quick Launch toolbar.

Install New Programs

During the Windows installation, the installation utility added any Windows programs to the Start, Programs menu. If you installed Windows 98 over a previous edition of Windows, the installation utility added any programs that you installed in your previous Windows version to the Start, Programs menu.

If those programs do not appear on the menu, or if you have a new program you want to install, you can run the installation routine from Windows 98. The *Guided Tour* shows you how to install a typical Windows program.

> The steps for installing programs vary from one program to another. However, all Windows programs come with an Install or Setup file that you can run to start the installation. Typically, when you run the file, Windows displays a series of dialog boxes that lead you through the installation process.

Check Disk Space Before Installing

Before you install any new program, you should make sure you have enough free space on your hard disk. The program's package should specify the required disk space. In addition, you should have 30 megabytes or more of free disk space that Windows and your programs can use as *virtual memory*. Virtual memory is disk space that Windows uses as additional memory.

To check your disk space, click **My Computer**, and then right-click the icon for your hard disk and choose **Properties**. My Computer displays the total size of the disk and the amount of free space remaining. ▶If you don't have enough free space, see "Optimize Your System," starting on page 493.◀

> Most Windows programs follow a standard installation procedure that sets up an icon for running the program. The procedure for installing a DOS program is typically a little more complicated, however. ▶For details, see "Install DOS Programs" on page 70.◀

Automate CD-ROM Installation

Many newer programs are packaged on a CD-ROM disc and support the Windows AutoPlay feature. To install the program, simply load the disc into the CD-ROM drive. Windows runs the AutoPlay utility, which typically displays a welcome screen and a button for installing the program. Follow the onscreen instructions, and you can skip the *Guided Tour*.

Install with the Start, Run Command or My Computer

The *Guided Tour* shows you the standard way to install programs in Windows using the Add/Remove Programs utility from the Windows Control Panel. However, there are alternative methods, which you may find to be quicker:

- Insert the installation disk or CD-ROM, click the **My Computer** icon, and click the icon for the drive that contains the installation disk. Then click the **Install** or **Setup** icon.

- Insert the installation disk or CD-ROM and select **Start**, **Run**. Click the **Browse** button, change to the drive that contains the installation disk, and click the **Setup** or **Install** file. Then click **OK**.

Guided Tour Install a Program with Add/Remove Programs

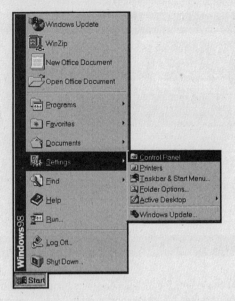

1 Click the **Start** button, point to **Settings**, and click **Control Panel**.

2 The Control Panel window appears. Click **Add/Remove Programs**.

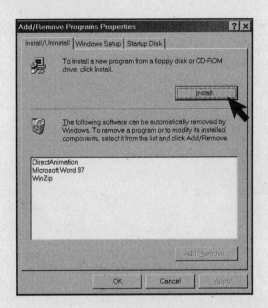

3 The Add/Remove Programs Properties dialog box appears with the Install/Uninstall tab in front. Click the **Install** button.

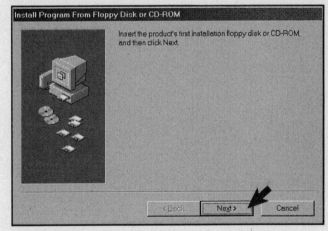

4 The Install Program from Floppy Disk or CD-ROM dialog box appears, prompting you to insert the installation disk. Insert the floppy disk or CD-ROM disc and click the **Next** button.

(continues)

Guided Tour   Install a Program with Add/Remove Programs

(continued)

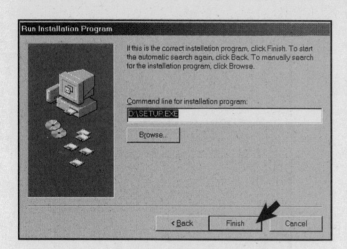

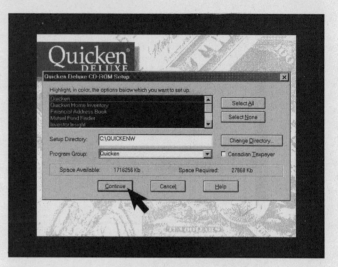

5 Windows searches any disks in your floppy drive and CD-ROM drive for the Setup or Install file, and then it displays the file's name. Click the **Finish** button.

6 At this point, the installation utility takes over and leads you through the installation process, which varies from program to program. Follow the onscreen instructions.

Uninstall Programs

When you buy a new computer, it seems as though it has an endless supply of hard disk space. A one-gigabyte hard drive seems big until you install Windows 98 and a few programs that take up 80 megabytes each. It's easy to install programs on your hard drive. So you install a program, use it for a few months, lose interest, and find a new program to install. Pretty soon, your disk is full.

It's tempting to just delete the folder that contains the program's files. That gets rid of the program, right? Not entirely, especially if the program you're trying to get rid of is a Windows program. When you install a Windows program, it commonly installs files not only to the program's folder, but also to the \WINDOWS folder, the WINDOWS\SYSTEM folder, and other folders. It also adds settings to the Windows Registry, which are not removed unless you follow the proper uninstall routine. To remove the program completely, you must use Windows' Add/Remove Programs utility.

Remove Windows Programs

When you install a program that's designed to work under Windows, it typically adds its name to a list of programs you can remove. This list is displayed in the Add/Remove Programs dialog box. If you have a Windows program that is on the list of programs you can uninstall, follow the *Guided Tour* to remove the program. If you are unsure whether the program is on the list, the *Guided Tour* shows you how to check.

Run the Program's Setup Utility

If the name of the program you want to remove does not appear in the Add/Remove Programs list, you may be able to use the program's own setup utility to remove the program. Use one of the following methods:

- Use My Computer or Windows Explorer to display the contents of the folder for the program you want to remove. If you see a **Setup** or **Install** icon, double-click it, and follow the onscreen instructions to remove the program. If there is no Setup or Install icon, close the My Computer or Windows Explorer window.

- Click the **Start** button, point to **Programs**, and point to the program's menu name. Look on the submenu that appears for a **Setup**, **Install**, or **Uninstall** option. If the menu has such an option, select it and then follow the onscreen instructions to remove the program.

In many cases, the program's setup utility allows you to choose whether you want to remove the entire program or only selected components. If you use the program but do not use its advanced features, you can save disk space by removing only the components you do not use.

If you don't see a Setup or Install button, the best thing to do is to obtain a program that's designed especially to help you remove other programs from your hard drive. Remove-It and Clean Sweep are two of the more popular programs. However, these programs are most useful if you install them *before* installing other programs, so the uninstall program can record all changes they make to your system.

Guided Tour   Remove Windows Programs

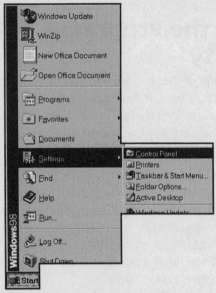

1 Click the **Start** button, point to **Settings**, and click **Control Panel**.

2 Click the **Add/Remove Programs** icon. The Add/Remove Programs Properties dialog box appears.

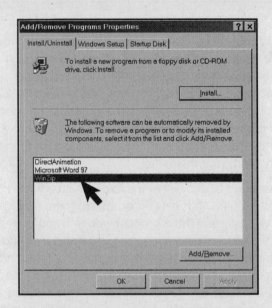

3 Click the **Install/Uninstall** tab if it is not already selected. At the bottom of the screen is a list of programs you can have Windows uninstall. Click the name of the program you want to remove.

4 Click the **Add/Remove** button.

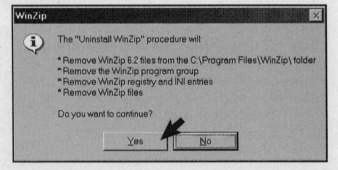

5 One or more dialog boxes will lead you through the uninstall process, asking for your confirmation. Follow the onscreen instructions to complete the process.

If the application you removed has a shortcut icon on the desktop, you might have to delete it manually. Right-click the icon, select **Delete**, and confirm the deletion. ▶See "Create Shortcuts to Disks, Folders, and Files" on page 114 for details.◀

Configure the Start Menu

A program's installation utility typically places the program on the Start, Programs menu or one of its submenus. During the installation, you might be given the opportunity to select the submenu in which you want the program to appear.

After you install a program, you might find that you have to work your way through several layers of submenus to run programs you commonly use. To fix this problem, you can customize the Start menu by creating your own submenus and by moving submenus or programs to suit your needs. You can also move programs to the top of the Start menu so you don't have to deal with submenus. The following *Guided Tour* shows you various ways to configure your Start menu.

Before you start, you should realize that the Start menu is actually a folder that contains shortcuts and

subfolders. You can open the Start Menu folder in My Computer or Windows Explorer (\WINDOWS\START MENU) and configure the menu by copying and moving shortcuts. See "Configure the Start Menu with Windows Explorer" in the *Guided Tour* for instructions on how to rearrange the Start menu using Windows Explorer.

> If your system is set up for multiple users and you are asked to enter your Windows login name when you start Windows, your Start folder will be in a different location. Check the \Windows\Profiles*yourname* folder, where *yourname* is the name you enter to log in.

Guided Tour   Rearrange the Start Menu with Drag and Drop

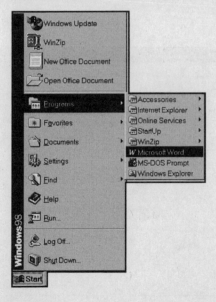

1 Windows 98 allows you to drag programs and submenus to rearrange them. Click **Start**, point to **Programs**, and point to the submenu or program you want to move.

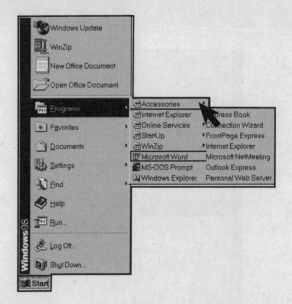

2 Drag the submenu or program up or down on the menu to the desired position. A horizontal line appears, showing where the program or submenu will be moved. Click the left mouse button. The program or submenu is moved to the new location.

(continues)

Guided Tour Rearrange the Start Menu with Drag and Drop   *(continued)*

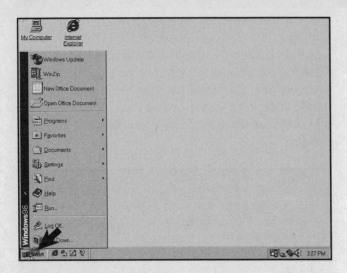

3 To place a program at the top of the Start menu, drag its icon from the Windows desktop, My Computer, or Windows Explorer over the Start button. Then release the mouse button.

4 Click the **Start** button to make sure the icon is at the top of the Start menu. (You can drag items listed at the top of the Start menu to rearrange them.)

Guided Tour Add a Program to the Start Menu

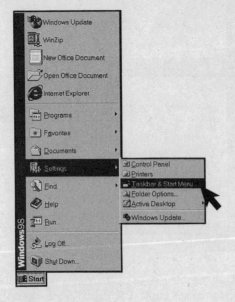

1 Click **Start**, point to **Settings**, and click **Taskbar & Start Menu**.

2 The Taskbar Properties dialog box appears. Click the **Start Menu Programs** tab.

3 The Start Menu Programs options appear. Click the **Add** button.

Guided Tour Add a Program to the Start Menu

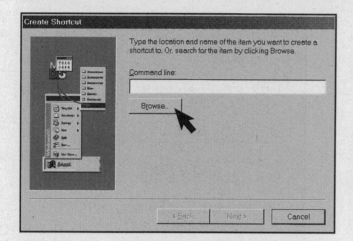

4 The Create Shortcut dialog box appears, prompting you to specify the location and name of the file that runs the program. Click the **Browse** button.

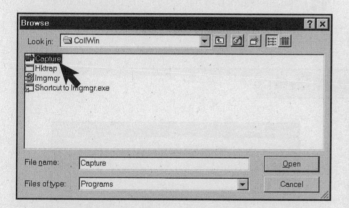

5 In the Browse dialog box, change to the drive and folder that contain the file that executes the program. Select the file and click **Open**.

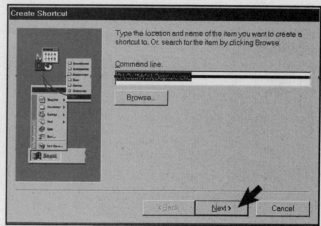

6 You are returned to the Create Shortcut dialog box, and the selected file's location and name appear in the Command Line text box. Click **Next**.

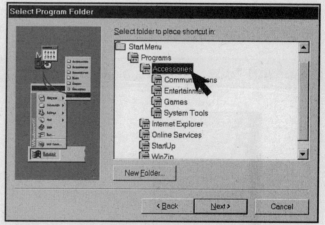

7 The Select Program Folder dialog box appears. Each program folder represents a submenu on the Start menu. (Optional) To place the program in a new folder (so it will appear on its own submenu), select the folder in which you want the new folder to appear (select the Programs folder to make a submenu on the Start, Programs menu). Click **New Folder** and type a name for the folder.

8 Select the folder in which you want the program placed (the menu on which you want it to appear) and click **Next**.

(continues)

Guided Tour   Add a Program to the Start Menu

(continued)

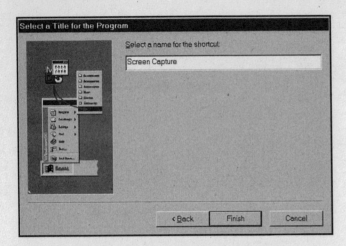

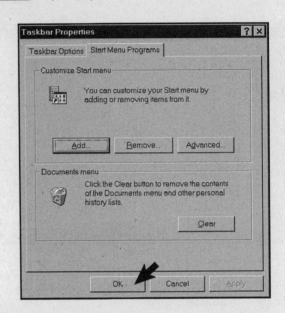

9 Windows prompts you to name the shortcut. Type the program's name as you want it to appear on the menu.

10 If you must choose a program icon, click **Next**, choose the desired icon, and click **Finish**. Otherwise, simply click the **Finish** button.

11 You are returned to the Taskbar Properties dialog box. Click **OK** to save your changes. The program is now listed on the specified menu or submenu.

Guided Tour   Remove an Item from the Start Menu

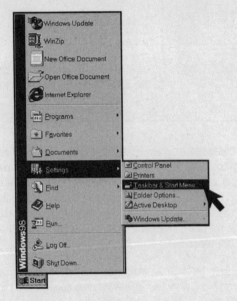

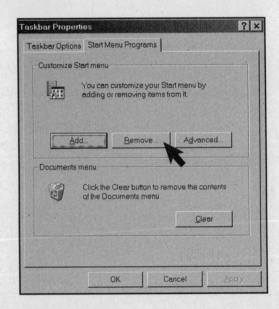

1 Click **Start**, point to **Settings**, and click **Taskbar & Start Menu**.

2 The Taskbar Properties dialog box appears. Click the **Start Menu Programs** tab.

3 The Start Menu Programs options appear. Click the **Remove** button.

Guided Tour Remove an Item from the Start Menu

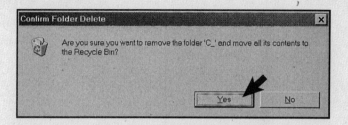

7 If you selected a program to remove, the program is automatically removed from the menu. If you selected a folder, the Confirm Folder Delete dialog box appears, as shown above. Click **Yes**.

4 The Remove Shortcuts/Folders dialog box appears. To display the contents of a folder, click the **plus sign** (+) next to its name.

5 Click the program or folder you want to remove.

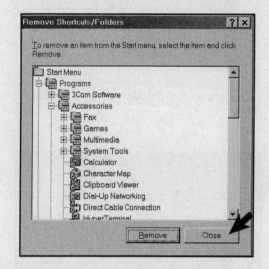

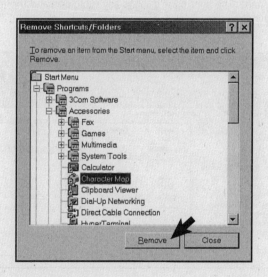

8 Click **Close** to return to the Taskbar Properties dialog box. Click **OK** to close the Taskbar Properties dialog box.

6 Click the **Remove** button.

Guided Tour Configure the Start Menu with Windows Explorer

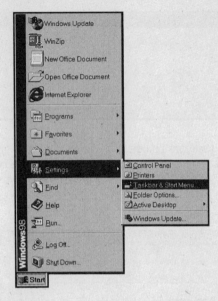

1 Click **Start**, point to **Settings**, and click **Taskbar & Start Menu**.

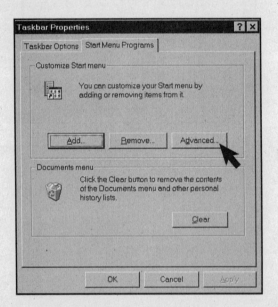

2 The Taskbar Properties dialog box appears. Click the **Start Menu Programs** tab.

3 The Start Menu Programs options appear. Click the **Advanced** button.

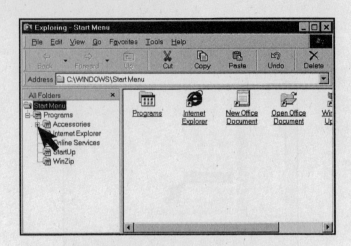

4 Windows Explorer starts and displays the contents of the Start Menu folder. The left pane displays a list of folders in the Start Menu folder. The right pane displays the contents of the currently selected folder (the Start Menu folder, in this figure). To display subfolders of a folder, click the **plus sign** (+) next to the folder's name.

5 To view the contents of a folder, click its name in the left pane. The right pane displays any subfolders and shortcuts stored in the selected folder.

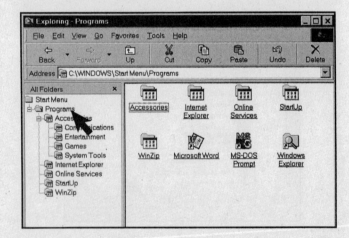

6 To create a new folder, click the name of the folder within which you want the new folder created.

Guided Tour Configure the Start Menu with Windows Explorer

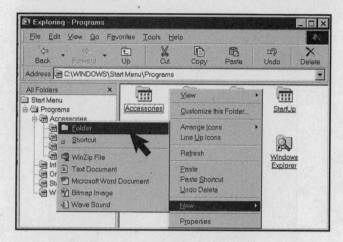

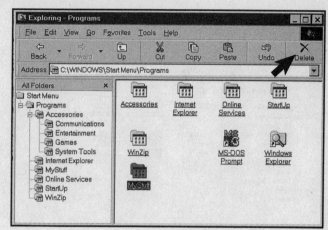

7 Right-click a blank area in the right pane, point to **New**, and select **Folder**.

8 A new folder appears named New Folder. Type the desired name of the folder, and then press **Enter** or click a blank area to rename the folder.

11 To remove a shortcut or folder, click its name in the left pane or point to it in the right pane and then click the **Delete** button in the toolbar. If a confirmation dialog box appears, click **Yes**.

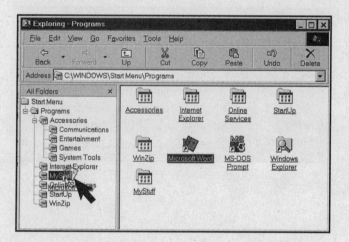

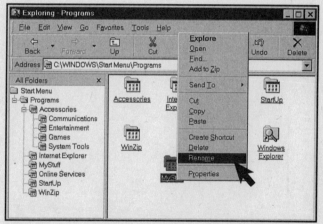

9 To move a shortcut from one folder to another, display the shortcut you want to move in the right pane, and display the destination folder in the left pane.

10 Drag the shortcut from the right pane over the destination in the left pane and release the mouse button.

12 To rename a folder or shortcut, right-click the shortcut and select **Rename**. The name appears highlighted.

To quickly select a folder or shortcut to be renamed, select the item and press **F2**.

13 Type a new name for the shortcut or folder, and then press **Enter** or click a blank area in the window.

(continues)

Guided Tour Configure the Start Menu with Windows Explorer *(continued)*

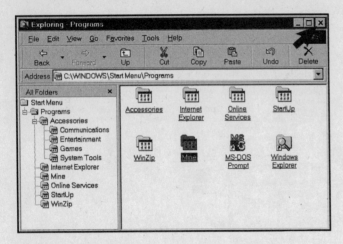

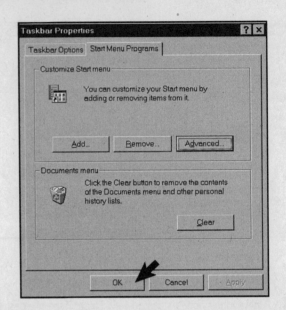

14 When you are done configuring the Start menu, click the **Close** button in the upper-right corner of the Windows Explorer window.

15 This returns you to the Taskbar Properties dialog box. Click **OK** to close it.

To create a desktop shortcut for any program on the Start menu, first open the Start Menu folder in Windows Explorer, and then open the folder that contains the program's shortcut. Using the right mouse button, drag the shortcut over a blank area of the desktop and release the mouse button. Click **Create Shortcut(s) Here**.

Configure the Taskbar

The taskbar at the bottom of the Windows screen displays the Start menu, the Quick Launch toolbar, buttons for any program windows that are currently open, and the system tray, which displays the current time and icons for any programs that are running in the background. ▶To use the taskbar, see "Switch Between Active Programs" on page 46.◀

In addition to providing a means for quickly switching between running programs, the taskbar contains a Quick Launch toolbar that allows you to run programs with a single mouse click. Initially, this toolbar contains buttons for quickly returning to the Windows desktop, running Internet Explorer (the Web browser), and accessing the Channel Bar. However, you can drag shortcuts for other programs to the Quick Launch toolbar to make them easily accessible, as well.

You can also move the taskbar to the top or side of the screen to suit your taste, resize the toolbar, hide the toolbar when you are working in your program windows, and even turn on additional toolbars that act like the Quick Launch toolbar. The following *Guided Tour* shows you how to take control of your taskbar.

> Many of the features described in the *Guided Tour* are new to Windows 98. Even if you are familiar with the taskbar options from Windows 95, you should take the *Guided Tour* to learn about the new features. The taskbar is a powerful tool for accessing all the programs and other resources on your system.

Guided Tour   Move and Resize the Taskbar

1 A vertical bar separates the Quick Launch toolbar from the rest of the taskbar. Drag the bar to provide more or less space for the Quick Launch toolbar.

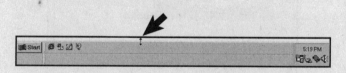

2 To make the taskbar larger, drag the top of the taskbar up. To make it smaller, drag down.

3 To move the taskbar, drag it up, down, left, or right. The figure above shows the taskbar moved to the right side of the screen.

(continues)

Guided Tour   Move and Resize the Taskbar   *(continued)*

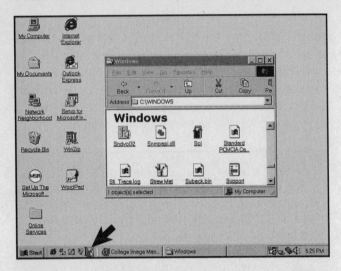

4 You can add shortcuts to the Quick Launch toolbar. Drag a shortcut from the Windows desktop or from My Computer or Windows Explorer to a blank area of the Quick Launch toolbar.

5 As you drag over the Quick Launch toolbar, an insertion point appears, showing you where the icon will be placed. When the insertion point is in the desired position, release the mouse button. The shortcut is added to the Quick Launch toolbar.

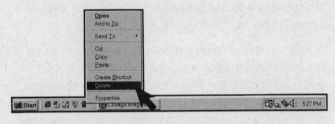

6 To remove a shortcut from the Quick Launch toolbar, right-click the shortcut and select **Delete**.

7 In the Confirm File Delete dialog box, click **Yes**.

Guided Tour   Set the Taskbar Options

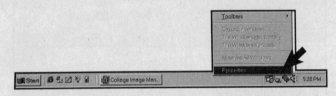

1 Right-click a blank area of the taskbar and select **Properties**.

2 The Taskbar Properties dialog box appears, displaying the Taskbar Options tab in front. To keep the taskbar in front of any open program windows, make sure **Always on Top** is checked.

Guided Tour Set the Taskbar Options

(continued)

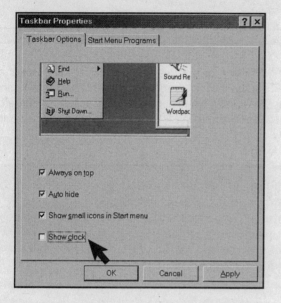

3 To have the taskbar disappear when you are working in a program window, click **Auto Hide** to place a check in its box. When this option is enabled, you can bring the taskbar into view by pointing to the edge of the screen where the taskbar is positioned (the bottom of the screen, unless you moved the taskbar).

4 To display smaller icons on the Start menu, select **Show Small Icons in Start Menu** to place a check in its box. This gives each menu and submenu more room for displaying menu and program names.

5 The clock in the system tray (right side of the taskbar) displays the current time. By default, the time is on. To turn off the time display, select **Show Clock** to remove the check from its box.

6 Click **OK** to save your settings and close the Taskbar Properties dialog box.

Guided Tour Turn Toolbars On or Off

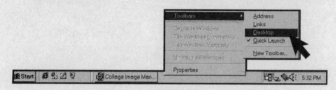

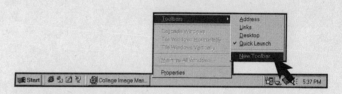

1 To turn on the Desktop toolbar, which displays all the shortcuts on the Windows desktop, right-click the taskbar, point to **Toolbars**, and select **Desktop**.

3 You can create a toolbar for any folder on your system. To do so, right-click the taskbar, point to **Toolbars**, and select **New Toolbar**.

(continues)

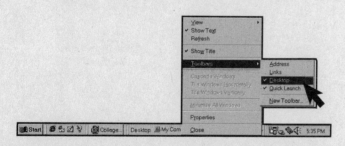

2 To turn the Quick Launch or Desktop toolbar off, right-click the taskbar, point to **Toolbars**, and select **Quick Launch** or **Desktop**.

Guided Tour Turn Toolbars On or Off *(continued)*

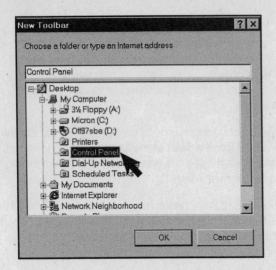
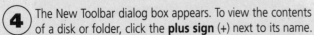
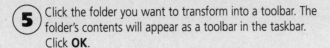

6 Windows transforms the selected folder into a toolbar and displays the folder's contents. If the toolbar contains more icons than it has room to display, an arrow appears on the left or right side of the toolbar. Click the arrow to bring other icons into view.

If you add several toolbars, you might want to make your taskbar larger to accommodate them. If you make the taskbar larger, consider turning on Auto Hide, so the taskbar does not get in the way when you are working with your programs.

4 The New Toolbar dialog box appears. To view the contents of a disk or folder, click the **plus sign** (+) next to its name.

5 Click the folder you want to transform into a toolbar. The folder's contents will appear as a toolbar in the taskbar. Click **OK**.

Run Programs Automatically with Task Scheduler

Task Scheduler is a new Windows tool that allows you to set up programs to run and perform specific tasks automatically at a specified date and time. If you use Task Scheduler, it runs whenever you start Windows, and it remains in the background. When the scheduled time arrives, Task Scheduler launches the designated program, which then performs the specified task.

Like most programs that run in the background, Task Scheduler displays an icon in the system tray (on the right end of the taskbar) when it is running. You can double-click the Task Scheduler icon to view a list of

scheduled tasks. You can then pause Task Scheduler to prevent it from automatically running programs (if you are currently working with another program).

Task Scheduler is particularly useful for automating system management tasks, such as backing up files on your hard disk, optimizing your hard disk, and checking disks for errors. ▶See "Maintain Your Computer" on page 405 and "Optimize Your System" on page 493 for details.◀

The *Guided Tour* shows you how to use Task Scheduler to automate your system and how to control Task Scheduler when it is running.

Guided Tour Schedule Programs to Run Automatically

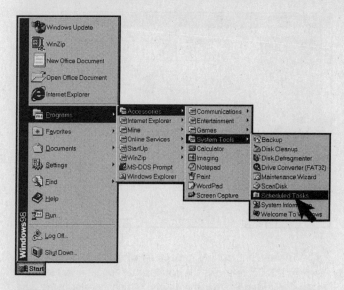

① Click the **Start** button, point to **Programs**, **Accessories**, **System Tools**, and click **Scheduled Tasks**.

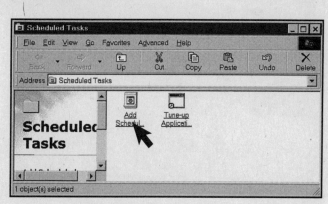

② The Scheduled Tasks window appears. Click **Add Scheduled Task**.

(continues)

Guided Tour Schedule Programs to Run Automatically   *(continued)*

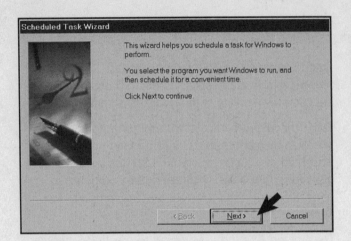

3 The Scheduled Task Wizard appears. Click the **Next** button.

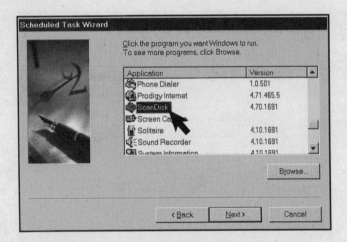

4 The Scheduled Task Wizard prompts you to select the program you want to set up from a list of installed programs. Click the program that you want Task Scheduler to run automatically. Click **Next**.

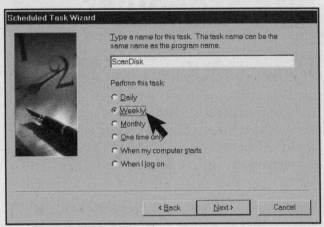

5 Type the name of the program as you want it to appear in the task list (or accept the original program name). Select the desired schedule for running the program: **Daily**, **Weekly**, **Monthly**, **One Time Only**, **When My Computer Starts**, or **When I Log On**. Click **Next**.

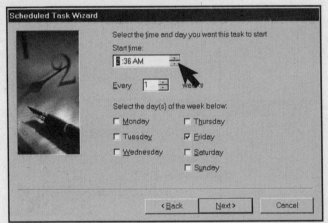

6 The resulting options depend on what you selected in step 5. This figure shows the options that appear if you selected Weekly in step 5. Enter the desired settings to specify the time and days you want the program to run. Click **Next**.

Guided Tour   Schedule Programs to Run Automatically

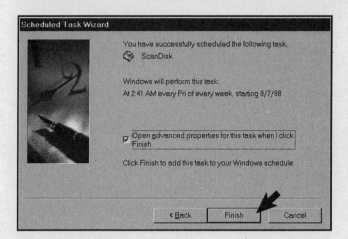

7 The last Scheduled Task Wizard dialog box appears. (Optional) To enter preferences that control the program's operation, select **Open Advanced Properties for This Task When I Click Finish**, click **Finish** and proceed to step 8; otherwise, just click the **Finish** button.

8 If you chose to set advanced properties, the properties dialog box for the selected program appears. Click the **Settings** button. (This button is not available for all applications.)

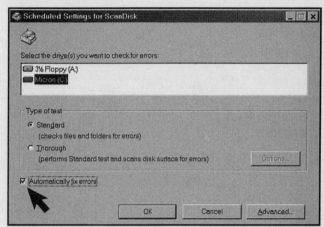

9 The Scheduled Settings dialog box appears. This dialog box is different for each program. The figure above shows the options for ScanDisk. Enter your preferences and click **OK**.

> Some programs prompt you for instructions or confirmation. If you schedule a program to run at a time when you will not be using your computer, you must make sure you set up the program to proceed without displaying prompts, if possible.

10 (Optional) To enter advanced settings, click the **Settings** tab and enter your preferences. For example, you can have Task Scheduler start the task only if your computer is not in use or terminate the task after a specified amount of time. Click **OK**.

(continues)

Guided Tour Schedule Programs to Run Automatically

(continued)

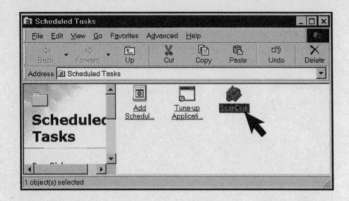

11 The selected program appears in the task list. Click the **Close** (X) button to close Task Scheduler but keep it running in the background.

Guided Tour Pausing and Stopping Task Scheduler

1 When Task Scheduler is running, its icon appears in the system tray. You can pause it to prevent scheduled programs from running when you are working in another program. To do so, right-click the Task Scheduler icon and select **Pause Task Scheduler**.

2 A red X symbol appears on the Task Scheduler icon. To reactivate Task Scheduler, right-click the icon and select **Continue Task Scheduler**.

3 To view a list of scheduled programs, double-click the Task Scheduler icon.

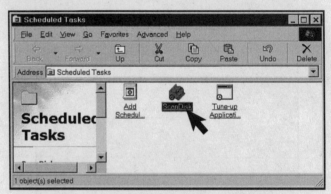

4 Icons for your scheduled tasks appear. To change the properties of a scheduled program, click its icon.

Guided Tour Pausing and Stopping Task Scheduler

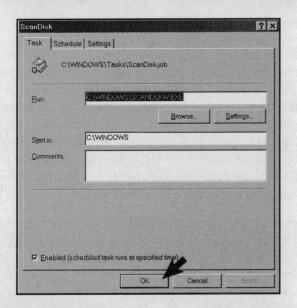

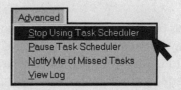

7 To turn off Task Scheduler so it will no longer run programs automatically, open the **Advanced** menu and select **Stop Using Task Scheduler**.

8 Click the **Close** (X) button to close the Task Scheduler window.

To turn Task Scheduler back on, first run it by choosing **Start, Programs, Accessories, System Tools, Scheduled Tasks**. Then open the **Advanced** menu and choose **Start Using Task Scheduler**.

5 The properties dialog box appears, displaying three tabs for changing the program's properties, scheduled time, and advanced settings. Enter your preferences and click **OK**.

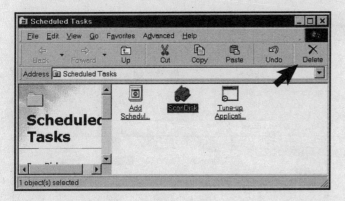

6 To remove a program from the list, point to it and click the **Delete** button.

Install DOS Programs

Up to this point, you have been working with Windows programs, which are relatively easy to install and run. However, you might still have some old DOS programs, such as computer games, that you would like to run on your computer. The good news is that you can still run most of your DOS programs; some might run even better under Windows. The bad news is that installing your DOS programs and setting them up could be a bit complicated.

The first step is to install the DOS program. Although the procedure for installing Windows programs varies depending on the program, all Windows programs have a setup or install utility that initiates the installation in a fairly standard way. Most DOS programs have their own installation utility that works just like a Windows setup utility. With some DOS programs, however, the installation may consist of copying the files from floppy disks to a separate folder on your hard disk. The *Guided Tour* shows you both installation procedures.

DOS, pronounced "dawss," is short for Disk Operating System. Before Windows, when you started your computer, the first thing you saw was the DOS prompt, which looked like c:\>. You typed commands at the prompt to run programs and perform other tasks, such as deleting and copying files. (Microsoft's version of DOS is called MS-DOS.)

If you have a DOS program on a CD-ROM disc, you may not want to install the program because it may require too much hard disk storage. Try creating a shortcut icon for the program file that is on CD. ►See "Create Shortcuts to Disks, Folders, and Files" on page 114.◄

Guided Tour Run a DOS Installation Utility

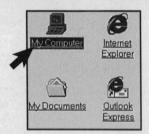

1 Load the DOS program CD into the CD-ROM drive or insert the first floppy disk of the set into the floppy disk drive. Click **My Computer** on the Windows desktop.

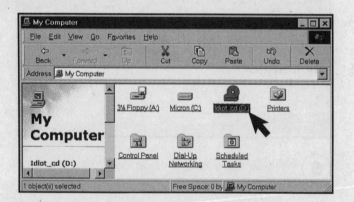

2 The My Computer window appears, displaying icons for disk drives on your computer. Click the icon for the drive that contains the CD or floppy disk.

Guided Tour Run a DOS Installation Utility

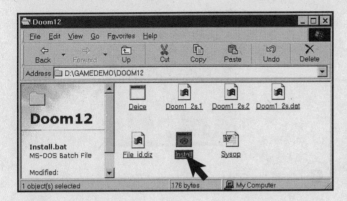

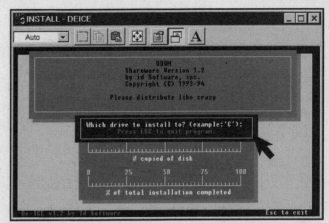

3 Most programs have a Setup or Install file. Click the file to run the installation utility. If the disk has folders labeled Disk1, Disk2, Disk3, and so on, change to the **Disk1** folder and click the **Setup** or **Install** file. If the program does not have a Setup or Install file, skip to the next *Guided Tour*, "Install a Program Manually."

4 The setup utility appears in its own DOS window. Follow the onscreen instructions to complete the setup.

Guided Tour Install a Program Manually

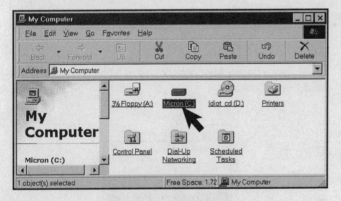

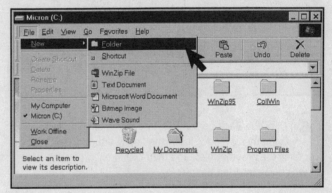

1 Open the My Computer window and click the icon for the hard disk on which you want to install the DOS program.

2 My Computer displays the contents of the selected disk. Open the **File** menu, point to **New**, and click **Folder**.

(continues)

Guided Tour Install a Program Manually

(continued)

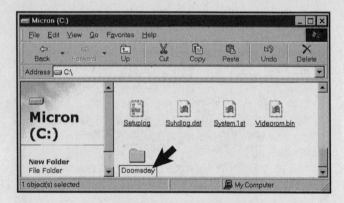

3 My Computer creates a new folder called New Folder. Type a descriptive name for the folder and press **Enter**.

> When naming a folder for a DOS program, try to adhere to the old DOS 8-character name limit (no spaces). Although the Windows 98 version of DOS can handle long filenames, this version still has trouble with some long names.

4 Click the **Back** button to return to the opening My Computer window. Insert the floppy disk or CD-ROM that contains the program files, and then click the icon for the drive in which you inserted the disk.

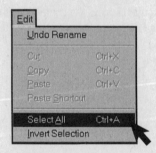

5 My Computer displays the contents of the disk. Open the **Edit** menu and choose **Select All**. All folders and files on the disk appear highlighted.

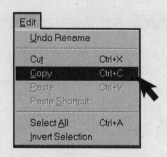

6 Open the **Edit** menu and select **Copy**.

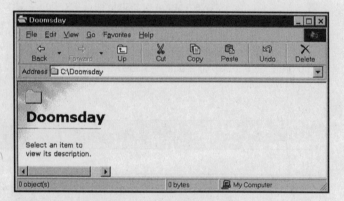

7 Change back to the disk and folder you created for the new program. My Computer displays the contents of the folder, which is empty.

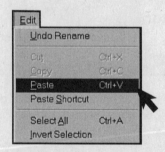

8 Open the **Edit** menu and select **Paste**. My Computer pastes all files and folders copied in step 7 to the new folder. Repeat steps 5–9 for each program disk.

Guided Tour Install a Program Manually

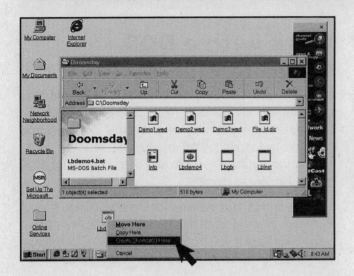

9 When all the files are in the new folder, you should have one file for running the program. The figure above shows the generic icon used for DOS programs. Use the right mouse button to drag the icon to the Windows desktop, release the mouse button, and select **Create Shortcut(s) Here**.

You can place an icon for your DOS program on the Start, Programs menu. ▶See "Configure the Start Menu" on page 53 for instructions.◀

Run DOS Programs

When you run a DOS program, Windows creates a separate "virtual" computer for running the program and provides the program with the memory and other resources it needs to run efficiently. Windows runs the program in its own window, allowing you to switch between DOS and Windows programs as easily as you switch from one Windows program to another.

Although most DOS programs run well under Windows 98, some need additional memory and require special settings. If you have trouble running your DOS program, right-click the DOS program's icon, choose Properties, and try adjusting the program's properties to give it additional memory and resources. Check the program's documentation for details on how to run it effectively in Windows.

Work with a DOS Program Window

When you run a DOS program from Windows, the program appears in a window that's similar to a Windows program window. The upper-right corner of the window has buttons for minimizing, maximizing, restoring, and closing the window. You can also drag a corner or side of the window to resize it.

When maximizing or resizing DOS windows, you should be aware that not all DOS programs can display a full-screen window. If you maximize a window and it does not fill the entire screen, don't panic—it's normal.

In addition to the standard window controls, Windows displays a special toolbar at the top of the DOS window. The following table lists the buttons on that toolbar and provides a brief description of each button.

DOS Window Toolbar Buttons

Button	Name	Description
Auto ▼	Font	Lets you select the font size for displayed text. The Auto setting automatically adjusts the font size when you resize the window.
⬚	Mark	Turns on Mark mode, which allows you to use your mouse to select text you want to copy or move to another document.
🗐	Copy	Copies the selected text to the Windows Clipboard, so you can paste it into other documents.
📋	Paste	Inserts the contents of the Windows Clipboard into the currently displayed document.
⛶	Full Screen	Displays the program in Full-Screen mode instead of in a window. This button is not available in some programs.
📄	Properties	Displays the Properties dialog box for the program.
🗗	Background	By default, this button is active, preventing the program from doing anything when you are working in other programs. If you want the program to be able to perform tasks in the background, click this button to turn it off.
A	Font	Displays a dialog box for changing the font size for displayed text. This button performs the same function as the Font drop-down list on the left end of the toolbar.

Go to the MS-DOS Prompt

Some DOS programs simply cannot run under Windows 98, no matter which special settings you enter. If the program will not run, try restarting your computer in MS-DOS mode, as explained in the *Guided Tour*, and then running the program from the DOS prompt.

Some programs, especially games, may require that your computer use special startup commands to create an environment in which the program will run. If the program requires special startup commands, create a floppy system disk ►as explained in "Format Floppy Disks" on

page 129.◄ Copy the CONFIG.SYS and AUTOEXEC.BAT files from your hard disk to the floppy disk, and then edit those files on the floppy disk to insert the required startup commands.

See the program's documentation to determine which commands are required.

There's a quick way to go to the DOS prompt. Open the **Start** menu, point to **Programs**, and click **MS-DOS Prompt**.

Guided Tour   Run a DOS Program

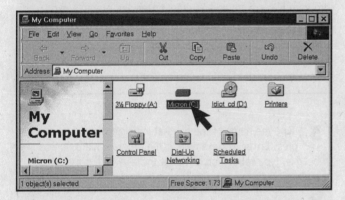

1 Open the My Computer window and click the icon for the disk that contains the DOS program. Then click the icon for the program's folder.

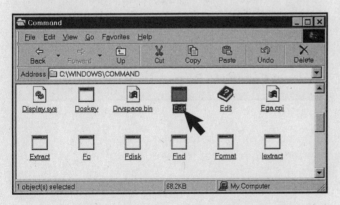

2 My Computer displays the contents of the selected folder. Click the icon for the file that initializes the program.

Names of files that initialize programs end in .EXE, .COM, or .BAT. To view filename extensions in My Computer, open its **View** menu, select **Folder Options**, click the **View** tab, and click **Hide File Extensions for Known File Types** to remove the check from its box. Click OK.

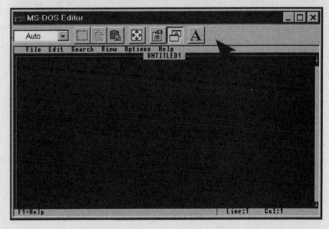

3 The DOS program starts and appears in a window. If the program has its own toolbar, you can use the toolbar to enter commands that affect only this program. ►To exit the program correctly, see "Exit DOS Programs" on page 77.◄

Guided Tour Restart in MS-DOS Mode

1 Open the **Start** menu and select **Shut Down**.

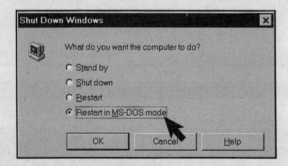

2 The Shut Down Windows dialog box appears. Select **Restart in MS-DOS Mode** and click **OK**.

```
C:\>d:
```

3 Windows shuts down and restarts, displaying the DOS prompt. If the program is on a drive other than C, type the drive's letter followed by a colon (for example, **d:**) and press **Enter**.

```
C:\>d:
D:\>cd\rebel
```

4 If the file that runs the program is in a separate folder, type **cd** followed by the name of the folder in which the program files are stored and press **Enter**. For example, type **cd\rebel** and press **Enter**.

```
D:\>rebel
```

5 Type the name of the file that initializes the program and press **Enter**. For example, if the program file is named rebel.exe, type **rebel** (you can omit the .exe) and press **Enter**.

6 The program runs in full-screen mode. When you are done using it, exit the program. Then type **exit** and press **Enter** to restart your computer with Windows 98.

> You can start your computer without starting Windows 98. After you turn on your monitor and system unit, wait for a beep. As soon as you hear your computer beep, press the **F8** key. Windows displays a list of startup options. Select **Command Prompt Only**.

Exit DOS Programs

Although you can run DOS programs inside windows, DOS program windows do not provide the same fail-safe system you find in Windows program windows. If you click the Close (X) button in the upper-right corner of a Windows program window, Windows prompts you to save any changes you have made to your documents before exiting.

In DOS program windows, the warning is a little less informative. It simply tells you that Windows cannot

automatically shut down the program. It does not remind you to save changes to open documents. If you do not heed the warning, you can close the DOS program from Windows and risk losing changes you have made to documents.

To avoid such risks, you should exit the DOS program using its Quit or Exit command, as shown in the *Guided Tour*.

Guided Tour Exit a DOS Program

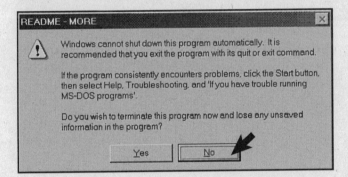

1 If you click the **Close** (X) button in a DOS program window, this warning dialog box may appear. Click the **No** button to cancel and return to the DOS program window.

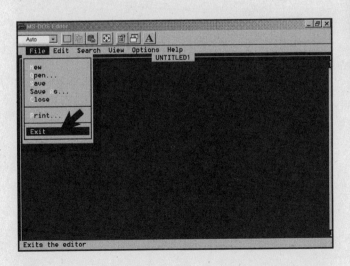

2 To properly exit a DOS program, use the program's **File**, **Exit** or **File**, **Quit** command. The procedure for exiting DOS programs varies, so check the program's documentation.

In many DOS programs, you can press the **Esc** key to display a menu of options that includes the Exit or Quit command.

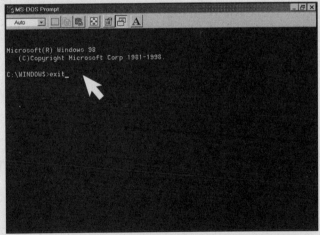

3 After you exit a DOS program, the DOS program window may remain open, displaying the DOS prompt. Type **exit** at the prompt and press **Enter**.

4 Windows closes the DOS program window, and you can continue working in Windows.

HOW TO...

Manage Disks, Folders, and Files

Picture your computer as an office. It has a desktop on which you work, and it is packed with "filing cabinets." In the case of your computer, each disk is a huge filing cabinet containing several drawers and folders in which you store your program and document files.

To stay organized, you need to be able to access your disks, folders, and files; delete and move folders and files; and create new folders to store your files in logical groups. Windows 98 offers two tools to help you stay organized: My Computer and Windows Explorer. In this section, you will learn how to use these important and useful tools.

What You Will Find in This Section

Understand Data Storage

Whenever you install a program or save a document you created, one of your disk drives stores the data magnetically on a disk, in a way similar to that in which a tape recorder stores sounds on a tape. Your system uses *filenames* to identify each program or document file. When you turn your computer off, the files remain intact, and you can later run your program files or open your document files from the disk.

A typical hard disk can store thousands of files. If you stored all your files in one folder on the disk, finding your files later would be nearly impossible. Because of this, your operating system, Windows, allows you to create *folders* on your disks. You can then store related files in assorted folders, making them easy to find and manage.

Understand Folders and Paths

To use folders, you must first understand the way Windows structures the folders. Each disk contains one directory called the *root directory*, which can store files and folders (other directories). You can create folders in the root directory. These folders act as the first level of folders on the hard disk. When you click a disk icon, the names of these folders appear. You can create folders inside these first-level folders to create *subfolders*.

> Because floppy disks typically store few files, you rarely need to use folders to group files on a floppy disk. However, you can create and use folders on floppy disks, just as you can on hard disks.

As you create folders and subfolders, your folder list can become somewhat long. Here's an example of what a typical folder list might look like:

```
C:\
    \Documents
        \Finance
            \Investments
            \Loans
            \Analysis
        \Diary
        \Soccer Notes
        \PTA
```

To open a folder on a disk, you must work through the various layers of folders to access the desired subfolder. You can do this by clicking folders or by entering a *path* to the desired file or folder. A path specifies the location of a file or folder, including the drive letter and a complete list of folders that leads to the specified subfolder or file. For example, the path to the Analysis folder above is as follows:

```
C:\Documents\Finance\Analysis
```

Work with Icons

Windows uses *icons* to identify the various resources on your computer, displaying distinctly different icons for your disks, folders, program files, document files, and shortcuts. Use the following table to identify the icons you encounter.

Windows 98 Icons

Icon	Icon Type	Description
	Hard disk drive	Represents a hard disk. Click the icon to view the contents of the disk.
	Floppy disk drive	Represents a floppy disk drive. Make sure the drive has a formatted disk in it before you click this icon.
	CD-ROM drive	Represents a CD-ROM drive. Make sure the drive has a CD in it before you click this icon.

Icon	Icon Type	Description
📁	Folder	Represents a folder. Click the icon to view the contents of the folder.
🖐	Program	Represents the file that executes a particular program. The appearance of the program icon varies depending on the program. To run the program, click its icon.
📄	Document	Represents a data file, typically a file you have created. The icon looks like a piece of paper with the corner folded over. If Windows "knows" which program was used to create the document, it displays the program's logo on the icon. Otherwise, Windows displays a generic document icon like the one shown here.
🖼	Shortcut	Represents a shortcut that points to a program or document file on your disk. The appearance of the shortcut icon varies depending on the program. Note the arrow in the lower-left corner of the icon. Shortcut icons always display this arrow.

Guided Tour Explore the Disk and Folder Structure

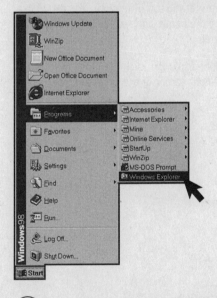

1 To understand the structure of your disks and folders, view the structure in Windows Explorer. Click the **Start** button, point to **Programs**, and click **Windows Explorer**.

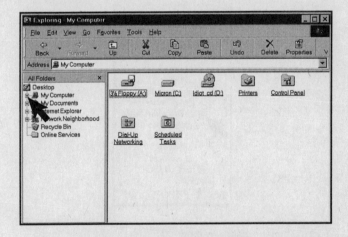

2 The Desktop represents the highest level folder on your computer. My Computer contains icons for your disk drives and folders. If there is a plus sign next to My Computer, click the plus sign to view the contents of My Computer.

Windows displays the plus (+) and minus (–) symbols next to disk and folder icons so you can quickly expand and collapse folder lists. When you click the plus sign next to a folder, the icon changes to show an open folder, the folder's subfolders appear below it, and the plus sign is replaced by a minus sign. You can then click the minus sign to collapse the list.

(continues)

Guided Tour   Explore the Disk and Folder Structure   *(continued)*

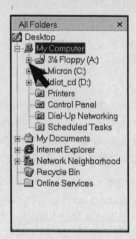

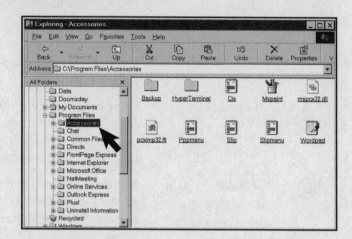

3 If your disk icon has a plus sign next to it, click the plus sign to view a list of folders on the disk.

5 To view the contents of a folder, click the folder's name. The right pane displays the files and folders in the selected folder.

6 As you can see, the folder list now looks like a family tree, with the drive letter at the top of the tree. You can hide a list of folders by clicking the minus sign next to the folder or disk icon at the top of the tree.

7 When you are done exploring, click the **Close** (X) button in the upper-right corner of the Windows Explorer window.

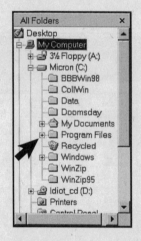

4 The list expands to show the first level of folders on the disk. To view the folders in a particular folder, click the plus sign next to the folder's icon.

Work in Web View

If you have worked with file management tools in previous versions of Windows, you are accustomed to double-clicking disk and folder icons to display their contents and clicking folders and files to select them.

Windows 98 has revamped its desktop, My Computer, and Windows Explorer so that it acts more like a Web page. ▶You will learn more about the Web in "Use Windows 98 on the World Wide Web" on page 217.◀ To successfully navigate My Computer, Windows Explorer, and your Windows desktop, however, you must know the basics of Windows 98's new Web View, and you must make sure Web View is turned on.

In Web View, you no longer click an icon to select it. Instead, you simply point to the icon. To access a drive, open a folder or file, or run a program, you no longer need to double-click; instead, you point to the desired icon and click once. If this is your first encounter with Windows, you should pick up these techniques fairly quickly. However, if you are accustomed to working in previous versions of Windows, you may have to shed your old habits and learn new techniques.

Because the remaining instructions in this section assume you have Web View turned on, take the *Guided Tour* to make sure that it is on and to change any additional Web View settings.

Guided Tour Turn On Web View

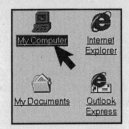

1 Click or double-click **My Computer** on the Windows desktop. If My Computer runs with a single click, Web View is on.

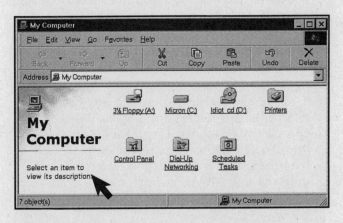

2 The My Computer window appears. If Web View is on, a vertical listing containing information about the window appears on the left side of the window (as shown above).

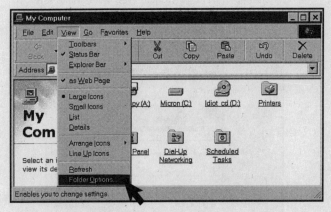

3 Open the **View** menu and select **Folder Options**.

(continues)

Guided Tour Turn On Web View *(continued)*

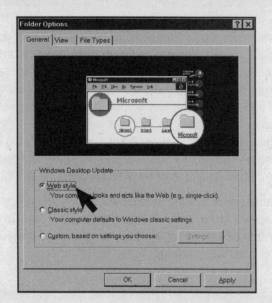

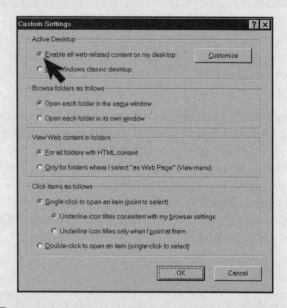

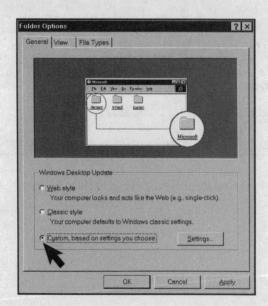

4 The Folder Options dialog box appears, displaying the General tab in front. To work in Web View, make sure **Web Style** is selected. To use My Computer as you did in Windows 95, select **Classic Style**.

5 To change any additional settings, click **Custom Based on Settings You Choose**, and then click the **Settings** button.

6 The Custom Settings dialog box appears. Under Active Desktop, make sure **Enable All Web-Related Content on My Desktop** is turned on so you will have single-click access to desktop icons.

7 Under Browse Folders as Follows, select **Open Each Folder in the Same Window**. If you select **Open Each Folder in Its Own Window**, Windows 98 opens a new window for each drive or folder you select—which can quickly clutter your screen.

8 In the View Web Content in Folders area, choose **For All Folders with HTML Content**.

9 Under Click Items as Follows, choose **Single-Click to Open an Item (Point to Select)**. (The instructions in this section assume this option is on.)

10 Click **OK** to save your changes.

If you simply cannot get used to pointing to select files and folders and single-clicking to open them, change to Classic View. If you do that, however, when you're working through the instructions in this section, you must single-click when you're instructed to point and double-click when you're instructed to click.

Navigate My Computer

Windows provides two tools for managing your folders and files: My Computer and Windows Explorer. My Computer provides quick access to your disks and folders, displaying icons for all the disks on your computer. Windows Explorer, ►described in "Navigate Windows Explorer" on page 87◄, is a better tool for copying and moving files and managing your folders.

When you click the My Computer icon, a window appears, displaying icons for all the disks on your computer, plus icons for system management tools you

might frequently access, including the Windows Control Panel and Printers. To view the contents of a disk, you simply click its icon. You can then click a folder icon to display the folder's contents, or you can click a file icon to run a program, open a document, or use a utility in the Control Panel.

The following *Guided Tour* introduces you to My Computer and shows you how to navigate your disks and folders. Detailed instructions on how to copy, move, and rename folders and files are provided later in this section.

Guided Tour   View Disk and Folder Contents in My Computer

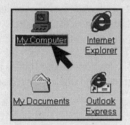

1 Click the **My Computer** icon (it's usually in the upper-left corner of the desktop).

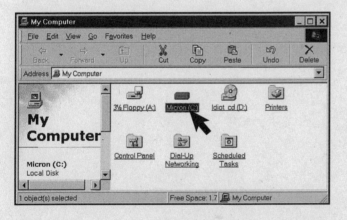

2 The My Computer window appears, displaying icons for your floppy drive (if present), hard disk drive(s), CD-ROM drive (if present), Control Panel, Printers, Scheduled Tasks, and Dial-Up Networking. To view the contents of a disk, click its icon.

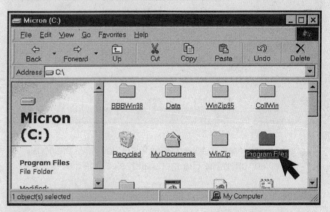

3 My Computer displays the first level of folders on the disk and any files stored in the root directory of the disk. To display the contents of a folder, click its icon.

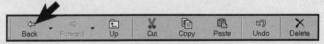

4 As you move through folders, the Back button becomes active. Click the **Back** button to back up to the previous folder or disk or all the way back to the initial display.

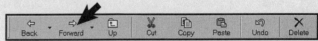

5 After you back up for the first time, the Forward button becomes active. Click **Forward** to move ahead to the next folder. You can use the Forward button to move ahead only to folders you have previously opened.

(continues)

Guided Tour View Disk and Folder Contents in My Computer *(continued)*

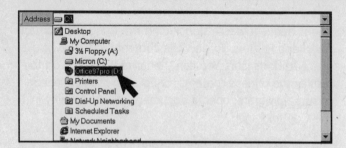

6 To quickly change to a different disk or folder, open the **Address** drop-down list and select the desired disk or folder.

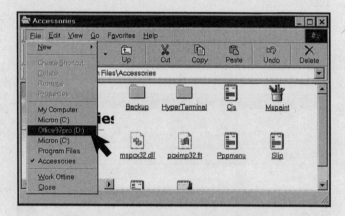

7 To quickly return to a disk or folder you have previously viewed, open the **File** menu and select the disk or folder.

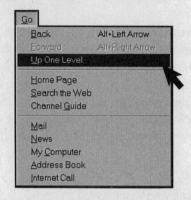

8 The Go menu contains the Back and Forward commands along with the Up One Level command. To move up to the previous level in the folder list, open the **Go** menu and select **Up One Level**.

9 The menus in My Computer contain many commands for accessing Internet features. ▶You can learn more about these options in "Master the Active Desktop," starting on page 301.◀ For now, ignore these options.

10 When you finish exploring your folders and files, click the **Close** (X) button in the upper-right corner of the My Computer window.

Navigate Windows Explorer

Windows Explorer is a more advanced folder- and file-management tool than My Computer. It displays a window consisting of two panes. The left pane displays a list of disks and folders on your computer. The right pane displays the contents of the selected folder. You can click disk and folder icons, just as you can in My Computer, to display the contents of a disk or folder. In addition, you can drag folders and files from one pane to another to quickly copy or move them to other folders or disks.

If you worked with Windows Explorer (or My Computer) in Windows 95, the biggest improvement you will notice is that the toolbar is different. To make your computer as easy to navigate as the World Wide Web, Microsoft redesigned the toolbar by adding a Back and Forward button that allows you to quickly back up to

the previous folder or disk. The toolbar also contains an Address text box/drop-down list into which you can type the path to a folder. You can also use Windows Explorer to open and display Web pages (➤see "Navigate the Web with Windows Explorer" on page 306◀).

The steps you take to display the contents of disks and folders in Windows Explorer differ quite a bit from the steps you take in My Computer. To help you see the differences, the following *Guided Tour* shows you the basics of using Windows Explorer to access the disks, folders, and other resources on your system.

> If you are moving up from Windows 3.x to Windows 98, you will find that Windows Explorer is very similar to File Manager.

Guided Tour View Disk and Folder Contents in Windows Explorer

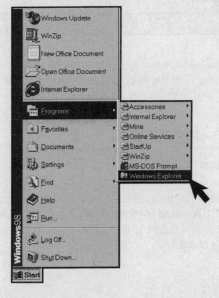

1 To run Windows Explorer, click the **Start** button, point to **Programs**, and click **Windows Explorer**.

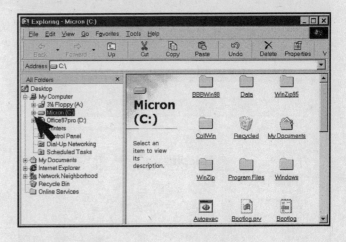

2 The folder list on the left displays icons for all the disks and folders on your system. To display the folders on a disk or the subfolders inside another folder, click the plus sign next to the disk's or folder's icon.

(continues)

Guided Tour View Disk and Folder Contents in Windows Explorer

(continued)

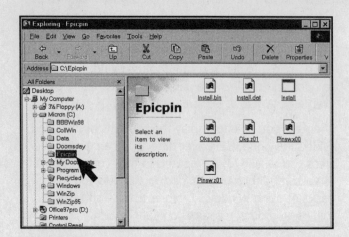

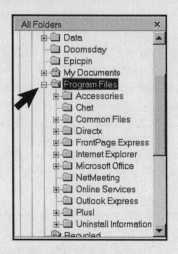

3 Windows Explorer expands the folder list, displaying the folders on the disk or subfolders in the selected folder. To display the contents of a folder, click its name.

> When an item is highlighted in the left pane, you can use the up or down arrow key to move the highlight over a different disk or folder icon. The contents of the selected disk or folder are displayed in the right pane.

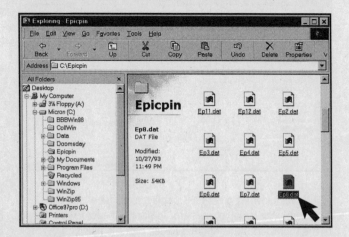

4 When you click a folder, the folder's contents appear in the right pane. You can click a folder in the right pane to open it, or you can click a file icon to run a program or open a document.

5 To stop displaying the folders on a disk or the subfolders in a folder, click the minus sign next to the drive or folder icon. This collapses the list so you can work with other folders.

6 Windows Explorer hides the folders and displays a plus sign next to the drive or folder icon, indicating that the folder list has been collapsed.

7 As you move through folders, the Back button becomes active. Click the **Back** button to back up to the previous folder or disk or all the way back to the initial display.

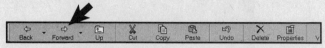

8 When you back up, the Forward button becomes active. Click **Forward** to move ahead to the next folder. You can use the Forward button to move ahead only to folders you have previously opened.

> ## Guided Tour View Disk and Folder Contents in Windows Explorer

9 To quickly change to a different disk or folder, open the **Address** drop-down list and select the desired disk or folder.

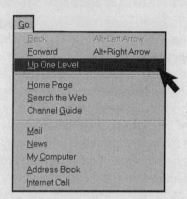

11 The Go menu contains the Back and Forward commands along with the Up One Level command. To move up to a previous level in the folder list, open the **Go** menu and select **Up One Level**.

12 When you finish experimenting in Explorer, click the **Close** (X) button in the upper-right corner of the window.

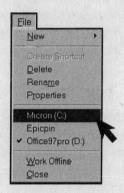

10 To quickly return to a disk or folder you have previously viewed, open the **File** menu and select the disk or folder.

Control Folder and File Views

My Computer and Windows Explorer initially list files alphabetically by name, so you can find a file if you know its name. My Computer displays large icons for files, and Windows Explorer displays small icons. Although this is usually the most useful way to organize files, you can change the way files are displayed to make them more manageable. For example, you might want to list files by type in order to keep program and document files separate. You might also want to display small icons to fit more filenames on the screen.

The View menu contains the following options for controlling the way files are displayed:

- **Large Icons** displays big icons, which are useful indicators of file types.

- **Small Icons** displays tiny icons, displaying more filenames in the window. In this view, files are listed in several newspaper-like columns. If you drag a selection box around the files, the selection snakes from the bottom of the left column to the top of the right column. You cannot select a rectangular group of files.

- **List** displays tiny icons but arranges the icons in tabular columns. You can drag a selection box around a rectangular group of files.

- **Details** displays tiny icons and information about each file, including its size and the date on which it was created. Details view is most useful when you need information about a file.

The View, Arrange Icons menu contains additional options for positioning the icons:

- **By Name** arranges the file list in alphabetical order, displaying folder names first.

- **By Type** arranges the file list in alphabetical order according to filename extension. For example, a file named letter.doc will appear before a file named letter.xls. Folder names appear first. ▶See "Configure My Computer or Windows Explorer" on page 90 for details about hiding and displaying filename extensions.◀

- **By Size** displays small files first, followed by larger files.

- **By Date** displays the most recently modified files first.

- **Auto Arrange** is a check mark option that tells My Computer or Windows Explorer to automatically rearrange the file list whenever you insert or move a file. This option is especially useful in Large Icons view, where icons can overlap if you move one icon on top of another.

The View, Line Up Icons option arranges the icons in columns and rows without changing their relative positions in the list. The *Guided Tour* lets you experiment with the various views to see how they affect the way folders and files are displayed.

Use the Toolbar

The Standard toolbar at the top of My Computer and Windows Explorer contains several controls for changing file views, navigating your folders, and copying, moving, and deleting files. The following table provides descriptions for these controls.

Configure My Computer or Windows Explorer

In addition to changing the appearance and arrangement of the file list, you can use the View, Folder Options command to display a dialog box for additional configuration options. The Folder Options dialog box has the following three tabs:

- **General** lets you turn Web View on or off. In Web View, you can open folders, run programs, and open documents with a single mouse click. ▶See "Work in Web View" on page 83 for details.◀

- **View** provides options for making all your folders look alike, displaying or hiding system files, displaying the path in the title bar, and hiding filename extensions for known file types. By default, filename extensions are hidden, and you can tell what kind of file you are dealing with by looking at its icon.

Standard Toolbar Controls

Icon	Control Name	Purpose
Micron (C:)	Address	Lists all the disks and folders on your computer. Use the Address list to quickly change to a disk or move back up the folder list.
	Back	Displays the previously opened disk or folder. This button doubles as a drop-down list, which displays a brief history of disks and files you recently opened. (Click the downward-pointing arrow on the right side of the button to display the list.)
	Forward	Moves ahead to a disk or folder you've already viewed after you've clicked the Back button to back up. This button also doubles as a drop-down list.
	Up	Moves up one level in the folder list. For example, if you open the \Data\Letters folder, clicking Up will display the contents of the \Data folder.
	Cut	Removes the selected folder or file from its current location, allowing you to paste it in a different folder.
	Copy	Creates a copy of the selected folder or file so you can paste it on another disk or into another folder.
	Paste	Inserts the cut or copied file(s) or folder(s) onto the currently active disk or into the active folder.
	Undo	Reverses the previous action. This option is useful if you delete a file or folder by mistake.
	Delete	Moves the currently selected file(s) or folder(s) to the Recycle Bin.
	Properties	Displays information and settings for the selected disk, file, or folder.
	Views	Opens a drop-down menu offering the same options you find on the View menu: Large Icons, Small Icons, List, and Details.

It's a good idea to keep system files hidden so you do not accidentally delete them.

- **File Types** displays a list of document file types that are associated with programs on your computer. When a document file type is *associated*

with a program, you can open the document file by clicking on it. Windows runs the associated program, which then opens the document.

The *Guided Tour* shows you how to access the Options dialog box and change some common settings.

Guided Tour Control the File and Folder Display

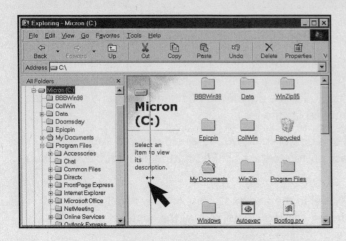

1 In Windows Explorer, you can drag the vertical bar that separates the left and right panes to change their relative sizes.

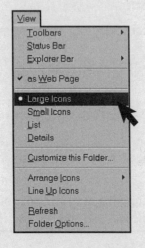

2 To view large icons in Windows Explorer or My Computer, open the **View** menu and select **Large Icons**.

3 In Windows Explorer, large icons appear in the right pane (as shown in this figure). In My Computer, all the icons in the window appear large. To return to the small icon display, open the **View** menu and select **Small Icons**.

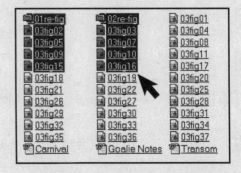

4 In Small Icons view, folders are displayed at the top of the window, followed by files. You can drag a selection box around a rectangular group of files or folders.

5 To change to List view, open the **View** menu and select **List**.

Guided Tour Control the File and Folder Display

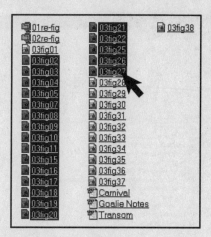

6 In List view, folders appear at the top of the left column, and folders and files are arranged in newspaper-like columns. If you drag a selection box around folders or files, the selection extends from the bottom of one column to the top of the next.

7 To view information about your files, open the **View** menu and select **Details**.

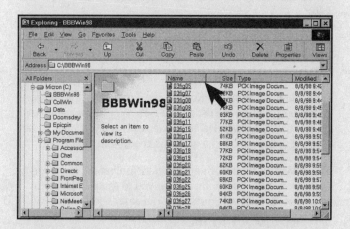

8 Details view displays not only the file's name but also its size, its type, and the date it was last modified. You can drag the lines that separate the column headings, as shown here, to resize the columns.

In Details view, you can sort files by clicking the desired column heading above the file list. For example, to list files by date, click the **Modified** heading. Clicking the heading again reverses the sort order; for example, if the most recently modified files are listed first, clicking **Modified** again lists the most recently modified files last.

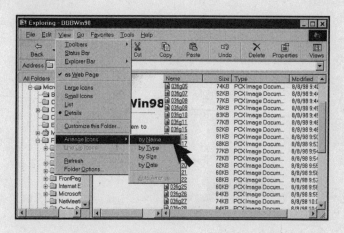

9 To specify the way My Computer or Windows Explorer sorts the folders and files, open the **View** menu, point to **Arrange Icons**, and select **By Name**, **By Type**, **By Size**, or **By Date**.

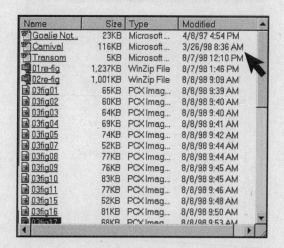

10 The figure above shows files and folders arranged by date in Details view. You can cycle through the various views (Large Icons, Small Icons, and so on) by clicking the **Views** button in the toolbar. Or you can click the arrow to the right of the Views button to select the desired view from a menu.

If text labels are turned on, the toolbar in My Computer and Windows Explorer might not display all the buttons. To display all the buttons, open the **View** menu, point to **Toolbar**, and select **Text Labels**. This turns text labels off. After that, if you're not sure what a button does, point to it to display a pop-up label with the button's name.

Guided Tour Configure My Computer or Windows Explorer

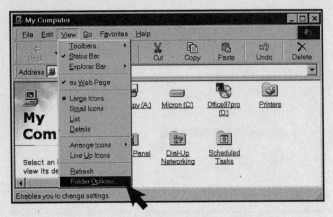

1 In My Computer, open the **View** menu and select **Folder Options**. (You can select the same option in Windows Explorer.)

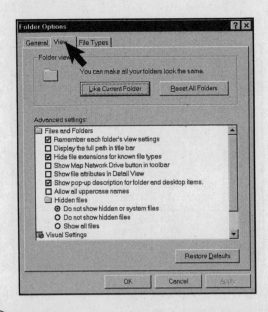

2 The Folder Options dialog box in My Computer has three tabs. The General tab allows you to turn on Web View (Web Style). ▶See "Work in Web View" on page 83 for details.◀ Click the **View** tab.

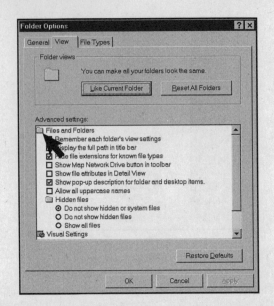

3 In the Advanced Settings box, select the desired options under Files and Folders:

Remember Each Folder's View Settings tells Windows to use the selected view settings for each folder each time you open the folder.

Display the Full Path in Title Bar displays the path (the location and name of the selected folder or file) in the window's title bar.

Hide File Extensions for Known File Types hides the last three characters following the period in a file's name. If you are accustomed to working with filename extensions and you want to see them, click this option to remove the check from its box.

Show Map Network Drive Button in Toolbar displays a special button in the toolbar that allows you to assign a drive letter to a network drive or folder so you can easily select it in My Computer or Windows Explorer.

Show File Attributes in Detail View displays file attributes (indicating if files are marked as System, Hidden, or Read-Only files) when you turn on Details view. ▶See "View Disk, Folder, and File Properties" on page 121 for details about file attributes.◀

Show Pop-Up Description for Folder and Desktop Items displays a brief description of the selected object on the Windows desktop or in My Computer or Windows Explorer when you point to the object.

Allow All Uppercase Names allows you to use all uppercase characters to name folders and files. By default, Windows uses a mix of upper- and lowercase characters.

Guided Tour Configure My Computer or Windows Explorer

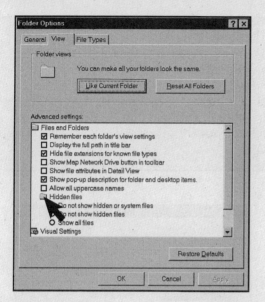

④ In the Advanced Settings box, select one of the following options under Hidden Files: **Do Not Show Hidden or System Files** (the default setting), **Do Not Show Hidden Files**, or **Show All Files**.

> If you choose to show all files, be careful when deleting files. If you delete a system file, you might disable Windows and make it impossible to start your computer.

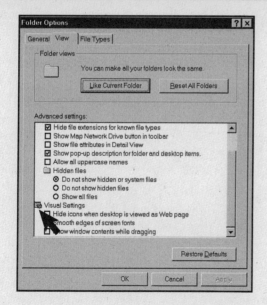

⑤ In the Advanced Settings box, choose any of the following options under Visual Settings:

Hide Icons When Desktop Is Viewed as a Web Page hides shortcut icons when View as Web Page is turned on. Windows displays only the name of each icon, and it's underlined to indicate that it is a link.

Smooth Edges of Screen Fonts makes the characters look more finished, but it might slow down your system slightly.

Show Window Contents While Dragging displays the window and its contents as you drag it. If you turn this option off, as you drag the window, only an outline of the window moves; when you release the mouse button, the window moves to where the outline is.

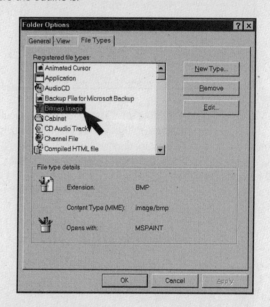

⑥ Click the **File Types** tab. The Registered File Types list displays document file types that are associated with programs on your computer.

> When you install a program, it registers itself with Windows to create a file association with the document file types you use the program to create. You rarely, if ever, have to edit file types, unless you prefer to use a particular program to open a certain type of file. When you install Windows 98 and anytime you install a new program, the installation could change some of your file associations. ►See "Create and Edit File Associations" on page 125 for details.◄

(continues)

Guided Tour Configure My Computer or Windows Explorer

(continued)

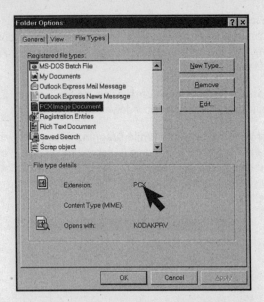

MIME stands for Multipurpose Internet Mail Extension, a standard for transferring files over Internet connections. Windows uses the MIME type for the same purpose it uses file-name extensions: to determine which program to use to open a file of a particular type. MIME types are specified for relatively few file types.

7 To determine which program is associated to a particular file type, click a file type in the list. The File Type Details box (near the bottom of the tab) displays the document file's extension, the name of the associated program, and the file's MIME type (if applicable).

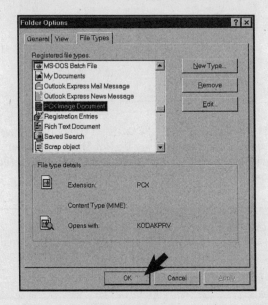

8 When you finish exploring the various options and making your desired changes, click **OK**.

Select Files and Folders

Before you can start copying, moving, renaming, or deleting folders and files, you must learn the various techniques for selecting files and folders. Selecting an individual item is easy: You point to it. However, you can use several less-intuitive techniques for selecting multiple files. The following table lists these techniques, and the *Guided Tour* provides some hands-on training.

> If you selected Classic Style or turned off single-click access, you must use **Ctrl+***click* or **Shift+***click* to select multiple files or folders instead of using **Ctrl+***point* or **Shift+***point*.

Techniques for Selecting Multiple Files or Folders

Technique	Description
Edit, **Select All** or **Ctrl+A**	To select all files displayed in the window, open the **Edit** menu and choose **Select All** or press **Ctrl+A**.
Shift+*point*	To select adjacent files or folders, point to the first item, and then hold down the **Shift** key and point to the last item in the group.
Ctrl+*point*	To select nonadjacent files or folders, point to the first item, and then hold down the **Ctrl** key and point to each additional item. You can also use **Ctrl+***point* to deselect files.
Drag	To select adjacent files, move the mouse pointer to the outside corner of a file, press and hold down the mouse button, and then drag. A selection box appears as you drag. Any files or folders inside the box are highlighted.
Edit, **Invert Selection**	Select the files you do not want to work with, and then open the **Edit** menu and choose **Invert Selection**. The selected files become deselected, and the unselected files become highlighted.

Guided Tour Select Folders and Files

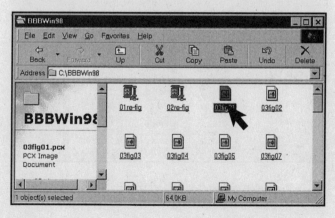

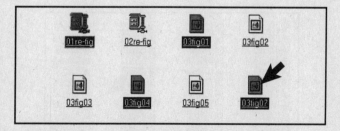

2 To select additional nonadjacent folders or files, hold down the **Ctrl** key and point to their names or icons.

(continues)

 To select a single folder or file, point to its name or icon.

Guided Tour   Select Folders and Files   *(continued)*

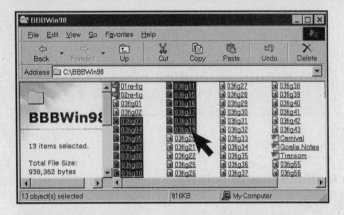

3 To select a group of adjacent files, point to the first file in the group, and then hold down the **Shift** key and point to the last file. The figure above illustrates this technique in List view. Note that the selection continues from the bottom of one column to the top of the next.

4 The figure above shows the **Shift**+*point* technique used in Small Icons view. Note that the selection consists of a rectangular group of files.

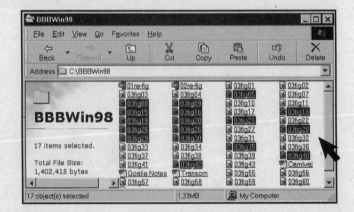

5 You can drag a selection box around the desired files. First position the mouse pointer slightly above and to the left or below and to the right of the first file you want to select.

6 Hold down the left mouse button and drag to the opposite corner until all of the desired files and folders are highlighted. Then release the mouse button.

7 If you need to select most of the files but they're non-adjacent, select those files you *do not* want to work with and then open the **Edit** menu and select **Invert Selection**. The selected files become unselected, and all other files become selected.

8 To deselect all selected files, click a blank area inside the window where the files and folders are displayed.

Create, Rename, and Move Folders

As you learned earlier in this section, it is important to store your files in folders to organize them and make them more manageable. Your hard disk already has several folders that are created and used by Windows 98, including \Windows, \Program Files, and \Accessories. In addition, whenever you install a program, it typically creates its own folder or collection of folders and uses those folders for storing its program files.

To organize and manage the document files you create, you need to create and use your own folders and subfolders. These folders serve a dual purpose: They keep your documents separate from the many program files already on your disk, and they store your files in logical groups to make them easy to find later. For example, you might create a folder called \Data that contains

subfolders such as \Finances, \Resumes, \Evaluations, and \Diary. These folders might contain subfolders that further subdivide your files into groups.

In order to take control of your files, you must know the basic steps required to create, move, and rename folders. The following *Guided Tour* leads you step by step through these important tasks.

> Be careful about deleting, renaming, and moving program folders. Windows and most programs store files in specific folders that the programs require to function properly. Deleting, renaming, or moving a program folder or file might incapacitate the program.

Guided Tour   Create a Folder

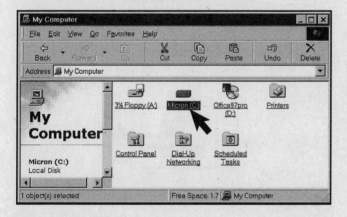

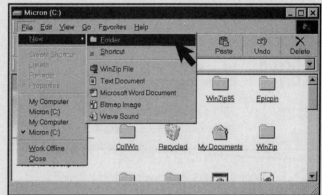

1 Open the drive or folder in which you want the new folder placed. For example, to create a new folder on the first folder level on drive C, click the icon for drive C, as shown above.

2 Open the **File** menu, point to **New**, and click **Folder**.

(continues)

Guided Tour Create a Folder

(continued)

3 A new folder named "New Folder" appears at the end of the file list.

4 Type the desired name for the folder (up to 255 characters, including spaces) and press **Enter**. When you type the first character "New Folder" is deleted and is replaced by the name you type. After you press Enter, the newly named folder appears.

Another way to create a new folder is to right-click a blank area inside the window, point to **New**, and select **Folder**.

Guided Tour Rename a Folder

1 To change a folder's name, right-click its icon and select **Rename**.

3 When you type the first character, the original name is deleted and is replaced by the new name you type.

4 Press **Enter**, and the folder icon appears with its new name.

2 A box appears around the folder's name, and the name appears highlighted. Start typing the new name.

Guided Tour Move Folders in Windows Explorer

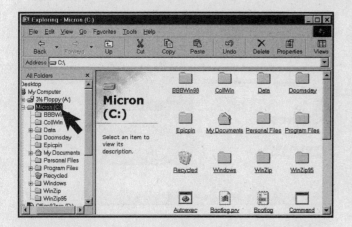

1 Windows Explorer is a great tool for moving folders. In the left pane, display the icon for the drive or folder to which you want to move one or more folders.

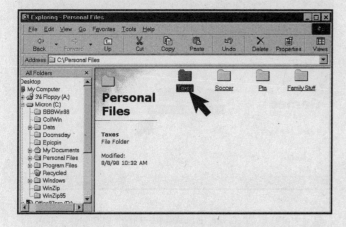

2 In the right pane, display the icon(s) for the folder(s) you want to move and select the folder(s).

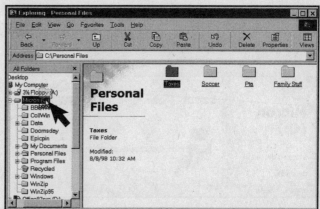

3 Position the mouse pointer over one of the selected folders, press and hold down the left mouse button, and then drag the folder over to the icon for the destination disk or folder (in the left pane). Release the mouse button when the desired destination disk or folder is highlighted.

> If you are moving folders to another folder on the same disk, you can simply drag one of the selected folders. To move folders to a different disk, hold down the **Shift** key and drag. Otherwise, Windows will copy the folders instead of moving them.

4 The folder(s) disappear from the right pane. Click the plus sign (+) next to the destination disk or folder (if needed). As you can see, the folders now appear on the destination disk or within the destination folder.

Guided Tour Move Folders with My Computer

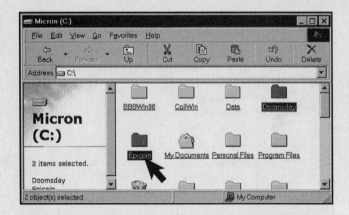

1 Because My Computer does not have two panes, you must use the Cut and Paste commands to move folders. Select the icon(s) for the folder(s) you want to move.

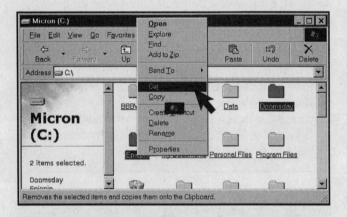

2 Right-click one of the selected icons and choose **Cut**. The icons appear transparent to indicate that they have been cut.

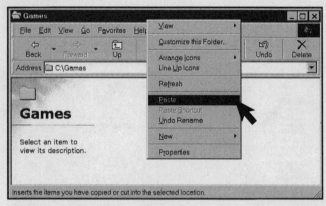

3 Change to the disk or folder into which you want the cut folder(s) moved. Then right-click a blank area inside the window and select **Paste**.

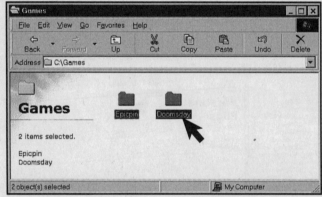

4 The cut folders are removed from their original location and are placed on the destination disk or in the destination folder.

You can display two My Computer windows, one that displays the contents of the destination disk or folder and another that displays the icon(s) for the folder(s) you want to move. You can then drag the folder icons into the destination window.

Copy, Move, and Rename Files

In your real office, you frequently copy documents you want to distribute or modify, and in many cases you probably keep backup copies in case the original documents are lost or destroyed. You might also move a paper document from one folder to another to reorganize your documents, or you might rename documents to make them easier to find and distinguish from other documents.

You can perform similar tasks with your digital files. For example, you can copy files to a floppy disk to share them with friends or colleagues, copy files so you can modify the copies without changing the originals, move files from one folder to another to reorganize them, or even give your files new names to make them easier to identify.

As the *Guided Tour* shows, the best tool to use for copying and moving files is Windows Explorer. Using its two-paned window, you can easily drag selected files

from the right pane to a disk or folder displayed in the left pane. If you prefer to use My Computer, you can drag and drop files by opening two My Computer windows, or you can use the Cut, Copy, and Paste commands.

The following *Guided Tour* leads you through these standard file-maintenance tasks so you can have more control over the files on your computer.

> Be careful when copying or moving files. If the destination disk or folder already contains a file with a name matching a file that you are copying or moving to it, Windows displays a warning asking if you want to replace the existing file with the file you're copying or moving. You might want to cancel the operation and rename one of the files before proceeding.

Guided Tour   Move Files

1 In Windows Explorer's right pane, select the files you want to move.

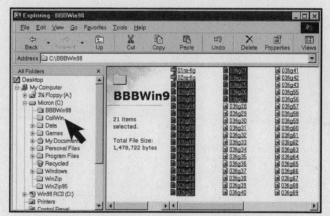

2 In the left pane, display the icon for the disk or folder to which you want to move the files. Do not click the disk or folder icon; doing so will change the contents of the right pane.

(continues)

Guided Tour Move Files

(continued)

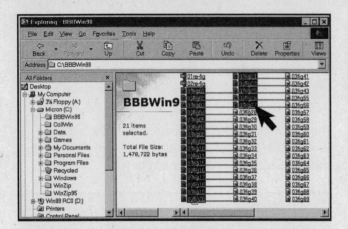

3 Point to one of the selected files in the right pane and press and hold down the left mouse button. (To move the files to a different disk, hold down the **Shift** key; otherwise, Windows Explorer assumes that you want to copy the files.)

4 Drag the files over to the icon for the destination disk or folder displayed in the left pane. When the correct destination icon is highlighted, release the mouse button. Windows Explorer moves the files.

As you drag files or folders, Windows displays a plus sign (+) next to the mouse pointer to indicate when you are copying files. No plus sign appears when you are moving files.

If the folder list in the left pane is collapsed, and you cannot see the destination folder, rest the mouse pointer on a disk or folder icon that has a plus sign next to it to expand the folder list. Expand the list as needed until you see the destination folder, and then drop the files in it. (This works only when you are moving or copying files.)

Guided Tour Copy Files

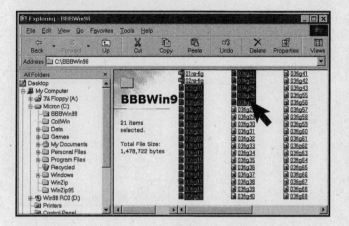

1 In Windows Explorer's right pane, select the files you want to copy.

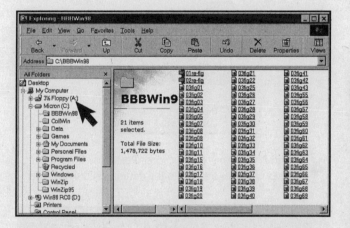

2 In the left pane, display the icon for the disk or folder to which you want to copy the files. Do not click the disk or folder icon; doing so will change the contents of the right pane.

3 Point to one of the selected files in the right pane and press and hold down the left mouse button. (To copy the files to a folder on the same disk, hold down the **Ctrl** key; otherwise, Windows Explorer assumes that you want to move the files.)

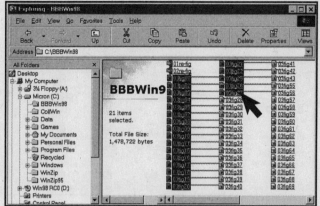

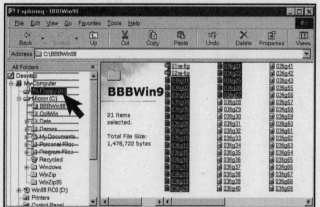

4 Drag the files over the icon for the destination disk or folder displayed in the left pane. When the correct destination icon is highlighted, release the mouse button. Windows Explorer copies the selected files to the destination disk or folder.

Guided Tour Copy and Move Files with My Computer

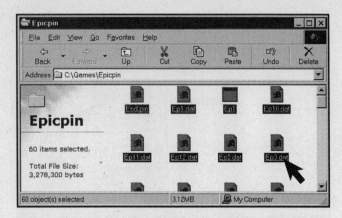

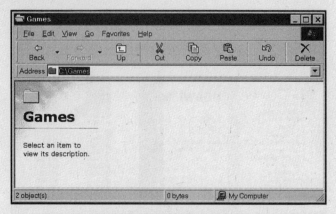

1 To copy or move files with My Computer, first select the files you want to copy or move.

3 Change to the drive and open the folder in which you want to paste the files.

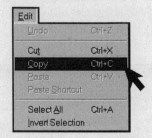

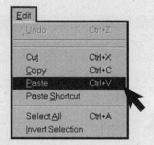

2 Open the **Edit** menu and choose **Cut** (to move the files) or **Copy** (to copy the files). If you cut the files, ghost images of the files appear. (If you don't paste the files the ghosts will remain.)

4 Open the **Edit** menu and choose **Paste**. My Computer copies or moves the files to the destination disk or folder.

You can cut files by pressing **Ctrl+X** or copy them by pressing **Ctrl+C**. You can also right-click a selected file and choose **Cut** or **Copy** from the context menu. To paste files, press **Ctrl+V**, or right-click a blank area in the window and choose **Paste**. These shortcuts work in both Windows Explorer and My Computer and in most Windows programs.

Guided Tour   Rename Files

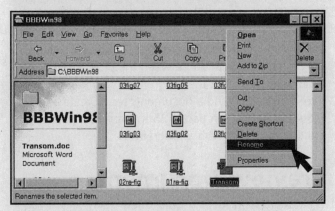

3 When you type the first character, the original name is deleted and is replaced by the new name you type.

4 Press **Enter**, and the file icon appears with its new name.

1 To change a file's name, right-click its icon and select **Rename**.

2 A box appears around the file's name, and the name appears highlighted. Start typing the new name.

Run Programs and Open Documents

Although you can run a program by clicking its shortcut or selecting it from the Start menu and you can open documents using the program's File, Open command, sometimes it is more convenient to run programs and open documents from My Computer or Windows Explorer. For example, if you're not sure where you stored a document, you can browse for it in Windows Explorer and then quickly open it by clicking its icon.

The *Guided Tour* shows you how to run programs and open documents from My Computer and Windows Explorer.

Understand File Associations

When you choose to open a document from My Computer or Windows Explorer, Windows automatically runs the program associated with the selected document type, and then the program opens the document. When you install a program, it typically sets up the required association between the program and the document types that the program can handle. ►If you have trouble opening a document, see "Create and Edit File Associations" on page 125 to learn how to associate the document with a program.◄

Preview Documents

Windows also includes a Quick View utility, which you can use to preview the contents of a document. Quick View is useful when you are organizing files on your hard drive and are unsure about the contents of a file. It also helps you determine what a document contains before you choose to open it. This can really be a time-saver because you can open the correct document on the first try instead of having to open several to find the one you want. The *Guided Tour* shows you how to preview documents with Quick View.

Guided Tour Run a Program

1 In My Computer or Windows Explorer, change to the appropriate disk and open the folder that contains the program files for the program you want to run.

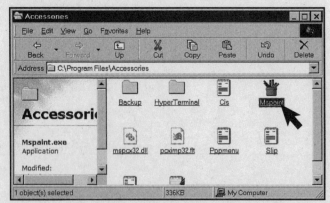

2 Click the icon for the file that executes the program. (Program icons typically appear as colorful pictures. Document icons appear as a piece of paper with a corner folded over.) Windows runs the program and displays its window.

Guided Tour Preview a Document with Quick View

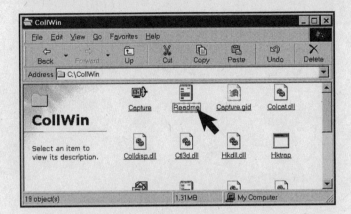

1 Display the icon for the document file you want to preview. The icon might be on the Windows desktop, or it might be displayed in My Computer or Windows Explorer.

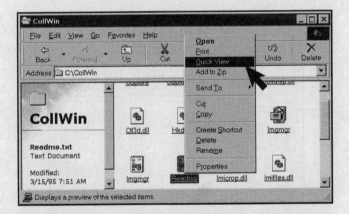

2 Right-click the icon and select **Quick View**. If Quick View is not on the context menu, Windows has no viewer for the selected file type. (To view a graphic file, right-click it and choose **Preview**.)

Quick View is not installed during a typical Windows installation. To install it, open the **Control Panel**, run **Add/Remove Programs**, click the **Windows Setup** tab, double-click **Accessories**, and click the check box next to **Quick View**. Then click **OK** to return to the Add/Remove Programs Properties dialog box, click **OK** to close the dialog box, and follow the onscreen instructions.

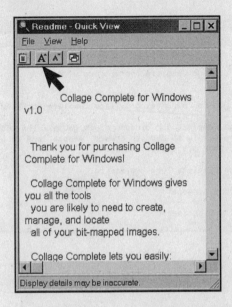

3 The document appears in the Quick View window. You can click the **Increase Font Size** or **Decrease Font Size** button to enlarge or shrink the displayed type size.

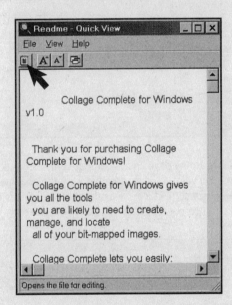

4 To open the document in its associated program, click the **Open File for Editing** button.

(continues)

Guided Tour Preview a Document with Quick View

(continued)

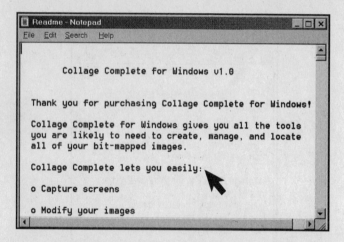

5 Quick View opens the program associated with this document file type, and the program opens the document.

6 To close the Quick View window, click its **Close** (X) button.

Guided Tour Open a Document

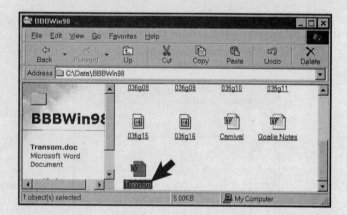

1 Change to the drive and folder that contains the document you want to open, and then click the document's name or icon. (Document icons typically appear as sheets of paper with one corner folded over.)

3 If the document's file type is not associated with a program, Windows displays the Open With dialog box. ▶See "Create and Edit File Associations" on page 125 for details on how to proceed.◀

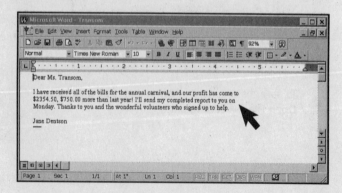

2 If the document's file type is associated with a specific program, Windows runs the program, and the program opens and displays the document.

Find Files and Folders

In a perfect world, people would be careful about organizing their documents in folders and giving document files logical names. However, the world is less than perfect, and most of us are too busy to arrange our files neatly in folders. Shortly after we save files, we forget their names and where we stored them.

Fortunately, Windows has a search tool that you can use to track down your files and folders by searching for their names or contents. You simply enter a portion of the file or folder name, and Windows presents a dialog box listing all the files and folders that match your entry. You can choose to search in a particular folder, in all the folders on a disk, or in all the folders on all disks.

You can initiate a search in three ways: by selecting **Find**, **Files or Folders** from the Windows **Start** menu, by selecting **Tools**, **Find**, **Files or Folders** in Windows Explorer, or by selecting **File**, **Find** in My Computer. The *Guided Tour* shows you how to initiate a search from the Start menu.

Search for Partial Names

If you know the name of a file, finding the file is easy. You simply enter the file's complete name to find an exact match. However, if you've given a file a long name, you might remember only a portion of the name. In such a case, you can enter the part you remember. Windows will find all the files with names that contain the specified string of characters.

In addition, you can use *wild cards* in your search. A wild card is a character that stands in for one or more characters you cannot remember. You can use two wild cards: the asterisk (*) and the question mark (?). The asterisk represents any group of successive characters. For example, to find all files whose names end with "Notes" you might enter the search string "*notes." Windows would then find files with names such as

Soccer Notes.doc, Financial Notes.txt, and Mynotes.wpf. The question mark wild card stands in for one individual character. For example, if you searched for "??notes," Windows would find Mynotes.wpf but would skip Soccer Notes.doc and Financial Notes.txt.

The *Guided Tour* shows a couple examples of wild cards used in a search.

> To find files of a particular type, enter the file-name extension. For example, to find all files with the .DOC extension, enter ***.doc** as your search string.

Search File Contents

If you have completely forgotten the name you gave one of your documents, the search tool can help you locate the file based on its contents. To find a file, you can type a portion of the file's name as explained earlier, or you can leave the File Name text box blank. You then type one or two unique words that are contained in the document. For example, to find a file that contains information about your mutual funds, you might search for "mutual fund." Windows then searches the contents of the files in the specified folder or drive, looking for the word or phrase you typed. The *Guided Tour* shows you how to search for files by their contents.

> Although you can search the contents of a file for a particular string of text, any text in a picture (graphic file) is not stored as text in the file. In other words, don't bother searching the contents of graphic files for text.

Guided Tour Search for Files and Folders by Name

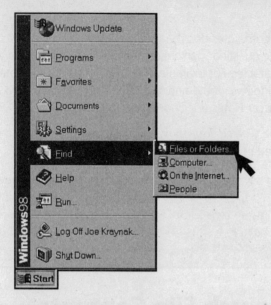

1 Click the **Start** button, point to **Find**, and select **Files or Folders** (or press **Ctrl+F** in My Computer or Windows Explorer).

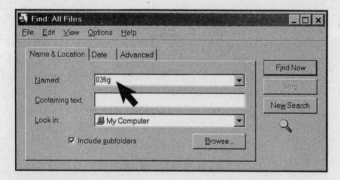

2 The Find: All Files dialog box appears with the Name & Location tab in front. If you know all or part of the name of the folder or file you want to search for, type it in the **Named** text box.

3 To search for files that contain a unique word or phrase, type the word or phrase in the **Containing Text** text box.

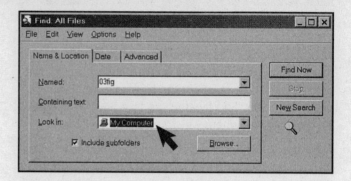

4 Open the Look In drop-down list, and select the disk or folder where you think the file is stored. To search in all folders on all of your disks, choose **My Computer**.

5 By default, Windows will search all the subfolders of the currently selected folder. If you selected a folder in the previous step, and you do not wish to search its subfolders, click **Include Subfolders** to remove the check from its box.

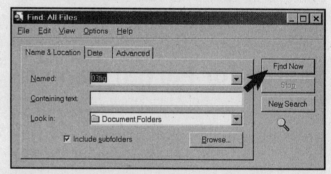

6 Click the **Find Now** button. Windows searches the selected drive(s) and folder(s) for files or folders that match your search criteria. When it finishes, it displays a list of all the files and folders it found at the bottom of the dialog box.

Guided Tour Search for Files and Folders by Name

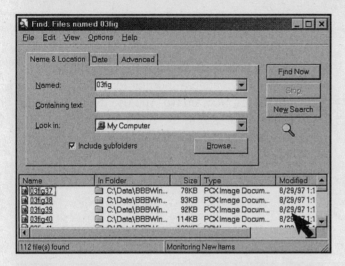

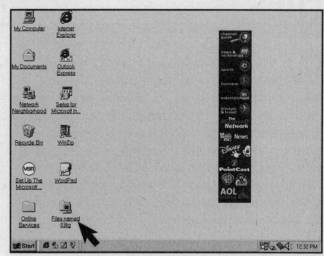

7 In the list of matching files and folders, you can select, cut, copy, delete, or open folders and files, just as if you were working in My Computer. You can even drag files or folders from the list to the Windows desktop to create shortcuts.

9 When you save a search, Windows places an icon for the search on the desktop. To perform the same search, click the icon.

10 When you are done searching for files and folders, click the **Close** (X) button in the upper-right corner of the Find window.

> If the search does not provide the desired results, edit your search instructions and click the **Find Now** button. To start over from scratch, click the **New Search** button to delete all search instructions you entered. Then perform the new search.

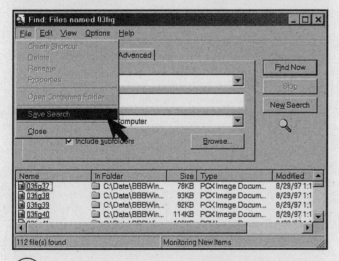

8 You can save your search entries to save yourself time if you think you might want to perform the same search later. Open the **File** menu and select **Save Search**.

Create Shortcuts to Disks, Folders, and Files

Whenever you find yourself running Windows Explorer or My Computer to access the same disk, run the same program, or open the same folder or file time and again, it's a good sign that you can save time by placing a shortcut for it on the Windows desktop. Then, instead of sifting through a long list of folders to find and open the folder or file, you can simply click its shortcut. You can also assign a key combination to the shortcut so you can quickly open it by pressing the key combination instead of using the mouse.

The steps you take to create a shortcut are the same whether you are creating a shortcut for a disk, folder, document file, or program file. You use the right mouse button to drag the icon to the Windows desktop, and then you select **Create Shortcut(s) Here** from the context menu. The *Guided Tour* walks you through the process.

Guided Tour   Create a Shortcut

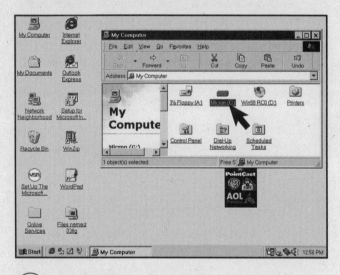

1 In My Computer, Windows Explorer, or the Find window, display the icon for the disk, folder, or file for which you want to create a shortcut. (Make sure you can still see a blank part of the desktop.)

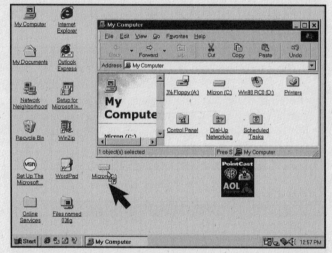

2 Point to the disk, folder, or file icon, hold down the right mouse button, and drag the icon to the Windows desktop. Release the mouse button.

Guided Tour Create a Shortcut

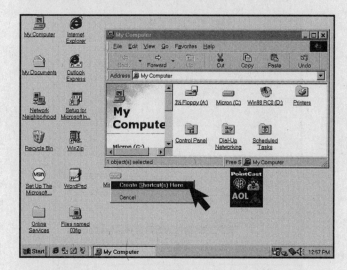

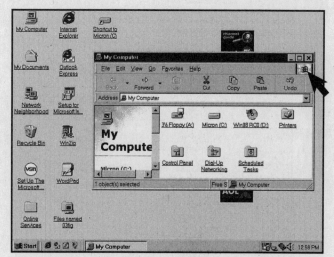

3 From the context menu that appears, select **Create Shortcut(s) Here**.

4 Windows places a shortcut icon for the selected disk, folder, or file on the desktop. You can click the shortcut to display the disk or folder contents in My Computer, to open the file, or to run the program.

Guided Tour Change a Shortcut's Properties

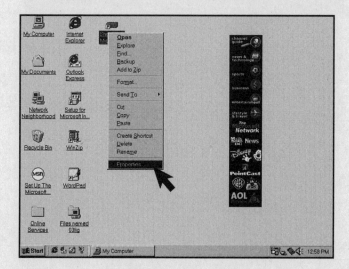

1 Right-click the shortcut and select **Properties**.

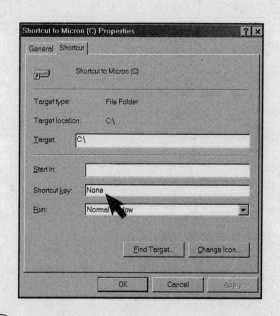

2 Windows displays the Properties dialog box for the selected shortcut. To assign a shortcut key to the icon, click in the **Shortcut Key** text box.

(continues)

Guided Tour   Change a Shortcut's Properties   *(continued)*

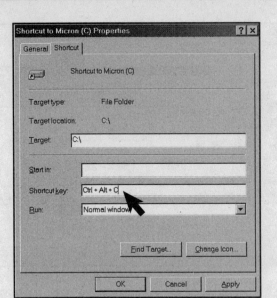

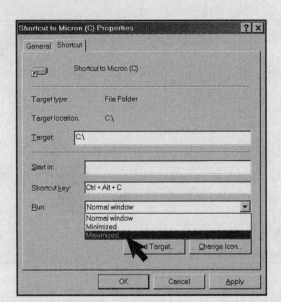

3 Press the key you want to use in combination with Ctrl+Alt to activate this shortcut. For example, if you press C, Ctrl+Alt+C appears in the text box, as shown here. You cannot use Esc, Enter, Tab, Spacebar, Print Screen, Backspace, or Delete.

4 Open the Run drop-down list and select the window size that you want the program to initially open in: **Normal Window**, **Minimized**, or **Maximized**. ▶See "Move and Resize Windows" on page 21.◀

5 Click **OK** to save your changes and close the dialog box.

Delete and Undelete Using the Recycle Bin

The Recycle Bin is your safety net when you delete folders and files. Whenever you delete folders or files, they are moved to the Recycle Bin just as if you had moved them to a different folder on your hard disk. Even if you turn off your computer, the deleted files remain safe until you empty the Recycle Bin.

There are two ways to place files in the Recycle Bin: You can drag files or folders from My Computer or Windows Explorer over the Recycle Bin icon, or you can use the Delete command. Either method places the files in the Recycle Bin. The *Guided Tour* shows both techniques for deleting files and folders.

Recover Deleted Files and Folders

Because the Recycle Bin acts as a folder, you can open it and drag files and folders out of it if you decide you want to restore them. You can also use the Recycle Bin's **File**, **Restore** command to automatically undelete files and folders and restore them to their original locations on your disk.

Of course, this temporary storage area does take up valuable hard disk space. So when you decide that you will never again need the files it contains, you can empty the Recycle Bin to permanently delete the files. The *Guided Tour* provides instructions.

Change the Recycle Bin's Properties

Although the *Guided Tour* stops short of showing you how to change the properties of the Recycle Bin, you might want to check out the properties after you master the Windows basics. By changing the Recycle Bin's properties, you can disable the Recycle Bin if you want the files and folders you delete to be permanently removed from your disk immediately. You can also specify the maximum amount of disk space allotted for temporary storage. Then if you delete more files than the Recycle Bin has room to store, it automatically removes the oldest files from your disk to make room for the newer files.

To check out the Recycle Bin's properties, right-click the **Recycle Bin** icon and choose **Properties**. To stay on the safe side, however, avoid changing any of the properties until you gain confidence in your ability to avoid accidental file deletions.

If you decide to change properties, do not turn off *both* the Display Delete Confirmation Dialog Box option and the Do Not Move Files to the Recycle Bin option. Turning off both options eliminates all safeguards. If you turn off both options, when you choose to delete an item, Windows permanently removes it from your disk without warning—and you have no recourse.

Guided Tour   Delete Files and Folders with Drag and Drop

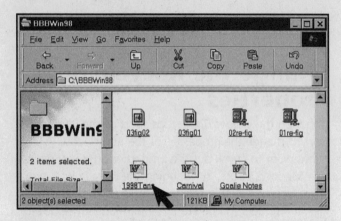

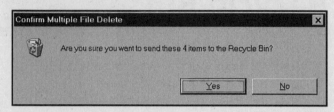

4 Windows displays the confirmation dialog box, prompting for your approval. If you are sure you want to delete the items, click **Yes**; otherwise, click **No**. If you click Yes, the folder is removed from your hard drive and placed in the Recycle Bin.

1 Open My Computer or Windows Explorer and resize the window so that you can see the Recycle Bin on the Windows desktop.

2 Select the file(s) or folder(s) you want to delete.

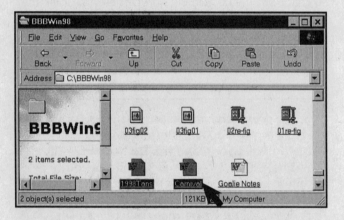

3 Drag one of the selected items from My Computer or Windows Explorer over to the Recycle Bin icon. Then release the mouse button.

Guided Tour   Use the Delete Command

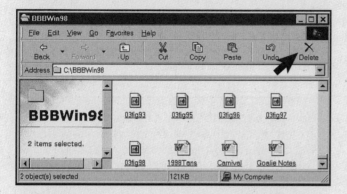

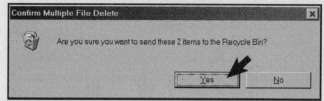

3 The Confirm File or Confirm Folder Delete dialog box appears, asking if you are sure. Click **Yes** to confirm the deletion or **No** to cancel it. If you click Yes, the selected items are moved to the Recycle Bin.

1 Open My Computer or Windows Explorer and select the file(s) or folder(s) you want to delete.

2 Click the **Delete** (X) button in the toolbar, or press the **Delete** key. (You can also select **File**, **Delete** or right-click one of the selected items and choose **Delete**.)

Guided Tour   Restore Files and Folders

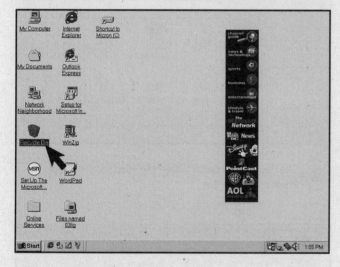

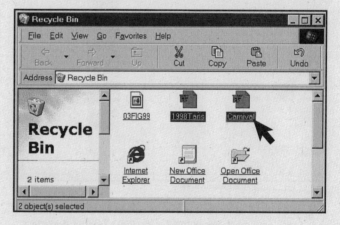

1 Click the **Recycle Bin** icon on the Windows desktop to view the contents of the Recycle Bin.

2 The contents of the Recycle bin appear inside the My Computer window. Select the file(s) and folder(s) you want to restore.

(continues)

Guided Tour Restore Files and Folders

(continued)

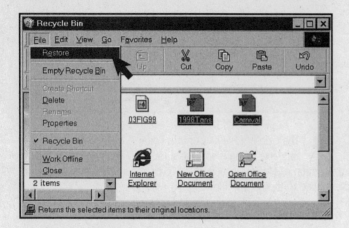

3 Open the **File** menu and select **Restore**, or right-click one of the selected files or folders and select **Restore**. Windows removes the selected items from the Recycle Bin and moves them to their original locations.

> You can also restore items by dragging them from the Recycle Bin in Windows Explorer or My Computer to the desktop or to another folder or disk on your computer. Or, you can use the Cut, Copy, and Paste commands to move the items.

Guided Tour Empty the Recycle Bin

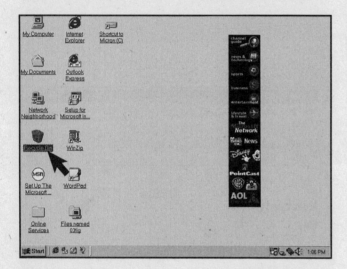

1 To permanently remove files or folders from your hard disk, you must empty the Recycle Bin. Click the **Recycle Bin** icon on the desktop.

> A quicker way to empty the Recycle Bin is to right-click its icon and choose **Empty Recycle Bin**. You can do this from the Windows desktop or in My Computer or Windows Explorer.

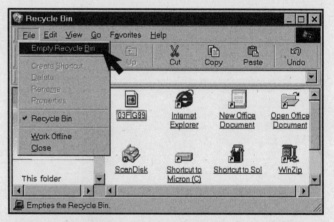

2 The Recycle Bin opens. Open the **File** menu and select **Empty Recycle Bin**.

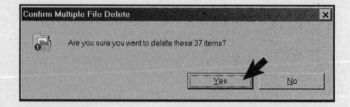

3 The Confirm Multiple File Delete dialog box appears, warning you that all the items in the Recycle Bin will be deleted. Click **Yes** to confirm the deletion or **No** to cancel it. If you click Yes, the Recycle Bin is emptied, and the icon changes to show an empty wastebasket.

View Disk, Folder, and File Properties

Each disk, folder, and file on your computer has properties that indicate the item's name, date, settings, and attributes. The properties vary depending on the selected item, as explained in the following list:

- *Disk properties* display the disk's label (name), the total amount of storage space on the disk, and the amounts of used and free space. The Properties dialog box also has a Tools tab that provides easy access to disk maintenance tools, including ScanDisk and Backup.

- *Data file properties* display the file's attributes: System, Hidden, Read-Only, and Archive. The System attribute marks files that you should not alter or delete. My Computer and Windows Explorer hide system files to prevent accidental deletions, and Windows displays a special warning if you attempt to delete or modify a system file. The Hidden attribute keeps the file hidden to prevent accidental deletions. Read-Only lets you open the file but does not allow you to save changes to it. Archive is used to determine if a file has changed since you last backed it up. If the file has changed, the Archive attribute is turned on, indicating to the backup program that this file needs to be backed up.

- *Folder properties* are similar to data file properties and include the four attributes described above. However, the folder Properties dialog box has one additional option: Enable Thumbnail View. With this option on, My Computer and Windows Explorer can display small pictures of certain data files. For example, if you have an image stored as a .PCX graphic file, My Computer can display a tiny replica of the image in the file list in place of the standard document icon for .PCX files.

- *Program file properties* vary depending on the type of program. For DOS programs, the Properties dialog box contains several tabs full of options. For Windows programs, the properties include the standard file attributes, along with information about the program's version number.

- *Shortcut properties* allow you to change the settings for a shortcut. For example, you can specify a shortcut key combination for running the associated program, and you can specify the size of the window that appears when you first run the program.

- *Network sharing properties* are available for disks, files, and folders on a network. If you work on a network, the Properties dialog box has a Sharing tab that contains settings with which you specify whether or not the item is shared or requires a password for access.

The *Guided Tour* explains how to display the Properties dialog box for disks, folders, and files on your computer and shows you what to expect in the various Properties dialog boxes.

Guided Tour Display Disk, Folder, and File Properties

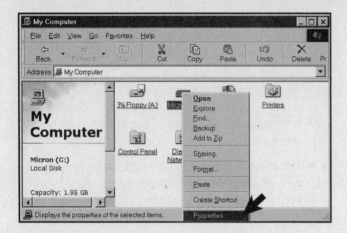

1 To display disk properties, right-click a disk icon and select **Properties**.

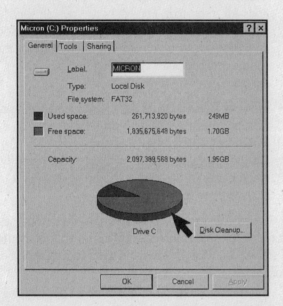

2 Click the **General** tab if necessary to display the disk's label (name) and a pie chart that shows the amounts of total, used, and free disk space.

▶For more information about the disk maintenance tools in Windows 98, see "Check for and Repair Disk Problems" on page 416 (ScanDisk), "Improve CD-ROM and Hard Drive Performance" on page 502 (Disk Defragmenter), and "Back Up Files" on page 432 (Backup).◀

3 Click the **Tools** tab. This tab contains information about when the disk was last checked for errors (using ScanDisk), backed up (using Backup), and defragmented (using Disk Defragmenter). The buttons on this tab provide quick access to these essential disk maintenance tools.

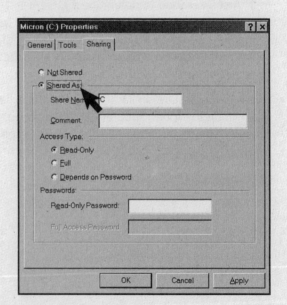

4 The Sharing tab appears only if you are working on a network and you share files and programs with others on the network. If it's available, click the **Sharing** tab to see the sharing properties for the selected item. ▶See "Share Resources" on page 394 for details.◀ Click **OK** to close the dialog box.

Guided Tour Display Disk, Folder, and File Properties

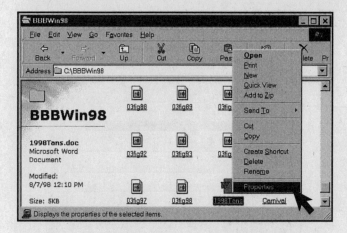

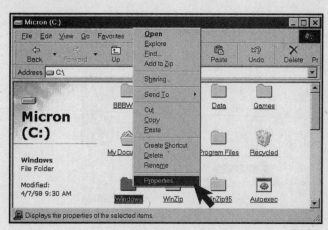

5 Right-click a data file and select **Properties** to view the file's attributes.

7 Right-click a folder and select **Properties**.

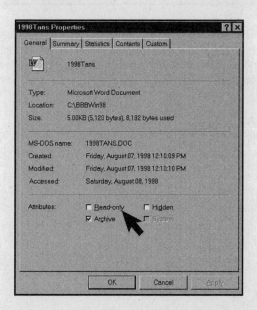

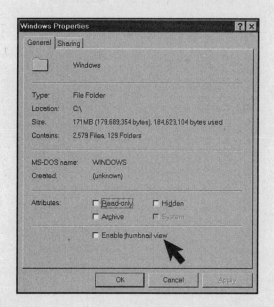

6 The Properties dialog box for a data file displays the file's name and size, as well as the dates when it was created, last modified, and most recently opened. In addition, the dialog box displays the file's attributes, which you can change. Click **OK** to close the dialog box.

8 The Properties dialog box for a folder looks very similar to the dialog box for data files. Turn on **Enable Thumbnail View** if you want to see small replicas of the files in this folder in place of standard icons. Click **OK** to close the dialog box.

(continues)

Guided Tour Display Disk, Folder, and File Properties *(continued)*

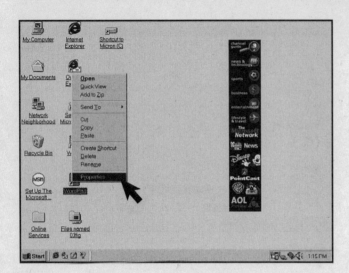

9 Right-click a shortcut and select **Properties**.

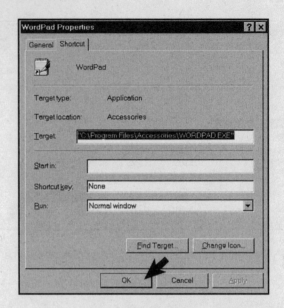

10 The shortcut's Properties dialog box allows you to assign a keystroke for running the program and to set the size of the window that the program uses on startup. Click **OK** to close the dialog box.

Create and Edit File Associations

Whenever you choose to open a document file, display a graphic image, play an audio or video clip, or open any other type of data file outside of the program used to create it, Windows checks the Windows Registry to determine which program to use to open the file.

If the Registry contains a record that associates files of the selected type with a specified program, Windows runs the associated program, which then opens the selected file. When you install a program, it typically adds its name to the Registry automatically and associates itself with data files of a particular type. In most cases, you don't have to deal with file associations.

If a document file you click is not associated with a program, Windows displays a dialog box prompting you to select the program you want to use to open the document. This allows you to quickly set up the file association on-the-fly, as shown in the *Guided Tour*.

The *Guided Tour* also shows you how to edit file associations. Why would you want to edit an existing file association? During installation, some programs automatically associate themselves to file types that they can open, without asking for your permission. Because only one program can be associated to any one file type, this can foul up your existing file associations. To correct the problem, you must edit the association.

Guided Tour Create File Associations On-the-Fly

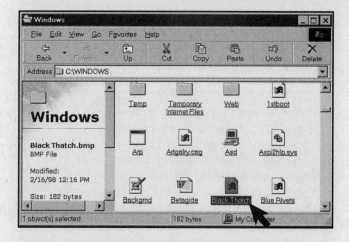

1 Click the icon for the document file you want to open. (You can click the icon in My Computer, in Windows Explorer, or on the Windows desktop.)

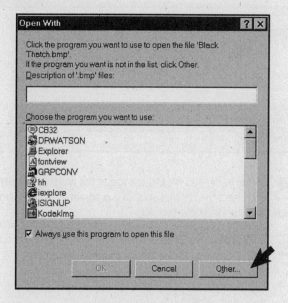

2 If the selected file type is not associated with a program, the Open With dialog box appears, prompting you to select an installed program. If the program is in the list, select it and skip to step 6. If the program is not in the list but you know it is available, click the **Other** button and proceed with step 3.

(continues)

Guided Tour Create File Associations On-the-Fly *(continued)*

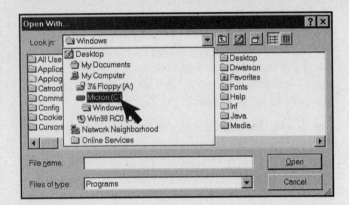

3 A second Open With dialog box appears. Open the **Look In** drop-down list and select the disk on which the program is stored.

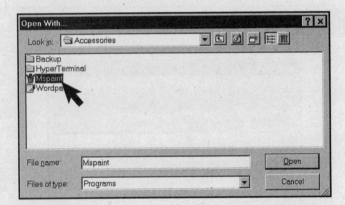

4 In the folder and file list, change to the program's folder and select the file that starts the program. The file's name appears in the File Name text box.

5 Click **Open**. This closes the second Open With dialog box and returns you to the first Open With dialog box.

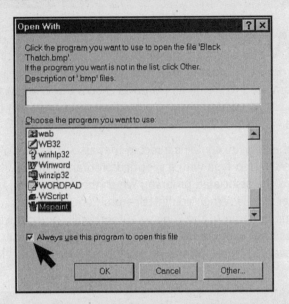

6 To permanently associate files of this type with the selected program, make sure there is a check mark in the **Always Use This Program to Open This File** check box.

7 Click **OK**. Windows runs the specified program, which then opens the document.

If the selected program is incapable of opening files of the specified type, one of two things will happen. The program might run and then display an error message indicating that it cannot open the file, or it might open the file and display the codes used to format the document. Be sure you choose the correct program for the selected file type.

Guided Tour Edit a File Association

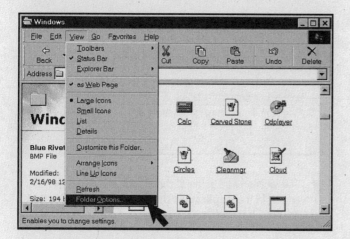

1 In My Computer or Windows Explorer, open the **View** menu and select **Folder Options**.

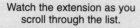

Watch the extension as you scroll through the list.

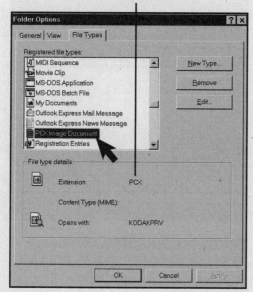

2 Click the **File Types** tab. Then use the down arrow key to scroll through the list of registered file types. Keep your eye on the Extension entry in the File Type Details area to determine the file type.

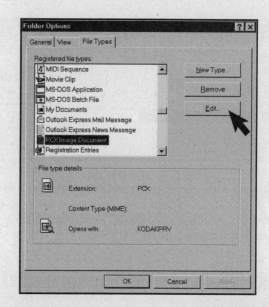

3 Highlight the file type you want to associate with a different program, and then click the **Edit** button.

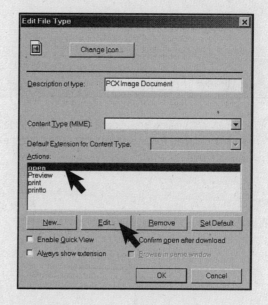

4 In the **Actions** box, click **open**, and then click the **Edit** button.

(continues)

Guided Tour Edit a File Association *(continued)*

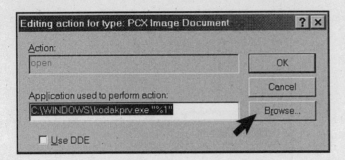

5 In this dialog box, the entry in the Application Used to Perform Action text box shows the location and name of the program currently associated with this file type. Click the **Browse** button to select a different program.

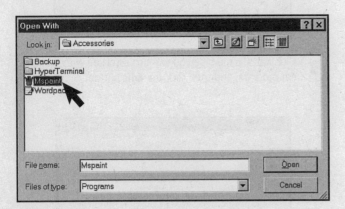

6 The Open With dialog box appears. Change to the desired program's disk and folder, select the file that starts the program, and click **Open**.

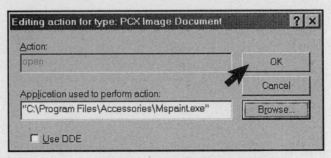

7 The location and name of the file you selected now appear in the **Application Used to Perform Action** text box. Click **OK**.

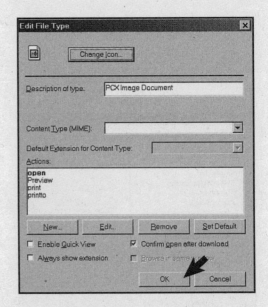

8 You are returned to the Edit File Type dialog box. Click **OK** to save your change.

9 In the Options dialog box, click **OK**. Now when you choose to open documents of this type, Windows will use the new associated program to open the files.

You can also use options on the File Types tab to remove file associations or to create new associations. Be careful when creating new file associations, though. Only one program can be assigned the task of opening a particular file type. Therefore, before you create a new type, you should remove the existing file type from the Registered File Types list.

Format Floppy Disks

With the increased popularity of the Internet and email, people are relying less and less on floppy disks to exchange files. Instead of handing a floppy disk or sending files on disk by standard mail to a friend or colleague, you can simply send files over the phone lines much faster and easier. However, you might still use floppy disks to store copies of important files or to exchange files if you do not yet have an Internet connection.

Before you can use a floppy disk to store files, you must *format* the disk (unless you purchased preformatted disks). You may also want to format a disk to erase any files on the disk or to ensure that an old disk is properly formatted. Whatever the case, the *Guided Tour* shows you how to format floppy disks in Windows.

> Formatting a floppy disk erases any data the disk may contain. Format only blank disks or disks that contain files you will never again need. To see if a disk contains files, insert it in your floppy disk drive and switch to that drive with My Computer or Windows Explorer.

Understand Disk Size and Capacity

Floppy disks come in two standard sizes: 3.5" and 5.25". The 5.25" disks are all but extinct. The 3.5" disks can store different amounts of data based on their *density*. A high-density disk can store 1.44 megabytes of data. A low-density disk can store 720 kilobytes. The total amount of data a disk can store is referred to as the disk's *capacity*. Most floppy disk drives are high-capacity drives (5.25" 720 kilobyte drives or 3.5" 1.44 megabyte drives), which can handle both low- and high-capacity floppy disks.

When formatting a floppy disk, you should be aware of the disk's capacity. If you format a high-capacity disk as a low-capacity disk or vice versa, the disk will not store data reliably.

Create a System Disk

When formatting a floppy disk, you can choose to make it a system disk so you can use it to start your computer if necessary. Your C: hard disk is formatted as a system disk. If you created an Emergency Startup disk when you installed Windows, it is also formatted as a system disk.

In the past, it was a good idea to format a floppy disk as a system disk in case you could not start your computer from its hard disk. However, the Windows 98 Emergency Startup disk works better, offering tools to help you recover your system files. ▶If you have not yet created an Emergency Startup disk, see "Create and Use an Emergency Disk" on page 442.◀

Although you might not want to format a disk as a system disk for backup purposes, you might still want to create floppy system disks if you commonly run DOS programs, especially games that do not run well under Windows. You can create a separate system disk for each game that contains special startup commands. You can then use the floppy disk to start your computer instead of starting with Windows. The *Guided Tour* shows you how to use a special option to create a system disk when formatting.

Guided Tour Format a Floppy Disk

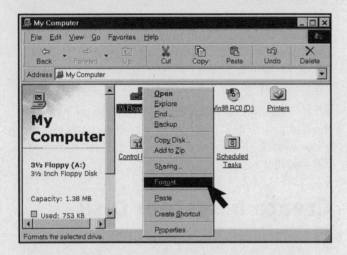

1 Insert the floppy disk into your computer's floppy disk drive. In My Computer or Windows Explorer, right-click the drive's icon and select **Format**.

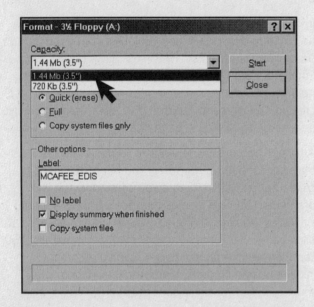

2 The Format dialog box appears. Open the **Capacity** drop-down list and select the setting that matches the floppy disk's capacity (not the drive's capacity).

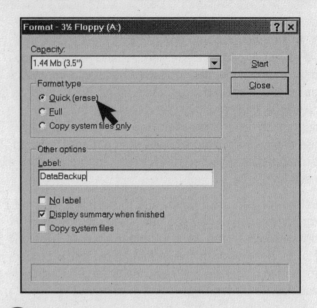

3 Select the desired format type: **Quick** or **Full**. Quick is useful for reformatting a disk; it simply erases any files or folders from the disk. You must choose Full for unformatted disks, but it is also useful for refreshing old disks.

4 Click in the **Label** text box, and then type a name for the disk (up to 11 characters) or select **No Label**.

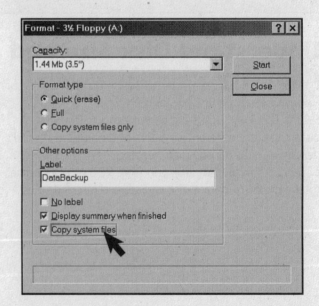

5 To give this disk the capability to start your computer, click **Copy System Files** to place a check mark in its box.

6 Click the **Start** button.

Guided Tour Format a Floppy Disk

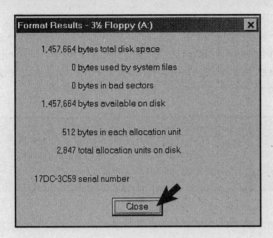

Format Results - 3½ Floppy (A:)

1,457,664 bytes total disk space

0 bytes used by system files

0 bytes in bad sectors

1,457,664 bytes available on disk

512 bytes in each allocation unit

2,847 total allocation units on disk

17DC-3C59 serial number

Close

7 Windows formats the disk and displays summary information about the disk. Click **Close** to close this information box.

8 You are returned to the Format dialog box, which you can use to format another floppy disk. When you finish formatting disks, click the **Close** button.

If a disk has serious defects, Windows might not be able to successfully format the disk, and will display a warning message. It's a good idea to just discard the disk instead of trying to use it to store data.

ipp1al

Copy Floppy Disks

If you purchase a program on floppy disks, it is a good idea to copy the original disks and use the copies to install the program. By using the copies instead of the originals, you prevent any accidental damage to the original disks.

Before you copy disks, you should write-protect them. If you hold a 3.5" disk label-edge up with the label facing away from you, you will see a write-protect tab in the upper-left corner of the window. Slide the tab so you can see through the little hole that the tab covers. Many program disks come write-protected or have the write-protect tab permanently removed. After write-protecting the disks, follow the *Guided Tour* to copy them.

> The floppy disks you use as the copies do not have to be formatted, but the disk copying will proceed faster if they are.

Guided Tour Copy a Floppy Disk

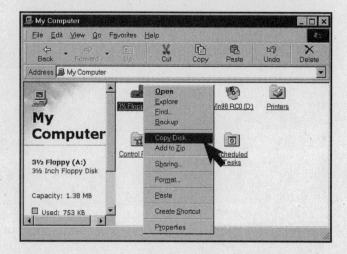

(1) Insert the disk you want to copy in your computer's floppy disk drive. In My Computer or Windows Explorer, right-click the drive's icon and select **Copy Disk**.

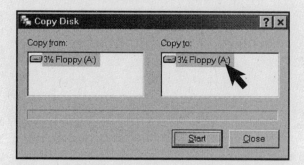

(2) The Copy Disk dialog box appears. If you have two floppy disk drives of the same size and capacity, you can select one drive in the **Copy From** list and select the other drive in the **Copy To** list, so you won't have to swap disks out of the same drive. If you do this, insert the blank floppy disk into the drive you selected under Copy To.

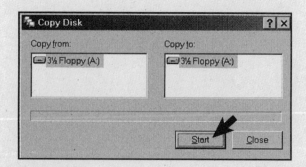

(3) Click the **Start** button. Windows copies all files on the disk to a temporary storage area on your hard drive and displays the progress of the operation.

Guided Tour Copy a Floppy Disk

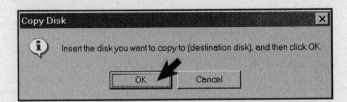

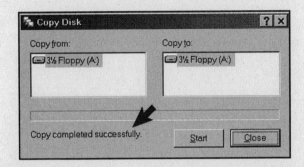

4 When Windows has completely copied the disk, it displays a dialog box telling you to insert the destination disk (if you are using only one disk drive). Remove the original floppy disk from the drive and insert a blank floppy disk. Click **OK**.

When copying disks, do not mix up the source (original) and destination (blank) disks. If the original disks are not write-protected, you could end up copying a blank disk over an original disk, completely destroying any files that were on the original disk.

5 Windows writes the copied data to the blank floppy disk, creating a duplicate disk. When the copy operation is complete, "Copy Completed Successfully" appears in the lower-left corner of the Copy Disk dialog box.

6 Remove the duplicate disk from the drive. If you are done copying disks, click **Close**. If you want to copy additional disks, repeat the steps.

HOW TO...

Create and Print Documents

Unless you purchased your computer to use solely as a game machine and entertainment center, you will probably want to use it to create documents, including letters, reports, greeting cards, images, spreadsheets, graphs, and presentations. In fact, most of the programs that you will use in Windows 98 are designed to help you create and print documents.

In order to use these programs, you must learn the basic tasks of creating, editing, saving, opening, and printing documents. Fortunately, all Windows programs use the same or similar commands for performing these tasks. Once you learn the steps for performing a task in one Windows program, you will know how to perform the same task in any Windows program.

What You Will Find in This Section

Create a Document

Most programs automatically create a new document when you start the program. On startup, the program displays a blank document window in which you can start typing, drawing, or entering data. The document starts as a blank sheet of paper and typically expands as you type, allowing you to create a multipage document.

As you create the document, the program stores it in your computer's electronic memory (RAM, short for random-access memory), which is a temporary storage area. In order to preserve your data, you must name your document and save it as a file on your computer's hard disk. ►You will learn how to do this in the next task, "Save a Document," on page 139.◄

After you save the document and close its window, the program typically displays a blank screen with no document window. In order to continue working on something else, you must either open a saved document or create a new document. Creating a new document opens a blank document window in which you can start working.

In most programs, you create a new document by using the File, New command. In some programs, this automatically opens a blank document window. Other programs may display a dialog box prompting you to specify the type of document you want to create. For example, Microsoft Word allows you to select from several templates for creating letters, faxes, memos, and other types of documents. A *template* (an electronic boilerplate) contains all the formatting required for the document and may even contain some sample text.

The *Guided Tour* shows you two common ways to create a new document in a typical Windows program. The *Guided Tour* also provides instructions on how to create a new document from My Computer or Windows Explorer.

> In most Windows programs, you can work on several documents at the same time. This allows you to refer to one document while working on another or to quickly copy and paste data from one document to another. ►See "Work with Two or More Documents" on page 155.◄

Guided Tour Create a New Document

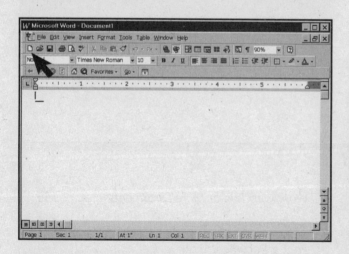

1 If the program has a New button in its toolbar, as shown above, click the button to create a generic document, no questions asked.

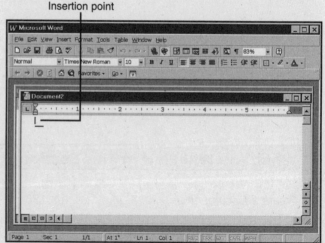

2 A blank document window appears immediately. If you are working in a standard word processing or spreadsheet program, a blinking insertion point appears in the upper-left corner of the window, indicating where text will be inserted when you type.

Guided Tour Create a New Document

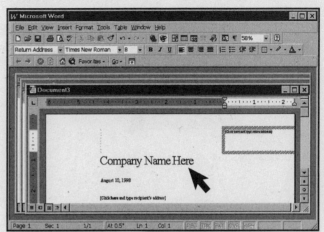

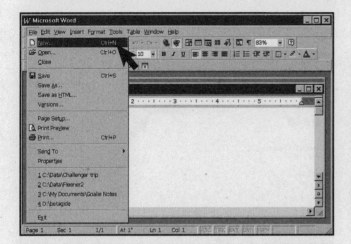

3 In most Windows programs, you can start a new document by using the File, New command. Open the **File** menu and select **New** or try pressing **Ctrl+N**.

5 The program opens a new document window. This figure shows Microsoft Word's letter template. You can edit the document ▶as explained in "Edit a Document" on page 144.◀

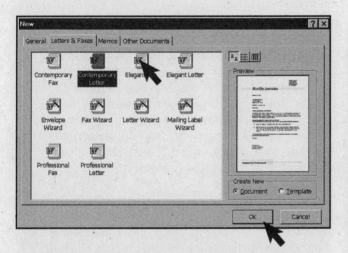

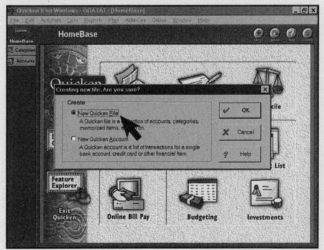

4 If the program displays a dialog box prompting you to select a template, choose the desired template and click **OK**. This figure shows Microsoft Word's New dialog box. Most programs that offer a template option also let you create a blank document if you prefer to start from scratch.

6 Although the File, New command typically opens a blank document, the document type varies from program to program. For example, if you select File, New in Quicken (a financial program), Quicken asks if you want to create a new file or a new account, as shown in the figure above.

Guided Tour Start a New Document from a Folder

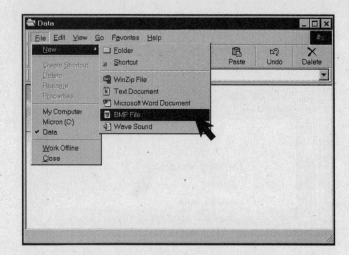

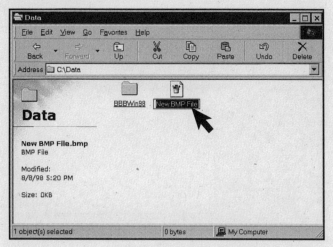

1 Run My Computer and open the folder in which you want the new document created.

2 Open the **File** menu and point to **New**.

3 A list of registered document types appears. Click the type of document you want to create.

4 Windows creates an icon for the new document and highlights its name. To rename the document, type the desired name and press **Enter**. You can now click the icon to open it in its associated program.

Not all programs add their names to the File, New submenu. If the document type you want to create is not on the File, New submenu, the document type might not be associated with the right program or the program might not have added its name to the File, New submenu. ▶To check your file associations, see "Create and Edit File Associations" on page 125.◀

You can also create new documents by right-clicking a blank area in My Computer or Windows Explorer and then pointing to **New** on the context menu.

Save a Document

As you type, draw, or enter data to create a document, your computer saves your work in RAM (random-access memory). RAM is an electronic area that stores your work as long as your computer's power is on. If you turn your computer off or if power is interrupted for any reason, everything stored in RAM is immediately erased.

Whenever you install a program, the installation utility places the files necessary for running the program on your hard disk, which is a permanent storage medium. When you run the program, its instructions are stored in RAM, where the computer can access them more quickly.

To store your work permanently, you must save it as a file on your computer's hard disk. The hard disk drive acts as a tape recorder for your data, but instead of storing your data on tapes, the hard drive stores it on disks. When you turn off your computer, the data remains on the hard disk, and you can "play back" the data later.

Why Save Documents?

In most Windows programs, you use the File, Save command or click the Save button to save your work. The first time you choose to save your work (document), you must select the disk and folder where you want the document stored, and you must enter a name for the document (a *filename*). After you have saved a file, subsequent saves are much easier. You simply enter the File, Save command, and your program updates the file automatically; the program already knows the file's name and location. The *Guided Tour* shows you how to save a document for the first time.

In some cases, you might want to save a copy of the file so you can edit it without changing the original document. To save a copy of a file, you use the Save As command, as shown in the *Guided Tour*. This displays the Save As dialog box, which prompts you to choose a different drive or folder for the file and/or give it a name.

You cannot store two files with the same name on the same disk in the same folder. If you save a new file to a folder that already contains a file of the same name, the new file replaces the old file, completely deleting it. Don't be alarmed, though—most programs display a warning message before replacing the existing file with the new one.

Filename Rules

If you have worked with documents in old DOS programs, you know that DOS does not provide much flexibility with filenames. DOS restricts names to eight or fewer characters (no spaces) and an optional extension of up to three characters, such as BOOKMARK.DOC. In Windows 98 (and Windows 95) you can use long filenames, up to 255 characters including spaces. The only characters you cannot use are the following:

$$\backslash \ / \ ? \ : \ * \ '' \ < \ > \ |$$

Navigate Folders

When you choose to save a document for the first time, the Save As dialog box appears and displays the contents of the current disk and folder. You can use this dialog box to change to a different folder and enter a filename for your document.

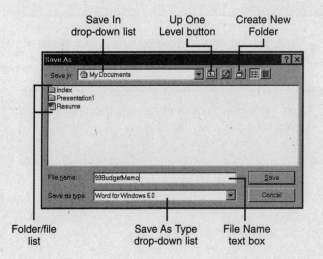

Save In drop-down list · Up One Level button · Create New Folder · Folder/file list · Save As Type drop-down list · File Name text box

At first this dialog box might seem a bit difficult to maneuver. Use the following controls to change to the desired disk and folder and to name your document:

Save In is a drop-down list that displays the available disks on your computer. Open this list and select the name or icon for the disk on which you want to save the file.

Folder/file list displays the contents of the currently selected disk or folder. To open a folder, double-click its icon.

Up One Level moves up one level in the folder list. For example, if the C:\Data\Vacation folder is open and you click Up One Level, the contents of the Data folder are displayed.

Create New Folder creates a new folder on the current disk or in the current folder. You can then enter a name for the new folder and double-click its icon to activate it.

File Name text box is where you type a name for your document. If the File Name text box already has an entry in it, double-click the entry and type a new name to replace it.

Save As Type drop-down list allows you to save the document in a format that can be used by another program. For example, if you've created a report using Microsoft Word and you want to share the file with a person who uses a different word processor, such as WordPerfect, you can save your document in that word processor's format—as a WordPerfect file, for example.

Guided Tour Save a File for the First Time

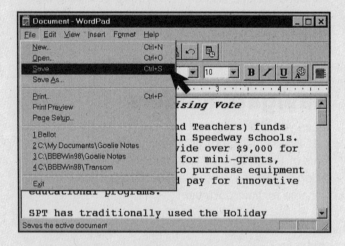

1 With the document the you want to save open onscreen, open the **File** menu and select **Save**.

> Most Windows programs have a shortcut key combination for saving files. In most cases, you can press **Ctrl+S**.

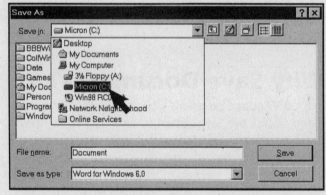

2 The Save As dialog box appears. Open the **Save In** drop-down list and click the name or icon for the disk on which you want to save the document.

Guided Tour Save a File for the First Time

Up One
Level button

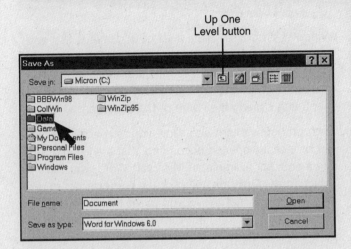

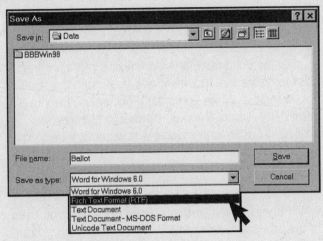

3 The contents of the disk appear in the folder/file list. In the folder list, click or double-click a folder to open it. Continue clicking folder icons until you have opened the folder in which you want to save the document.

4 If you go too far down the folder/file list, click the **Up One Level** button to move up one level in the list.

6 To save the file for use in a different program, open the **Save As Type** drop-down list and select the file format for the desired program.

7 Click the **Save** or **OK** button. Your program saves the document on the specified drive, in the currently selected folder, using the file name you entered.

> To close a document after saving it, simply click the **Close (X)** button in the upper-right corner of the document window. ▶For details, see "Open and Close Windows" on page 18.◄

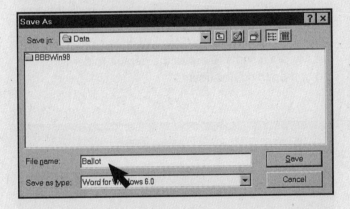

5 Double-click in the **File Name** text box and type the name you want to give the document.

Open a Saved Document

When you save and close a document, your computer stores it safely on disk. If you decide to edit or print the document later, you must run the program used to create the document and then open the saved document file. When you open a document, the program reads it from the disk, stores it in memory, and displays it onscreen in a document window, where you can work on it or print it.

In most programs, you use the File, Open command to open a document. This displays the Open dialog box, which is very similar to the Save As dialog box you used in the previous *Guided Tour*. It contains a Look In drop-down list, which allows you to select the disk where the document file is stored, and a folder/file list from which you open the folder the file is stored in and select the file. The Open dialog box might also contain a Files of Type drop-down list that allows you to specify the file's format. The *Guided Tour* shows you how to open a document using the Open dialog box.

Shortcuts for Opening Documents

Most Windows programs allow you to bypass the File, Open command by pressing **Ctrl+O**. In addition, many

Windows programs create a list of documents that you have recently opened and worked on and display that list at the bottom of the File menu. In those programs, you can open a document simply by opening the **File** menu and clicking the name of the document.

Such programs might also allow you to specify the number of recently opened documents that are listed on the File menu. For example, in Microsoft Word, you can select **Tools**, **Options** and click the **General** tab to display a spin box that allows you to set the number of recently opened files that Word keeps track of (from 0 to 9 documents).

Default File Locations

If you store most of the documents you create in a single folder, you might be able to tell your program to open that folder whenever you choose to save or open a document. By setting a default folder, you save yourself the trouble of always having to select the disk and folder in which you want the file stored. Check the program's documentation to determine how to set a default document folder. (Many Windows programs use the My Documents folder as the default folder for saving and opening documents.)

Guided Tour   Open a Document

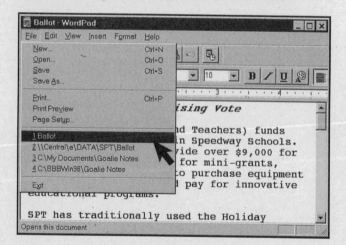

1 Many programs keep a list of recently opened files on the File menu, To open a document you've used recently, open the **File** menu and click the name of the document.

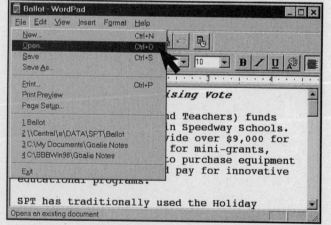

2 The standard way to open a document is to use the File, Open command. Open the **File** menu and select **Open**.

Guided Tour Open a Document

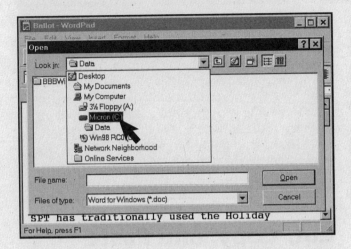

3 The Open dialog box appears, displaying a list of files and folders on the current drive. Open the **Look In** drop-down list and select the disk on which the document is stored.

Up One
Level button

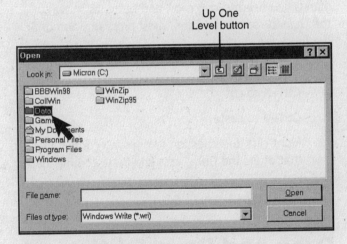

4 In the folder/file list, click or double-click a folder to open it. Continue clicking or double-clicking folder icons until you have opened the folder in which the document is stored.

5 If you go too far down the folder/file list, click the **Up One Level** button to move up one level in the list.

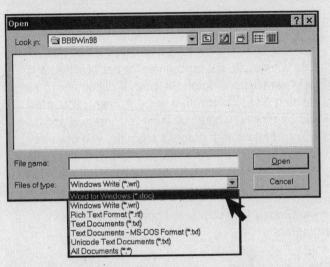

6 If the document was created in a program other than the program you are using to open it, open the **Files of Type** drop-down list and select the file format for the desired file.

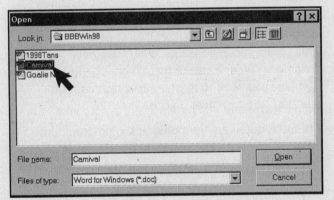

7 Click or double-click the name of the document you want to open. Its name becomes highlighted, and the program might automatically open it.

8 If the program does not automatically open the file, click the **Open** button. The program opens the document and displays it in its own document window.

Edit a Document

Once a document is open, you can edit it by deleting, inserting, moving, and copying text and other data. Of course, the procedures for performing such tasks vary depending on the type of document you are creating. For example, in a text document, you insert text by clicking where you want text inserted and then typing the text. In a graphics program, you use the mouse to paint or draw objects in the desired locations. In a spreadsheet, you type data into *cells* (the boxes that are formed by the intersection of columns and rows).

The *Guided Tour* shows you how to edit text and graphics.

Select Text and Other Objects

In many cases, you will need to do more than simply delete or insert a few characters or words. You may need to cut an entire paragraph, move it to a different location in your document, or rearrange the objects (lines, ovals, rectangles, and so on) that make up a drawing. In order to make these more significant modifications, you need to master a few techniques for selecting text and other objects.

The techniques vary from program to program, but there are some standard procedures you can follow:

- Drag over text to highlight it.

- In a spreadsheet, click in a cell to select a single entry. Drag over adjacent cells to select multiple entries.

- Click a drawing object to select it. *Handles* (little squares) appear around the object. You can drag a handle to resize the object or drag the object to move it. (**Ctrl**+*click* additional objects to select them.)

- Drag a selection box around several drawn objects.

- Press **Ctrl+A** to select all text or objects in the document. (This is a fairly universal shortcut in Windows programs.)

Most programs offer additional techniques for selecting text and objects. In many programs, you can hold down the **Shift** key and use the arrow keys to extend the highlight. Other programs allow you to double-click to highlight a word, triple-click to highlight a paragraph, or **Ctrl**+*click* to highlight a sentence. Check your program's Help system to learn about additional shortcuts.

Cut, Copy, and Paste

After you have highlighted a chunk of text or selected one or more objects, you can cut and paste the selection to move it, or you can copy and paste the selection to duplicate it. The Edit menu contains all the commands you need to cut, copy, and paste, as shown in the *Guided Tour*. In addition, most programs also offer the following shortcuts:

Ctrl+C to copy

Ctrl+X to cut

Ctrl+V to paste

Right-click the selection to display a context menu that offers the Cut, Copy, and Paste commands

Some programs offer additional keystrokes. Check your program's documentation or Help system for details.

Drag-and-Drop Editing

The most intuitive way to move text or other objects is to use the mouse. Position the mouse pointer over the selection and then press and hold down the left mouse and drag the selection to the desired location. When you release the mouse button, the selection is moved to the new location.

To copy the selection instead of moving it, hold down the **Ctrl** key and drag. A plus sign appears next to the mouse pointer, indicating that you are copying the selection. When you release the mouse button, a duplicate copy of the selection is inserted in the document.

Guided Tour Edit a Text Document

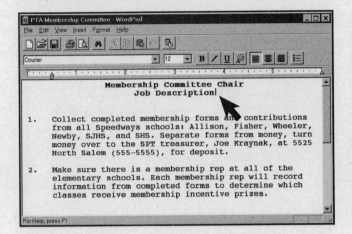

1 A blinking insertion point shows where any text you type will be inserted. To move the insertion point, use the arrow keys, Page Up, and Page Down, or click in the desired location.

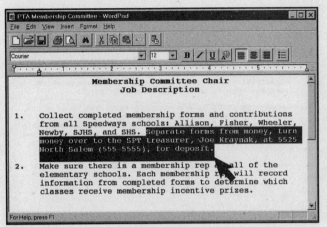

3 To select text, move the insertion point to the beginning of the text you want to select, press and hold down the left mouse button, and drag to the end of the desired text.

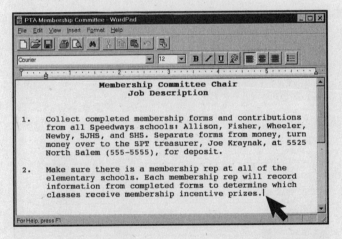

2 The insertion point moves to the selected position. You can use the **Backspace** key to delete characters to the left or **Delete** to remove characters to the right. To insert text, start typing.

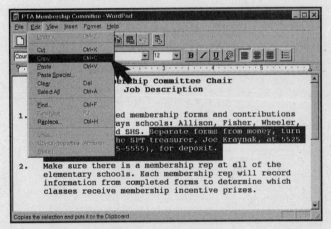

4 To copy the selection, open the **Edit** menu and choose **Copy**. To cut the selection (to move it), open the **Edit** menu and select **Cut**.

(continues)

Most programs offer two typing modes: Insert and Typeover. In Typeover mode, new characters replace existing characters as you type. In most programs, you can switch between typing modes by pressing the Ins key or by double-clicking the OVR indicator in the status bar. If neither of these techniques work, check the program's Help system.

Guided Tour Edit a Text Document

(continued)

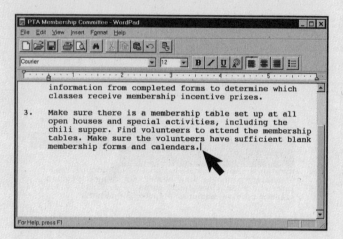

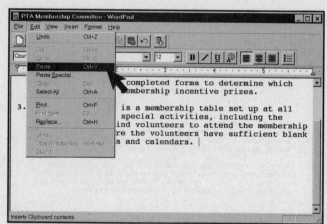

5 Move the insertion point to where you want the cut or copied text inserted. (You can use the arrow keys or click with the mouse.)

6 Open the **Edit** menu and select **Paste**. The cut or copied data is pasted at the location of the insertion point.

Guided Tour Edit a Spreadsheet

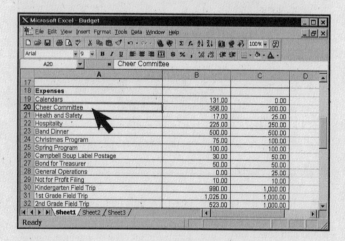

1 In most spreadsheets, when you click in a cell, the entire cell entry is selected. You can type a new entry to replace the current entry.

2 To edit an entry instead of replacing it, double-click the cell. You can then use the **Backspace** and **Delete** keys to delete individual numbers or characters.

Guided Tour Edit a Spreadsheet

3 You can also edit a cell entry by typing your changes in the input box and pressing **Enter**. (Older spreadsheet programs may offer only this one way of editing or entering cell contents.)

4 To select multiple cells in a spreadsheet, click the first cell you want to select and then drag over the adjacent cells.

5 You can select a row or column by clicking the row number at the left of a row or the column letter at the top of a column. Drag over row numbers or column letters to highlight multiple rows or columns.

Most spreadsheet programs display a *marquee* around the target area when you're moving cells.

6 To move the highlighted cells, rows, or columns, position the mouse pointer over the selection, press and hold down the left mouse button, and drag the selection to the desired location. To copy the selection, hold down the **Ctrl** key and drag.

Guided Tour   Select, Move, and Copy Drawn Objects

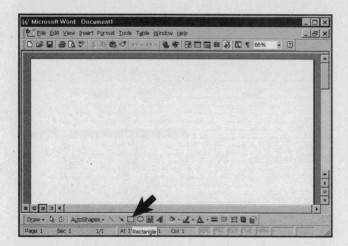

1 To draw an object in most drawing programs, first click a button for the type of object you want to draw (line, rectangle, oval, arrow, and so on).

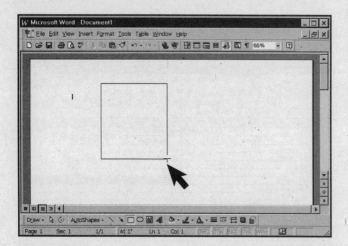

2 Position the mouse pointer where you want the object inserted, hold down the left mouse button, and drag to create the object.

These steps show how to create objects using simple drawing tools included with Microsoft Word. With a *drawing program*, each object has its own identity and is defined by handles. In *painting programs*, you cannot click an object to select it. You must drag a selection box around an area of the painting. ►See "Create Images in Paint" on page 177.◄

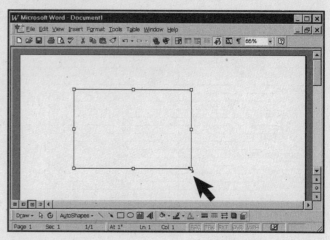

3 When you release the mouse button, the object appears with handles to define its size and dimensions. You can drag a handle to resize the object, or you can drag the object to move it.

Handles appear around an object only when the object is selected. When you click outside the object or start drawing something else, the handles disappear.

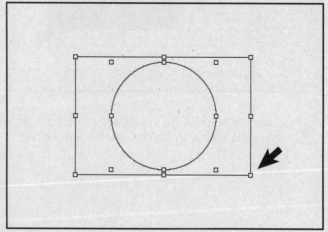

4 To select an object, click it. Handles appear around it. To select additional objects, **Ctrl**+*click* or **Shift**+*click* them (depending on the program).

Guided Tour   Select, Move, and Copy Drawn Objects

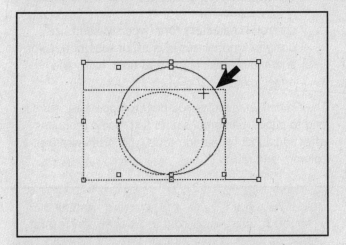

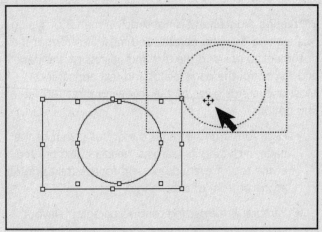

5 To resize one or more selected objects, drag one of the handles. Drag a top handle to change the object's height, a side handle to change its width, or a corner handle to change both the height and width proportionally.

6 To move one or more selected objects, position the mouse pointer over any one of the selected objects, press and hold down the left mouse button, and drag the object(s) to the desired location. To copy the object(s), hold down the **Ctrl** key and drag.

Format a Document

Creating a document is not simply a matter of typing text and drawing objects. You must also *format* the document to position the text and objects on the page and to control the page layout and text appearance. Most documents give you the following three formatting options:

- *Page formatting* controls the overall layout of the page, including its margins, *headers* (text printed at the top of every page), and *footers* (text printed at the bottom of every page).

- *Paragraph formatting* controls paragraph layout, including how far the paragraphs are indented from the left and right margins, the space before and after the paragraphs, and whether the paragraphs are formatted as numbered or bulleted lists.

- *Character formatting* controls the appearance of each letter, number, or symbol in the text. You can

control a character's *font* (type style and size), *position* (normal, superscript, or subscript), color, and *enhancements* (such as bold, italic, and underlining).

The *Guided Tour* shows you how to apply basic formatting to pages, paragraphs, and text. Some programs offer additional formatting tools, such as newspaper columns and tables.

> Most programs have a formatting toolbar that contains buttons for the most common formatting options. These toolbar buttons typically allow you to change the type style and size; make text bold, italic, or underlined; align paragraphs (left, center, or right); and create bulleted or numbered lists.

Guided Tour   Format a Page

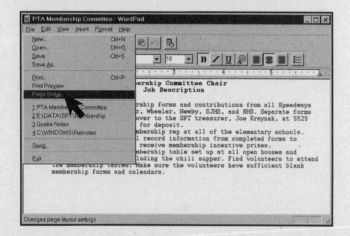

1 Open the document you want to format. Then open the **File** menu and select **Page Setup** (or a similar option for entering page settings).

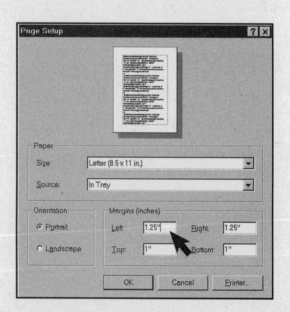

2 The page setup dialog box generally offers several settings for controlling the page layout. (This picture shows the WordPad version.) If necessary, click the tab for the margin settings. Enter the desired settings for the top, bottom, left, and right margins.

Guided Tour Format a Page

Most printers designate *unprintable regions* near the edges of the paper. When setting margins, do not set them so narrow that your text or other data ends up in an unprintable region.

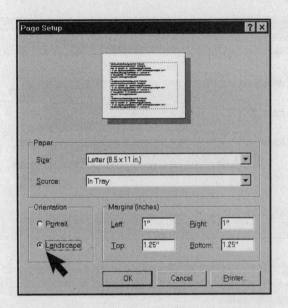

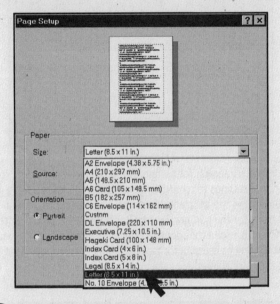

3 The Page Setup dialog box should have settings for the paper size. Make sure the program is set up to use the same size paper that is in your printer.

4 The paper orientation setting allows you to print in *portrait* or *landscape orientation*. For letters, reports, and similar documents, you want to print in portrait orientation. For wide documents, select **Landscape** orientation to print sideways on the page.

5 Advanced programs might offer additional page setup options for controlling the placement of headers and footers or for printing on envelopes, mailing labels, and so on. For example, Microsoft Word allows you to print a different header and footer (or none at all) on odd- and even-numbered pages.

6 When you are done entering your page setup settings, click the **OK** button.

Guided Tour Format Paragraphs

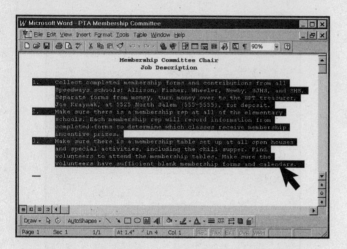

1 To apply paragraph formatting, move the insertion point to the paragraph you want to format, or highlight two or more paragraphs.

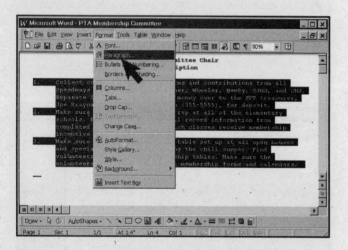

2 Open the **Format** menu and choose **Paragraph** (or a similar option for entering paragraph format settings).

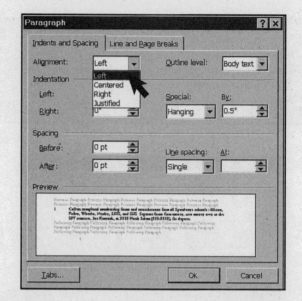

3 The paragraph formatting dialog box generally offers several settings for controlling the paragraph layout. (This picture shows the Microsoft Word version.) Select the desired alignment for the paragraph(s): **Left**, **Center**, or **Right**. (Center alignment is useful for adding a document title on the first page. Right alignment is useful for placing a date in the upper-right corner of a document.)

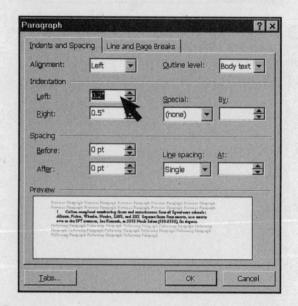

4 To indent a paragraph from the left or right margin, enter the distance you want the left or right side of the paragraph to be indented.

Guided Tour Format Paragraphs

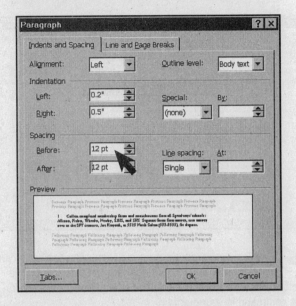

5 To insert additional space above or below the paragraph, type the desired amount of space (typically measured in *points*) in the **Spacing Above** or **Spacing Below** text box or its equivalent. (A point is 1/72 of an inch.)

6 Some programs offer advanced paragraph formatting options for controlling the way a paragraph is divided at a page break. For example, checking the **Widow/Orphan Control** option in Microsoft Word prevents a single line of a paragraph from being stranded at the bottom or top of a page.

7 After entering the desired paragraph settings, click **OK**.

Guided Tour Format Text

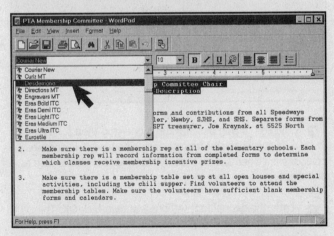

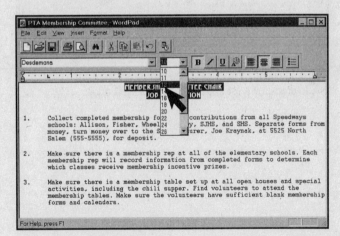

1 You can enter text formatting settings before typing text, or you can format existing text by highlighting it and applying the formatting. Highlight some text you want to format.

2 The easiest way to apply formatting is to use the formatting toolbar—if your program has one. Open the **Font** list and select the desired type style. (If your program does not have a formatting toolbar, skip to step 6.)

3 Open the **Font Size** drop-down list and select the desired type size (in points).

(continues)

Guided Tour   Format Text

(continued)

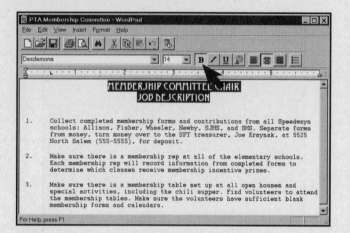

(4) Click the **Bold**, **Italic**, or **Underline** button to add any desired text enhancements. (You can click a button again to remove the enhancement.)

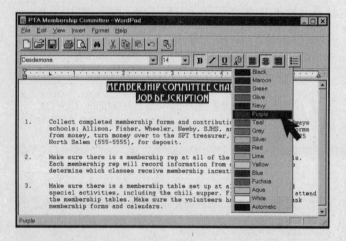

(5) To change the color of the text, open the **Font Color** drop-down list and choose the desired color.

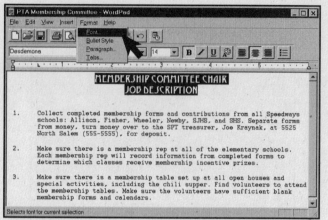

(6) If your program does not have a formatting toolbar or you need to apply text formatting that's not available on the toolbar, open the **Format** menu and select **Font** (or the equivalent command in your program).

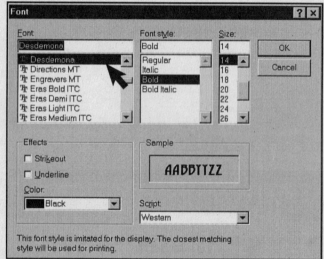

(7) The Font dialog box provides a one-stop shop for all the available character formats, including type style and size, color, enhancements, and, in some cases, special effects such as animation.

(8) Enter the desired font settings and then click **OK**. The program immediately applies the font settings to the selected text.

Work with Two or More Documents

In most cases, you will work with one document at a time. You'll type a letter, write a report, reconcile your checkbook, or perform some other single task. However, work sometimes requires that you juggle two or more documents. For example, you might need to copy a graph from a spreadsheet and paste it into a report, or copy an outline and paste it into a blank document so you can develop it into a chapter or report.

To work with two or more documents at a time, you need to know how to juggle program and document windows and cut, copy, and paste data between documents. The *Guided Tour* shows you how to perform these basic tasks in most Windows programs.

Sharing Data in Windows

Whenever you cut or copy data from one document, it is placed on the *Windows Clipboard*, where it is stored until you cut or copy another selection. You can then use the Edit, Paste command to paste the data into the same document or a different document. The Clipboard handles the data exchange behind the scenes, so you don't have to work with it directly. ▶To view the contents of the Clipboard, see "Share Data Between Applications with Clipboard Viewer" on page 199.◀

In addition, Windows provides an environment called *OLE* (*object linking and embedding*) for advanced data sharing with programs that support it. With OLE (pronounced oh-LAY), you can paste data from one document (the source) into another document (the destination) as a *linked object*. Whenever you update the source document, the changes automatically appear in the destination document. The *Guided Tour* shows you how to share data dynamically between two documents with OLE.

You can exchange data by using the Windows desktop. Drag the selected data to a blank area of the Windows desktop to create a *scrap*. An icon for the scrap appears on the desktop. You can then drag the scrap into another document to insert the copied data.

Compatible File Formats

Whenever you save a document, the program stores it in a *file format* that includes program-specific codes. These codes tell the program how to display and print the document. You rarely (if ever) work with these codes directly. However, if you need to open the document in a different program, you should be aware of the differences between file formats.

Don't confuse file formats with paragraph and text formatting, discussed earlier in this chapter. A file format is sort of like a secret code that the program uses. If you try to open the file in a program that doesn't understand the secret code, the program might not open the file or might display strange symbols on the screen. Likewise, if you try to insert a picture that's stored in a format your word-processing program does not *support* (understand), the picture might not appear in your document.

Most advanced programs provide support for common file formats. When you open a file created in a different program, the current program automatically converts the file into its native format. If the program does not support the format of the document you are trying to open, it might not be able to open the document.

If you cannot open a document you created in one program in another program, try using the original program to save the document in a format that the other program supports. To do so, use the **File, Save As** command and select a supported format from the **Save As Type** drop-down list.

Guided Tour Work with Two Documents in the Same Program

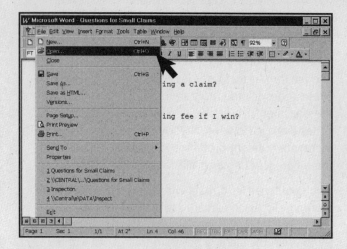

1 Use the **File**, **Open** command to open two or more documents in your program. ▶See "Open a Saved Document" on page 142.◀

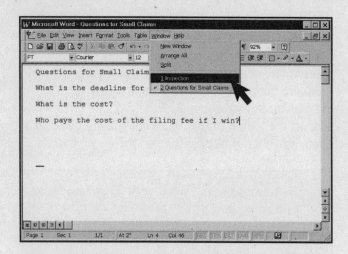

2 If the document windows are maximized, the program displays only the most recently opened document. Open the **Window** menu and click the name of the desired document to move its window to the front.

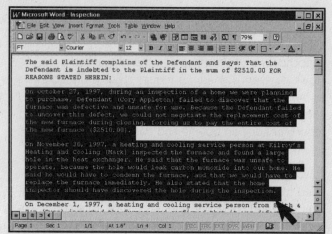

3 To copy data from one document and insert it into another, first select the text or other data you want to copy.

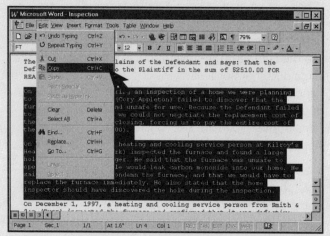

4 Open the **Edit** menu and choose **Copy**. The selected data is placed on the Windows Clipboard.

Guided Tour Work with Two Documents in the Same Program

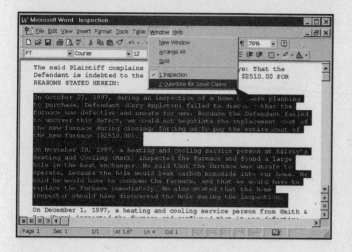

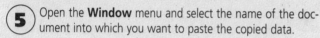

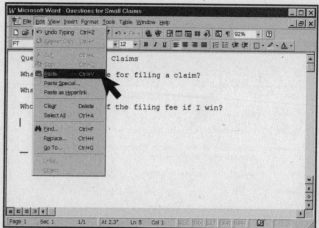

5 Open the **Window** menu and select the name of the document into which you want to paste the copied data.

6 The selected document is moved to the front. Position the insertion point where you want the data inserted. Then open the **Edit** menu and choose **Paste**. The data from the Clipboard is inserted.

Guided Tour Exchange Data Between Programs

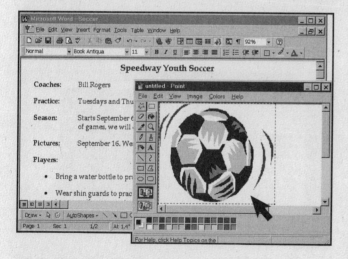

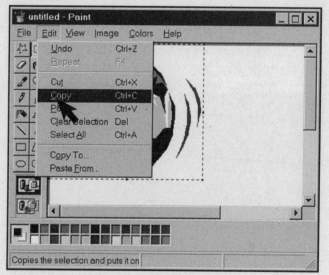

1 Run both programs and open the two documents you want to use.

2 In the source document, select the data you want to insert into the destination document. Then open the **Edit** menu and choose **Copy**.

(continues)

Guided Tour Exchange Data Between Programs *(continued)*

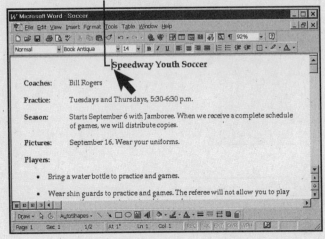

The graphic of the soccer ball will be inserted here.

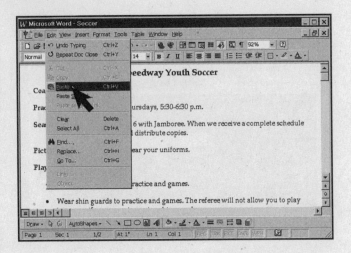

3 In the destination document, position the insertion point where you want the copied data inserted.

4 Open the **Edit** menu and choose **Paste**. The copied data is inserted into the document at the location of the insertion point.

Guided Tour Paste Data as a Link with OLE

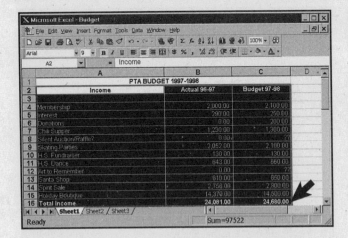

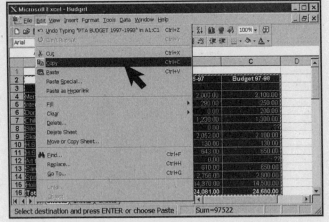

1 Open the source document and highlight the data you want to copy. (In this figure, the cell that says "Income" *is* highlighted along with the others, but Excel doesn't reverse the colors for the first cell selected.)

2 Open the **Edit** menu and choose **Copy**. The data is placed on the Windows Clipboard.

Guided Tour   Paste Data as a Link with OLE

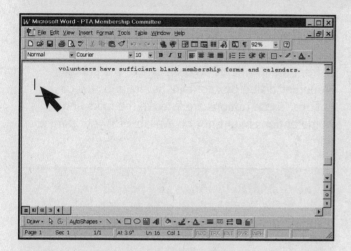

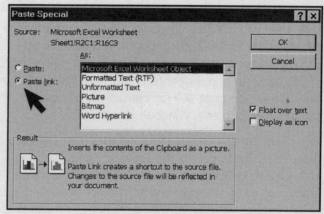

3 Open the destination document and position the insertion point where you want to insert the copied data.

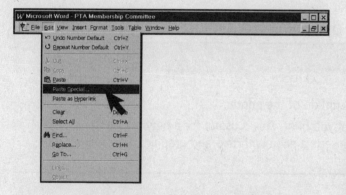

4 Open the **Edit** menu and choose **Paste Special**. If the Paste Special command is not available, the program does not support dynamic data sharing, but you can still use the Edit, Paste command.

5 The Paste Special dialog box appears. Click **Paste Link**.

6 In the **As** list, select the desired format in which to insert the data. (Format options vary depending on the type of data you are pasting.)

7 Click **OK**, and the data is inserted. Whenever you edit the data in the original (source) document, the pasted data will automatically be updated in the destination document.

If you paste data using Edit, Paste instead of Edit, Paste Special, the data is not automatically updated in the destination document when you edit the source document. However, you can usually edit the data right inside the destination document. In some cases, you can edit the pasted data by double-clicking the data in the destination document. This displays the data in the program you used to create it.

Set Printer Options

When you installed Windows, the setup program should have led you through the process of setting up your printer. ▶If your printer was not connected or you chose to skip the printer setup, see "Set Up a New Printer" on page 369 for instructions on how to set up a new printer in Windows.◀

When you install a printer, Windows uses the printer's default settings to control the paper size and type, text and graphics quality, and other properties of the printer. Before you print, you might want to check and change some of these settings to increase the speed or quality at which your printer prints.

The *Guided Tour* leads you through the basic steps for changing your printer's default properties. If you used special software that came with your printer to set it up,

the dialog box you use to change your printer's properties might look much different. If you installed the printer from the Windows 98 disks or CD, the Printer Properties dialog box contains several tabs full of options. Those options are listed in the following table (some options might not be available for your particular printer).

> The *Guided Tour* shows you how to change the default settings for your printer. Enter settings to control the way *most* documents are printed. You can change the settings for individual documents when you print them. ▶See "Print a Document" on page 164.◀

Printer Options

Option Name	Description
General	
Comment	Optional entry that provides a description of the printer.
Separator Page	Inserts a page after each document you print. This is useful for a network printer that several people are using. The Full setting inserts a page with text and graphics; the Simple setting inserts a page with text only.
Details	
Print to the Following Port	Specifies the port on the back of your computer to which the printer is connected. If you receive an error message indicating that the port you are trying to print to is unavailable (but you know the printer is turned on), try printing to a different port. Most printers connect to the LPT1 port.
Print Using the Following Driver	Specifies the *printer driver* you want to use. The driver tells Windows how to communicate with the printer. When you set up a printer in Windows, the driver is automatically installed. However, you might need to update or change the driver if you are having severe printing problems.
Not Selected	Tells Windows how long to wait before displaying an error message when your printer is not connected or turned on.
Transmission Retry	Tells Windows how long to wait before displaying an error message when Windows has trouble sending data to your printer.
Color Management	
Profiles Currently Associated with This Printer	Allows you to assign a color profile to your color printer, which provides greater control of how colors are displayed in print.

Option Name	Description
Sharing (Network Only)	
Not Shared	Marks your printer as an unshared resource.
Shared As	Allows you to share the printer that is connected to your computer with other computers on the network. If you choose Shared As, you must enter a name for your printer. You can also specify a password to prevent unauthorized printing.
Paper	
Paper Size	Specifies the size and type of paper you are printing on (such as standard 8.5-by-11 inch paper or a #10 envelope).
Orientation	Sets the print direction. You can print in Portrait or Landscape (sideways) orientation.
Paper Source	Specifies the paper tray to use for printers that have more than one paper tray.
Media Choice	Specifies the paper type. For example, your printer might be able to print on plain or glossy paper or transparencies.
Copies	Specifies the default number of copies of a document. Because you usually set the number of copies each time you print, consider leaving this set to 1.
Unprintable Area	Specifies the distance from the edges of the paper where the print head cannot physically reach.
Graphics	
Resolution	Sets the number of dots per inch that the printer uses for printing images. With higher resolution, print quality is higher, but printing takes longer and uses more ink or toner.
Dithering	Specifies how shading is handled. Fine dithering shades with many small dots, which creates smoother shading.
Intensity	Sets the darkness of the print.
Fonts	
Cartridges	Specifies the number of print *cartridges* installed. Some printers allow you to add fonts and memory to the printer using cartridges. Fonts stored on cartridges typically print faster than *soft fonts* (fonts generated from software).
TrueType Fonts	Tells the printer how to handle *TrueType fonts*, an advanced type of software font that you can set to any size. The Print TrueType as Graphics setting generates the highest text quality. Treating TrueType fonts as outline soft fonts provides for faster printing but lower quality. Printing TrueType fonts as bitmaps provides slow, high-quality printing.
Device Options	
Print Quality	Typically gives you three options: Normal (medium speed and quality), EconoFast (low-quality, but fast), and Presentation (high-quality, but slow).
Printer Memory	Displays the amount of memory typically installed in the printer by the manufacturer. If you add memory by installing a memory board or cartridge, you must change the Printer Memory setting here. Do not specify more memory than your printer has.
Page Protection	If your computer has a great deal of memory, you might be able to turn on page protection to use a portion of memory as a buffer area for large or complex documents.
Printer Memory Tracking	Specifies how conservatively or aggressively your printer driver should monitor the printer's memory usage. If you receive an error message when you try to print a large or complex document, you might want to enter a more aggressive setting. However, doing so could overload your printer's memory and result in garbled output.

Guided Tour Change the Default Printer Settings

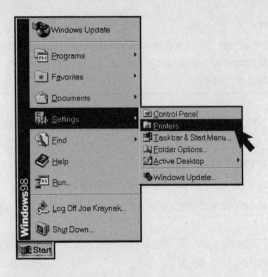

1 Click the **Start** button, point to **Settings**, and click **Printers**.

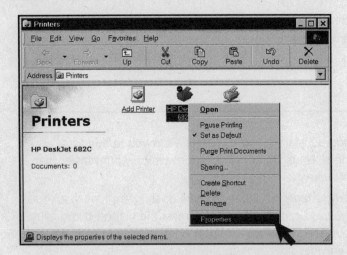

2 The Printers window appears, displaying icons for all printers installed in Windows. Right-click the printer whose properties you want to change and choose **Properties**.

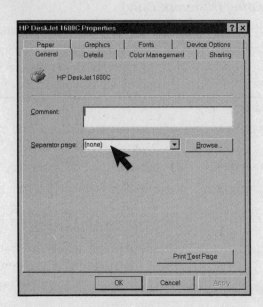

3 The Properties dialog box for the selected printer appears, displaying the General tab in front. Enter any desired settings on the General tab, as explained in the previous table.

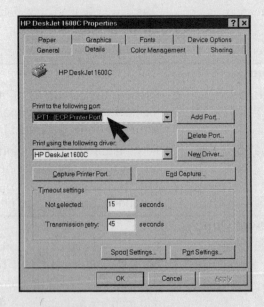

4 Click the **Details** tab to display settings that allow Windows to communicate with your printer. If Windows is not communicating with the printer, change the necessary settings as explained in the previous table.

5 If you have a color printer, you can click the **Color Management** tab to view a list of color profiles. To add a profile, click the **Add** button, choose the desired profile, and click **Add**.

Guided Tour   Change the Default Printer Settings

6 If the printer connected to your computer is the network printer, click the **Sharing** tab, select **Shared As**, and type a name for the printer in the **Share Name** text box.

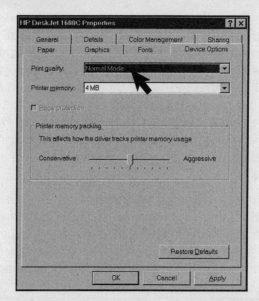

7 Click the **Paper** tab to check the paper settings. Enter your preferences, as described in the previous table. For example, if you have a printer with two or more paper trays, you might want to specify which is the default tray.

8 Click the **Graphics** tab and enter your preferences to specify how you want your printer to print images.

9 Click the **Fonts** tab and enter settings to specify how you want your printer to print text.

10 Click the **Device Options** tab and enter settings to adjust the print quality and the way Windows manages your printer's memory.

11 When you're satisfied with your settings on all the tabs, click **OK**.

Print a Document

Although it is becoming common to share documents electronically via email or by publishing them on the World Wide Web, paper is still the most popular medium. In order to create a paper document, you must open it in the program you used to create it (or a compatible program) and then use the program's File, Print command to start printing. The program then transmits the document to the printer to create the desired output.

Most programs provide two ways to print. You can click the **Print** button on the program's toolbar to print a single copy using the printer's default properties. To print more than one copy or to change the printer properties for this document, you use the **File**, **Print** command to open a dialog box in which you can enter your preferences. The following *Guided Tour* shows you how to print using both methods.

Many programs offer a *print preview* feature that lets you display the document the way it will appear in print. Previewing a document before you print it can save time, effort, and supplies spent in reprinting—if it's a long document and you forgot to put in page numbers, for example. You can usually access the print preview feature by clicking a print preview button or by choosing **File**, **Print Preview**.

Guided Tour Print Quickly Using the Print Button

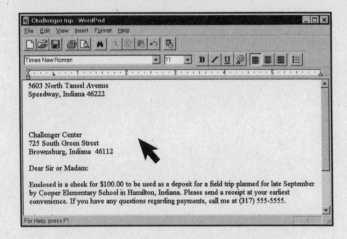

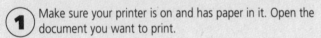

1 Make sure your printer is on and has paper in it. Open the document you want to print.

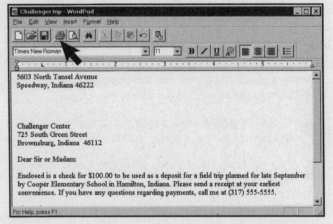

2 Click the **Print** button in the program's Standard toolbar. Windows immediately transmits the document to the printer, and the printer starts to print it.

Guided Tour Change the Printer Settings for One Document

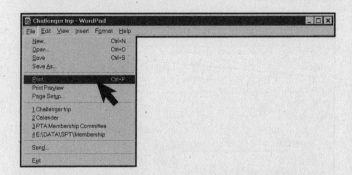

1 Open the document you want to print, and then open the **File** menu and select **Print**.

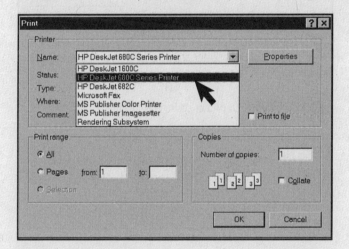

2 The Print dialog box appears. If your computer is set up to use more than one printer, open the **Name** drop-down list and choose the name of the printer you want to use.

Some of the options shown in these steps might not be available in the Print dialog box for older Windows applications.

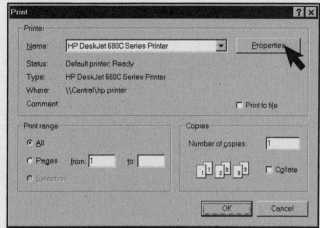

3 Click the **Properties** button.

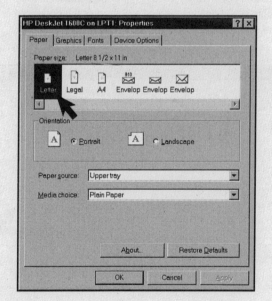

4 The Properties dialog box appears, displaying many of the same tabs you encountered in the previous task. Enter the desired settings and click **OK**.

(continues)

Guided Tour Change the Printer Settings for One Document *(continued)*

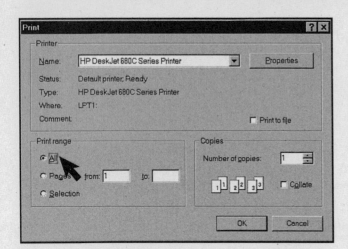

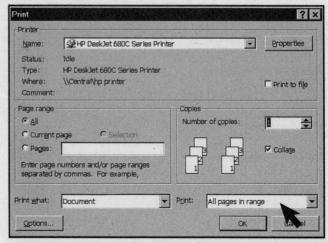

5 You are returned to the Print dialog box. Under Print Range, specify the portion of the document you want to print: **All**, **Pages from ___ to ____**, or **Selection**. (Selection is available only if you highlighted a portion of the document before selecting the Print command.)

7 The Print dialog box in some programs contains additional printing options. Enter any additional settings, such as printing pages in reverse order.

8 Click **OK**. Your printer starts printing the document.

Error messages are common during printing. ▶If you receive an error message, see "Printers and Printing" on page 545 to figure out what to do about it.◀

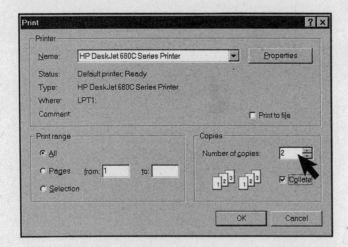

6 Under Copies, enter the number of copies you want to print. To have your printer collate the copies, click **Collate**. (The Collate option varies depending on the program. Some programs print all copies of page one, followed by all copies of page two, and so on. Other programs collate by printing the first copy of all pages, then the second copy of all pages, and so on.)

Manage Print Jobs

Most printers are set up for *background printing*. When you enter the Print command, the program saves instructions on how to print the document to a temporary file. Windows then feeds (*spools*) the instructions to the printer when the printer is ready to receive them. This allows you to continue to work in other programs as the document is printed.

However, print spooling does make it a little more difficult to manage the actual printing. Because Windows is busy feeding instructions to your printer, you can run into problems when you are printing several documents and you need to pause or cancel the printing operation.

Fortunately, Windows has a tool called *Print Manager* that displays the names of all the documents currently

being printed. You can use Print Manager to remove one or more documents from the *queue* (the waiting line), to rearrange documents in the queue, and even to pause printing. The *Guided Tour* shows you how to display Print Manager and use it to control the printing operation.

> If you are using a printer that is physically connected to a different computer on a network, you might not have control of the print jobs. You will still be able to display Print Manager, but you will not be able to pause, cancel, or rearrange print jobs in the queue.

Guided Tour   Control Document Printing

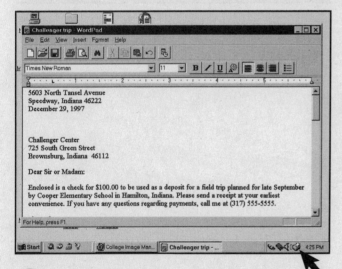

1 When you start printing, the Print Manager icon appears in the system tray (at the right end of the Windows taskbar). Double-click the **Print Manager** icon.

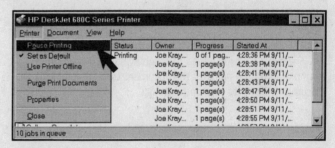

2 Windows displays the print queue window, which contains a list of documents currently being printed. To pause printing, open the **Printer** menu and select **Pause Printing**. A check mark appears next to the Pause Printing option.

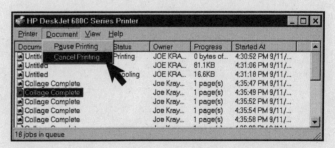

3 To remove a document from the print queue, click the document's name, open the **Document** menu, and select **Cancel Printing**.

(continues)

Guided Tour Control Document Printing

(continued)

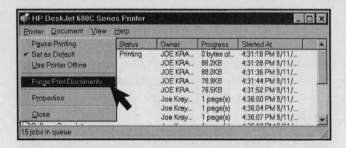

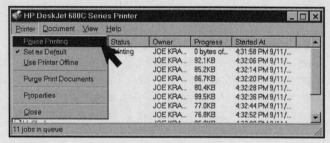

4 To remove all documents from the print queue and cancel printing altogether, open the **Printer** menu and select **Purge Print Documents**.

6 To resume printing (if you paused it), open the **Printer** menu and select **Pause Printing** again to remove the check mark.

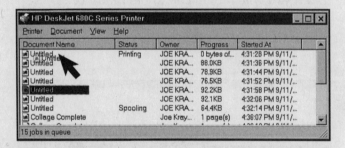

Because your printer has its own memory, it will not immediately stop printing when you choose to cancel or pause printing. Depending on the amount of memory installed in your printer, it might print one or more pages before it stops.

5 To move a document up or down in the print queue (to move a rush job ahead of others waiting to print, for example), drag the name of the document up or down in the list. Documents closer to the top print first.

HOW TO...

Use the Windows 98 Accessories

Although Windows 98's main role is to act as an operating environment in which you run your other programs, it also comes with its own programs that you can use immediately to write letters and other simple documents, paint pictures, perform calculations, program your modem to dial the phone for you, play games, record and play sounds, and even play audio CDs on your CD-ROM drive.

Because each of these programs is robust and offers some fairly advanced features, this book cannot cover each program in great detail. However, in this section, you will learn how to run the Windows accessories and use each program's basic tools to perform common tasks, create standard documents, and even have some fun with games.

As you create and edit documents by using some of the Windows accessories (including WordPad and Paint), you may need to refer to the following tasks: ▶"Create a Document," on page 136; "Save a Document," on page 139; "Edit a Document," on page 144; "Format a Document," on page 150; and "Print a Document," on page 164.◀

What You Will Find in This Section

Type Documents with WordPad

Personal computers started out as not much more than fancy typewriters. What made them attractive was that you could type a document, save it, and then edit it later to correct grammatical errors and typos without having to retype the entire document or mar its appearance with a bottle of Liquid Paper.

Although computers have become more useful for performing other tasks, such as reconciling checkbook balances, creating graphs, and managing data, people still use word processing programs to type and print documents more than they use any other type of program.

Windows comes with a basic word processing program called *WordPad* that you can use to type, format, and print documents, such as letters and reports. The following *Guided Tour* shows you how to create and format a simple document in WordPad.

You can open and revise the documents you create in WordPad in almost any word processing program, so if you decide to move up to a more robust word processing program later (such as WordPerfect or Microsoft Word), you won't have to retype the documents you created in WordPad.

Format Your WordPad Document

WordPad has some standard tools for formatting documents (changing the look and layout of the text). The Formatting toolbar includes drop-down lists for changing the type style and size; making text bold, italic, or underlined; changing the text color; aligning paragraphs

Formatting Toolbar Controls

Control	Name	Description
Times New Roman	Font	Displays a list of type styles from which to choose.
10	Font Size	Displays a list of type sizes from which to choose.
B	Bold	Makes text bold.
I	Italic	Makes text italic.
U	Underline	Underlines text.
A	Color	Displays a list of colors from which to choose.
	Align Left	Positions all lines in a paragraph flush against the left margin.
	Center	Positions all lines in a paragraph at an equal distance between the left and right margins.
	Align Right	Positions all lines in a paragraph flush against the right margin.
	Bullets	Transforms selected paragraphs into a bulleted list.

left, right, or center; and transforming paragraphs into bulleted lists. The Formatting Toolbar Controls table describes these drop-down menus and buttons.

The Format menu contains additional options for changing the appearance and layout of your text. It contains four options: Font (for changing type style, size, and color, and for adding enhancements such as bold), Bullet Style (does the same thing as the Bullet button in the toolbar), Paragraph (for controlling paragraph alignment and indents), and Tabs (for setting the tab stop positions).

Tab stops mark the positions to which the insertion point moves when you press the Tab key. For example, if you set a tab stop at every inch, the insertion point moves one inch to the right each time you press the Tab key.

WordPad also displays a ruler just above the document viewing area that you can use to set tab stop positions and paragraph indents. The ruler has triangular margin markers at its left and right ends. You drag the right margin marker to indent the right side of a paragraph. The left margin marker is a little trickier. It has two triangles and a box. Drag the top triangle to indent only the first line of the paragraph. Drag the bottom triangle to indent all lines of the paragraph except the top line (creating a *hanging indent*). Drag the box below the triangle to indent all lines in the paragraph. The *Guided Tour* shows this tool in action.

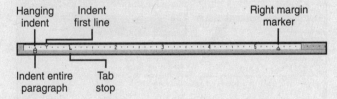

Insert Images and Other Objects

As you create documents, you might need to insert graphic images, sounds, the date and time, and other items. For example, you might want to create a simple logo in Paint and then insert it at the top of a business letter, or you might want to add a clickable sound icon so that the reader receives a recorded message with the letter.

WordPad has a tool you can use to quickly insert the current date and time from your computer into a

document. You can also use basic copy and paste techniques (➤as explained in "Edit a Document" on page 144◄) to insert text, graphics, or other objects copied from another document. In addition, WordPad's Insert, Object command lets you use any shared program installed on your computer to create and insert an object (such as an image) on-the-fly. The *Guided Tour* shows you how to use the Insert, Object command.

Shared programs are programs you can open and use from your other Windows programs. In Windows 98, programs share computer code, so if you choose to insert a bitmapped image in WordPad, Paint's tools appear inside the WordPad window, allowing you to paint a picture right inside your document. The technology that enables two programs to share data dynamically is called *OLE* (pronounced "Oh-lay," which is short for *Object Linking and Embedding*).

Set WordPad's Options

By default, WordPad is set up to display the toolbar, format bar, and ruler; to display measurements in inches (as opposed to centimeters, points, or picas); and to automatically *wrap* text between the left and right margins. When word wrap is on, WordPad automatically starts a new line of text whenever the insertion point reaches the right margin. You can also turn *automatic word selection* on or off. With automatic word selection on, WordPad extends the highlight over entire words as you drag over text.

You can change any of these options for the various document file types you create with WordPad. To do so, open the **View** menu, select **Options**, and click the tab for the desired document type. Enter your preferences and click **OK**.

Windows also comes with a text-only editor, called Notepad, that allows you to create unformatted documents. Notepad is also used to display text files, whose names end in .TXT. Many programs come with text-only documents, such as README.TXT, which contain useful information. You simply click the file in My Computer, and Notepad opens it. To run Notepad without opening a file, choose **Start, Programs, Accessories, Notepad**.

Guided Tour Type and Format a WordPad Document

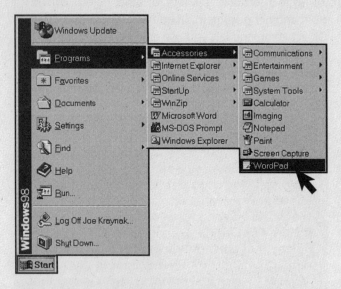

1 Click the **Start** button, point to **Programs** and then **Accessories**, and click **WordPad**. WordPad starts and displays a blank document window.

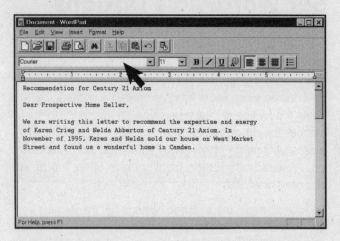

2 Type your document. You can use the drop-down lists and buttons in the Formatting toolbar to format text as you type it.

3 To format existing text, first highlight the text by dragging over it. ▶For details on how to select text, see "Select Text and Other Objects" on page 144.◀

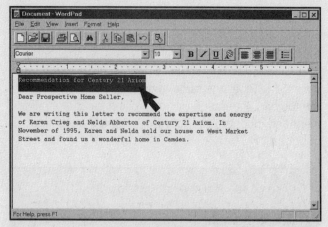

If you make a mistake while editing or formatting your document, you can undo the last action you performed by clicking the **Undo** button in the toolbar or by choosing **Edit, Undo**.

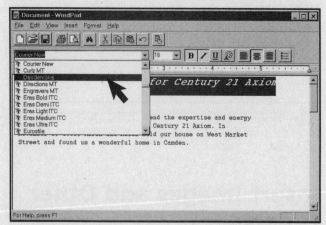

4 Use any of the controls in the Formatting toolbar to change the appearance or position of the selected text. See the table "Formatting Toolbar Controls" for details.

Guided Tour Type and Format a WordPad Document

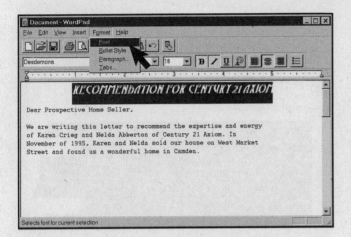

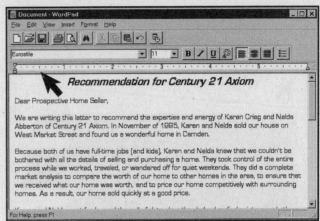

5 For additional control over text and paragraph formatting, open the **Format** menu and select the desired option: **Font**, **Bullet Style**, **Paragraph**, or **Tabs**.

7 The ruler allows you to quickly add tab stops and change paragraph indents. To set a tab stop, click in the bottom part of the ruler where you want to insert the tab stop.

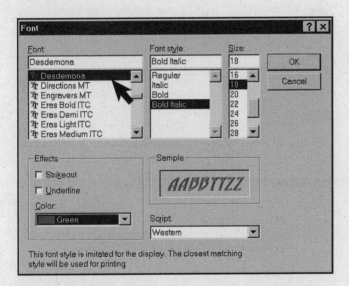

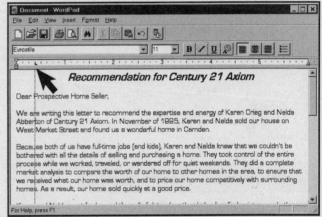

6 Most options on the Format menu display a dialog box that allows you to enter your preferences. The Font dialog box is shown here. Enter the desired settings and click **OK**. (Keep an eye on the Sample box as you make changes to see how your text will look with the selected settings.)

8 The tab stop appears as an L. You can remove the tab stop by dragging it off of the ruler. You can move the tab stop by dragging it to the left or right. Notice the dashed, vertical line that appears below the tab stop when you click it; this line helps you position the tab.

(continues)

Guided Tour Type and Format a WordPad Document

(continued)

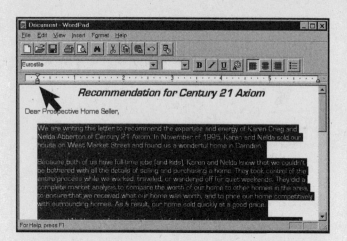

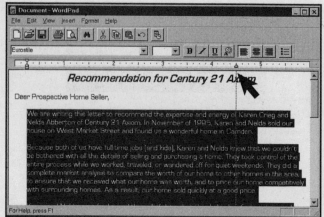

9 To indent the current paragraph or selected paragraphs, click the little box below the left margin markers and drag it to the right. (You can drag the top triangle to indent only the first line of the paragraph(s), or you can drag the bottom triangle to indent all lines except the first line, creating a hanging indent.)

10 To indent the right side of the current paragraph or selected paragraphs, click the right margin marker and drag it to the left.

11 When you finish creating your document, save it ▶as explained in "Save a Document," on page 139.◀

> Eventually you will want to save and probably print the document you create. ▶See "Save a Document" on page 139 and "Print a Document" on page 164 for details.◀

Guided Tour Insert Objects

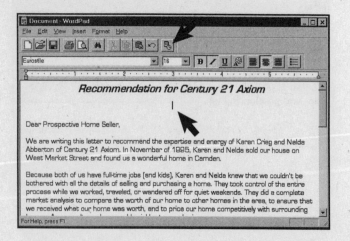

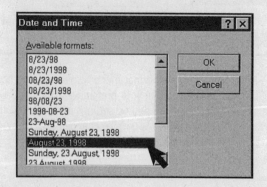

1 To insert the date and/or time, position the insertion point where you want the date or time inserted, and then click the **Date/Time** button.

2 The Date and Time dialog box prompts you to select a format. Click the desired format and click **OK**. WordPad inserts the date and/or time based on your computer's internal clock.

Guided Tour   Insert Objects

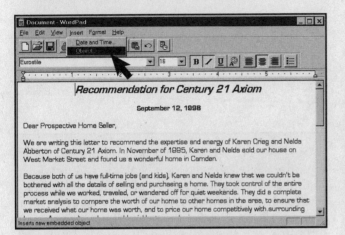

③ To insert an object from a shared program, position the insertion point where you want the object inserted. Then open the **Insert** menu and choose **Object**.

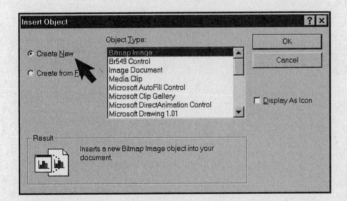

④ The Insert Object dialog box prompts you to select the type of object you want to insert. The list of object types varies depending on the programs installed on your computer. By default, Create New is selected; it allows you to create an object from scratch.

⑤ In the **Object Type** list, click the type of object you want to insert. In this example, Bitmap Image is selected. This will run Paint, which you can use to draw a picture. Click **OK**.

Because Paint and WordPad support OLE, you can paint a picture directly in the WordPad window.

The WordPad   Paint's
title bar   menu bar

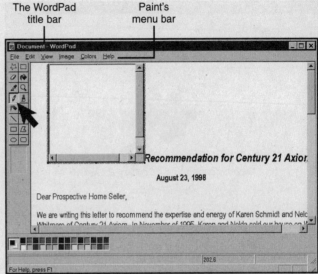

⑥ A Paint drawing window appears in your WordPad document, the WordPad menu bar changes to the Paint menu bar, and Paint's drawing tools appear on the left. Use Paint's tools to create your picture. ▶See "Create Images in Paint" on page 177.◀

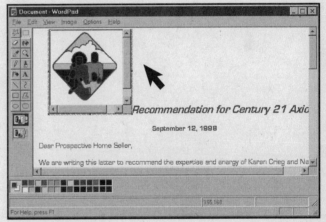

⑦ When you finish creating your picture, click anywhere outside the picture window (but still inside the WordPad document).

(continues)

Guided Tour Insert Objects *(continued)*

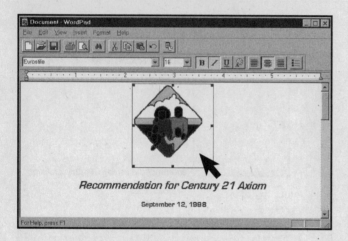

8 You are returned to WordPad, and the picture (or other object you created) is inserted in your document. To edit the object at any time, double-click it. To change its size or location, click the object and use the handles that appear, ▶as described in "Select, Move, and Copy Drawn Objects" on page 148.◀

The Insert Object dialog box also has an option called Create from File. You can use that option to insert an object that you have already created and saved. Simply select **Create from File** and then click the **Browse** button and select the file you want to insert.

Create Images in Paint

If you have some artistic skills, you can use Paint to transform your mental images into pictures. You can create logos for your business letters, create your own clip art, and even paint pictures for your home or office. And if you have kids, they will spend hours playing with Paint and using it to create illustrations for their classroom reports.

When you start Paint, it displays a blank page on which you can start drawing. You select the line or shape you want to draw from the Paint toolbox, choose a color, and then drag the mouse pointer over the page to create the line or shape, as shown in the *Guided Tour*. By using various shapes and colors, you create pictures or illustrations. The following table lists the available Paint tools and provides a brief description of each tool.

Paint Tools

Tool	Name	Description
	Free-Form Select	Allows you to highlight an irregularly shaped area of your picture for cutting or copying.
	Select	Allows you to highlight a rectangular area of your picture for cutting or copying.
	Erase/Color Eraser	Transforms the mouse pointer into an eraser that you can use to delete lines or colors.
	Fill With Color	Transforms the mouse pointer into a "can of paint" that you can tip inside an object to fill the object with the selected color.
	Pick Color	Lets you "lift" a color from your picture so you can use the same color for another line or shape.
	Magnifier	Zooms in on an area of the picture, so you can edit the individual dots (*pixels*) that make up the lines and colors.
	Pencil	Lets you draw irregularly shaped thin lines.
	Brush	Lets you stroke color on your screen; you can choose different thicknesses for your brushstrokes.
	Airbrush	Transforms the mouse pointer into a "paint can" that you can use to spray-paint the page.
	Text	Lets you place an insertion point on the page and type titles, labels, and other text.
	Line	Lets you draw a straight line.
	Curve	Lets you draw a curved line.
	Rectangle	Lets you draw rectangles and squares.

(continues)

Paint Tools Continued

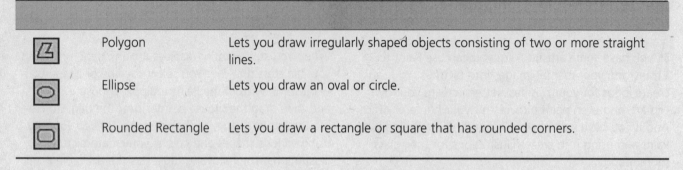

	Polygon	Lets you draw irregularly shaped objects consisting of two or more straight lines.
	Ellipse	Lets you draw an oval or circle.
	Rounded Rectangle	Lets you draw a rectangle or square that has rounded corners.

The Paint window also has a color palette (called the *Color Box*) for choosing the foreground and background colors you want to use, as well as a palette whose tools change depending on the object you want to draw. For example, if you click the Line button, the palette displays various line thicknesses. If you click a button for a shape, such as a rectangle, the palette provides tools for creating an outline (which has no color inside), a filled shape (consisting of a line that defines the shape and a

color shading), or a filled shape with no outline. Take the *Guided Tour* to learn how to use the Paint tools.

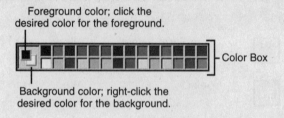

Foreground color; click the desired color for the foreground.

Color Box

Background color; right-click the desired color for the background.

Guided Tour Paint a Picture

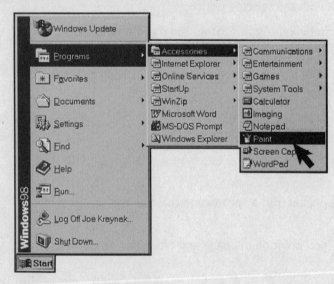

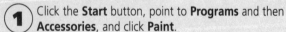

1 Click the **Start** button, point to **Programs** and then **Accessories**, and click **Paint**.

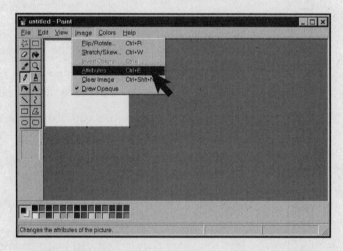

Changes the attributes of the picture.

2 Before you start painting, you should specify the desired size of the painting. Open the **Image** menu and choose **Attributes**.

Guided Tour Paint a Picture

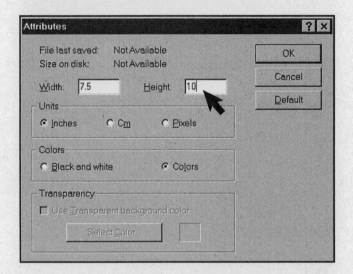

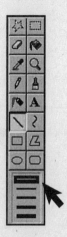

5 In the line thickness list, click the desired line thickness.

3 The Attributes dialog box initially displays the image size in pixels (screen dots). Under Units, click **Inches**, and then enter the desired width and height for the picture in the **Width** and **Height** text boxes. Click **OK**.

6 In the **Color Box**, click the desired color.

It's tempting to set the image size as 8.5-by-11 inches. However, your printer probably cannot print to the edge of the page. Subtract one inch from the dimensions to include a 1-inch border. If you are creating a picture that will be displayed onscreen, choose **Pixels** as the unit of measurement and enter your screen's resolution (for example, 800×600).

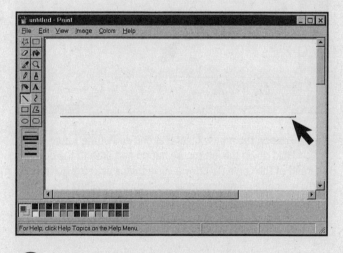

7 Position the mouse pointer at one end of the future line. Hold down the left mouse button and drag to the opposite end of the line. To draw a line that is perfectly horizontal, vertical, or at a 45-degree angle, hold down the **Shift** key while dragging.

4 To draw a line, click the **Line** button.

(continues)

Guided Tour Paint a Picture

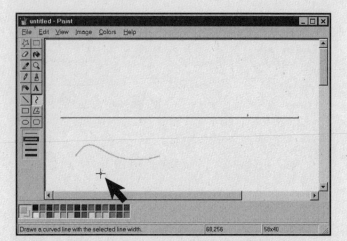

8 To draw a curve, click the **Curve** button and choose the desired line thickness and color.

10 When you release the mouse button, a straight line appears. You can now drag twice to define the curve. Move the mouse pointer to one side of the line and drag in the direction that you want the line to curve. Repeat this step to add another curve to the line.

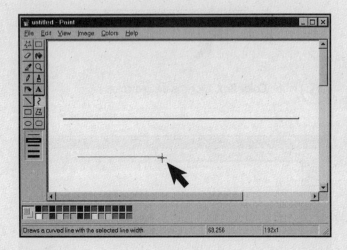

9 Position the mouse pointer at one end of the future curve. Hold down the left mouse button and drag to the opposite end of the curve. To draw a curve that is perfectly horizontal, vertical, or at a 45-degree angle, hold down the **Shift** key while dragging.

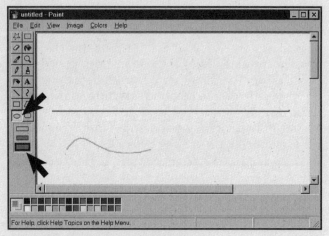

11 To create a rectangle, ellipse, or rounded rectangle, click the button for the desired shape.

12 From the fill style list, choose **Outline** (the top option) to draw an outline, **Filled** (the middle option) to create an outline that's filled with a color, or **No Outline** (the bottom option) to create a filled object without an outline.

13 In the **Color Box**, single-click the desired color for the shape's outline and right-click the color you want to use to fill in the shape.

Guided Tour   Paint a Picture

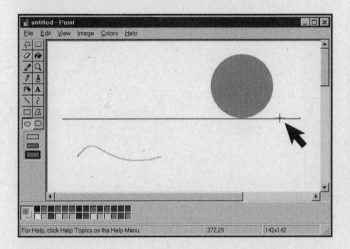

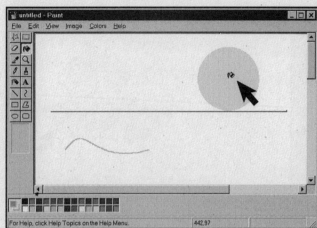

14 Position the mouse pointer where you want one corner or edge of the object to appear, hold down the left mouse button, and drag to the opposite corner or edge. To create a perfect circle or square, hold down the **Shift** key while dragging.

16 Move the mouse pointer inside the shape or area you want to fill with color and click the left mouse button. The entire object is filled with the selected color.

15 To fill any shape or enclosed area with color, click the **Fill With Color** button, and then choose the desired color from the Color Box.

If the shape or area you're filling is not *completely* enclosed (all edges connected), the fill color will "leak out." If this happens, select **Edit, Undo** to remove the fill color, and then fix the gap(s) and try again.

17 To spraypaint the screen, click the **Airbrush** button, and then choose the desired thickness of the spray and the color you want to use.

(continues)

Guided Tour Paint a Picture *(continued)*

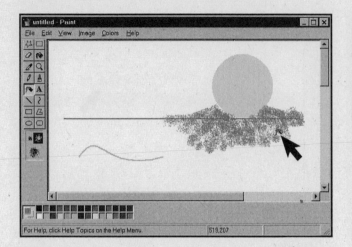

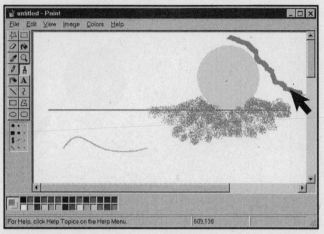

18 Drag over the painting to "spray" paint on it. The faster you drag, the lighter the coverage. (Drag with the left mouse button to paint using the foreground color; use the right mouse button to paint with the background color.)

20 Position the mouse pointer at one end of the future line, hold down the left mouse button, and drag to create a solid line of any shape. (You can drag with the right mouse button to use the background color.)

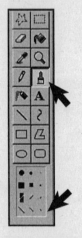

19 To draw irregularly shaped lines, you can use the Pencil or Brush button. For this example, click the **Brush** tool. Then choose the desired brush thickness and style and the desired color.

21 To use a color that is already in your picture, click the **Pick Color** button. This feature is great for modifying existing drawings with special colors that don't appear in the Color Box palette.

The Pencil and Brush tools are very similar. Both allow you to draw lines of any shape. However, the pencil tool creates only very thin lines. If you select the Brush tool, you can choose different brush thicknesses and styles.

Guided Tour Paint a Picture

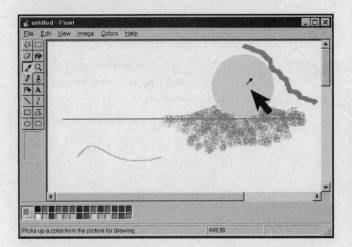

22 Single-click the color you want to use as the foreground color, or right-click a color to use it as the background color. The Color Box automatically changes to display the selected color(s).

After you pick up a color, Paint returns to the tool you were using before you clicked the Pick Color button. If you want to pick up both a new foreground color and a new background color, use the tool to pick one color, and then click the Pick Color button again before attempting to pick up the other color.

23 To add text to your painting, click the **Text** button.

24 In the palette at the bottom of the toolbox, you can choose to have the text appear in a box that is shaded with the selected background color, or in a clear box so that anything behind the text will show through.

25 In the Color Box, single-click the color you want to use for the text and right-click the color you want to use as the text box background (if any).

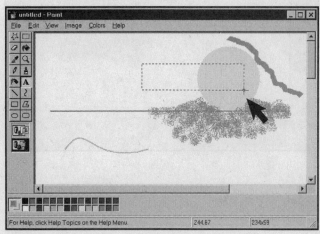

26 Position the mouse pointer where you want one corner of the text box to appear, hold down the left mouse button, and drag to the opposite corner.

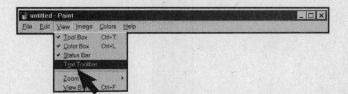

27 If the Fonts toolbar is not displayed, open the **View** menu and choose **Text Toolbar**.

28 From the Fonts toolbar, choose the desired type style, size, and enhancements.

(continues)

Guided Tour   Paint a Picture

(continued)

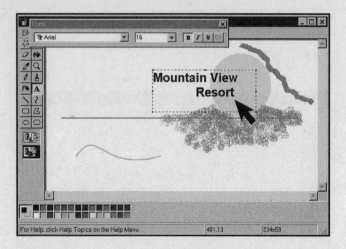

29 A text box appears, with an insertion point in the upper-left corner. Type your text.

30 Continue to add objects to the page as necessary to create your picture. Be sure to save your work, ▶as explained in "Save a Document" on page 139.◄

Guided Tour   Edit a Picture

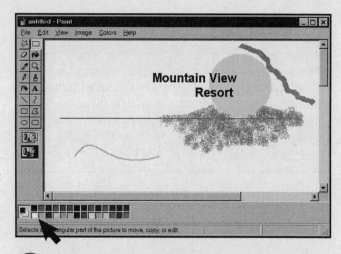

1 To cut or copy a rectangular area of your picture, click the **Select** button.

To open the file in which you stored your picture, use the **File, Open** command ▶as explained in "Open a Saved Document," on page 142.◄

2 When you cut a selected area of a picture, the background color is inserted in that area. For example, if the background color is green and you cut a rectangular area, that area will appear as a green rectangle. If you want a white area to appear, right-click the white color swatch in the Color Box.

Guided Tour Edit a Picture

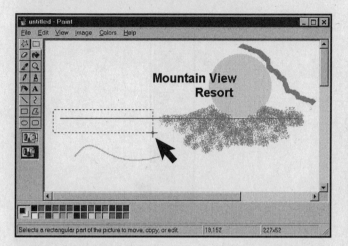

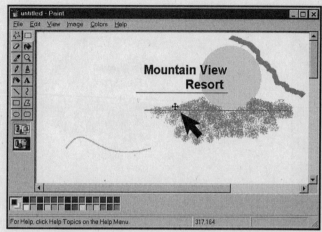

③ Position the mouse pointer at one corner of the area you want to select, hold down the left mouse button, and drag to the opposite corner. A dashed line appears around the selected area.

⑥ Position the mouse pointer over the selection, hold down the left mouse button, and drag it to the desired location. If you don't like the placement, click and drag it again. The selection is still active until you click another button in the toolbox or click outside the selected area.

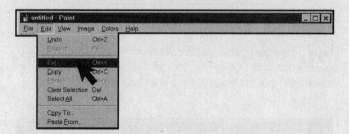

④ Open the **Edit** menu and choose **Cut** or **Copy**. The selected area is placed on the Windows Clipboard.

> After selecting an area, you can drag it to move it or **Ctrl+***drag* to copy it.

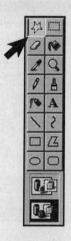

⑦ To select an irregularly shaped area of your picture, click the **Free-Form Select** button.

(continues)

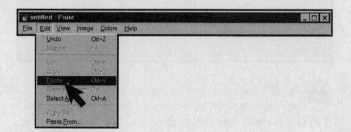

⑤ To paste the cut or copied area onto your picture, open the **Edit** menu and select **Paste**. The selection is inserted in the upper-left corner of the window.

Guided Tour Edit a Picture *(continued)*

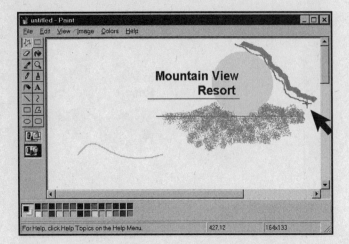

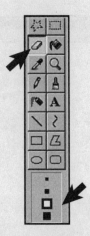

8 Move the mouse pointer to an edge of the area you want to select, hold down the left mouse button, and drag around the edge of the area. When you release the mouse button, a dotted rectangle appears around the selected area.

10 To erase a portion of your picture, click the **Erase/Color Eraser** button. Choose the desired size of the eraser from the style list at the bottom of the toolbox.

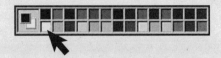

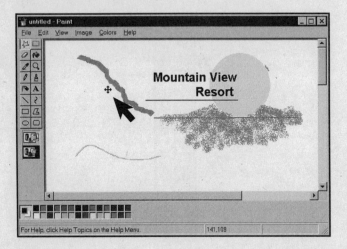

9 Position the mouse pointer over the selection, hold down the left mouse button, and drag the selection to the desired location. (To copy the selection instead of moving it, hold down the **Ctrl** key while dragging.)

11 The eraser paints just like the brush. Right-click the desired color in the Color Box; you can choose the white color swatch to have the eraser leave a plain background.

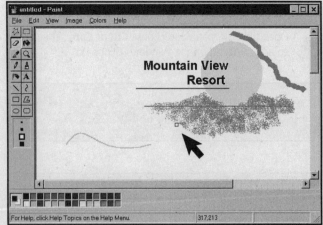

12 Position the mouse pointer over the area of the picture you want to erase. Hold down the left mouse button and drag over the area. Any lines or colors you drag over are replaced with the selected color.

Guided Tour   Edit a Picture

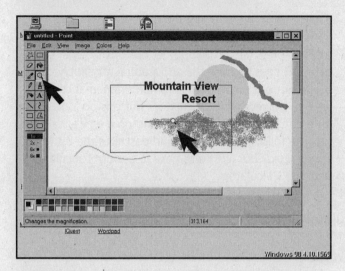

13 To work with individual pixels (the dots that make up the painting), click the **Magnifier** button and click the area of the picture you want to zoom in on.

14 Paint enlarges the view of the selected area. Use the Paint tools to draw or erase in this zoomed view. The Brush tool is especially useful for editing individual pixels.

15 To zoom out, click the **Magnifier** button and click in the magnified area again.

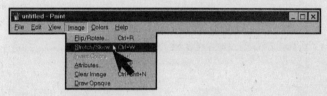

16 Open the **Image** menu to access additional options for editing your picture, including Attributes (to change the size and dimensions of the picture), Flip/Rotate (to flip the picture or rotate it around its center point), and Stretch/Skew (to stretch the picture). The best way to learn about these features is to experiment on a sample drawing.

Perform Calculations

Everyone has at least one calculator for performing daily tasks, such as calculating the total due on a bill or reconciling a checkbook register. Usually the calculator is hidden somewhere under a stack of papers on the kitchen table or a desk. The Windows Calculator is much more convenient. You can always find it on the Start, Programs, Accessories menu.

You use the Windows Calculator as you use any calculator. You press (click) the number buttons to enter values, and then you use the add, subtract, multiply, and divide buttons to perform common mathematical calculations. However, the Calculator's buttons do look a little different from the buttons you find on a typical calculator. The following table lists and describes the buttons. The *Guided Tour* illustrates how to perform calculations with the Calculator.

Windows Calculator Buttons

Button	Name	Function
/	Divide	Divides the current number by the next number you enter.
*	Multiply	Multiplies the current number by the next number you enter.
-	Subtract	Subtracts the next number you enter from the current number.
+	Add	Adds the next number you enter to the current number.
=	Total	Displays the result of the operation you performed on two numbers.
sqrt	Square Root	Determines the square root of the current number.
%	Percent	Determines the percentage that one number is of another number. Enter the first number, click the Percent button, enter the second number, and click the Percent button again.
1/x	Reciprocal	Determines the reciprocal value of a number (the value when you divide one by the number).
Backspace	Backspace	Works like the Backspace key in a text document, removing the number you just typed. You can Backspace out the entire entry, if you like.
CE	Clear Entry	Deletes the entry you are currently keying in.
C	Clear All	Deletes the entire operation, allowing you to start from scratch.
MS	Memory Store	Stores the current number in memory so you can insert it in a later calculation.
MR	Memory Recall	Inserts the number that is currently stored in memory.

Button	Name	Function
M+	Memory Add	Adds the current number to the value currently stored in memory and stores the result in memory.
MC	Memory Clear	Deletes any number currently stored in memory.

You can display a more complex version of the calculator that includes additional buttons for determining sines, cosines, logarithms, exponents, and averages and for performing higher mathematical equations. To access those functions, open the Calculator's **View** menu and choose **Scientific**.

You can view a description of any calculator button by right-clicking it and selecting **What's This?**

Guided Tour   Perform Simple Equations

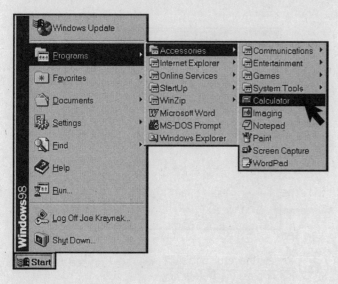

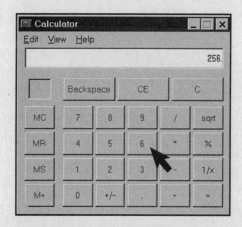

1 Click the **Start** button, point to **Programs** and then **Accessories**, and click **Calculator**.

2 The Calculator appears. Click the number buttons to insert the first value in the equation or use the number keys on your keyboard or numeric keypad (to use the keypad, make sure that the Num Lock button on your keyboard is turned on).

(continues)

Guided Tour Perform Simple Equations

(continued)

3 The number you enter is displayed at the top of the Calculator. Click the button for the operation you want to perform: addition, subtraction, multiplication, or division. In this figure, a multiplication operation is being performed.

4 Click the number keys or use your keyboard to enter the second value in the equation. The number is displayed at the top of the Calculator.

5 Click the **Total** (=) button. The result of the operation appears at the top of the Calculator. Repeat steps 2–5 to perform a series of calculations.

6 To clear the result and start over, click the **Clear All** button or press the **Delete** key.

Guided Tour Perform Simple Equations

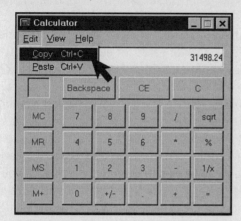

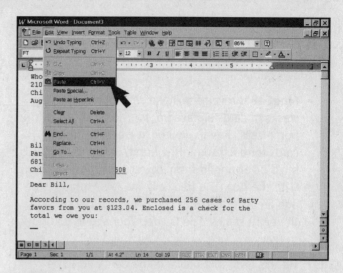

7 To insert the result in one of your documents, open the **Edit** menu and choose **Copy**. This places the result on the Windows Clipboard.

8 Open the document into which you want to insert the copied value, position the insertion point where you want to insert the value, and then open the **Edit** menu and select **Paste**.

You can also copy numbers *into* the Windows Calculator for use in calculations to help ensure accuracy. In the document containing the number, select the number and choose **Edit, Copy** or press **Ctrl+C**. Then return to the Calculator window and choose **Edit, Paste** or press **Ctrl+V** to paste the number.

9 When you finish performing calculations, click the **Close** (X) button in the upper-right corner of the Calculator window.

Play Games

Windows isn't all business. When you need a break from the daily grind, you can play any of several Windows games:

- **FreeCell** is reverse Solitaire. You start with eight stacks of cards all face up, four free cells, and four home cells. To win, you must create a stack of cards for each suit in the home cells and the cards must be arranged from lowest to highest starting with the Ace. The free cells act as temporary storage areas for cards as you rearrange the cards on the eight stacks. The *Guided Tour* shows you how to play.

- **Hearts** is a multi-player game designed to be played on a network; however, you can play against the three computer players. In Hearts, low score wins. You try to give your hearts (each worth one point) and the Queen of Spades (worth 13 points) to the other players, or you try to win all of the hearts and the Queen of Spades to score zero and penalize the other players 26 points each. See the *Guided Tour* to learn how to play.

- **Minesweeper** is a game of strategy in which several mines are hidden under a grid of tiles. You overturn the tiles in an attempt to find out where the mines are located. If you turn over a tile that's hiding a mine, you lose. See the *Guided Tour* for a quick explanation of the game.

- **Solitaire** doesn't need much explanation. This old favorite is just like the card game. You start out

with seven stacks of cards, and you must end up with a stack of cards for each suit starting with the Ace. Because the rules of Solitaire are common knowledge, we have decided to skip it in the *Guided Tour*. In the Windows version, you drag the cards from place to place (or double-click to let Windows help you) and click the deck to deal new cards. Windows can also keep score (select **Game**, **Options** to change the setup). If you win the game or play a timed game using certain card decks of those available, watch for some interesting animations.

Solitaire was originally included in Windows to provide a completely safe environment in which users could practice using the mouse. It's still a very practical method, especially for teaching kids to use the mouse without risking them hurting anything.

If the Games submenu does not appear on the Start, Programs, Accessories menu, the games were not installed. To add them, open the **Control Panel**, run **Add/Remove Programs**, click the **Windows Setup** tab, and install the desired games. (The games are listed under Accessories.)

Guided Tour   Play FreeCell

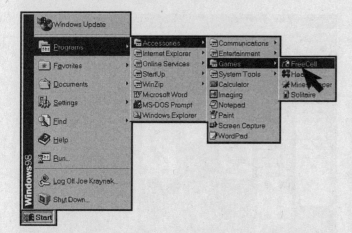

1 Click the **Start** button, point to **Programs**, **Accessories**, and then **Games**, and click **FreeCell**.

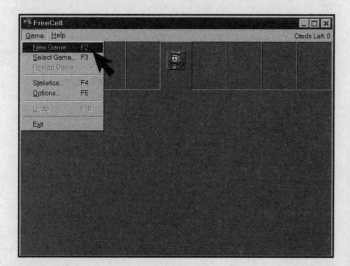

2 A blank FreeCell window appears. Open the **Game** menu and choose **New Game**.

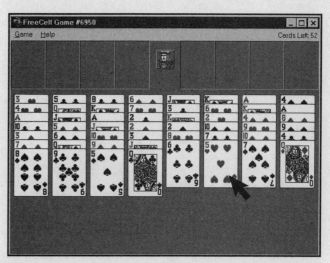

3 FreeCell deals eight stacks of cards, all face up. Look at the bottom of each stack to determine if you can move a card of one color (black or red) onto a card that is one level higher and of an opposite color that's at the bottom of a different stack (such as moving a red 5 onto a black 6). Click the card you want to move.

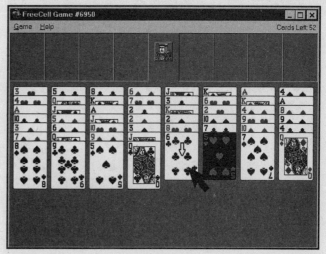

4 Move the mouse pointer over the card on which you want to move the selected card and click. When you move the mouse pointer over the card, a down arrow appears, indicating that the move will be allowed. If the move is illegal, no pointer appears.

(continues)

Guided Tour Play FreeCell *(continued)*

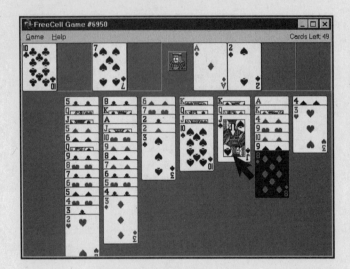

5 You can move more than one card at a time. For example, if there is a blackjack at the bottom of one stack, you can move a red 10, black 9, and red 8 as a group to the Jack, assuming that you have open free cells or blank stack space in which to place the cards before they reach the final target.

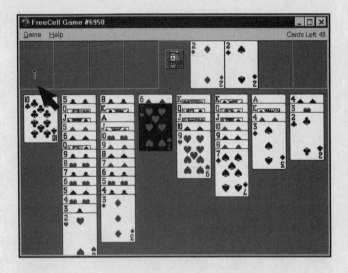

6 If you have no moves, drag a card from one of the stacks to a blank free cell in the upper-left corner. (The goal is to remove cards that you cannot play to uncover cards you can play.) You can also use the free cells to rearrange cards and create future moves.

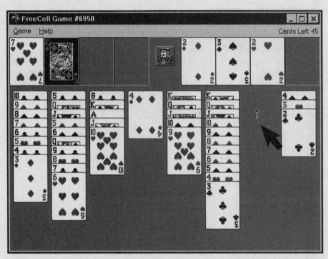

7 If you have a blank stack, you can start a new stack in its place by dragging one or more cards. (It's a good idea to start a new stack with a fairly high card or with a card that will give you a move.)

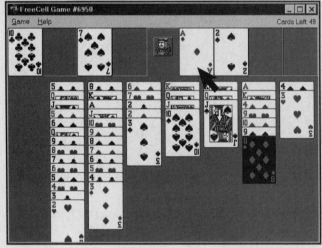

8 When you uncover an Ace, it is automatically added to one of the four home spaces in the upper-right corner, and any exposed cards that can be moved to the Ace are automatically added in order: 2, 3, 4, and so on.

Guided Tour Play FreeCell

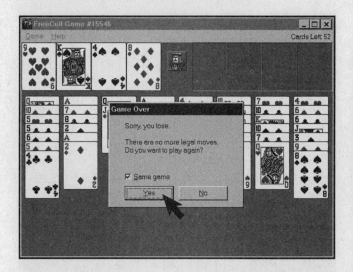

9 If you fill up all the home spaces and cannot move a card to one of the other seven stacks or to a home stack, you lose, and FreeCell lets you know. Click **Yes** to play another game.

10 You win when you complete all four home stacks. Yeah! Click **Yes** to play again (it's addictive).

Guided Tour Play Hearts Against the Computer

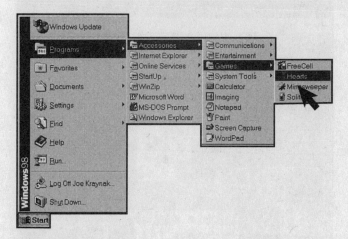

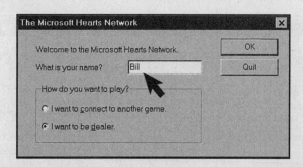

1 Click the **Start** button, point to **Programs**, **Accessories**, and then **Games**, and click **Hearts**.

2 The Microsoft Hearts Network dialog box asks for your name. Type your name in the **What Is Your Name?** text box.

3 Click **OK**.

If you're connected to a network, you can play Hearts with other people on the network. To do so, click **I Want to Connect to Another Game** and click **OK**. You must then enter the name of the dealer's computer and click **OK** again. (Each computer on a network has a unique name to identify it.) If you just want to play against the computer, choose **I Want to Be Dealer** and click **OK**.

(continues)

Guided Tour Play Hearts Against the Computer *(continued)*

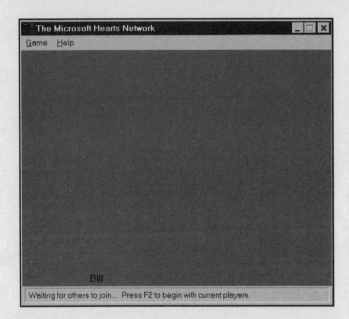

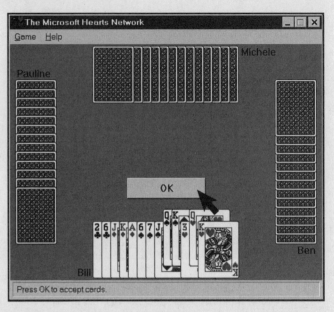

4 If you are on a network, the message "Waiting for Others to Join…" appears in the status bar. Press the **F2** key to start a game against three computer players. If you're not on a network, this step doesn't apply to you; skip to step 5.

7 Click **OK** to take the new cards. If one of the other players has the two of clubs, he or she plays it. If you have the two of clubs, double-click it to start playing.

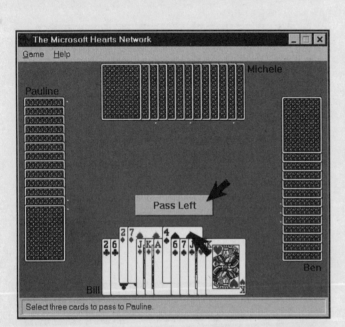

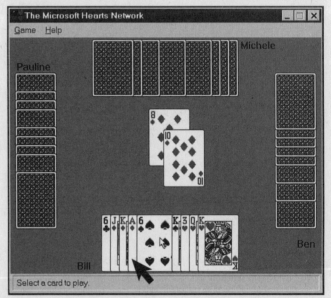

5 Click three cards to pass to the player on your left. As you click cards, they pop up out of the pile. To deselect a card, click it again. (For every fourth deal, no cards are passed.)

6 Click **Pass Left**. Each computer player selects three cards and passes them left, so you end up with three different cards.

8 Moving clockwise, each player clicks a card of the same suit to play. If the player does not have a card of the same suit, he or she can play any card (except in the first round, in which the player cannot play a heart or the Queen of Spades).

Guided Tour Play Hearts Against the Computer

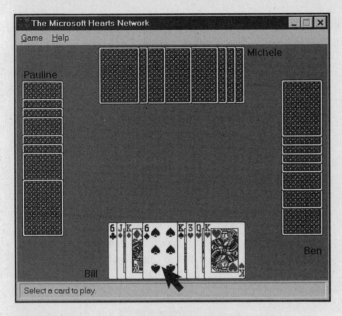

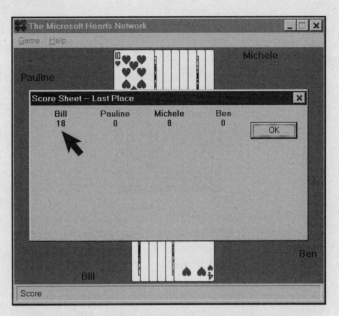

9 The person who plays the highest card of the same suit as the first card played takes the trick (wins all the cards) and plays the next card. You cannot lead with a heart unless someone has played a heart in a previous round.

10 At the end of each hand, you get a point for each heart you acquired and 13 points for the Queen of Spades. Low score wins. However, if you win all of the hearts *and* the Queen of Spades (you "shoot the moon"), you score zero, and each of the other players is penalized 26 points. Click **OK**. Play continues until one player scores 100 points.

Guided Tour Play Minesweeper

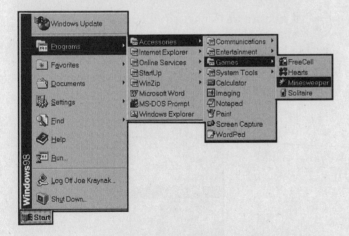

1 Click the **Start** button, point to **Programs**, **Accessories**, and then **Games**, and click **Minesweeper**.

2 The Minesweeper grid appears, displaying an 8-by-8 tile grid (64 tiles) with 10 hidden mines.

3 The first move is the hardest. Click a tile where you think no mine is hidden.

(continues)

Guided Tour   Play Minesweeper *(continued)*

4 If you are lucky, the tile flips over and displays a blank or a number. The number represents the number of mines that are next to the space. Use this number to formulate an educated guess as to which tile to flip next.

> If you flip a tile that reveals a blank (meaning no mines surround the tile), Minesweeper automatically flips any tiles that surround the blank to speed up game play.

5 (Optional) To mark a tile that you think is hiding a mine, right-click it to flag it. Right-click again to place a question mark on the tile. To remove the flag, right-click the tile again.

> If you have flagged all the mines touched by a square containing a number, you can "clear around" the number square by pointing to it and clicking both mouse buttons to expose the remaining blanks or numbers. This helps you uncover a huge section at a time and can really improve your game time.

6 Continue flipping tiles until you have flipped all the tiles except the 10 that are hiding mines. When you successfully complete the task, Minesweeper flips the remaining tiles to reveal the location of the mines. If you have the fastest time for this level, type your name and click **OK**.

7 If you flip a tile that has a mine under it, Minesweeper automatically marks it as exploded (surrounded by red) and flips the tiles that are hiding the remaining mines.

8 To play a new game, click the yellow smiley face or "frowney" face.

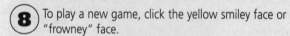

9 To start a more complex game (with more mines and tiles) open the **Game** menu and select **Intermediate**, **Expert**, or **Custom** (to enter your own grid size and number of mines).

Share Data Between Applications with Clipboard Viewer

Although the Windows Clipboard usually does its job behind the scenes, acting as a way station for cut and copied data, you can open it to view its contents.

When you open the Clipboard Viewer, it displays the most recently cut or copied data. You can save this data

as a file for use in other documents. You can also open a saved document to place it on the Clipboard and then insert it into a document using the Edit, Paste command. The *Guided Tour* shows you how to use the Clipboard Viewer.

Guided Tour View the Clipboard Contents

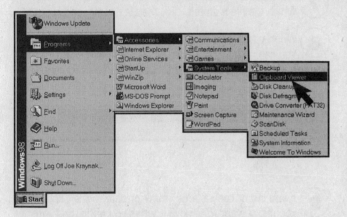

1 Click the **Start** button, point to **Programs**, **Accessories**, **System Tools**, and click **Clipboard Viewer**.

If Clipboard Viewer is not on the System Tools menu, you may not have installed it. To do so now, open the **Control Panel**, run **Add/Remove Programs**, click the **Windows Setup** tab, and use the available options to install the Clipboard Viewer. The Clipboard Viewer is included in the System Tools category.

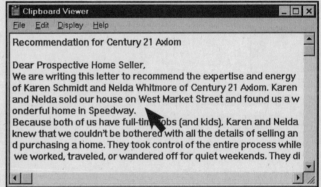

2 The Clipboard Viewer window appears, displaying the data you have most recently copied or cut from a document. If you have not cut or copied data from a document since you started Windows, the Clipboard Viewer window is blank.

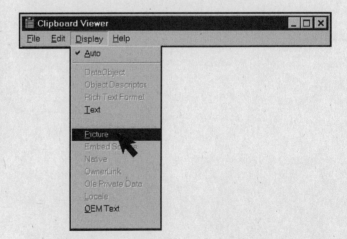

3 The Clipboard Viewer is set up to automatically display data in the format that it deems best. If the data is displayed incorrectly, you can open the **Display** menu and select a different format.

(continues)

Guided Tour View the Clipboard Contents

(continued)

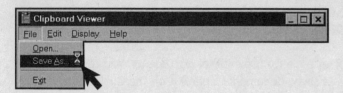

4 To save the contents of the Clipboard to a file, open the **File** menu and choose **Save As**.

5 The Save As dialog box appears. Type a name for the file, select the disk and folder you want to save it to, and click **OK**. ▶See "Save a Document" on page 139 for details.◀

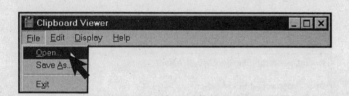

6 To open a document saved as a Clipboard file, open the **File** menu and choose **Open**.

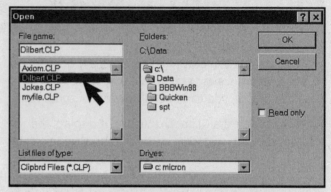

7 The Open dialog box appears. Select the disk and folder in which the file is stored, click the file's name, and click **OK**.

8 When you open a file, the Clipboard displays its contents. You can now use the **Edit**, **Paste** command in any program to insert the contents of the Clipboard in a document.

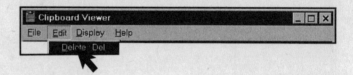

9 If you cut or copy a large chunk of data to the Clipboard, you might want to remove it when you're finished with it to free up some memory. Open the **Edit** menu and choose **Delete**.

10 When you are done with the Clipboard Viewer, click the **Close** button in the upper-right corner of the window to exit.

Play Audio CDs

If you have a CD-ROM drive that can play audio CDs (some older CD-ROM drives do not have this capability), you can use the Windows CD Player to play your favorite music CDs and other audio CDs. CD Player provides you with a control panel that looks and acts like one you might find on a real CD player. You simply click on the onscreen buttons to play, stop, pause, and eject your disc. CD Player also has some fancy features that allow you to select tracks, play them in a random order, and even change the volume and balance.

Playing an audio CD in Windows 98 is easy. You stick the CD in the CD-ROM drive, and Windows starts CD Player and plays the disc. You can then click on the CD Player's **Minimize** button to minimize the window and work on other tasks, and the CD continues to play. To use CD Player's controls to stop, pause, restart, or eject the disc, take the *Guided Tour*.

Like most CD players, the Windows CD Player is completely programmable. You can edit the play list to play only the tunes you want to hear and in the order you want to hear them. The *Guided Tour* provides step-by-step instructions on how to edit the play list.

Some newer audio CDs are actually multimedia CDs, which include information about the artists, music video clips, and pictures. Don't be surprised if you insert the CD and a program interface pops up on your screen. To play the music, run CD Player by choosing **Start, Program, Accessories, Entertainment, CD Player.**

Guided Tour   Play an Audio CD

① When you insert an audio CD, CD Player starts automatically and starts playing the CD. The CD Player starts as a minimized window. Click the CD Player button in the taskbar to display it.

② To change the volume, open the **View** menu and choose **Volume Control**.

③ The Volume Control dialog box appears. Drag the **Volume Control** up to increase volume or down to decrease it. You can also adjust the volume by dragging the **CD Audio Volume** control. Click the **Close** button when you are done.

You can also adjust the volume by double-clicking the Volume icon (the speaker) on the right end of the taskbar. Or, right-click the icon and choose **Open Volume Controls** or **Adjust Audio Properties**. You might need to use two or more volume controls to achieve the right volume.

(continues)

Guided Tour Play an Audio CD

(continued)

4 You can pause, restart, stop, or choose a specific track on the CD by clicking the following buttons:

Pause stops playing the CD at the current track.

Resume restarts the CD after you pause it.

Stop stops playing the CD.

Next Track skips to the next tune.

Previous Track starts playing the previous tune.

Skip Forwards moves forward in the current track (to play your favorite drum solo, for example).

Skip Backwards moves back in the current track.

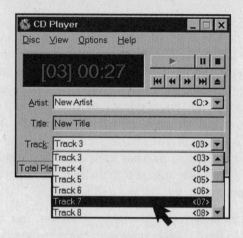

5 To select a specific tune, open the **Track** drop-down list and click the desired tune.

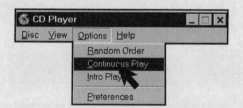

6 To have the CD play over and over, open the **Options** menu and choose **Continuous Play**.

7 To eject the CD, click the **Eject** button. You can click the CD Player's **Close** button to exit.

Guided Tour   Program the Play List

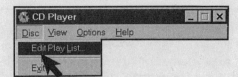

1 Open the **Disc** menu and select **Edit Play List**.

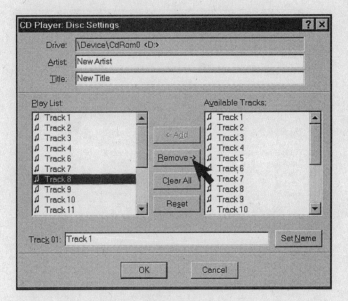

2 The CD Player: Disc Settings dialog box appears. To remove one track from the Play List, click the track listing and click **Remove**. The track is removed from the Play List, but still appears in the Available Tracks list, so you can add it later.

3 You can remove all tracks from the Play List by clicking on the **Clear All** button.

4 To add all the tracks from the Available Tracks list to the Play List, click on the **Reset** button.

5 To add a single track to the Play List, click the track you want to add (in the Available Tracks list) and click the **Add** button. You can add the track more than once to have the song play several times.

6 To move a track in the Play List, click it, drag it up or down in the list, and then release the mouse button.

7 Click **OK** when you finish editing the play list.

Guided Tour Name the Tracks

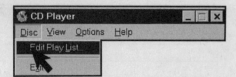

1 Open the **Disc** menu and choose **Edit Play List**.

When naming artist, title, and tracks, you can type anything you like—you don't have to use the "real" names or titles. (This is especially helpful for The Artist Formerly Known as Prince.)

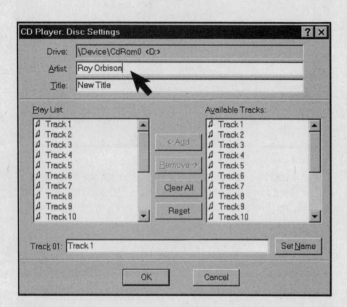

2 The CD Player: Disc Settings dialog box appears. In the **Artist** text box, type the name of the group or artist.

4 Click **Track 1** in the Available Tracks list.

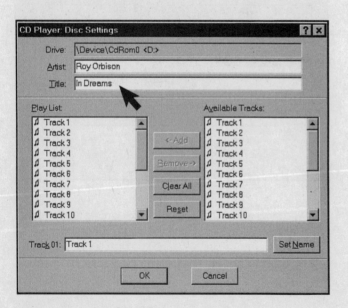

3 Click in the **Title** text box, and type the CD's title.

Guided Tour   Name the Tracks

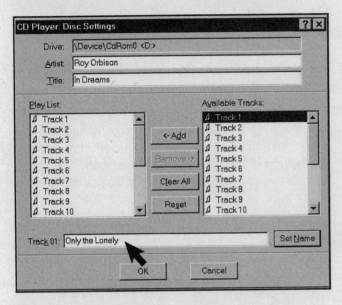

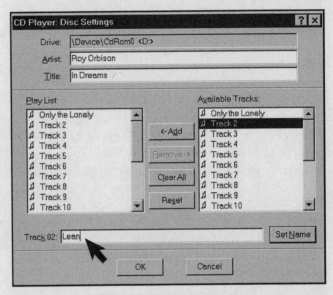

5 In the **Track 01** text box, drag over "Track 1," type the song or track name, and press **Enter**. CD Player highlights the next track number and lets you name it.

6 Type the name for the next track and press **Enter**. Repeat this step to name all the tracks.

7 Click the **OK** button. CD Player saves your changes for this CD. Whenever you play this CD, the Play List for this CD will be in effect, complete with names instead of the track numbers. If you insert a new CD (one for which you did not enter track names), CD Player uses track numbers.

CD Player can play tracks in a random order to add some variety to a CD you listen to frequently. Open the **Options** menu and choose **Random Order**.

Play and Record Sounds with Sound Recorder

If you have a sound card (such as Sound Blaster) and a microphone or CD-ROM drive that plays audio CDs (through your sound card), you can use the Windows Sound Recorder to record music, your voice, or any other sound and store it as a file. Then you can attach the sounds to certain events and have Windows play the sounds whenever those events occur. For example, you can have a specific short piece of music play whenever you start Windows.

The Sound Recorder lets you record a sound and save it in a .WAV file. To start the Sound Recorder and record a sound, take the *Guided Tour*. The *Guided Tour* shows you how to record your voice or other sounds using a microphone and how to record clips from audio CDs.

Guided Tour Record a Sound with Your Microphone

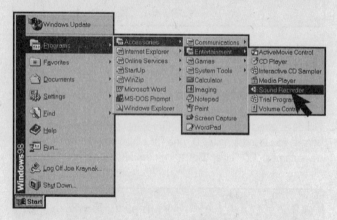

1 Click the **Start** button, point to **Programs, Accessories, Entertainment**, and click **Sound Recorder**.

2 The Sound Recorder window appears. When you are ready to record, click the **Record** button and start talking, playing music, or making other sounds into the microphone.

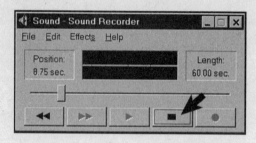

3 When you're done talking, click the **Stop** button.

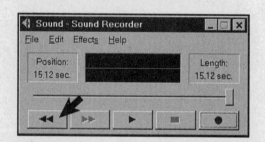

4 To play back the recording, click the **Seek To Start** button to return to the beginning of the recording.

Guided Tour Record a Sound with Your Microphone

(5) Click **Play**, and the recorded sound begins to play.

(6) To save the recording as a file, open the **File** menu and choose **Save**.

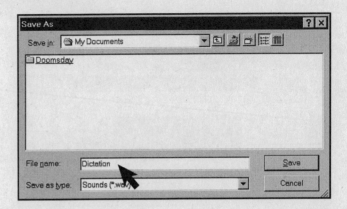

(7) The Save File dialog box appears. Type a name for the file in the **Name** text box, select the folder in which you want to save the file, and click the **Save** button.

Guided Tour Record from an Audio CD

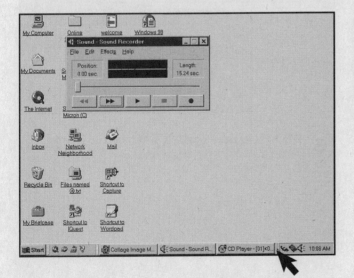

(1) Insert the CD that has the audio clip you want to record. CD Player starts and begins to play the first track. Click the **CD Player** button in the taskbar to view the CD Player window, ▶as explained in "Play Audio CDs" on page 201.◀

(2) Click the **Pause** button.

(continues)

Guided Tour Record from an Audio CD

(continued)

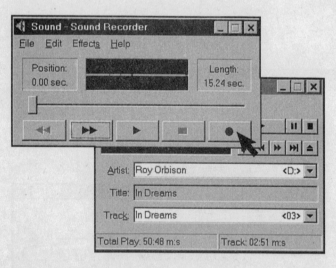

3 Open the **Track** drop-down list and choose the track that you want to record.

4 Run Sound Recorder, click the **Record** button, and quickly perform the next step.

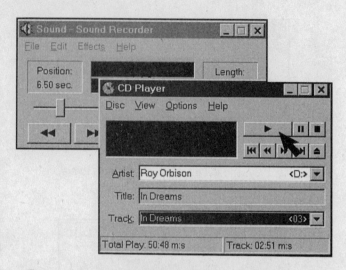

5 Switch to CD Player and click the **Resume** button. CD Player starts playing the selected track, and Sound Recorder records it.

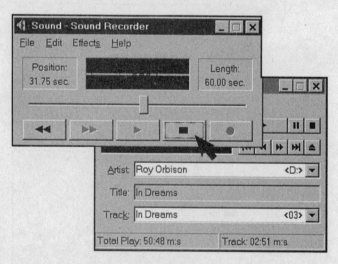

6 When you're done recording, switch back to Sound Recorder and click the **Stop** button.

Guided Tour Record from an Audio CD

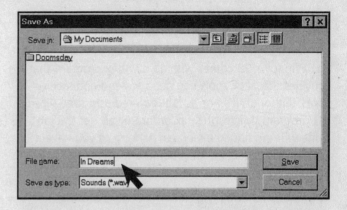

7 To save the recording as a file, open the **File** menu and choose **Save**.

8 The Save As File dialog box appears. Type a name for the file in the **File Name** text box, select the drive and folder in which you want to save the file, and click the **Save** button.

Send and Receive Faxes

To send and receive faxes in Windows 3.x, you had to purchase a special fax program such as WinFax PRO. But Windows 98 comes with its own fax program that provides the basic tools you need to send and receive faxes. Although it's not as full-featured as a specialized fax program, Microsoft's fax program can get the job done with no added expenses. As long as you have a modem that's capable of sending and receiving faxes, you can fax right now.

The Windows Compose New Fax Wizard provides a quick and easy way to send a fax. You start the wizard, and it displays a series of dialog boxes that you respond to. The wizard then dials the recipient's phone number and sends the fax. To send a fax with the Compose New Fax Wizard, take the *Guided Tour*.

> If the fax options described in the *Guided Tour* are unavailable, you may not have installed Microsoft Fax. To do so now, open the **Control Panel**, run **Add/Remove Programs**, click the **Windows Setup** tab, click **Microsoft Fax**, and click **OK**. You will have to insert the Windows 98 installation CD to continue.

Fax a Document File

If you choose to attach a file to your fax in the *Guided Tour*, it might take the wizard a while to transform the attachments into faxable data. The wizard runs the program used to create the file and then works with that program to turn the text into a graphic image that a fax machine can print.

There are several other ways to run the Compose New Fax Wizard and use it to transmit a fax. The following list explains these alternative methods:

- Run Windows Messaging (**Start**, **Programs**, **Windows Messaging**). Then open the **Compose** menu and select **New Fax** to start the wizard.

Start with step 2 and proceed through the *Guided Tour* to complete the operation.

- To fax files, select one or more files you want to fax in Windows Explorer or My Computer. Right-click on the name of one of the selected files, move the mouse pointer over **Send To**, and then click **Fax Recipient**. Start with step 2 and proceed through the *Guided Tour* to send the fax. (If you use this method, the wizard does not display a dialog box to ask you to attach files.)

- Some programs (such as Microsoft Word) have a Send To command on the File menu. If yours does, open the document you want to fax, and then select **File**, **Send To**, **Fax Recipient**. This starts Fax Wizard, which prompts you to enter the recipient's name and fax number. Enter the requested information, and then click the option for sending the fax.

- If you want to fax from a program that does not have a Send To, Fax Recipient command, select Microsoft Fax as your printer, and then use the program's Print command to print as you normally would. ▶See "Set Up a New Printer" on page 369 for instructions on how to set up a printer in Windows.◀

Receive a Fax

To receive a fax, you use Windows Messaging, a powerful communications program that can manage all your email and fax messages. To use Windows Messaging to receive an incoming fax, you can set it up to answer the phone automatically (after a specified number of rings), or you can enter a command to have it answer the phone now. The *Guided Tour* shows you what to do.

Guided Tour Send a Fax

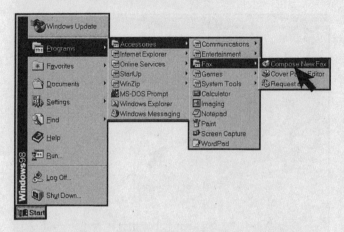

1 Click the **Start** button, point to **Programs**, **Accessories**, **Fax**, and click **Compose New Fax**.

The first time you run Microsoft Fax, the Inbox Setup Wizard appears, prompting you to configure Windows Messaging. Under Use the Following Information Services, turn off Microsoft Mail unless you are on a network that has a Microsoft Mail server, and make sure that Microsoft Fax is checked. Follow the onscreen instructions to complete the setup.

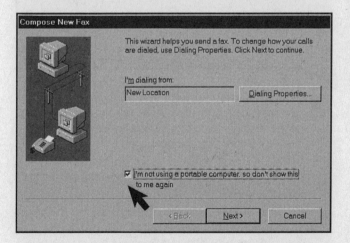

2 The Compose New Fax Wizard appears. If you take your computer on the road to different area codes, you can click **Dialing Properties** and change your current area code. If you do not take your computer on the road, click **I'm Not Using a Portable Computer...**, so the Wizard will not display this dialog box again. Click **Next**.

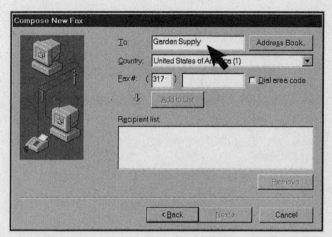

3 The Wizard prompts you to enter the name and fax number of the person to whom you are sending this fax. Type the name of the person or company.

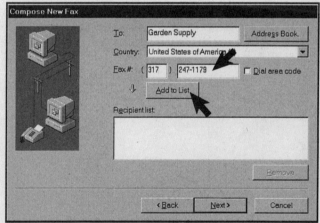

4 Click in the **Fax #** text box and type the fax phone number. (If you are faxing to a different area code, type the area code in the area code text box.)

5 Click the **Add to List** button to insert the person's name in the Recipient List, and then click the **Next** button.

(continues)

Guided Tour Send a Fax *(continued)*

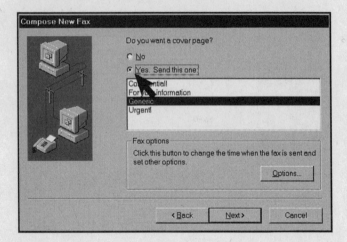

6 The Wizard displays a dialog box that asks whether you want to attach a cover page. To attach a cover page, click **Yes...** and select the type of cover page you want to use. Click the **Next** button.

8 Click in the **Note** area and type any message that you want on the cover page. Click the **Next** button.

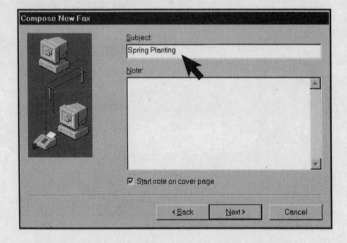

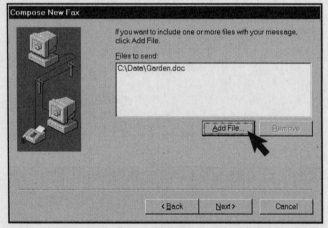

7 The next dialog box allows you to type a description of the fax. Type the fax description in the **Subject** text box.

9 The wizard asks if you want to attach a document file to the outgoing fax. To attach a file, click the **Add File** button, use the resulting dialog box to select the file you want to send, and click **Open**. Click the **Next** button.

Attached files are transmitted as document files, not as faxed pages. Therefore, the recipient must have a program that can open the attached document files. To send a document file as faxed pages, print the document using Microsoft Fax as your printer.

Guided Tour   Send a Fax

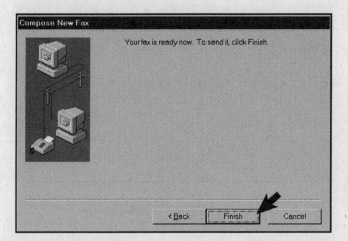

10 The wizard displays a dialog box indicating that it is nearly ready to send the fax. Click the **Finish** button. The wizard creates the cover page, transforms any attached files into faxable data, dials the recipient's fax number, and sends the fax.

> If the fax is not successfully transmitted, you can try again later. To do so, run Windows Messaging (**Start, Programs, Windows Messaging**), double-click the name of the fax message, and click **Send Again**.

Guided Tour   Receive a Fax

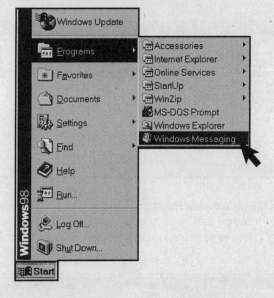

1 Click the **Start** button, point to **Programs**, and click **Windows Messaging**.

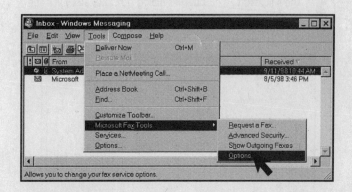

2 The Windows Messaging window opens and displays the contents of the Inbox. Open the **Tools** menu, point to **Microsoft Fax Tools**, and click **Options**.

(continues)

Guided Tour   Receive a Fax

(continued)

3 The Microsoft Fax Properties dialog box appears. Click the **Modem** tab.

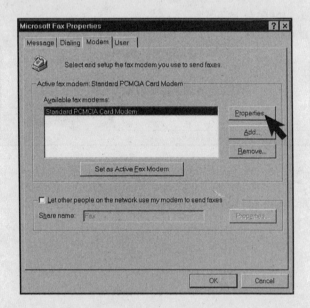

4 In the Available Fax Modems list, click the name of the modem you want to use for incoming faxes (assuming you have more than one modem). Then click the **Properties** button.

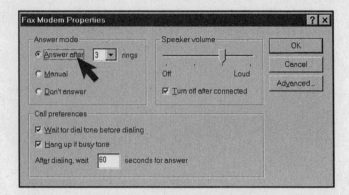

5 The Fax Modem Properties dialog box appears. Under Answer Mode, choose **Answer After ___ Rings** and select the desired number of rings from the drop-down list. Click **OK**.

6 This returns you to the Microsoft Fax Properties dialog box. Click **OK**.

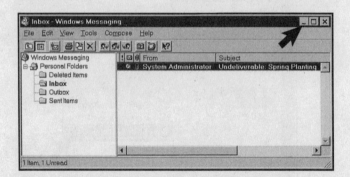

7 Leave Windows Messaging running so that it can answer incoming calls. You can minimize the window and use other Windows programs while Windows Messaging is running.

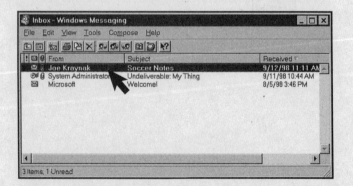

8 When a fax arrives, Windows Messaging answers and receives the fax. It displays the name of the fax in the Inbox. Double-click the name of the fax to display it in Kodak Imaging.

Guided Tour Receive a Fax

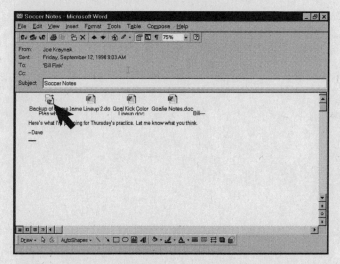

9 If the fax has attached files, icons for the attachments appear on the cover page. Double-click an icon to open the document in its associated program.

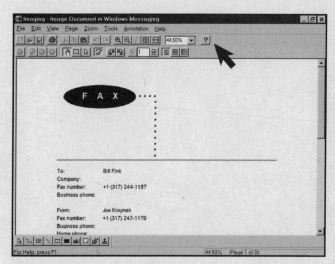

11 Use the buttons in the toolbar to print the fax, zoom in, and zoom out.

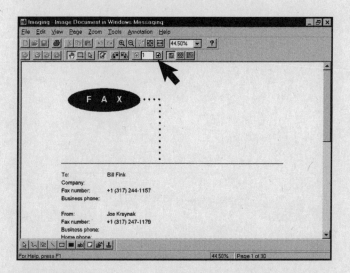

10 If the fax consists of two or more pages, you can click the **Next Page** button to flip pages.

HOW TO...

Use Windows 98 on the World Wide Web

One of the greatest new features of Windows 98 is its support for the Internet. On the Internet, you can pull up multimedia Web pages from anywhere in the world, send and receive email messages, read and post messages in newsgroups (electronic bulletin boards), and even chat online with other people by typing and sending messages.

Windows 98 features a suite of Internet programs, including Internet Explorer (for Web pages), Outlook Express (for email and newsgroups), FrontPage Express (for creating and publishing your own Web pages), and Microsoft Chat. This section shows you how to use Internet Explorer to navigate the Web and how to use FrontPage Express to create and publish a simple Web page.

What You Will Find in This Section

Access Commercial Online Services

Commercial online services, such as America Online, Prodigy, and The Microsoft Network, have popularized online communications. Through these services, you can access news, weather, investment services, technical support, online businesses, the Internet, chat groups, and much, much more.

If you have already set up an account with one of these services, Windows 98 is set up to use it. If you have not yet set up an account, you have two options. Either you can use Windows 98 to set up an account with a commercial online service (America Online, AT&T WorldNet, CompuServe, Prodigy Internet, or The Microsoft Network), or you can set up a simple Internet connection through an independent *Internet service provider* (*ISP*).

Commercial services give you the best of both worlds. All commercial services include Internet support. In addition, they provide high-quality content that you can receive only by subscribing to the service. For example, America Online features special news and financial areas that you cannot access from a simple Internet connection. However, commercial services typically charge a little more than ISPs.

The *Guided Tour* shows you how to set up an account with some of the major commercial online services. You will need a credit card number to set up an account with any of the available online services. ▶To set up an account with an ISP, see "Set Up Your Internet Connection" on page 220.◀

Guided Tour Connect to a Commercial Online Service

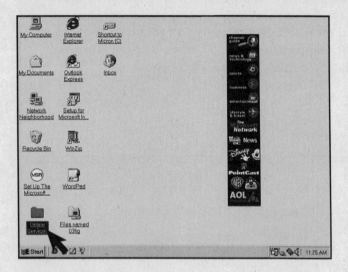

1 Return to the Windows desktop and click the **Online Services** folder.

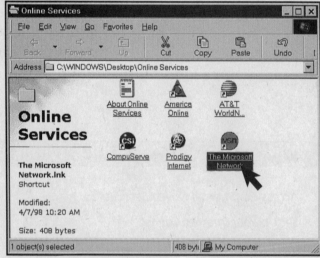

2 A My Computer window appears, displaying shortcuts to the major commercial online services: AOL (America Online), AT&T WorldNet, CompuServe, Prodigy Internet, and The Microsoft Network. Click the icon for the desired service.

Guided Tour Connect to a Commercial Online Service

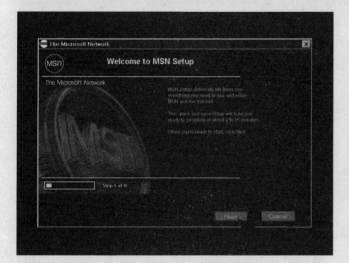

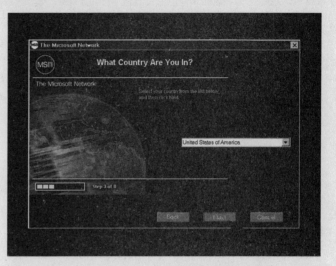

3 What happens next depends on the service you selected. For example, if you chose The Microsoft Network, the window shown above appears, prompting you to sign up. If you selected CompuServe, a dialog box appears, asking if you want to install the CompuServe software.

4 Follow the onscreen instructions to establish an account. In most cases, the setup procedure dials a toll-free number to connect you to the service, gather account information (name, address, credit card number), and provide a list of local access phone numbers from which you can choose.

Set Up Your Internet Connection

If you set up an account with a commercial online service, you already have an Internet connection. Check the program's Help system to learn how to access the Internet from the service. If you chose not to use a commercial service, you can access the Internet through an independent Internet service provider (ISP). The service provider typically gives you a local phone number for your computer to dial. This connects you to the service provider's network, which is tied into the Internet.

ISPs do not offer their own menu of special services. They provide a simple connection to the Internet. You must then use other programs (called *client software*) to access Internet features. For example, you might use Internet Explorer to navigate the World Wide Web and use Outlook Express to send and receive email messages.

Because the Internet Explorer suite is included with Windows 98, this book focuses on the programs that comprise the suite. You can use other Internet client software in Windows 98, such as Netscape Navigator (a very popular Web browser) and Eudora (a popular email client).

To set up your Internet connection through an ISP, you must first contact a local ISP and gather the information you need in order to enter the correct *connection settings*. The connection settings tell your computer and modem how to dial into the service provider's computer and establish communications. To find a service provider, check your phone book, local user groups, computer-related publications, or computer stores, or ask a friend or colleague to recommend a service.

Once you have found a service, call the service to set up an account. You will need to set up a payment plan and gather the following information:

Username: This is the name that identifies you to the ISP's computer. It is typically an abbreviation of your first and last name. For example, Bill Fink might use bfink as his username. You can choose any name you like, as long as it is not already being used by another user.

Password: The ISP might allow you to select your own password or it might assign you a password. Be sure to write down the password in case you forget it. Without the right password, you will not be able to connect to the service provider's computer.

Connection Type: Most ISPs offer SLIP (Serial Line Internet Protocol) or PPP (Point-to-Point Protocol). Point-to-Point Protocol is easier to set up and provides faster data transfer, so if you're given a choice, choose PPP.

Domain Name Server: The domain name server is a computer that's set up to locate computers on the Internet. Each computer on the Internet has a unique number that identifies it, such as 197.72.34.74. Each computer also has a *domain name*, such as www.whitehouse.com, which makes it easier for people to remember the computer's address. When you enter a domain name, the domain name server looks up the computer's number and locates it.

Domain Name: This is the domain name of your service provider's computer (for example, internet.com). You will use the domain name in conjunction with your username as your *email address* (for example, bfink@internet.com).

News Server: The news server allows you to connect to any of thousands of *newsgroups* on the Internet to read and post messages. Newsgroups are electronic bulletin boards for special interest groups. The news server name typically starts with "news" and is followed by the service provider's domain name (for example, news.internet.com). ►See "Set Up Your News Server Account" on page 348.◄

Mail Server: The mail server is in charge of electronic mail. The mail server's name typically starts with "mail" followed by the service provider's domain name (for example, mail.internet.com). ►See "Set Up Your Email Account" on page 322.◄

POP Server: The POP (Post Office Protocol) server is in charge of incoming email messages. When an email message addressed to you arrives, the POP server stores it in your *electronic mailbox*. You can then use an email program to retrieve and display your messages. The POP server's name typically starts with "pop" followed by the service provider's domain name (for example, `pop.internet.com`).

SMTP Server: The SMTP (Simple Mail Transfer Protocol) server is responsible for handling outgoing email messages. When you address, compose, and send an email message, the SMTP server transmits the message to the recipient's electronic mailbox. The SMTP server's name typically starts with "smtp" or "mail," followed by the service provider's domain name (for example, `smtp.internet.com.`)

Email Address: If you plan to receive email messages, you need an email address. Your address typically begins with your username, followed by

an at sign (@) and the domain name of your service provider (for example, `bfink@internet.com`).

Once you have the information you need, take the following *Guided Tour* to enter that information using the Internet Connection Wizard included with Windows 98. The wizard prompts you to enter each piece of information required to establish a connection with your ISP. The wizard then creates a Dial-Up Networking icon you can click to establish your connection.

> If you cannot find a local ISP, the Internet Connection Wizard will prompt you to pick from a list of popular ISPs. However, these services may not be local, and you might incur additional phone charges when connecting to them. See the second half of the following *Guided Tour* for details.

Guided Tour   Establish a Connection to Your ISP

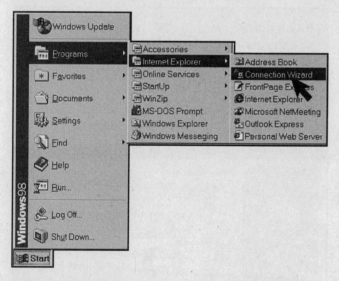

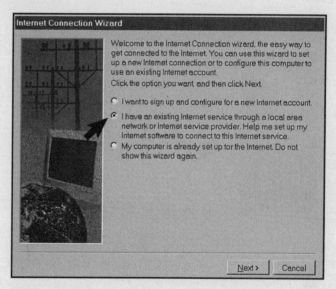

1 Click the **Start** button, point to **Programs** and then **Internet Explorer**, and click **Connection Wizard**.

2 The Setup options appear. To enter settings for your ISP, click **I Have an Existing Internet Service...** and click **Next**.

(continues)

Guided Tour   Establish a Connection to Your ISP   *(continued)*

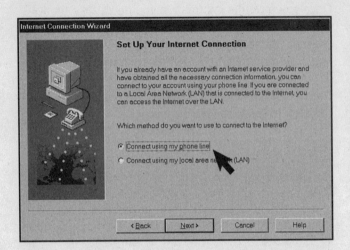

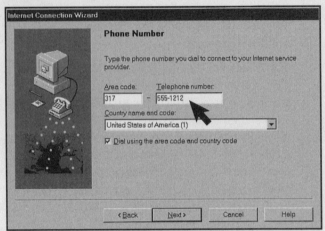

3 The wizard now prompts you to specify the type of connection you want to set up. If you are going to dial your service provider with a modem, choose **Connect Using My Phone Line**. If your computer is on a network and you are connecting through the network, click **Connect Using My Local Area Network (LAN)**. Click **Next**.

5 You are now asked to enter the phone number to dial to connect to the service provider's computer. Type the phone number in the **Telephone Number** text box. If the number is outside your area code, enter the area code in the **Area Code** text box. Click **Next**.

If you do not need to dial the area code and country code to connect to your service provider, remove the check mark next to **Dial Using the Area Code and Country Code** option in step 5.

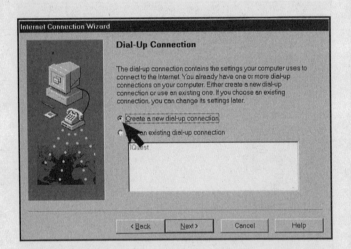

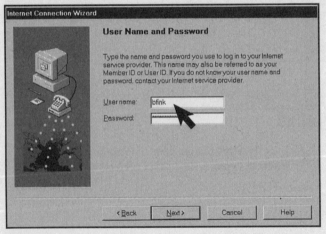

4 You are now prompted to set up a new account. Click **Create a New Dial-Up Connection** and click **Next**. (You may be prompted to install additional files from the CD before this dialog box appears; follow the onscreen instructions.)

6 The Wizard prompts you to enter your username and password. Type your user name in the **User Name** text box and then click in the **Password** text box and type your password. Click **Next**.

Guided Tour Establish a Connection to Your ISP

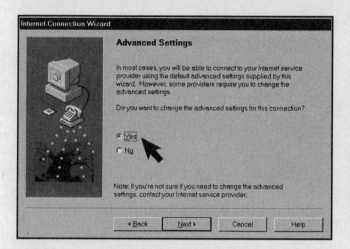

7 You are now asked if you want to change the advanced settings. Click **Yes**, so you can at least check the settings before you continue. Click **Next**.

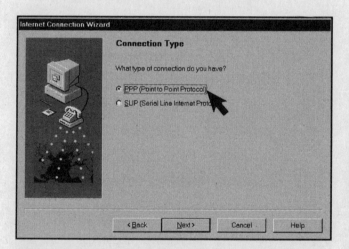

8 The wizard asks you to specify the type of connection: SLIP (Serial Line Internet Protocol) or PPP (Point-to-Point Protocol). Choose the connection type specified by your service provider and click **Next**.

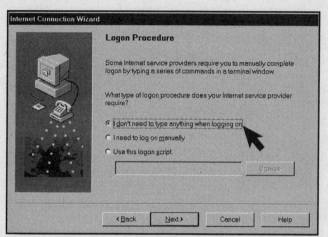

9 You are now asked to specify the type of logon procedure. Most service providers allow Windows Dial-Up Networking to enter your name and password for you, so leave **I Don't Need to Type Anything When Logging On** selected. If your service provider requires you to log on manually or use a special logon script (usually supplied by the service provider), select one of the other options. Click **Next**.

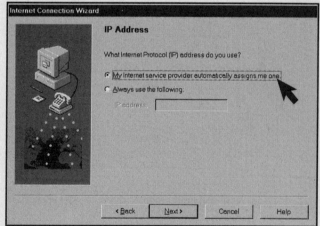

10 The wizard prompts you to enter your IP (Internet Protocol) address. This address, which most ISPs assign automatically when you log on, identifies your computer on the Internet. If your ISP assigned you a permanent address, select **Always Use the Following** and type your address in the **IP Address** text box. Click **Next**.

(continues)

Guided Tour Establish a Connection to Your ISP *(continued)*

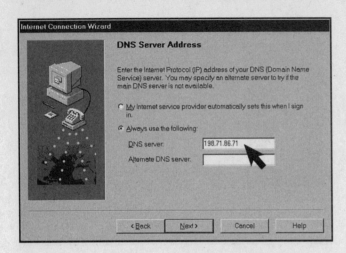

11 You are now prompted to enter the address of the Domain Name Server. If your service provider specified a DNS address, choose **Always Use the Following** and enter the DNS address in the **DNS Server** text box. Click **Next**.

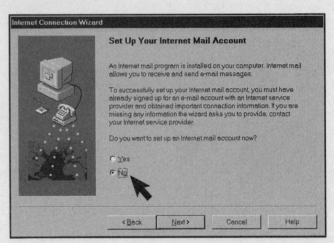

13 The wizard asks if you want to set up your email account. Click **Yes** or **No**, and then click **Next**. ▶If you choose Yes, refer to "Set Up Your Email Account" on page 322 for details.◀ You can set up your email account later.

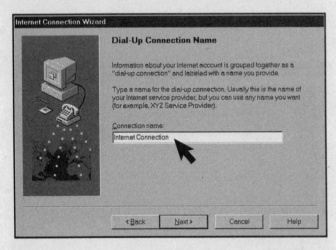

12 You are now prompted to enter a name for the connection. Type a descriptive name for your ISP and click **Next**.

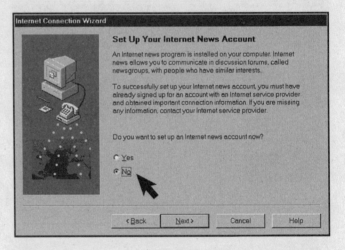

14 The wizard asks if you want to set up your news server account. Click **Yes** or **No**, and then click **Next**. ▶If you choose Yes, refer to "Set Up Your News Server Account" on page 348 for details.◀ You can set up your news server account later.

Guided Tour Establish a Connection to Your ISP

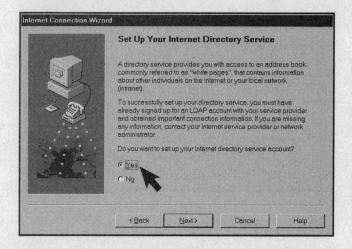

If you had a different Web browser installed in Windows before upgrading to Windows 98, that browser might run automatically and display the Dial-Up Connection dialog box, prompting you to connect to the Internet when you click Finish. If you prefer to use Internet Explorer instead of that browser, exit your Web browser and choose **Start, Programs, Internet Explorer, Internet Explorer**. When you're asked if you want to make Internet Explorer your default Web browser, click **Yes**.

15 The wizard asks if you want to set up your directory service account. A *directory service* is like a white pages phone book, which can help you locate the addresses, phone numbers, and email addresses of other people. Click **No**, and then click **Next**.

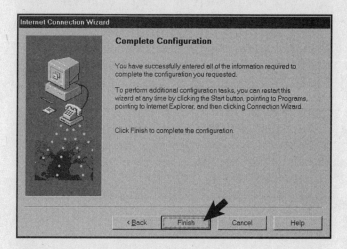

16 The Complete Configuration dialog box informs you that you have entered all the required information. Click **Finish**. (If you had to install additional files earlier, you might be prompted to restart your computer.)

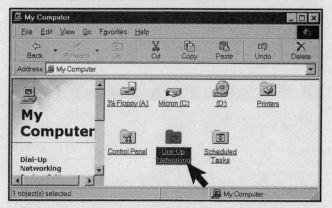

17 Open My Computer and click the **Dial-Up Networking** icon.

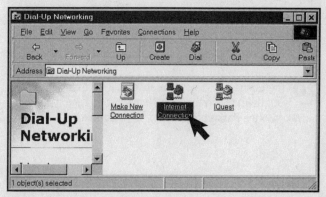

18 The Dial-Up Networking folder contains icons for any ISPs for which you have set up connections. Drag the icon for your ISP to a blank area of the Windows desktop.

(continues)

Guided Tour Establish a Connection to Your ISP *(continued)*

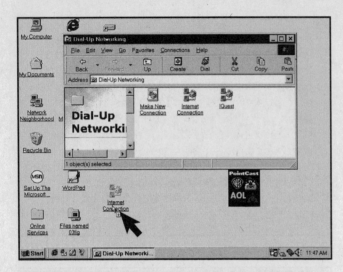

19 A copy of the icon appears on the desktop. Click it to dial into your service provider's computer.

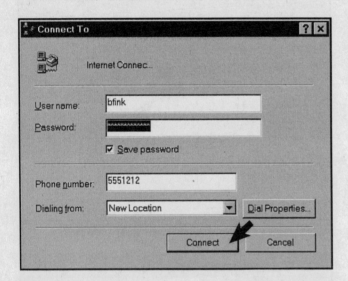

20 The Connect To dialog box appears. If necessary, enter your username in the **User Name** text box and type your password in the **Password** text box. Click **Connect**.

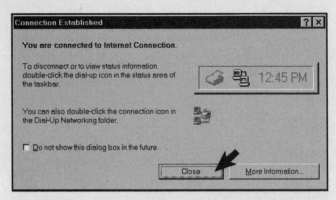

21 Using your modem, Dial-Up Networking dials the number, establishes the connection with your service provider, and displays a dialog box indicating that the connection was established. Click **Close**. ▶You can now proceed to the task "Use Internet Explorer" on page 229 to open and view Web pages.◀

Closing the Connect To dialog box does not disconnect you from the Internet. To disconnect, right-click the Internet connection icon in the system tray (at the right end of the taskbar) and choose **Disconnect**.

To change any of the Internet connection settings you entered, right-click the icon for your Internet connection in the Dial-Up Networking folder and choose **Properties**.

Guided Tour Find an ISP and Set Up a New Account

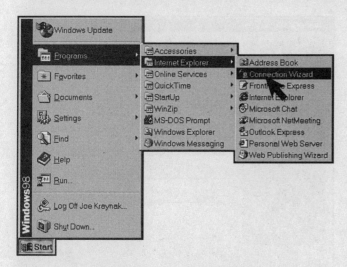

1 Click the **Start** button, point to **Programs** and then **Internet Explorer**, and click **Connection Wizard**.

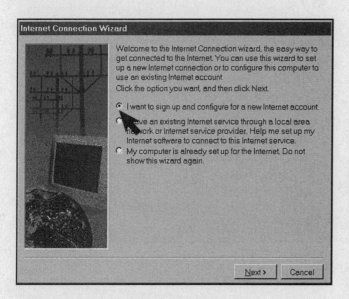

2 The Setup Options appear. To find and select a new ISP, click **I Want to Sign Up and Configure for a New Internet Account**. Click **Next**.

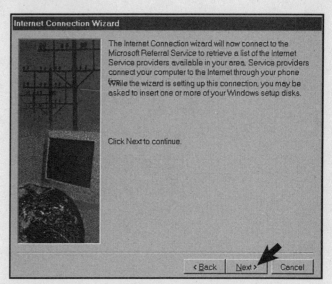

3 The next screen appears, indicating that you might need your Windows Setup Disk(s). Click **Next**.

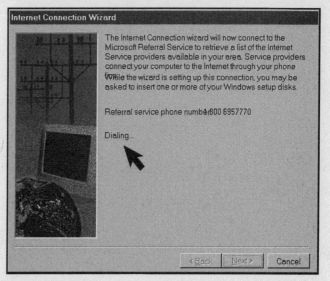

4 The wizard dials a toll-free number to connect you to Microsoft's Internet Referral Service and downloads a list of local Internet Service Providers.

(continues)

Guided Tour Find an ISP and Set Up a New Account *(continued)*

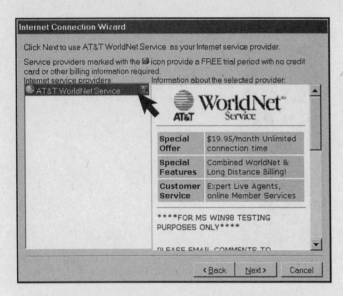

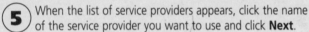

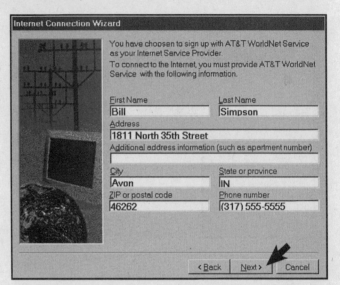

(5) When the list of service providers appears, click the name of the service provider you want to use and click **Next**.

(6) Follow the onscreen instructions, which vary from one provider to another, and enter the requested information.

When you have completed the setup, an icon for the service provider appears in the Dial-Up Networking folder. In My Computer, click **Dial-Up Networking**, and then click the icon for the service provider to display the Connect To dial box. Click the **Connect** button to establish your connection. In most cases, Windows will automatically prompt you to connect (or automatically dial) when you start any Internet program, such as Internet Explorer or Outlook Express.

Use Internet Explorer

The Dial-Up Networking connection you set up in the previous *Guided Tour* simply establishes the required Internet connection. It opens the line of communication between your computer and a computer that is wired to the Internet. After you establish a connection, you can use specialized client software to access the various features of the Internet: the World Wide Web, email, newsgroups, chat, and so on.

One of the more popular features of the Internet is the World Wide Web (the Web, for short). The Web stores millions of multimedia pages that contain text, pictures, audio and video clips, interactive presentations, games, and other interesting offerings. To open these pages and skip from one page to another, you use a client program called a *Web browser*. Windows 98 has a popular Web browser called Internet Explorer.

When you start Internet Explorer, it automatically opens Microsoft's home page, a page that contains

information from Microsoft Corporation. The page also contains icons, images, and highlighted text that act as *links*. Links point to other pages on the Web. To move from one page to another, you click a link. The *Guided Tour* shows you how to run Internet Explorer and use it to open Web pages.

> When you open Web pages, Internet Explorer frequently displays dialog boxes warning you of possible security risks, prompting you to download program updates or add-ons, and informing you that it cannot find a particular Web site or page. If Internet Explorer cannot find a page, try clicking the link or re-entering the page's address. ▶To decide how to handle the security warnings, see "Change Your Security Settings," on page 279.◀

Guided Tour   Start Internet Explorer

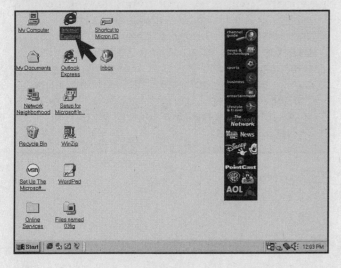

1 Click the **Internet Explorer** icon on the Windows desktop.

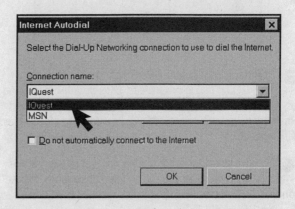

2 The Microsoft Internet Explorer window and Internet Autodial dialog box appear. Open the **Connection Name** drop-down list and choose the Dial-Up Networking connection you created for your service provider. Click **OK** and skip to step 6. If the Autodial dialog box does not appear, proceed with step 3.

(continues)

Guided Tour Start Internet Explorer

(continued)

If the Autodial dialog box does not appear, you might receive a warning message indicating that Internet Explorer could not load the opening Web page. Open Internet Explorer's **View** menu, choose **Internet Options**, and click the **Connection** tab. If you are using a modem, make sure **Connect to the Internet Using a Modem** is selected, click the **Settings** button, and enter your Internet connection preferences. Click **OK** to save your changes.

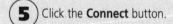

6 Windows dials your service provider's phone number and establishes the connection. The Dialing Progress dialog box displays the status of the connection and then minimizes itself when the connection is established.

3 If Autodial is turned off, you might see the Dial-Up Connection dialog box instead. Enter your username and password in the appropriate dialog boxes. To have Windows remember your password, click **Save Password** to place a check mark in its box.

4 To have Windows automatically connect to your service provider whenever you run an Internet program, choose **Connect Automatically** to place a check mark in its box.

5 Click the **Connect** button.

The first time you run Internet Explorer, it loads Microsoft's home page and displays a warning indicating that the site is trying to send information to your computer. This information, called a *cookie*, is like an ID badge that lets the site know who you are. The site uses the badge to greet you with personalized messages content. You can accept or reject the cookie and still connect to the Web site. ▶See "Enter Advanced Settings" on page 272 for more information about cookies and other security issues.◀

Guided Tour Start Internet Explorer

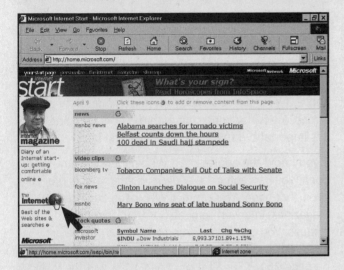

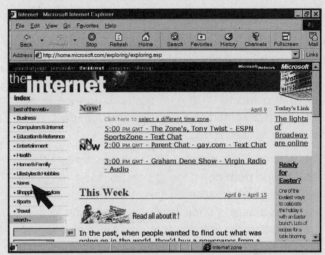

7 Internet Explorer opens and displays Microsoft's home page. To display a different page, click a link (underlined text or a special image or icon). You can tell if something is a link by resting the mouse pointer on it. If the pointer is over a link, the pointer turns into a hand.

8 When you click a link, Internet Explorer opens the page that the link points to, whether that page is stored at the same Web site or on another Web site anywhere in the world. For details about navigating Web pages, see the next task, "Browse the World Wide Web."

When the mouse pointer is over a link, the address of the page to which the link points appears on the left end of the status bar (at the bottom of the window).

The figures in this section display Internet Explorer as it appears on an 800×600dpi screen with Large Fonts turned on, so you can read the screen text in the figures. Using Large Fonts, however, causes two buttons on the toolbar (Print and Edit) to be hidden. The right side of your toolbar should have a Print and Edit button. ▶To learn how to change your display resolution and display font size, see "Change Display Properties" on page 406.◀

Browse the World Wide Web

The Web works much like a multimedia encyclopedia on CD. You select a topic of interest, and the encyclopedia displays a page of relevant information. The page typically contains text, images, and highlighted text that points to other related articles on the CD. You click the highlighted text, and the encyclopedia opens and displays the related information.

The Web provides a similar interface and similar tools for jumping from one page to another. Most pages contain highlighted text, called *links*, that are typically displayed as blue and underlined. You click a link to open the page that the link points to. Links may also appear as icons or graphics. Some pages even contain graphics, called *image maps*, that contain multiple links; you click various areas of the image map to activate different links. The *Guided Tour* shows you how to navigate the Web with links.

> To give the Web page you are viewing more screen space, click the **Fullscreen** button in the toolbar. This hides the Internet Explorer title bar, menu bar, and status bar. The toolbar remains onscreen, but the button names are hidden. To return to the normal view, click the **Fullscreen** button again.

Enter Page Addresses

Each Web page has a unique address that starts with http://. HTTP is short for *Hypertext Transfer Protocol*, which is the set of rules that govern data transfer on the Web. In an address, http:// is followed by the domain name of the computer on which the Web page is stored. For example, the address for the White House Web site is `http://www.whitehouse.gov`. Following the domain name is the path to the folder in which the Web page file is stored and the name of the file. For instance, the address of a specific page at the White House Web site might be `http://www.whitehouse.gov/WH/glimpse/top.html`. (HTML stands for Hypertext Markup Language, which is the set of codes used to format Web pages.)

When typing Web page addresses, you can omit the http:// at the beginning of the address; Internet Explorer supplies it for you. When entering the path to the folder or the filename, case is important. In the example above, typing /wh instead of /WH would result in an error. Case is not important with the domain name, but it is important in folder names and filenames.

If you know the address of a Web page you want to open, you can enter the address in Internet Explorer to open that page. You can get Web page addresses in magazines, in advertisements, or from friends and colleagues. You can also search for pages by name or topic, ▶as explained in "Find Information on the Web" on page 261.◀ For a list of quality sites, visit the Web page for this book at `http://www.mcp.com/info/0-7897/0-7897-1513-9/`.

Work with Frames

Some Web sites divide the Internet Explorer window into two or more *frames*, each of which can display part of a Web page. Frames are typically designed to help you navigate the site. For instance, in a two-framed window, an outline of the site might appear in the left frame. When you click a topic in the left frame, the right frame displays the associated page.

Frames are fairly intuitive. However, when you need to go back to a previous page, you must click the Back button several times to step back through the frames. In addition, when you print a framed document, you have to set several additional options, including whether to print the frames individually or as they appear onscreen. ▶See "Print Web Pages" on page 241 for details.◀

Tap the Power of Your Keyboard

The nature of the Web, with its links, buttons, and forms, nearly makes the mouse a necessity. However, Microsoft has built in enough quick keys in Internet Explorer 4 to make it possible to wean yourself from the mouse. The following table provides a comprehensive list of Internet Explorer's quick keys.

Internet Explorer 4's Quick Keys

Press	To
Ctrl+O	Open a Web page
Ctrl+N	Open a new Internet Explorer window
Alt+←	Go back to the previous page
Alt+→	Go to the next page (if you backed up)
Esc	Stop loading a page
F5	Refresh (reload) a page
Tab	Move from link to link
Shift+Tab	Move backward from link to link
Shift+F10	Display a shortcut menu for the selected link
Ctrl+Tab	Move from frame to frame
Ctrl+Shift+Tab	Move backward from frame to frame
↑	Scroll toward the top of a page
↓	Scroll toward the bottom of a page
Page Up	Scroll up one screenful at a time
Page Down	Scroll down one screenful at a time
Home	Go to the beginning of the Web page
End	Go to the end of the Web page
Ctrl+S	Save the current Web page
Ctrl+P	Print the current Web page
Ctrl+X	Cut selected text
Ctrl+V	Paste cut or copied text
Ctrl+C	Copy selected text
Ctrl+A	Select all text on the Web page
Ctrl+F	Find specific text on the page

Guided Tour Navigate the Web

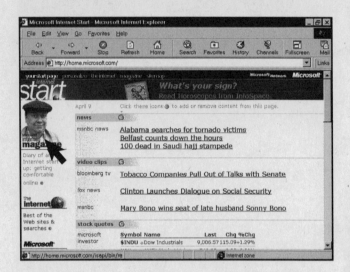

1 When you run Internet Explorer, it automatically opens Microsoft's home page. Click a link to open a different page.

If you had a previous version of Internet Explorer on your computer before installing Windows 98, the new version of Internet Explorer uses the settings from the previous version. So if you had Internet Explorer set up to load a different page on startup, Internet Explorer will also open that page instead of Microsoft's home page.

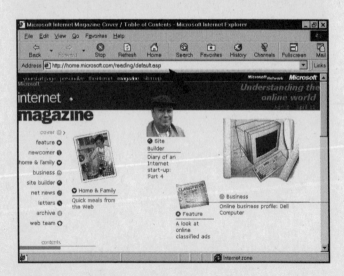

2 Internet Explorer opens the page and displays its address in the **Address** text box.

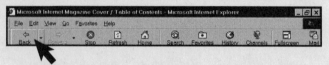

3 As you move from page to page, the Back button becomes active. Click the **Back** button anytime to move back to the previous page. ▶See "Return to Web Sites You've Already Visited" on page 243 for details on how to return to pages.◀

4 Some pages contain relatively large graphics called image maps. Each area of the image acts as a separate link. Click an area of the image to activate its link.

Guided Tour Navigate the Web

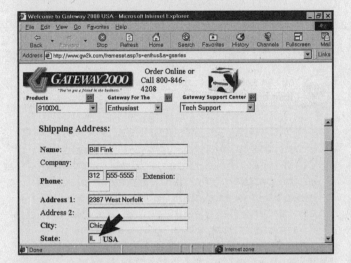

The Address text box employs the AutoComplete feature. If you start typing the address of a page you have already visited, Internet Explorer automatically enters the rest of the address for you. Then all you have to do is press **Enter**.

5 Some Web pages are forms that you can fill out to submit information or order products online. Complete a form as you would enter information in a dialog box, and then click the **Submit** button (or its equivalent).

Before entering information on a form, you should be aware of the security issues involved. ▶See "Change Your Security Settings" on page 279 for details.◀

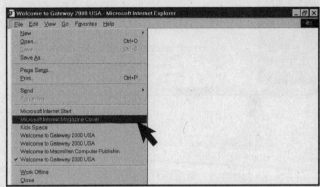

7 Internet Explorer's File menu stores a list of pages you have recently visited. To return to a page, open the **File** menu and click the name of the desired page.

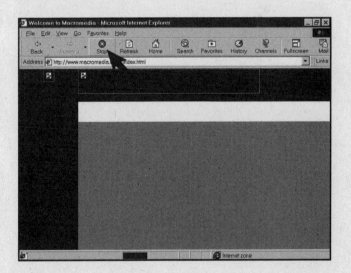

6 If you know the address of a specific page, you can open it by clicking in the **Address** text box, typing the page's address (for example, www.mcp.com), and pressing **Enter**. The Address text box also doubles as a drop-down list you can use to return to previously visited pages.

8 If a page is taking too long to load, you can click the **Stop** button to terminate the transfer. Internet Explorer loads text first and then graphics. In most cases, you will be able to see all of the text, but images might be missing.

(continues)

Guided Tour Navigate the Web *(continued)*

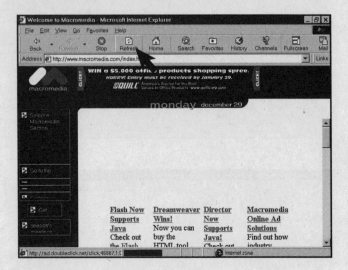

9 If you stopped a transfer or the page did not completely load for some reason, click the **Refresh** button to have Internet Explorer open the page again.

10 You can exit Internet Explorer at any time by clicking its **Close** button.

Some links point to audio or video clips or to other types of files. Internet Explorer or one of the programs included with it can play most types of audio and video files. If you encounter a file type that Internet Explorer does not support, a dialog box appears, prompting you to save the file to disk, cancel, or set up a program for playing it. ▶See "Play Audio, Video, and Other Active Content" on page 265 for details.◀

Save Web Pages and Files

As you wander the Web, you might encounter pages that you want to keep for reference or cool images and clips that you want save for future enjoyment. Internet Explorer allows you to save Web pages and other files to your hard disk. You can then open the pages later from disk or open the downloaded (copied) files.

The *Guided Tour* shows you how to save Web pages and other files to a disk and how to open Web pages from disk instead of from the Internet. When saving a Web page, you have the choice of saving it as an HTML or text-only document. The HTML document will appear as it does on the Web, with links and character

formatting intact but without the pictures. Text-only saves the document as unformatted text.

If you choose to save the page as an HTML document and you want the pictures to appear on the page, save the pictures to the same folder in which you saved the page. To save an image or other object, right-click the image or link and choose **Save Target As**.

Many sites on the Internet also offer shareware programs you can download, install, and use for a specified trial period. Check out Stroud's list at `cws.internet.com` or clnet's shareware link at `www.shareware.com`.

Guided Tour   Save a Web Page

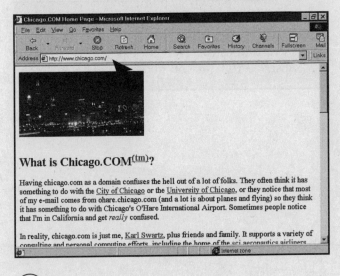

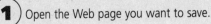

1 Open the Web page you want to save.

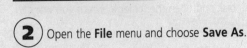

2 Open the **File** menu and choose **Save As**.

(continues)

Guided Tour Save a Web Page

(continued)

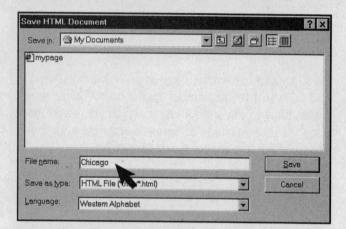

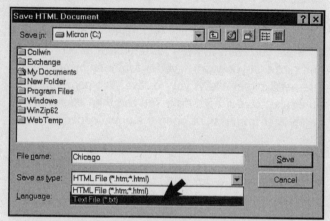

3 The Save HTML Document dialog box appears. In the **File Name** text box, type a name for the page.

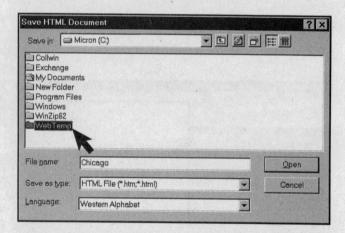

4 Use the **Save In** drop-down list and the folder list to choose the disk and open the folder in which you want to save the file.

5 (Optional) To save the page as a text-only document (no fancy Web page formatting), open the **Save as Type** drop-down list and choose **Text File**.

6 Click **Save**. Internet Explorer saves the Web page as a file, dropping any images the page has.

The best way to have Internet Explorer save the Web page and its images is to set up a subscription to the Web page. ▶See "Subscribe to Sites" on page 250.◄

Guided Tour Open a Saved Web Page

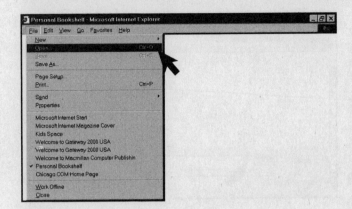

1 Open the **File** menu and click **Open** or press **Ctrl+O**.

3 Change to the disk and folder in which you saved the Web page file and select the file. Click **Open**.

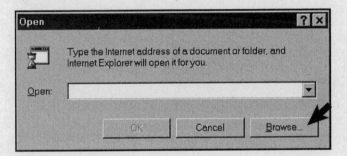

2 The Open dialog box appears. Click the **Browse** button.

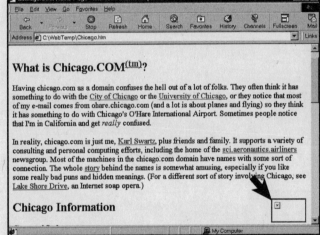

4 Click **OK**, and Internet Explorer opens and displays the Web page. Note that placeholders take the place of images.

Guided Tour Save a Link or File

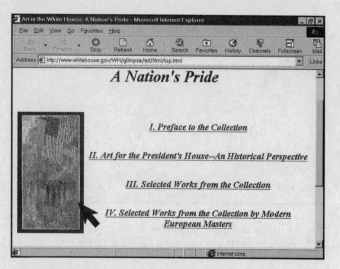

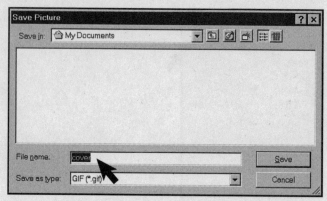

4 The Save As dialog box appears. Choose the disk and folder in which you want to store the file, type a name for the file, and click **Save**.

1 Open the page that has the image you want to save or a link to the file you want to save.

2 Right-click the image or link.

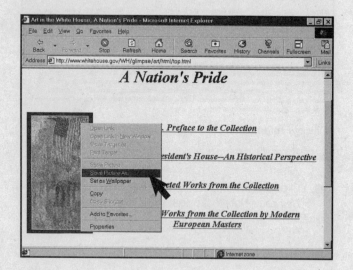

3 A context menu appears, displaying a couple of save options. To save a picture, click **Save Picture As**. To save another type of file, choose **Save Target As**.

Print Web Pages

Web pages are much more dynamic and interactive than their equivalent paper publications. They connect you to other pages with links, they provide video clips and presentations to capture your interest and convey information visually, and some pages even talk or sing to you with digitized recordings.

However, you might come across a page that you want to save as a printout. Perhaps you want to share it with a friend or relative who does not have an Internet connection, or you want to tuck it away in your files for future reference. In such cases, you can print the page from Internet Explorer. The following *Guided Tour* shows you just what to do.

Guided Tour   Print a Web Page

1 Open the page you want to print. Make sure your printer has paper and is turned on.

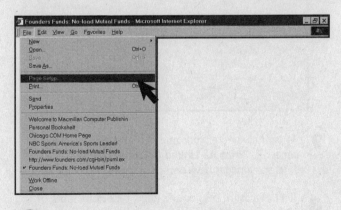

2 Open the **File** menu and choose **Page Setup**.

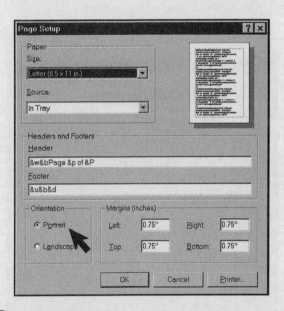

3 The Page Setup dialog box appears, showing the default page settings. Select the desired paper size and page orientation (portrait or landscape) and enter the desired margin settings. ➤See "Print a Document" on page 164 for details.◄ Click **OK**.

(continues)

Guided Tour Print a Web Page *(continued)*

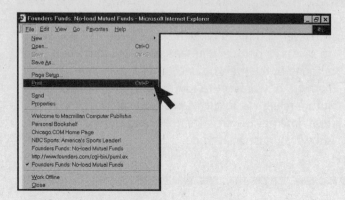

4 Open the **File** menu and choose **Print**.

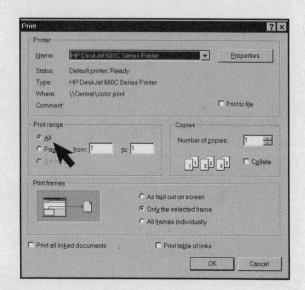

5 The Print dialog box appears. Under Print Range, choose **All**. (You can choose to print specific pages, but guessing which page contains what you want is difficult.)

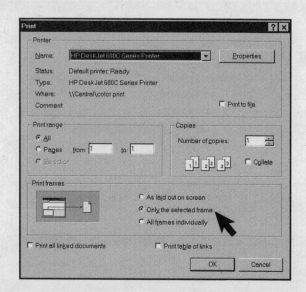

6 If the Print Frames options are available, use them to specify how you want the frames printed: **As Laid Out on Screen**, **Only the Selected Frame**, or **All Frames Individually** (which prints the frames on separate pages).

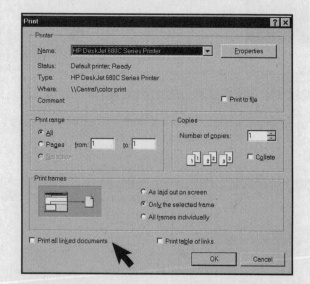

7 To print all the Web documents that are linked to this page, click **Print All Linked Documents**. (Be careful with this option; some pages have dozens of links.)

8 To print a list of links on this page, click **Print Table of Links**.

9 Click **OK**. Internet Explorer prints the document as specified.

Return to Web Sites You've Already Visited

As you move from one page to another, Internet Explorer keeps track of the pages you've visited. You can then return to pages by clicking the Back or Forward button. You can also select the desired page from any of several drop-down lists. The Back and Forward buttons and the Address text box all double as drop-down lists. You click the arrow to the right of the button or text box to view the names or addresses of the most recently opened pages. You can then choose a page from the list to quickly reopen it. The *Guided Tour* shows you what to do.

Use the History Bar

In addition to the Back, Forward, and Address drop-down lists, Internet Explorer features a History Bar. The History Bar contains a complete list of pages you have visited in the last 20 days. The History Bar is very similar to the folder list that appears on the left side of the Windows Explorer window. You click the day or week during which you visited the Web site, and then click the Web site's name to view a list of pages you viewed at that site. You can then quickly visit a page by choosing it from the list. The *Guided Tour* shows you how to display and use the History Bar.

Work with Cached Pages

Whenever you open a Web page, Internet Explorer stores it and any related files, such as graphics, in a temporary folder on your hard disk. This temporary storage area is called the *cache* (pronounced "cash"). The next time you open the page, Internet Explorer opens the file from your hard disk and updates the page, if necessary. This makes the page pop up on your screen much more quickly because Internet Explorer does not have to download the entire page from the Web.

Sometimes, however, Internet Explorer does not automatically update the page. If you suspect that you are viewing old information, click the **Refresh** button to have Internet Explorer update the page.

> Internet Explorer is set up to use a certain percentage of your hard disk space for the cache. You can clear the cache and change the percentage by opening the **View** menu and selecting **Internet Options**. The cache settings are listed under Temporary Internet Files. ▶See "Configure Internet Explorer" on page 272 for details.◀

Guided Tour Revisit Web Pages

1 When you click a link to load another page, the Back button becomes active. Click the **Back** button to return to the previous page.

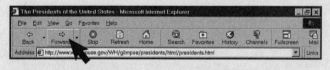

2 After you back up, the Forward button becomes active. Click the **Forward** button to move ahead to the next page.

(continues)

Guided Tour   Revisit Web Pages

(continued)

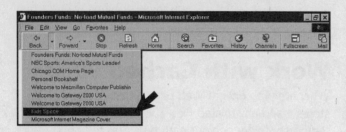

3 The Back and Forward buttons double as drop-down lists. Click the arrow to the right of one of these buttons to open a drop-down list of pages you have visited. Then click the desired page to return to it.

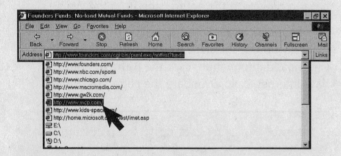

4 The Address text box also acts as a drop-down list. Click the arrow to the right of the **Address** text box, and then click the name or address of the desired page.

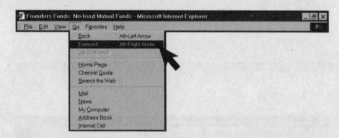

5 The Go menu also has options for moving back and forward. Open the **Go** menu and choose **Back** or **Forward** to return to a page.

6 To revisit a page you have visited some time ago, click the **History** button.

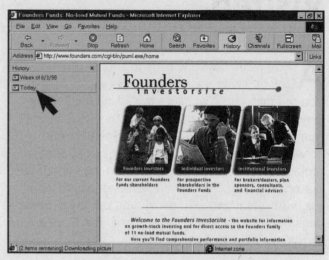

7 The History Bar appears as a separate frame on the left side of the window. Click a day or week to view a list of Web sites you visited during that time period.

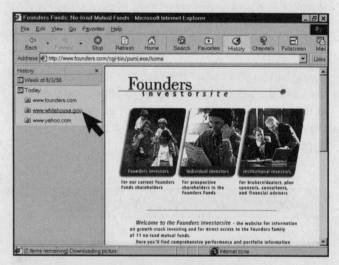

8 From the list of Web sites that appears, click the Web site that contains the page you want to revisit.

Guided Tour Revisit Web Pages

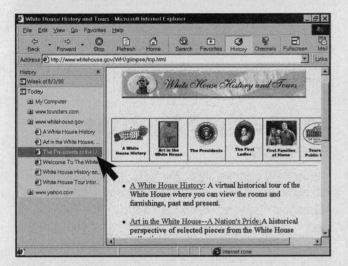

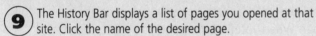

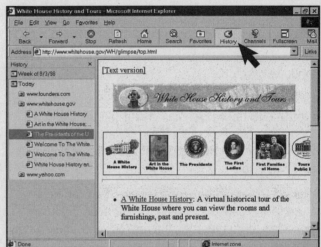

⑨ The History Bar displays a list of pages you opened at that site. Click the name of the desired page.

⑩ The page's contents appear in the right frame. To hide the History Bar, click the **History** button in the toolbar.

Create a List of Your Favorite Sites

In "Create Shortcuts to Disks, Folders, and Files" (►on page 114◄), you learned how to create icons for applications and documents and place them right on the Windows desktop.

Internet Explorer allows you to create shortcuts for your favorite Web pages. You can create shortcuts on the Windows desktop or place them on Internet Explorer's Favorites menu or the Quick Links toolbar, as shown in the *Guided Tour*.

After you create a shortcut to a page, you can quickly return to the page by clicking the shortcut. If you are connected to the Internet, Internet Explorer immediately loads the page. If you are not connected, the Connect To dialog box appears, prompting you to connect. Do so, and Internet Explorer runs and loads the page.

Organize Your Favorites Menu

The Favorites menu is yours to arrange and rearrange to your liking. You can delete favorites, create new submenus, and move items from the Favorites menu to your submenus.

To perform any of these management tasks, you first have to open the Organize Favorites window. Open the **Favorites** menu and click **Organize Favorites**. The

Favorites window is nearly identical to My Computer. You'll use the same techniques you learned in "Manage Disks, Folders, and Files" (►on page 79◄) to organize your favorites.

Locate the Favorites Menus

Internet Explorer has three Favorites menus: one in the toolbar, one on the Windows Start menu, and one that appears as a browser bar when you click the Favorites button. These menus are nearly identical. If you click the Favorites button, the menu appears as a browser bar on the left side of the Internet Explorer window. You can browse your favorite pages by selecting them from this bar. When you find the page you want, click the Favorites button again to close the bar and give your page some elbow room.

Make Your Own Button Bar

Internet Explorer has a Links toolbar (also called the Quick Links toolbar) to which you can add buttons to your favorite Web sites. The *Guided Tour* shows you how to display this timesaving toolbar and add your own buttons to it.

Guided Tour Add Shortcuts to the Windows Desktop

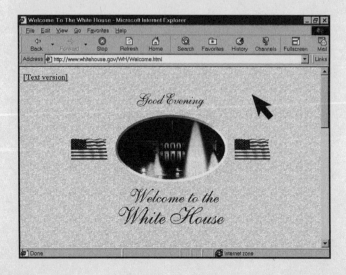

1 To create a shortcut for a page, open the page in Internet Explorer.

Guided Tour Add Shortcuts to the Windows Desktop

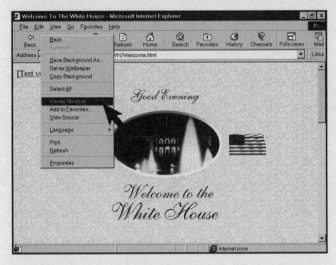

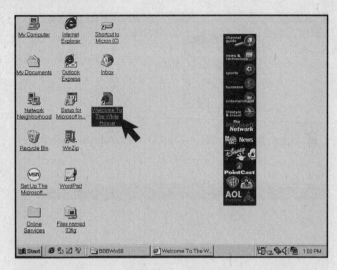

2 Right-click a blank area of the page or a link on the page and choose **Create Shortcut**.

4 Internet Explorer places a shortcut icon on the Windows desktop. Click the icon whenever you want to load the page.

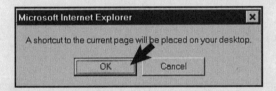

3 The Microsoft Internet Explorer dialog box informs you that a shortcut to the current page or link will be placed on the desktop. Click **OK**.

Guided Tour Add Shortcuts to the Favorites Menu

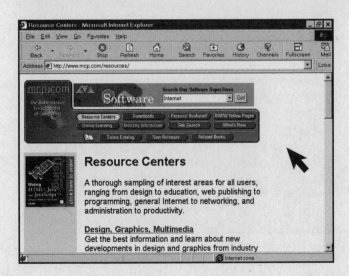

1 Open the Web page you want to mark as a favorite.

(continues)

Guided Tour Add Shortcuts to the Favorites Menu (continued)

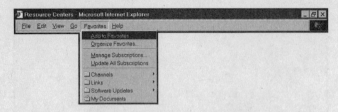

2 Open the **Favorites** menu and select **Add to Favorites**.

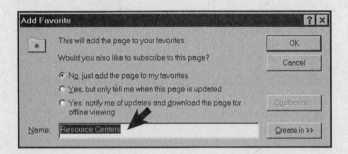

3 The Add Favorite dialog box appears. You can type a new name for the page in the **Name** text box, but you don't have to.

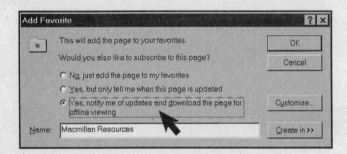

4 (Optional) Click **Yes, Notify Me of Updates and Download the Page for Offline Viewing** to subscribe to this Web page and have updated versions of the page automatically delivered to you. ▶See "Subscribe to Sites" on page 250.◀

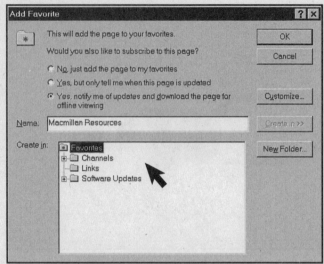

5 (Optional) To add the page to a submenu instead of to the main Favorites menu, click the **Create In** button and select the desired submenu from the **Create In** list.

6 Click **OK**.

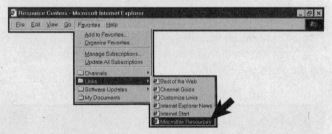

7 To quickly open a favorite page, open the **Favorites** menu and point to the submenu on which you placed the favorite (if necessary). Then click the page's name.

To place a shortcut on the top of the Start menu, drag the desired link over the **Start** button and release the mouse button. Open the **Start** menu, and you'll see the shortcut. You can also drag shortcuts onto the Quick Launch toolbar inside the Windows taskbar. ▶See "Configure the Start Menu," on page 53, for details.◀

Guided Tour Create Quick Link Buttons

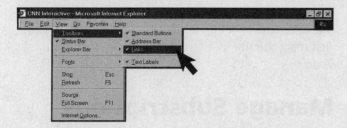

1 To view the Links toolbar, open the **View** menu, point to **Toolbars**, and make sure there is a check mark next to **Links**.

2 The bar initially appears to the right of the Address text box. To bring its existing buttons into view, double-click **Links**.

3 You can drag the bar down to display it as a separate toolbar.

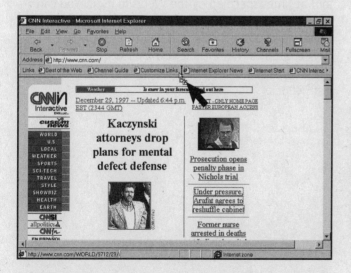

4 When the toolbar is in view, you can drag a link or shortcut icon over the Links toolbar to add it to the toolbar. A vertical line appears, showing where the button will be placed. Release the mouse button.

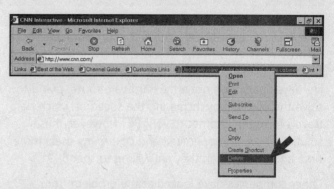

5 To delete a button, right-click it and choose **Delete**.

6 To move a button, drag it.

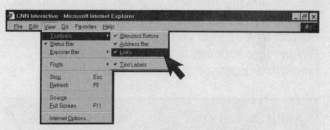

7 To hide the Links toolbar, open the **View** menu, point to **Toolbars**, and click **Links** to remove the check mark.

Links are nothing more than favorites that are placed in the \Favorites\Links folder. To rename a button, first display the contents of the Links folder in the Organize Favorites window. Then click the link, click the **Rename** button, and type the desired name for the button.

Subscribe to Sites

Several companies, including Microsoft, have been busy working on ways to speed up the Internet. Cable companies, modem manufacturers, and PC satellite developers have gone the hardware route, trying to solve the problem by increasing the speed at which data travels from the Internet to your PC. However, these solutions have an upper limit and cost many users more time and money than they are willing to spend.

Other companies have looked at the problem from a software standpoint and have developed the clever notion of *push content*. With push content, you subscribe to sites and have the Web sites broadcast updated content to your computer while you are working or sleeping. You can then disconnect from the Internet and view your pages offline. In the following sections, you will learn how to have updated Web pages delivered to your computer.

"Subscribing" sounds as if you will have to start paying an annual subscription fee for the Web pages you used to get for free. Actually, subscribing—in most cases—is free. To subscribe to a Web page, you create a shortcut or favorite and then enter settings that tell Internet Explorer how often to update the page. Internet Explorer then connects to the Web at the specified time(s) and downloads the updated page for you.

> Although you don't pay to subscribe to a site, you might incur additional connect time charges depending on how your ISP and phone company charge you. If they charge by the minute or hour, Internet Explorer can rack up huge bills.

The best time to set up a site subscription is when you first mark the site as a favorite, as shown in the *Guided Tour*.

Manage Subscriptions

As you subscribe to sites, Internet Explorer stores icons for the subscribed sites in the Windows\Subscriptions folder. You can open this folder from Internet Explorer by opening the **Favorites** menu and choosing **Manage Subscriptions**. This opens the Subscriptions window, which looks like My Computer. The window's toolbar contains two additional buttons for updating subscriptions: Update (to download current content from the selected site) and Update All (to download the current content from all subscribed sites). You can also change the subscription settings for a subscribed site, as shown in the *Guided Tour*.

Set Update Schedules

When you subscribe to a site, Internet Explorer downloads updated content according to the publisher's recommended schedule or the daily, weekly, or monthly schedule you set up in Internet Explorer. Unless you choose otherwise, Internet Explorer uses the publisher's recommended schedule and downloads updated content at times specified by the Web site itself. You can choose to have Internet Explorer download content daily, weekly, or monthly, and you can specify the days and times that Internet Explorer downloads updated pages. The *Guided Tour* provides step-by-step instructions.

Guided Tour Subscribe to a Web Site

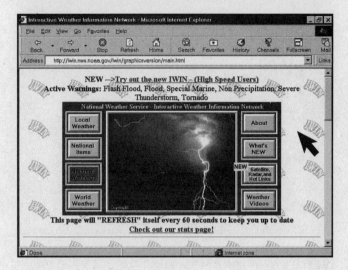

1 Open the page you want to subscribe to.

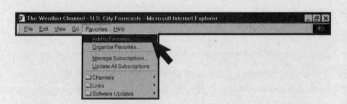

2 Open the **Favorites** menu and select **Add to Favorites**.

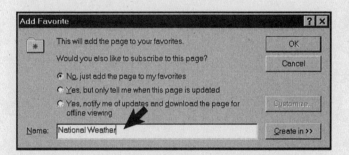

3 The Add Favorite dialog box appears. Drag over the page's name in the **Name** text box and type a name for the shortcut as you want it to appear on the Favorites menu. (You can click **Create In** to place the favorite on a submenu.)

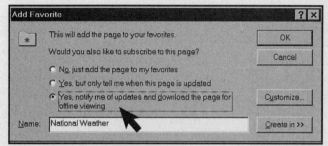

4 Choose **Yes, Notify Me of Updates and Download the Page for Offline Viewing**. This tells Internet Explorer to automatically download this page at the scheduled time (which you learn to set in the following steps).

5 Click the **Customize** button.

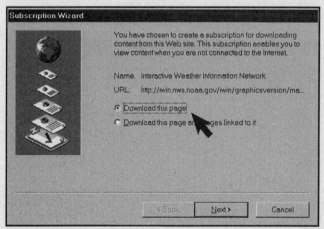

6 The Subscription Wizard starts, informing you that Internet Explorer will download updated content. Click **Download This Page** or **Download This Page and All Pages Linked to It**. Click **Next**.

Be careful about choosing Download This Page and All Pages Linked to It. Some pages are linked to several other pages. If you give Internet Explorer the okay to automatically download linked pages, you could end up with a packed hard drive.

(continues)

Guided Tour   Subscribe to a Web Site

(continued)

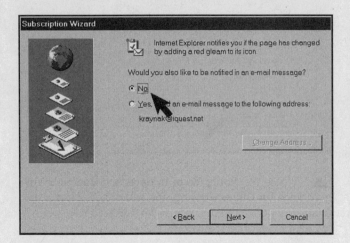

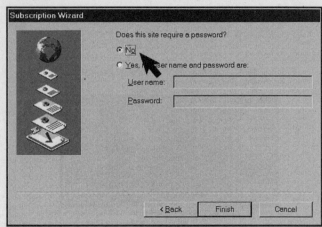

7 The wizard asks if you would also like to be notified via email. Click **No** or **Yes**. If you select Yes, you can click **Change Address** and specify the email address to which you want update notifications sent. Click **Next**.

10 The wizard now asks if you need to enter a login name and password to access the site. Click **No**, or click **Yes** and enter your login name and password. Click the **Finish** button.

11 This returns you to the Add Favorite dialog box. Click **OK**.

If you choose to have Internet Explorer download content at times when you don't normally use your computer, you must leave your computer on.

8 You are now asked how often you would like Internet Explorer to download updates. Open the **Scheduled** drop-down list and choose the desired schedule: **Daily**, **Weekly**, or **Monthly**.

9 To have Internet Explorer automatically dial into your Internet service provider at the scheduled time, choose **Dial As Needed If Connected Through a Modem**. Click **Next**.

Guided Tour Manage Subscriptions

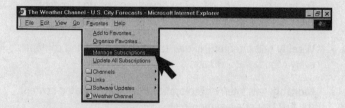

1 Open the **Favorites** menu and choose **Manage Subscriptions**.

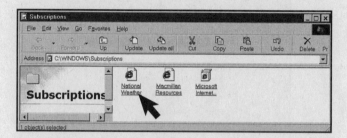

2 The Subscriptions window appears. Point to a subscription icon to select it. (You can select additional icons by **Ctrl+***pointing* to them.)

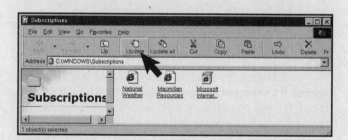

3 To update selected subscriptions, click the **Update** button.

4 To update all subscriptions, click the **Update All** button.

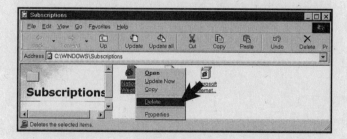

5 To delete a subscription, right-click it and choose **Delete**.

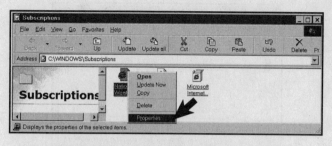

6 To change the properties of a subscription, right-click it and choose **Properties**.

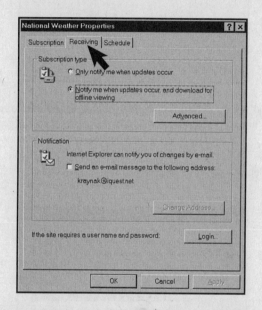

7 The Properties dialog box appears. Click the **Receiving** tab. The Receiving tab lets you modify the subscription settings you entered when you first subscribed to the site. Enter the desired settings.

(continues)

Guided Tour Manage Subscriptions *(continued)*

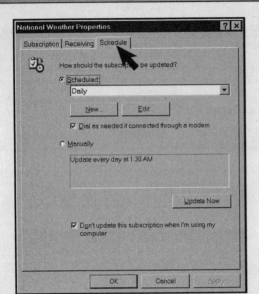

Daily tells Internet Explorer to download updated content every day at 4:30 a.m.

Weekly tells Internet Explorer to download updated content every Monday at 2:30 a.m.

Monthly tells Internet Explorer to download updated content the first day of every month at 4:30 a.m.

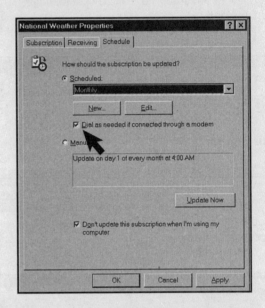

8 Click the **Schedule** tab. Then choose **Scheduled** to have Internet Explorer automatically download updated content, or choose **Manually** to download updates only when you choose the Favorites, Update All Subscriptions command in Internet Explorer.

10 You are returned to the Properties dialog box. If you connect to the Internet with a modem, choose **Dial as Needed if Connected Through a Modem** to place a check in its box. This tells Internet Explorer to automatically connect to your Internet service provider at the scheduled time.

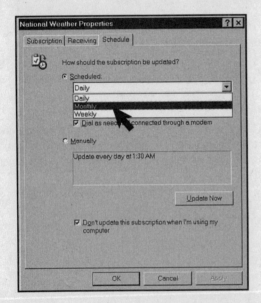

If your modem makes a lot of noise when it dials, it could wake you up. To mute it, open the **Control Panel**, click **Modems**, select your modem, and click **Properties**. Then click the **Connection** tab and click the **Advanced** button. In the **Extra Settings** text box, type **atm0** (zero, not the letter *O*). Then save the new setting.

9 If you chose Scheduled in the previous step, open the **Scheduled** drop-down list and choose one of the following options:

Publisher's Recommended Schedule (available only if the publisher has a recommended schedule) tells Internet Explorer to download updated contents according to the schedule specified by the publisher of the Web page.

Guided Tour   Manage Subscriptions

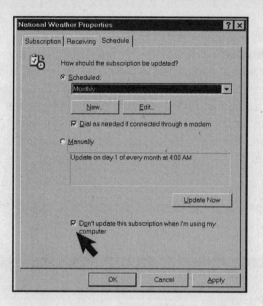

11 If you do not want Internet Explorer to download updates when you are using your computer, click **Don't Update This Subscription When I'm Using My Computer** to place a check mark in its box. (This prevents Internet Explorer from interrupting your work and using system resources that your other programs might need.)

12 Click **OK**.

You can create custom schedules that include a list of days and times when you want Internet Explorer to download updates. In step 10 of the *Guided Tour*, click **New**, type a name for the new schedule, and enter the desired settings.

Navigate the Web Offline

If you recently visited a Web page or set up a subscription to a site, you can go offline with Internet Explorer and open the page from your hard drive. This saves you time and any connect charges you might incur by staying connected to the Internet.

When you go offline, as shown in the *Guided Tour*, you can still select pages from the Favorites menu, enter page addresses, or click links just as if you were working online, but now Internet Explorer loads the pages from the disk cache instead of from the Web. If you point to a link whose page is not in the cache, the international symbol for no (a circle with a line through it) appears next to the hand pointer. If you click a link or enter the address of a page that is not in the cache, Internet Explorer displays a dialog box asking if you want to go online.

Guided Tour View Pages Offline

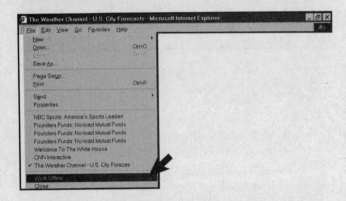

1 To work with Internet Explorer offline, open the **File** menu and select **Work Offline**.

If Internet Explorer is not set up to dial automatically, you'll get the Dial-Up Connection dialog box, which has an option for working offline.

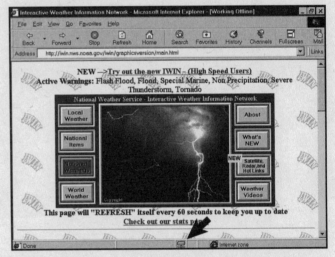

2 An icon appears in the status bar, indicating that the network connection has been broken. You can navigate the Web as you normally do, clicking links and entering page addresses.

Guided Tour View Pages Offline

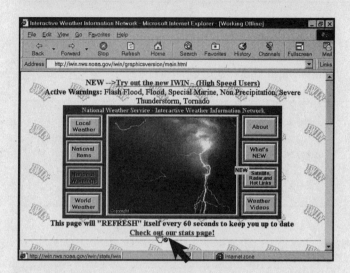

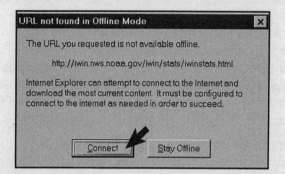

3 If you point to a link whose page is not on your hard disk, a circle with a line through it appears next to the hand pointer.

4 If you click a link or enter the address of a page that has not been saved to your hard disk, Internet Explorer displays a dialog box asking if you want to go online. Click the **Connect** button to go online, or click the **Stay Offline** button to cancel your request.

When you go offline, Internet Explorer does not "hang up" your modem. If you want to disconnect, you must close your Dial-Up Networking connection manually. However, offline browsing can still save you some time when you are connected. When you are offline and connected, Internet Explorer does not check for updated pages and does not load updates, which increases the page loading speed considerably.

Tune In to the Web with Channels

In a concentrated effort to transform your computer monitor into a TV set, Web developers have come up with some innovative tools. Microsoft's entry into this wave of the future is the Channels feature, a tool that enables you to create your own channel changer for the Web.

With Channels, you can tune in to the best sites the Web has to offer. Channel Guide comes with a Channel Finder that allows you to select from popular sites and then place those sites on the channel changer. To view a

site, you simply click a button on the channel changer; it's just like flipping channels on your TV set! The *Guided Tour* shows you what to do.

The Channels feature is relatively new and might not work as smoothly as opening standard Web pages in Internet Explorer. Expect to encounter more warnings and confirmation dialog boxes than you normally see.

Guided Tour   Channel Surf

1 To channel surf, you first need to display the Channel browser bar in Internet Explorer. Click the **Channels** button in the toolbar. (You can also use the Channel Bar on the Windows desktop.)

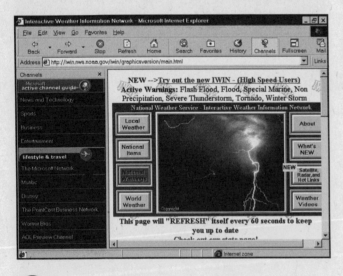

2 The Channel Bar contains several buttons for specific sites and content categories, including Entertainment and Business. Click the button for a site or category that interests you.

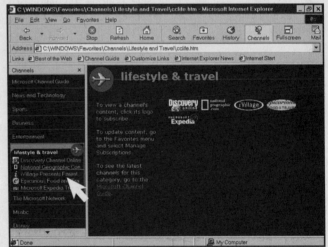

3 The right frame displays the contents of the selected site or category. In some cases, additional buttons appear in the Channel Bar, allowing you to access other pages at the site. You can click these buttons as well. Navigate the page as you normally would.

Depending on how the site is set up, it might open the page in fullscreen view and hide the Channel Bar. To bring the Channel Bar back into view, roll your mouse pointer to the left side of the screen. To return to normal view, click the **Fullscreen** button in the toolbar.

Guided Tour Channel Surf

Drag this bar to make the Channel Bar wider or narrower

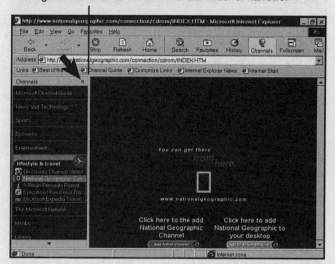

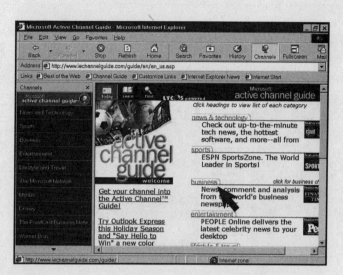

4 The Channel Bar takes up valuable screen space. To hide it, click its **Close** (X) button or click the **Channels** button in the toolbar.

6 The right frame displays additional content categories. Click the desired category to view the available channels in that category.

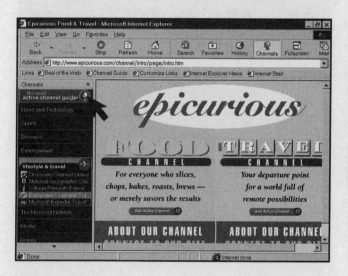

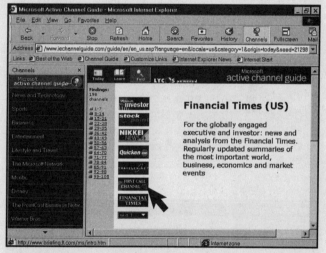

5 Redisplay the Channel Bar. At the top of the bar is a button labeled Microsoft Channel Guide. Click the **Microsoft Channel Guide** button to view additional channels registered with Microsoft.

7 Links for the available channels appear in the right frame. Click the link for the desired channel.

(continues)

Guided Tour Channel Surf *(continued)*

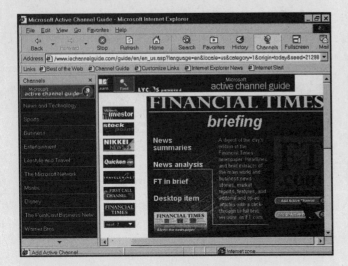

8 The right frame displays a preview of the site. To add the site to your Channel Bar, click the **Subscribe** or **Add Active Channel** link or its equivalent. (Not all pages use "Subscribe" or "Add Active Channel" as the name of the link for adding a channel.) You can click the Back button to return to the previous channel.

Some sites might offer two links: one for adding a channel and another for adding an Active Desktop component to your Windows desktop. ▶For details about using desktop components, see "Add and Remove Active Desktop Components" on page 311.◀

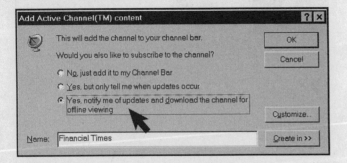

9 The Add Active Channel Content dialog box appears. Enter your subscription preferences ▶as explained in "Subscribe to Sites" on page 250.◀ Click **OK**.

10 The selected channel is added to the Channel Bar. To tune in to a site, click its button in the Channel Bar. (The Channel Bar also appears on the Windows desktop.)

To remove a button from the Channel Bar, right-click it and choose **Delete**.

Find Information on the Web

Wandering the Web appeals to the freewheeling side of all of us. We open a page and then click links to satisfy our urge to be more impulsive and to experience the unknown.

That's great if you have an infinite amount of time, a patient disposition, and little concern for reaching a specific destination. However, if you need to research a topic, find out about a recent film release, or check on arrivals or destinations at the airport, wandering with links will just pull you deeper into the Web.

When you need to find specific information in a hurry, you must be able to use Internet search forms. These fill-in-the-blank forms enable you to search for Web pages by topic. You simply enter a few words to specify the topic and then click a Search or Submit button to start the search. The search tool looks through its index to find pages that match your search instructions. It then displays a list of links you can click to load those pages.

Internet Explorer features its own Search Bar that contains links to the most popular and useful search tools on the Web. The *Guided Tour* shows you how to use the Search Bar.

Guided Tour Search for Web Pages

1 Click on the **Search** button in Internet Explorer's toolbar.

Occasionally, Microsoft offers online updates for Internet Explorer tools such as the Search Bar. Don't be surprised if you choose one of these tools and encounter a dialog box prompting you to update it.

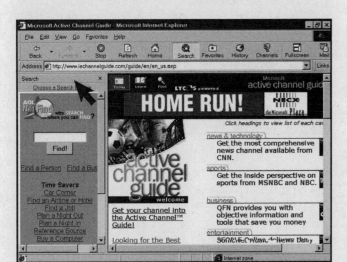

2 Internet Explorer selects a search tool for you and displays it in the left frame. To use a different search tool, click **Choose a Search Engine** or click the link for the desired search tool in the right pane.

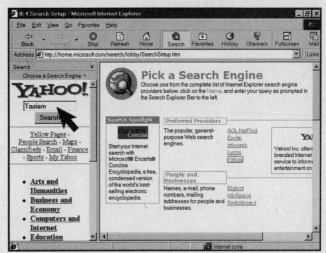

3 The left frame displays the page for the selected search tool. Click in the text box for entering your search words and type one or more words to specify what you are looking for. Some search services also display categories in the Search Bar that you can click if you want to narrow your search.

 Click the **Search** button or its equivalent.

(continues)

Guided Tour Search for Web Pages

(continued)

Because search tools use forms, Internet Explorer might display a security warning when you try to submit your search instructions. Internet Explorer doesn't know if you are entering a credit card number or searching for information about planting a rose garden. Just click **Yes** to continue. ▶See "Change Your Security Settings," on page 279 for more information.◀

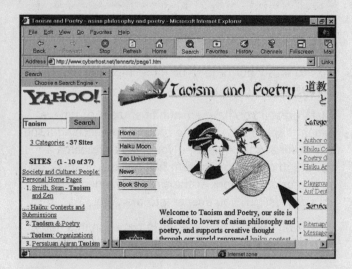

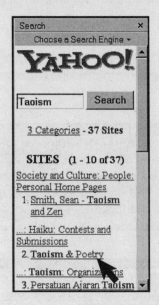

5 The search tool looks for pages that match your search word(s) and displays a list of links in the left frame. Click a link to load the associated page.

6 The right frame displays the contents of the page. You can continue clicking links in the left frame to load other pages.

7 When you find the page you want, you can click the Search Bar's **Close** (X) button or the **Search** button in the toolbar to hide the Search Bar.

You can access search tools from the Windows Start, Find submenu. Click the **Start** button, point to **Find**, and choose **On the Internet**. The Start, Find submenu also has options for searching for Files and Folders, Computers (on a network), and People (using Internet phone books). ▶See "Use the Address Book" on page 340 to learn how to search for people on the Internet.◀

Add Components to Internet Explorer

When you installed Internet Explorer, the installation placed the most common Internet Explorer components on your hard disk. However, you can install additional components for playing media files and accessing other Internet features.

Most of these components or add-ons are *ActiveX controls*, additional programming code that increases the capability of Internet Explorer. The great feature of

ActiveX is that it is automatic. When you choose to download an ActiveX control, Internet Explorer displays a dialog box asking for your confirmation. After you give your okay, Internet Explorer automatically downloads and installs the control without your intervention.

To take an inventory of your system to determine which components are already installed and to install missing components, follow the *Guided Tour*.

Guided Tour Install Additional Internet Explorer Components

1 Open Internet Explorer's **Help** menu and choose **Product Updates**. (If Microsoft moved the page, connect to the Internet Explorer home page at www.microsoft.com/ie and look for the appropriate link.)

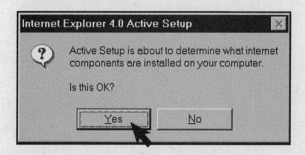

2 Microsoft's components download site initializes the Internet Explorer 4.0 setup and displays the Internet Explorer 4.0 Active Setup dialog box, asking for your confirmation. Click **Yes**.

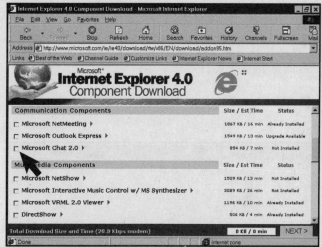

3 Active Setup takes an inventory of your system and displays a list of installed and uninstalled components. To install a component or upgrade, click its check box. You can select more than one check box. Click **Next**.

Guided Tour Install Additional Internet Explorer Components
(Continued)

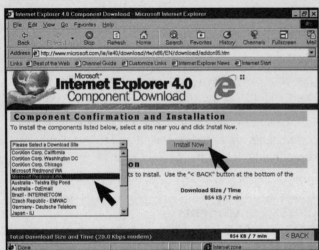

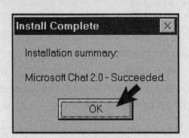

7 When installation is complete, the Install Complete dialog box appears. Click **OK**. (You might need to restart your computer, depending on the component(s) you installed.)

4 The Components Download page appears. Open the drop-down list near the top of the page and choose a download site near you.

5 Click **Install Now**.

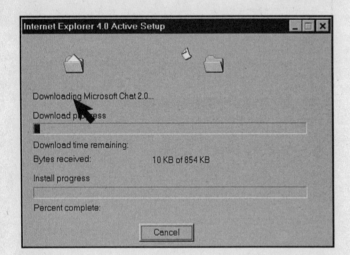

6 The Internet Explorer 4.0 Active Setup dialog box appears, displaying the progress of the download and installation. (This might take some time, depending on the size and number of components you chose and on the speed of your Internet connection.)

Play Audio, Video, and Other Active Content

Internet Explorer isn't just a cruise liner for the Web. Microsoft has built into its latest Web browser the capability to display most graphic file types, almost any sound file, and more video file types than just about any dedicated video player can handle. However, Internet Explorer cannot play all file types. To play a file type that it cannot handle, Internet Explorer needs a special program: a *helper application, plug-in,* or *ActiveX control.*

Not very long ago, Web browsers relied solely on helper applications to play file types that the Web browsers could not handle, such as video clips. Helper applications (*helper apps* or *viewers* for short) are small programs that typically take up little memory and run very fast. Whenever you try to play a file on the Internet that the Web browser cannot handle, the browser downloads the file and runs the helper app assigned to that file type, which then opens and "plays" the file.

To integrate viewers with Web browsers and make them easier to install and set up, Web browser creators have come up with alternatives to helper apps. One such alternative is the *plug-in.* Plug-ins are additional computer code that typically increase the built-in capabilities of the Web browser. Unlike helper apps, which are separate applications, most plug-ins become part of the Web browser, making it much more efficient for playing media files.

In addition to plug-ins, Internet Explorer allows you to use ActiveX controls to play media files. Unlike plug-ins, which you have to download and install, ActiveX controls install themselves, typically when you choose to play a particular file type. All you have to do is give your okay to install the control.

Which is best? Here's a quick rundown:

- ActiveX controls are the winners, hands down. ActiveX controls install themselves and are designed to work with Internet Explorer.

- Plug-ins are an excellent alternative to ActiveX controls. If you can find an ActiveX control that does the same thing, use it instead. Internet Explorer does support Netscape Navigator plug-ins, so if you can't find an equivalent ActiveX control, go with the plug-in.

- Helper apps are good if you want to download a media file and play it later or modify it. You won't need to fire up your Web browser to play the file.

ActiveX controls, which come from unlicensed sites, do pose a security risk. Before giving your okay to download and install an ActiveX control, make sure Internet Explorer displays its certificate. If Internet Explorer shows that the control is not certified, cancel the download. ▶See "Change Your Security Settings," on page 279 for more information.◀

File Types That Internet Explorer Can Play

Internet Explorer has built-in players for most of the file types you will encounter on the Web. The following table lists the file types that Internet Explorer or one of its many components can play.

Media File Types That Internet Explorer Supports

Program or Plug-In	Description	File Types
Internet Explorer	Web browser	.html, .htm (Web page) .txt (text only) .gif (graphic) .jpg, jpeg, jpe, .jfif (graphic) .xbm (graphic) .au .aif, .aiff, .aifc .snd, .wav .mid, .midi, .rmi Java applets JavaScriptVRML
ActiveMovie	Video Player	.avi, mpeg, .mov
ActiveX VRML	VRML Player	.wrl .wrz

Download and Install Plug-Ins

You can download (copy) plug-ins from various Internet sites and then install them for use with Internet Explorer. In most cases, if you visit a Web site that has file types that most Web browsers cannot play, the site has a link you can click for downloading the required plug-in. The Web also has some sites that act as plug-in warehouses, offering reviews of various plug-ins along with links for downloading the plug-ins. Check out the following sites:

TUCOWS at www.tucows.com is one of the best places to go for Internet-related software. TUCOWS offers a thorough list of the best software, along with ratings, reviews, and links for downloading the software.

Stroud's at cws.internet.com is my favorite shareware site, allowing me to browse through several categories of the top Internet software. Stroud's contains links for helper applications, plug-ins, and ActiveX controls.

HotWired's Webmonkey at http://www.hotwired.com/webmonkey/ provides a thorough list of players for both Mac and Windows platforms.

clnet's Shareware Central at www.shareware.com presents plug-ins and helper apps you might not find elsewhere.

Although not as easy to install as ActiveX components, plug-ins are fairly easy to set up and use. You simply run the program's installation utility and follow the onscreen instructions. The installation utility associates the plug-in with file types that it can play, so you do not have to create the association manually. ▶See "Install New Programs" on page 48.◀

Set Up Helper Applications

Helper applications are a little difficult to set up. First, you install the helper application as you would install any program. Then you must associate the program with the file types you want it to play. ▶See "Install New Programs" on page 48 to learn how to install a helper application. See "Create and Edit File Associations" on page 125 for instructions on creating file associations.◀

Guided Tour Install ActiveX Controls

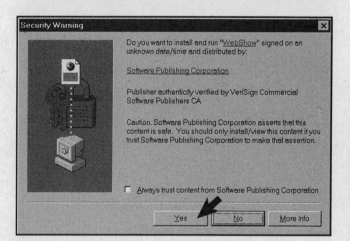

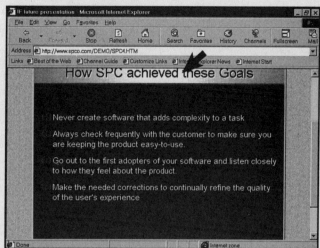

1 When you click a link to play a file type that requires an ActiveX control, Internet Explorer displays a dialog box asking if you want to download and install the control. If the dialog box indicates that the control is certified, click **Yes**; otherwise, click **No** to cancel the download.

2 Internet Explorer automatically downloads the control, installs it on your computer, and starts to play the media file.

Guided Tour Download and Install Plug-Ins

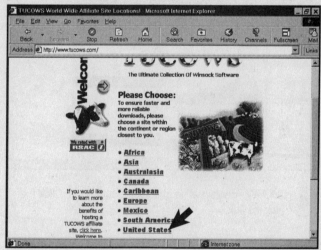

1 One of the best places to find plug-ins is at TUCOWS. Click in the **Address** text box, type **www.tucows.com**, and press **Enter**.

2 Internet Explorer connects to TUCOWS and displays its opening Web page. Follow the trail of links to a TUCOWS site near you. You will need to click the link for your country and then click the link for your state or locality.

(continues)

Guided Tour Download and Install Plug-Ins *(continued)*

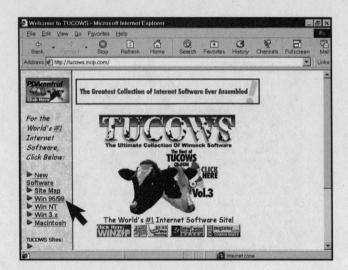

3 Click the Win 95/98 link.

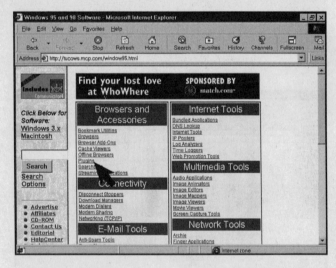

4 TUCOWS displays a list of software categories. Click the **Plugins** link.

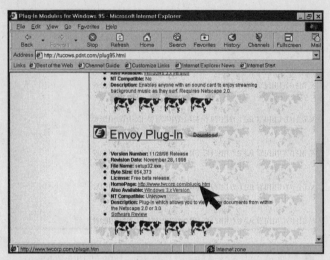

5 TUCOWS displays a list of available plug-ins. Click the link for downloading the plug-in. (You might have to follow a trail of links to the download site and then click the link for the plug-in.)

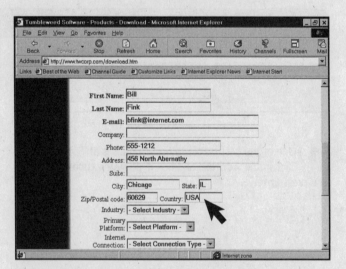

6 Some sites require you to register before downloading. Complete the registration form and click the button to submit it.

Guided Tour   Download and Install Plug-Ins

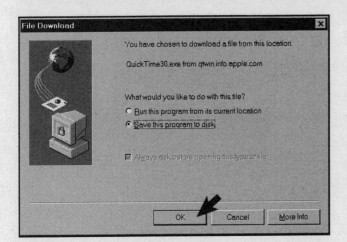

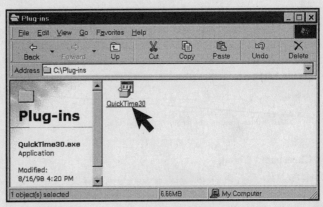

10 Exit Internet Explorer and open My Computer or Windows Explorer. Change to the disk and folder in which you saved the downloaded program file, and then click the file.

7 The File Download dialog box appears, asking if you want to download the program file or run it. Click **Save This Program to Disk** and click **OK**.

To create a new folder, click the Create New Folder button.

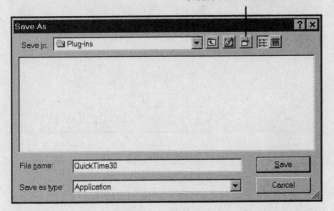

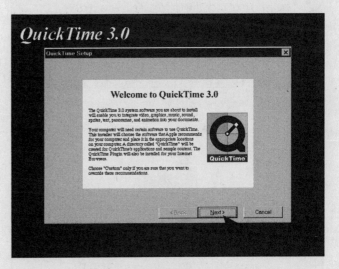

8 The Save As dialog box appears. Choose the disk and folder in which you want to store the file. Click **Save**.

11 The installation utility starts. Follow the onscreen instructions to install the plug-in.

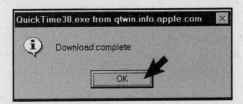

9 Internet Explorer downloads the file and places it in the specified folder (this may take some time, depending on the file's size). When the Download Complete dialog box appears, click **OK**.

Most plug-ins come as EXE files that you can run. Older plug-ins may be packaged as ZIP files, which you first must decompress. If you encounter a ZIP file, first download and install a program called WinZip. After installing WinZip, click the ZIP file you downloaded. WinZip displays a list of files in the zipped file. Double-click the **Setup.exe** or **Install.exe** file to run the installation utility.

Guided Tour Play Media Files

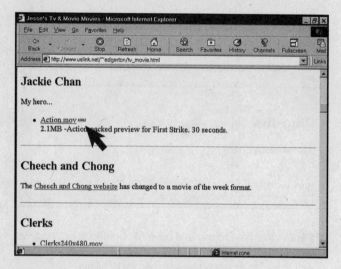

3 In other cases, Internet Explorer downloads the file and launches the associated plug-in, component, or helper application, which plays the file in its own window.

1 To play a media file, load the page that contains the media clip or click the link for the media clip.

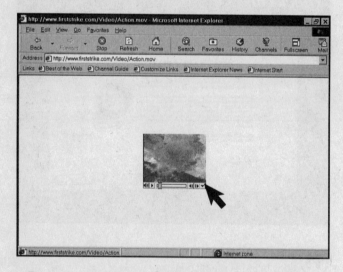

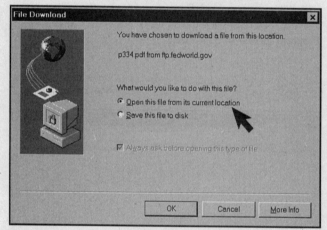

4 If you click a link to a file that Internet Explorer cannot play or that is not associated with a program, the File Download dialog box appears. Click **Open This File from Its Current Location** and click **OK**.

2 If Internet Explorer can play the file, it does. In many cases, the media file plays right on the page you're viewing. These file types are called *embedded files*.

Guided Tour   Play Media Files

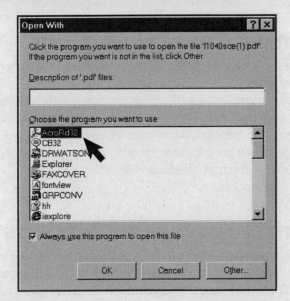

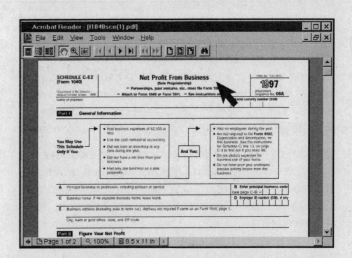

6 Internet Explorer launches the associated plug-in or helper application. The program opens and plays the file.

5 The Open With dialog box appears, prompting you to choose the program you want to use to open this type of file. Scroll down the list and click the program you want to use. Click **OK**.

You can associate file types only with programs already installed on your computer. If you encounter a file type that no program on your computer can play, you must first install the required plug-in or helper application before you can associate it with a file type.

Configure Internet Explorer

Although Internet Explorer is set up to run immediately with settings that anyone can use, Internet Explorer allows you to customize it to make it look and act the way you want it to. You can enlarge the viewing area by turning toolbars off, change the screen colors, load pages without loading graphics, and much more.

You can change most settings by opening the **View** menu, selecting **Internet Options**, and then clicking the tab for the set of options you want to change: General, Security, Content, Connection, Programs, and Advanced. The *Guided Tour* provides detailed instructions on how to change the most common settings. However, this *Guided Tour* skips the Security and Content options. ▶Security is covered in "Change Your Security Settings" on page 279, and Content is covered in "Censor the Internet" on page 283.◀

Enter General Settings

The General settings are the most helpful of the bunch. They allow you to change the page that Internet Explorer loads on startup, clear temporary Internet files off your hard disk, clear the History list, and specify the colors and fonts you want Internet Explorer to use for pages when no color scheme or fonts are specified. As you work through the *Guided Tour*, focus on the General options.

Enter Advanced Settings

The Advanced settings are too numerous to describe in the *Guided Tour*. If you decide to look at the Advanced settings, refer to the following table for descriptions of the available options.

Advanced Settings

Option Name	Description
Accessibility	
Move System Caret...	Tells an accessibility aid, such as a screen reader, to move the system caret (an onscreen pointer) to focus on significant areas of the page.
Always Expand Alt Text...	Expands the space occupied by an image to display all alternate text that the Web page author included, in the event that you chose to turn off image display. (See "Show Pictures," in the "Multimedia" section of this table.)
Browsing	
Disable Script Debugging	Turns off warning messages for built-in scripts that are not working properly on pages.
Show Channel Bar at Startup...	Displays the Channel Bar on the Windows desktop even if you turn off the Active Desktop.
Launch Channels in Full Screen...	Opens channels in a fullscreen window.
Launch Browser in Full Screen...	Opens Internet Explorer in a fullscreen window when you start it.
Use AutoComplete	Enables Internet Explorer to automatically complete a page address you are typing for a page you have already visited. This is a valuable time-saver.
Show Friendly URLs	Tells Internet Explorer to display an abbreviated address for the current page in the status bar.
Use Smooth Scrolling	Makes the page flow more smoothly when you are scrolling up or down.

Option Name	Description
Enable Page Transitions	Tells Internet Explorer to fade out the current page when fading in the next page for smoother page transitions.
Browse in a New Process	Tells Internet Explorer to start fresh whenever you run it to avoid conflicts with other programs.
Enable Page Hit Counting	Allows Web sites to automatically track your page-viewing history at their site. Many Web sites track usage for research purposes.
Enable Scheduled Subscription...	Allows Internet Explorer to download updated content for subscribed sites automatically.
Show Welcome Message Each Time...	Displays the Internet Explorer welcome message each time you run Internet Explorer.
Show Internet Explorer on the...	Displays the Internet Explorer shortcut icon on the Windows desktop.
Underline Links	Specifies whether you want Internet Explorer to display a line under linked text.

Multimedia

Show Pictures	Tells Internet Explorer to display all graphic images on a page. If you turn this off, pages load much more quickly but without images.
Play Animations	Tells Internet Explorer to automatically play any animations on a page. Again, turning this off makes pages load more quickly.
Play Videos	Tells Internet Explorer to automatically play any embedded video clips.
Play Sounds	Allows Internet Explorer to automatically play any background audio clips.
Smart Image Dithering	Smooths the rough edges of images to improve their appearance.

Security

Enable Profile Assistant	Allows Internet Explorer to pass any personal information that you enter about yourself to Web sites that request it.
PCT 1.0	PCT (Private Communications Technology) is a security standard that encrypts any information you enter on a form to protect it from prying eyes.
SSL 2.0 and 3.0	SSL (Secure Socket Layer) is another security standard that protects sensitive information from being intercepted and read.
Delete Saved Pages When Browser...	Deletes any cached pages to prevent people from determining what you accessed when you used Internet Explorer.
Do Not Save Encrypted Pages...	Prevents any encrypted pages from being saved to your disk.
Warn If Forms Submit Is Being...	Displays a warning if you submit information via a form and the form tries to reroute it through other Internet sites.
Warn If Changing Between Secure...	Tells Internet Explorer to display a warning whenever you move from a secure Web site to an insecure Web site.

Advanced Settings   Continued

Option Name	Description
Check for Certificate Revocation	Tells Internet Explorer to check a site's certificate to determine if it has been revoked before trusting the site. ►See "Change Your Security Settings" on page 279 for more information about security settings.◄
Warn About Invalid Site...	Displays a warning if there is some evidence that a secure site's certificate has been tampered with.
Cookies	Tells Internet Explorer to accept or reject cookies. Cookies consist of data that a Web site stores on your computer to help identify you in the future or keep track of products you are ordering online.

Java VM (Virtual Machine)

Java JIT Compiler Enabled	Tells Internet Explorer to automatically compile and run Java applets (small programs embedded on Web pages). (A compiler transforms programming instructions into a language that your computer and operating system can understand).
Java Logging Enabled	Tells Internet Explorer to log the activity of any Java applet to help you track down problems and trace security breaches.

Printing

Print Background Colors...	Tells Internet Explorer to print not only the text and graphics on a page but also any background colors or images.

Searching

Autoscan Common Root Domains	Allows Internet Explorer to search other domains for a particular Web site in the event that you typed the wrong root domain. For instance, if you entered www.whitehouse.com, and Internet Explorer found no such site, it would automatically replace .com with other root domains (.edu, .gov, and so on) to find the site.
Search When URL Fails	Tells Internet Explorer to search for Web sites with similar addresses when you enter an address that does not work.

Toolbar

Show Font Button	Turns on the Font button, which allows you to choose the type size used for Web page text.
Small Icons	Displays smaller buttons in the toolbar so more buttons fit and the toolbar takes up less screen space.

HTTP (HyperText Transfer Protocol) 1.1 Settings

Use HTTP 1.1	Gives Internet Explorer the okay to load pages that support the HTTP 1.1 standard.
Use HTTP 1.1 Through Proxy...	Tells Internet Explorer to load pages that support HTTP 1.1 only through a proxy server. A proxy server is a middleman used to secure a system (usually a network).

Guided Tour   Customize Internet Explorer

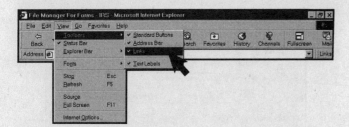

1 You can turn any of Internet Explorer's toolbars on or off. Open the **View** menu, point to **Toolbars**, and choose the toolbar you want to turn on or off: **Standard Buttons**, **Address Bar**, or **Links**. (You can hide the button names by choosing **Text Labels**.)

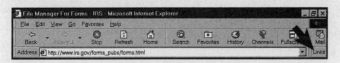

2 To maximize the Links toolbar, double-click the word **Links**.

3 You can drag the toolbar's name up or down to move it. Or, drag the vertical bar next to the toolbar's name to resize the toolbar.

4 To change additional options, open the **View** menu and choose **Internet Options**.

5 The Internet Options dialog box appears with the General tab in front. To have Internet Explorer start with a different page, type its address in the Home page, Address text box. (To use the page that is now displayed in the browser window as the starting page, click the **Use Current** button.)

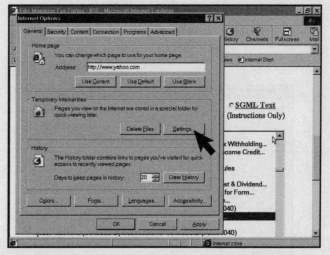

6 Under Temporary Internet Files, click the **Settings** button.

(continues)

Guided Tour   Customize Internet Explorer   *(continued)*

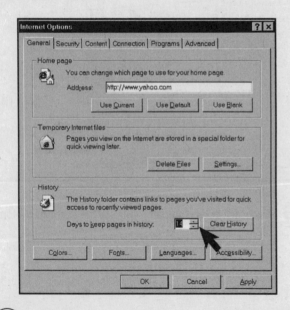

7 The Settings dialog box appears. Under **Temporary Internet Files Folder**, drag the slider to the left to decrease the amount of disk space set aside for cached pages or to the right to increase the amount of space.

8 By default, Internet Explorer is set up to check for newer versions of cached pages each time you start Internet Explorer. To ensure that you are always viewing the latest content, choose **Every Visit to the Page**. To speed up Internet Explorer, choose **Never**. Click **OK**.

9 In the **History** section, use the spin box to set the number of days you want Internet Explorer to keep track of pages you have visited. (The higher the number, the more disk space is used.)

10 To change the default colors used for text, links, or page backgrounds, click the **Colors** button.

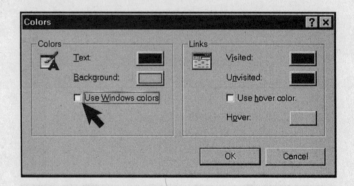

11 The Colors dialog box appears. To change the text and background colors, click **Use Windows Colors** to remove the check mark. Click the **Text** or **Background** button and choose the desired color.

12 Under Links, click the **Visited** or **Unvisited** button and choose the desired color for link text. (You can also choose **Use Hover Color** and then pick the color you want to use for a link when the mouse is over it.) Click **OK**.

The colors you choose for text, backgrounds, and links affect only those pages that do not specify a color scheme. If the page has a specified color scheme, that color scheme will override your settings.

Guided Tour   Customize Internet Explorer

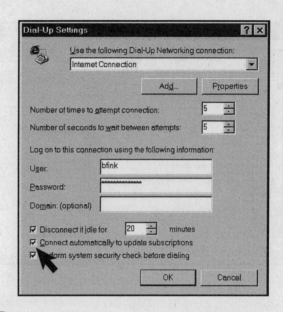

13 If you are using a modem to connect to the Internet, click the **Connection** tab and click the **Settings** button.

16 To have Internet Explorer automatically dial your modem to download content from subscribed sites at the specified times, click **Connect Automatically to Update Subscriptions** to place a check in its box.

17 To prevent Internet Explorer from prompting you for your username and password before dialing, click **Perform System Security Check Before Dialing** to remove the check mark from its box. Click **OK**.

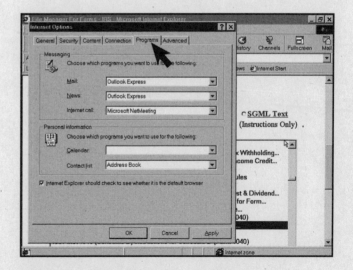

14 The Dial-Up Settings dialog box appears. You can specify the number of times your modem should attempt to dial your Internet service provider and the number of seconds to wait before each attempt.

15 To have Internet Explorer automatically hang up when your Internet connection has been idle for some time, choose **Disconnect if Idle for ___ Minutes** and enter the desired number of minutes. (Or, remove the check mark to prevent automatic disconnects.)

18 Click the **Programs** tab. This tab lists the programs Internet Explorer should launch to access other Internet features. By default, Internet Explorer is set up to use Outlook Express for email and newsgroups. If you have a different newsreader or email program you would rather use, choose it from the drop-down lists.

(continues)

Guided Tour Customize Internet Explorer *(continued)*

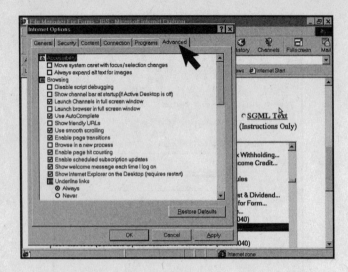

19 Click the **Advanced** tab to access the advanced options. Refer to the table preceding this *Guided Tour* for descriptions of these options. Enter your preferences.

20 Click **OK** to save your settings.

Change Your Security Settings

As you send data and receive active content on the Web, Internet Explorer supervises your actions and the actions of the remote server and warns you of any risky activity. Whenever you submit a form, Internet Explorer displays a dialog box, warning you that you are sending data over a remote network connection and asking if you want to proceed. If a Web site tries to send you an ActiveX control or Java applet (which could potentially contain a computer virus), Internet Explorer either displays a warning or prevents the application from downloading or running on your computer.

If you receive a warning dialog box, you can usually prevent similar warnings from appearing in the future by selecting the **In the Future, Do Not Show This Warning** option before giving your okay.

Another way to control these warnings is to set up *security zones*, a new feature in Internet Explorer 4. Each zone has different security settings, allowing you to relax the security settings for sites that you trust and tighten security settings for untrusted or untested sites. Internet Explorer offers the following four security zones:

- *Local Intranet* allows your network administrator to set up a list of restricted Internet sites and to enter security settings to prevent users throughout your company from accessing risky content.

- *Trusted sites* allow you to turn off the security warnings for sites you trust. This prevents you from being inundated with warning messages at the sites you visit most frequently.

- *Internet* allows you to specify security settings for untested sites. When you wander off to sites you do not frequent, you may wish to tighten security.

- *Restricted sites* lets you create a list of sites you do not trust and tighten security for those sites. For example, you might want to prevent a particular site from automatically installing and running programs on your computer.

The *Guided Tour* shows you how to add and remove sites from the Trusted Sites, Internet, and Restricted Sites zones.

Add Sites to the Local Intranet Zone

If you have a network connection, your network administrator is in charge of setting the security levels for trusted and untrusted sites. Because of this, the procedure for adding sites to the Local Intranet list is different from the procedure in the *Guided Tour*. When you select the Local Intranet zone and click the **Add Sites** button, Internet Explorer displays a dialog box offering three options:

- **Include All Local (Intranet) Sites Not Listed in Other Zones** adds all the sites on your (internal) intranet. Because these sites are controlled internally, you can be fairly certain that they do not pose a security risk.

- **Include All Sites That Bypass the Proxy Server** adds all Internet sites that you do not have to access using a proxy server. A proxy server stands between the Internet and the local network to prevent unauthorized transfers. If your network administrator deems a site safe, it might not have to go through the proxy server so you can treat it as a Local Intranet site.

- **Include All Network Paths (UNCs)** adds all intranet sites that are actually paths to network servers and other computers on your network.

Enter Zone Security Levels

To specify a security level for a zone, open the **View** menu, select **Internet Options**, and click the **Security** tab. Open the **Zone** drop-down list, select the zone whose security level you want to change, and then select the desired level:

- **High** prevents you from submitting any information by way of form, even a search form. If you complete a form and click the button to submit it, nothing happens. In addition, Internet Explorer won't play Java applets, download ActiveX controls, or transfer any other potentially harmful programs or scripts to your computer. The High setting is useful for sites you place on the Restricted Sites list.

- **Medium** turns on prompts, so Internet Explorer displays dialog boxes whenever you attempt to send data or download scripts or other active content. The Medium setting is useful for the Internet zone, where you might want to be prompted before doing anything risky.

- **Low** turns off the prompts, allowing you to submit information using a form and allowing sites to send you active content. The Low setting is good for Trusted sites, where you are fairly certain that nothing bad is going to happen.

- **Custom** allows you to enter specific security settings. For example, you might want to prevent active content from being automatically downloaded to your computer, but you don't want a dialog box popping up on your screen every time you fill out a form.

If you select Custom, click the **Settings** button to display the Security Settings dialog box, which lists all the settings. Open the **Reset To** drop-down list near the bottom of the dialog box and select the desired security level; for instance, you might select **Medium** to turn on prompts for most actions. Then select the desired security settings for each activity. The following list provides a brief explanation of each category:

ActiveX Controls and Plug-ins: These programs add capabilities to Internet Explorer for playing sounds, video clips, and other files that Internet Explorer cannot play itself. You should keep Prompt on for Unsigned ActiveX controls because these controls have not been registered as coming from a secure source. Enable both Signed ActiveX controls and Run ActiveX controls and plug-ins. You will learn more about ActiveX controls and plug-ins in Part 3.

Java: Java is another programming language used to play active Web content. Again, signed Java controls are from trusted, registered providers, so you can set this option to Enabled. Sandboxed Java is a secure form of Java, which prevents access to system files and other vulnerable system resources; for those you can safely leave the Enable setting on. Java Permissions allow you to specify the level of system access you want Java applets to have: Low, Medium, High, or Disable. As you will see in later sections, Java adds a great deal of activity and interactivity to Web pages so you don't want to completely disable it; Medium is a good setting.

Scripting: Scripting is programming code that is built into Web pages to create animations and interactive objects. Because scripts are built into most pages on the Web, you should Enable Java scripts and Active scripts. Set Script ActiveX controls that are not marked safe to Prompt or Disable.

User Authentication: These are advanced options for connecting to servers that require you to enter a username and password to connect.

Downloads: This allows you to prevent remote systems from automatically sending you font files or other files. If you want to view special fonts used on a page, keep Font files set to Enable or Prompt. You should keep File download set to Prompt or Disable because files from untrusted sources may carry viruses.

Miscellaneous: The major option in this category is Submit form data. If you want to be prompted every time you submit a form, turn on Prompt; otherwise, turn on Enable. It's also pretty safe to set Drag and drop components to the desktop to Enable, because you must initiate the drag-and-drop operation. Keep Launching applications and files set to Prompt.

Guided Tour Add Sites to the Security Zones

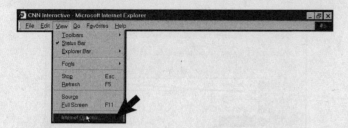

1 To access the security settings, open the **View** menu and select **Internet Options**.

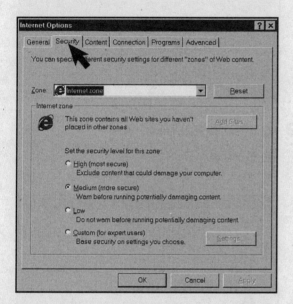

2 The Internet Options dialog box appears. Click the **Security** tab.

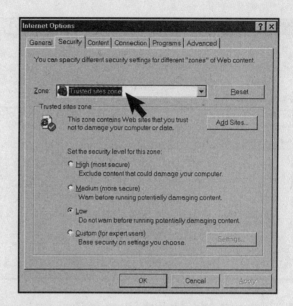

3 You can add and remove sites from three of the four security zones: Local Intranet, Trusted sites, and Restricted sites. Open the **Zone** drop-down list and select the zone to which you want to add sites.

4 Click the **Add Sites** button.

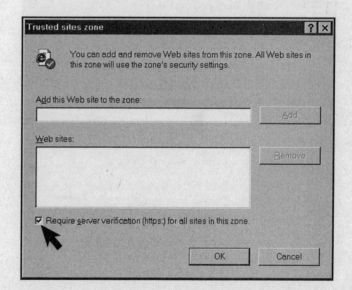

5 The resulting dialog box shows a list of sites in the selected zone, which should be empty because you haven't specified any sites. Click **Require Server Verification (https:) for All Sites in This Zone** to remove the check mark. With this option on, you can't add many sites to the zone.

(continues)

Guided Tour Add Sites to the Security Zones (continued)

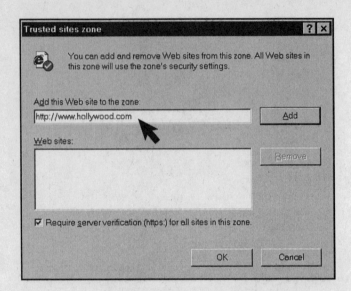

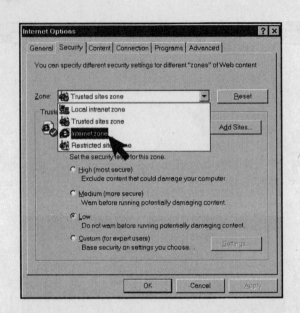

6 Click in the **Add This Web Site to the Zone** text box, type the site's address, and click the **Add** button. Repeat this step to add more sites to the zone. (You must type http:// at the beginning of the page address.)

9 To change the security level for a zone, open the **Zone** drop-down list and choose the zone whose security level you want to change.

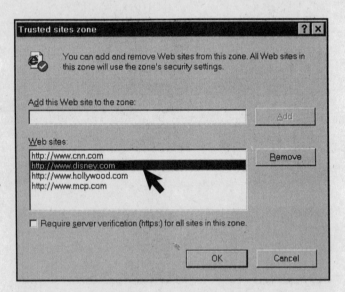

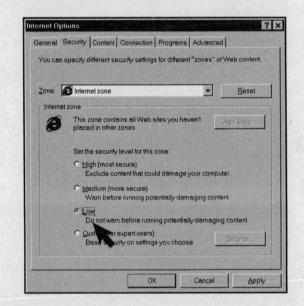

7 To remove a site from the zone, click its address in the **Web Sites** list and click the **Remove** button.

8 Click **OK** to close the zone dialog box and return to the Internet Options dialog box.

10 Choose the desired security level as explained previously: **High**, **Medium**, **Low**, or **Custom**. If you choose Custom, click the **Settings** button, enter your preferences, and click **OK**.

11 Click the **OK** button to save your list of sites and your security settings.

Censor the Internet

The Internet is a virtual world, providing access to some of the best that our society has to offer: literature, music, creative arts, museums, movies, and medicine. However, like any world, the Internet also has its share of pornography, obscenity, and violence.

Over the years, people have debated the issue of whether the government (we, the people) should control the Internet and prohibit people from transmitting

any material that might be considered offensive by some impartial third party. As society wrestles with this issue, and as the courts overrule each other, the offensive material remains readily available.

Fortunately, Internet Explorer has a built-in censor that allows you to block access to offensive material from your end. The *Guided Tour* shows you how to enable and customize the censor.

Guided Tour   Enable the Censor

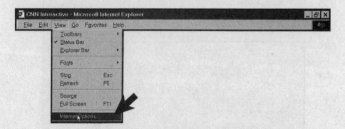

1 Open the **View** menu and choose **Internet Options**.

2 Click the **Content** tab. Under Content Advisor, click the **Enable** button.

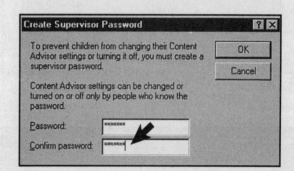

3 The Create Supervisor Password dialog box appears. Enter your password and click **OK**. If this is the first time you have used the Content Advisor, the dialog box contains a **Confirm password** text box. Type your password again before clicking **OK**.

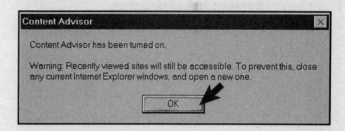

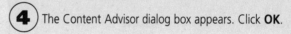

4 The Content Advisor dialog box appears. Click **OK**.

(continues)

Guided Tour Enable the Censor

(continued)

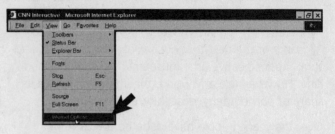

8 To turn off the content advisor, open the **View** menu and choose **Internet Options**.

5 You are returned to the Internet Options dialog box. Click **OK**.

6 As a test, click in the **Address** text box and type the address of a page that you know has material that some people would consider offensive. In this example, www.playboy.com has been typed. Press **Enter**.

9 Click the **Content** tab and click the **Disable** button under Content Advisor.

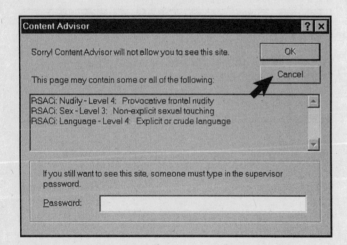

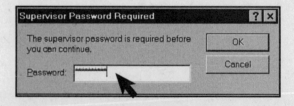

10 The Supervisor Password Required dialog box appears. Type your password and click **OK**.

11 Another dialog box appears, informing you that you have disabled the content advisor. Click **OK** to return to the Internet Options dialog box, and then click **OK** to save your change.

7 You should see the Content Advisor dialog box shown here, displaying a list of reasons why you have been denied access to this site. Click **Cancel**.

Guided Tour Change the Ratings Levels

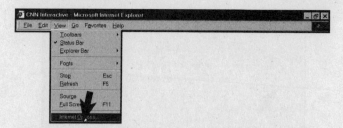

1. To change the ratings restrictions, open the **View** menu and select **Internet Options**.

2. Click the **Content** tab and click the **Settings** button.

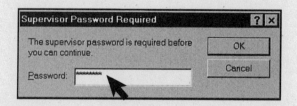

3. The Supervisor Password Required dialog box appears. Type your password and click **OK**.

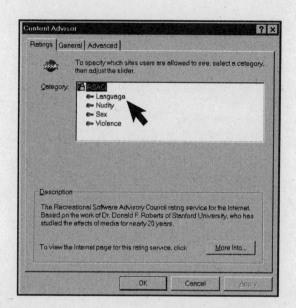

4. The Content Advisor dialog box appears, allowing you to change the restrictions. On the Ratings tab, click on the category of offensive material whose restriction level you want to change: Language, Nudity, Sex, or Violence.

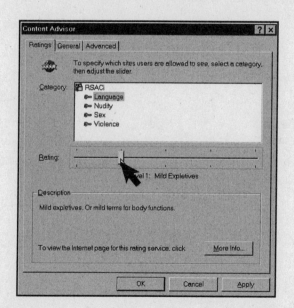

5. A slider appears below the category list; drag the slider to the right to relax the restrictions or to the left to tighten the restrictions. You can repeat steps 4 and 5 for each of the four categories.

(continues)

Guided Tour Change the Ratings Levels

(continued)

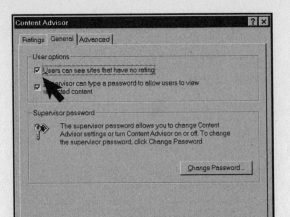

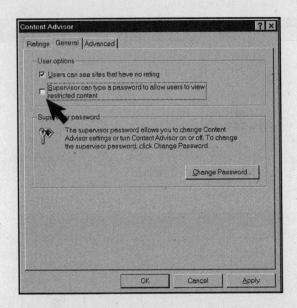

6 Click the **General** tab to change a couple other restrictions. To allow users to visit unrated sites, choose **Users Can See Sites That Have No Rating**. This option is useful if Internet Explorer is blocking access to inoffensive pages that you or your kids need to access.

7 By default, **Supervisor Can Type a Password to Allow Users to View Restricted Content** is turned on. You can turn this off to prevent the appearance of the Supervisor Password Required dialog box when a user attempts to access a restricted page.

8 Click **OK** to save your settings.

Make a Simple Web Page with FrontPage Express

The Web is great. At any time of the day or night, you can hit the Web and pull up pages containing text, pictures, video clips, animations, and a host of other media. Now it's time for you to make your mark on the Web. Maybe you want to post your résumé, educate the world, publish a collection of photographs, brag about your family, or simply provide a list of links to other pages that you find interesting.

Whatever the case, you want to publish a Web page, but you don't know where to start. Well, you've come to the right place. The *Guided Tour* shows you how to create a personal Web page using FrontPage Express, a desktop publishing program for the Web.

Understand Web Pages

Although most Web pages appear to contain text and pictures, what they really contain are text and *HTML tags*. The text appears just like any text in a word-processing or desktop publishing program. The HTML (*Hypertext Markup Language*) tags serve other functions, including controlling how the text appears; inserting pictures, sounds, and video clips; and linking the page to other pages. For example, you might use the bold tags like this `<b>This is bold</b>`, to make text appear bold. The following tag inserts a link:

```
<a href="http://www.folkartmuse.org">
American Folk Art Museum</a>
```

Just imagine that not too long ago, people were creating Web pages by typing all their text and HTML tags in a simple text editor, such as Windows Notepad!

Webtop Publishing with FrontPage Express

The Web wasn't built by people typing HTML codes in Notepad. If it were, the Web wouldn't be half the size it is today. To crank out all those Web pages, Web authors use professional Web page layout applications (called *HTML editors*). With one of these high-powered editors, all you have to do is type your text, format it, and drop in a couple pictures, just as you do in your favorite word processing application. The editor handles all the HTML tags for you—behind the scenes.

In the following *Guided Tour*, you will use Internet Explorer's built-in HTML editor, FrontPage Express, to create your own Web page and modify it.

Guided Tour Create a Personal Web Page

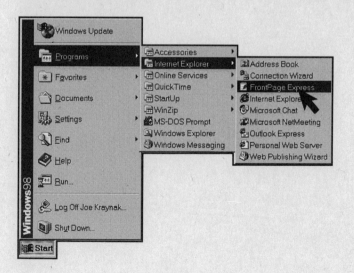

1 To run FrontPage Express, click the **Start** button, point to **Programs** and then **Internet Explorer**, and click **FrontPage Express**.

(continues)

Guided Tour Create a Personal Web Page *(continued)*

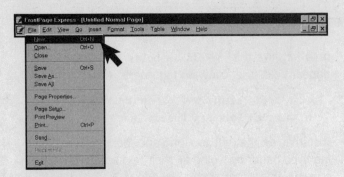

2 FrontPage Express appears, displaying a blank Web page. Open the **File** menu and select **New**.

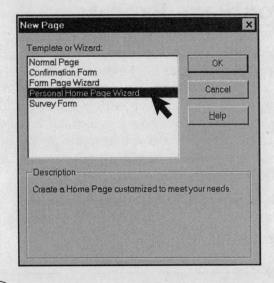

3 The New Page dialog box appears, displaying a list of the FrontPage templates and wizards. Select **Personal Home Page Wizard** and click **OK**.

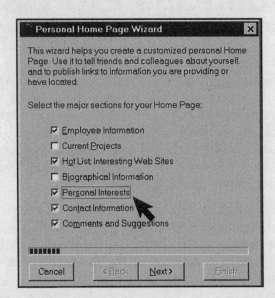

4 The first Personal Home Page Wizard dialog box appears, prompting you to select the contents of your home page. Select each section you want to include on your home page. Each item you select will appear as a heading on your page. Click **Next**.

Keep in mind that you can edit the headings later. If a heading does not exactly match what you had in mind, select it anyway and edit it later.

Guided Tour Create a Personal Web Page

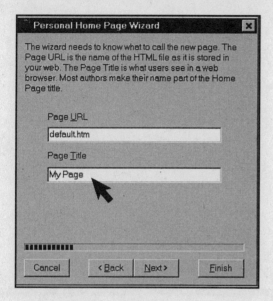

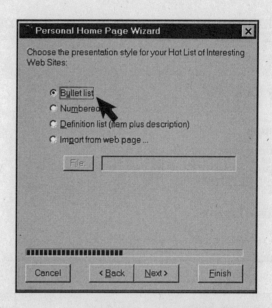

5 You are now asked to name the page. In the **Page URL** text box, type the name of the page (its filename). The name should have the filename extension .htm or .html. In the **Page Title** text box, type the name of the page as you want it to appear in the title bar when a visitor opens the page in his Web browser. Click **Next**.

Many service providers require that you use a specific filename for your Web page, such as default.htm or index.htm. Check with your service provider.

6 The remaining dialog boxes vary depending on the content you selected in step 4. For example, if you chose to include a list of links, the wizard asks if you want the list presented as a bullet list, numbered list, or definition list. Follow the onscreen instructions to make your selections.

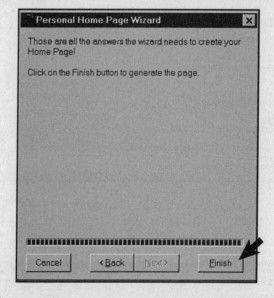

7 When the last dialog box appears, click **Finish**.

(continues)

Guided Tour   Create a Personal Web Page

(continued)

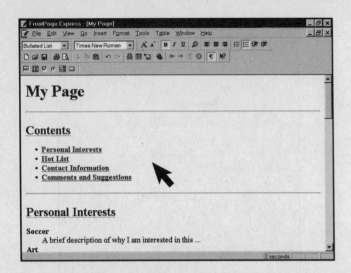

8 The wizard creates your home page and displays it in FrontPage Express, where you can edit it.

Guided Tour   Insert Links

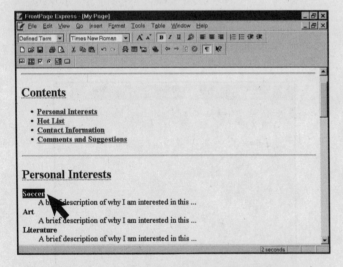

1 Drag over the text that you want to use as the link. This is the text the visitor will click to activate the link.

2 Click the **Create or Edit Hyperlink** button in the Standard toolbar (or press **Ctrl+K**).

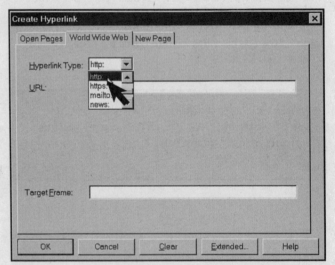

3 The Create Hyperlink dialog box appears, with the World Wide Web tab up front. Open the **Hyperlink Type** drop-down list and select **http:** to point to a Web page.

You can create links to other Internet resources. For example, you can choose to point to a file on your hard drive, an FTP server, or email address (mailto:).

Guided Tour Insert Links

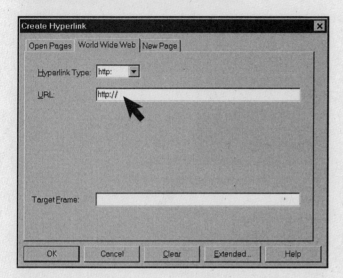

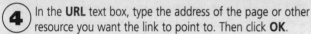

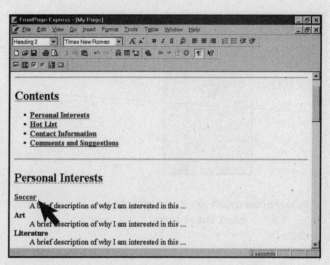

4 In the **URL** text box, type the address of the page or other resource you want the link to point to. Then click **OK**.

5 FrontPage Express converts the selected text into a link and displays the text as blue and underlined.

> One of the easiest ways to add links and images to your Web page is to drag them from a page displayed in Internet Explorer onto your page displayed in FrontPage Express. However, before using any original text or images, you should get written permission from the person who created the Web page.

Guided Tour Insert an Image

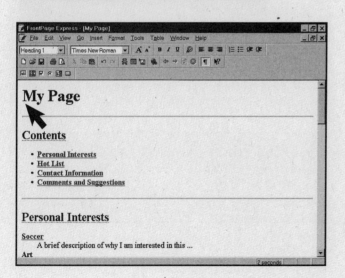

1 Position the insertion point where you want the graphic image inserted.

(continues)

Guided Tour Insert an Image

(continued)

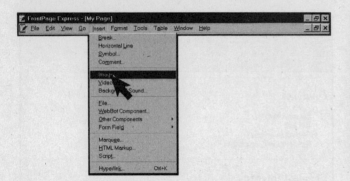

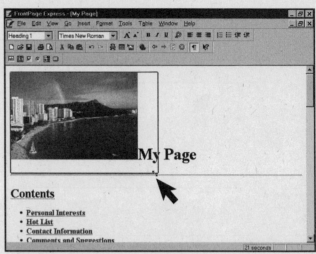

(2) Open the **Insert** menu, and select **Image**. (To save a step, click the **Insert Image** button in the Standard Buttons toolbar.)

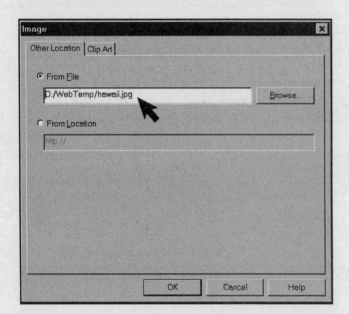

(4) The selected image or video clip is inserted. You can drag the image to move it, or you can drag one of its handles to resize it.

> To change the properties of an image, right-click it and choose **Image Properties**. Check out the Insert menu for additional items you can add to your Web page, including horizontal lines, video clips, background sounds, and scrolling marquees.

(3) The Image dialog box appears, prompting you to select a file. You can specify the location and name of a file on the Web or on your hard drive. Take one of the following steps:

To use a file that's on your hard drive, make sure **From File** is selected, click the **Browse** button, and select the graphic file you want to use. Click **OK**.

To use a file that's stored on a Web server, click **From Location**, type the file's address and name in the text box, and click **OK**.

Guided Tour Insert and Format Text

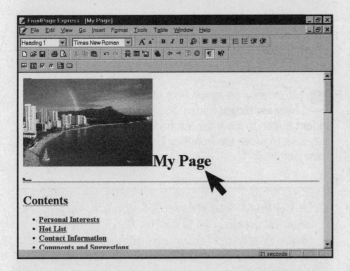

1 To insert additional text, position the insertion point where you want the text inserted. To create a new paragraph, move the insertion point to the end of an existing line and press **Enter**.

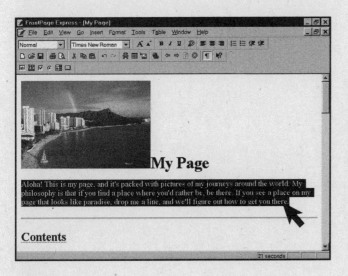

2 Type the text and then drag over it to select it.

3 To transform text into a heading, open the **Change Style** list and choose the desired heading level. You can also choose to make the text normal or transform it into a list item.

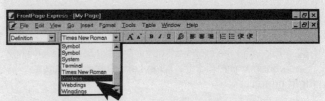

4 To change the type style, open the **Change Font** list and choose the desired type style. You can use the **Increase Text Size** or **Decrease Text Size** button to change the text size.

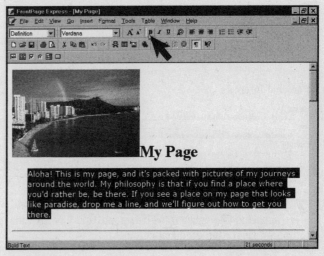

5 To add text enhancements, click the **Bold**, **Italic**, or **Underline** button. You can change the text color by choosing clicking the **Text Color** button and choosing the desired color.

(continues)

Guided Tour Insert and Format Text

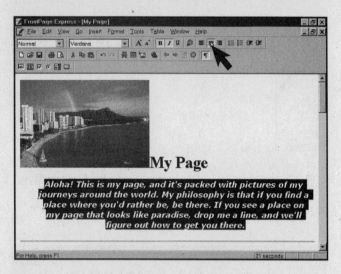

6 To control the alignment of the text between the left and right margins, click the **Align Left**, **Center**, or **Align Right** button.

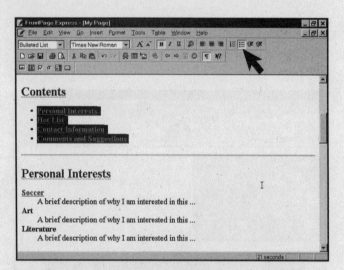

7 To transform two or more paragraphs into a bulleted or numbered list, highlight the paragraphs and then click the **Numbered List** or **Bulleted List** button.

8 To indent a paragraph from the left margin, click the **Increase Indent** button. You can click the **Decrease Indent** button to move the text back to the left margin. (You may have to widen the FrontPage Express window to see both of those buttons.)

This *Guided Tour* showed you how to apply basic formatting to text. The Format menu contains additional options, including Background, which allows you to add a background image to your page and change the overall text and background colors.

Place Your Page on the Web

When you finish creating your Web page, you must place it on a Web server where other people can open and view it with their Web browsers. In the past, the only way to place a page on a Web server was to use a separate FTP (File Transfer Protocol) program. However, FrontPage Express comes with its own file transfer program, called WebPost, that you can access simply by entering the File, Save As command.

WebPost works along with the Web Publishing Wizard to lead you through the process of placing your page on the Web, as shown in the *Guided Tour*. If you have trouble publishing your Web page using the File, Save As command, run the Web Publishing Wizard from the Start, Programs, Internet Explorer menu. In some cases, using the Web Publishing Wizard by itself is easier than using the File, Save As command.

> If the Web Publishing Wizard is not on the Start, Programs, Internet Explorer menu, you must install it. To do so, open the Windows **Control Panel**, click the **Add/Remove Programs** icon, and click the **Windows Setup** tab. Click **Internet Tools** and then click the **Details** button. Click the check box next to **Web Publishing Wizard** and click **OK**. Click **OK** and follow the onscreen instructions to complete the installation.

Find a Home for Your Page

Unless you've been working directly on a *Web server* (a computer that stores Web sites where people browsing the Web can see them), you will have to take the additional step of *publishing* your Web pages.

Before you start, you need to make sure you have somewhere to store your Web page. The best place to start is with your Internet service provider. Most providers make some space available on their Web servers for subscribers to store personal Web pages. Call your service provider and find out the following information:

- Does your service provider make Web space available to subscribers? If not, maybe you should change providers.

- How much disk space do you get, and how much does it cost (if anything)? Some providers give you a limited amount of disk space, which is usually plenty for one or two Web pages, assuming you don't include large audio or video clips.

- Can you save your files directly to the Web server or do you have to upload files to an FTP server?

- What is the URL of the server you must connect to in order to upload your files? Write it down.

- What username and password do you need to enter to gain access to the server? (This is typically the same username and password you use to connect to the service.)

- In which directory must you place your files? Write it down.

- What name must you give your Web page? In many cases, the service lets you post a single Web page, and you must call it **index.html** or **default.html**.

- Are there any other specific instructions you must follow to post your Web page?

- After posting your page, what will its address (URL) be? You'll want to open it in Internet Explorer as soon as you post it.

If you are using a commercial online service, such as America Online, you may have to use its commands to upload your Web page and associated files.

If your service provider does not offer Web page service, fire up Internet Explorer, connect to your favorite search page, and search for places that allow you to post your Web page for free. These services vary greatly. Some services require you to fill out a form, and then the service creates a generic Web page for you (you can't use the page you created in FrontPage Express). At others, you can copy the HTML-coded document (in Notepad or WordPad) and paste it in a text box at the site. A couple of other places will let you send them your HTML file and associated files. Find out what's involved.

You will save yourself some time and trouble by placing your Web page and all graphic files and any other associated files in a single folder separate from other files. The Web Publishing Wizard can then transfer all the required files as a batch to your Web server. Make sure you use the correct filename for your Web page file, as specified by your service provider.

Check and Test Your Web Page

Before you place your page on the Web, where millions of people can check it out, you should check it just as you would check any document you intend to make

public. First, check the page for spelling errors or typos. FrontPage Express does not have a spelling checker, so ask a few of your friends or colleagues to proofread your page. (The full version of FrontPage includes a spelling checker.)

You should also open your page in your Web browser and check to make sure it looks right. Check the position and appearance of graphics, make sure your text contrasts with any background colors you have used, and, most importantly, click every link to make sure it pulls up the correct linked page.

Guided Tour   Save Your Page to a Web Server

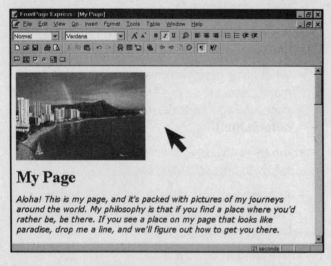

1 Establish your Internet connection and use FrontPage Express to open the page you want to place on the Web.

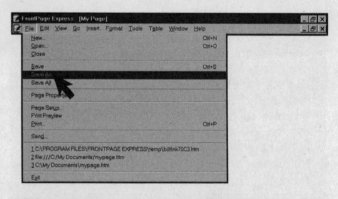

2 Open the **File** menu and select **Save As**.

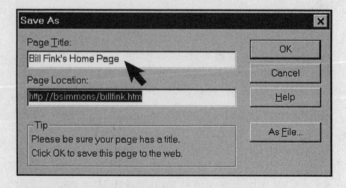

3 The Save As dialog box appears, displaying the title and location of your Web page file. You can type a new title for your Web page. Click **OK**.

Guided Tour Save Your Page to a Web Server

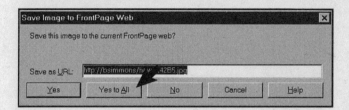

(4) If you used any images or other files in your Web page, a dialog box appears, asking if you want to save these files to the Web server. Click **Yes to All**.

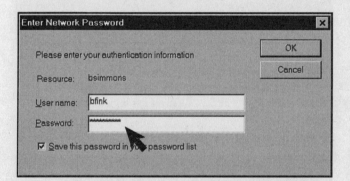

(5) The Enter Network Password dialog box appears, prompting you to enter your username and password. Type your username in the **User Name** text box, click in the **Password** text box, and type your password. Click **OK**. (FrontPage Express is set up to save your password, so you won't need to enter it the next time you publish a Web page.)

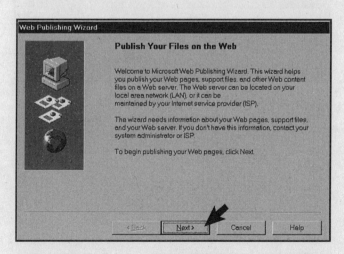

(6) The Web Publishing Wizard appears, displaying an explanation of what you are about to do. Click **Next**.

(7) The wizard prompts you to type a name for your Web server. Type a brief descriptive name (you do not need to type the server's domain name at this point). Click **Next**.

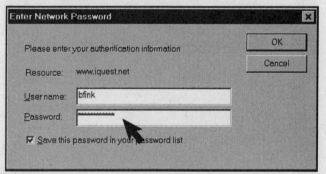

(8) You might be prompted to enter your username and password again. If prompted to type your username, type your username in the **User Name** text box, click in the **Password** text box, and type your password. Click **OK**.

(continues)

Guided Tour Save Your Page to a Web Server *(continued)*

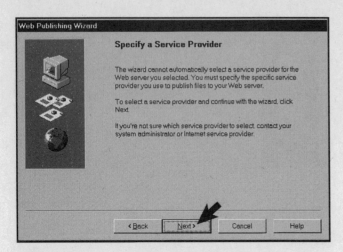

(9) The wizard indicates that it cannot automatically select a Web server. Click **Next**.

(10) The wizard prompts you to select your service provider. If you are unsure, select **HTTP Post** to place your files directly on a Web server, **FTP** to upload them to an FTP server, or one of the other options for your special Web server. Click **Next**. You are now prompted to enter information about the server.

(11) Enter the server's name and any special command you need in order to upload your page to the Web server. Your service provider should have supplied this information. Click **Next**.

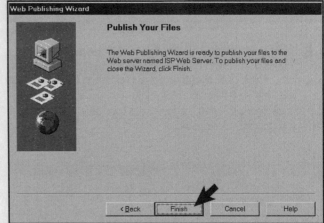

(12) The final dialog box appears, indicating that the wizard is ready to publish your Web page. Click **Finish**.

Guided Tour Save Your Page to a Web Server

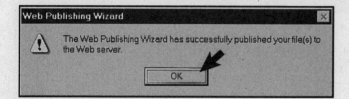

13 The wizard dials into your service provider (if you are not yet connected) and uploads your Web page and all associated files to the Web server. Dialog boxes appear showing the progress. The dialog box shown above appears when the process is complete. Click **OK**.

If you receive an error message indicating that the wizard was unable to publish the files, you might have entered the wrong username or password, typed the wrong Web server address, or selected the wrong service provider. Check with your service provider to ensure that you have the correct information, and then repeat the steps. If you still have trouble, run the Web Publishing Wizard from **Start, Programs, Internet Explorer**, and use the wizard to transfer your files to the Web or an FTP server.

HOW TO...

Master the Active Desktop

Ever since the Web became popular, Microsoft has been toying with the idea of integrating the personal computer with the Web. Microsoft wants you to be able to navigate your local PC, network, and company intranet just as easily as you can navigate remotely stored Web pages. (An *intranet* is simply a network that is set up like the Internet, but is typically closed to Internet traffic.)

To help achieve this goal, Microsoft invented the Active Desktop, an automated Windows desktop that not only gives you access to your programs and documents, but also acts as an information center. You can place live components on the desktop to display up-to-the-minute news, weather, sports, and other media right on the Windows desktop.

As you work through this section and learn about the various Windows desktop enhancements, keep in mind that all the changes are designed to make your PC act like the Web and to make it easier to configure your desktop for the way you work.

What You Will Find in This Section

Tour the Active Desktop

The idea behind the Active Desktop is that it provides a seamless connection between the Web, your company's network, and your local PC. The "active" part is that you can quickly and easily configure your desktop to make it look and act the way you want it to.

One of the great new features of the Active Desktop is that it allows you to place components (*desktop components*) of any size and dimensions on your desktop. In other words, you can go beyond shortcut icons and add larger objects such as stock tickers, scrolling news

headlines, and email notification boxes right on your desktop. With desktop components, you have complete control of their size and position. You can even set up desktop components to receive automatic updates from the Web during the day.

The *Guided Tour* provides a brief orientation to the major features of the Active Desktop. The remaining *Guided Tours* in this section show you how to tap the power of the Active Desktop and configure it.

Guided Tour   Use the Active Desktop

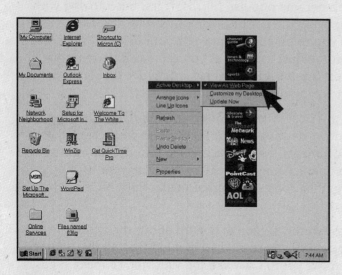

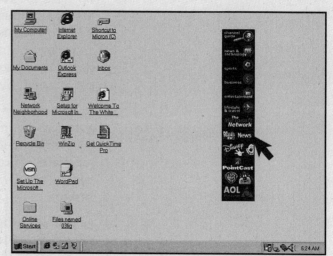

1 Before you tour the Active Desktop, make sure it is on. To do so, right-click a blank area of the desktop, point to **Active Desktop**, and make sure there is a check mark next to **View As Web Page**. ▶See "Work in Web View" on page 83, for additional instructions.◀

2 The first thing you might notice about the new Windows desktop is that it has a Channel Bar. This desktop component provides links to high-quality active Web sites. ▶See "Tune In to the Web with Channels" on page 258.◀

Guided Tour Use the Active Desktop

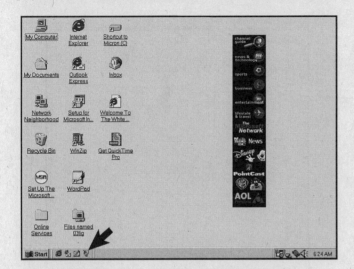

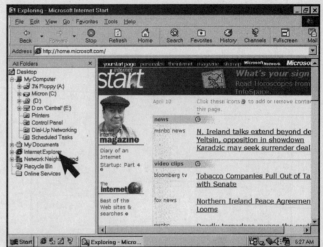

3 The new taskbar has a Quick Launch toolbar that provides quick access to Internet Explorer, Outlook Express, and Channels. It also contains the Show Desktop button, which returns you to the desktop when you are working in other programs. (Show Desktop minimizes all open program windows to clear the desktop.)

5 In addition to helping you manage disks, folders, and files, Windows Explorer allows you to navigate the Web. Click **Internet Explorer** in the folder list to use the contents pane (on the right) for displaying Web pages.

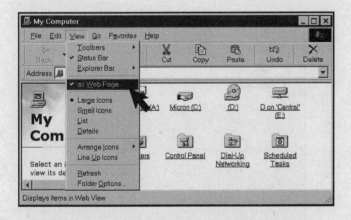

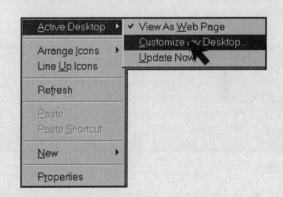

4 Although they are not part of the desktop itself, My Computer and Windows Explorer are considered part of the Active Desktop. Open the **View** menu and make sure there is a check mark next to **As Web Page**. ▶See "Work in Web View" on page 83.◀

6 Right-click a blank area of the Windows desktop, point to **Active Desktop**, and choose **Customize My Desktop**.

(continues)

Guided Tour   Use the Active Desktop *(continued)*

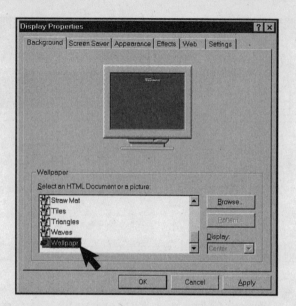

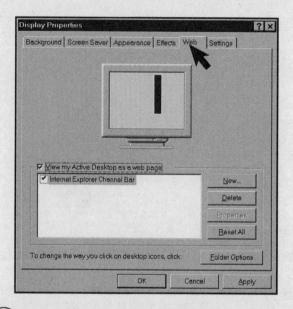

7 The Background tab in the Display Properties dialog box has an option for using a Web Page background instead of the standard Windows backgrounds. ▶See "Use Web Page Wallpaper" on page 315 for details.◀

8 Click the **Web** tab in the Display Properties dialog box to view options for displaying your desktop as a Web page and for adding desktop components. ▶See "Add and Remove Active Desktop Components" on page 311.◀

Your copy of Windows 98 may already be set up to use Web page wallpaper. For instance, if you purchased a new computer with Windows 98 on it, it may have wallpaper showing the manufacturer's logo.

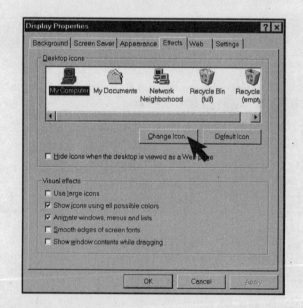

9 Click the **Effects** tab in the Display Properties dialog box to view options for customizing the appearance of your desktop icons. Click the **OK** button to close this dialog box.

Guided Tour Use the Active Desktop

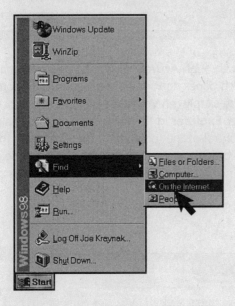

10 The Start menu has a few new features as well. Click the **Start** button and point to **Find**. In addition to options for finding files and folders and searching your own computer, the Find submenu has an option called On the Internet that you can use to perform Internet searches and an option called People that's useful for tracking down individuals.

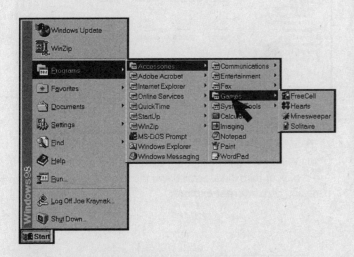

11 You can now rearrange items on the Start menu by dragging and dropping them. Click the **Start** button and point to the folder or program you want to move.

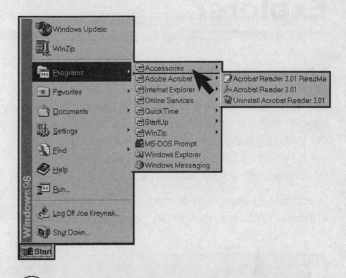

12 Hold down the left mouse button and drag the item to the desired position in the menu system. A horizontal insertion point appears, showing where the item will be moved to. Release the mouse button.

> You can right-click an item on the Start menu or one of its submenus to display a context menu offering additional options.

> The Start menu also contains the Favorites submenu, which contains a list of pages you have marked as favorites. In addition, you can enter the **Start**, **Run** command and enter a page address in the Run dialog box to quickly run Internet Explorer and open the specified page.

Navigate the Web with Windows Explorer

Windows Explorer has the same enhancements you find in My Computer. Windows Explorer provides one-click access to programs and files and offers the Internet Explorer toolbar, which you can use to browse the Web or your company's intranet. ▶For details about using Windows Explorer to manage files, see "Navigate Windows Explorer" on page 87.◀

In addition to improved file management tools, Windows Explorer is completely integrated with Internet

Explorer through ActiveX, allowing you to open and view Web pages right inside the Windows Explorer window. You simply run Windows Explorer and click **Internet Explorer** in the folder list. Internet Explorer takes control of the toolbar and the right pane to display Web pages and the tools you need to navigate them. The *Guided Tour* shows you how to get started.

Guided Tour View Web Pages in Windows Explorer

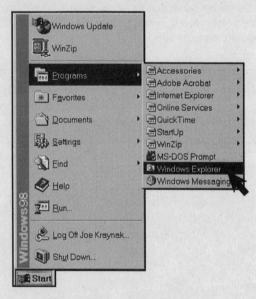

1 Open the **Start** menu, point to **Programs**, and click Windows Explorer.

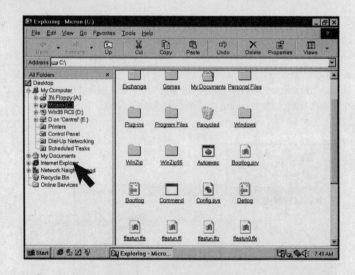

2 Windows Explorer appears, displaying the contents of one of your hard disks. Scroll down the folder list in the left pane and click **Internet Explorer**.

Guided Tour View Web Pages in Windows Explorer

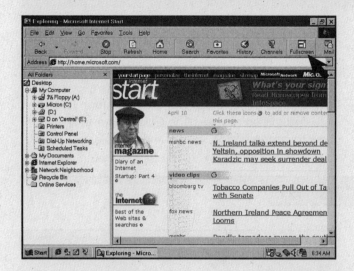

3 The right pane displays Internet Explorer's opening Web page. Note that Internet Explorer's toolbar replaces Windows Explorer's toolbar.

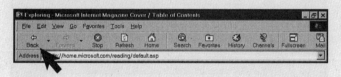

4 Click the **Back** button to redisplay the contents of your computer. You can then click the **Forward** button to return to the Web page.

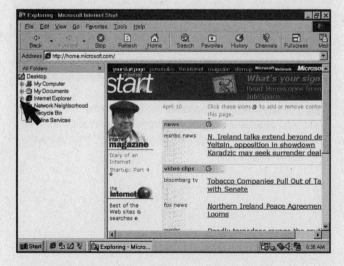

5 Click the plus sign next to **Internet Explorer** (in the left pane).

6 One or more links to helpful pages about Internet Explorer appear below Internet Explorer in the left pane. Click a link to load its page.

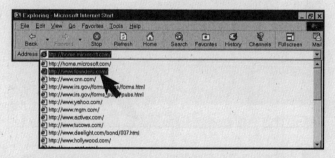

7 The Address text box allows you to enter both Web page addresses and paths to your disks and folders. In addition, you can open the **Address** drop-down list to select folder views or Web pages you have recently accessed.

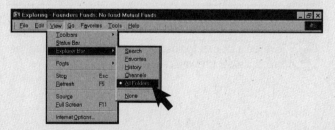

8 To turn the folder list off, click its **Close** (X) button. To turn it back on, select **View**, **Explorer Bar**, **All Folders**.

Use the New Taskbar Toolbars

Not to be outdone by the Start button, the taskbar has a couple of new features as well. Just to the right of the Start button is a new toolbar (called Quick Launch) that initially contains icons for running Internet Explorer, Outlook Express (for email), and Channels and for quickly returning to the Windows desktop.

You can take control of this new toolbar and your new taskbar in several ways. You can move or resize the toolbars, drag an icon over a toolbar to add it to the toolbar, turn on additional toolbars, remove toolbars, change their appearance, and even transform folders into customized toolbars. The *Guided Tour* shows you how to customize the taskbar and its toolbars.

Guided Tour　Customize the Taskbar and Toolbars

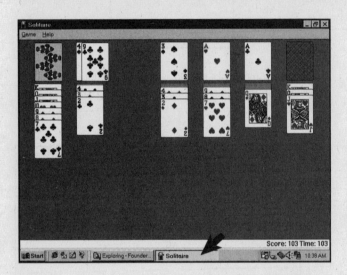

1 When you run a program, a button for it appears in the taskbar. You can use the button to toggle a program: Click the button to bring the program window to the front, and then click it again to minimize the window.

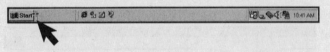

2 To resize a taskbar toolbar, such as Quick Launch, drag the toolbar's slider (the vertical bar).

3 To move a toolbar, drag the slider to the left or right of another toolbar's slider.

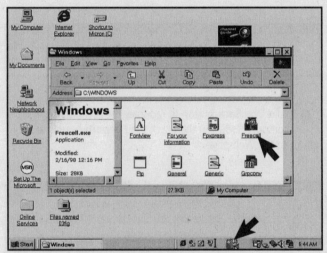

4 To add buttons to a toolbar for quick access to documents and programs, drag an icon from the desktop or from My Computer or Windows Explorer over the toolbar. Then release the mouse button.

Guided Tour Customize the Taskbar and Toolbars

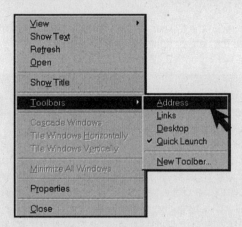

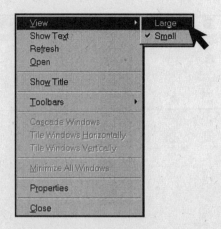

⑤ To add a toolbar to the taskbar, right-click a blank area of the toolbar, point to **Toolbars**, and choose any of the following options:

Address places the Address text box on the taskbar. You can enter the address of a Web page into this text box to quickly open a page.

Links inserts a bar that contains buttons pointing to helpful Web pages. You can add buttons for your own favorite pages.

Desktop displays a toolbar containing buttons for all the shortcuts on your Windows desktop.

Quick Launch displays another copy of the toolbar that contains the icons for Outlook Express and Internet Explorer. (You don't need more than one of these toolbars.)

New Toolbar lets you transform a folder into a toolbar. For example, you can choose **New Toolbar**, and choose **Control Panel** to create a toolbar that contains icons for all the tools in the Windows Control Panel.

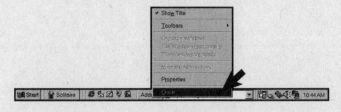

⑥ To remove a toolbar, right-click on a blank area of the toolbar and select **Close** from the context menu.

⑦ To view larger icons in the toolbar, right-click a blank area of the toolbar, point to **View**, and select **Large**.

⑧ To turn text descriptions of the toolbar buttons on or off, right-click a blank area of the toolbar and select **Show Text**.

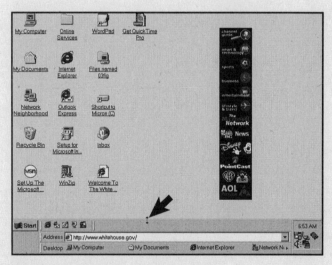

⑨ If the taskbar becomes overcrowded, you can drag the top of the taskbar upward to enlarge it.

(continues)

Guided Tour Customize the Taskbar and Toolbars *(continued)*

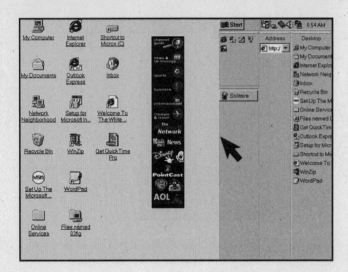

10 To move the taskbar, drag a blank area of the taskbar to the top, left, or right side of the screen.

If your taskbar takes up too much screen space, consider turning on Auto Hide. Right-click a blank area of the taskbar, select **Properties**, make sure there is a check mark next to **Auto Hide** and **Always On Top**, and click **OK**. This hides the taskbar while you are working on other things. Whenever you want to use the taskbar, simply move the mouse pointer to the bottom of the screen or to the edge of the screen where your taskbar hangs out.

Add and Remove Active Desktop Components

Although you probably won't notice right away, your new desktop consists of two layers: an *HTML layer* and an *icon layer*. HTML (short for Hypertext Markup Language) is a system of codes used to format Web pages. By using HTML to control your desktop, Internet Explorer transforms your desktop into a Web page. This allows you to place active desktop components that are HTML-friendly right on your desktop as *frames* (windows that contain Web pages and other Web content).

Before you can add desktop components, first make sure the Active Desktop is turned on. Right-click a blank

area of the Windows desktop, point to **Active Desktop**, and, if View as Web Page does not have a check mark next to it, click **View As Web Page**. When you know for sure that the Active Desktop is on, take the *Guided Tour* to add or remove desktop components.

Be careful when using automatically updated desktop components. If your phone company or ISP charges you by the minute or hour, these automatic updates can become costly.

Guided Tour   Add a Desktop Component

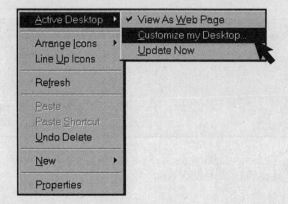

1 Right-click a blank area of the Windows desktop, point to **Active Desktop**, and click **Customize My Desktop**.

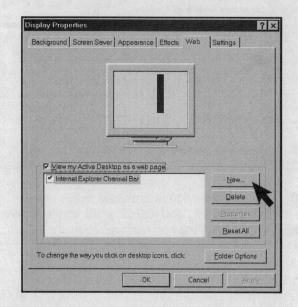

2 The Display Properties dialog box appears. Click the **Web** tab.

3 The Web options allow you to view the desktop as a Web page and add components. Click **New**.

(continues)

Guided Tour Add a Desktop Component *(continued)*

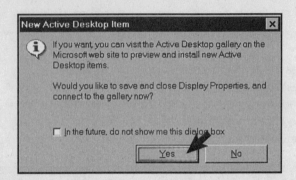

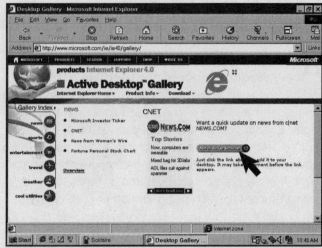

4 The New Active Desktop Item dialog box appears, asking if you want to go to the Active Desktop Gallery. Click **Yes**.

6 A page appears, describing the component and displaying a link or button for downloading it. Click the link or button to download it and place it on your desktop.

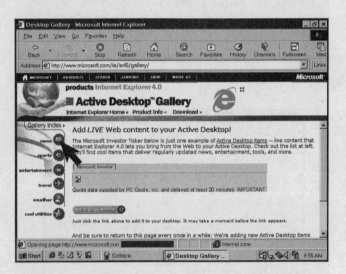

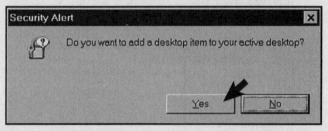

5 This runs Internet Explorer and connects you to the Internet if you are not already connected. Internet Explorer loads the Active Desktop Gallery Web page. Follow the trail of links to the desktop component you want.

7 Internet Explorer displays a dialog box, asking for your confirmation. Click **Yes**.

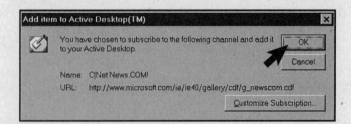

8 A second dialog box appears, indicating that Windows will set up a subscription for this component. (You can click Customize Subscription and choose an update schedule, ►as explained in "Subscribe to Sites" on page 250.◄) Click **OK**. (You may encounter additional confirmation dialog boxes, depending on the site's content.)

Guided Tour Add a Desktop Component

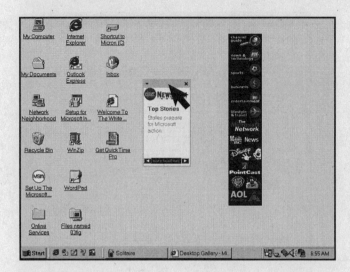

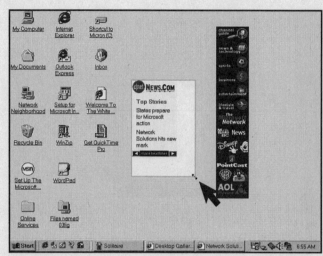

9 Internet Explorer downloads the component and places it on the desktop. To move a component, point to its title bar to display a gray bar at the top of the window. Then drag the gray bar to move the component.

10 To resize a component, drag one of the corners of its frame to the size you want, and then release the mouse button.

11 To shut down the component, and prevent it from automatically connecting to the Internet to download updated content, click its **Close** button. (The component may connect without displaying a modem icon in the system tray, so you won't even know you're connected.)

You can change the subscription settings for a desktop component at any time. In the Display Properties dialog box, click the **Web** tab. Click the component whose subscription settings you want to change and click the **Properties** button.

Guided Tour Remove a Desktop Component

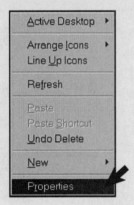

1 Right-click a blank area of the desktop and choose **Properties**.

2 The Display Properties dialog box appears. Click the **Web** tab.

3 The Web tab contains a list of desktop components, as shown above, including the Channel Bar. To turn off a component, click its check box to remove the check mark.

4 To completely remove a component, select it, and then click the **Delete** button. Click **Yes** to confirm.

5 Click **OK** to save your changes.

The Folder Options button at the bottom of the Web tab gives you access to a dialog box that allows you to turn off Web View for My Computer and the Windows desktop. ▶See "Work in Web View" on page 83.◀

Use Web Page Wallpaper

Windows 98 comes with several wallpaper designs that you can use in place of the default Microsoft wallpaper. Most of these designs are stored as bitmapped graphic images (BMP files) and were included with previous versions of Windows. Many people like to customize their Windows backgrounds by creating their own designs in Paint.

In addition to the bitmapped graphics, Windows 98 comes with several designs stored as Web pages. You can use one of those Web page files as your Windows

wallpaper by following the *Guided Tour*. You can also use any Web page you have downloaded from the Internet.

> You can download any Web page or create your own Web page and use it as a Windows background. Be sure you save the page and any graphic images that are embedded on the page. The best way to do this is to open the page in FrontPage Express and save it to your disk. If you save the page from Internet Explorer, graphics are not saved.

Guided Tour   Use Web Page Wallpaper

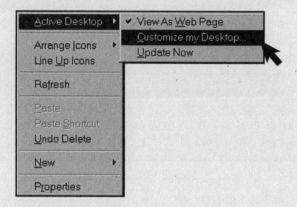

1 Right-click a blank area of the desktop, point to **Active Desktop**, and select **Customize My Desktop**.

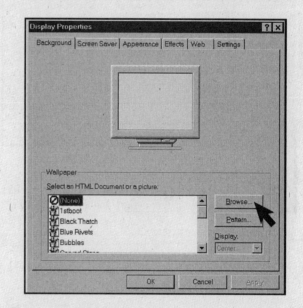

2 The Display Properties dialog box appears with the Background tab in front. Under Wallpaper, click **Browse**.

(continues)

Guided Tour Use Web Page Wallpaper *(continued)*

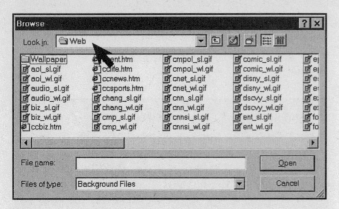

3 The Browse dialog box appears. Change to the
Windows\Web or **Windows\Web\Wallpaper** folder.

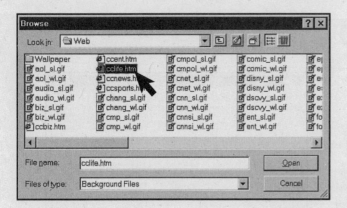

4 A list of Web pages and GIF image files appears (Web
page designs appear with the Internet Explorer icon beside
them). Click the desired wallpaper design, and then click **Open**.

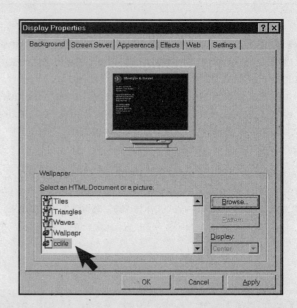

5 The selected design appears in the Wallpaper list and in
the preview area. Repeat steps 4 through 6 until you find
the design you want, and then click **OK**.

You can download updated content for your
Web page wallpaper and for any desktop
component. Right-click a blank area of the
desktop, point to **Active Desktop**, and click
Update Now.

Turn On the Channel Screen Saver

If you have worked with channels very much, you may have noticed that their content is much more dynamic than the content of standard Web pages. Many channels display content that looks more like something you would see on TV or at the movies than something you'd see on the Web.

To take advantage of this dynamic content, consider using your favorite channel as a screen saver. To use the Channel screen saver, you must first subscribe to channels, ►as explained in "Tune In to the Web with Channels" on page 258.◄ Then take the *Guided Tour* to turn on the screen saver.

> **Guided Tour**   Use the Channel Screen Saver

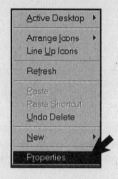

1 Right-click a blank area of the desktop and choose **Properties**.

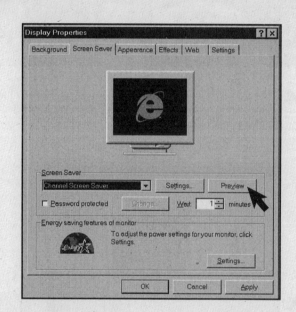

3 Click the **Preview** button to see how the screen saver will appear when active.

(continues)

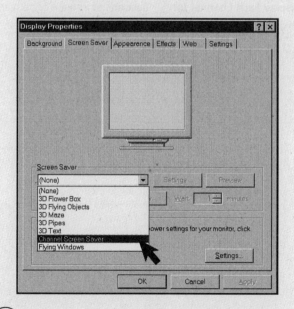

2 The Display Properties dialog box appears. Click the **Screen Saver** tab. Then open the **Screen Saver** drop-down list and select **Channel Screen Saver**.

Guided Tour Use the Channel Screen Saver *(continued)*

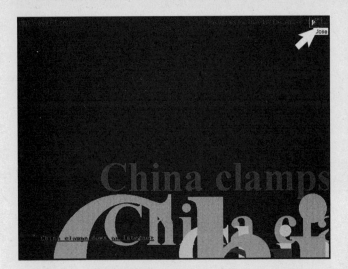

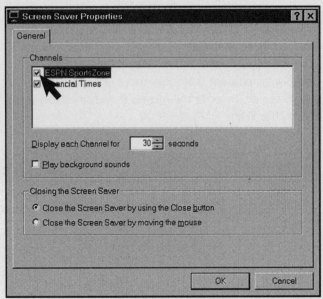

4 The preview shows the screen saver in action. Point to the upper-right corner of the screen and click the **Close** (X) button to close the screen saver.

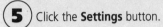

5 Click the **Settings** button.

6 The General tab displays a list of channels that will appear when the screen saver kicks in. You can prevent any of the channels from appearing by clicking their check boxes to remove the check marks.

7 By default, the screen saver displays the URL (address) of each channel for 30 seconds. Click the arrows next to **Display Each Channel for ___ Seconds** to increase or decrease the amount of time the URL is displayed.

Guided Tour Use the Channel Screen Saver

8 Under Closing the Screen Saver, you can choose to have the screen saver close when you move the mouse. The default setting, **Close the Screen Saver By Using the Close Button**, keeps the screen saver running even when you move the mouse.

9 Click the **OK** button to save your settings. This returns you to the Display Properties dialog box.

10 Enter any other screen saver preferences you want, such as password protection and the number of minutes of inactivity that will cause the screen saver to kick in. (Be careful assigning a password. If you assign a password and then forget it later, you won't be able to access your computer.)

11 Click **OK** to save your changes.

HOW TO...
Use Outlook Express for Email and Newsgroups

The two most efficient ways to communicate with other people on the Internet are to use email and newsgroups. Email (electronic mail) allows you to send and receive messages across the Internet to anyone else who has an Internet connection and an email account. The messages fly across the Internet in a matter of seconds or minutes and can contain text, images, or other attached files.

Newsgroups are electronic bulletin boards where you can post messages and read and reply to messages posted by other people. There are more than 20,000 Internet newsgroups, covering every topic imaginable—from investing to tattoos.

Internet Explorer 4 comes with an email program and newsreader called Outlook Express. You use the same interface to send and receive both email and newsgroup messages. In this section, you will learn how to use Outlook Express to send, receive, and manage email and newsgroup messages.

What You Will Find in This Section

Set Up Your Email Account

Before you can use the email features in Outlook Express, you must enter settings to specify which mail server it should use and how to connect to it. The mail server is like a post office, acting as an email distribution center. In order to send and receive email, you first have to connect to your mail server. Your Internet service provider should give you access to its mail server and provide you with the server's address.

The first time you run Outlook Express, it runs the Internet Connection Wizard, which leads you through the process of setting up your mail server. Take the *Guided Tour* to run Outlook Express for the first time and set up your mail server connection.

Guided Tour Enter Connection Settings for an Email Account

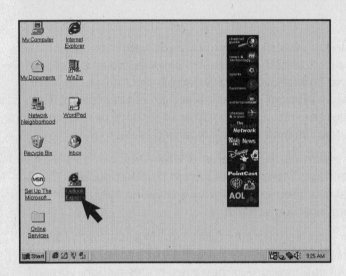

1 To start Outlook Express, click the **Outlook Express** icon on the Windows desktop or click the **Launch Outlook Express** icon in the Quick Launch toolbar.

You can also run Outlook Express by selecting it from the **Start, Programs, Internet Explorer** menu or by choosing **Go, Mail** in Internet Explorer. (You can also run Outlook Express by choosing **Go, Mail** in Windows Explorer or My Computer.)

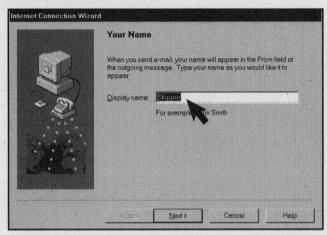

2 The first Internet Connection Wizard dialog box appears. Type your name as you want it to appear on messages you send. (This can be your real name or a nickname.) Click **Next**.

If the Internet Connection Wizard does not appear, select **Tools, Accounts,** and click the **Mail** tab. Click the **Add** button and select **Mail** to add a new mail server.

Guided Tour Enter Connection Settings for an Email Account

3 Type your email address so people can reply to your messages. Your email address is usually all lowercase and starts with your username (such as, jsmith@iway.com). Click **Next**.

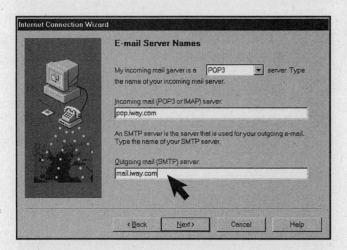

4 You are now prompted to type the address of the mail server used for incoming and outgoing mail. Open the drop-down list at the top of the dialog box and select the type of server used for incoming mail: **POP3** or **IMAP**.

5 Type the addresses of the incoming and outgoing mail servers:

Incoming Mail (POP3 or IMAP): POP is short for Post Office Protocol, the POP server is like your neighborhood post office. It receives incoming messages and places them in your personal mailbox. IMAP (short for Internet Message Access Protocol) is similar to POP but offers additional features, such as allowing you to search the contents of messages on the mail server and retrieve only the messages you want. The address usually starts with pop or "imap" (for example, pop.iway.com).

Outgoing Mail (SMTP): Short for Simple Mail Transfer Protocol, the SMTP server is the mailbox into which you drop your outgoing messages. It's actually your Internet service provider's computer. The address usually starts with mail or smtp (for example, mail.iway.com).

Then click **Next**.

6 If the server requires you to log on, select one of the following logon settings:

Log On Using if your mail server requires you to enter a name and password to connect. Enter the required name and password in the appropriate text boxes.

Log On Using Secure Password Authentication (SPA) if your mail server requires you to connect using a digital certification.

Click **Next**.

(continues)

Guided Tour Enter Connection Settings for an Email Account *(continued)*

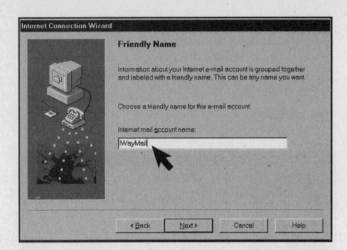

7 You are prompted to enter a "friendly" name for this account. Type a brief name to help you recognize the account, and click **Next**.

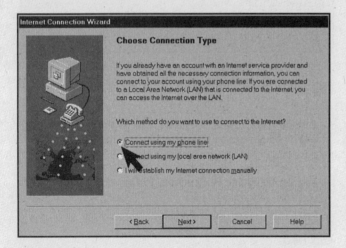

8 You are now prompted to specify how you connect to the Internet. Click **Connect Using My Phone Line** or **Connect Using My Local Area Network (LAN)** to specify how you connect to the Internet. Click **Next.**

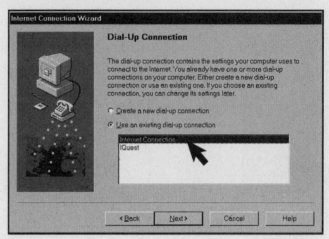

9 If you chose to connect using your phone line, click **Use an Existing Dial-Up Connection** and click the Dial-Up Networking connection you use to connect to the Internet. Then click **Next**.

10 Click the **Finish** button.

Guided Tour Enter Connection Settings for an Email Account

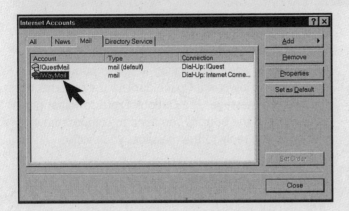

11 The Internet Accounts dialog box may appear, showing the name of the mail server you added. To use this account as the default (if you have more than one email account), select the account name and click **Set as Default**. Click **Close**, and you are returned to the Outlook Express window.

> If the Internet Accounts dialog box does not appear, select **Tools, Accounts**, and click the **Mail** tab.

Tour Outlook Express

Outlook Express provides a communications hub from which you can access both email messages and newsgroups. The Outlook Express window consists of three panes. The left pane contains a list of folders for incoming and outgoing mail, sent items, deleted items, drafts of mail you're creating, and newsgroups. The top right pane displays descriptions of the messages in the currently selected folder. The bottom right pane displays the contents of the selected message. This provides an integrated message area where you can quickly switch between Outlook Express Mail and News. It also allows you to manage your messages as easily as you manage files on your hard drive.

As you will see later in this section, you can easily read messages by first selecting the folder in which the message is stored and then clicking the description of the message. The lower-right pane displays the contents of the selected message. The Outlook Express toolbar provides most of the buttons you need to compose new messages and reply to the messages you receive.

The *Guided Tour* shows you how to start Outlook Express, navigate its window, and change its layout to suit your tastes.

Guided Tour   Navigate Outlook Express

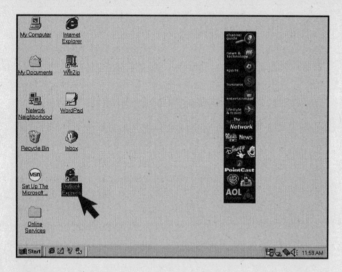

1 Click the **Outlook Express** icon on the Windows desktop.

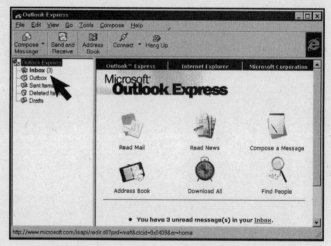

2 The Outlook Express window appears. The folder list displays icons for the Inbox, Outbox, Sent Items, Deleted Items, Drafts (of messages you are composing), and any default newsgroups. Click the **Inbox** icon or click the **Read Mail** icon.

Guided Tour   Navigate Outlook Express

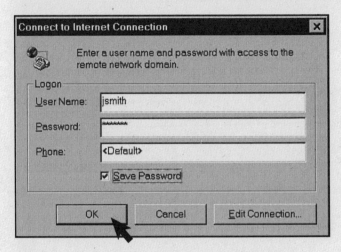

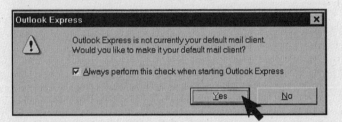

3 If Outlook Express is set up to automatically dial your Internet service provider, the Connect To dialog box appears, prompting you to connect. Enter your user name and password and click **OK** or **Connect**.

4 If Outlook Express is not set up to be used as your default email program, this dialog box appears. Click **Yes**.

If Windows is set up to use Windows Messaging as the default email program, you may encounter a series of dialog boxes prompting you to set up the Windows Messaging Inbox. Follow the onscreen instructions to complete the operation.

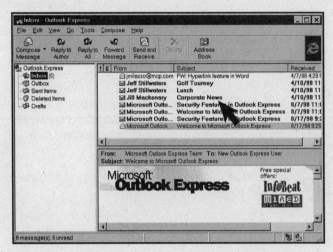

5 Outlook Express displays a three-paned window. The upper-right pane displays a list of descriptions for messages you have received. If this is the first time you've used Outlook Express, you will have only a couple sample messages that are included with the program.

6 Click a message's description to display its contents.

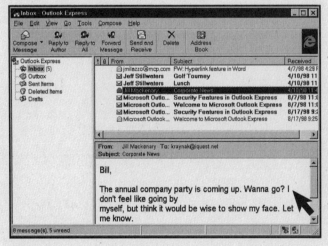

7 The contents of the message appears in the lower-right pane. You can use the scroll bar to bring additional text into view.

(continues)

Guided Tour   Navigate Outlook Express   *(continued)*

8 Outlook's toolbar contains buttons for composing and replying to messages, forwarding messages to other recipients, sending and receiving messages, deleting messages, and displaying the address book.

9 You can close Outlook Express at any time by clicking its **Close** (X) button.

You can customize the Outlook Express window by resizing the panes. Drag the bar that separates the left and right panes or the top and bottom panes to change their relative sizes. To change the layout of the Outlook Express window more dramatically, open the **View** menu, choose **Layout**, and enter your preferences.

Read Incoming Messages

Whenever someone sends you a message, it doesn't automatically pop up on your screen. Instead, it sits inside the equivalent of your P.O. box on your service provider's computer (the mail server). You need to use Outlook Express to log in to the mail server and fetch the mail.

To retrieve your mail, run Outlook Express and click the **Send and Receive** button, as shown in the *Guided Tour*. Outlook Express logs in to the mail server and checks for messages. If you have no new messages,

No new messages appears in the status bar. If you do have messages, Outlook Express displays their descriptions in the upper-right pane. To read a message, click its description or double-click to view the message in its own window.

If the message has a file attached to it, a paper clip icon appears to the left of the message. ▶See "View and Save File Attachments" on page 338 to learn how to work with attached files.◀

Guided Tour Retrieve Email Messages

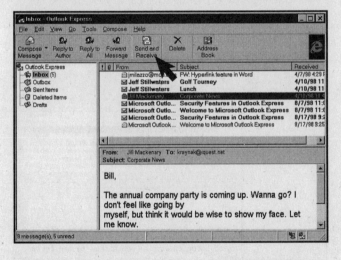

1 Run Outlook Express and click the **Send and Receive** button.

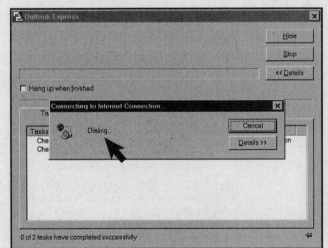

2 If you're not connected to the Internet, Outlook Express establishes a connection with the mail server. The Connecting To dialog box displays the progress.

(continues)

Guided Tour Retrieve Email Messages

(continued)

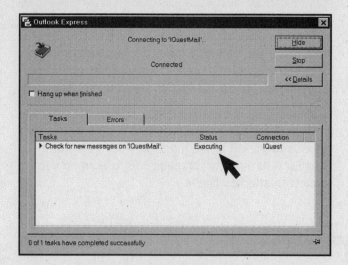

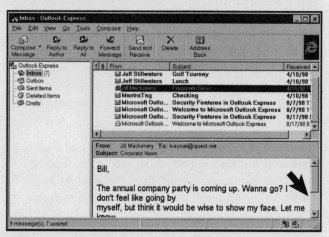

3 When the Internet connection is established, Outlook Express checks for incoming messages.

5 The contents of the selected message appears in the lower-right pane. Use the scroll bar to view any text not displayed in the window.

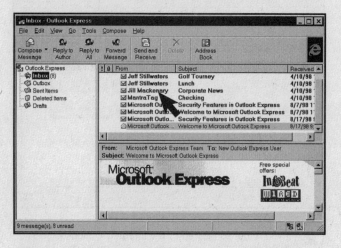

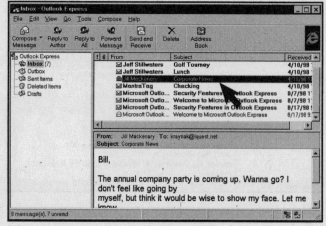

4 If you have no new messages, No new messages appears in the status bar. If you do have messages, Outlook Express displays their descriptions (called *message headers*) in the upper-right pane. To read a message, click its description.

6 To view the message in its own window, double-click its description.

Guided Tour Retrieve Email Messages

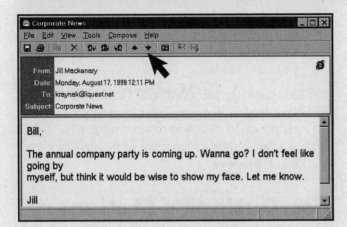

7 Outlook Express opens a new window displaying the message contents. To display the contents of the next or previous message, click the up or down arrow button in the toolbar. (You can click the **Print** button to create a paper copy of the message, if desired.)

8 Click the window's **Close** (X) button to close the message window and return to the Outlook Express main window.

Send Messages and Replies

Once you start to receive messages, you will no doubt feel compelled to reply to those messages and initiate correspondence with your friends, relatives, and business associates. To do this, you *compose* a message and send it.

As you'll see in the *Guided Tour*, composing a basic text message is fairly simple. You click the **Compose** button, type the person's address, type a brief description of the message, and then type the message itself. Click the **Send** button, and you're done.

Replying to a message you received is even easier because you do not have to address the message or type a description of it. You select the message, click the **Reply to Author** or **Reply to All** button, type the contents of the message, and click **Send**.

> Depending on how Outlook Express is set up, it might send email messages automatically, or it might place them in the Outbox folder until you click Send and Receive to instigate the process. To change the setting for sending messages, open the **Tools** menu, choose **Options**, and click the **Send** tab. Click the **Send Messages Immediately** option to turn it on or off, and then click **OK**.

Send Files and Shortcuts

You can send shortcuts that point to your favorite Web pages and any type of file (documents, graphics, even programs). There are a few ways to send shortcuts and files:

- Drag the shortcut or the icon that represents the file into the message area. When you release the mouse button, the icon is placed in a new pane below the message area in the New Message window.

- Right-click the shortcut (a link on a Web page) or on the icon for the file you want to copy, and select the **Copy** command. Right-click in the message area in the New Message window, and select **Paste**.

- To insert a file, open the **Insert** menu and select **File Attachment**, or click the **Insert File** button

(the button with the paper clip) in the toolbar. Use the Insert Attachment dialog box to select the file you want to send.

You can repeat the process to insert additional shortcuts and files into your message. You can also right-click in the new pane and click **Add** to insert additional files. To remove a file or shortcut from the pane, right-click it and choose **Remove**.

Use Outlook's Stationery

Outlook Express introduces a new concept to email that has long been a staple of standard mail: stationery. With stationery, you can send birthday greetings, announcements, invitations, or simple messages with graphics.

To use the stationery that comes with Outlook Express, open the **Compose** menu, point to **New Message Using**, and click on the desired stationery. (You can also click the down-arrow button on the Compose Message button and select the desired stationery.) Outlook Express displays the New Message window, which contains a background graphic.

> Before you use stationery, you should know that Outlook Express uses HTML (Web page) tags (codes) to format and add graphics to your messages. If the recipient uses an email program that does not support HTML, he or she cannot view the graphics and might receive a collection of HTML tags or an HTML file attachment instead.

Format Email Messages with HTML Codes

You can spruce up your message by using HTML codes. This allows you to specify the color of your text, select different fonts, insert bulleted lists, center text, and so on. If the recipient is using Outlook Express or another email program that can display HTML-coded email, your message will appear as a simple Web page. If the recipient's email program can't handle HTML codes, the message will appear as simple text with an HTML file attached. The recipient can then open the attached file in a Web browser.

To create an HTML mail message, display the New Message window, open the **Format** menu, and select **Rich Text (HTML)**. The HTML toolbar appears. To format existing text, drag over it, and then use the buttons and drop-down lists to select the desired formatting. Or, select the desired format before you begin typing. Then send the message as you normally would. The following table provides descriptions of the buttons in the Formatting toolbar.

HTML Toolbar Buttons

Button	Name	Description
Arial	Font	Changes the type style.
10	Font Size	Changes the type size.
	Style Tag	Formats paragraphs to make them headings, lists, or normal paragraphs.
B	Bold	Makes text bold.
I	Italic	Makes text italic.
U	Underline	Underlines text.
	Font Color	Changes the text color.
	Formatting Numbers	Transforms selected paragraphs into a numbered list.
	Formatting Bullets	Transforms selected paragraphs into a bulleted list.
	Decrease Indentation	Moves all lines of an indented paragraph to the left, closer to the left margin.
	Increase Indentation	Moves all lines of a paragraph to the right, farther from the left margin.
	Align Left	Pushes all lines of a paragraph against the left margin.
	Align Center	Centers all lines of a paragraph between the left and right margins.
	Align Right	Pushes all lines of a paragraph against the right margin.
	Insert Horizontal Line	Inserts a horizontal line to graphically divide your message into sections.
	Insert Hyperlink	Inserts a hyperlink that the recipient can click to open a Web page or access some other Internet resource.
	Insert Picture	Displays a dialog box prompting you to specify a graphic file to include in your message.

To enter the default setting for composing your email messages (plain text or HTML), open the **Tools** menu, choose **Options**, and click the **Send** tab. Under Mail Sending Format, click **HTML** or **Plain Text** to pick the desired default format. You can still change the option for individual messages by selecting the desired setting from the **Format** menu.

You can enter settings to control the way in which the spell checker performs its job. Open the **Tools** menu in the main Outlook Express window (not in the New Message window), choose **Options**, and click the **Spelling** tab. You can then enter settings to tell the spell checker to always check spelling before sending a message or to ignore certain text strings, such as all uppercase. Enter the desired settings and click **OK**.

Check for Typos and Spelling Errors

In the past, you had to rely on your own typing skills and keen editorial eye to ensure error-free email messages. Now you can have the spell checker check your messages for you and suggest corrections.

To check for typos and spelling errors, open the **Tools** menu and choose **Spelling**. The spell checker looks over your words. If the spell checker finds a questionable spelling (anything that is not listed in its spelling dictionary), it stops on the word and usually displays a list of suggested corrections. If the word is correct, you can choose to ignore it. If the word is misspelled, you can choose a correction from the list, or you can type your own correction.

Compose Messages Offline

If you have several messages to send, you can compose them offline to reduce your connect time charges. To compose mail offline, simply run Outlook Express without connecting to the Internet. Compose your message as shown in the *Guided Tour*. Then instead of clicking the Send button, open the **File** menu and click **Send Later**. This places the message in the Outlook Express Outbox folder. You can repeat the process to add messages to the Outbox.

When you're ready to send the messages you've composed, establish your Internet connection and click the **Send and Receive** button in the Outlook Express toolbar. This sends all the messages in the Outbox and checks for incoming mail.

Guided Tour   Reply to a Message

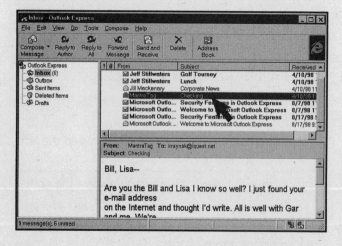

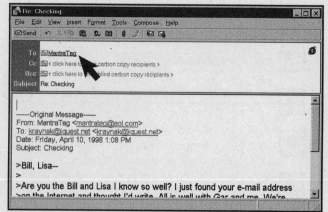

1 Run Outlook Express and click the message you want to reply to.

2 Click the **Reply to Author** button (to reply to the author) or the **Reply to All** button (to reply to the author and all recipients of the author's original message, except yourself).

3 The composition window appears and Outlook Express automatically inserts the email address(es), a description of the message, and the contents of the original message.

Guided Tour Reply to a Message

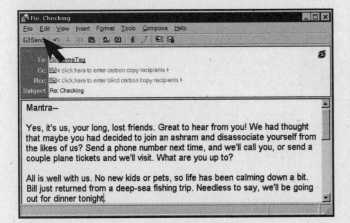

4 Type your reply above the original message and then click the **Send** button.

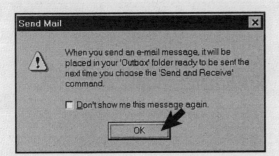

5 If Outlook Express is set up to send messages immediately, it sends the message. Otherwise, Outlook Express displays the Send Mail dialog box shown here, indicating that the message will be placed in the Outbox. Click **OK**.

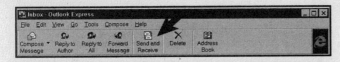

6 You can compose and send additional messages and replies to store them in the Outbox. When you are ready to send the messages, click the **Send and Receive** button.

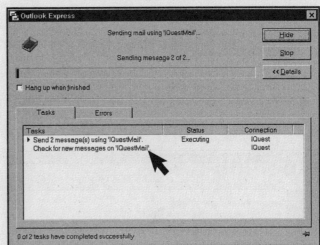

7 Outlook Express connects to your mail server and transmits the email message. A dialog box appears, displaying the progress of the operation.

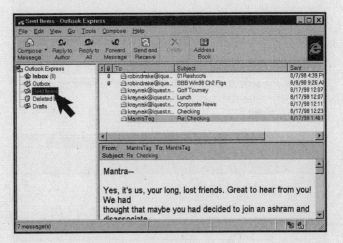

8 To make sure your messages were successfully transmitted, click the **Sent Items** folder in the folder list. The upper-right pane displays a list of messages that were successfully sent.

You can perform similar steps to forward a message. Forwarding sends a duplicate of the original message to another recipient. Instead of clicking Reply to Author in step 2, click **Forward Message**. You must then enter the email address of the person to whom you want to forward the message. You can type additional text in the message area. Click **Send**.

Guided Tour   Compose a New Message

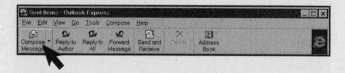

1 Run Outlook Express and click the **Compose Message** button.

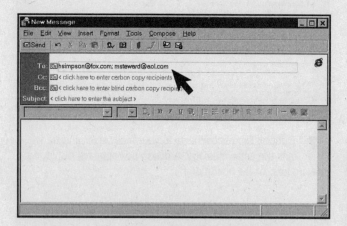

2 The New Message dialog box appears. In the **To** text box, type the email address of the person to whom you want the message sent. If you want to type additional addresses, separate them with a semicolon and a space.

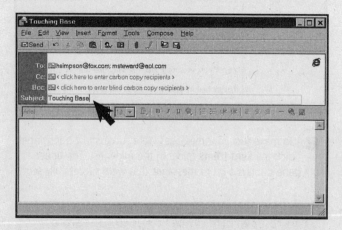

3 Click in the **Subject** text box and type a brief description of the message.

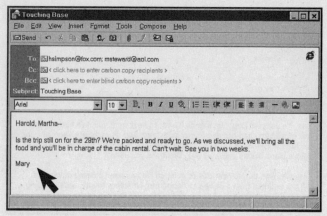

4 Click in the message area and type the contents of your message.

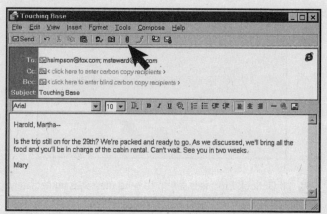

5 To attach a file to your message, click the **Insert File** button.

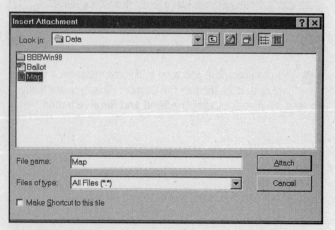

6 The Insert Attachment dialog box prompts you to choose the file you want to send. Change to the drive and folder that contains the file, click the file's name, and click the **Attach** button.

Guided Tour   Compose a New Message

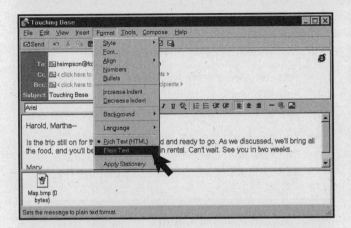

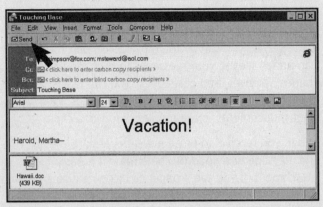

7 The attachment appears as an icon in a new pane below the message area. Repeat steps 5 and 6 to add more attachments if necessary.

8 Open the **Format** menu and choose the desired format for the message: **Rich Text (HTML)** or **Plain Text**.

11 Click the **Send** button.

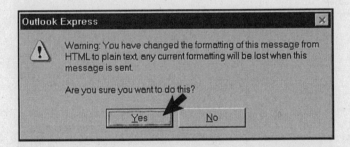

9 If the default format is set to Rich Text (HTML) and you chose Plain Text, a dialog box appears, prompting you to confirm your choice. Click **Yes**.

12 If Outlook Express is set up to send messages immediately, it sends the message. Otherwise, Outlook Express displays the Send Mail dialog box shown here, indicating that the message will be placed in the Outbox. Click **OK**.

13 You can compose and send additional messages and replies to store them in the Outbox. When you are ready to send the messages, click the **Send and Receive** button.

10 If you chose to send a rich text (HTML) message, use the HTML Formatting toolbar to format your message, insert images or horizontal lines, or add hyperlinks as desired.

View and Save File Attachments

Email is useful for sending more than simple text messages. As you saw in the previous *Guided Tour*, you can attach files to your messages to exchange files with friends, relatives, and colleagues. You can use email to exchange any type of file, including graphics, Web pages, documents, program files, and video clips.

When you receive an email message, look to the left of the message description to determine if it has a file attachment. If you see a paper clip icon next to an email message, there's more to the message than what's displayed in the preview pane. Double-click the description of the message to open it in its own window. You should now see an icon that represents the attached file.

You have two options for working with the file, both of which are shown in detail in the *Guided Tour*:

- You can save the file to a folder on your hard drive and then open it later in one of your applications. To do so, right-click the icon and select **Save As**.

- You can open the file, assuming it is of a file type that has been associated with an application. To do so, double-click the icon to open the file.

> You can set file associations from My Computer or Windows Explorer. Open the **View** menu, choose **Folder Options**, and click the **File Types** tab. ▶See "Create and Edit File Associations" on page 125 for details.◀

Guided Tour View and Save Attachments

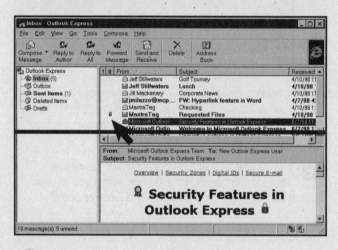

1 Look to the left of the message descriptions for a paper clip icon, which indicates that the message has an attached file. Click the message description.

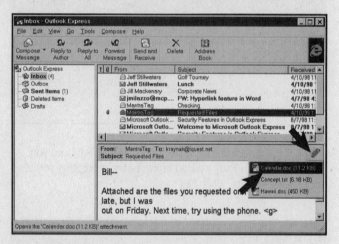

2 The contents of the message appear in the preview pane, and the paper clip icon appears in the header bar above the pane. Click the paper clip icon.

3 A context menu appears, displaying the names of all attached files. Click the file's name to open it in its associated program.

Guided Tour View and Save Attachments

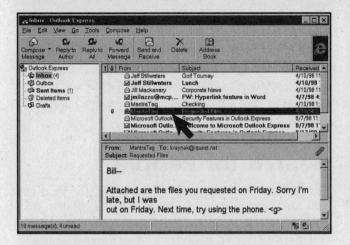

4 Another way to display the contents of a message is to double-click the message description to view the message in its own window.

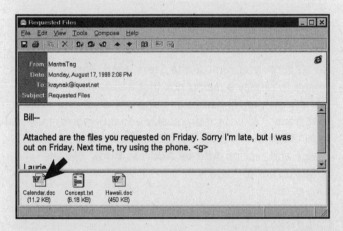

5 The message window displays a new pane at the bottom, containing icons for any attached files. Right-click the icon for the file you want to work with.

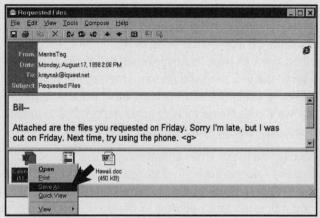

6 A context menu appears, providing commands for opening, printing, and saving the file. To save the file, click **Save As**.

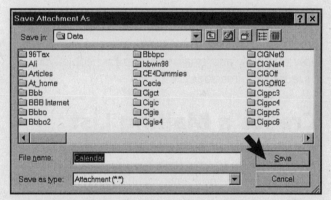

7 The Save Attachment As dialog box appears. Change to the disk and folder in which you want to save the file. (You can also rename the file at this point.) Click **Save**.

8 When you finish reading your messages, click the message window's **Close** (X) button.

Use the Address Book

Even if you have a photographic memory and you can rattle off every email address you've ever seen, you don't want to have to retype a person's email address every time you send the person a message. It's much easier to select the address from a list. Outlook Express allows you to create a list of email addresses and insert those addresses in your messages and replies.

To create a list of email addresses, you use the Outlook Express Address Book. To display the address book, click the **Address Book** button or press **Ctrl+Shift+B**. To add a person's email address to the book, click the **New Contact** button, and then fill out the requested information. All you really have to enter is the person's name and email address. If you want a more comprehensive entry, however, you can add the person's home address, phone number, fax number, cellular phone number, company information, and any other information you want to store. The *Guided Tour* leads you through the process step by step. The *Guided Tour* also shows you how to quickly add email addresses for people who have sent you messages.

Create a Mailing List

If you're collaborating on a project with several people, you might need to send identical messages to everyone in the group. Adding names manually to the To text box

can become tedious. To save time, you can create a group of recipients. Whenever you need to send an identical message to everyone in the group, you simply select the group's name instead of selecting each person's name. The *Guided Tour* shows you how to create a mailing list.

Search for People

The Internet has several electronic "phone books" that you can use to search for a person's email address. You can connect to various people-search tools using Internet Explorer. Following is a list of popular people-search tools:

- Four11 at `four11.com`
- Bigfoot at `bigfoot.com`
- WhoWhere? at `whowhere.com`
- InfoSeek at `infoseek.com`

In addition, you can use the **Start**, **Find**, **People** command to display a dialog box that allows you to search for people's email addresses using any of several online directories. You can then quickly add a person's email address to the Address Book by selecting the person's name and clicking **Add to Address Book**. See the *Guided Tour* for details.

Guided Tour Add an Email Address to the Address Book

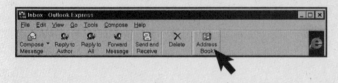

1 Run Outlook Express and click the **Address Book** button or press **Ctrl+Shift+B**.

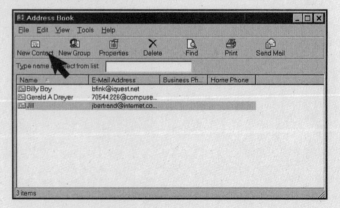

2 The Address Book window appears. Click the **New Contact** button.

Guided Tour Add an Email Address to the Address Book

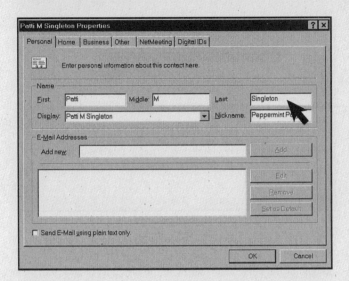

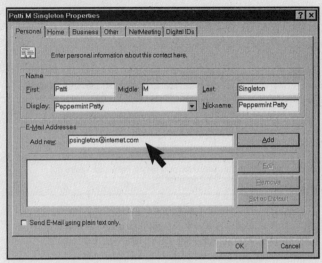

3 The Properties dialog box prompts you to enter information about the person. Type the person's first name, middle initial (optional), and last name in the appropriate text boxes.

4 (Optional) Click in the **Nickname** text box and type the person's nickname.

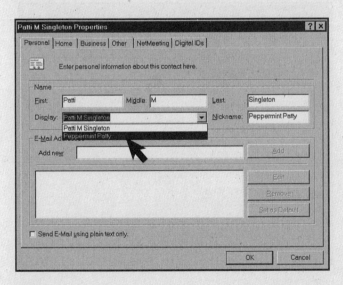

5 (Optional) Click in the **Display Name** text box and type the person's name as you want it to appear in the Address Book, or open the drop-down list and select the person's full name or nickname.

6 Under E-Mail Addresses, click in the **Add New** text box and type the person's email address. Click the **Add** button. If the person has more than one email address, repeat this step to insert additional addresses.

7 If you inserted more than one email address for the person, click the address you will use most often and click the **Set As Default** button.

8 To send only plain text messages to this person, click **Send E-Mail Using Plain Text Only** to place a check mark in the box.

9 You can use the Home, Business, Other, NetMeeting, and Digital IDs tabs to enter additional contact information about the person. Then click **OK**.

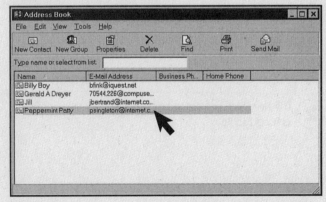

10 You are returned to the Address Book window, and the person's name and email address are displayed. Repeat this *Guided Tour* as necessary to enter additional email addresses. Click the **Close** (X) button when you finish.

Guided Tour Add an Address from an Incoming Message

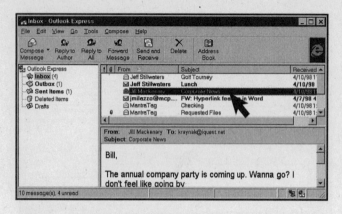

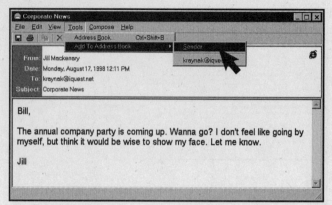

1 The easiest way to add an address to the Address Book is to lift it from a message you've received. Double-click the message's description to display it in its own window.

2 The message appears. Open the **Tools** menu, point to **Add to Address Book**, and click **Sender** (to add the address of the person who sent you the message) or click the email address of another person who received the message (the recipients are listed below Sender).

Guided Tour Insert an Address from the Address Book

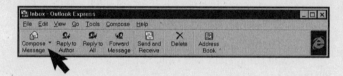

1 Click the **Compose Message** button to start a new message.

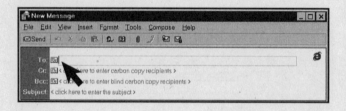

2 The New Message dialog box appears. Click the card file icon next to **To**.

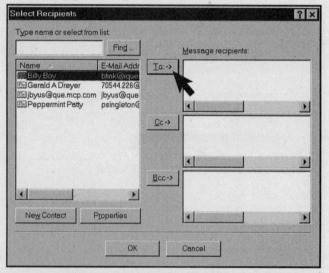

3 The Select Recipients dialog box appears. In the list of email addresses, click the name or address of the person to whom you want to send the message, and then click the **To** button.

Guided Tour   Insert an Address from the Address Book

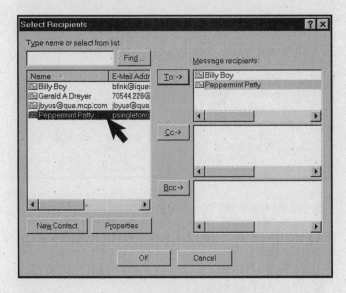

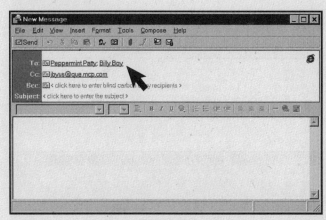

7 You are returned to the New Message dialog box, and Outlook Express inserts the selected names or email addresses in the To, Cc, and Bcc text boxes. Compose and send the message, ▶as explained in "Send Messages and Replies" on page 332.◀

4 The person's name or address is added to the Message Recipients list. Repeat the steps to address the message to additional recipients. (To remove a name or address from the Message Recipients list, click it and press the **Delete** key.)

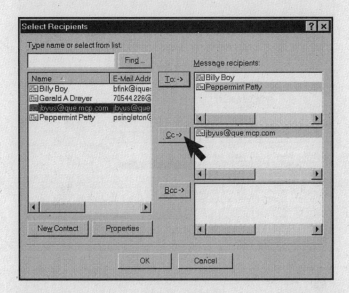

5 To send a copy of the message to another person's attention, click the person's name or address in the list of email addresses and click the **Cc** (Carbon Copy) button. The **Bcc** (Blind Carbon Copy) button allows you to send a copy of the message to someone else without the main recipient knowing about it.)

6 When you finish adding addresses, click **OK**.

Guided Tour Search for an Email Address

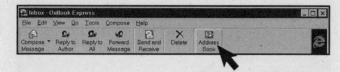

1 Run Outlook Express and click the **Address Book** button or press **Ctrl+Shift+B**.

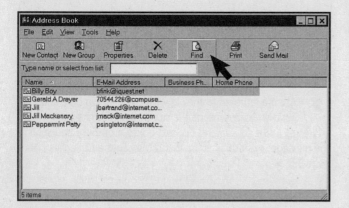

2 The Address Book window appears. Click the **Find** button.

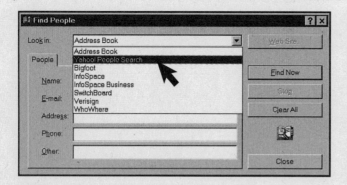

3 The Find People dialog box appears. Open the **Look In** drop-down list and choose the online directory you want to search.

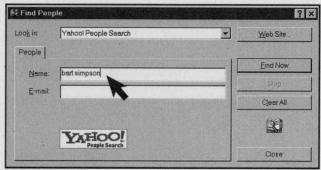

4 In the **Name** text box, type the person's name. You can type the person's full name, last name only, or initial and last name. The more detailed the entry, the more focused the search will be.

5 Click the **Find Now** button.

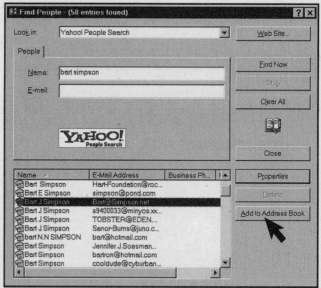

6 Outlook Express connects to the online directory. If the directory finds some names and email addresses that match your entry, it displays a list of names and email addresses in a separate panel at the bottom of the dialog box. Click the name of the person you want to add to the Address Book, and then click the **Add to Address Book** button.

Guided Tour Search for an Email Address

If you keep receiving error messages indicating that the search is taking too long, increase the timeout setting for the service. To do this, open the Address Book's **Tools** menu and choose **Accounts**. Click the name of the service and click **Properties**. Click the **Advanced** tab and make sure the **Search Timeout** is set to at least 1 minute.

If the search fails to produce any entries, try entering a shorter version of the person's name (perhaps only the person's last name). You can also try to use a different online directory; not all of them have the same listings. Another option is to click the **Web Site** button to go to the directory's Web page, where you might find additional search options and instructions.

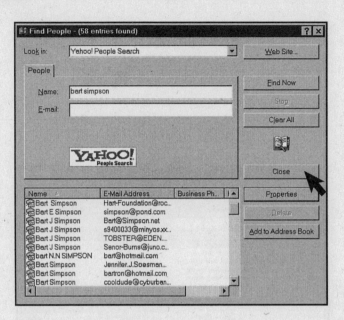

8 You are returned to the Find People dialog box. You can insert additional names from the list into your Address Book. Click the **Close** button when you are done.

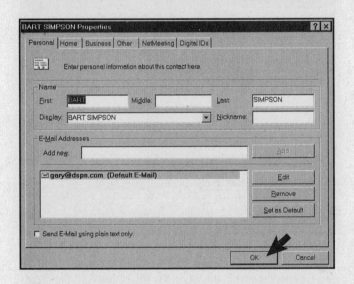

7 The Properties dialog box for the selected person appears, displaying the person's name and email address. Enter any additional information as desired, and then click **OK**.

Guided Tour Create a Mailing List

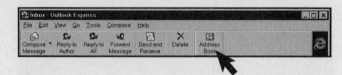

1 Run Outlook Express and click the **Address Book** button.

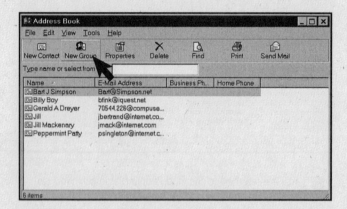

2 The Address Book window appears. Click the **New Group** button.

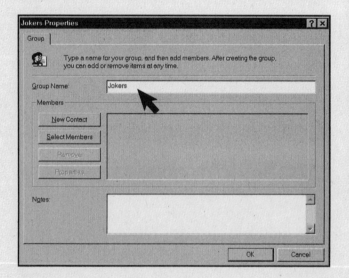

3 The Properties dialog box appears. In the **Group Name** text box, type a name for the group.

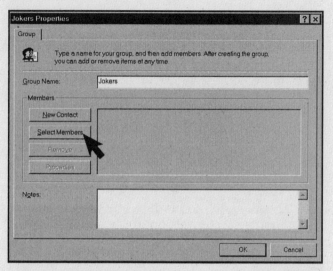

4 Click the **Select Members** button to display a list of people in your address book.

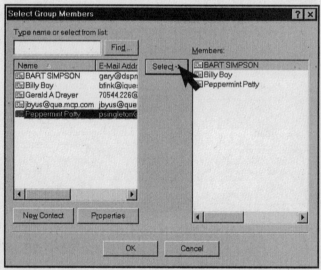

5 To add a person's name to the group list, double-click the person's name in the list on the left, or highlight the name and click the **Select** button; repeat this step to add other people to the group.

6 When you finish adding names, click the **OK** button.

7 You are returned to the Address Book window. Click **OK**.

Guided Tour   Create a Mailing List

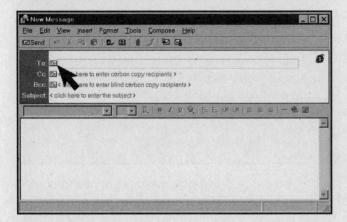

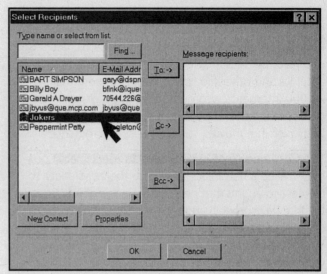

8 To send a message to everyone in the group, display the New Message window and click the card file icon next to the **To** box.

9 The Select Recipients dialog box appears. From the list on the left, select the name of the *group* to which you want to send the message. (You can send the message to additional recipients that are not in the group.) Click **OK**.

10 Compose and send the message as you normally would.

Set Up Your News Server Account

Newsgroups are discussion groups where people can share knowledge, insights, and concerns. Users can find help, ask and answer questions, and even post graphics and other file types. There are more than 20,000 Internet newsgroups, covering such topics as politics, current events, software, automobiles, pets, body piercing, movies, supermodels, and romance.

To access a newsgroup, you need to use a special program called a *newsreader*. You use the newsreader to connect to an Internet news server, subscribe to your favorite newsgroups, and read messages posted by others. You can then reply to someone's posting or start a discussion by posting your own question or message. Windows comes with its own newsreader: Outlook Express.

A *newsgroup* is an online bulletin board where people can read posted messages and post replies or start discussions. A *newsreader* is a program that allows a person to visit a newsgroup and read and post messages. The *news server* is a feature of the Internet, which makes newsgroups accessible.

Before you can read and post messages in newsgroups, you must first connect to a news server. Your Internet service provider should have given you the address of its news server. The address typically looks something like `news.internet.com`. You must then enter this address in your newsreader so it can connect to the news server. The *Guided Tour* shows you how to enter the settings required to connect to your news server.

Guided Tour   Enter News Server Settings

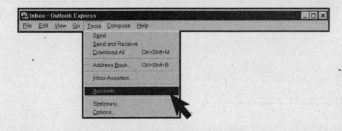

1 Run Outlook Express, and then open the **Tools** menu and select **Accounts**.

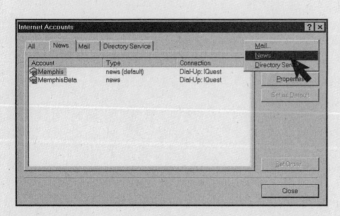

2 The Internet Accounts dialog box appears. Click the **News** tab.

3 The News tab lists any installed news servers. Click the **Add** button and select **News**.

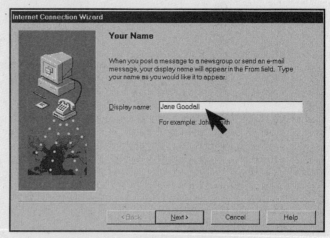

4 This starts the Internet Connection Wizard. Type your name as you want it to appear when you post messages to a newsgroup. (This can be your real name or, if you prefer to remain anonymous, a nickname.) Click **Next**.

Guided Tour Enter News Server Settings

5 Type your email address so people can reply to the messages you post by sending you email messages. Click **Next**.

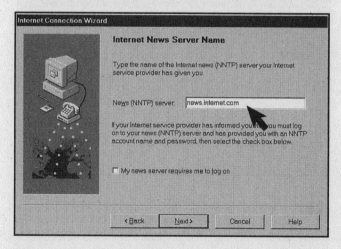

6 You are now prompted to type the address of your news server. In the **News (NNTP) Server** text box, type your news server's address (for instance, `news.internet.com`).

7 If your news server requires you to log on using your username and password, select **My News Server Requires Me to Log On**. Click **Next**.

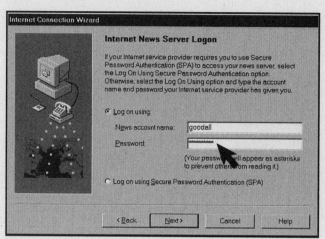

8 If the server requires you to log on, select one of the following logon settings:

Log On Using if your news server requires you to enter a name and password to connect. Enter the required name and password in the appropriate text boxes.

Log On Using Secure Password Authentication (SPA) if your news server requires you to connect using a digital certification.

Click **Next**.

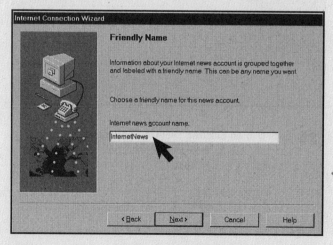

9 The wizard prompts you to enter a friendly name for your news server. Type a descriptive name for the server and click **Next**.

(continues)

Guided Tour Enter News Server Settings   *(continued)*

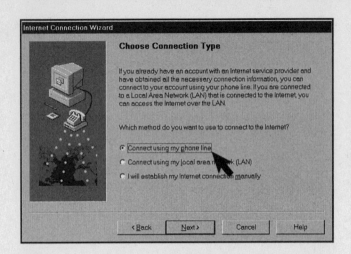

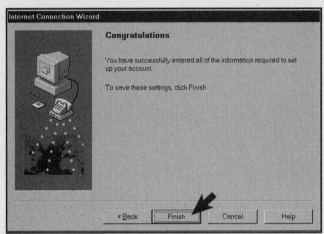

10 Click **Connect Using My Phone Line** or **Connect Using My Local Area Network** to specify how you connect to the Internet. Click **Next.**

12 Click the **Finish** button.

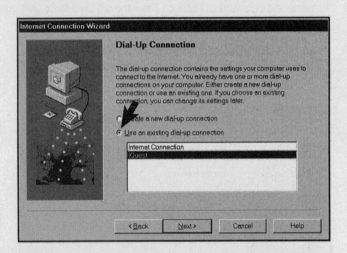

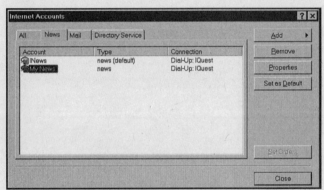

11 Click **Use an Existing Dial-Up Connection**, and then click the Dial-Up Networking connection you use to connect to the Internet. Click **Next**.

13 The Internet Accounts dialog box appears, showing the name of the news server you added. To make this your default news server, click its name and click the **Set as Default** button. Then click **Close**.

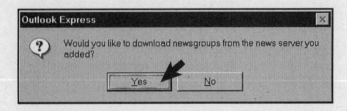

14 The Outlook Express dialog box appears, asking if you want to download a list of newsgroups from the server. Click **Yes**.

Guided Tour Enter News Server Settings

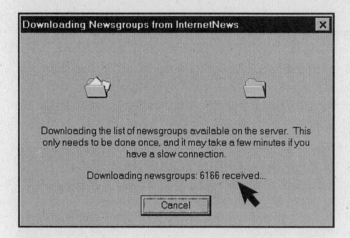

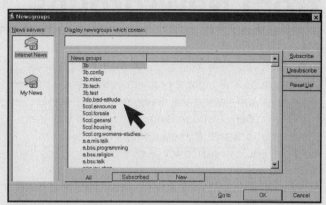

15 Outlook Express starts to download the list of available newsgroups from your Internet service provider's news server and displays a dialog box showing the progress.

16 After downloading the list of available newsgroups, Outlook Express displays a list of their names. ▶See "Find, Subscribe to and Unsubscribe fromNewsgroups" on page 352 to learn what to do next.◀

The list of newsgroups will contain some newsgroup names that you may find offensive. If you have children who use your computer, you may wish to block access to some of these newsgroups. ▶See "Censor the Internet" on page 283 for details.◀

Outlook Express allows you to set up more than one news server. However, only one server acts as the default server. If you've set up more than one server, you must mark it as the default server before you can use it to open newsgroups. Display the Internet Accounts dialog box, click the **News** tab, select the server, and click the **Set as Default** button.

Find, Subscribe to, and Unsubscribe from Newsgroups

When you have a list of more than 20,000 news-groups, the biggest problem you face is narrowing the list and finding the newsgroups that interest you. Fortunately, Outlook Express provides a tool that allows you to search for newsgroups by name. For example, you can search for all of the newsgroups that deal with gardening by typing "garden." Outlook Express then narrows the list of newsgroups to display only those newsgroups that have "garden" or "gardening" in their names.

When you find the newsgroups that interest you, you can *subscribe* to them. This places the newsgroups on a shorter list of subscribed newsgroups so you can access

them more quickly later. The following *Guided Tour* shows you how to search for newsgroups that interest you, subscribe to them, and unsubscribe from news-groups that no longer interest you.

Subscribing to a newsgroup is not like sub-scribing to a Web site. When you subscribe to a newsgroup, Outlook Express does not auto-matically download newsgroup messages on a specified schedule. Subscribing simply places the newsgroup on a list of newsgroups that interest you.

Guided Tour   Find Newsgroups

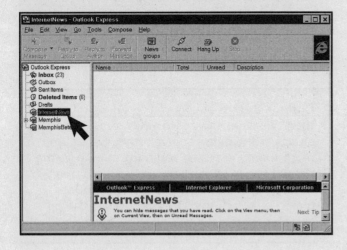

1 Run Outlook Express and click the icon for your news server in the folder list.

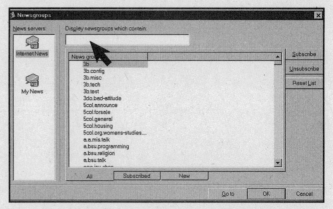

2 The Newsgroups dialog box displays a list of all available newsgroups. In the **Display Newsgroups Which Contain** text box, type a word that describes the topic you're inter-ested in.

Guided Tour   Find Newsgroups

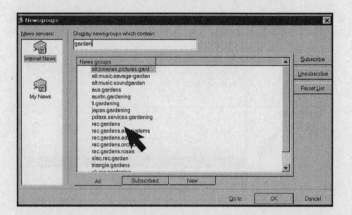

3️⃣ Outlook Express filters out any newsgroups whose names do not contain the text you typed and displays a short list of newsgroups whose names do contain the text you typed.

Guided Tour   Subscribe to and Unsubscribe from Newsgroups

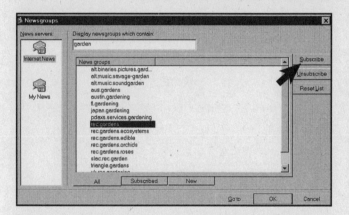

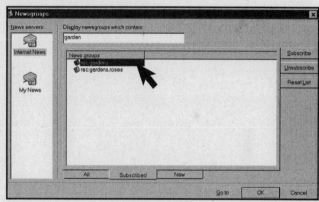

1️⃣ In the Newsgroups dialog box double-click the name of the newsgroup to which you want to subscribe, or click the newsgroup and click the **Subscribe** button. Repeat this step to subscribe to additional newsgroups.

3️⃣ A list of all subscribed newsgroups appears. To unsubscribe from a newsgroup, double-click its name or select it and click the **Unsubscribe** button.

4️⃣ When you are done setting up your newsgroup subscriptions, click the **OK** button.

(continues)

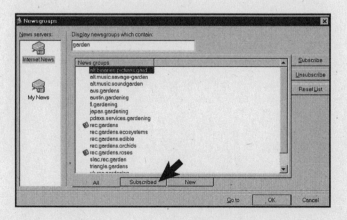

2️⃣ A newspaper icon appears next to the name of each subscribed newsgroup. Click the **Subscribed** tab.

Guided Tour Subscribe to and Unsubscribe from Newsgroups *(continued)*

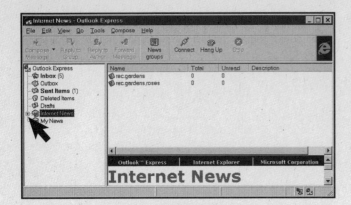

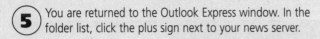

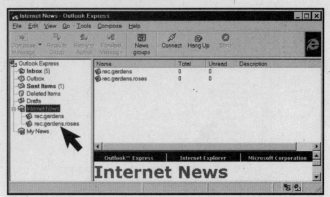

5 You are returned to the Outlook Express window. In the folder list, click the plus sign next to your news server.

6 A list of all the subscribed newsgroups appears. Click the name of the newsgroup to display a list of messages posted in that newsgroup. ▶See "Read Newsgroup Messages" on page 355 for details on reading messages.◀

Read Newsgroup Messages

When you click the name of a subscribed newsgroup, the newsreader displays a list of *headers*, descriptions of the posted messages. Outlook Express displays the header list in the upper-right pane and the contents of the selected message in the lower-right pane. To read a message, you either click its header or double-click to display the message in its own window. The *Guided Tour* shows you how to display the contents of newsgroup messages.

In some newsgroups, such as those on games and graphics, messages often have file attachments. ▶To view and save attached files, see "View and Save File Attachments" on page 338.◄ The procedure for attaching files to your own messages is the same as that for attaching files to outgoing email messages. ▶See "Send Files and Shortcuts" on page 332.◄

Follow a Discussion

Occasionally, someone will post a message that inspires a long discussion or at least a couple replies. When this happens, Outlook Express keeps the related messages together so you can follow the discussion. To the left of the original message, you'll see a plus sign (+). Click the plus sign to display the related messages. You can then read those messages by clicking them.

When you click the plus sign, it turns into a minus sign. When you finish viewing the messages, you can click the minus sign to collapse the list of replies so that only the original message appears in the list of messages.

Find and Sort Newsgroup Messages

If you connect to a newsgroup that contains hundreds of messages, you might have trouble sifting through the list to find messages on specific topics. To help, you can use the **Edit**, **Find Message** command. This displays a dialog box that allows you to search for messages by topic or for messages posted by a particular person. You can also sort messages, as shown in the *Guided Tour*.

Guided Tour   Read Posted Messages

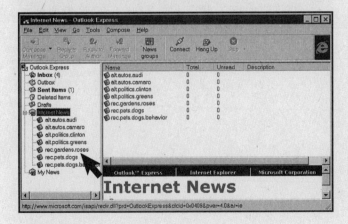

1 In the folder list, click the name of a subscribed newsgroup.

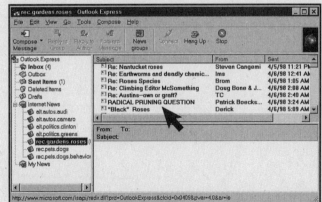

2 Outlook Express displays a list of message headers (descriptions). Click the header of the message you want to read.

(continues)

Guided Tour Read Posted Messages

(continued)

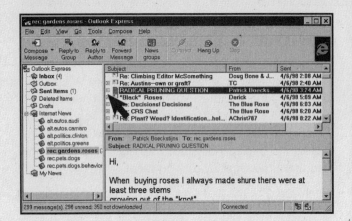

3 The contents of the message appear in the lower-right pane. If a message has a plus sign next to it, click the plus sign to view a list of message headers for replies to the message.

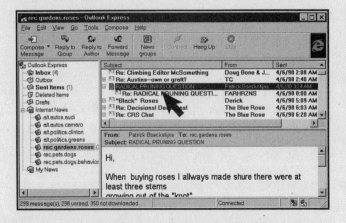

4 The replies are listed below the original message. Click a reply message's header to view the contents of the reply. (You can click the minus sign next to the original message to hide the list of replies.)

5 To view a message in its own window, double-click its header.

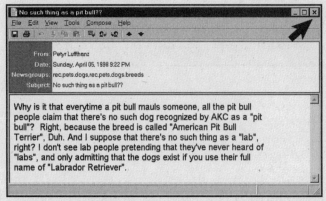

6 Outlook Express opens the message in its own window and displays its contents. Click the up or down arrow button in the toolbar to display the previous or next message. Click the window's **Close** (X) button when you are done.

Guided Tour   Read Posted Messages

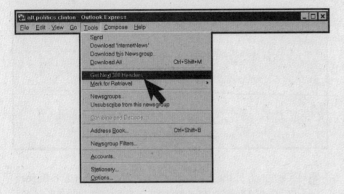

7 By default, Outlook Express downloads the first 300 message headers in the newsgroup. To download the next 300 message headers, open the **Tools** menu and choose **Get Next 300 Headers**.

To have Outlook Express download more or fewer message headers, open the **Tools** menu and choose **Options**. In the Options dialog box, click the **Read** tab. Use the **Download ___ Headers at a Time** spin box to set the number of headers you want Outlook Express to download at one time. Click **OK**.

8 Outlook Express downloads the additional headers and displays them in the upper-right pane.

When you click a newsgroup, Outlook Express downloads and displays only the message headers. It does not download the message contents until you select the message. To read messages offline, use the **Tools**, **Download** options to download the newsgroup messages. Then click the **Hang Up** button in the toolbar to disconnect, and you can read the messages offline.

Guided Tour   Sort Messages

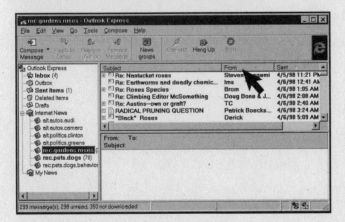 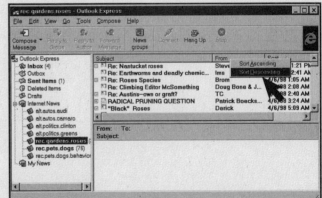

1 Right-click the heading for the column you want to sort (for example, right-click **From**).

2 A context menu appears, allowing you to sort in Ascending order (A to Z, 1 to 10) or Descending order (Z to A, 10 to 1). Select the desired sort order. Outlook Express rearranges the message descriptions to conform to the specified sort order.

Guided Tour Find Messages

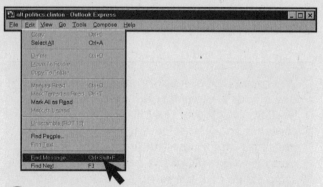

1 Select the newsgroup that contains the message you want to search for. Then open the **Edit** menu and select **Find Message**.

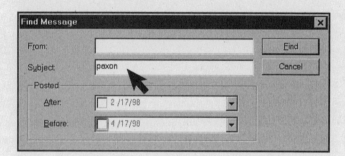

2 The Find Message dialog box appears. Take one of the following steps:

To search for messages posted by a specific person, enter the person's username in the **From** text box.

To search for messages on a particular topic, click in the **Subject** text box and type one or two unique terms to indicate what you are searching for.

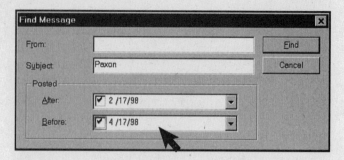

3 (Optional) In the Posted section, use the **After** and **Before** options to search for messages posted only between specified dates.

4 Click the **Find** button.

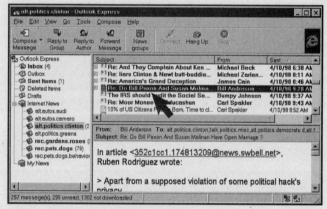

5 Outlook Express performs the specified search and highlights the description of the first message it finds that matches your search instructions. To find another message that matches your search instructions, open the **Edit** menu and select **Find Next** (or press **F3**).

Post Messages and Replies

Posting a reply or starting a discussion is as easy as sending an email message. You click a button to post your reply or message, enter a description of the message, type the message itself, and then click the **Post** button. However, you do have a few choices on how to post your reply or message:

- Post your reply or message publicly to have it appear in the list of messages so all visitors of the newsgroup can read it.

- Post your reply privately by sending an email message to the person who posted the original message. The person will then receive your reply without having to check the newsgroup. Sometimes, a person specifically requests that you reply via email.

- Post your reply publicly and privately via email. This places your message in the newsgroup so all visitors can read it, and it also sends a copy via

email to the person who posted the original message.

Before you post messages to a newsgroup, familiarize yourself with the newsgroup. Hang out for a while, and spend some time reading existing messages to obtain a clear idea of the focus and tone of the newsgroup. Reading messages without posting your own messages is known as *lurking*. Newsgroups encourage lurking because it provides you with the knowledge you need to respond intelligently and to avoid repeating what has already been said. If the newsgroup has a FAQ (frequently asked questions) list, read it to learn of the newsgroup's rules and regulations.

Take the following *Guided Tour* to post a reply or start your own discussion.

Guided Tour Post a Reply

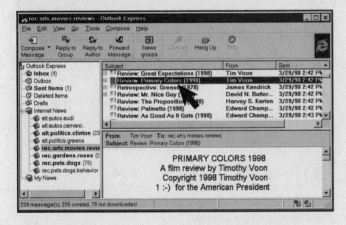

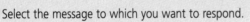

1 Select the message to which you want to respond.

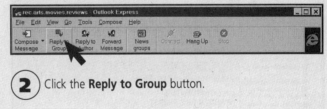

2 Click the **Reply to Group** button.

(continues)

Guided Tour Post a Reply

(continued)

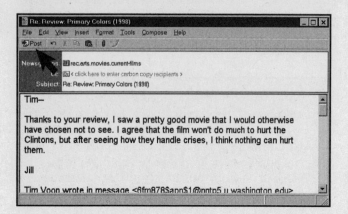

3 A new message window appears, and the newsgroup's address and the subject description are filled in for you. Type your message in the message area at the bottom of the window.

Click the **Post** button, and your newsreader sends your reply as instructed.

You can format your message using HTML tags to make it look like a Web page. Open the **Format** menu and choose **Rich Text (HTML)**. This displays the HTML Formatting toolbar, which you can use to format your message. Note, however, that the other people in the newsgroup might be using a newsreader that does not support HTML.

Guided Tour Reply Via Email

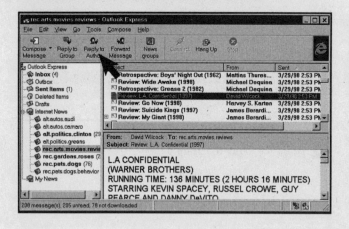

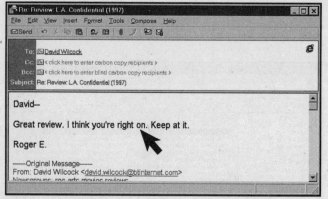

1 Select the message to which you want to respond.

2 Click the **Reply to Author** button.

3 Outlook Express displays a new message window, and the person's email address and the subject description are already filled in for you. Type your message in the message area at the bottom of the window.

Guided Tour Reply Via Email

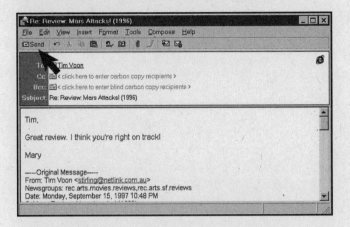

4 Click the **Send** button, and your email program sends your reply to the specified email address.

Guided Tour Start a Discussion

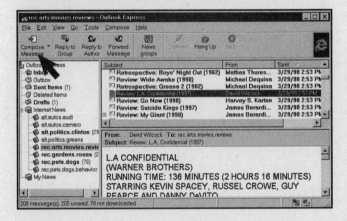

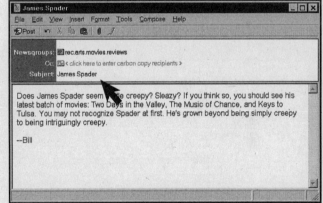

1 Select the newsgroup in which you want to post your message.

2 Click the **Compose Message** button.

3 The window that appears is very similar to the window you use to reply to messages, except that in this dialog box, the Subject text box is blank. Click in the **Subject** text box, and then type a description for your message.

4 Click in the big message area and type your message.

5 Click the **Post** button. Your message is posted in the active newsgroup. You can now check the newsgroup on a regular basis to see if anyone has replied to your message.

HOW TO...
Install Hardware

When you purchased your computer, you might have thought that it had everything necessary to satisfy you well into the 21st Century. Well, computer technology changes rapidly, and as you learn more about computers, you might start to realize that your computer is not as powerful and well-equipped as you had hoped. Maybe you got stuck with a "free" black-and-white printer or a dinky 15-inch monitor. Or maybe now that you have started to use the Internet, you have found that your 14.4Kbps modem just can't keep up with the Web.

Whatever the case, at some point you will want to upgrade your computer to make it more powerful and to take advantage of additional computing features. Fortunately, Windows 98 can help you install your new equipment. Windows 98's Add New Hardware Wizard can detect the new hardware you install and lead you through the process of setting it up. This section shows you how to use the Install New Hardware Wizard and other tools to enter the required settings for your upgrades.

What You Will Find in This Section

Install New Hardware

Depending on your computer and on the upgrade, upgrading can be easy or difficult. Plugging in a printer or joystick is a fairly easy operation. You simply plug the device into a *port* (outlet) on the back of your computer. Adding memory chips, a hard disk drive, or an internal modem is more difficult, however, because you must remove the system unit cover and tinker with the insides of your computer. And if your computer or the upgrade device is not Plug and Play-compatible, you might have to adjust settings on the device to prevent it from conflicting with other devices.

> Plug and Play (commonly abbreviated PnP) is a computer technology that makes it possible for you to connect a device to your computer without having to enter settings for the device. Windows and most new devices support Plug and Play technology, and Microsoft is working to implement more Plug and Play enhancements throughout the computer industry.

The following sections provide useful information about obtaining upgrades and installing devices on your computer. For details on how to install a specific device, check your computer's documentation and the instructions that came with the device itself. After you have successfully installed the device, you must install the necessary *driver* for that device, as shown in the *Guided Tour*.

A driver is a computer program that provides the instructions Windows needs to use the device. To install a hardware driver in Windows, you use the Add New Hardware Wizard, as shown in the *Guided Tour*. Although Windows comes with updated drivers for most common devices (including printers, modems, and mice), devices commonly come with their own drivers. If the driver is old, you can obtain a new driver by calling the manufacturer or by downloading the updated driver from the company's Web site. See ▶"Find Technical Support" on page 483.◀

> The steps in the *Guided Tour* might vary, depending on how your system is set up. The Add New Hardware Wizard first checks for Plug and Play devices and then for non-Plug and Play devices. If it does not detect a new Plug and Play device on your computer, it skips the steps required to install a new device.

Mail Order Upgrades

The best place to start shopping for upgrades is through the dealer from which you purchased your computer. This might not be the best place to *buy* upgrade components, but it is the best place to begin looking. Find out which components you need and the types of components that are compatible with your system. Get a price to use for comparison purposes.

With that information in hand, call the following mail-order companies for prices:

- **USA Flex** at **800-723-0334** is a good place to shop for printers, graphics cards, CD-ROM drives, scanners, and modems.

- **First Source** at **800-468-9866** or www.first-source.com is an excellent place to buy memory and processor upgrades. They offer quality products at reasonable prices, and their sales staff can help you figure out what you need for your particular system.

- **Computer Discount Warehouse** at **800-886-4239** or www.cdw.com offers a wide selection of software, multimedia and processor upgrades, monitors, and input devices.

Safety Precautions

Before you start installing hardware, you should be aware of some safety precautions. Because so many delicate electrical components reside inside your computer, and because working with electricity can be dangerous, you have to be careful. Follow these standard precautions:

- Check your computer's warranty before you do anything. Some companies require you to buy upgrades from them or send your computer to them for any upgrades. If you perform the upgrade yourself and the computer breaks down later, your warranty may no longer be valid. This is especially important if you are upgrading a notebook PC.

- Make sure all the parts of your computer are turned off and unplugged.

- Before you start, touch a metal part of the system unit to discharge any static electricity from your body. Better yet, go to an electronics store and buy a grounding strap. Attach the strap (usually to your wrist) and to ground (a metal part of your computer will work).

- New computer parts usually come in antistatic bags. Before handling a part, touch a metal part of the system unit case to discharge static electricity from your body.

- Keep parts in their electrostatic bags (not on top of the bags) until you are ready to use them.

- If the parts have warranty seals, be careful not to break them. Breaking a seal could invalidate the warranty. If the system unit case is sealed, check the warranty before breaking the seal.

- Hold parts by their edges and mounting brackets. Avoid touching any components or solder on the parts.

- Never slide parts over your work surface. This can build up a static charge in the part.

- Keep plastic, vinyl, furs, and Styrofoam out of your work area.

- If your upgrade part arrives on a cold day, let it warm to room temperature before installing it. Any condensation on the new part could damage your system.

- If you drop a stray screw inside the system unit, stick some tape on a pencil eraser and retrieve the screw; don't use your fingers or a magnet.

- When removing the cover from your system unit, make sure you don't bump any cables loose or pinch them when you replace the cover.

Install an Expansion Board

Many upgrades require you to "install" an expansion board (also called a *circuit board* or *card*). An expansion board is an integrated circuit board that plugs into the main circuit board (the *motherboard*) inside your system unit. An internal modem is an expansion board. A sound card is an expansion board. In some cases, you might even have to install an expansion board to add a floppy drive, CD-ROM drive, or hard disk drive to your system.

If your computer and the expansion board are Plug and Play-compatible, you can install the board without changing any settings on the board itself. Windows 98 can automatically change the settings on Plug and Play devices to make them work on your computer.

However, many expansion boards on the market do not conform to the rules of Plug and Play. With these types of boards, you have to make sure that the new board will not use the same settings as an existing board. Typically, there are three settings you need to consider:

- **IRQ** stands for *interrupt request* and is a number that enables a device to demand attention from the central processing unit. If two devices have the same IRQ, they demand attention at the same time, confusing the CPU.

- **DMA channel** is a path to your computer's RAM. Most computers have eight DMA (Direct Memory Access) channels. If two devices share one DMA channel, usually only one device gains access to RAM. The other device simply won't work.

- **I/O port address** is a designation that allows a device to take input and output information at a certain location. As with IRQs and DMAs, if two devices use the same I/O setting, problems occur.

You change these settings on the expansion board by flipping tiny switches or by sliding jumpers over or off of wire posts on the card. The documentation that comes with the card shows how to position the switches or jumpers to change the interrupt, DMA channel, and I/O port setting for the card. The documentation should also show the default settings for these switches; if default positions are not given, write them down before changing them on the card.

> Try installing the expansion board with the factory settings (don't change anything). If the board doesn't work or if it causes another device to stop working, start flipping switches or rearranging the jumpers as instructed in the documentation. (Change only one setting at a time.)

To install an expansion board, first remove the system unit cover. The expansion slots are located on the motherboard near the back of the system unit (where your printer and monitor plug in). Find an expansion slot that matches the size of the board you need to plug in. If you're installing an expansion board (such as an internal modem or sound card) that requires an external connection, remove the metal cover near the expansion slot.

To install the expansion board, insert the contacts at the bottom of the board into one of the expansion slots, and then press down on the card while rocking it gently back and forth. Expect the fit to be snug, but don't push so hard that you crack the board. Make sure the board is seated securely in the socket and that it is not leaning against any other boards (this could cause the board to short circuit). Secure the board in place using the screw you removed from the cover plate. When you're done, replace the system unit cover.

Guided Tour   Run the Add New Hardware Wizard

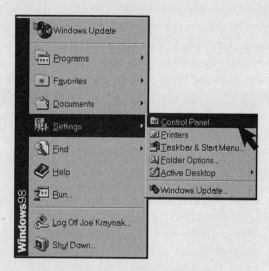

1 Exit all running programs. Then click the **Start** button, point to **Settings**, and click **Control Panel**.

2 The Control Panel window appears. Click the **Add New Hardware** icon.

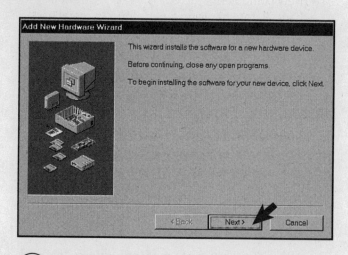

3 The Add New Hardware Wizard appears, informing you about what the wizard will do. Click the **Next** button.

Guided Tour Run the Add New Hardware Wizard

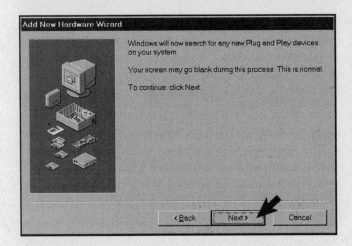

4 The next dialog box indicates that Windows will search for Plug and Play devices. Click **Next**.

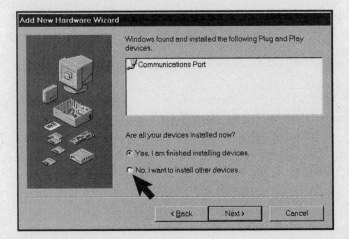

5 If Windows finds a Plug and Play device, it displays the name of the device and asks if all the devices you want to install are listed. If Windows did not detect the device you just installed, click **No, I Want to Install Other Devices**. Click **Next**.

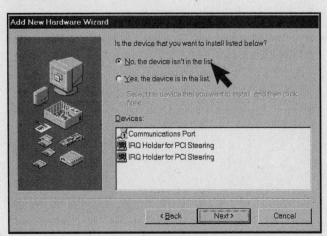

6 If the wizard detected other devices, it displays a list of them and asks if the device you want to install is in the list. If the device is not in the list, click **No, the Device Isn't in the List**. If the device is in the list, click **Yes, the Device Is in the List** and click the name of the device. Click **Next**.

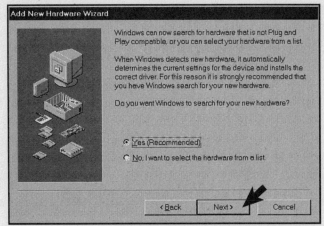

7 The wizard asks if you want it to search for any non Plug and Play devices on your system. Make sure **Yes (Recommended)** is selected, and then click the **Next** button.

(continues)

Guided Tour Run the Add New Hardware Wizard *(continued)*

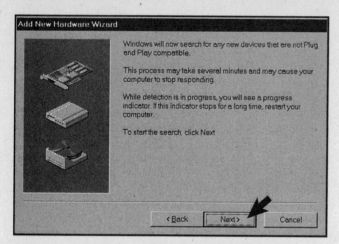

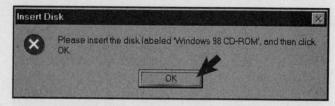

10 Windows might prompt you to insert the Windows 98 CD, a Windows 98 setup disk, or a disk that came with the device. The wizard installs the new device. If the device conflicts with another device in your system, Windows displays a dialog box informing you of the conflict and offering to help you resolve it.

8 The wizard informs you that it will now search for any new non Plug and Play devices. Click the **Next** button to have the wizard perform the search. It then searches your computer for any new hardware that's installed. This may take several minutes.

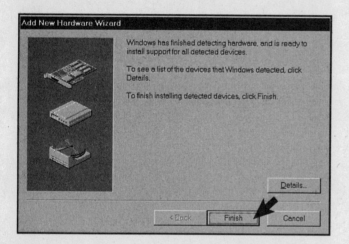

9 Wait until the detection process is complete, and then click the **Finish** button.

Set Up a New Printer

One of the most common ways to upgrade your computer is to change printers. There are several good inkjet and laser printers on the market that double as scanners, fax machines, and copy machines. And these feature-packed printers are priced nearly the same as their obsolete siblings.

Adding a new printer to your system has always been fairly easy. You connect the printer to the parallel printer port on the back of your computer using a printing cable and then plug the printer into an electrical outlet.

After installing the printer, however, you must enter settings in Windows to tell Windows which port the printer is connected to and to install a printer driver. The printer driver provides instructions that tell Windows how to communicate with the printer. Most printers come with their own printer driver on a floppy disk. For those printers that do not have their own driver, Windows has a wide selection of drivers to choose from.

To install the driver and enter additional settings in Windows, you can use the Add Printer Wizard, as shown in the *Guided Tour*.

Guided Tour Add a Printer

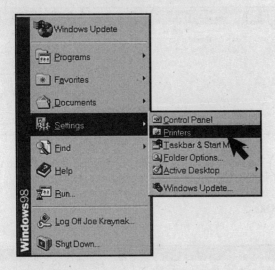

1 Click the **Start** button, point to **Settings**, and click **Printers**.

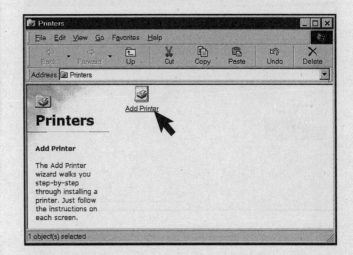

2 My Computer opens and displays the Printers folder. Click the **Add Printer** icon.

(continues)

Guided Tour Add a Printer *(continued)*

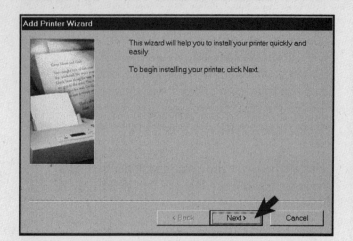

3 Windows starts the Add Printer Wizard, which informs you of what it is about to do. Click **Next**.

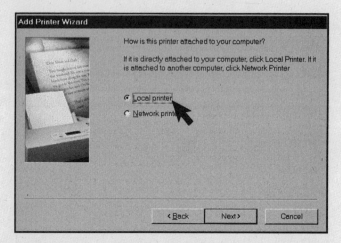

4 If you are connected to a network, the wizard asks if you want to install a local or network printer. (A network printer is a printer that is already installed on another computer on the network.) Click **Local Printer** or **Network Printer** and click **Next**.

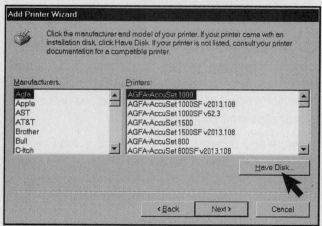

5 The wizard displays a list of manufacturers and printers. If your printer came with its own driver, click **Have Disk**. If the printer did not come with its own driver, skip to step 7.

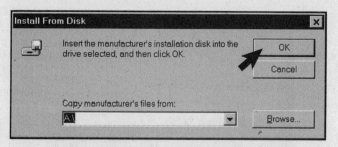

6 The Install From Disk dialog box appears. Insert the printer installation disk in your computer's CD-ROM or floppy drive, select the drive letter from the drop-down list, and click **OK**.

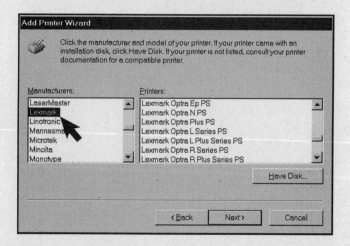

7 In the Manufacturers list, click the name of the printer's manufacturer.

Guided Tour　Add a Printer

8 The Printers list displays the models produced by the selected manufacturer. Click the printer model that matches your printer. If no model in the list is an exact match, pick the closest model name and number. Click **Next**.

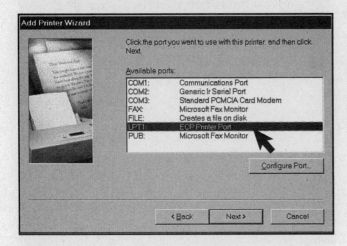

9 The wizard prompts you to specify the port to which the printer is connected. Choose **LPT1** if you connected the printer to the parallel port. Choose one of the COM ports if the printer is connected to a serial port. Click **Next**.

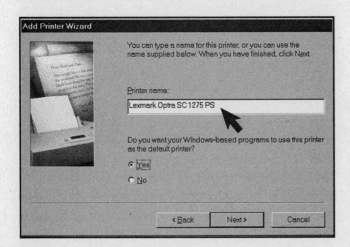

10 You are now prompted to type a name for the printer. Type the name as you want it to appear in the Printers folder.

11 To use this printer as the default for printing from all of your Windows programs, click **Yes** near the bottom of the dialog box. Click **Next**.

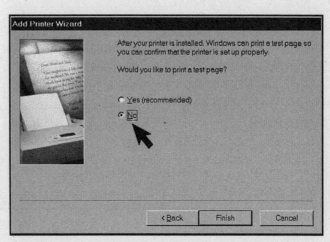

12 The wizard asks if you would like to print a test page. Click **Yes** or **No**. Then click **Finish**.

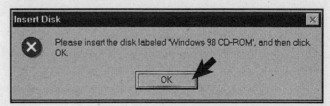

13 If the driver for the selected printer has not been installed, Windows prompts you to insert the Windows 98 CD-ROM disc or installation disk. Insert the CD-ROM disc or installation disk and click **OK**.

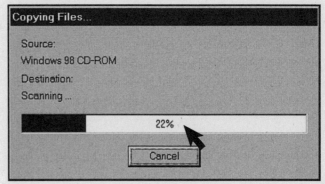

14 Windows copies the printer driver and any additional files from the CD-ROM disc or floppy disk to the hard disk drive.

(continues)

Guided Tour   Add a Printer

(continued)

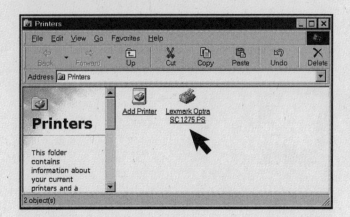

If you chose to install a printer driver included on the Windows installation disc or disk and Windows informs you that it cannot find the necessary file, click the **Browse** button and change to the **\Drivers\Printers** folder on the disc or disk.

15 You are returned to the Printers folder, which now contains an icon for the installed printer.

Configure a Mouse or Joystick

You probably already have a mouse connected to your computer, or you wouldn't have made it this far through the book. Because Windows is so point-and-click dependent, a mouse or other pointing device (such as a touchpad or trackball) is an essential tool. And if you have a fancy computer game, you might find that a joystick is equally essential. To fly a virtual airplane and shoot alien ships out of the sky, you need a device that gives you more control than a mouse does.

Installing the device itself is fairly easy because you do not have to remove the system unit cover to install an expansion board. Most mice plug in to the serial port or a special mouse port (PS/2) at the back (or front) of your computer. To install a joystick, you plug it in to the game port on the back of your computer. (Most sound cards include a port for plugging in one or more joysticks.) After connecting the device, run the Add New Hardware Wizard to install its driver, ▶as explained in "Install New Hardware" on page 364.◀

Once you have installed the device, take the *Guided Tour* to configure it. The first part of the *Guided Tour* shows you how to configure your mouse. The second part shows you how to calibrate your joystick.

> Many mouse and joystick manufacturers update their Windows drivers to improve them and fix bugs. Visit the manufacturer's Web site to determine if there is an updated driver for your device. You can then download the driver file and install it using the Add New Hardware Wizard.

Guided Tour   Configure Your Mouse

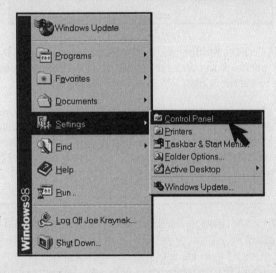

1 Click the **Start** button, point to **Settings**, and click **Control Panel**.

2 My Computer opens the Windows Control Panel. Click the **Mouse** icon.

(continues)

Guided Tour   Configure Your Mouse   *(continued)*

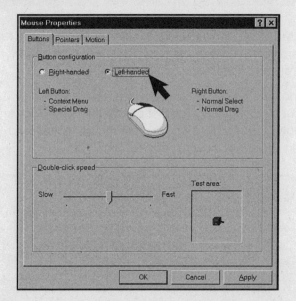

3 The Mouse Properties dialog box appears with the Buttons tab in front. If you are left-handed, click **Left-Handed**. This setting switches the buttons so that you click with the right button and "right-click" with the left button.

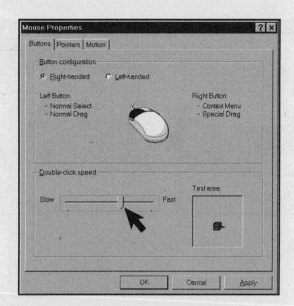

4 To change the speed at which you must click twice for a double-click, drag the **Double-Click Speed** slider to the left or right. You can double-click the jack-in-the-box to determine if you like the new setting.

You can also change the appearance of your mouse pointer. Click the **Pointers** tab and then open the **Scheme** drop-down list and select the desired mouse pointer collection.

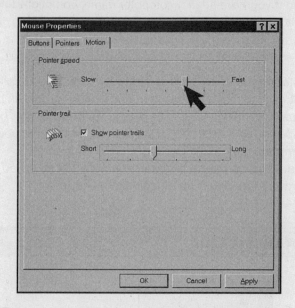

5 Click the **Motion** tab. To change the speed at which the pointer moves across the screen, drag the **Pointer Speed** slider to the left or right.

6 To have the mouse pointer leave a shadow as you move it, click **Show Pointer Trails** and use the slider to make the trails long or short. (This option is especially useful for notebook computers because the mouse pointer commonly disappears if you move the mouse fast.) Click **OK**.

Your Mouse Properties dialog box might have additional tabs or settings, depending on the mouse. If you have a Microsoft IntelliPoint Mouse, for instance, the Mouse Properties dialog box contains options for automating the mouse and configuring the wheel that sits between the left and right mouse buttons.

Guided Tour Calibrate Your Joystick

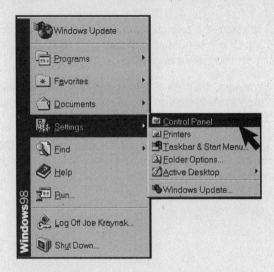

1 Click the **Start** button, point to **Settings**, and click **Control Panel**.

2 My Computer opens the Windows Control Panel. Click the **Game Controllers** icon.

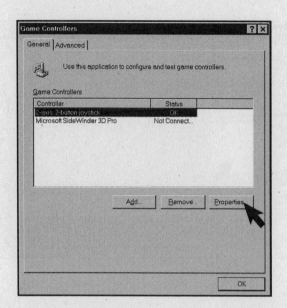

3 The Game Controllers dialog box appears. If you have more than one joystick connected to your computer, click the joystick you want to calibrate and click the **Properties** button.

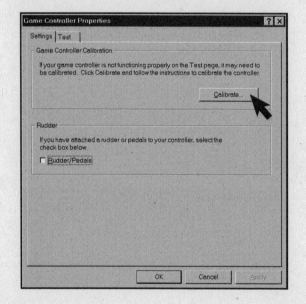

4 Click the **Calibrate** button.

(continues)

Guided Tour Calibrate Your Joystick   *(continued)*

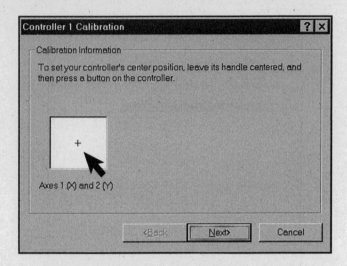

5 This starts the calibration procedure. Move the joystick and click its buttons as instructed. Click **Next** after performing each step in the calibration.

6 When you are done, Windows displays a message indicating that the calibration has been successfully completed. Click **Finish**.

7 You are returned to the Properties dialog box. Click **OK** to return to the Game Controllers dialog box, and then click **OK** to save your changes.

Install and Configure a Modem

Before you can connect to an online service or play around on the Internet, you must install a modem. The modem dials into the online service, establishes communications, and sends and receives data electronically. To receive data, the modem translates the analog signals, which travel through the phone lines, into digital signals that your computer can understand. To transmit data, the modem translates digital signals from your computer into analog signals.

The procedure for connecting a modem to your computer varies depending on the type of modem. If you have an external modem, you connect the modem to a serial port on the back of your computer using a serial cable. You must then plug the modem into an electrical outlet. An internal modem is an expansion board that plugs into an expansion slot inside the system unit. ▶See "Install an Expansion Board" on page 365 for details.◀

After connecting the modem to your computer, you must connect it to a phone line. Your modem should have two jacks: one to connect the modem to a phone jack in your home or office and another to connect the modem to a phone (so you can still use the phone to place phone calls). Use a standard phone cable to connect the modem to the phone jack and to your phone (if desired).

If you are using the same phone line for your modem and phone and you have call waiting, disable it before using the modem to dial your online service. Otherwise, if someone calls you while your modem is "talking," your modem will be disconnected. You typically disable call waiting by dialing *70 before making your connection. The *Guided Tour* shows you how to set up your modem to dial this number before placing a call. When your modem hangs up the phone, call waiting is automatically turned back on.

Guided Tour   Install a Modem

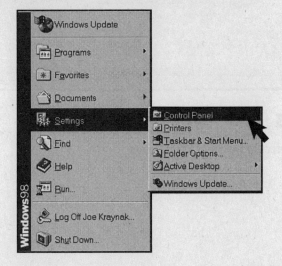

1 If you have an external modem, make sure it is turned on. Then click the **Start** button, point to **Settings**, and click **Control Panel**.

2 My Computer opens the Windows Control Panel. Click the **Modems** icon.

(continues)

Guided Tour Install a Modem *(continued)*

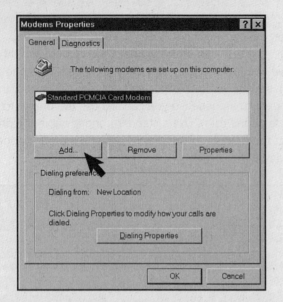

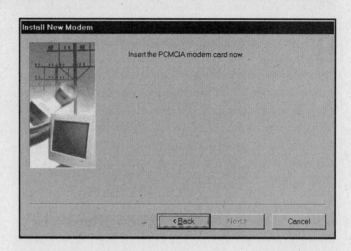

5 If you are installing a PCMCIA modem card, this dialog box appears. Insert the modem card in your computer's PCMCIA slot and click **Next**. (You may have to perform additional steps using the Add New Hardware Wizard.)

3 If you already set up a modem during the Windows installation, the Modems Properties dialog box, click **Add**. If you did not set up a modem, the Install New Modem Wizard starts automatically, so you don't have to click Add.

> If you are replacing a modem, select the old modem in the Modems Properties dialog box and click **Remove**. This will prevent any conflicts with the new modem.

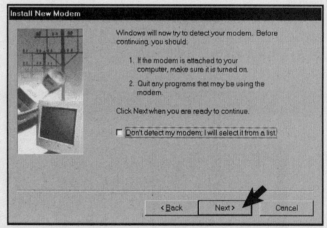

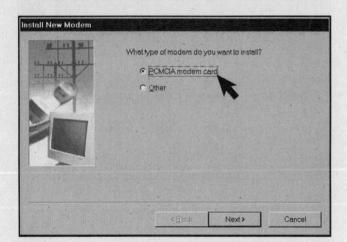

6 Windows offers to automatically detect the modem. If you would rather select your modem from a list, click **Don't Detect My Modem...**. Click **Next**.

4 If you have a notebook computer with PCMCIA slots, this dialog box appears. If you are installing a PCMCIA modem card, click **PCMCIA Modem Card**; otherwise, click **Other**. Click **Next**.

Guided Tour   Install a Modem

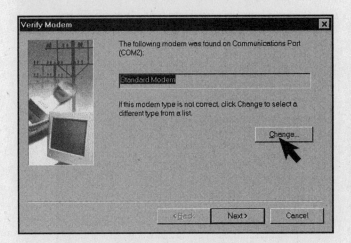

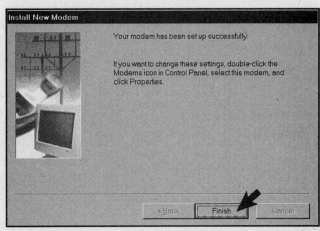

7 Windows displays the name of the modem it detected and the COM port the modem is using. If the modem type is incorrect, click the **Change** button and proceed to step 7. Otherwise, click **Next** and skip to step 9.

9 Windows displays a dialog box indicating that the modem has been successfully installed. Click **Finish**. (Windows might prompt you to insert the Windows installation disk or the disk that came with your modem. Follow the onscreen instructions.)

> If Windows cannot detect your modem, it displays a dialog box telling you so. Click **Next** and proceed to step 7 to select your modem from a list.

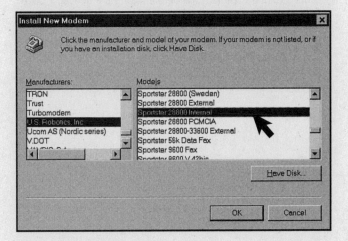

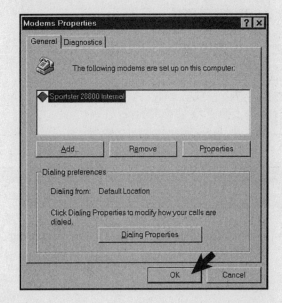

8 Windows displays a list of modem manufacturers and models. Select the manufacturer from the **Manufacturers** list and select the modem model in the **Models** list. (If the modem came with its own installation disk, click **Have Disk** and follow the onscreen instructions.) Click **Next**.

10 You are returned to the Modems Properties dialog box, where Windows displays the name of the installed modem. Click the **OK** button.

Guided Tour   Enter Dialing Preferences

1 Click the **Modems** icon in the Windows Control Panel.

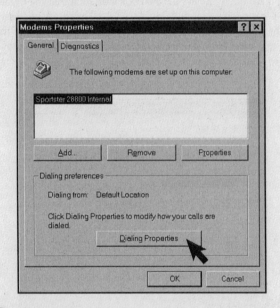

2 In the Modems Properties dialog box, click the **Dialing Properties** button.

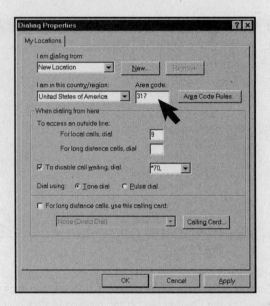

3 The Dialing Properties dialog box appears. Type your area code in the **Area Code** text box. This tells your modem to dial an area code only when the required area code differs from yours.

4 In the When Dialing from Here section, enter any numbers you must dial to access an outside line. For example, you might have to dial 9 to get any outside line. DO NOT type "1" in the For Long Distance Calls, Dial text box. Type a number only if you need to dial a special code before dialing the generic 1 commonly required for placing long-distance calls.

5 If you have call waiting, click to place a check mark next to **To Disable Call Waiting, Dial ___**, and then enter the number required to disable call waiting in your area. (This is usually ***70**.)

Guided Tour Enter Dialing Preferences

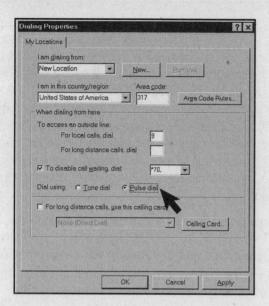

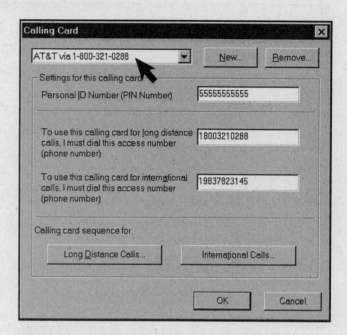

6 If you have rotary phone service (you can hear clicks instead of tones when you dial your phone), click **Pulse Dial**.

7 If you plan to use a calling card to place long distance calls, click to place a check mark next to **For Long Distance Calls, Use This Calling Card**, and then click the **Calling Card** button.

8 In the Change Calling Card dialog box, enter the requested calling card information. Click **OK**.

9 You are returned to the Dialing Properties dialog box. Click **OK** to return to the Modem Properties dialog box, and then click **OK** to save your settings.

Configure Multimedia Devices

Most new computers meet the current multimedia standards. They come complete with a CD-ROM drive, sound card, speakers, and microphone, and they have the memory, disk storage, and processing power needed to play audio and video clips and handle audio and video input. If you have an older computer, the following list will help you determine if your computer meets the *minimum* requirements for a multimedia PC. At the time this book was being written, the current standard was MPC3, which specified the following minimum configuration:

- A 75MHz Pentium processor

- SVGA (super video graphics array) monitor

- 8 megabytes of memory

- 540 megabyte hard drive with a 15-millisecond access time and 1.5 megabyte per second transfer rate

- 1.44 megabyte floppy drive

- 4X (quad speed) CD-ROM

- 16-bit stereo sound card with decent speakers

Once you know what you need, where do you get it? You have two options: Buy a multimedia upgrade kit, or buy the components separately. The easiest option is to go with the kit. That way, you know that the CD-ROM drive and sound card will work together and that you'll get all the cables and software you need to get the system up and running. Most upgrade kits also include a small collection of CDs so you get immediate gratification. Creative Labs, IBM, and Sony offer upgrade kits for under $700.

Assuming that you're shopping for something *new*, don't settle for a 4X CD-ROM drive or a 16-bit sound card. Look for an 8X or 12X CD-ROM drive or one of the new DVD drives and a wavetable sound card. That way, your equipment won't be obsolete in a year.

To upgrade to multimedia, you install a CD-ROM (or DVD) drive and a sound card. ▶See "Install New Hardware" on page 364 to learn how to set up your new equipment in Windows.◀ The following *Guided Tour* shows you how to configure your multimedia devices after they're installed.

Guided Tour   Enter Multimedia Settings

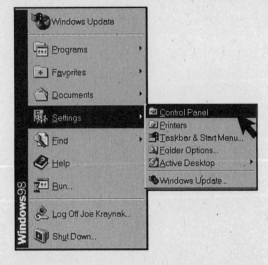

1 Click the **Start** button, point to **Settings**, and click **Control Panel**.

2 My Computer opens the Windows Control Panel. Click the **Multimedia** icon.

Guided Tour Enter Multimedia Settings

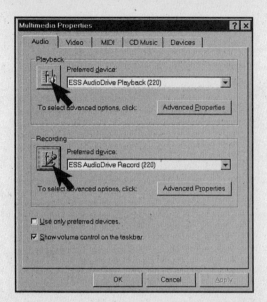

3 The Multimedia Properties dialog box appears with the Audio tab in front. To change the speaker or recording volume for your sound card, click the **Playback** or **Recording** button.

> For additional volume controls, right-click the speaker icon on the taskbar system tray and choose **Adjust Audio Properties.** You can use the volume control on your sound card, as well, to adjust the playback volume.

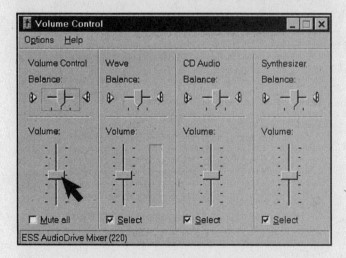

4 Drag the desired volume control slider(s) up to increase volume or down to decrease volume. When you are finished making your volume adjustments, click the **Close** (X) button.

5 To change the recording quality, open the **Preferred Quality** drop-down list and select the desired quality: · **CD Quality** (high), **Radio Quality** (medium), or **Phone Quality** (low). You can click the **Customize** button for finer control.

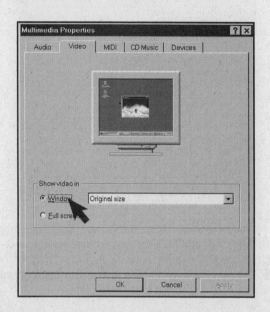

6 Click the **Video** tab and choose to display video clips in a **Window** or **Full Screen**. Although Full Screen is appealing, clips that are not designed for full-screen display look blocky when displayed full screen.

(continues)

Guided Tour   Enter Multimedia Settings

(continued)

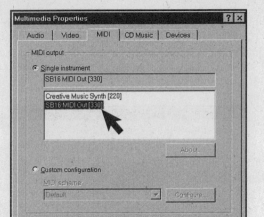

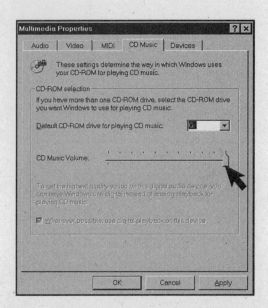

7 If you have a MIDI (Musical Instrument Digital Interface) device, such as a MIDI keyboard, connected to your computer, click the **MIDI** tab and enter the desired settings for the device. You can click the **Add New Instrument** button to add a MIDI device that's connected to the MIDI port.

8 Click the **CD Music** tab and drag the **CD Music Volume** slider to the left or right to adjust the audio output for the CD player. (This adjusts both the volume for the headphone jack on the CD player and the signal the CD player sends to the sound card.)

Most sound cards have a MIDI port. You plug a MIDI device, such as a music keyboard or synthesizer, into the port. You can then record your music.

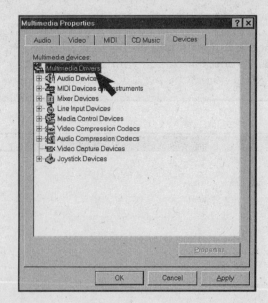

9 Click the **Devices** tab to view a list of multimedia devices that are connected to your computer. You should avoid changing the properties of a device unless you are having problems using it.

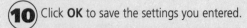

10 Click **OK** to save the settings you entered.

HOW TO...

Hit the Road with Portable Computers

Portable computers are becoming more and more powerful. Most notebook computers now include at least 16 megabytes of RAM, a one- or two-gigabyte hard disk, a CD-ROM drive and sound card, and several ports and expansion slots for installing additional equipment. Many notebooks are powerful enough to be used as replacements for desktop computers.

To keep up with these powerful new portable computers, Windows includes many features designed specifically for notebook computers, including Plug and Play support for PCMCIA cards, a power-saving utility, and programs for connecting to your desktop computer and for logging on to your network via modem. In this section, you will learn how to use these features to harness the power of your notebook computer.

What You Will Find in This Section

Add and Remove PCMCIA Cards

If you have ever installed an expansion board in a desktop computer, you know how inconvenient it is to upgrade your computer. You must remove the cover from your system unit, remove the cover plate at the back of the computer, install the board, and then put everything back together again. And if the board conflicts with other devices on your computer, you have to flip the hood again and use jumpers or DIP switches to change the card's settings.

Most newer notebook computers make it much easier to upgrade by using PCMCIA cards. Short for *Personal Computer Memory Card International Association*, PCMCIA is an organization that has developed a set of standards for small devices that plug directly into expansion slots on the *outside* of the computer. These cards are about the size of credit cards, and you can insert them when the power is on. It's sort of like inserting a disk in a floppy disk drive.

PCMCIA cards were originally designed to allow users to add memory to their notebook computers without having to open the case. Recent advances in the standards have allowed manufacturers to design other types of PCMCIA cards. You can now use a PCMCIA card to add a fax modem, network adapter, hard disk drive, and even a game port to your notebook. And because Windows supports Plug and Play PCMCIA, you can swap cards in and out of the slots without turning off the computer and without having to worry about setting jumpers or DIP switches to prevent hardware conflicts. The *Guided Tour* shows you just how easy it is.

When you are shopping for a PCMCIA card, you need to know the differences in the three types of cards. They are all the same length and width, but their height varies:

- Type I cards (up to 3.3mm thick) are used primarily to add memory to a computer.

- Type II cards (up to 5.5mm thick) are typically used to add a fax modem, network adapter, or CD-ROM drive (the drive is connected to the PCMCIA card with a cable).

- Type III cards (up to 10.5mm thick) are usually used to add a hard disk drive.

Your notebook computer should have one or more PCMCIA slots. The slots also come in three types:

- Type I slots can use only one Type I card.

- Type II slots can use one Type I card or two Type II cards.

- Type III slots can use one Type III card or one Type I card and a Type II card.

You can insert the card whether the power is on or off. When you insert the card with the power on, Windows automatically detects it and runs the Add New Hardware Wizard, which leads you through the process of installing a driver for the card.

Ideally, you should be able to insert and remove PCMCIA cards without having to turn off your computer or restart it. This is called *hot plugging*. However, some older PCMCIA cards and notebook computers may not support the latest PCMCIA standards, which allow for hot plugging. To prevent damaging your notebook PC or PCMCIA card, check the manufacturer's documentation to determine if it is safe to exchange cards while your system is running.

Guided Tour Insert a PCMCIA Card

1 Turn on your computer and insert the PCMCIA card (label up) into one of the PCMCIA slots on your computer. If you have two empty slots, typically marked 0 and 1, use the number 0 (top) slot first. The card should be firmly seated in the slot, but don't force it.

2 If the card requires you to connect a cable or phone line, plug the cable or phone line into the opening on the card.

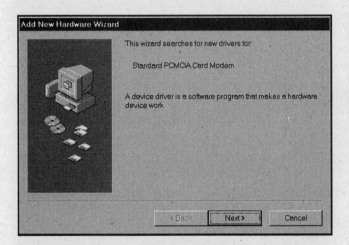

3 Windows sounds a two-tone beep (a medium tone followed by a high tone). If this is the first time you've inserted the card, Windows runs the Add New Hardware Wizard. Click **Next**.

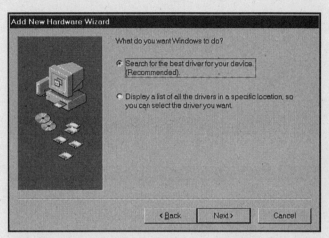

4 The wizard asks if you want to search for the best driver for the device or display the drivers on a specific disk. Click **Search for the Best Driver for Your Device** and click **Next**.

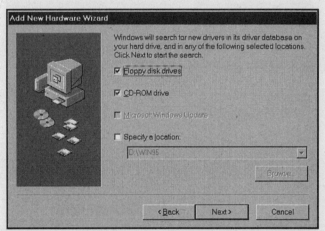

5 The wizard displays a list of all of the locations it will search. If the device came with an installation disk or CD, insert it into the floppy disk drive or CD-ROM drive, and select **Floppy Disk Drives** and **CD-ROM Drive**. The Microsoft Windows Update option tells the wizard to search the Web, although this option may not be available. Click **Next**.

You may want to check the Specify a Location option, if you downloaded an updated driver from the Web site of the manufacturer of the device, so you can specify the location of the file on your hard disk.

(continues)

Guided Tour Insert a PCMCIA Card *(continued)*

If you have not yet registered your copy of Windows 98, the Microsoft Windows Update option will be unavailable (grayed out). See ►"Update Windows" on page 420 for more information about Microsoft Windows Update.◄

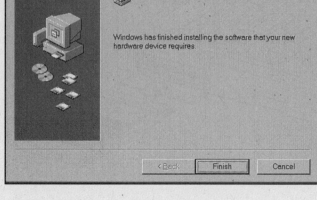

6 The wizard locates the required driver and displays its name. Click **Next**.

7 The wizard displays a message indicating that it has successfully installed the driver. Click **Finish**.

Guided Tour Remove a PCMCIA Card

1 Click the PC Card (PCMCIA) Status icon in the system tray, and then choose the **Stop...** option for the card you want to remove.

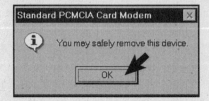

2 A dialog box appears, indicating that it is safe to remove the card. Click **OK**.

3 Press the Eject button next to the PCMCIA card. The card pops out of the slot, and Windows emits a two-toned beep (a high tone followed by a medium tone). Pull the card out of the slot.

Windows manages your PCMCIA cards automatically, keeping track of shared memory and sounding a beep whenever you insert or remove a card. However, you can change the settings for your PCMCIA cards. Right-click the **PC Card (PCMCIA) Status** icon in the system tray on the right end of the taskbar and choose **Adjust PC Card Properties**.

Synchronize Your Notebook and Desktop with Briefcase

If you have both a notebook and desktop computer, you probably need to transfer files from your desktop computer to your notebook computer to take work with you on trips. If you edit the files on your notebook computer, you must then copy them back to the desktop computer to ensure that you have the most recent versions on both computers.

Of course, you can exchange files between your notebook and desktop computers by using My Computer or Windows Explorer to transfer the files with a floppy disk. However, this is not the most efficient or secure method. If you happen to forget which files are the most recent, you run the risk of replacing the new versions with older ones.

Fortunately, Windows offers a convenient tool for safely transferring files between computers: Briefcase. With Briefcase, you open an electronic "briefcase," copy the

desired files to it, and then drag the Briefcase icon over your floppy disk icon. Windows copies all the files in the Briefcase to the floppy disk. Briefcase is useful not only for transferring files between a notebook and desktop PC, but also between any two PCs (for instance, between your and your colleague's PCs.)

Briefcase also keeps track of file versions to help prevent the chance of overwriting newer files with their older versions. When you copy files back to your desktop computer, Briefcase indicates which files are newer and helps you decide which files should be updated.

> Briefcase can store only as much data as will fit on a floppy disk. If you need to transfer more data, you must create a new Briefcase, as shown in the *Guided Tour*.

Guided Tour Transfer Files from Desktop to Notebook

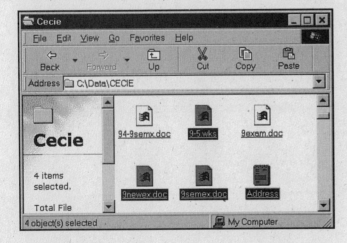

① In Windows Explorer or My Computer, select the folder(s) or file(s) you want to place in your Briefcase.

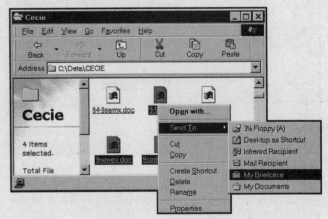

② Right-click one of the selected items, point to **Send To**, and click **My Briefcase**.

(continues)

Guided Tour   Transfer Files from Desktop to Notebook   *(continued)*

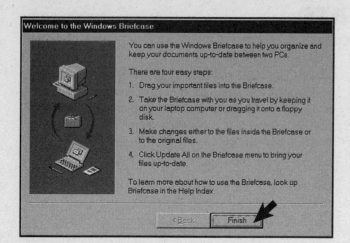

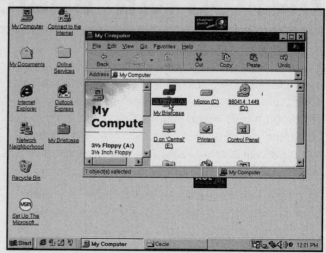

3 The Welcome to the Windows Briefcase dialog box displays a brief overview of how to use Briefcase. (If Briefcase was used on this computer before, this dialog box will not appear.) Click **Finish**, and Windows copies the selected items to your Briefcase.

6 Drag the My Briefcase icon over the floppy disk icon and release the mouse button. Windows moves My Briefcase and its contents to the floppy disk.

7 Eject the disk and pack it with your notebook computer.

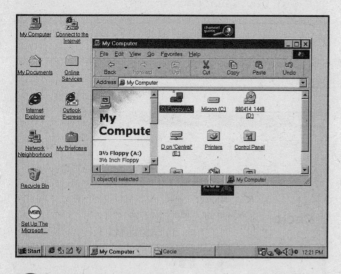

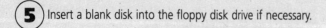

4 In Windows Explorer or My Computer, display the icon for your floppy disk drive. Move and resize the window so you can see the My Briefcase icon.

5 Insert a blank disk into the floppy disk drive if necessary.

Guided Tour Use Your Briefcase on the Road

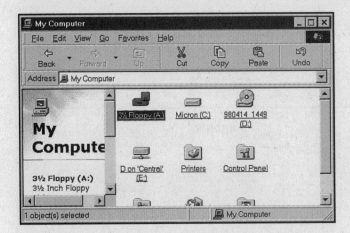

1 Turn on your notebook computer and insert the floppy disk. In Windows Explorer or My Computer, click the icon for the floppy disk drive.

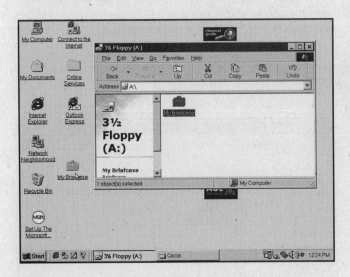

2 The contents of the disk are displayed. Drag the My Briefcase icon onto the Windows desktop. Windows moves My Briefcase and its contents to the desktop.

If you already have a My Briefcase icon on your Windows desktop, Windows displays a warning indicating that it will be replaced. If your Briefcase is empty, go ahead and replace it. Otherwise, cancel the operation and rename My Briefcase on the floppy disk before moving it to the desktop.

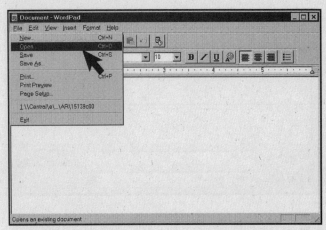

3 To open a file from the Briefcase, run the program you want to use to open the file and choose its **File**, **Open** command.

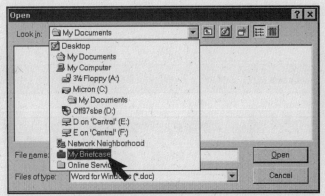

4 The Open dialog box prompts you to choose a file. Open the **Look In** drop-down list and choose **My Briefcase**.

(continues)

Guided Tour   Use Your Briefcase on the Road   *(continued)*

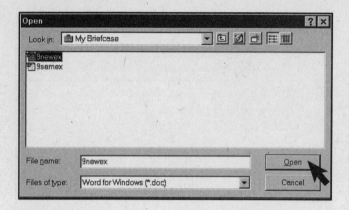

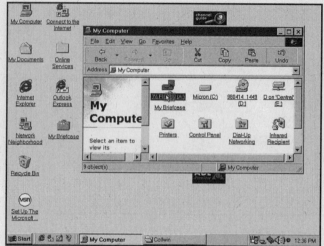

5 Choose the file you want to open and click the **Open** button. The program opens the file and displays its contents. Enter your changes and save the file.

6 When you are ready to end your trip, insert a disk into your notebook's floppy drive. Drag the **My Briefcase** icon over the icon for your floppy drive and release the mouse button. Windows copies the briefcase to the floppy disk.

Guided Tour   Returning My Briefcase to Your Desktop Computer

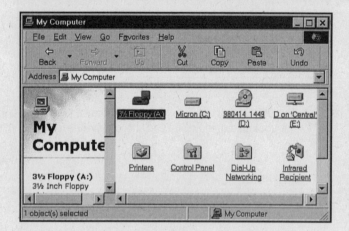

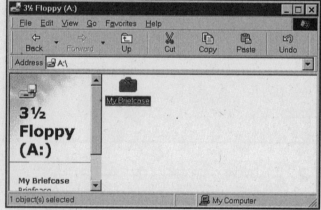

1 When you return from your trip, insert the Briefcase floppy disk into your desktop PC's floppy disk drive. In My Computer or Windows Explorer, click the icon for the floppy disk drive.

2 Drag the My Briefcase icon from My Computer or Windows Explorer onto the Windows desktop. Then click the **My Briefcase** icon to display its contents.

Guided Tour Returning My Briefcase to Your Desktop Computer

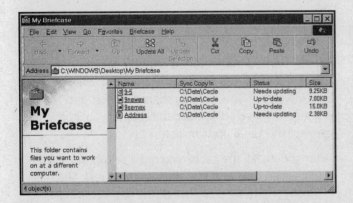

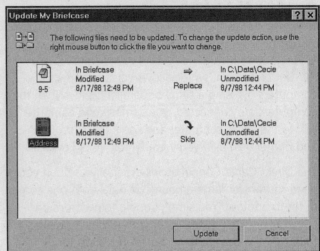

③ The My Briefcase window displays the folders and files in the Briefcase. Open the **Briefcase** menu and choose **Update All** (or click **Update All** in the toolbar).

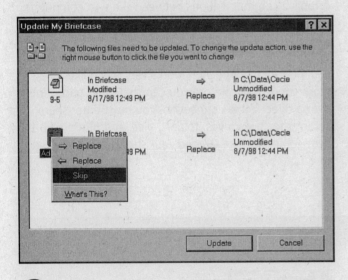

⑤ After marking any files you want to skip, click the **Update** button. Windows updates the files automatically.

You can also transfer files between a notebook and desktop computer by connecting the parallel or serial ports on the two computers with a special cable, as explained in the next section, "Link Your Notebook and Desktop Computers." You can then copy files using My Computer or Windows Explorer or by dragging My Briefcase from one computer to the other.

④ The Update My Briefcase window displays a list of the old and new versions of all of the files. To prevent a file from being updated, right-click it and choose **Skip**.

Link Your Notebook and Desktop Computers

Windows includes a feature called Direct Cable Connection, which allows you to connect two computers by using a serial or parallel cable. When the computers are connected, you can use one computer to link to the other computer and use its files, programs, and printer, just as if you were typing at its keyboard.

The Direct Cable Connection is especially useful if you need to transfer large amounts of data from one computer to another. You simply copy a folder from one computer, switch to the other computer, and paste the folder on the desired hard disk. You can do this between a notebook and desktop computer, between two desktop computers, or between two notebook computers.

Set Up a Connection

To set up a direct cable connection, you must first connect the serial or parallel ports on the two computers. To connect the serial ports, you must have a *serial null-modem cable* (sometimes called a *file transfer cable*), a special serial cable that is designed for direct data transfers instead of modem communications. Connecting the

parallel ports is the preferred method because they transfer data 10–15 times faster than the serial ports do. However, if you want to share a printer and the printer is connected to the parallel port, you'll have to connect the serial ports instead.

After you install the cable, you must set up one computer as the *host* and the other as the *guest*. The host is usually the more powerful of the two computers. If you are connecting a desktop and notebook computer, for example, the desktop computer will typically be the host. The *Guided Tour* shows you how to connect the two computers and set up Direct Cable Connection to establish communications between the two computers.

Share Resources

A direct cable connection works very much like a network connection. Before you can share files and printers over a direct cable connection, you must enter share settings for disk drives, folders, files, and printers on the host computer. The *Guided Tour* shows you just what to do.

Guided Tour Set Up a Direct Cable Connection

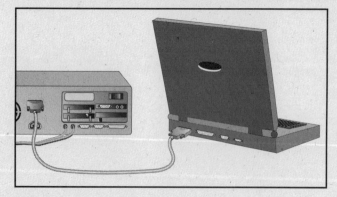

1 Connect your two computers using a standard parallel printer cable or a serial null-modem cable.

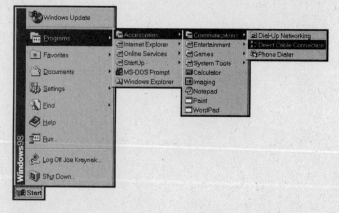

2 On the host computer, click the **Start** button, point to **Programs, Accessories, Communications**, and then click **Direct Cable Connection**.

Guided Tour Set Up a Direct Cable Connection

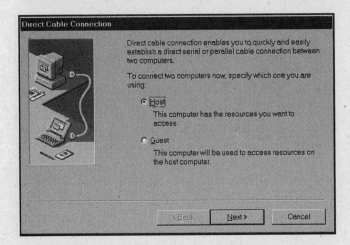

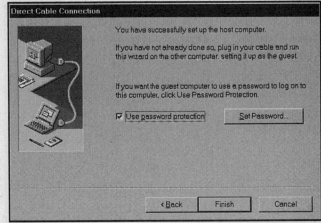

3 The Direct Cable Connection Wizard appears. Click **Host** and click **Next**.

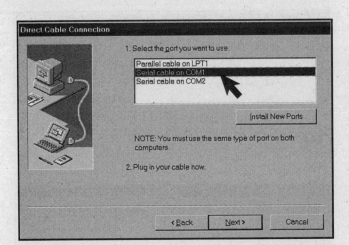

4 You are prompted to pick the port into which you plugged the cable. Select the port and click **Next**.

5 (Optional) To prevent unauthorized access to your computer, choose **Use Password Protection**. Then click the **Set Password** button, enter the password in the two text boxes, and click **OK**.

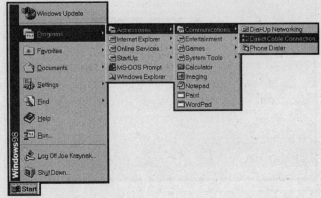

6 On the guest computer, click the **Start** button, point to **Programs**, **Accessories**, **Communications**, and click **Direct Cable Connection**.

(continues)

Guided Tour Set Up a Direct Cable Connection

(continued)

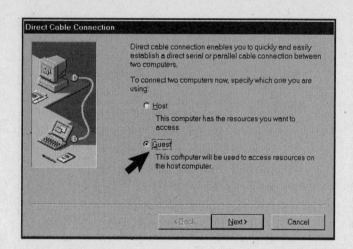

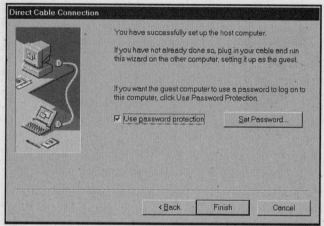

7 The Direct Cable Connection Wizard starts. Click **Guest** and click **Next**.

9 Go back to the host computer and click **Finish**.

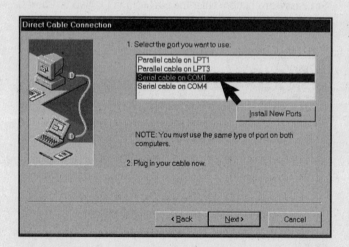

10 The host computer displays a dialog box, indicating that it is waiting for the guest computer to connect.

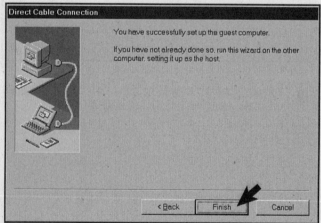

8 You are prompted to pick the port into which you plugged the cable. Select the port and click **Next**.

11 On the guest computer, click **Finish**.

Guided Tour Set Up a Direct Cable Connection

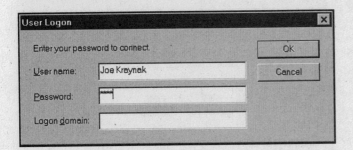

If you run into trouble connecting your computers with Direct Cable Connection, the problem may be caused by a conflict with your Dial-Up Networking (Internet) connection. Try disconnecting from the Internet.

12 If you set password protection on the host computer, a dialog box appears on the guest computer, prompting you to enter the password. Type the password and click **OK**.

Guided Tour Share a Disk or Folder on Your Computer

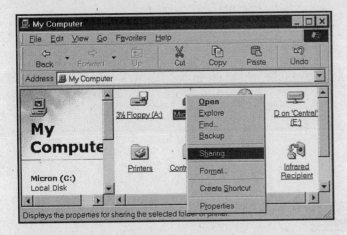

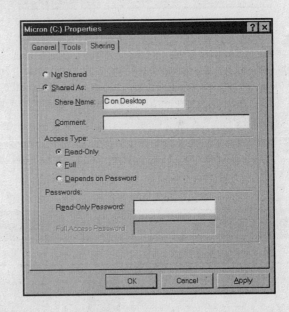

1 Run My Computer or Windows Explorer. Then right-click the icon for the disk or folder you want to share and choose **Sharing**.

If the Sharing option is not on the context menu, you may need to install File and Printer Sharing. In the Windows Control panel, click the **Network** icon. Click File and Print Sharing and make sure both sharing options are checked. You'll need to insert your Windows CD to complete the installation.

2 The Properties dialog box for the selected disk or folder appears with the Sharing tab in front. Click **Shared As**.

3 The **Share Name** text box automatically displays the drive's letter or the folder's name as it will appear on the other computer. You can type a different entry in this text box, if desired.

4 (Optional) Type any additional information in the **Comment** text box.

(continues)

Guided Tour Share a Disk or Folder on Your Computer *(continued)*

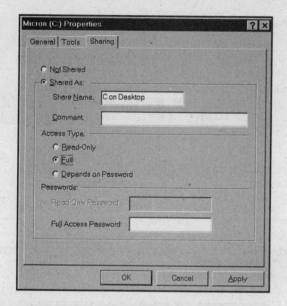

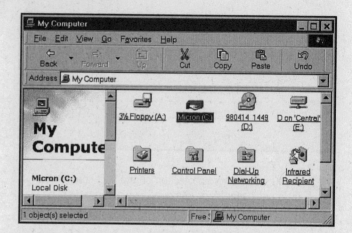

7 You are returned to My Computer or Windows Explorer, and a hand appears as part of the icon for the shared disk or folder. The next *Guided Tour* shows you how to access the disk or folder from the other computer.

5 Under Access Type, choose the desired share option: **Read-Only** (to allow the other computer to open and copy files, but not delete, rename, change, or replace them), **Full** (to make the disk act just as it would if it were installed on the other computer), or **Depends on Password** (to use a different password for read-only or full access).

6 Leave the Password text box(es) blank, so you won't have to enter a password to access the shared disk or folder. Click **OK**.

> To terminate sharing, right-click the icon for the disk or folder and choose **Sharing**. On the General tab of the Properties dialog box, select **Not Shared** and click **OK**.

Guided Tour Access a Shared Disk or Folder

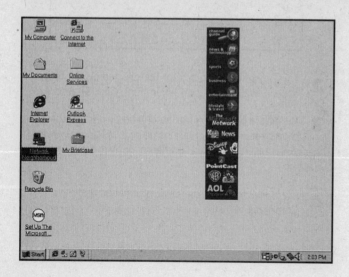

1 Once you mark a disk or folder as shared on one computer, you can display its contents on the other computer. On the computer you are using to access the shared disk or folder, click the **Network Neighborhood** icon on the Windows desktop.

Guided Tour Access a Shared Disk or Folder

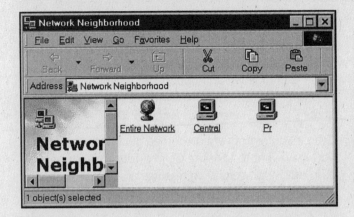

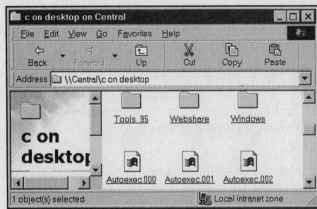

2 My Computer opens the Network Neighborhood and displays icons for both computers. Click the icon for the computer you want to access.

4 Folders and files appear as if they were on your computer. If you have full access to the disk and folder, you can copy files from one computer to the other.

Shared disks are
displayed as folders

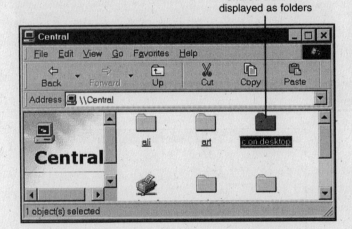

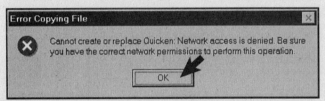

5 If you try to enter a command that you do not have permission to enter, an error message appears, indicating that the network has denied you access. Click **OK**.

3 A folder is displayed for each shared disk and folder on the other computer. Click the icon for the disk or folder you want to access.

To make a disk on one computer appear right inside the My Computer window and in the Save and Open dialog boxes in your programs, *map* the drive to your computer. To map a drive, right-click its icon in the Network Neighborhood, choose **Map Network Drive**, and choose a letter for the drive. You can choose Reconnect at Logon to have Windows call up that drive whenever you start Windows.

Save Energy

Although a computer doesn't consume quite as much energy as an energy hog like a central air conditioner, it does use quite a bit of energy over the long haul, especially if you keep your computer running all the time. In addition, if you're running a notebook PC on battery power, if the PC is running even when you're not, it keeps using energy until the battery goes dead.

To help, Windows has a power-saving feature that can help reduce the amount of energy your computer uses. These features can double the life of your notebook PC's battery and help trim your electric bill by powering down your monitor and hard disk drive after a specified amount of time. You can even turn on warnings to have Windows notify you when the battery is running down, so you can save your work and shut down Windows before the battery goes dead.

To change any of the power saving settings in Windows, you use the Power Management utility in the Control Panel. When you click the Power Management icon, a dialog box appears, presenting you with two sets of power-saving options: options for when the computer is plugged in and options for when it is running on batteries. You simply enter the desired settings, as shown in the *Guided Tour*, and click **OK**.

Even if you're not very concerned about saving power, you may want to take the *Guided Tour* to learn how to turn off the power-saving features or increase the time that Windows waits before going on standby.

If your computer is going to be inactive for more than a couple of hours, you should turn it off to conserve even more energy. Although Windows can save a great deal of power by shutting down your monitor and hard disk drive, your computer still consumes power even when these components are powered down.

Guided Tour   Enter Power-Saving Settings

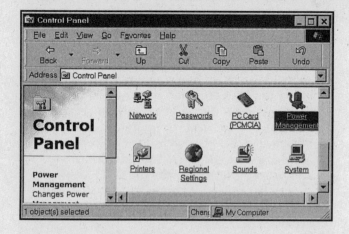

1 Open the **Control Panel** and click the **Power Management** icon.

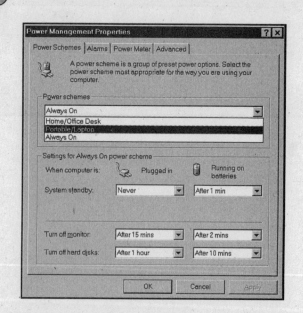

2 The Power Management dialog box appears. For a notebook PC, the dialog box will appear as shown above; for desktop PCs, the dialog box has no options for running on batteries. Open the **Power Schemes** drop-down list and choose **Home/Office Desk**, **Portable/Laptop**, or **Always On** (to disable the power-saving features).

Guided Tour Enter Power-Saving Settings

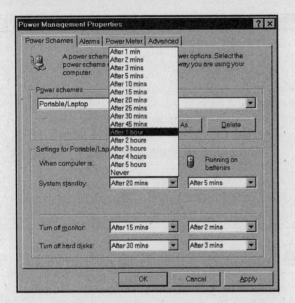

Consider increasing the number of minutes or hours of inactivity for the Plugged In options so that Windows does not shut down your computer after only a few minutes of inactivity. You may want to decrease the setting under Running on Batteries to conserve additional energy on a notebook PC.

3 Open the **System Standby** drop-down list (unavailable for desktop PCs) and choose the number of minutes or hours of inactivity you want to pass before Windows puts your computer in Standby mode (turning off the monitor and hard drive, but ready to leap into action). (On a notebook PC, you have two drop-down lists for choosing the number of minutes of inactivity: Plugged in and Running on Batteries. You can use either or both drop-down lists.)

5 Open the **Turn Off Hard Disks** drop-down list and choose the number of minutes or hours of inactivity you'll allow to pass before Windows turns off the hard disk drives.

(continues)

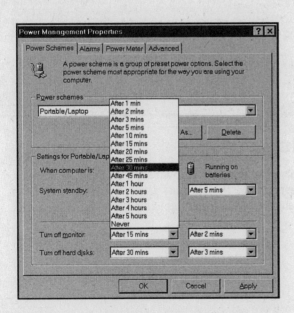

4 Open the **Turn Off Monitor** drop-down list and choose the number of minutes of inactivity you'll allow to pass before Windows turns off the monitor. Again, on notebook PC, you can choose from either or both of two lists.

Guided Tour Enter Power-Saving Settings *(continued)*

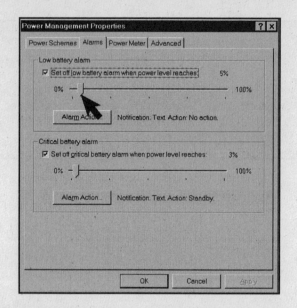

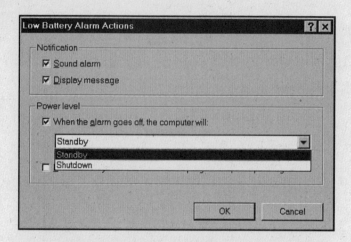

9 Under Power Level, click **When the Alarm Goes Off, the Computer Will**, and then open the drop-down list and choose **Standby** or **Shutdown**. Standby keeps Windows running, but turns off the monitor and hard disk drives.

6 (Notebook PC only. If you have a desktop PC, skip to Step 12.) Click the **Alarms** tab. By default, Windows displays a message whenever the battery power level reaches 5% and 3%. You can drag the sliders to the right to be notified sooner or to the left to be notified later.

7 To change the way Windows notifies you of low battery power, click one of the **Alarm Action** buttons.

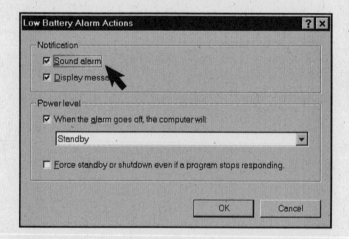

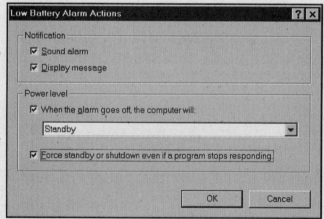

10 To force your notebook computer to go into Standby or Shutdown mode even if a program is not responding, click **Force Standby or Shutdown Even if a Program Stops Responding.** (This can cause data loss, however, so you may want to leave this option off.) Click **OK.**

8 In the Low Battery Alarm Actions dialog box, turn on **Sound Alarm** if you want Windows to sound an alarm when the battery power drops to the specified level. The text alarm is on by default, but you can turn it off.

Guided Tour Enter Power-Saving Settings

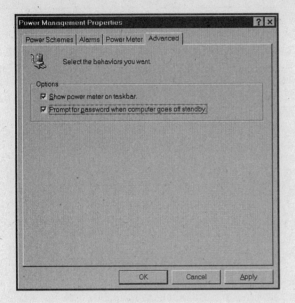

11 Click the **Advanced** tab. **Show Power Meter on Taskbar** is on by default. You should leave this option on, so you can easily see the battery power level in the system tray.

12 To prevent unauthorized use of your computer when it goes off standby, choose **Prompt for Password When Computer Goes Off Standby**. Click **OK**.

If you leave Show Power Meter on Taskbar turned on, a battery icon appears in the system tray (on the right end of the taskbar). To see how much power is left, rest the mouse pointer on the icon. If your notebook is plugged in, Windows displays a plug icon.

HOW TO...

Maintain Your Computer

Some computer maintenance is like VCR maintenance: You have to keep your computer and the area around it dust free, clean the floppy disk drive, pick out dust balls from your mouse, wipe the monitor, and check your cable connections regularly.

Most computer maintenance, however, is software related. As you use your computer, the hard disk drive can become packed with files you don't use. You need to clear them from your system to create room for your programs and data files. In addition, you should check your hard disk drive and repair any errors on it, back up your files, and make sure you have the latest Windows 98 updates installed. You should also have an emergency disk at hand just in case your computer fails to start with Windows.

In this section, you will learn all the tasks you need to perform to keep your computer in peak operating condition.

What You Will Find in This Section

Change Display Properties

When you installed Windows, the installation automatically selected a monitor type for you and set the color of the desktop background. Unless you have stumbled across the Display icon in the Control Panel, you might think that you are stuck with the colors and appearance of your screen. The truth is that you have almost complete control over the appearance of Windows.

To change the look of your desktop or the resolution (quality) of the display, you can click the **Display** icon in the Control Panel or right-click a blank area of the desktop and choose **Properties**. In either case, the Display Properties dialog box appears, presenting tabs for changing the desktop colors, controlling the appearance of icons, turning on a screen saver, and increasing or decreasing the display resolution. The *Guided Tour* shows you just what to do.

As you work through the *Guided Tour*, you should know that some of the options require additional system resources. Turning on a Windows wallpaper graphic and using background patterns and screen savers take up memory. If your system seems sluggish after you turn on an option, consider turning the option off.

Install a Video Driver

Your computer's display is controlled by two components: the monitor and the display adapter (the expansion board into which you plug the monitor). For your monitor to work correctly, Windows must have the correct video driver installed for your display adapter and monitor. When you installed Windows, the installation utility automatically selected and installed a video driver that should work. If you are satisfied with the appearance of Windows and your other programs, you should not change the video driver. Picking the wrong driver might blank your screen, making it impossible for you to use your computer.

However, if Windows is not displayed properly or if you know that your monitor is capable of displaying a higher-quality picture, you should install the driver that came with your monitor or an updated driver designed specifically for your monitor and display adapter. Many

companies make updated video drivers available on their Web sites. You can also check for updated video drivers using the Add New Hardware Wizard. The *Guided Tour* provides step-by-step instructions.

Change the Screen Resolution

Most monitors are capable of displaying at various resolutions and colors. For example, an SVGA (Super Video Graphics Array) can display at 640×480, 800×600, or 1024×768 pixels (or higher). A *pixel* is an onscreen dot. The more pixels, the higher the resolution and display quality. Monitors can also display a range of colors: 16, 256, High Color (16-bit), or True Color (32-bit). Increasing the number of colors also increases the display quality.

If you notice that graphics or video clips look grainy on Web pages or in your documents, you should check the screen resolution and color settings, as shown in the *Guided Tour*. You can also decrease the resolution to display larger icons and menus if you have difficulty seeing these objects or to increase the overall speed of your computer.

Use a Screen Saver

A screen saver is a utility that blanks your monitor or displays a moving picture on it when your computer has been inactive for a specified amount of time. In the past, screen savers protected the monitor by preventing a screen from burning its image into the video tube. Current video tubes are less susceptible to damage from an unchanging display.

However, screen savers are still useful for preventing passersby from reading a file that's currently displayed on your monitor and for providing a low level of password protection. With a password-protected screen saver, a person must enter the correct password to turn off the screen saver and return to Windows. Windows comes with several screen savers you can use. Take the *Guided Tour* to turn on one of these screen savers.

Guided Tour Open the Display Properties Dialog Box

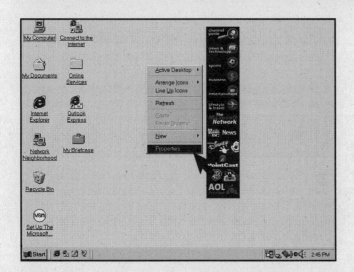

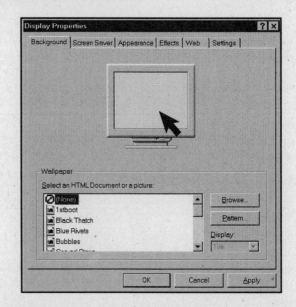

1 You will use the Display Properties dialog box to enter your Windows display preferences. To display this dialog box, right-click a blank area of the Windows desktop and choose **Properties**.

2 The Display Properties dialog box appears. Whenever you change a display option, the Preview area displays the Windows desktop as it will appear with the current settings. Use this dialog box in the following sections of the *Guided Tour* to enter your preferences.

Guided Tour Change the Windows Background

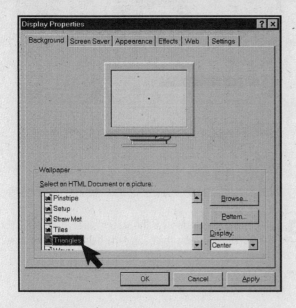

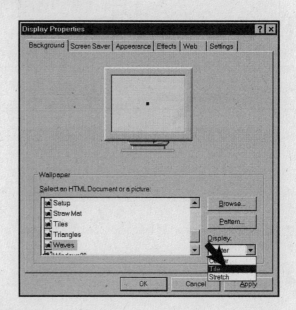

1 In the Display Properties dialog box, on the background tab under Wallpaper, choose the design you want to use as your Windows wallpaper.

2 Open the **Display** drop-down list and choose **Center** (to display the selected design in the center of the desktop) or **Tile** (to repeat the design as needed to cover the desktop).

(continues)

Guided Tour Change the Windows Background

(continued)

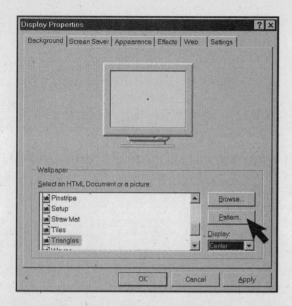

Tile is the best option for most of the prefab wallpaper designs because they are so small. You can also use the Stretch option to make the small graphic fill the screen, but the image may appear blurry or distorted. If you want to use a large graphic you obtained from the Web or another source, choose **Center**.

3 If you chose Center, click the **Pattern** button, choose a pattern to fill in any blank space around the design, and click **OK**. (The pattern will appear behind any icon names, so make sure you choose a pattern that won't make the icon names unreadable.) Click **OK** to save your changes.

Guided Tour Turn on a Screen Saver

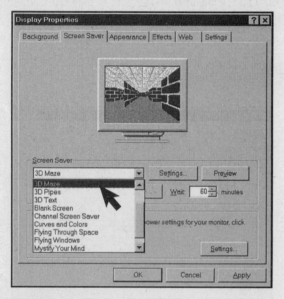

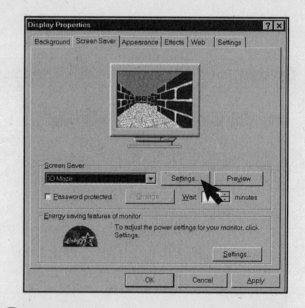

1 In the Display Properties dialog box, click the **Screen Saver** tab.

2 Open the **Screen Saver** drop-down list and choose the desired screen saver.

3 The preview area displays the screen saver in action. Click the **Settings** button to change the behavior of the screen saver.

Guided Tour Turn on a Screen Saver

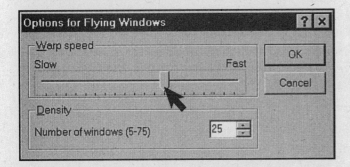

4 The available options vary depending on the screen saver you selected. Enter the desired settings for the screen saver you chose. For example, if you chose Flying Windows, you can enter the desired number of flying windows and the speed at which they fly. Click **OK**.

> Don't be surprised if your screen saver automatically goes blank. The Windows power saving features, described in ▶"Save Energy," on page 400◀, may turn off the monitor automatically, shutting down your screen saver.

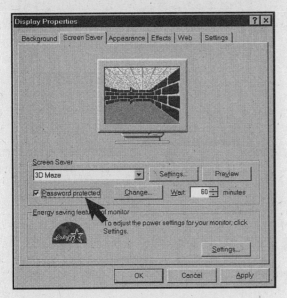

5 To protect your computer against unauthorized use, click **Password Protected** and click the **Change** button.

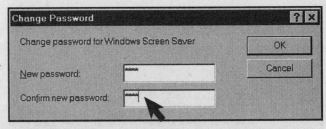

6 In the Change Password dialog box, type the password you want to use. Then click in the **Confirm New Password** text box and retype the password. Click **OK**.

> Write down your password and store it in a safe place, in case you forget it. However, the screen-saver password is easy to bypass. You shut down your computer, restart it, and then turn off the password option in the Display Properties dialog box before the screen saver kicks in.

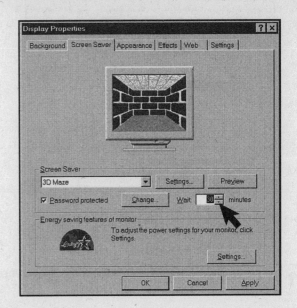

7 Use the **Wait** spin box to specify the number of minutes of inactivity that should pass before the screen saver kicks in. Click **OK**.

(continues)

Guided Tour   Turn on a Screen Saver

(continued)

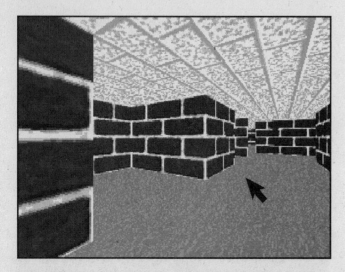

8 When the specified period of inactivity passes, the screen saver starts. Move your mouse or press a key to turn it off and return to the desktop. If you turned on password protection, you are prompted to enter your password. Type the password and click **OK**.

Guided Tour   Change the Windows Colors

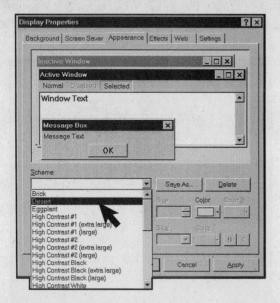

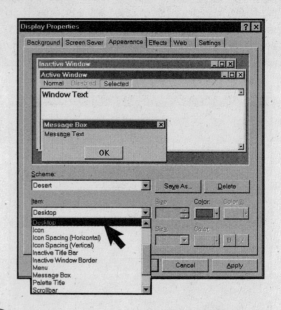

1 In the Display Properties dialog box, click the **Appearance** tab.

2 Open the **Scheme** drop-down list and choose the desired color scheme. The preview area displays the appearance of Windows with the selected color scheme. Try out several schemes until you find a color scheme that has most of the colors you want.

3 To change the color of an individual item (such as a title bar or the Windows desktop), click on the item in the preview area or select the item from the **Item** drop-down list.

Guided Tour Change the Windows Colors

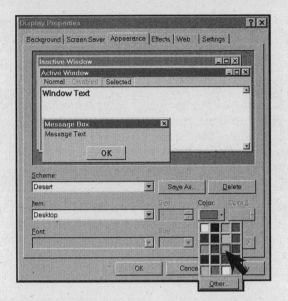

4 Open the **Color** drop-down list and choose the desired color.

5 For some items, you can change the size of the item. Use the **Size** spin box to make the object larger or smaller.

6 If the item contains text, you can change the font, size, and color of the text and make the text bold or italic.

7 Repeat steps 3 through 6 to change the appearance of additional items. When you finish, click **OK**.

Guided Tour Change the Look of Windows Icons

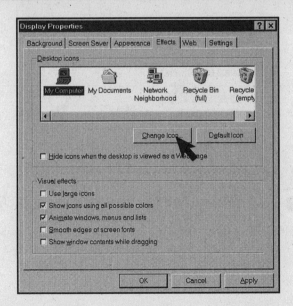

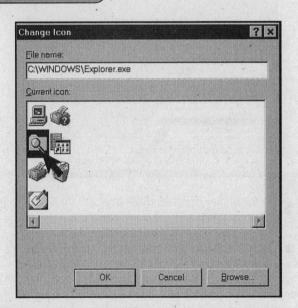

1 In the Display Properties dialog box, click the **Effects** tab. To change a desktop icon, click the icon in the **Desktop Icons** list and click the **Change Icon** button.

2 In the **Current Icon** list, click the icon you want to use, and then click **OK**.

(continues)

Guided Tour Change the Look of Windows Icons *(continued)*

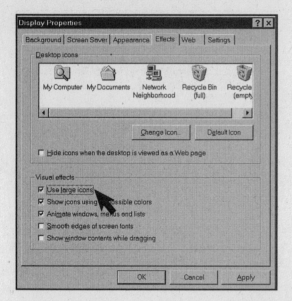

The icon selection is limited. You can click the **Browse** button and look for additional files that contain icons. Files that end in .exe, .dll, and .ico commonly contain additional icons. Before looking for icons, however, enter the **View, Folder Options** command in My Computer. Then click the **View** tab and remove the check box next to **Hide File Extensions for Known File Types**.

3 Under Visual Effects, select any other desired options. (The Use Large Icons setting is particularly helpful for people with vision problems.) Click **OK**. Repeat steps 2 and 3 to change other desktop icons.

Guided Tour Adjust Screen Colors and Resolution

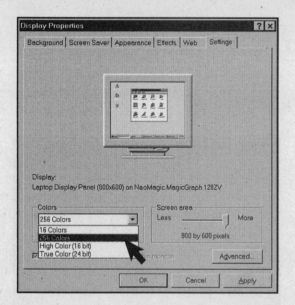

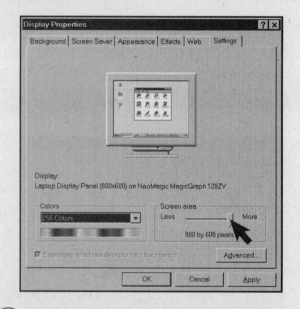

1 In the Display Properties dialog box, click the **Settings** tab.

2 Open the **Colors** drop-down list and choose the desired number of colors. Although a higher number of colors improves the appearance of graphics and video, it also requires more processing power and system resources. 256 is a good choice for most purposes. If you surf the Web, choose the 16-bit color option.

3 Drag the **Screen Area** slider to the left or right to specify the desired resolution. A higher resolution enables Windows to fit more on the screen by making the objects smaller. On the other hand, if you have trouble seeing the text, try a lower resolution. 800×600 is the best setting for general use. Click **OK**.

Guided Tour Install a New Video Driver

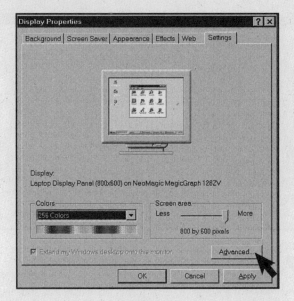

1 In the Display Properties dialog box, click the **Settings** tab and click the **Advanced** button.

2 In the Properties dialog box for your monitor, click the **Adapter** tab and click the **Change** button.

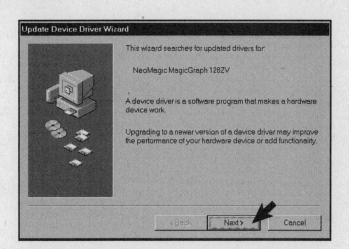

3 The Upgrade Device Driver Wizard appears. Click **Next**.

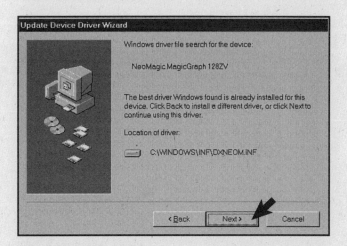

4 **Search for a Better Driver...** is already chosen. Click **Next**.

(continues)

Guided Tour Install a New Video Driver

(continued)

5 If you have a floppy disk or CD-ROM with the new video driver on it, insert the disk, and then turn on **Floppy Disk Drives** or **CD-ROM Drive**. (Remove the check marks from these boxes if you don't have a disk.)

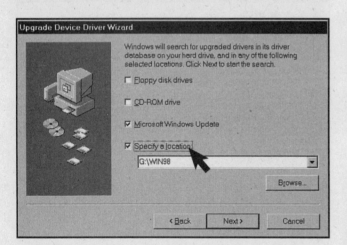

6 If you downloaded an updated driver from the Internet and saved it to a folder on your hard disk, click **Specify a Location**. Then click the **Browse** button, choose the folder, and click **OK**. Click **Next**.

If you have not yet registered your copy of Windows 98, the Microsoft Windows Update option will be unavailable (grayed out). See ►"Update Windows" on page 420 for more information about Microsoft Windows Update.◄ Before you register, make sure you have a licensed copy of Windows, or the software pirate police might come a-knockin' at your door.

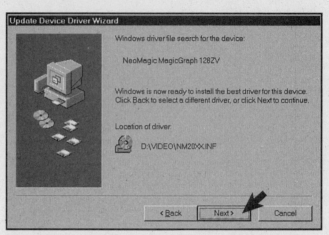

7 Windows searches the specified disks, folders, and Microsoft's Web site for the best video driver for your system. If Windows locates a better driver, this dialog box appears, indicating the location of the driver. Click **Next**.

If the best driver for the device is already installed, a dialog box appears telling you that. You can then back up and choose to select a device driver (which is a little risky if you don't know which device to select), or you can cancel the operation.

8 Windows indicates that it has successfully installed the updated device driver. Click **Finish**.

Guided Tour Install a New Video Driver

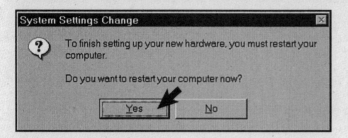

9 You are prompted to restart your computer. Save your work, exit any running programs, and click **Yes**.

What about that Web tab? The Web tab contains options for installing Active Desktop components on the Windows desktop. See ▶"Add and Remove Active Desktop Components," on page 311 for details.◀

Check for and Repair Disk Problems

Any time you turn off your computer without using the Windows Start, Shut Down command, any time Windows locks up, or any time your computer shuts down as the result of a power outage, files and folders can become damaged or your computer can simply lose track of temporary files. This can cause your computer to run more slowly and crash more frequently in the future.

In addition, an old disk (hard or floppy) can start to develop bad *sectors* (storage areas on a disk), making these storage areas unreliable. If your computer saves part of a file to a bad sector or one that is going bad, you run the risk of losing that portion of the file and perhaps the entire file. And if the sector stores a system file, you might not even be able to start your computer or run Windows.

To clean up your disk, recover lost files, delete useless file fragments, and block out any bad sectors, you should run a Windows utility called ScanDisk whenever

your system crashes or you experience unexplained program errors. You can also run ScanDisk on damaged floppy disks to recover files and repair a disk that your computer is indicating is unreadable.

Although this sounds like a complicated operation, repairing disks with ScanDisk is as simple as running just about any program. You simply run ScanDisk, pick the disk you want to check, and specify whether you want ScanDisk to do a Standard or Thorough check. If you tell ScanDisk to automatically fix errors, it does its job without asking you for any input or confirmation.

The *Guided Tour* shows you how to run ScanDisk and use it to repair common disk errors.

> If you start your computer after shutting it down improperly, Windows automatically runs ScanDisk on startup and repairs any disk problems.

Guided Tour Check Files and Folders for Errors

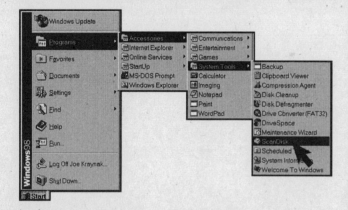

1 Click the **Start** button, point to **Programs**, **Accessories**, **System Tools**, and click **ScanDisk**. (If you are using ScanDisk to check and repair a floppy disk, insert it in the disk drive.)

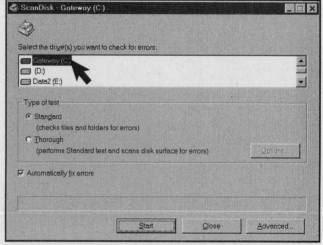

2 ScanDisk displays a list of disk drives. Click the disk drive that contains the files and folders you want to check and repair.

Guided Tour Check Files and Folders for Errors

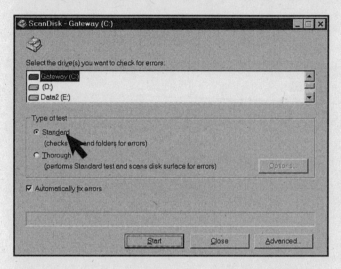

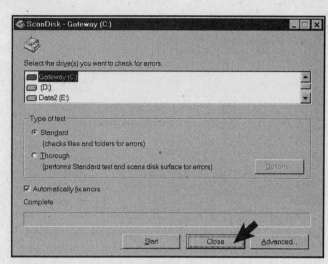

3 To check files and folders for errors, without checking the actual surface of the disk, click **Standard**.

4 To have ScanDisk proceed without prompting for your input, click **Automatically Fix Errors** to place a check mark in its box.

5 Click the **Start** button.

7 You are returned to ScanDisk's opening window. You can repeat steps 2 through 6 to check and repair files and folders on additional disks. Click the **Close** button when you are done.

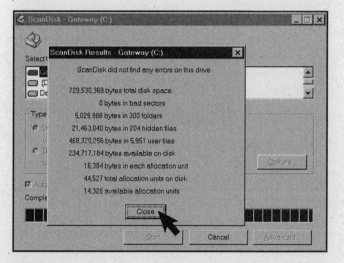

6 ScanDisk checks the files and folders on the selected disk for errors and repairs any damaged files or folders. It displays a dialog box showing the results. Click the **Close** button.

Guided Tour   Check for Defects on a Disk

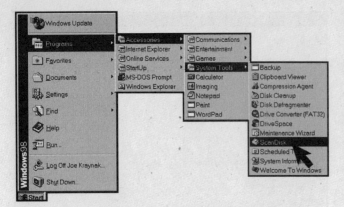

1 Click the **Start** button, point to **Programs**, **Accessories**, **System Tools**, and click **ScanDisk**. (If you are using ScanDisk to check and repair a floppy disk, insert the disk in the disk drive.)

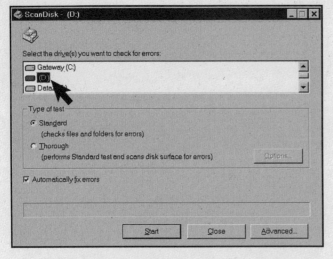

2 ScanDisk displays a list of disk drives. Click the disk drive that contains the disk you want to check and repair.

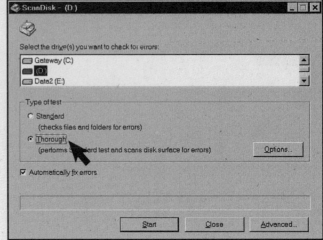

3 Click **Thorough** to repair folders and files and to check for any defective areas of the disk and attempt to recover data stored on those areas.

4 Click the **Options** button.

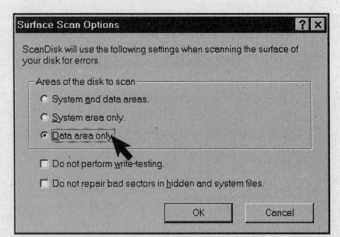

5 In the Surface Scan Options dialog box, choose the areas of the disk you want to scan: **System and Data Areas** (the most thorough check), **System Area Only**, or **Data Area Only**.

Guided Tour Check for Defects on a Disk

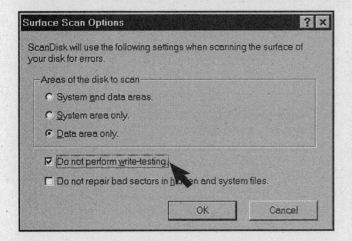

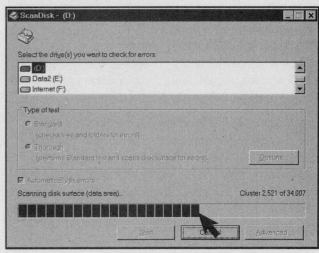

6 To prevent ScanDisk from performing write-testing, turn off **Do Not Perform Write-Testing**. Write-testing writes sample data to each sector and then reads it to determine if the sector is properly storing data. This takes a great deal of time, but it ensures that your disk can reliably store data.

7 To prevent ScanDisk from repairing bad sectors in system areas, turn off **Do Not Repair Bad Sectors in Hidden and System Files**. Click **OK**.

> To repair a bad sector, ScanDisk moves data stored on that sector to a different sector. This can cause problems if your computer or a program is set up to look for that data on a specific sector.

9 ScanDisk performs a standard check to repair any damaged files or folders, and then starts checking your disk for defective sectors. (This can take several minutes.)

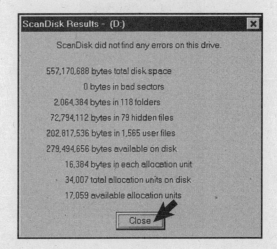

10 ScanDisk checks the files and folders on the selected disk for errors and repairs any damaged files or folders. It displays a dialog box showing the results. Click the **Close** button.

11 You are returned to ScanDisk's opening window. You can repeat steps 2 through 10 to check and repair files and folders on additional disks. Click the **Close** button when you are done.

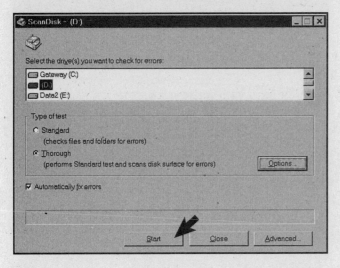

8 You are returned to ScanDisk's opening window. Click the **Start** button.

Update Windows

As you work with Windows, Microsoft stays busy perfecting its product, developing new drivers, and improving its performance. To use the latest version of Windows, you should check for and install updates on a regular basis (at least every couple of months).

In the past, you had to check Microsoft's Web site for updates, download the updates, and install them on your computer. In Windows 98, the process is much easier. You simply run the Windows Update utility from your computer. Windows connects you to the Microsoft Web site, checks for updates, and then downloads and installs any available updates.

The *Guided Tour* shows you how to run Windows Update and use it to upgrade your copy of Windows 98.

Because Microsoft is constantly working on improving the Windows Update feature, and because Windows Update runs on the Internet (not from your copy of Windows), the steps you must take may differ from those in the *Guided Tour*. Whenever you work on the Internet, be prepared to remain flexible.

Guided Tour Update Your Copy of Windows 98

1 Click the **Start** button and choose **Windows Update**.

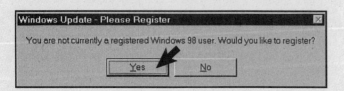

2 Windows runs Internet Explorer, connects you to the Internet, loads the Microsoft Windows Update page, and asks if you want to register. Click **Yes**. (If you're using a bootleg copy of Windows 98, don't register it. Instead, get a legal copy and then you won't have to worry about registering.)

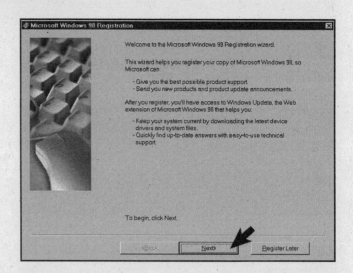

3 The Registration Wizard appears. Click **Next**.

4 The Registration Wizard indicates that your responses will be sent to Microsoft and its affiliates. Click **Next**.

Guided Tour Update Your Copy of Windows 98

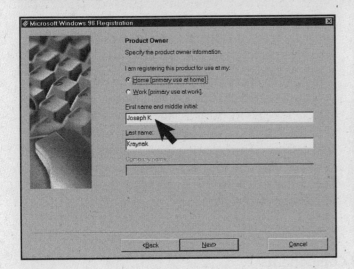

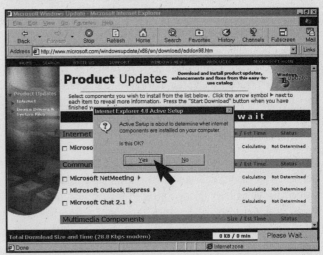

5 You are prompted to enter your name. Choose **Home** or **Work**, enter the requested information, and click **Next**. Then follow the remaining instructions from the Registration Wizard to complete the process.

7 Internet Explorer runs the online Update Wizard and checks for updates at Microsoft's Web site. The Active Setup dialog box asks for permission to check your system. Click **Yes**.

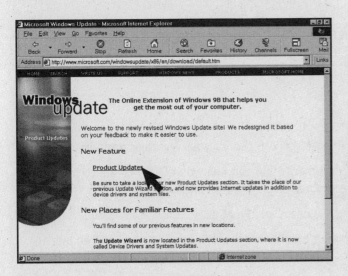

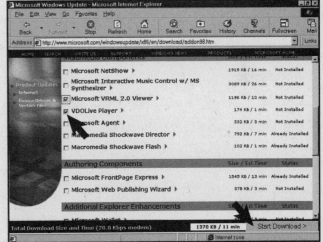

6 After you register, you are returned to Internet Explorer, which displays the Update Wizard page. Click the **Product Updates** link. (If you're prompted to confirm the download and installation of a control, click **Yes**.)

8 A list of uninstalled components and newer versions of installed components appear. You can click a category on the left to view a different group of components. To install the new or updated component, click its check box. You can click more than one check box.

9 Click the **Start Download** button in the lower-right corner of the screen.

Add and Remove Windows Components

If you performed a typical installation of Windows, the installation placed the most common Windows components on your computer. To save disk space, a typical installation does not install Windows components that most people will not need, such as Direct Cable Connection, networking support, and additional sound schemes and wallpaper.

However, if you find that a component discussed in this book is not on your system, you can easily add it by using the Windows Setup tab in the Add/Remove Programs dialog box. In addition, if your computer is running low on disk space, you can quickly remove Windows components that you never use.

Windows components are organized by category. When you want to add or remove a component, you must select the category (such as Internet Tools) and then click the Details button to view a list of components in that category. The following table contains a section for each category and then lists the components you will find in that category. The *Guided Tour* shows you how to add and remove Windows components.

Windows 98 Components

Component	Description
Accessibility Options	
Accessibility Options	Includes special keyboard, sound, display, and mouse options for people with mobility, visual, or hearing impairments.
Accessibility Tools	Offers a screen magnifier and additional options for changing the behavior of the mouse.
Accessories	
Calculator	Performs mathematical calculations.
Desktop Wallpaper	A collection of background images you can use for your Windows desktop.
Document Templates	A collection of predesigned documents that can help you quickly create common documents in your Windows programs.
Games	Includes Minesweeper, Hearts, Solitaire, and FreeCell.
Imaging	A program that displays common graphic images, allows you to edit and enhance images, and provides scanner support.
Mouse Pointers	A collection of alternative mouse pointers.
Paint	Lets you create your own paintings and graphic images.
Quick View	Allows you to preview common types of document files without having to open them.
Screen Savers	A collection of animated screens for protecting your monitor during long pauses in computer activity.
Windows Scripting Host	An advanced tool for automating tasks in Windows.
WordPad	Allows you to create and print typed documents.

Component	Description
Communications	
Dial-Up Networking	Connects your computer to another computer or the Internet via modem.
Dial-Up Server	Allows your computer to answer incoming phone calls and share resources with another computer via modem.
Direct Cable Connection	Allows you to connect two computers using a special cable and share resources between them.
HyperTerminal	Allows your computer to dial into another computer via modem.
Microsoft Chat	A program that allows you to enter chat rooms where groups of people hang out and type messages to each other. (➤ See "Chat on the Internet" on page 486.◄)
Microsoft NetMeeting	Allows you to place a voice phone call over an Internet connection.
Phone Dialer	Dials a phone number for you. You can then pick up the phone and start talking.
Virtual Private Networking	Allows you to securely connect to private networks over a public (Internet) connection.
Desktop Themes	
Various	Includes a collection of desktop themes that control the appearance of the Windows desktop, mouse pointers, screen savers, and background sounds. (➤ See "Change Your Desktop Theme" on page 457.◄)
Internet Tools	
FrontPage Express	Allows you to create and publish Web pages electronically.
VRML Viewer	Displays and helps you navigate interactive, three-dimensional worlds on the Internet.
Wallet	Allows you to perform electronic transactions securely over the Internet.
Personal Web Server	Configures your computer to act as a Web server, allowing you to test your Web pages before placing them on the Web.
Real Audio Player	Allows you to play Real Audio recordings that you might encounter on the Web. These recordings play immediately after you click a link for the recording, so there is no delay while your Web browser downloads the clip. It's similar to listening to a radio.
Web Publishing Wizard	Leads you step by step through the process of transferring a page (or a collection of pages) to a Web server.
Web-Based Enterprise Management	Includes components that system administrators can use to manage and troubleshoot servers.
Outlook Express	
N/A	Microsoft's Internet email program, which is installed by default.

Windows 98 Components   Continued

Component	Description
Multilanguage Support	
N/A	Adds support for foreign languages, including Baltic, Cyrillic, and Greek.
Multimedia	
Audio Compression	Supports audio compression to help keep recorded audio files small.
CD Player	Allows you to play audio CDs in Windows.
Macromedia Shockwave	Includes Shockwave Director and Flash, two very useful programs for playing media files on the Web.
Media Player	Plays common audio and video file types.
NetShow	Plays NetShow multimedia files, which provide a TV/radio-like quality to Web page presentations.
Sound Schemes	A collection of audio clips that you can apply to Windows events, such as warning messages and Windows shut down.
Sample Sounds	A collection of audio clips that you can use to test the audio output of your computer.
Sound Recorder	A tool for recording sounds from a microphone, audio CD, or other audio input device.
Video Compression	Supports video compression to help keep recorded video files small.
Volume Control	A convenient tool for setting the volume of speakers, microphones, and other audio input and output devices on your computer.
Online Services	
Various	Allows you to quickly connect to and set up an account for popular online services, including America Online and The Microsoft Network.
System Tools	
Backup	Copies files from your hard-disk drive, compresses them, and stores them on floppy disks or a backup drive.
Character Map	Allows you to insert special characters and symbols in documents.
Clipboard Viewer	Displays the contents of the Windows Clipboard, which you use to copy and paste data between documents.
Disk Compression	Tools for compressing the files on your hard disk so they take up less space.
Drive Converter	Converts file storage on your computer to FAT32, so you can store more files on a disk without compressing files.
Group Policies	Provides support for workgroups on a network.
Net Watcher	Enables you to monitor your network and its connections.
System Monitor	Tracks system performance.

Component	Description
Resource Meter	Displays system resources so you can determine if your system is running low on resources.
WinPopup	Lets you send and receive messages over a network connection.

WebTV for Windows

WaveTop Data Broadcasting	Adds WaveTop capability to your TV tuner, so you can receive specialized Web content through your computer's TV tuner without having to use a separate Internet Service Provider.
WebTV for Windows	Supports TV tuner cards, allowing your computer to display standard TV broadcasts on your computer. Also supports Web TV broadcasts and program guides without a TV tuner card.

Guided Tour   Add and Remove Windows Components

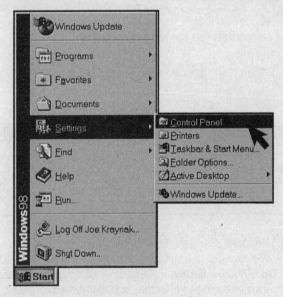

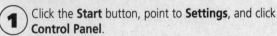

2 The Control Panel opens. Click **Add/Remove Programs**.

(continues)

1 Click the **Start** button, point to **Settings**, and click **Control Panel**.

Guided Tour Add and Remove Windows Components

(continued)

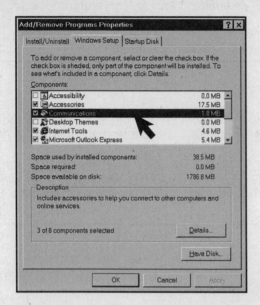

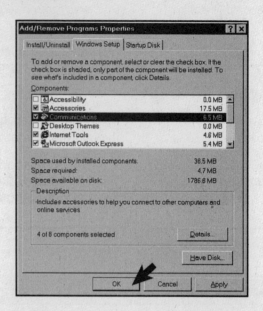

3 In the Add/Remove Programs Properties dialog box, click the **Windows Setup** tab.

4 In the **Components** list, click the category that contains the component you want to install or remove, and then click the **Details** button. (To install all of the components in a category, click the category's check box and skip to step 6.)

6 You are returned to the Add/Remove Programs Properties dialog box. Repeat steps 4 and 5 if necessary to mark other components you want to add or remove.

7 When you're satisfied with your choices, click **OK**.

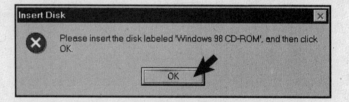

8 Windows displays a message telling you to insert the Windows CD or installation disk. Insert the disk or CD and click **OK**. Windows displays a dialog box indicating the progress of the installation. When it finishes, you might need to restart Windows.

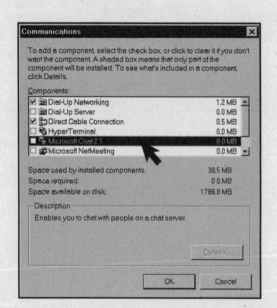

5 A list of components in the selected category appears. Click the check box next to each component you want to add or remove. A check mark indicates the component is or will be installed. No check mark indicates that the component is not installed or, if installed, will be removed. Click **OK**.

Add and Remove Fonts

As you know from formatting documents, a *font* is a collection of characters of a specific type style and size. For example, Courier 10-point is a font. (Fonts are measured in points; there are approximately 72 points in an inch.) By using different fonts, you can enhance the appearance of your typed documents.

The available fonts depend on which fonts you have installed on your computer and printer. The following list describes the various types of fonts you will encounter:

- **Printer fonts.** Your printer has some basic fonts installed, which the printer can access directly for quick printing. Check your printer's manual to determine which fonts came with it. You can also determine which fonts are printer fonts by looking at the fonts names in Windows. Windows marks printer fonts by displaying a printer icon next to the font's name.

- **Cartridge fonts.** Many printers have a port into which you can plug a cartridge that contains additional printer memory or additional fonts. These fonts act as printer fonts. Windows also displays a printer icon next to the names of these fonts.

- **Soft fonts.** Many programs come with their own fonts, which you can install and use in that program and, in some cases, in other programs.

- **TrueType fonts.** Windows and many Windows programs come with special soft fonts called *TrueType* fonts. Unlike traditional fonts, which require a special font for each type size, TrueType fonts are *scalable,* giving you more flexibility with resizing fonts. Windows displays a TT symbol next to the names of TrueType fonts.

Although you cannot change the fonts on your printer (except by adding a cartridge), you can install or remove fonts in Windows. You might want to install a font that you have purchased or downloaded from the Internet. You can also install additional fonts from the Windows CD-ROM. The *Guided Tour* shows you how to use the Windows Font Manager to install additional fonts.

If you are running low on disk space, you should consider removing fonts that you do not use. The Windows Font Manager allows you to preview fonts and then quickly remove them from your system. It can also display a list of fonts that are similar to help you decide which fonts you can live without. The *Guided Tour* shows you just what to do.

> Do not remove the font named MS Sans Serif. Windows uses this font, which is easy to read, to display text in its windows, menus, and dialog boxes. If you remove this font, Windows will use a different font, which might not display all onscreen text.

Guided Tour Add Fonts

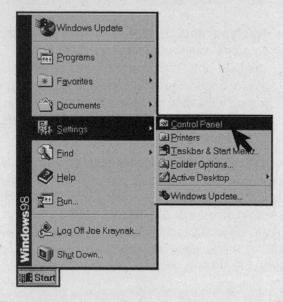

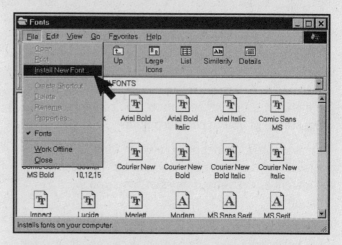

3 The Fonts window displays an icon for each installed font. Open the **File** menu and choose **Install New Font**.

1 If necessary, insert the disk or CD that contains the font you want to install. Then click the **Start** button, point to **Settings**, and Click **Control Panel**.

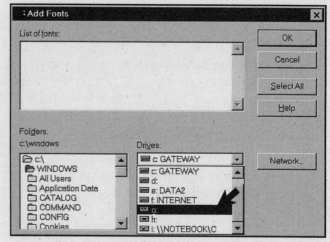

4 The Add Fonts dialog box prompts you to specify the location of the new font. Open the **Drives** drop-down list and choose the disk drive where the fonts are stored.

2 In the Control Panel, click the **Fonts** icon.

Guided Tour Add Fonts

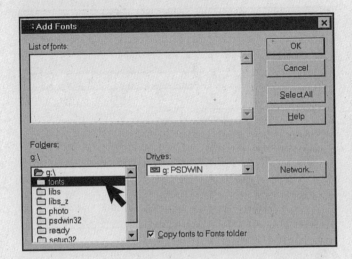

5 In the **Folders** list, double-click the folder in which the font is stored. (You may have to double-click subfolders to access the fonts.)

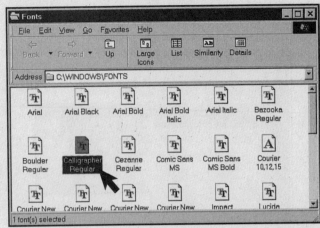

8 Windows copies the fonts to your hard disk and places them in the Windows\Fonts folder. Icons for the new fonts are added to the Fonts window.

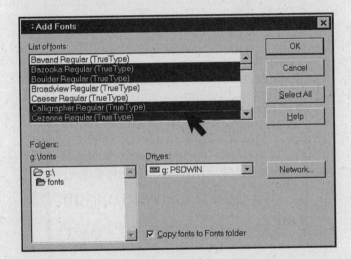

6 The names of the available fonts appear under List of Fonts. Click the font you want to install. To select additional fonts, **Ctrl+**_click_ their names. To install all of the fonts in the list, click the **Select All** button.

7 Make sure **Copy Fonts to Fonts Folder** is checked. Then click **OK**.

Guided Tour   Remove Fonts

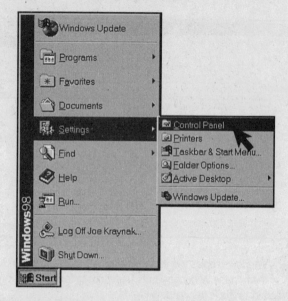

(1) Click the **Start** button, point to **Settings**, and click **Control Panel**.

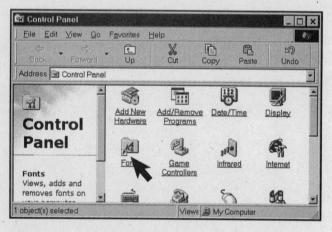

(2) In the Control Panel, click the **Fonts** icon.

You can click the **Similarity** button in the toolbar to group similar fonts; this allows you to trim the number of fonts while still giving you enough different fonts to use in your documents. Windows places the fonts that are similar to the currently selected font at the top of the list. To view fonts that are similar to a different font, open the **List Fonts by Similarity To** drop-down list and choose the desired font.

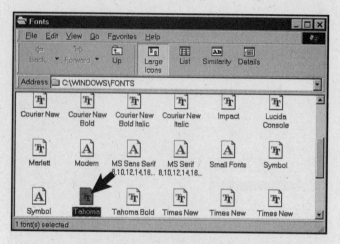

(3) Double-click the icon for the font you might want to delete so you can preview it before removing it.

(4) Windows displays sample text in the selected font. When you finish previewing the font, click the **Done** button.

Guided Tour Remove Fonts

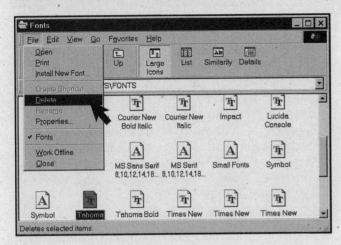

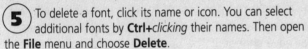

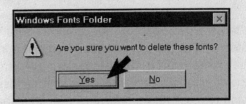

6 Windows prompts you to confirm the deletion. Click **Yes**.

5 To delete a font, click its name or icon. You can select additional fonts by **Ctrl+**_clicking_ their names. Then open the **File** menu and choose **Delete**.

Back Up Files

The most valuable part of your computer is not the system unit or the monitor. Your programs and data are much more valuable. You can replace the system unit, the monitor, the printer, and all the other devices, but trying to re-create your documents and databases can be nearly impossible. And re-entering all the configuration settings for your programs can be almost as difficult.

Because your data and program settings are so valuable, you should back up your files regularly and store your backups somewhere away from your computer. That way, if your computer is stolen or toasted in a fire, or if you accidentally delete a file or your hard-disk drive dies, you can restore your data and program files from your backups.

Backing up consists of copying selected folders and files from your hard disk to a set of floppy disks or to a special backup drive (typically a tape drive). The backup operation compresses the files so they take up less space. However, if you must back up a large amount of data, you should consider getting a special backup drive, so you can perform the backup without having to swap disks in and out of your floppy drive.

Windows comes with its own backup program that supports most backup devices, including floppy disk drives. Take the *Guided Tour* to back up the files from your hard disk. The *Guided Tour* shows you how to use the new Backup Wizard, which is the easiest way to back up files. However, if you have used Backup in Windows 95, you can cancel the wizard and enter backup settings yourself.

> Microsoft Backup is not installed by default. To install it, see ▶"Add and Remove Windows Components" on page 422.◀

When you back up your files, you must realize that the backups are only as good as they are recent. If you back up your files at the beginning of the month and then you lose some files at the end of the month, your backup files will not contain any of the changes you made to those files during the month. To successfully recover lost files, you must restore recent backup files.

> When shopping for a backup drive, look for a drive that can store at least half as much as your hard disk. If you have 2GB of data and program files and a tape backup that can handle only 100 MBtapes, you're going to have to swap tapes in and out of the drive during the backup operation, and you'll have a stack of tapes that are difficult to store. A good choice in backup drives is the Iomega Jaz drive, which can store 1–2GB per cartridge.

With that in mind, you should develop a practical backup strategy. You don't want to have to back up all your files every day, but you do want daily backups of files that have changed. The best way to accomplish this goal is to practice the following strategy:

1. Create a separate folder for the data files you create, and store all your data files in that folder or in subfolders of that folder. You can then easily back up your data without having to back up Windows or your programs.

2. Back up your entire system minus the Data folder on a monthly basis. (This gives you a backup of Windows and all your programs.)

3. Whenever you install a program or change your system settings, do an incremental backup of your system. An incremental backup copies only those files that have changed since the last full backup. This backup is *in addition to*, not *in place of*, the previous system backup.

4. Do a complete backup of your Data folder weekly. A complete backup copies all the files and subfolders in the Data folder.

5. Do an incremental backup of your Data folder daily. This ensures that your backup files contain the latest changes. You should have six incremental backups in the set; on the seventh day, do your full backup again. By following this system, you will avoid overwriting yesterday's backup set with today's backup set.

Guided Tour Back Up Your Entire System

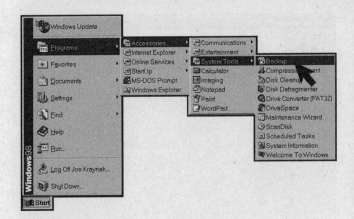

1 Click the **Start** button, point to **Programs**, **Accessories**, **System Tools**, and click **Backup**.

A dialog box may appear indicating that Backup did not find a special backup drive. If you know that a backup drive is installed, click **Yes** to run the Add New Hardware Wizard and set it up in Windows. If you don't have a special backup device, you can use your floppy disk drive for backups. If the message appears, simply click **No** and use your floppy disk drive.

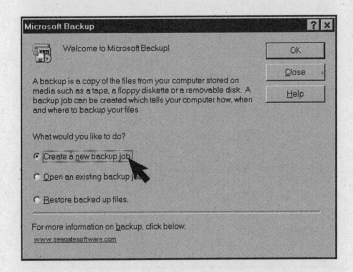

2 Backup prompts you to specify what you want to do. Choose **Create a New Backup Job** and click **OK**.

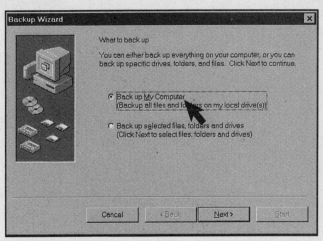

3 Backup prompts you to specify what you want to back up. Choose **Back Up My Computer** and click **Next**.

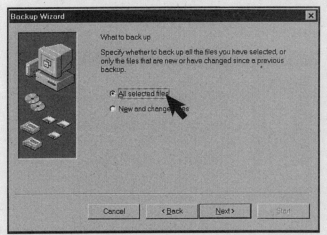

4 You are now prompted to back up all files or only those files that have changed since the last backup. Choose **All Selected Files** and click **Next**.

(continues)

Guided Tour Back Up Your Entire System *(continued)*

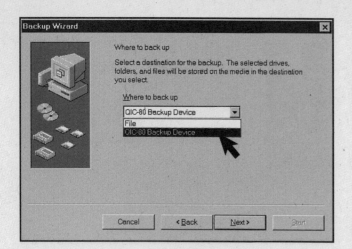

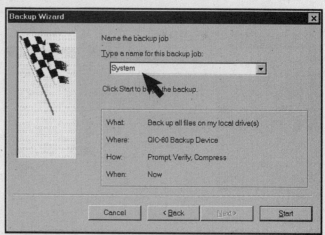

5 Backup prompts you to choose the type of backup device you want to use. Open the **Where to Back Up** drop-down list and choose the desired device type. (Again, File indicates another disk drive—a floppy or hard drive, for example.) Click **Next**.

7 You are prompted to type a name for the backup. Type a brief description, such as "System," and then click the **Start** button.

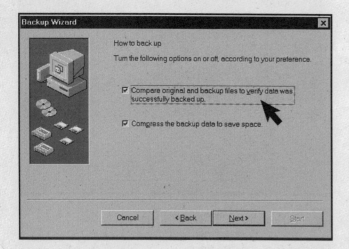

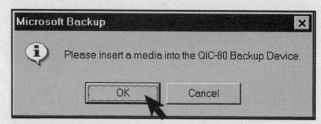

6 Backup indicates that it will compare files after the backup to verify the copies against the originals and that it will compress files in order to fit more on a disk or tape. Leave these two options on. Click **Next**.

8 Backup starts backing up the files and displays a dialog box telling you to insert a disk or tape in the selected drive. Insert the disk or tape and click **OK**. (You might have to swap disks or tapes during the backup operation if the amount of data to be backed up is more than one disk or tape can store.)

Now that you have a full backup of all the files on your hard disk, you can perform an incremental backup later to back up only those files that have changed since the full backup. To perform the incremental backup, rather than choosing All Selected Files in step 4, choose **New and Changed Files**. This appends backups for any new or changed files to the last tape or disk in the backup set.

Guided Tour Back Up Selected Folders and Files

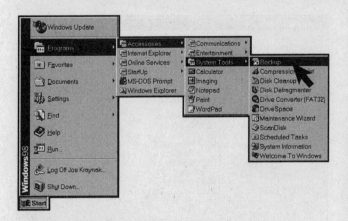

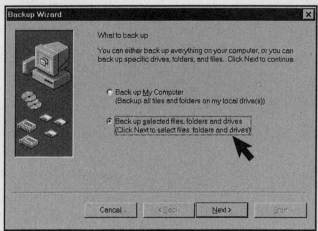

1 If Backup is not running, click the **Start** button, point to **Programs**, **Accessories**, **System Tools**, and click **Backup**. If Backup is running, open the **Tools** menu, choose **Backup Wizard**, and skip to step 3.

3 Backup prompts you to specify what you want to back up. Choose **Back Up Selected Folders, Files, and Drives** and click **Next**.

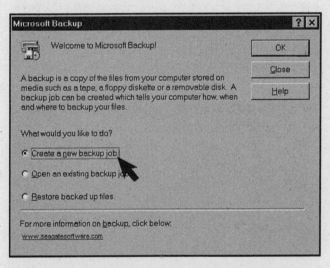

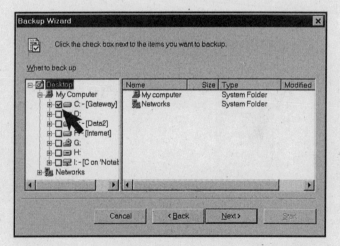

2 Backup prompts you to specify what you want to do. Choose **Create a New Backup Job** and click **OK**.

4 A list of all the hard disk drives on your system appears. To back up an entire disk, click the check box next to its letter. You can choose more than one disk.

(continues)

Guided Tour Back Up Selected Folders and Files *(continued)*

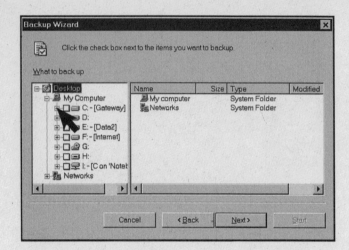

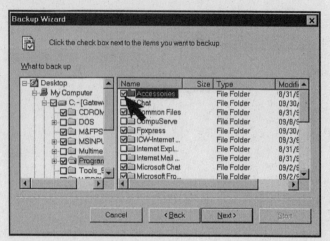

5 To back up one or more folders or files on a disk, click the **plus sign** (+) next to the letter of the disk on which the folders or files are stored.

7 If you click a folder's name, Backup displays its contents in the right pane. You can click the check boxes next to subfolder and file names to select them. When you select partial contents of a disk or folder, the check box next to the disk or folder appears gray with a check mark in it.

8 When you are finished selecting the disks, folders, and files you want to back up, click **Next**.

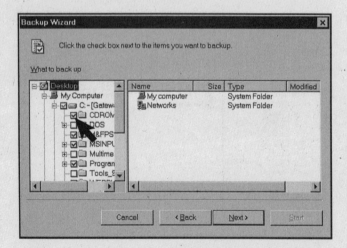

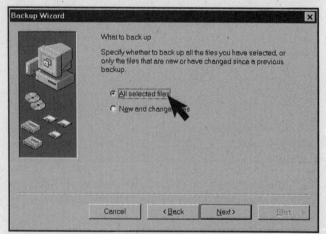

6 Backup displays a list of the folders. You can click the **plus sign** (+) next to a folder to display its subfolders. Click the check box next to a folder's name to select all the files in the folder. Or, click the folder's name to display its contents.

9 To back up all of the files on the selected disk or folder, choose **All Selected Files**. If you want to back up only those files that have been created or changed since the last backup, choose **New and Changed Files**. Click **Next**.

Guided Tour   Back Up Selected Folders and Files

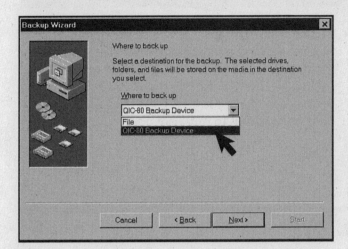

10 Backup prompts you to choose the type of backup device you want to use. Open the **Where to Back Up** drop-down list and choose the desired device type. (Again, File indicates a floppy disk drive.) Click **Next**.

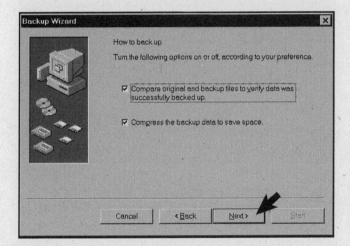

11 Backup indicates that it will compare files after the backup to verify the copies against the originals and that it will compress files in order to fit more on a disk or tape. Leave these two options on. Click **Next**.

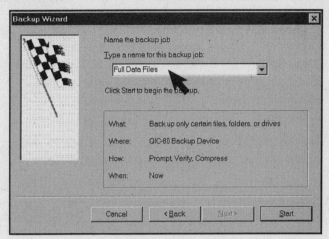

12 You are prompted to type a name for the backup. Type a brief description, such as "Full Data Files," and then click the **Start** button.

13 Backup starts backing up the files and displays a dialog box telling you to insert a disk or tape in the selected drive. Insert the disk or tape and click **OK**. (You might have to swap disks or tapes during the backup operation if the amount of data to be backed up is more than one disk or tape can store.)

> When you type a name for the backup, Backup stores the name and any selections you made. To perform the backup much more quickly next time, start Backup and cancel the wizard. This displays the main Backup window. Open the **Backup Job** drop-down list, choose the backup's name, and click the **Start** button.

Restore Files

Hopefully, you will never need the backup files you create. However, if your hard disk drive goes south or you accidentally delete an important file, you can use your backup disks or tapes to recover some or all of your work (depending on how recently you backed up the lost files).

Restoring files from your backups is just as easy as making the backups. Backup comes with its own Restore

Wizard, which can lead you step by step through the process, allowing you to specify which files you want to restore and warning you if you are about to replace an existing file. The *Guided Tour* shows you how to run the Restore Wizard and use it to restore files and folders from your backups to your hard disk.

Guided Tour Restore Files from Backups

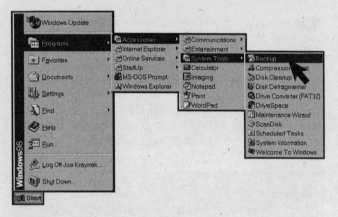

1 If Backup is not running, click the **Start** button, point to **Programs**, **Accessories**, **System Tools**, and click **Backup**. If Backup is running, open the **Tools** menu, choose **Restore Wizard**, and skip to step 3.

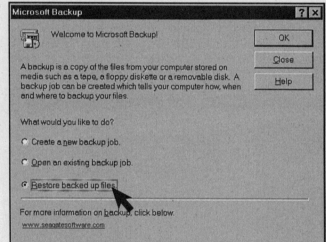

2 Backup displays a message asking what you want to do. Choose **Restore Backed Up Files** and click **OK**. (Insert the first disk or tape that has the backup files on it.)

Guided Tour Restore Files from Backups

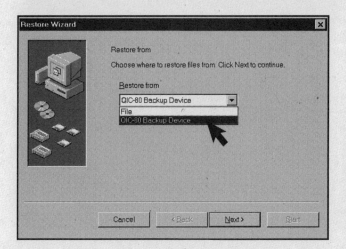

(3) The Restore Wizard starts, Open the Restore From drop-down list and choose the type of device you are using to restore files. Then click Next.

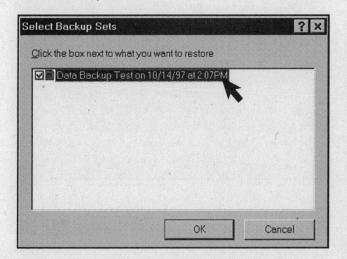

(4) Windows searches the specified restore device for the names of backups you performed and displays a list. Click the name of the backup set from which you want to restore files and click **OK**.

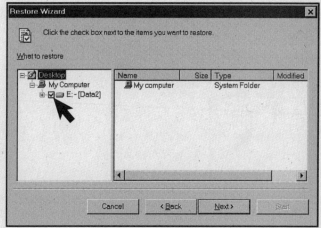

(5) Restore creates a list of the folders and files stored in the selected backup set and displays a list of disks that the files were backed up from. To restore all of the files on a disk, click the check box next to the disk's letter.

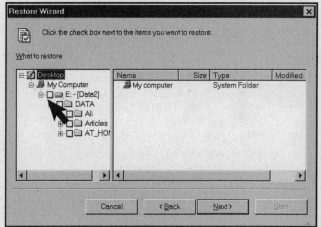

(6) To restore only selected folders or files, click the plus sign (+) next to the disk's letter.

(continues)

Guided Tour Restore Files from Backups   *(continued)*

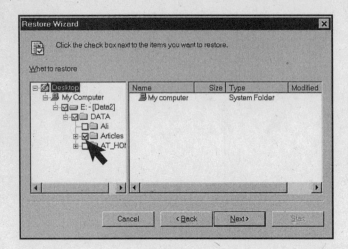

7 Restore displays a list of the folders. You can click the **plus sign** (+) next to a folder to display its subfolders. Click the check box next to a folder's name to select all the files in the folder. Or, click the folder's name to display its contents.

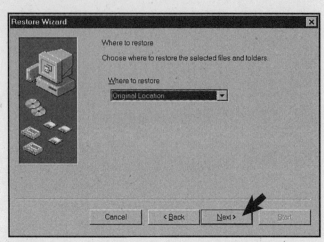

10 Restore prompts you to specify the drive and folder in which you want to restore the files. By default, Restore will place the files on the disk and folder from which they were backed up. Click **Next**.

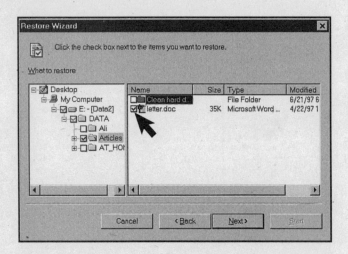

8 If you click a folder's name, Restore displays its contents in the right pane. You can click the check boxes next to sub-folder and file names to select them. When you select partial contents of a disk or folder, the check box next to the disk or folder appears gray with a check mark in it.

9 When you finish selecting the disks, folders, and files you want to back up, click **Next**.

If you are afraid of overwriting files on your hard disk with old backup files, open the **Where to Restore** drop-down list in step 10, choose **Alternate Location**, click the **Folder** icon, and choose a different disk or folder. Note, however, that Restore will prompt you before replacing any newer files on your hard disk with older versions.

Guided Tour   Restore Files from Backups

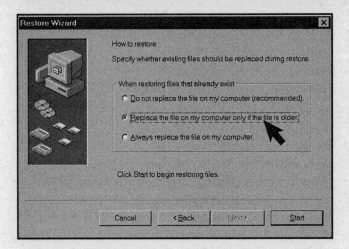

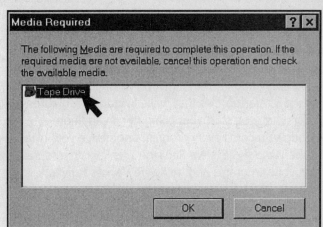

11 Restore asks if you want to replace files on your hard disk with files from the backup. Choose one of the following options: **Do Not Replace the File on My Computer** (safest), **Replace the File on My Computer Only If the File Is Older** (pretty safe), or **Always Replace the File on My Computer** (risky). Click the **Start** button.

12 The Media Required dialog box appears. Choose the media type on which the backup files are stored and click **OK**. Restore then copies the files from the backup disk or tape and places them on the specified drive and folder.

Create and Use an Emergency Disk

Windows 98 is a complex operating system that does a great deal of work behind the scenes to make it easier for you to use your computer. When you installed Windows, it automatically installed essential Windows startup files that make Windows run automatically when you start your computer. In addition, Windows records every program and device you install in the *Windows System Registry*. This Registry ensures that your programs and hardware devices function properly and work smoothly with other programs and devices on your system.

All of this is great until your hard-disk drive fails or the System Registry file becomes corrupted. When that happens, Windows is no longer as user friendly as the ads touted it. In fact, you won't be able to start Windows or even use your computer.

Fortunately, Windows comes with a utility that can create an emergency startup disk for you. You pop the disk into the floppy drive, restart your computer, and fix whatever problem caused Windows to crash.

When you installed Windows, Windows prompted you to make an emergency disk. If you skipped the procedure to save some time, you should make a disk right now. You should also make a new emergency disk whenever you install a new program or hardware device so the disk will contain the latest version of the System Registry. The *Guided Tour* shows you how to make a recovery disk after installing Windows and how to use it to get your system up and running when it fails.

Guided Tour   Make an Emergency Disk

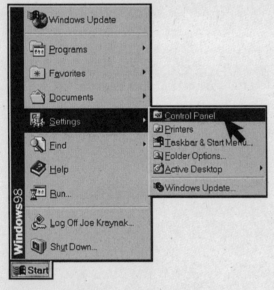

1 Click the **Start** button, point to **Settings**, and click **Control Panel**.

2 In the Control Panel, click **Add/Remove Programs**.

Guided Tour Make an Emergency Disk

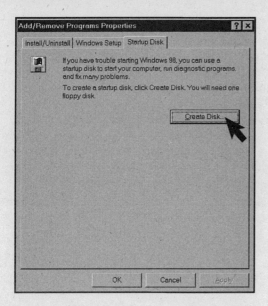

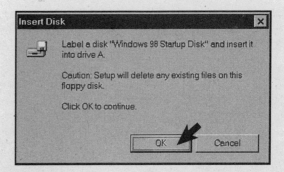

3 In the Add/Remove Programs Properties dialog box, click the **Startup Disk** tab and click the **Create Disk** button. (If you're prompted to insert the Windows 98 CD, insert it and click **OK**.)

4 Windows copies the files required for the startup disk and prompts you to insert a floppy disk. Insert a blank floppy disk or one that contains files you no longer need (it need not be formatted). Click **OK**.

5 Windows formats the disk (if needed) and copies the necessary recovery files to the disk. When you are returned to the Add/Remove Programs Properties dialog box, click **OK**.

Guided Tour Recover After a System Failure

1 If you cannot start your computer or Windows, insert the recovery disk into your computer's floppy disk drive. Restart your computer by pressing **Ctrl+Alt+Delete** or by turning the power off, waiting about 30 seconds, and turning the power back on.

2 Your computer restarts from the floppy disk. A menu might appear asking if you want to start with CD-ROM support. Choose the optin for CD-ROM support.

3 The DOS prompt appears as A:>. Type **c:** and press **Enter**.

4 This changes to drive C, and the c:> prompt appears. Type **cd\windows** and press **Enter**.

5 This changes to the Windows folder. Type **win** and press **Enter**.

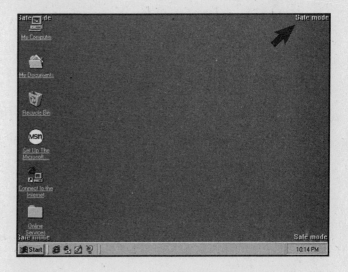

6 Windows typically starts in safe mode after a failure. In most cases, you can exit and restart Windows to have it automatically repair any problems that caused it to fail. ▶See "Start and Shut Down Windows" on page 10 for details.◀

Guided Tour Recover After a System Failure   *(continued)*

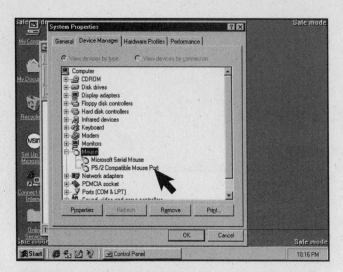

Windows stores a backup of the current System Registry on your hard disk; for that reason, even if the Registry file on your emergency disk is old or corrupt, Windows can restore the System Registry. When you shut down and restart Windows, it automatically checks the System Registry and replaces it with the backup if necessary. This is why shutting down and restarting Windows often corrects startup problems.

7 If Windows starts again in safe mode, you might need to change a video driver or mouse driver or change the Windows system settings. ▶See "Installation and Startup Issues" on page 528 for details.◀

PART 2

Do It Yourself...

In the first part of this book you learned the Windows basics. You learned how to navigate the Windows desktop; run programs; use the Windows accessories; copy, move, and delete files; take advantage of the Internet features; and other standard operating procedures to help you survive in Windows.

Now that you're comfortable with the basics, you're probably ready to put your newly acquired skills to the test, to apply your new skills to real-world tasks. That's what this part is all about. In this part, you get additional hands-on experience with the most common Windows features as you perform several *Do It Yourself* projects. Here, you'll learn how to use your modem to speed-dial phone numbers, use Desktop Themes to make working in Windows more fun, use the Windows utilities to optimize your system, and make practical use of the Internet.

To help you find projects that interest you, I grouped them in the following sections.

What You Will Find in This Part

DO IT YOURSELF

Customize Windows 98

T hroughout the *Guided Tours* in this book, you have already customized Windows 98 by changing the desktop properties, adding shortcuts to the Windows desktop, configuring the taskbar, choosing screen savers, and working in Web View. You might have also tinkered with hardware settings in the Control Panel.

The projects in this section show you how to customize Windows even further by using the Phone Dialer along with your modem to dial phone numbers for you, changing the sounds that Windows plays when certain events occur, setting up programs to run whenever you start your computer, configuring your mouse and keyboard, and preventing unauthorized use of your computer with passwords.

What You Will Find in This Section

Use Your Modem as a Programmable Phone

All new modems have at least two jacks: one to connect the modem to a phone jack and one to connect it to a phone. This allows you to establish your online connections and place regular phone calls using a single line. You don't have to disconnect the modem and plug in your phone every time you want to make a phone call.

Most people have their fancy programmable phone connected to a separate phone jack in their bedroom or kitchen. They install an additional phone jack in the office or den for their computer and then hook some cheap standard telephone to it. They then dial phone numbers manually on their computer phone.

Fortunately, manual dialing is unnecessary with Windows 98. Windows comes with an accessory called *Phone Dialer*, which allows you to enter phone numbers you dial often and then quickly dial those numbers when you click a single button. In this project, you learn how to program numbers into Phone Dialer and have it automatically dial phone numbers for you.

Do It Yourself Place Calls with Phone Dialer

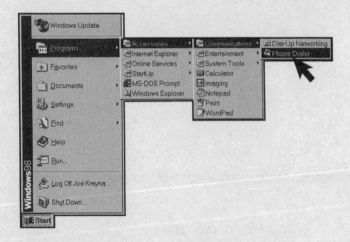

1 Click the **Start** button, point to **Programs**, **Accessories**, and **Communications**, and then click **Phone Dialer**.

2 To quickly dial a number, type it in the **Number to Dial** text box and click the **Dial** button.

Do It Yourself Place Calls with Phone Dialer

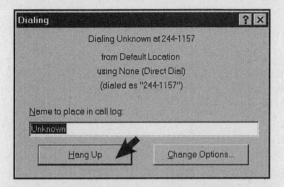

3 Phone Dialer starts to dial teh phone and displays teh Dialing dialog box. Pick up the phone and continue with the phone call just as if you had dialed manually.

4 When you finish talking, click the **Hang Up** button and hang up the phone.

Do It Yourself Program Numbers for Speed Dial

1 Click a blank button in the Speed Dial list.

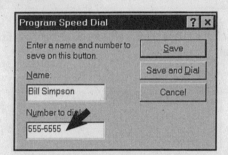

3 Click in the **Number to Dial** box and type the phone number.

4 Click the **Save** button.

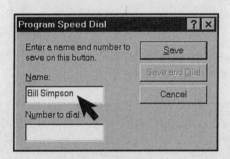

2 In the Program Speed Dial dialog box, type the name of the person or place you want to call.

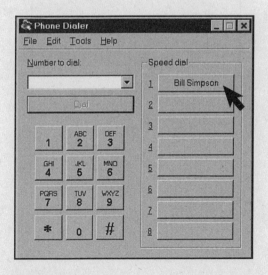

5 The Speed Dial list now contains a button labeled with the name of the person or place you entered in step 2. If you want to call that number, click the button to dial the number, and then pick up the phone when you see the Dialing dialog box.

Do It Yourself   Edit Speed Dial Numbers

1 Open the Phone Dialer's **Edit** menu and choose **Speed Dial**.

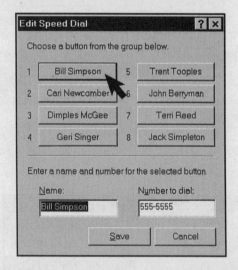

2 Click the button for the person or place whose information you want to change.

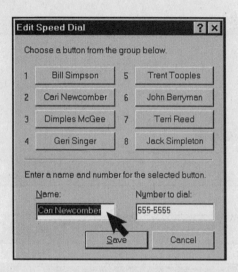

3 The name and current phone number appear in the text boxes at the bottom of the dialog box. To change the name, simply click in the **Name** box and type the new name.

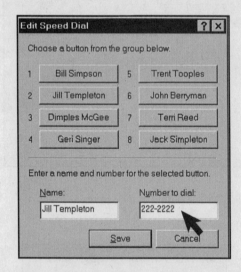

4 Click in the **Number to Dial** text box and type the new phone number. Click **Save**.

To further automate Phone Dialer, you can enter special dialing preferences. For example, if you have to dial a 9 before dialing any phone number, you can have Phone Dialer dial it for you for every call you place. To enter preferences, open the **Tools** menu and choose **Dialing Properties**.

Insert Special Characters and Symbols in a Document

Although your computer keyboard has keys for most of the characters you need to type in a document, it lacks many of the special characters and symbols such as © and ®, mathematical signs such as Σ, and fractions, such as ½ and ¼. To insert these signs and symbols in your documents, you can choose a font that contains these characters and then type them, assuming you know which keys to press to insert the correct characters.

If you don't know which keys to press, you can use Windows Character Map to preview the signs and symbols in a selected font, choose and copy the signs and symbols you want to use, and then paste them into

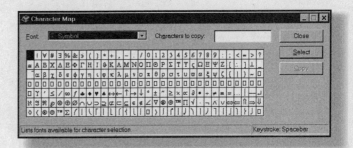

your document. In this project, you will learn how to use Character Map to insert these special characters in your documents.

Do It Yourself Copy Special Characters from Character Map

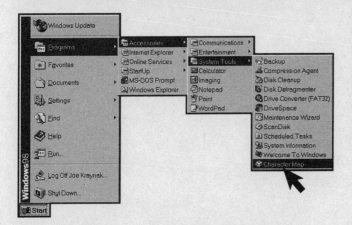

1 Click the **Start** button, point to **Programs**, **Accessories**, **System Tools**, and then click **Character Map**.

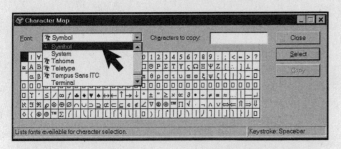

2 Character Map appears, with the Symbol font selected. Open the **Font** list and choose the desired font. Each font offers a different set of signs and symbols.

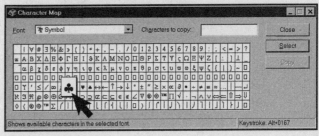

3 Point to a character or symbol and hold down the left mouse button to display a larger version of it.

4 Double-click a character or symbol to add it to the **Characters to Copy** text box, Repeat this step to insert additional characters and symbols, if desired.

5 Click the **Copy** button. The characters and symbols in the Characters to Copy text box are placed on the Windows Clipboard.

(continues)

Do It Yourself   Copy Special Characters from Character Map   *(continued)*

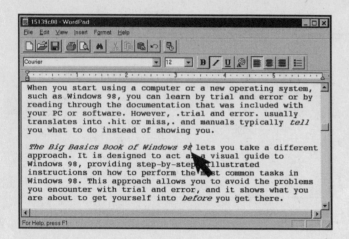

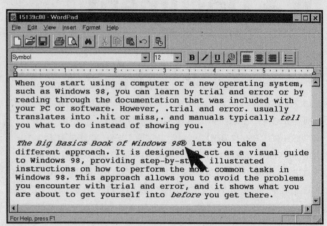

6 Switch to the document in which you want to insert the copied characters or symbols, and then position the insertion point where you want to insert them.

8 The copied character(s) and/or symbol(s) are inserted in the document. You can format them just as you can format any characters to change their size and attributes, but do not change the font style.

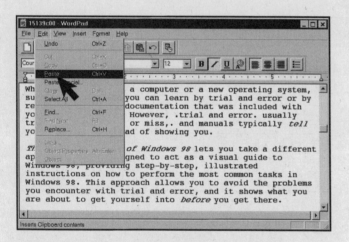

7 Open the **Edit** menu and choose **Paste** (or press **Ctrl+V**).

Choose a Different Sound Scheme

As you no doubt have noticed, Windows plays sounds when certain events occur, including when you start and exit Windows, open or close windows, and receive error messages. What you might not know is that you can change the sounds that Windows plays when these events occur. Windows comes with several sound schemes, each of which contains a collection of audio clips assigned to particular events.

To quickly change the sounds that Windows plays, you can choose one of the sound schemes. For example, you can choose the Jungle Sound Scheme to hear wild animals, rattlesnakes (in the jungle?), and other jungle sounds when you perform actions in Windows. In addition, you can change individual sounds by attaching a different sound to each event. You can even record sounds from an audio CD or by using a microphone, save the sounds as .WAV files, and create your own sound scheme, or use audio files that came with your favorite computer game or that you downloaded from the Internet.

The following project shows you how to select a different sound scheme and attach sounds to individual events. To use your own recorded sounds, first record the sounds and save them as .WAV files, ▶as explained in "Play and Record Sounds with Sound Recorder" on page 206.◀

Windows Sound Schemes are not installed during a typical installation. ▶To install additional sound schemes, see "Add and Remove Windows Components" on page 422.◀ Sound Schemes are in the Multimedia group.

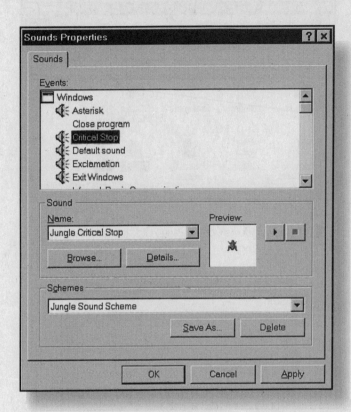

Do It Yourself Choose a Windows Sound Scheme

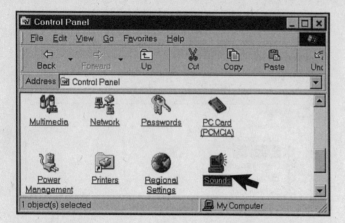

1 In the Windows Control Panel, click the **Sounds** icon.

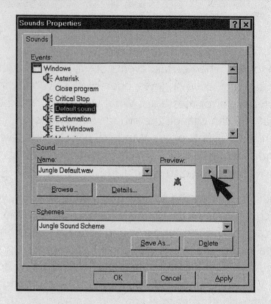

3 To preview the sound that is attached to an event, first click the event in the **Events** list.

4 Click the **Preview** button, and Windows plays the sound.

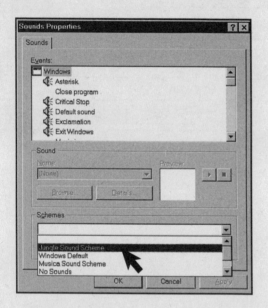

2 Open the **Schemes** drop-down list and choose the desired sound scheme.

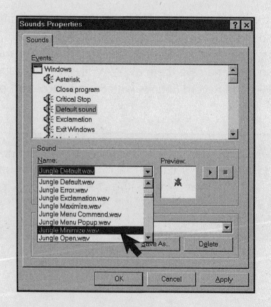

5 To apply a different sound (from any sound scheme) to the selected event, open the **Name** drop-down list and choose the desired sound.

Do It Yourself Choose a Windows Sound Scheme

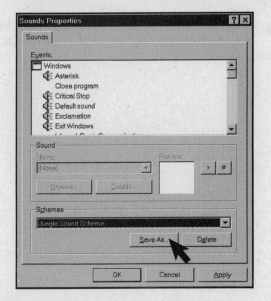

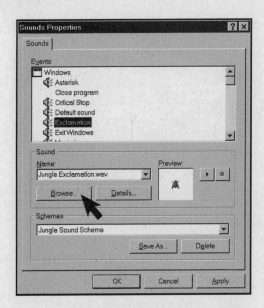

6 If you change a Windows sound scheme, you should save it under a different name so that the original sound scheme will remain intact. Click the **Save As** button.

8 To attach a sound you recorded or acquired to an event, click the event in the **Events** list and click the **Browse** button.

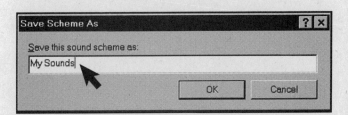

7 In the Save Scheme As dialog box, type a name for the new sound scheme and click **OK**.

9 In the Browse for Sound dialog box, change to the disk and folder in which you saved your sound, click its name, and choose **OK**.

(continues)

Do It Yourself Choose a Windows Sound Scheme

(continued)

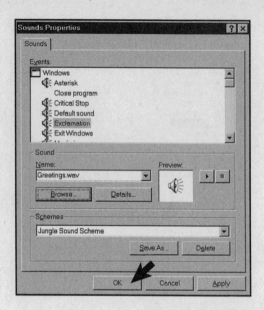

10 You are returned to the Sounds Properties dialog box. Enter any other changes as desired, and then click **OK**. Windows immediately activates the new sounds.

Change Your Desktop Theme

When most people start to play around in Windows, one of the first things they do is change the desktop colors and background. People seem to enjoy having control over their work environment, and this carries over to their personal computers. Chances are good that you have already changed the Windows desktop using the Desktop Properties dialog box (▶as explained in "Change Display Properties" on page 406◀).

In addition to the standard display properties, which were also available in Windows 95, Windows 98 comes with a collection of desktop themes. These themes change the appearance of nearly everything on the Windows desktop, including the icons used for My Computer and the Recycle Bin, the mouse pointer, program and document windows, dialog boxes, and the screen saver. For example, if you choose the Dangerous Creatures desktop, the Network Neighborhood icon changes into a tarantula, your mouse pointer becomes a jellyfish, and sharks and stingrays swim across your monitor when the screen saver kicks in.

The following project shows you how to choose a different desktop theme. Before you can perform the

project, however, you must install the desktop themes, which are not installed by default. The themes require over 30MB of free space if you install all of them, so you might want to install only one or two. ▶See "Add and Remove Windows Components" on page 422 for details.◀

Do It Yourself   Choose a Desktop Theme

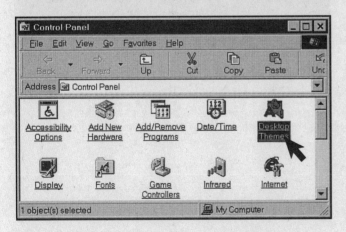

(1) In the Windows Control Panel, click the **Desktop Themes** icon.

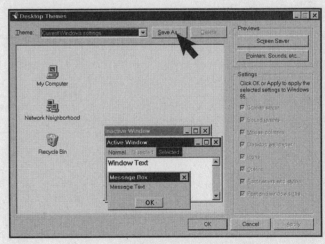

(2) In the Desktop Themes window, click the **Save As** button to save your current desktop settings as a starting point.

(continues)

Do It Yourself Choose a Desktop Theme *(continued)*

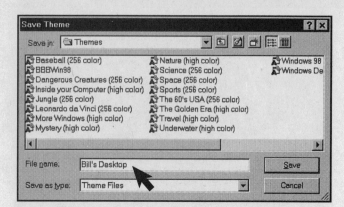

3 Type a name for the theme in the **File Name** text box, and then click the **Save** button.

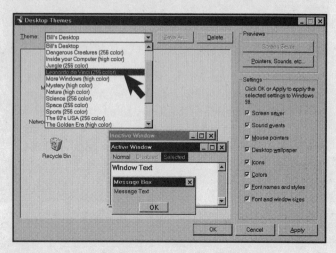

4 Open the **Theme** drop-down list and choose the desired desktop theme.

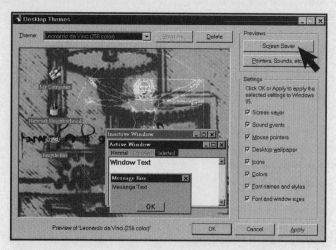

5 The selected theme appears in the preview area. To preview the screen saver, click the **Screen Saver** button.

6 Windows plays the screen saver. Move the mouse pointer or press a key to turn it off.

Do It Yourself   Choose a Desktop Theme

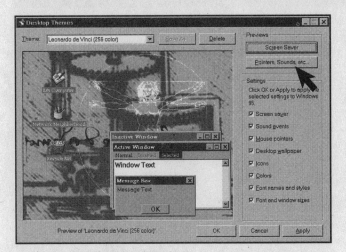

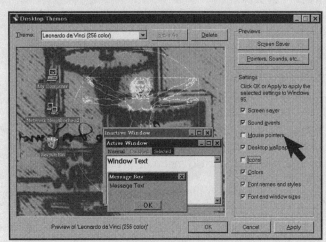

7 To preview mouse pointers, sounds, and icons, click the **Pointers, Sounds, etc.** button.

9 You can disable individual components of the desktop theme by clicking the name of each component to remove the check mark from its box. Click **OK** to save your settings.

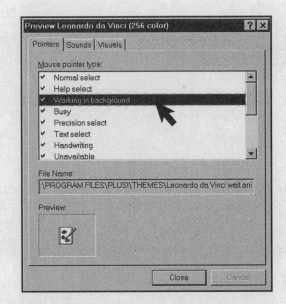

8 The Preview window appears. Click the tab for the type of object you want to preview: **Pointers**, **Sounds**, or **Visuals**. Double-click an item in the list to display it in the preview area or play a sound. When you're done, click the **Close** button.

Run Programs Automatically on Startup

If you always work with the same programs whenever you're working in Windows, you can set them up so that they start automatically whenever you start your computer. Windows 98 has a Startup menu, which you can open by clicking Start, Programs, StartUp. The menu might already contain icons for a few programs that need to run in the background. Windows runs any program on the StartUp menu automatically on startup.

To add a program to the StartUp menu, you use the Start Menu Programs tab in the Taskbar Properties dialog box. You might have already encountered this tab if you added programs to the Start menu in "Configure the Start Menu" ►on page 53◄. The process for adding a program to the StartUp menu is the same. The following project shows you just what to do.

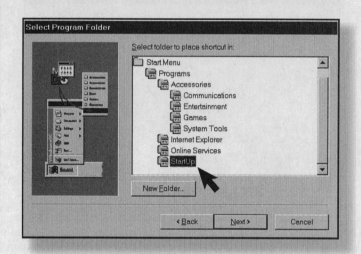

Do It Yourself Add a Program to the StartUp Menu

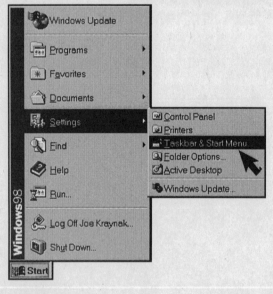

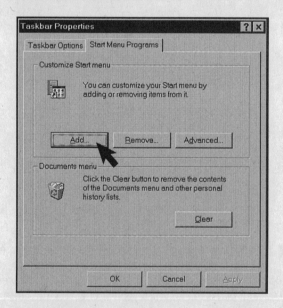

1 Click **Start**, point to **Settings**, and click **Taskbar & Start Menu**.

2 In the Taskbar Properties dialog box, click the **Start Menu Programs** tab.

3 Click the **Add** button.

Do It Yourself Add a Program to the StartUp Menu

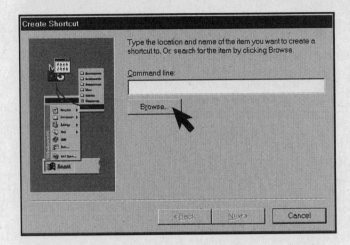

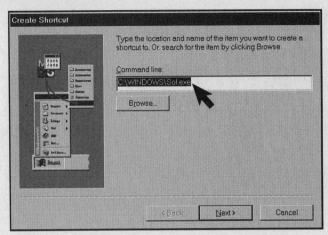

4 The Create Shortcut dialog box appears, prompting you to specify the location and name of the file that runs the program. Click the **Browse** button.

6 You are returned to the Create Shortcut dialog box, and the selected file's location and name appear in the Command Line text box. Click **Next**.

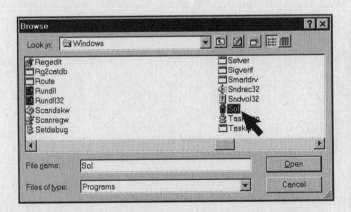

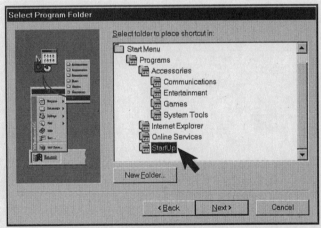

5 In the Browse dialog box, change to the drive and folder that contains the file that executes the program. Select the file and click **Open**.

7 Select Program Folder dialog box appears. Click the **StartUp** folder and click **Next**.

(continues)

Do It Yourself Add a Program to the StartUp Menu

(continued)

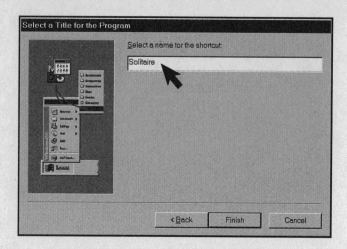

8 Windows prompts you to name the shortcut. Type the program's name as you want it to appear on the menu and click **Finish**.

9 You are returned to the Taskbar Properties dialog box. Click **OK** to save your changes. The program is now listed on the StartUp menu and will run automatically on startup.

Enter Keyboard Preferences

In "Configure a Mouse or Joystick" (►on page 373◄), you learned how to control the appearance and movement of the mouse pointer. Windows provides similar control for your keyboard, allowing you to enter preferences for the following options:

Repeat Delay. Controls the amount of time you have to hold down a key before it starts to repeat the keystroke.

Repeat Rate. Controls the speed at which a key repeats itself when you hold it down.

Cursor Blink Rate. Controls the rate at which the insertion point blinks.

Although the standard settings for these options probably work okay for you, you might notice as you work that you often type repeating characters, such as spaces or periods, or that you have to hold down the key for a relatively long time to make it repeat. You can change these settings to accommodate the way you work. The following project shows you what to do.

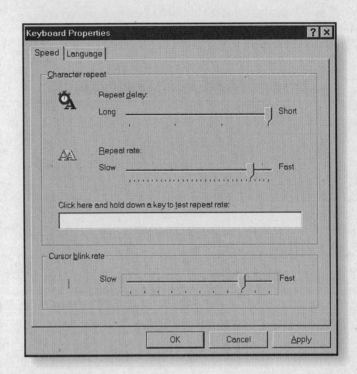

Do It Yourself   Enter Keyboard Properties

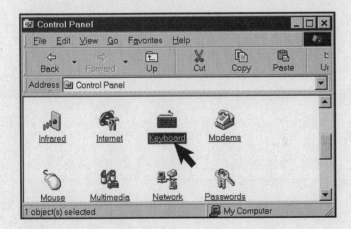

1 In the Windows Control Panel, click the **Keyboard** icon.

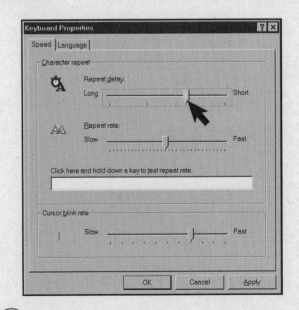

2 The Keyboard Properties dialog box appears with the Speed tab in front. To change the repeat delay, drag the **Repeat Delay** slider to the left to increase the delay or to the right to decrease it.

(continues)

Do It Yourself Enter Keyboard Properties

(continued)

3 To change the speed at which repeating characters are inserted, drag the **Repeat Rate** slider to the left to decrease the speed or to the right to increase it.

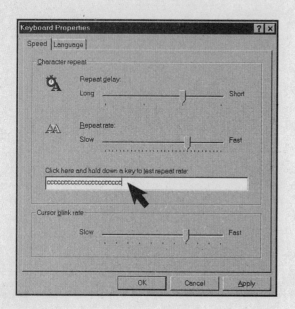

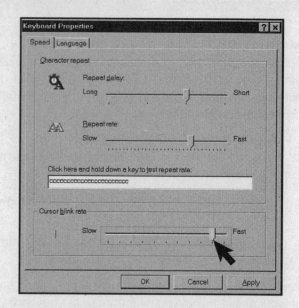

6 To change the speed at which the insertion point blinks, drag the **Cursor Blink Rate** slider to the left to decrease the speed or to the right to increase it. Click **OK** to save the settings.

4 To test the repeat rate, click in the text box below the sliders and hold down a key.

5 Repeat steps 3 and 4 as necessary to make any desired changes to the repeat rate and delay.

Password-Protect Your Computer

You learned how to use a screen saver password to protect your computer in the section "Change Display Properties" ►on page 406◄. This allows you to step away from your computer without having someone peek at your screen while you're away.

However, sometimes you must share your computer with coworkers or family members. When people share a computer, everyone needs access to it, and each person probably has a different idea about how to set up the Windows desktop and configure the work environment. This poses a problem. You don't want to have to reconfigure your system each time someone else messes with the Windows settings.

To solve this problem, Windows allows you to set up your system for more than one user. Each user is given a username and password that identifies him or her. When the person makes changes to the Windows desktop or the work environment, Windows saves the changes for that person. Each person can then configure Windows separately without affecting anyone else's settings.

The following project shows you how to enter usernames and passwords for logging on to Windows.

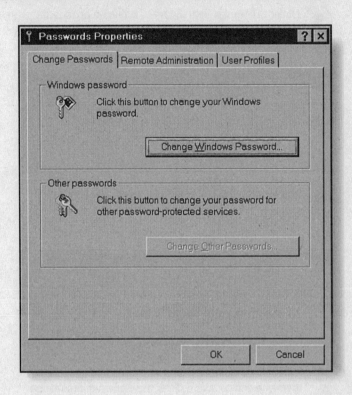

Do It Yourself   Set Up Windows for Multiple Users

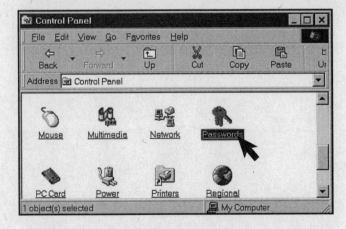

1 In the Windows Control Panel, click the **Passwords** icon.

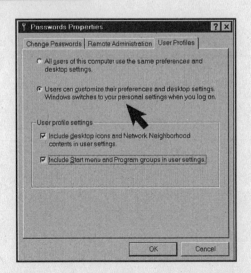

2 In the Passwords Properties dialog box, click the **User Profiles** tab and choose **Users Can Customize Their Preferences....**

(continues)

Do It Yourself Set Up Windows for Multiple Users *(continued)*

3 Under User Profile Settings, make sure both options are checked. Click **OK**.

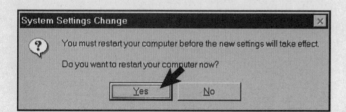

4 You are prompted to restart Windows. Close any programs you are currently running, and then click **Yes**.

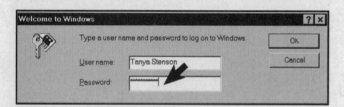

5 When Windows restarts, it prompts you to enter your username and password. Enter the requested information and click **OK**. (Each person using this computer should perform this step and the next one to log on.)

If you are not concerned about system security, and you want to simply set up your computer for multiple users, each person can leave the Password text box blank. To log on to Windows, the user simply enters his or her username.

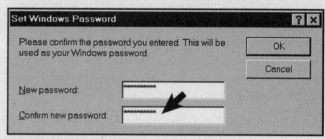

6 Windows prompts you to confirm your password. Type the password in the **New Password** and **Confirm New Password** text boxes and click **OK**.

7 Windows indicates that you have not logged on to this computer before and asks if you would like to save any settings you enter for the next time you log on. Click **Yes**.

DO IT YOURSELF

Use the Internet Tools

n "Use Windows 98 on the World Wide Web" ▶on page 217◀, you learned how to use the most important Internet tool, a Web browser, to open Web pages, play multimedia files, and skip around the Web. In "Use Outlook Express for Email and Newsgroups" ▶on page 321◀, you learned how to use Microsoft's email program to send and receive email messages and to read and post messages in newsgroups.

This section provides hands-on instructions for using these same Internet tools for practical purposes, such as job searches, shopping, and computing. In addition, the projects in this section introduce you to tools you have not yet encountered, including Microsoft Chat, which allows you to exchange typed messages instantly with people around the globe.

What You Will Find in This Section

Search for Jobs

Companies are flocking to the Web not only to market their products online, but also to find qualified employees who are computer-literate and know their way around the Internet. To tap into this growing job market, you need to know how to connect to the companies that are hiring, where to look for online job listings, and how to contact companies via email. It can also help if you have your résumé posted on the Web or in appropriate newsgroups.

This project does not focus on any one of the Internet tools included with Windows 98. Instead, it shows how to use several Internet tools (Internet Explorer, FrontPage Express, and Outlook Express) together to execute an effective and successful job search on the Internet.

Do It Yourself Locate Prospective Employers

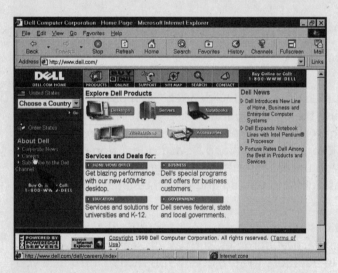

1 If you know which company you want to work for, connect to the company's home page (most large companies have their own home page on the Web) and look for a link labeled Employment or Jobs. Click the link.

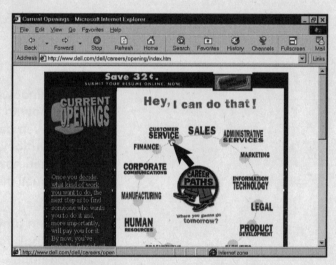

2 The Employment or Jobs link typically displays a page that lists current openings. If the page lists various categories, click the link for the desired category, and follow the trail of links to the desired ad.

Do It Yourself Locate Prospective Employers

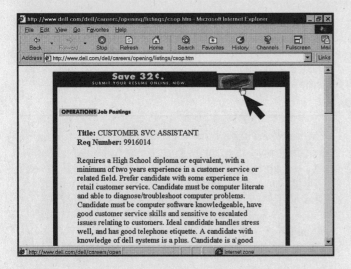

3 Eventually, you should reach a page that displays a description of the current opening. Read the job description, just as you would read it in your local newspaper. There might even be a link you can click to submit your résumé online.

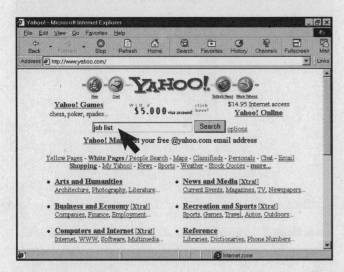

4 The Web also has several sites that publish job listings. Open your favorite Internet search tool, ▶as explained in "Find Information on the Web" on page 261◀, and search for **Job List**.

Because Yahoo organizes sites by category, it is one of the best search tools to use for finding job listings. Go to Yahoo at www.yahoo.com and search for **Jobs**. Several links for various job categories will appear, helping you narrow the search for your field of expertise.

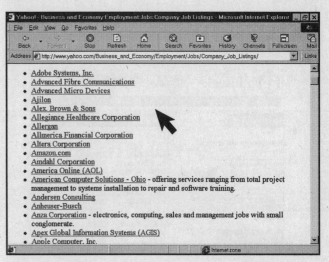

5 The search tool will find and display a long list of links to online job lists. Click the desired link.

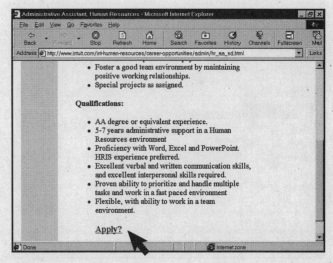

6 Most lists provide a job description, location, and contact information for the job. Jot down or print out the information you need. (The entry might also contain links to the company's home page and to an email address you can use for more information or to submit your résumé.)

(continues)

Do It Yourself Locate Prospective Employers

(continued)

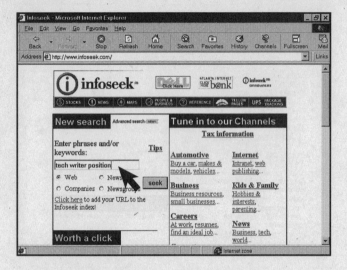

7 Another way to search is to use your favorite search tool to look for the desired job title, such as "tech writer" or "advertising assistant." Consider adding words such as "job," "wanted," "position," and "opening" to your search phrase or specify a state or city to narrow the search.

When you search by job title, expect to turn up a long list of links that have nothing to do with job openings. You might even find a few links for other people who are looking for the same job! If you find some of those, click the links to find out what other people are doing online to advertise themselves.

Do It Yourself Create a Web Page Résumé

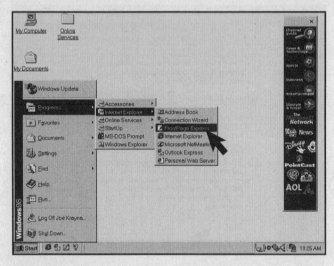

1 Click the **Start** button, point to **Programs** and then **Internet Explorer**, and click **FrontPage Express**.

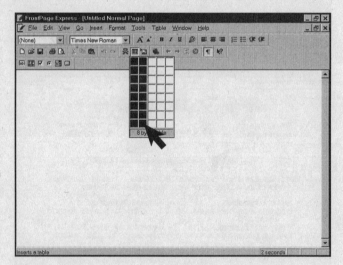

2 Now you will make a two-column table so you can insert categories and dates in the left column and details in the right column. Click the **Insert Table** button and drag down and to the right to select two columns and several rows.

Do It Yourself Create a Web Page Résumé

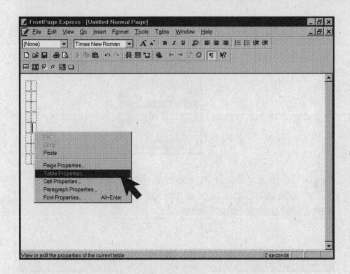

3 When you release the mouse button, FrontPage Express inserts the table. Right-click the table and choose **Table Properties**.

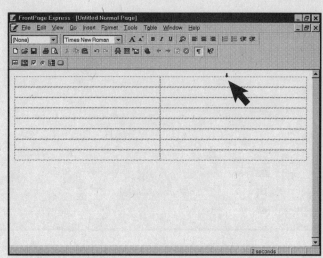

5 Move the mouse pointer above the right column so it appears as a down arrow, and then click to select the column.

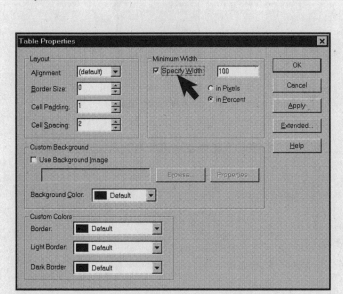

4 In the Table Properties dialog box, choose **Specify Width** and make sure the setting is 100 percent to make the table as wide as the page. Click **OK**.

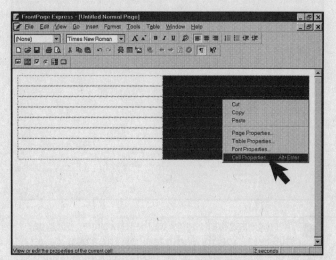

6 Right-click a selected cell and choose **Cell Properties**.

(continues)

Do It Yourself   Create a Web Page Résumé

(continued)

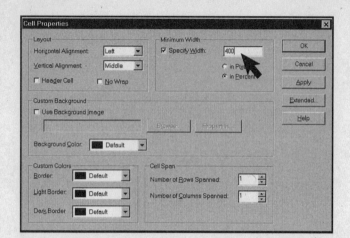

7 In the Cell Properties dialog box, click **Specify Width**, choose **In Percent**, and type **400** in the Specify Width text box. Click **OK**.

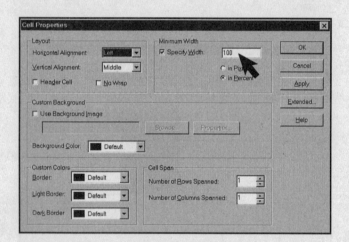

8 Repeat steps 5 through 7 for the left column, but type **100** in the **Specify Width** text box. This makes the left column one-fifth the width of the table and the right column four-fifths the width of the table.

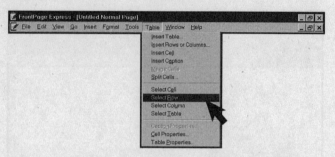

9 You should merge the top two cells to create a single, large cell. Click in one of the top cells, open the **Table** menu, and choose **Select Row**.

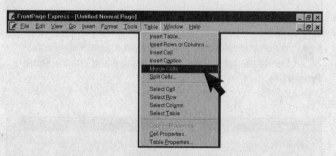

10 The two cells in the top row are highlighted. Open the **Table** menu and choose **Merge Cells**.

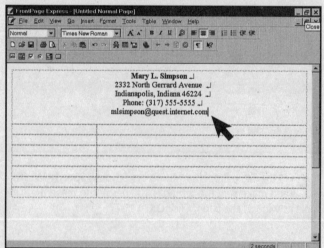

11 The two cells are merged to create a single cell. Type your name, address, phone number, and email address on separate lines (press **Shift+Enter** to start new lines). Then format the text as desired. (In this figure, all lines are centered and the name is bold.)

Do It Yourself   Create a Web Page Résumé

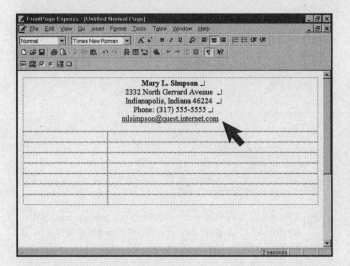

12 When you type your email address and press the spacebar, FrontPage Express automatically converts it into a link. Behind the link is **mailto:*youraddress***. This makes it convenient for prospective employers to contact you immediately via email.

If you are an artist, writer, or editor, or if you have additional documents that will help you land an interview, you can place samples of your work or any other documents on your Web site and add links that point to those documents. ▶See "Make a Simple Web Page with FrontPage Express" on page 287 to learn more about inserting links.◀

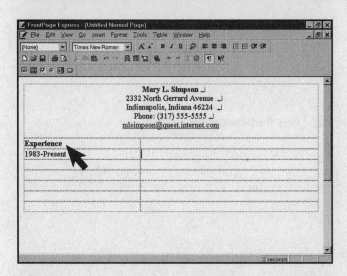

13 Click in the next cell down and to the left, click the **Bold** button, and type a category name, such as **Experience** or **Education**.

14 Press the **Down Arrow** key to move down to the next cell, click the **Bold** button, and then type the dates for the first entry in this category.

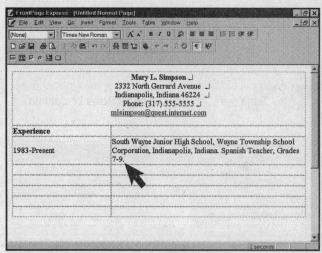

15 Click in the cell to the right of the date and type a brief description of your activities during that time period.

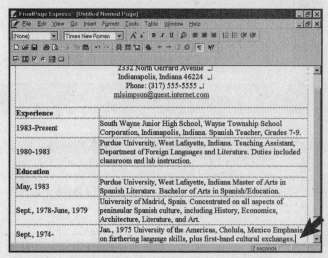

16 Repeat steps 13 through 15 to insert additional categories, dates, and descriptions.

(continues)

Do It Yourself Create a Web Page Résumé

(continued)

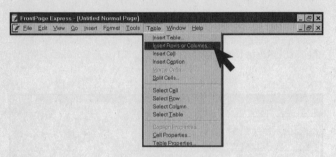

17 If you run out of rows, click in a cell in the last row, open the **Table** menu, and choose **Insert Rows or Columns**.

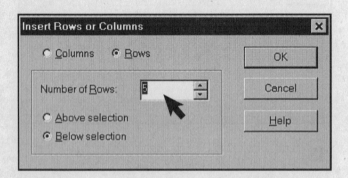

18 In the Insert Rows or Columns dialog box, make sure **Rows** is selected, and use the **Number of Rows** spin box to specify the desired number of rows. Click **Below Selection** and click **OK**.

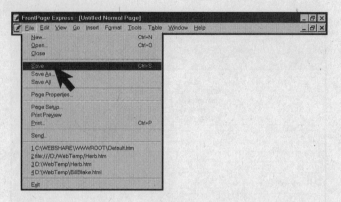

19 When you finish creating your résumé, use the **File**, **Save** command to publish it to your Web site. ►See "Place Your Page on the Web" on page 295.◄

Many job sites allow you to publish your résumé. In addition, you can email your Web résumé to prospective employers by attaching it to your email message. ►See "Send Messages and Replies" on page 332 for details.◄

Do It Yourself Find a Job in Newsgroups

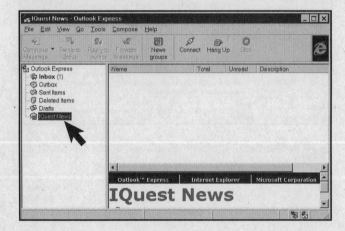

1 Another place you can look for jobs is in newsgroups. Run Outlook Express and click the icon for your news server. ►See "Set Up Your News Server Account" on page 348.◄

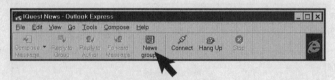

2 Click the **Newsgroups** button.

Do It Yourself Find a Job in Newsgroups

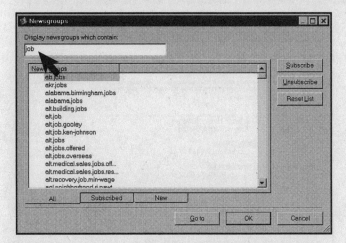

3 The Newsgroups window appears, displaying a list of all of the newsgroups available on the selected news server. In the **Display Newsgroups Which Contain** text box, type **job**.

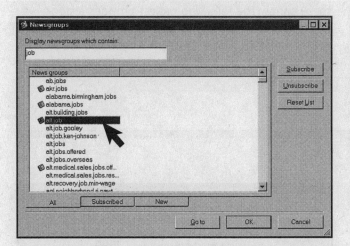

4 The list is filtered to show only those newsgroups whose names contain the word "job." To subscribe to some of those newsgroups, double-click their names. ▶See "Find, Subscribe to, and Unsubscribe from Newsgroups" on page 352.◀ Then click **OK**.

Many of the newsgroup names have abbreviations that specify the city, state, or organization that is hosting the newsgroup. For example, `chi.jobs` contains messages that pertain to jobs in the Chicago area. Other parts of the newsgroup name might state the type of job, such as `pdaxs.jobs.clerical` (for clerical positions) and `csd.academic-jobs` (for teaching positions).

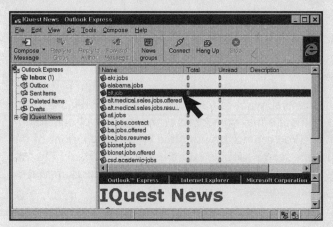

5 You are returned to the main Outlook Express window, where a list of the subscribed newsgroups appears. Double-click a newsgroup name to view its messages.

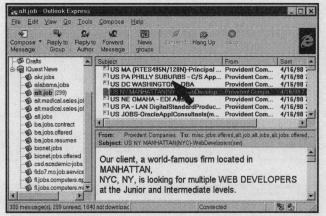

6 The message descriptions appear in the upper-right pane. Click a description to view its contents in the lower-right pane. ▶For details on reading and replying to newsgroup messages, see "Read Newsgroup Messages" on page 355 and "Post Messages and Replies" on page 359.◀

Find Relatives and Friends

In "Use the Address Book" ▶on page 340◀, you learned how to search for people's email addresses using various Internet search tools from the Outlook Express Address Book. However, there might be times when you want to track down a friend or relative to find out a mailing address or the person's phone number. You can do this using the Web-page versions of the same search tools you used earlier in this book. The following is a list of popular people-search tools and their Web addresses:

Four11 at four11.com

Bigfoot at bigfoot.com

Infospace at infospace.com

SwitchBoard at switchboard.com

WhoWhere? at whowhere.com

Yahoo at yahoo.com/search/people/

Although these search tools provide a fairly intuitive way of looking up phone numbers and addresses, you might not know what to expect when you connect to one of

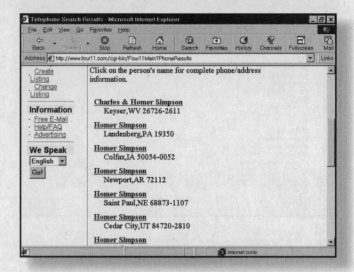

these pages. The following project provides a step-by-step example of how to use Four11 to search for people using an online directory. As you will see in the project, Four11 can even give you directions to the person's house!

Do It Yourself Find People with Four11

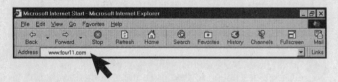

① Run Internet Explorer, type **www.four11.com** in the **Address** text box, and press **Enter**.

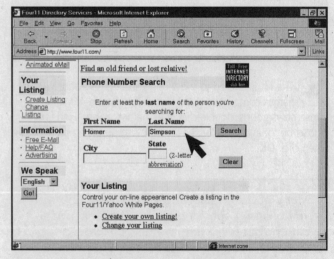

② The Four11 home page initially prompts you to search for email addresses or telephone numbers. Scroll down to the **Phone Number Search** form.

Do It Yourself   Find People with Four11

3 Type the requested information, including the person's first name, last name, and the city and/or state in which the person lives. (If the person has a unique last name, a last name entry might be all you need.) Click the **Search** button.

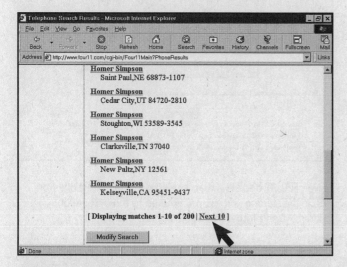

4 Four11 locates a list of people in its directory whose entries match the entry you typed. If the list is long, click the **Next 10** link at the end of the list to view more.

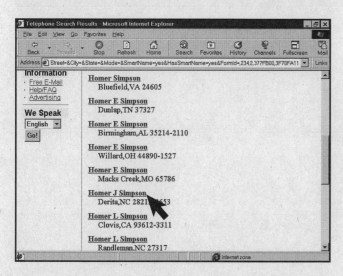

5 When you find the link for the person you're looking for, click the link.

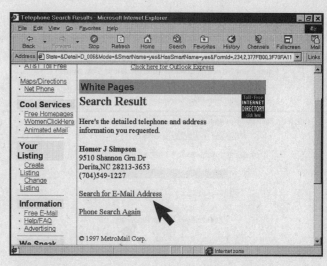

6 Four11 displays the person's street address and telephone number, along with links for searching for the person's email address.

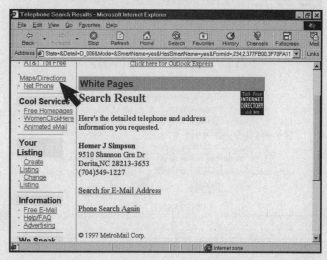

7 Once you have the person's street address, jot it down or select and copy it, and then click the **Map/Directions** link.

(continues)

Do It Yourself   Find People with Four11   *(continued)*

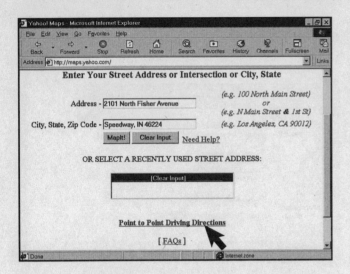

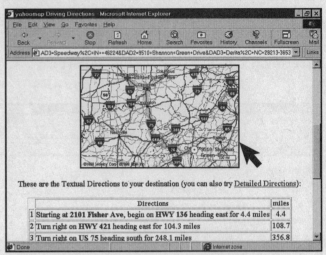

8 Scroll down the resulting page and click the **Point to Point Driving Directions** link.

11 Four11 displays a map plus step-by-step directions from the starting address you entered to the destination address. (Don't forget that you can print this page.)

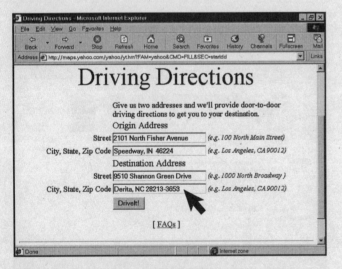

Be careful when following the directions. The directions Four11 provided for traveling from my home in Indianapolis to my parents' home in Chicago added an hour to the trip.

9 In the text boxes at the top, type the address, city, state, and ZIP code from which you would be departing (for instance, your home address).

10 In the text boxes at the bottom, type the destination address, city, state, and ZIP code (the address of the place you want to go). Click the **DriveIt!** button.

Shop for Products and Services

Purchasing items on the Internet offers some unique advantages. Because so many companies are attempting to establish themselves as the best places to shop, and because these companies do not have to pay a high overhead for renting store space, they often offer the best prices. In addition, you can often find products that you cannot find anywhere else, such as those rubber sunglasses mentioned on the AT&T Internet commercial, and other specialty items. And you can use most Internet search tools to track down these specialty items. Shopping online also allows you to place your order immediately, just as if you were ordering from a mail-order catalog.

However, you should also be careful when shopping online. If you give your credit card number to a con artist who knows how to set up a Web page, you might discover on your next statement that someone other than you has been doing a little shopping. Make sure you place orders at reputable companies that have a system in place for making secure transactions. Unless you have turned off the warning messages in Internet Explorer, Internet Explorer will indicate when you are moving from an insecure site to a secure site, and vice versa. If you have turned off the warnings, check the status bar for a padlock icon. The presence of this icon indicates that the site is secure.

Just in case you haven't bumped into any electronic shopping malls on the Web, this project shows you how to actively connect to some of the best malls and company Web sites. Before you begin, you might want to set your Visa card next to your keyboard. To buy anything from most companies on the Web, you must first enter billing information, including a credit card number.

Do It Yourself   Shop on the Web

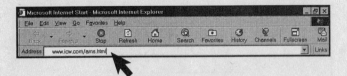

1 Run Internet Explorer, click in the **Address** text box, type **www.icw.com/ams.html**, and press **Enter**.

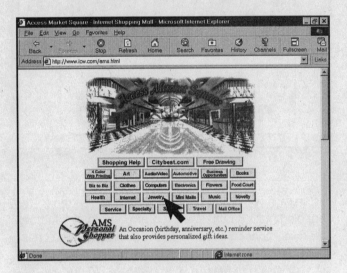

2 Internet Explorer takes you to Access Market Square, where you'll find links to clothing, electronics, art, flowers, and much more. Click a link for the desired product.

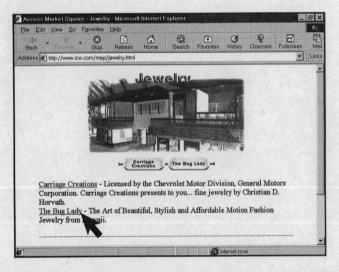

3 Access Market Square displays a list of companies on the Web that sell the selected product, along with descriptions of the companies and links that point to their sites. Click the desired link.

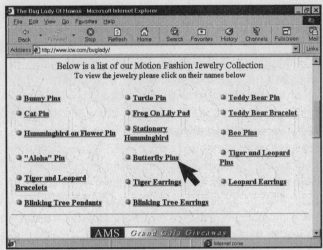

4 Because Access Market Square provides links to other online stores, the procedure for shopping varies depending on which store you're in. Follow the links as you would at any Web site.

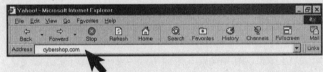

5 When you finish browsing the Access Market Square, visit CyberShop, one of the slickest online malls. Click in the **Address** text box, type **cybershop.com**, and press **Enter**.

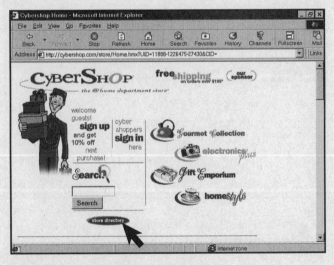

6 At CyberShop, click the **Store Directory** link.

Do It Yourself Shop on the Web

You can sign up at CyberShop to register for special deals and receive 10% off your first order. Click the **Sign Up** link and complete the resulting form to register.

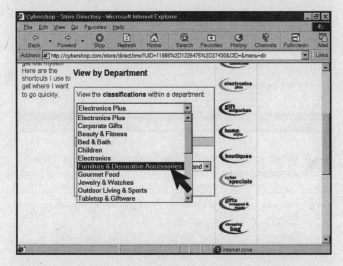

7 Scroll down the store directory page, open the **View the Classifications within a Department** list, and choose the desired product category. Then click the **Show Me!** button.

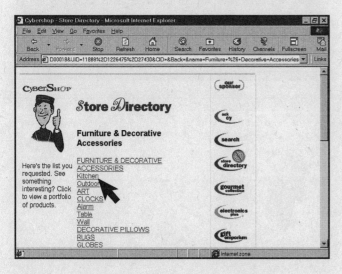

8 CyberShop displays a list of subcategories. Click the desired subcategory.

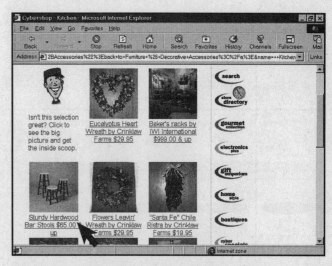

9 An online catalog appears, complete with pictures and prices of products in the selected category. To learn more about a product, click its link.

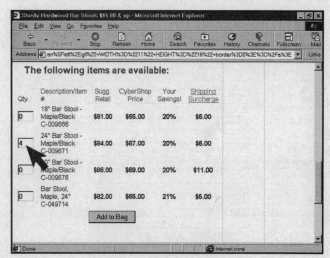

10 When you find an item you want to order, scroll down the page, click in the **Qty** text box, and type the number of items you want to order. Then click **Add to Bag**.

(continues)

Do It Yourself Shop on the Web *(continued)*

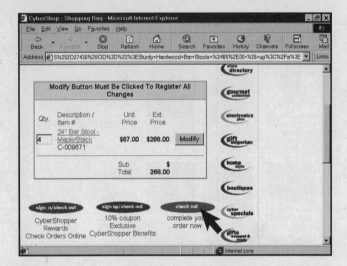

11 CyberShop displays the order details. You can continue shopping for other items and adding them to your bag. When you are done shopping, click the **Check Out** link.

14 When you are done at CyberShop, check out the following online malls:

Barclay Square at www.barclaysquare.co.uk
eShop at www.eshop.com/
Internet Shopping Network at www.isn.com/
Net Market at www.netmarket.com/

If you are looking for a specific product, use a Web search tool to look for that product. You'll probably find links to several companies that sell the product.

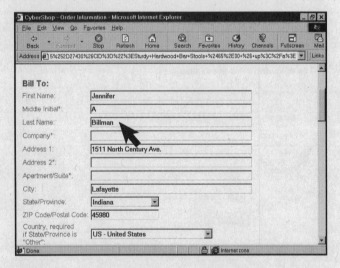

12 You are taken to the Check Out page. Note the padlock icon in Internet Explorer's status bar; this indicates that the site is secure.

13 An order form appears, prompting you to enter shipping and billing information. Complete the form and click **Continue**. Follow the onscreen instructions to submit your order.

Find Technical Support

Nearly every computer hardware and software company has its own Web site, where you can purchase products directly and find technical support for products you own. If your printer is not feeding paper properly, you're having trouble installing your sound card, you keep receiving cryptic error messages in your favorite program, or you have some other computer-related problem or question, you can usually find the solution on the Internet.

In addition, computer and software companies often upgrade their software and post updates and fixes on their Web sites for downloading. If you are having problems with a device, such as a printer or modem, you should check the manufacturer's Web site for updated drivers. If you run into problems with a program, check the software company's Web site for a *patch*, a program file that you install to correct the problem.

Although the following project cannot show you how to find technical support for specific problems, it does show you how to find help at Microsoft's Web site and what you can expect at the Web sites of hardware manufacturers, such as Gateway. The following table pro-

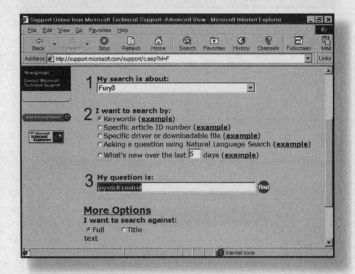

vides Web page addresses of popular software and hardware manufacturers to help you in your search. Most of the home pages listed have a link for connecting to the support page. If a page does not have a link to the support page, use its search tool to locate the page.

Computer Hardware and Software Web Sites

Company	Web Page Address	Company	Web Page Address
Acer	www.acer.com	Hitachi	www.hitachipc.com
Borland	www.borland.com	IBM	www.ibm.com
Broderbund	www.broderbund.com	Intel	www.intel.com
Brother	www.brother.com	Iomega	www.iomega.com
Canon	www.ccsi.canon.com	Lotus	www.lotus.com
Compaq	www.compaq.com	Micron Electronics	www.micronpc.com
Corel	www.corel.com	Microsoft	www.microsoft.com
Creative Labs	www.soundblaster.com	Motorola	www.mot.com/MIMS/ISPD/support.html
Dell	www.dell.com	NEC	www.nec.com
Epson	www.epson.com	Packard Bell	www.packardbell.com
Fujitsu	www.fujitsu.com	Panasonic	www.panasonic.com
Gateway	www.gw2k.com	Sony	www.sony.com
Hayes	www.hayes.com	Toshiba	www.toshiba.com
Hewlett-Packard	www.hp.com	US Robotics	www.usr.com

Do It Yourself Access Online Technical Support

1 In Internet Explorer's **Address** text box, type the address of the company whose tech support page you want to view and press **Enter**.

2 Internet Explorer loads the page. Click the **Support** link or its equivalent.

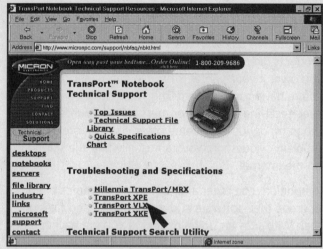

3 In most cases, the resulting page lists links to products or product categories. Follow the trail of links to the specific product you own.

4 When you see a link for the product, click it.

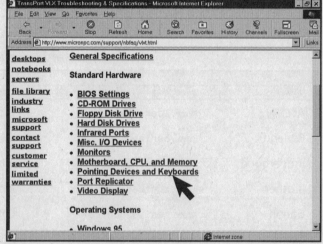

5 The resulting page might display additional links for components and software. Click the link for the component or software for which you need help.

Do It Yourself   Access Online Technical Support

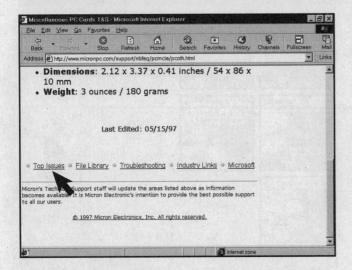

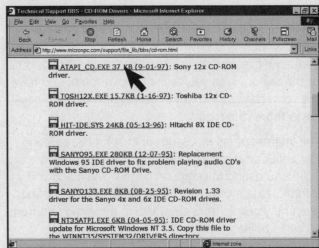

6 In many cases, the site has a link for viewing FAQs (frequently asked questions). Click the link to view a list of questions and problems that many users have with the product.

8 In some cases, the company might offer software you can download and install to correct a problem. ▶See "Save Web Pages and Files" on page 237 to learn how to download files.◀

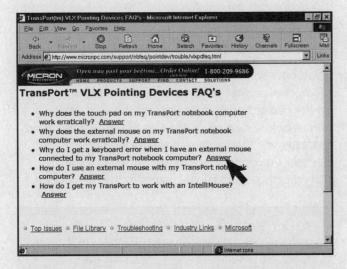

7 The FAQ list appears, displaying questions and answers. You might have to click a link to view the answer to a question in the list.

In addition to searching the Web for technical support, you might be able to find help in newsgroups from other users of the same product. Use Outlook Express to search for newsgroups that address the product you are using. In many cases, you can find an ongoing discussion that answers your question. If you can't find the answer in the newsgroup, post a description for the problem you are having, and ask other users for help.

Chat on the Internet

Although the Internet consists mostly of computers that store and serve up files for you to download and view, the Internet also has a social side. At any time of the day or night, you can enter chat rooms and have live conversations, via typed messages, with other people in those chat rooms.

The Internet offers thousands of chat rooms, covering just about any topic you can think of—from sports to politics to dating to computer games. You'll also find informal chat rooms where you can just hang out and meet new people from anywhere in the world and from all walks of life.

In this project, you will fire up Microsoft Chat and use it to access a chat room on the Internet. (If you are a parent, you should be aware that some chat rooms are for adults only. Supervise your kids if you choose to allow them to chat.)

> Microsoft Chat is not installed during a typical installation of Windows 98. To install it, ▶see "Add and Remove Windows Components" on page 422.◀ Microsoft Chat is listed in the Communications Components category.

Send a Message

Comic Chat displays a three-paned window. The upper-left pane (the largest) displays the ongoing discussion. The right pane displays a list of people in the room, a picture of your character, and an emotion wheel that allows you to change your character's posture and facial expression. The lower-left pane contains a text box from which you type and send a message. To send a message, type it in the text box and click one of the following buttons:

 Say displays your text in a balloon over your character.

 Think displays your text as a thought in a bubble above your character.

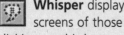 **Whisper** displays your text only on the screens of those people you select. Before clicking on this button, select the individuals you

want to include from the list in the upper-right corner of the screen.

 Action displays your text in a box in the upper-left corner of the comic strip frame.

If you have something to say to a specific person in the room, click on that person's name in the member list or on the person's character in one of the comic strip frames before clicking on the **Say** button. The selected character will then appear in the frame with you. You can select more than one person to speak to by **Ctrl+***click*ing on additional names in the member list.

> Instead of clicking on the buttons, you can press a key combination: **Enter** (Say), **Ctrl+T** (Think), **Ctrl+W** (Whisper), or **Ctrl+I** (Action).

If the comic strip frames are too large for your liking, you can change their size. Open the **View** menu, select **Options**, and click on the **Settings** tab. Open the drop-down list under **Page Layout**, and click on **3** or **4 Panels Wide**. Click **OK**.

Create a New Identity

Microsoft Chat is a unique chat program in that it displays the ongoing discussion in the form of a comic strip. When you start Comic Chat, it displays a dialog box asking you to pick a nickname, as shown in the project. Then you pick a chat server (a computer that hosts the chat rooms) and a chat room, and you can start chatting right away.

However, before you start to chat, you might want to change your identity. You want to do two things: enter information about yourself that you want other chatters to know, and pick a comic strip character. The second part of the project shows you how to change your identity.

Do It Yourself   Chat Live on the Internet

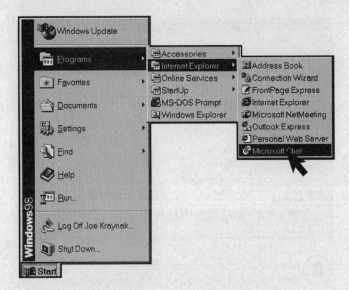

1 Click the **Start** button, point to **Programs** and then **Internet Explorer**, and click **Microsoft Chat**.

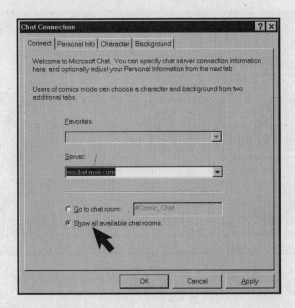

2 You are prompted to choose a chat server and chat room. A Microsoft Chat server is already selected. Click **Show All Available Chat Rooms**.

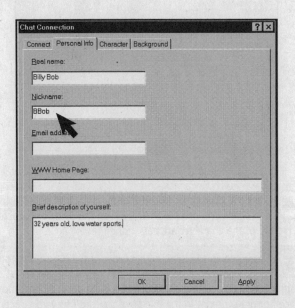

3 Click the **Personal Info** tab and change "Anonymous" in the **Nickname** text box to a name you want to be called in the chat room. (You can type additional information about yourself, but be careful about entering information that can help a person track you down.)

Your nickname will appear in the list of people in a particular room. The other information (your name and personal description) is provided only by request. If someone wants the information, the person simply enters a command to check your profile.

(continues)

Do It Yourself   Chat Live on the Internet

(continued)

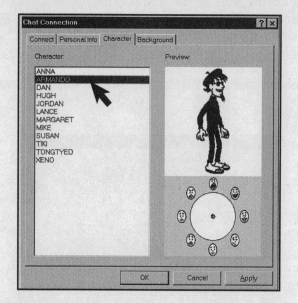

You can change your personal information, character, or comic strip background at any time. Open the **View** menu and choose **Options** or press **Ctrl+Q**.

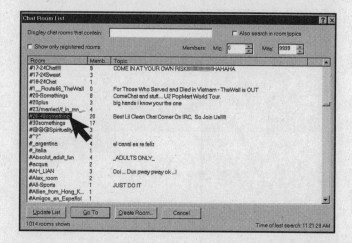

4 Click the **Character** tab. This displays a list of comic strip characters you can become. Click on the desired character. A picture of the character appears in the Preview area.

5 The wheel in the lower-right corner of the dialog box contains several attitudes you can use for your character—happy, angry, coy, bored, and so on. Click the desired demeanor (face), or drag the dot in the middle of the circle toward a face on the outside of the circle (where emotions are higher).

8 Microsoft Chat downloads a (long) list of room names from the server and displays them, along with the number of people in each room. Click the name of the room in which you want to chat and click **Go To**.

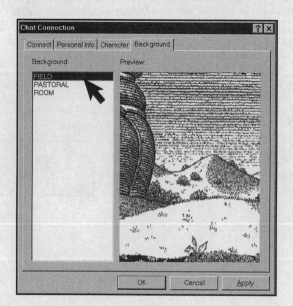

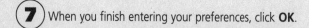

6 Click the Background tab and choose the desired background for the comic strip panels.

7 When you finish entering your preferences, click **OK**.

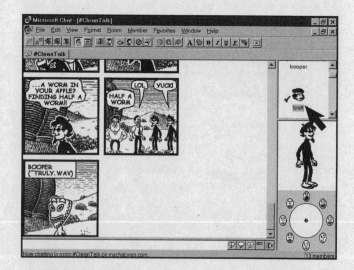

9 Microsoft Chat takes you to the selected room and displays the ongoing discussion as a comic strip.

10 To say something, first click the character you want to talk to in the member list (that character will appear in the comic strip frame with you). **Ctrl+***click* to choose additional members.

Do It Yourself   Chat Live on the Internet

11 Click in the message area, type your message, and click the **Say**, **Think**, **Whisper**, or **Action** button.

12 Comic Chat displays a new frame along with a bubble containing the message you sent.

13 To change your character's posture or facial expression, click an expression in the **Emotion Wheel** or drag the circle in the center of the wheel out toward the desired emotion.

14 To view personal information about someone in the chat room, right-click the person's character and choose **Get Profile**.

(continues)

Do It Yourself Chat Live on the Internet

(continued)

15 A new frame appears, displaying the person's character and any information the person entered about herself.

16 To talk privately with a person, you can whisper. Right-click the person's character in the member list and choose **Whisper Box**.

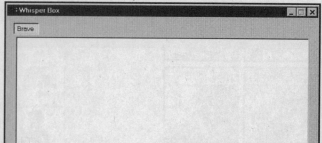

17 In the Whisper Box, type your message in the message area and click the **Whisper** button (or press **Ctrl+W**). The message is sent only to that person. Any messages the person sends back are displayed in the discussion area.

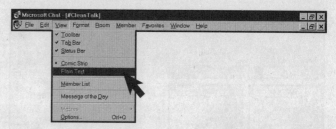

18 The comic strip takes up a great deal of screen space and makes it difficult to follow the discussion. You can switch to plain text mode. Open the **View** menu and choose **Plain Text**.

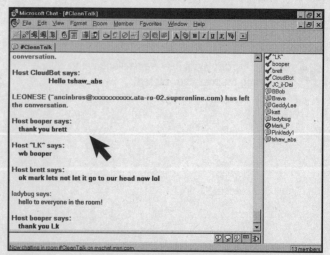

19 In plain text mode, no characters are displayed, but you can still see their names.

Do It Yourself Chat Live on the Internet

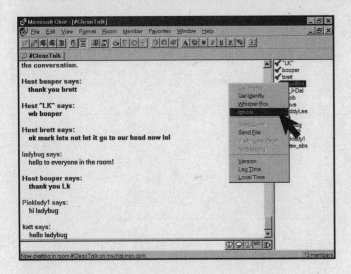

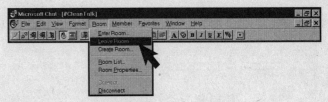

20 If a member is harassing you, you can choose to block any messages that person sends. Right-click the person's name in the member list and choose **Ignore**.

21 To leave the chat room you are currently in, open the **Room** menu and choose **Leave Room**.

22 To enter a different room, open the **Room** menu, choose **Room List**, and double-click the name of the desired room.

DO IT YOURSELF

Optimize Your System

Every month or so, computer manufacturers release new, improved computers that are faster. Unless you're independently wealthy, keeping up with the latest technology is impossible. You want your computer to run faster and more efficiently, but the cost is prohibitive. Fortunately, Windows 98 has several tools that can keep your computer running at least at *its* peak performance.

In this section, you will learn how to fine-tune your computer to make it run as fast and efficiently as it is capable of running. These projects show you how to automate tune-ups with the new Windows Maintenance Wizard, increase your hard disk space with the new Drive Converter, use some standard Windows tools to increase the performance of your hard disk drive, clear useless files from your hard drive, optimize your CD-ROM drive, and give your system a little more memory without you having to install more RAM.

What You Will Find in This Section

Use the Windows Maintenance Wizard

Your computer is like a car. As you install programs, wander the Web, and create documents, your system continually becomes slower and less efficient. If a program's installation utility automatically adds the program to the StartUp menu, Windows starts more slowly. When you wander the Web, Internet Explorer saves Web page files to your hard disk (without asking you), cutting down on available space. When you create and edit documents, programs often place temporary files on your disk that remain there until you delete them. And files on your hard disk continually become more and more fragmented as parts of files are stored on separate areas of the disk.

The Windows Maintenance Wizard can help you keep your computer in tip-top condition. It automatically performs a series of tests and corrections at scheduled times to check for problems on your hard disk, defragment files, delete temporary files (files that Windows and your programs use as they work but may "forget" to delete), remove programs from the StartUp menu that may slow down the initial Windows startup, and optimize your hard disk. With the Windows Maintenance Wizard, you will rarely have to go

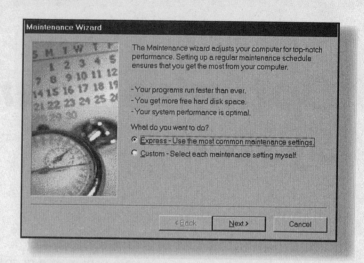

behind-the-scenes with Windows to perform such tasks manually.

The following project shows you how to run the Windows Maintenance Wizard and perform the customized setup to have it perform only the corrections you allow.

Do It Yourself Run and Configure the Maintenance Wizard

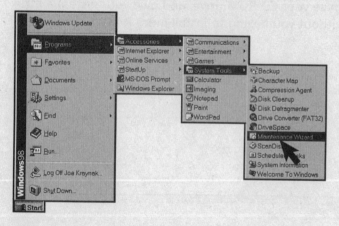

1 Click the **Start** button, point to **Programs**, **Accessories**, and then **System Tools**, and click **Maintenance Wizard**.

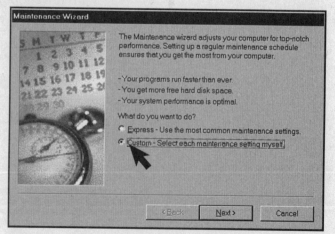

2 The Maintenance Wizard displays a brief description of itself. Choose **Custom** and click **Next**.

Do It Yourself Run and Configure the Maintenance Wizard

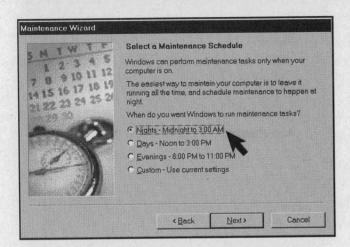

3 The Wizard asks when you want it to perform daily tune-ups. Choose the desired time (a time when you normally have your computer on but you are not using it). Then click **Next**.

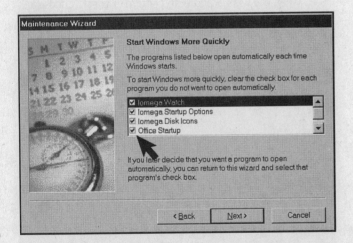

4 If your system has any programs that run automatically when you start Windows, the Wizard displays a list of those. To prevent any of these programs from starting, click its check box to remove the check mark. Click **Next**.

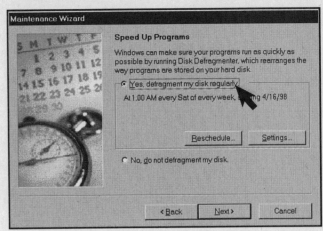

5 The Wizard can rearrange the program files on your hard disk to make programs run faster by defragmenting your disk. Leave **Yes, Defragment My Disk Regularly** turned on. Click the **Reschedule** button.

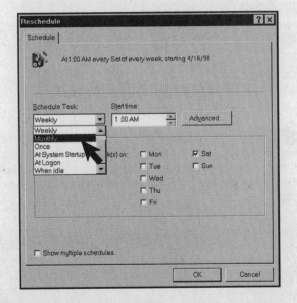

6 Enter settings in the Reschedule dialog box to specify when you want program files rearranged. If you rarely install new programs on your system, choose a weekly or monthly schedule. Click **OK**.

(continues)

Do It Yourself Run and Configure the Maintenance Wizard *(continued)*

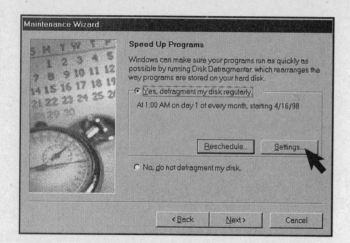

⑦ Click the **Settings** button.

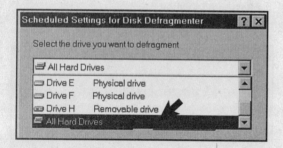

⑧ The Scheduled Settings for Disk Defragmenter dialog box asks which drives you want to optimize. Choose the disk drive on which you normally install programs or choose **All Hard Drives**. Click **OK**, and then click **Next** when you return to the wizard.

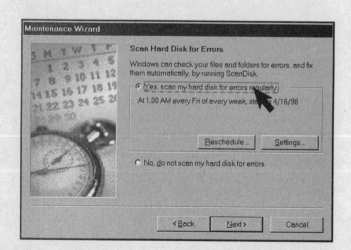

⑨ The wizard asks if you want ScanDisk to check your hard disk drives for errors. Make sure **Yes, Scan My Hard Disk for Errors Regularly** is selected. Click the **Reschedule** button.

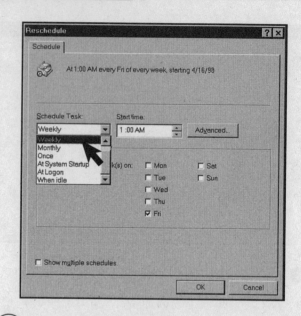

⑩ Enter settings in the Reschedule dialog box to specify when you want ScanDisk to perform its check. Choose a daily or weekly schedule to keep your disk drives running at peak performance. Click **OK**.

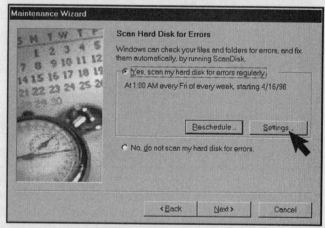

⑪ Click the **Settings** button.

Do It Yourself Run and Configure the Maintenance Wizard

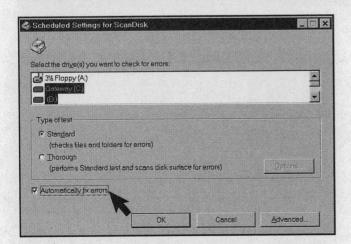

12 By default, ScanDisk is set up to check all your hard disk drives. If you have more than one hard disk drive and you want ScanDisk to check only certain drives, **Ctrl+**_click_ a drive to have ScanDisk skip it.

13 In the Type of Test area, leave **Standard** selected so ScanDisk will not test your hard disks for physical defects. (You can perform this check manually on a monthly or semi-monthly basis.)

14 Click **Automatically Fix Errors** to allow ScanDisk to perform its corrections without your intervention. Click **OK** and then click **Next** when you return to the wizard.

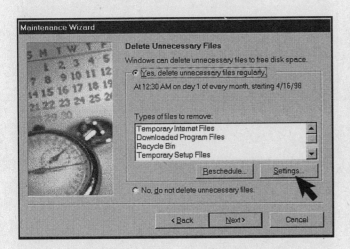

15 The wizard can automatically free up hard disk space by removing unneeded files. Click the **Settings** button.

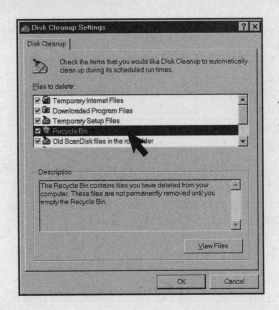

16 The wizard displays a list of file types it can delete. Click a file type to place a check in its box to mark those files for deletion, or remove the check mark to prevent those files from being deleted.

17 You can click the **Reschedule** button to change the schedule for deleting these files and click **OK**. When you return to the wizard, click the **Next** button.

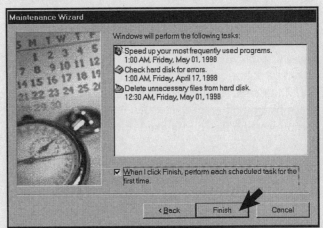

18 The wizard displays a list of optimization activities it will perform at the scheduled time(s). To have the wizard perform those activities now, choose **When I Click Finish...**.

19 Click the **Finish** button. Be sure to leave your computer on at the scheduled time so that Windows can perform the optimization activities at the scheduled time(s).

Increase Disk Space

As computers become more complex, program and document files are becoming larger and larger. Five years ago, a typical program would take up a couple megabytes of disk space. Today, each program can consume 10MB or more. In addition, as you explore the Internet, you will commonly encounter graphics and audio and video clips that are over 1MB!

As files become larger and as your own thirst for the latest programs and media increases, your hard disk quickly becomes packed. To help, Windows offers a few utilities that can help your hard drive use its storage space more efficiently: Drive Converter and DriveSpace.

To understand Drive Converter, you must first understand how older hard disk drives have stored data in the past. If you have a hard drive larger than 500MB, older operating systems (using FAT16) would use 32KB of hard drive space to store every file containing 32KB or less of data. For example, a 2KB file would still take up 32KB of disk space. You could partition your hard disk drive into units smaller than 500MB to make the operating system store files in 4KB chunks instead, saving you up to 40 percent of wasted space. However, partitioning the hard disk drive destroys any data the disk contains. FAT32 can perform the optimization without destroying data, as shown in this project.

The only problem with FAT32 is that it cannot increase disk drive space on smaller hard disks. If you have a 500MB or smaller hard disk drive, you must free up disk space using a different utility: DriveSpace. DriveSpace compresses the files on the hard drive so that they take

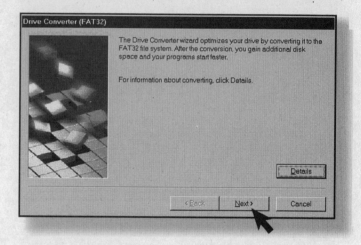

up less space when not in use (just like folded clothes take up less space than unfolded clothes). When you run a compressed program or open a compressed file, DriveSpace automatically decompresses it. Because DriveSpace must decompress files when you run a program or open a document, it slightly decreases overall system performance.

The following project shows you how to use Drive Converter and DriveSpace.

You cannot use DriveSpace on FAT32 drives. If you have a large hard drive (1 GB or more), use FAT32. If you have a smaller hard drive, use DriveSpace.

Do It Yourself   Convert a Hard Disk Drive to FAT32

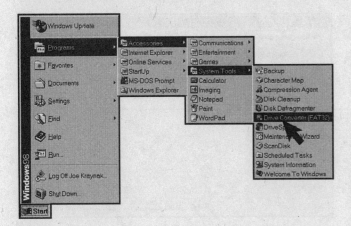

1 Click the **Start** button, point to **Programs**, **Accessories**, and then **System Tools**, and click **Drive Converter (FAT32)**.

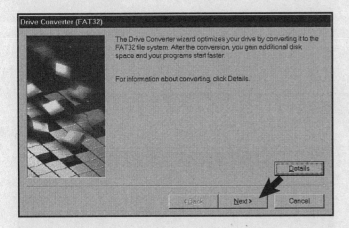

2 The Drive Converter Wizard displays a description of what it will do. Click **Next**.

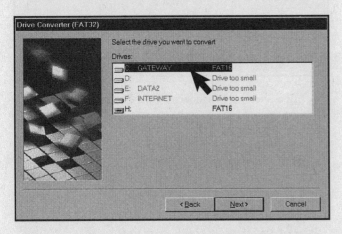

3 Drive Converter analyzes your hard disk drive(s) to determine which drive(s) are currently using FAT16. Click the drive you want to optimize and click **Next**.

If your hard disk drive is too small to use FAT32 or if it is already using FAT32, Drive Converter displays that information in the list.

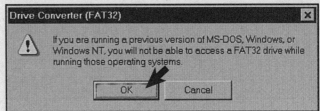

4 Drive Converter displays a warning indicating that you will not be able to access the converted drive using a previous version of Windows, MS-DOS, or Windows NT. Click **OK**.

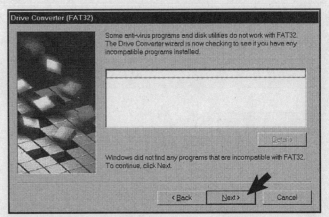

5 Drive Converter checks for any running programs that might interfere with its operation and displays a list of them. Close any of these programs and click **Next**.

(continues)

Do It Yourself Convert a Hard Disk Drive to FAT32 *(continued)*

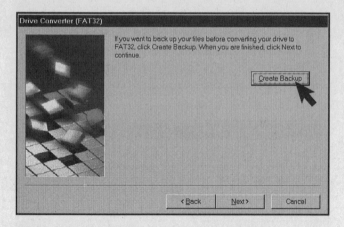

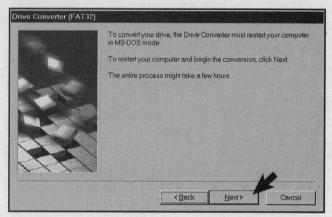

6 Drive Converter prompts you to back up the files on your hard disk before continuing. Click **Create Backup**, ▶and then refer to "Back Up Files" on page 432 for instructions on how to perform the backup.◀

7 When you return to Drive Converter, click **Next**.

8 Drive Converter indicates that it must restart your computer in MS-DOS mode. Close any programs you are currently running and click **Next**. The conversion may take more than one hour.

Do It Yourself Compress Disks with DriveSpace

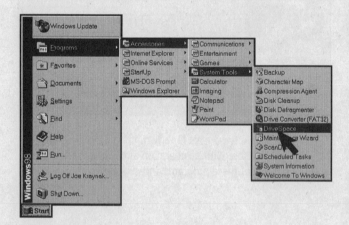

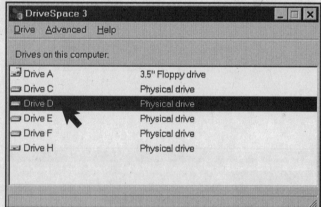

1 Back up all files on the hard disk drive you want to compress, ▶as explained in "Back Up Files" on page 432.◀ Click the **Start** button, point to **Programs**, **Accessories**, and then **System Tools**, and click **DriveSpace**.

2 The DriveSpace window appears. Choose the disk drive you want to compress. If you choose a floppy disk drive, insert the disk into the drive.

Do It Yourself Compress Disks with DriveSpace

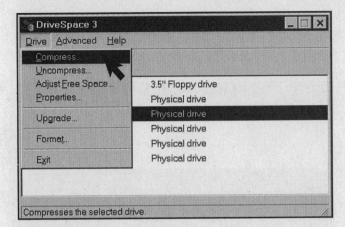

3 Open the **Drive** menu and choose **Compress**.

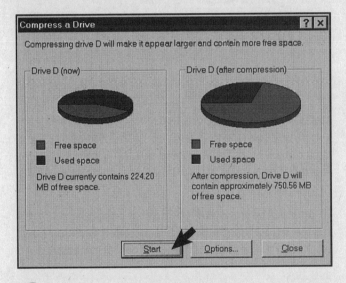

4 The Compress a Drive dialog box displays a graph of how much free space the drive currently has and how much it will have after compression. Click the **Start** button.

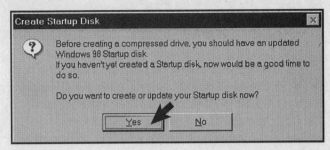

5 A confirmation dialog box appears, prompting you to create or update your Windows Startup disk before proceeding. Click **Yes** and follow the onscreen instructions to create a startup disk.

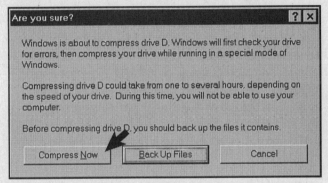

6 Another confirmation dialog box appears, prompting you to back up your files before proceeding, which you should have done in step 1. Click **Compress Now**.

7 Wait until the compression is complete. This can take from several minutes to several hours depending on the size of the hard disk.

Improve CD-ROM and Hard Drive Performance

Whenever you delete a file from your hard disk and whenever Windows removes a temporary file, a storage area on the disk becomes free for use again. The next time you save a file, Windows uses this free area to store as much of the file as will fit. It then saves the rest of the file in other storage areas. As you delete and save files, the files become more and more fragmented, and your hard disk drive must skip around the disk to read a file. This slows down the overall speed of your system.

To help, Windows 98 includes Disk Defragmenter. This useful utility reads files from the disk, positions important program files on the disk to make them run faster, and rearranges the parts of each file to place them in neighboring storage areas on the disk. This not only increases the speed at which programs run and files open, but it also leaves your disk with a large free storage area that Windows can use as virtual memory (disk space used as memory). And it reduces future file fragmentation.

To improve the overall performance of your hard disk drive, run Defragmenter on it regularly, as shown in the following project.

Windows also allows you to increase the speed of your hard drive and CD-ROM drive by configuring each drive's *read-ahead buffer*. With a read-ahead buffer, Windows reads data from the hard disk or CD and

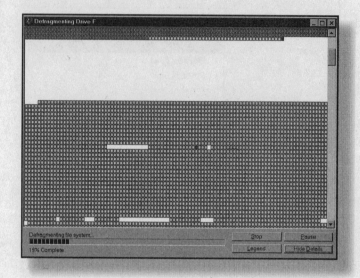

stores it in memory before that data is actually needed. When Windows needs the data, it can then access the data quickly from RAM instead of having to read it from the relatively slow drive. This increases the overall speed of your system.

To optimize your system, you should check the settings for the read-ahead buffers. This project shows you how to check your settings and adjust them if necessary.

Do It Yourself   Defragment Files on a Hard Disk

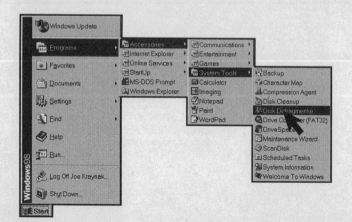

1 Click the **Start** button, point to **Programs**, **Accessories**, and then **System Tools**, and click **Disk Defragmenter**.

Do It Yourself Defragment Files on a Hard Disk

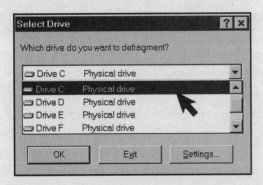

2 In the Select Drive dialog box, open the drop-down list and choose the disk drive you want to defragment.

3 Click the **Settings** button.

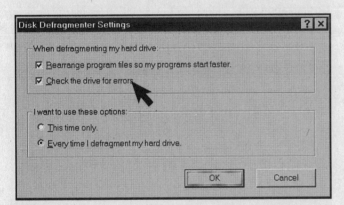

4 In the Disk Defragmenter Settings dialog box, make sure the first two options are checked. The first option tells Defragmenter to rearrange program files to make them run faster. The second option tells Defragmenter to check the disk for errors (and run ScanDisk if needed) before rearranging files. Click **OK**.

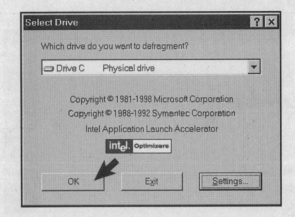

5 When you return to the Select Drive dialog box, click **OK**.

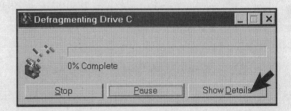

6 Defragmenter starts to defragment files on the selected drive and displays its progress. Click **Show Details** to see Defragmenter in action.

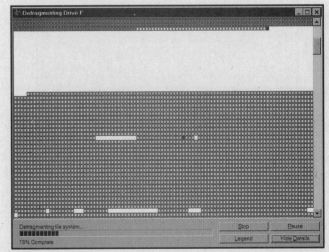

7 With Show Details, Defragmenter illustrates the operation by displaying tiny squares that represent each portion of a particular file.

Do It Yourself   Adjust the Read-Ahead Buffer

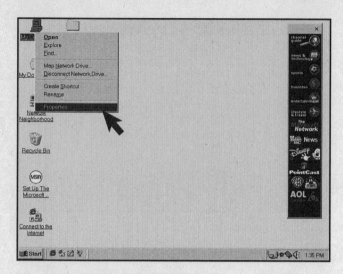

1 Right-click the **My Computer** icon on the Windows desktop and choose **Properties**.

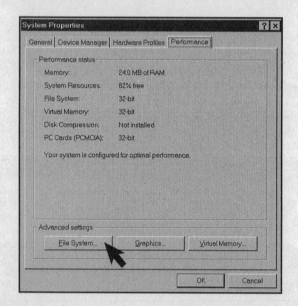

2 In the System Properties dialog box, click the **Performance** tab and click the **File System** button.

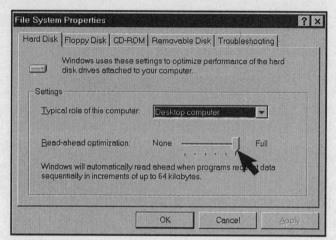

3 The File System Properties dialog box appears with the Hard Disk tab in front. Drag the **Read-Ahead Optimization** slider all the way to the right to set full optimization.

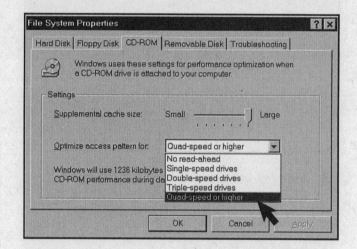

4 Click the **CD-ROM** tab. Then open the **Optimize Access Pattern For** drop-down list and choose the speed of your CD-ROM drive. For instance, if you have an 8X CD-ROM drive, choose **Quad-Speed or Higher**.

Do It Yourself Adjust the Read-Ahead Buffer

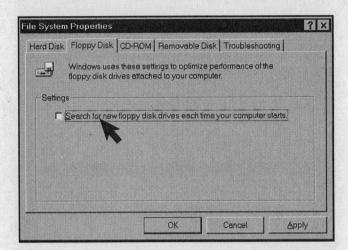

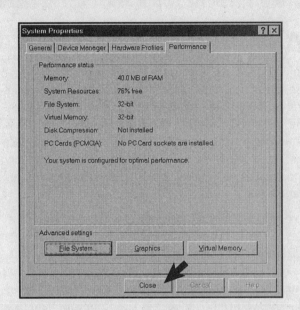

5 While you're in this dialog box, click the **Floppy Disk** tab and choose **Search for New Floppy Disk Drives Each Time Your Computer Starts** to turn it off. This increases the speed at which Windows starts. Click the **OK** button.

6 You are returned to the System Properties dialog box. Click the **Close** button to exit and save your settings.

Clean Up Your Hard Disk

As you learned earlier in this section, Internet programs and other programs scatter temporary files on your hard disk during their operation. After weeks of use, these programs can clutter your hard disk with several megabytes of useless files. This not only decreases the space you have for storing the files you need, it also slows down your system. Windows has less drive space for use as *virtual memory* (drive space used as memory), and it causes other files on your disk to become more fragmented.

To optimize your hard disk, you should remove useless files regularly. If you use the Windows Maintenance Wizard to clean up your disks at scheduled times, you do not have to clean them up yourself. However, if you chose not to schedule the Maintenance Wizard for regular use, you can clear useless files from your hard disk manually or by using the Disk Cleanup utility as shown in this project.

Disk Cleanup can increase the amount of free disk space by removing the following:

- Temporary Internet files

- Downloaded program files (program files you downloaded from the Internet)

- The contents of the Recycle Bin

- Old ScanDisk files (files that ScanDisk creates to allow you to recover lost data; usually these files contain nothing useful)

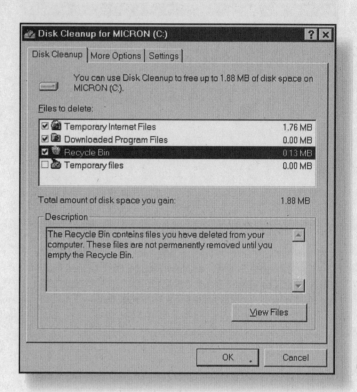

- Temporary files that your programs create and use during operation but do not delete when you exit

- Programs you no longer use

- Windows components that you do not use

Do It Yourself   Remove Unneeded Files from a Hard Disk

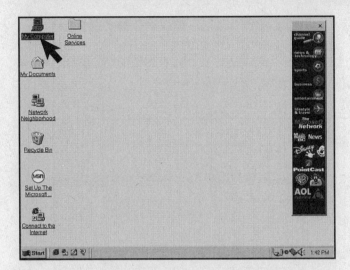

1 Click the **My Computer** icon on the Windows desktop.

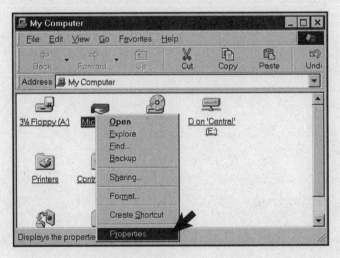

2 Right-click the icon for the disk you want to clean up and choose **Properties**.

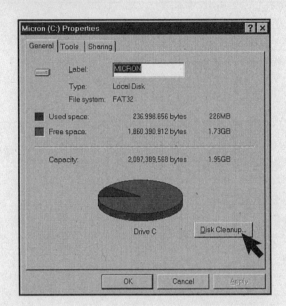

3 In the Properties dialog box, click the **Disk Cleanup** button.

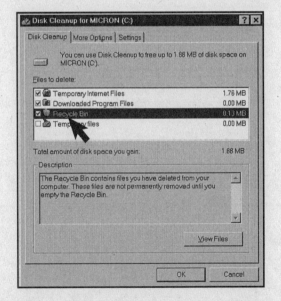

4 The Disk Cleanup dialog box for the selected disk drive appears. Click the check box next to each type of file you want to remove from the disk to place a check mark in its box.

(continues)

Do It Yourself Remove Unneeded Files from a Hard Disk *(continued)*

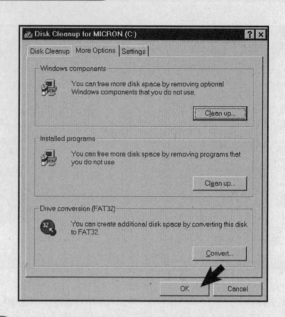

5 Click the **More Options** tab. To remove Windows components or uninstall programs you do not use, click the desired **Clean Up** button.

7 You are returned to the Disk Cleanup dialog box. Click **OK**, and Disk Cleanup automatically removes the specified files.

6 This displays the Add/Remove Programs Properties dialog box. ▶To remove Windows components, see "Add and Remove Windows Components" on page 422.◀ ▶To uninstall programs, see "Uninstall Programs" on page 51.◀ When you're done, click the **OK** button.

Clear the Documents Menu

Windows keeps a record of the last 15 documents you opened in your Windows programs and stores their names on the Start, Documents menu. You can quickly open a document you recently worked on by selecting it from the Documents menu. Windows then runs the program you used to create or edit the file, and the program opens the file.

Windows allows you to remove file names from the Documents menu. Although removing file names from the Documents menu does not significantly increase the speed at which Windows starts or operates, it does allow you to prevent someone from determining what you have been doing recently. This can be important if you are working on projects that you want to prevent prying eyes from quickly accessing on your computer. This project shows you how to clear file names from the Documents menu.

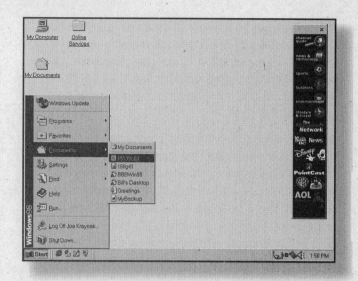

Do It Yourself Remove File Names from the Documents Menu

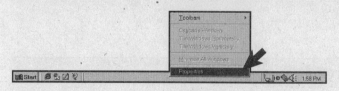

1 Right-click a blank area of the Windows taskbar and choose **Properties**.

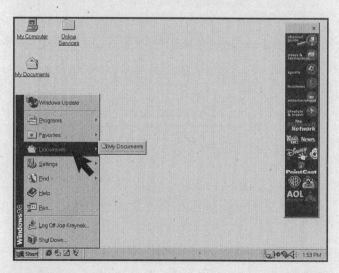

2 In the Taskbar Properties dialog box, click the **Start Menu Programs** tab. In the Documents Menu area, click the **Clear** button. Then click **OK**.

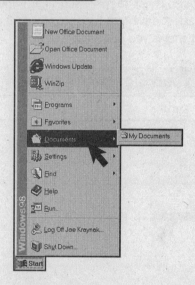

3 Windows automatically removes all file names (except the My Documents folder) from the Documents menu. To check it, click the **Start** button and point to **Documents**.

Increase Your System Memory

The best way to increase memory on your computer is to install additional physical memory (memory modules), as explained in "Install New Hardware" ▶on page 364◀. If your computer has less than 16MB of memory, you should seriously consider installing additional memory.

However, as you use Windows programs, Windows requires even more than the standard 16MB. To obtain this additional memory, Windows uses free space on your hard disk as *virtual memory*. With virtual memory, Windows uses a *swap file* to exchange data and program instructions between physical memory and your hard disk. Although virtual memory is significantly slower than physical memory, it does allow you to run larger programs and more programs than you could run without it.

To ensure that Windows is making optimal use of virtual memory, you should check the virtual memory settings in Windows. If you have more than one hard disk drive, you should also check to make sure that Windows is using the fastest drive that has the most free disk space. This project shows you just what to do.

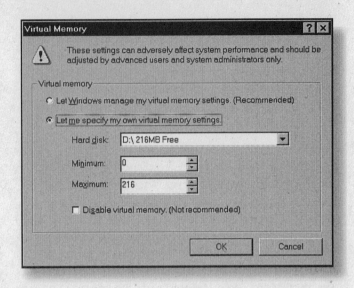

Do It Yourself   Adjust the Virtual Memory Settings

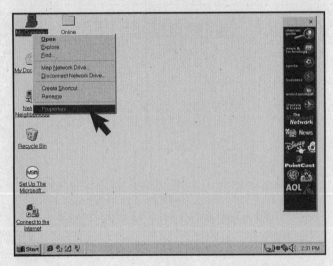

1 On the Windows desktop, right-click the **My Computer** icon and choose **Properties**.

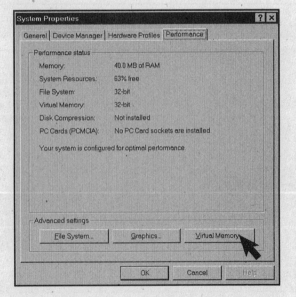

2 In the System Properties dialog box, click the **Performance** tab and click the **Virtual Memory** button.

Do It Yourself Adjust the Virtual Memory Settings

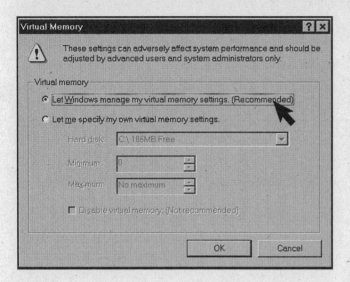

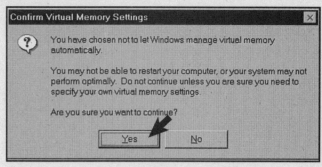

5 If you chose to specify settings yourself, Windows displays a warning. Click **Yes**.

3 If you have only one hard disk drive, leave **Let Windows Manage My Virtual Memory Settings** turned on.

If the hard disk drive has less than 30 MB of free space, you should run Disk Cleanup to remove unneeded files and programs and Windows components that you do not use. Otherwise, you might start to receive Out of Memory messages, Windows might run programs slowly, and your system might crash more frequently.

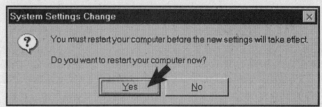

6 You are returned to the System Properties dialog box. Click the **Close** button, and then click **Yes** when you're prompted to restart your computer.

If you chose a different hard disk drive to use for virtual memory in step 4, Windows uses the drive but takes control of the virtual memory settings. If you recheck your settings, you will see that **Let Windows Manage My Virtual Memory Settings** is turned on.

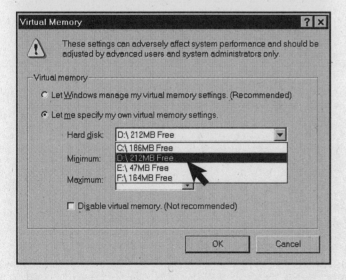

4 If you have more than one hard disk drive, choose **Let Me Specify My Own Virtual Memory Settings**. Then open the **Hard Disk** drop-down list and choose the fastest hard disk drive that has the most free space. Click **OK**.

PART 3

Quick Fixes

Computers rank right up there with indoor plumbing as one of the greatest products of human ingenuity. Like indoor plumbing, computers make life a little easier, and we sort of take them for granted—until, of course, something goes wrong. At that point, you just want to fling your computer out the window and dig through your attic to find your old typewriter.

But going back to the good old days isn't all that easy, and it's not even necessary. With the 101 Quick Fixes described in this section, you'll be able to track down the causes of the most common computer glitches, fix the problems yourself, and get your computer up and running in a hurry.

To use this section, look for your problem in the Quick-Finder tables. This part is broken down into sections, including Windows Programs, CD-ROM Drives, and Insufficient Memory, to help you quickly find the solution to your current computer problem.

What You Will Find in This Part

101 QUICK FIXES

Windows Programs

1. My Windows application has locked up my system.

In most cases, this is a random, minor problem. Unfortunately, tracking down the cause is tough. Sometimes a new device, such as a mouse or modem, can cause a systemwide problem. In other cases, you might be running two or more programs that interfere with one another. In still other cases, your system might not be locked up at all; the program might be performing a complex task that does not allow you to perform another task, cancel the operation, or even close the program. Try the following possible fixes:

- Wait a couple minutes for the program to complete whatever task it might be in the process of performing.

- If Windows is still locked up, press **Ctrl+Alt+Delete**. A list of currently running programs appears. Click the program that has (not responding) next to its name, and then click the **End Task** button. This usually closes the problem program and returns control to Windows.

- If pressing Ctrl+Alt+Delete does not work, try to save any work you've done in your other programs and exit them (to prevent losing documents or changes), and then press **Ctrl+Alt+Delete** again to try to close the problem program.

- If your system is still locked up, press **Ctrl+Alt+Delete**, and then click the **Shut Down** button or press **Ctrl+Alt+Delete** again. This restarts Windows. (If even that doesn't work, press the **Reset** button on your computer.)

- If one program consistently locks up your system, try reinstalling it.

In some cases, especially if you have to shut down Windows to correct the problem, Windows might place temporary files on your hard disk drive that cause your system to lock up in the future. After restarting from a lockup, you should always run ScanDisk to remove these files. Windows typically runs ScanDisk automatically when you start your computer after an improper shutdown. ►See "Check for and Repair Disk Problems" on page 416 for instructions.◄

If your computer continues to lock up regularly no matter which programs you are running, you should suspect a problem with your mouse driver, video driver, sound card, or modem. Check the manufacturer's online technical support area for updated drivers or troubleshooting information, ►as explained in "Find Technical Support" on page 483.◄ Also try running the Windows Hardware Troubleshooter, as explained in Quick Fix number 98.

2. I clicked the icon for a Windows program, but it didn't start.

If a Windows program does not start, either the program is not compatible with Windows 98 or one of its files has been deleted or damaged. If the program ran okay in a previous version of Windows, check with the manufacturer to determine if you need to upgrade to a more recent version of the program. Most programs designed for Windows 3.1 or Windows 95 should run as well, if not better, in Windows 98, but some programs might not be able to run at all.

You might also run into this problem if you move a program's folder or if you forget to insert the CD-ROM before running a program that requires the CD-ROM. In such cases, Windows displays a message indicating that the file the shortcut points to no longer exists. If you simply forgot to insert the CD, cancel the message, insert the CD into the CD-ROM drive, and click the shortcut again. If you moved a folder and Windows cannot locate it, take the following steps to point the shortcut to the correct file:

1. Right-click the shortcut and choose **Properties**.
2. In the Properties dialog box, type the path to the folder in which the program files are now stored, followed by the name of the file that runs the program.
3. Click **OK**.

3. I know I installed the program correctly, but I can't find it on the Start menu or the Windows desktop.

When you install most Windows programs, the installation utility creates a separate submenu for the program on the Start, Programs menu. However, other programs and Windows components might install themselves at the bottom of the Programs menu or on one of the existing submenus.

Check the top of the Start menu, the bottom of the Programs menu, and all the Program menu's submenus before you do anything else.

Rarely, programs do not add themselves to the Start menu or any of its submenus. In such cases, you must add the program yourself or create a shortcut for it on the Windows desktop. ▶To add a program to the Start menu or one of its submenus, see "Configure the Start Menu" on page 53.◀ ▶To add a shortcut to the Windows desktop, see "Create Shortcuts to Disks, Folders, and Files" on page 114.◀

4. Every time I try to open a particular document in one of my programs, I receive an error message.

If you are trying to open the file by choosing it from the bottom of the program's File menu, you might have moved the file since the last time you opened it. Try using the **File**, **Open** command. You can then change to the disk and folder in which the file is now stored and open it from there.

If you open a file and it locks up your computer, or if the application indicates that the file is in an incompatible format, you might have saved the file in a format the program does not support, or the file might have become corrupted. Try the following fixes:

- Open the file in the program in which it was created, and then save it in a compatible format.

- If you know the file is already in a compatible format, try running ScanDisk on the disk where the file is stored. ▶See "Check for and Repair Disk Problems" on page 416.◀

- As a last resort, try opening the file in WordPad or Notepad. The document will probably contain a bunch of formatting codes, but you can recover the raw data by copying and pasting it to a new document.

- You can also try viewing the contents of the file with Quick View. In My Computer or Windows Explorer, right-click the file's name and choose Quick View (if the option is available).

5. I tried to type a filename extension when saving my document, but the program wouldn't let me.

Many Windows programs automatically add the correct filename extension to the file's name when you save it. This prevents you from typing the extension incorrectly. If a program won't let you add a filename extension, simply omit it when naming the file and let the program do it for you.

In some cases, even though you type a filename extension, the program will add an extension anyway, and the filename will end up with two extensions, such as My Novel (Chapter 7).doc.doc. If this happens, use My Computer or Windows Explorer to rename the file, ▶as described in "Copy, Move, and Rename Files" on page 103.◀

6. I'm accustomed to using filename extensions to determine file types, but Windows doesn't display them.

Windows is trying to wean computer users from relying on the old three-character filename extensions to determine file types. Instead, Windows expects users to determine file types by looking at icons. My Computer can also display thumbnail views of selected files to help you determine which program was used to create the files.

However, if you are accustomed to determining file types from their filename extensions, icons are more confusing than helpful. To have Windows display filename extensions, take the following steps:

1. Click the **My Computer** icon on the Windows desktop.

2. Open the **View** menu and choose **Folder Options**.

3. Click the **View** tab.

4. Click **Hide File Extensions for Known File Types** to remove the check from its box and turn the option off.

5. Click **OK**.

DOS Programs

Problem	Quick Fix Number	Page
Can't run DOS game	7	518
DOS application locks up	8	519
Can't switch back to Windows	9	519
Can't switch to DOS	9	519
DOS program runs slowly	7	518
Mouse is disabled on return to Windows	11	520
Mouse, joystick, or sound card is disabled in DOS game	12	521

7. Each time I try to run my DOS game, I get kicked back to Windows.

Although most DOS games run well under Windows 98, some require more resources than Windows provides for DOS programs. Try the following fixes:

- In Windows, create a shortcut icon for running the DOS game, and then right-click the icon and choose **Properties**. Click the **Programs** tab and click the **Advanced** button. Choose **MS-DOS Mode** and click **OK**. Then click **OK** to save your changes. This gives the DOS program all available system resources. Try running the game again.

- Click the **Start** button, choose **Shut Down**, choose **Restart in MS-DOS Mode**, and click **OK**. Then try to run the program from the DOS prompt.

- If that doesn't work, restart Windows. As soon as your computer beeps, press and release the **F8** key. This displays the Microsoft Windows 98 Startup Menu. Choose **Command Prompt Only**, and then run the game from the DOS prompt.

If you are still having the same problem, move on to the next Quick Fix.

8. My DOS program locks up the system, and I can't do anything.

First, try the fixes described in problem 7. If those corrections do not solve the problem, it's possible that your DOS game needs more than conventional memory (the first 640 kilobytes of memory). Some games require additional memory in the form of *expanded memory*. To make expanded memory available, take the following steps:

1. Right-click the icon you use to run the DOS program and choose **Properties**.

2. Click the **Programs** tab and click the **Advanced** button.

3. Make sure **MS-DOS Mode** is on.

4. Click **Specify a New MS-DOS Configuration**.

5. Move the insertion point to the end of the line that reads DEVICE=C:\WINDOWS\HIMEM.SYS and press **Enter** to create a blank line.

6. Type **DEVICE=C:\WINDOWS\EMM386.EXE RAM**. This provides expanded memory for running programs that require it.

7. Click the **OK** button. When you return to the Properties dialog box, click **OK** to save your changes.

You can also use a separate startup disk for starting the computer when you want to play your game. To create such a disk, take the following steps:

1. Format the disk as a system disk (➤as explained in "Format Floppy Disks" on page 129◄).

2. Copy the Config.sys and Autoexec.bat files from disk C:\ to the floppy disk.

3. Run Windows Notepad and open the Config.sys file from the floppy disk.

4. Move the insertion point to the end of the line that reads DEVICE=C:\WINDOWS\HIMEM.SYS and press **Enter** to create a blank line.

5. Type **DEVICE=C:\WINDOWS\EMM386.EXE RAM**.

6. Open the **File** menu and choose **Save**.

7. In Windows Notepad, open the Autoexec.bat file from the floppy disk and type **REM** at the beginning of any line that runs a device driver you don't need for the game or a program that runs in the background. This prevents these programs from running and using conventional memory that the game may require.

8. Open the **File** menu and choose **Save**.

Insert the disk into your computer's floppy disk drive and restart your computer. When the computer starts, you will see the DOS prompt: A:\> instead of Windows. Change to the disk and folder that contains the DOS game files and enter the command for running the game. (If you don't know that command, refer to the game's documentation.)

9. My DOS program runs fine, but I can't return to Windows when I'm done.

When you run a DOS program in full-screen mode, you can usually return to Windows by pressing **Alt+Enter**. If the DOS program uses that keystroke for some other command, however, it might not return you to Windows. Try pressing **Alt+Tab**, **Alt+Esc**, or **Ctrl+Esc**. If you exit your DOS program and the DOS prompt is displayed, type **exit** and press **Enter**.

If you do not use the Alt+Enter keystroke in the DOS program, you can re-enable it in Windows by taking the following steps:

1. Right-click the icon for running the program and choose **Properties**.

2. Click the **Misc** tab.

3. In the Windows Shortcut Keys area, click **Alt+Enter** to place a check mark in its box.

4. Click **OK**.

10. When I exit my DOS program and return to Windows, I can no longer use my mouse.

Some DOS programs require a different mouse driver from the driver used by Windows, and sometimes that driver conflicts with the Windows mouse driver and disables it. The fastest way to reclaim mouse control in Windows is to restart Windows. To restart Windows without the help of your mouse, press **Ctrl+Esc** to open the Start menu, press the down arrow key to highlight **Shut Down**, and press **Enter**.

If you do not use the mouse in your DOS program, consider changing the DOS program's options to disable the mouse.

11. My DOS game seems to run okay, but sometimes I can't use my mouse or joystick, and sometimes the audio is disabled.

Many DOS games require that you specify the controller type you want to use: keyboard, mouse, or joystick. On the game's startup screen, look for a Configuration or Setup option on the menu and select it. Enter your preferences before you start playing. The Setup option should also allow you to specify a sound device to use or whether to turn audio on or off.

If changing these options doesn't fix the problem, restart your computer in MS-DOS mode and run the software that came with your sound card or controller. In most cases, the Windows drivers will not work under DOS. You must install the DOS drivers.

Check the documentation that came with your sound card and controller to determine if your start-up files (Config.sys and Autoexec.bat) require special commands. If they do, take the following steps to add the commands for your game to Config.sys and Autoexec.bat:

1. Right-click the icon you use to run the DOS program and choose **Properties**.

2. Click the **Programs** tab and click the **Advanced** button.

3. Make sure **MS-DOS Mode** is on.

4. Click **Specify a New MS-DOS Configuration**.

5. Type the required commands in the text areas below **CONFIG.SYS for MS-DOS Mode** and **AUTOEXEC.BAT for MS-DOS Mode**.

6. Click the **OK** button. When you return to the Properties dialog box, click **OK** to save your changes. Then run the game again.

CD-ROM Drives

Problem	Quick Fix Number	Page
No icon for CD-ROM drive	12	521
Error reading from CD-ROM disc	13	522
No audio from CD	14	522
CD does not AutoPlay in Windows	15	522
CD-ROM drive does not play audio CDs	14	522
Invalid drive specification	16	523
CD-ROM drive unavailable in DOS	16	523

12. My Computer and Windows Explorer do not display an icon for my CD-ROM drive.

If you just installed the CD-ROM drive, turn off your computer and check the cables that connect your CD-ROM drive to the motherboard or expansion board inside your computer. Also check the cable from the power supply to the CD-ROM drive to ensure that the connections are good. You might have jiggled a cable loose when you replaced the system unit cover.

Shut down Windows and restart your computer. Press the key to enter your computer's setup program. The required key is typically displayed onscreen when you first start your computer but before Windows loads. If it is not displayed, check your computer's documentation to determine which key to press.

The setup screen should display a menu showing the system's configuration. Look for an EIDE or IDE Adapter option. You should have one option for your hard disk drive and another for a second drive, typically the CD-ROM drive. Check the settings to make sure your computer recognizes the CD-ROM drive. Do *not* change the setting for the hard drive, because you will end up disabling it.

If the cables are properly connected and your computer recognizes the CD-ROM drive, Windows might be set up to use the wrong driver for your CD-ROM drive, or the driver might be corrupted. Take the following steps to reinstall the driver:

1. Open the Windows Control Panel and click the **System** icon.
2. In the System Properties dialog box, click the **Device Manager** tab.
3. Click the plus sign (+) next to **CD-ROM**.
4. Click the name of the CD-ROM driver to select it, and then click the **Remove** button. Click **OK** to remove the driver.
5. When you return to the System Properties dialog box, click **OK**, and then restart Windows.

Windows should restart and automatically run the Add New Hardware Wizard, which will lead you through the process of installing the required CD-ROM driver. If the Add New Hardware Wizard does not start, start it from the Control Panel. ►See "Install New Hardware" on page 364 for details.◄

13. When I insert a CD into the CD-ROM drive, I receive an error message indicating that Windows cannot read the disc.

If you are having problems with a single disc, the problem is probably the disc and not the drive. Make sure the printing on the disc is facing up; CD-ROM drives read from the bottom (unpainted side) of the disc. If the disc was positioned in the drive properly, check the bottom of the disc for dust, dirt, and scratches. If the disc is dusty, wipe it off with a lint-free cloth from the center to the outside edges. If the disc has something sticky on it, spray the disc with window cleaner and wipe it thoroughly, again going from the center to the outside edges.

If you are having problems with more than one disc, the reading mechanism in the CD-ROM drive might be dirty. Purchase a CD-ROM drive cleaning kit and use it to clean the reading mechanism. These kits typically contain a CD with some cleaning solution. You squirt the cleaning solution on the disc, insert it in the drive, and remove it when it stops spinning.

14. I know that my CD-ROM program has audio clips, but I can't hear them play.

In most cases, the CD-ROM drive is not at fault. The sound in Windows is just turned way down. Right-click the **Volume** icon in the Windows taskbar and choose **Open Volume Controls**. Make sure the Speaker, CD Player, and Wave volumes are at their maximum levels. Also, make sure the Mute check boxes are *not* checked. (If these controls are not displayed, open the **Options** menu, choose **Properties**, and turn on the controls.)

If those adjustments do not correct the problem, check the volume control on your CD-ROM drive and on your sound card. (If the sound card has a volume control, it is on the back of the sound card, where you plug in the speakers.) Also, make sure your speakers are plugged securely into the OUT jack on your sound card and that the speakers are plugged in and turned on.

The volume control on the CD-ROM drive typically controls only the headphone output, not the speaker output from your sound card. You can check your CD-ROM drive by plugging in a set of headphones and trying to play audio through the headphones. If you can hear audio through the headphones, you know that the problem is in either the sound card or the connection between the CD-ROM drive and the sound card.

If the audio does not play through the sound card, check the cable that connects the CD-ROM drive to the sound card. This cable typically has four wires connected to a small plug that you connect to the sound card *inside* your computer. Make sure the cable is in good condition and is securely connected.

15. I thought Windows was supposed to start playing CDs automatically when I insert them, but it doesn't.

Not all CDs have AutoPlay built into them. Many CDs act like floppy or hard disks: You must first enter a command or click an icon for the CD (in My Computer or Windows Explorer) to run the program or the installation utility.

Then again, maybe AutoPlay has been disabled on your computer. Take the following steps to make sure AutoPlay is on:

1. Open the Windows Control Panel and click the **System** icon.

2. Click the **Device Manager** tab.

3. Click the plus sign (+) next to **CD-ROM**, and then double-click the icon for your CD-ROM drive. This displays the CD-ROM drive's properties.

4. Click the **Settings** tab and make sure there is a check mark in the **Auto Insert Notification** check box. Click **OK**.

5. When you return to the System Properties dialog box, click **OK** to save your changes. You must then restart your computer.

> Some audio CDs contain not only music, but also multimedia presentations. If you insert an audio CD to play some tunes, don't be surprised if a program window pops up on your screen. To play the tunes, run CD Player from the **Start**, **Programs**, **Accessories**, **Entertainment** menu.

16. When I restart my computer in MS-DOS mode, I can't change to my CD-ROM drive.

When you install Windows 98, it automatically disables your CD-ROM driver in DOS to prevent conflicts between the DOS and Windows CD-ROM drivers. When you restart in MS-DOS mode, the required driver is not loaded. Therefore, when you try to change to the CD-ROM drive at the DOS prompt, you receive the `Invalid Drive Specification` error message.

To use your CD-ROM drive from the DOS prompt, take the following steps:

1. Copy the required driver files from the installation disk that came with your CD-ROM drive to a separate folder on your hard disk.

2. In My Computer, change to drive C.

3. Drag the Command.com file to a blank area on the Windows desktop and release the mouse button. This creates a shortcut called "Shortcut to MS-DOS Prompt."

4. Right-click the new shortcut icon and choose **Properties**.

5. Click the **Programs** tab and click the **Advanced** button.

6. Choose **MS-DOS Mode** and select **Specify a New MS-DOS Configuration**.

7. In the text areas below **CONFIG.SYS for MS-DOS Mode** and **AUTOEXEC.BAT for MS-DOS Mode,** type the commands for loading your CD-ROM driver. Check the documentation that came with your CD-ROM drive for the required commands.

> In most cases, Autoexec.bat requires a command such as C:\CDROM\MSCDEX.EXE /d:mscd001, and Config.sys requires a command such as DEVICE=C:\CDROM\ CDROMDRV.SYS /d:mscd001. C:\CDROM is the folder into which you copied the necessary CD-ROM driver files.

8. Click **OK**. When you return to the shortcut's Properties dialog box, click **OK** to save your settings.

When you want to use the CD-ROM drive from the DOS prompt, do not restart Windows in MS-DOS mode. Instead, click the shortcut icon you created. This shuts down Windows and starts it in MS-DOS mode automatically. Assuming you entered the correct commands, you should then be able to access the CD-ROM drive.

> The Windows emergency recovery disk you created when you installed Windows 98 has a standard CD-ROM driver on it. This comes in handy if you have to reinstall Windows 98 from a CD. Start your computer with the emergency recovery disk and choose the option for booting your computer with CD-ROM support.

Disk Drives

Problem	Quick Fix Number	Page
No floppy disk icon	17	524
No hard disk icon	17	524
Non-system disk or disk error	18	525
Insufficient space on disk	19	525
Can't access files on floppy disk	20	525
Cannot write to disk	21	526
Slow hard disk drive	22	526
Disk drive light stays on	22	526

17. I know I have a particular disk drive, but there's no icon for it in My Computer or Windows Explorer.

First, you should see if you can access the disk drive from DOS. Restart your computer in MS-DOS mode (**Start, Shutdown, Restart in MS-DOS Mode, OK**). If you are having trouble with a floppy disk drive, insert a formatted disk in the drive. At the DOS prompt, type the letter of the drive followed by a colon (for example, **a:**) and press **Enter**.

If you can access the drive from DOS but there's no icon for it in Windows, the problem is in Windows. Run the Add New Hardware Wizard to upgrade the driver or reinstall it. ▶See "Install New Hardware" on page 364.◀

If you cannot change to the drive from the DOS prompt and you receive the Invalid Drive Specification error message, your computer's record of the drive might have become corrupted. Restart your computer, wait until you hear a single beep, and then press the key for activating your computer's setup program (typically the F1 or F2 key). On the Setup screen, you should see a Diskette option. Make sure the correct letter is assigned to the drive (A or B) and that the correct capacity is specified (typically 1.44MB for a 3½-inch disk or 1.2MB for a 5¼-inch disk). Save your settings and exit Setup.

> Be careful when accessing your computer's setup program. This program contains all the settings that make devices work properly. If you pick the wrong setting for a device (such as your hard drive), you are likely to disable it. Before changing a setting, write down the current setting so you can change it back if necessary.

If you still cannot access the drive, the drive might be damaged or one of its cables might have shaken loose. Turn off your computer, open the system unit, and make sure that the power cable is securely connected to the power supply and that the data cable is securely connected to the motherboard or expansion board.

18. At startup, I see the `Non-System Disk` or `Disk Error` message.

This is a DOS error message that typically appears if you've forgotten to remove a disk from your computer's floppy disk drive. When you start your computer, Windows looks in drive A for a disk containing the startup files before it looks on the hard disk. If you leave a disk in the drive by mistake, Windows tries to start your computer using the files on that disk. Remove the disk and press **Enter** to continue.

If you did not leave a floppy disk in the drive by mistake, one of the startup files on your hard disk drive might have become corrupted. Restart your computer using the Windows Emergency disk you created in "Create and Use an Emergency Disk" ►on page 442◄. Then run ScanDisk on your hard disk drive to see if it can fix the disk. To run ScanDisk from the A:\> prompt, type **scandisk** followed by the letter of the drive you want to check (for example, **scandisk c:**) and press **Enter**.

If ScanDisk informs you that the disk drive letter is invalid, you have serious problems. Do not try to reboot your computer from the hard disk drive. Simply leave the computer running and seek help from a qualified technician.

19. When I try to install a program or copy files, I receive the `Insufficient Disk Space` message.

Your disk is packed with files and has no more room for additional files. If you are trying to copy files to your hard disk drive, you will first need to remove files from the disk. The easiest way to do that is to use the Windows Disk Cleanup utility. ►See "Clean Up Your Hard Disk" on page 506.◄ Alternatively, you can use the Windows Maintenance Wizard.

If you have a floppy disk that's packed with files, you must either remove some files from the floppy disk or copy the files to a different disk.

20. I can't open any of the files on my floppy disk.

First, check the obvious: Are the files you are trying to open compatible with the program you're trying to use to open them? For instance, you might not be able to open a particular type of graphics file in a word processing program, and you won't be able to read a Macintosh disk at all, unless the disk was formatted in a PC format on a Macintosh computer.

If you know that the files are compatible with the program you are using, the disk or the files on it might be corrupted. You can usually tell that a disk is corrupted if the disk drive grinds as it tries to read data from the disk. ►See "File Problems" on page 526 for more details.◄

21. When I try to copy files to a floppy disk, Windows won't let me.

Most floppy disks have a write-protect tab in the corner of the disk. If the tab is in the closed position (so the hole in the disk is not visible), you can copy files to the disk. If the tab is in the open position (you can see through the hole), you cannot copy files to the disk.

Before you remove write protection from the disk, check its contents in My Computer or Windows Explorer to determine what's on the disk. If the disk came with your computer or is part of a set of installation disks, it might be write-protected to prevent you from erasing important files. If you're trying to reuse a disk that's missing its write-protect tab, you can cover the hole with a small piece of adhesive tape. Be careful not to get the tape stuck in the drive, though.

22. My hard disk drive light stays on almost all of the time, and I can hear the drive working a lot. Is this normal?

If your computer is performing a complex, disk-intensive operation, such as defragmenting files on the hard drive, it is normal for the hard disk drive light to stay on. Otherwise, the light will flicker on and off as you work, whenever Windows needs to access data from the drive.

If the light stays on no matter how little you are doing on your computer, your system might be low on memory. If your computer has less than 16 megabytes of RAM, Windows needs to make greater use of disk space as virtual memory, and the light will stay on longer. If you have plenty of RAM installed, a program you exited might have left certain files running that are still present in memory. Try restarting your computer.

You should also check your hard disk to make sure it has at least 30 megabytes of free space for Windows to use as virtual memory. If it has less than that, Windows must swap data between the disk and RAM more often. In addition, run the Windows Disk Cleanup utility, ▶as explained in "Clean Up Your Hard Disk" on page 506◀, and defragment the files on your hard disk, ▶as explained in "Improve CD-ROM and Hard Drive Performance" on page 502◀. Or, you can use the Windows Maintenance Wizard to schedule automatic cleaning and defragmenting of your hard disk, ▶as described in "Use the Windows Maintenance Wizard" on page 494.◀

File Problems

Problem	Quick Fix Number	Page
Damaged files	23	527
Program can't open file	23	527
Lost files	24	527
Accidentally deleted files	25	527
Incompatible file formats	26	527
Accidental deletion in a document	27	527

23. I have successfully opened this file in the same program before, but now Windows says it cannot read the file.

The file has become *corrupted* (damaged). Exiting a program before saving your work can often corrupt a document file (or prevent any changes you entered from being saved). Occasional computer glitches can also affect documents.

Some programs automatically create a backup copy of each file you create. Check the folder in which you saved the file for a file that has the same name but a different extension, such as .BAK. If you find a backup copy, try opening it. It should contain the previous version of the document, which will be missing your latest changes.

Also, try running ScanDisk on the disk to which you saved the file. Perform a thorough check so ScanDisk can recover any data that is stored on defective areas of the disk.

24. I know I saved the file, but now I can't find it.

The best place to look for a lost document file is in the program you used to create it. Many programs list the names of recently opened files at the bottom of the File menu. Open the **File** menu and check the list for your file. To open the file, simply click its name. The Start, Documents submenu also contains a list of recently opened files.

If you still can't find the file, use Windows' **Start**, **Find**, **Files or Folders** command to track it down. ▶See "Find Files and Folders" on page 111.◀

25. I accidentally deleted a file. Can I get it back?

When you delete a file or folder, Windows places it in the Recycle Bin. To recover it, click the Recycle Bin icon on the Windows desktop, select the file or folder, and then open the **File** menu and choose **Restore**. Windows restores the file or folder to the same folder from which you deleted it. (You can also drag files and folders from the Recycle Bin to the Windows desktop or to a folder opened in My Computer or Windows Explorer.)

26. I created and saved a document in one program, and now I want to edit it in a different program. Can I?

Some programs support several file formats, making it possible for you to share documents with other people who use different programs. However, you usually can share only files created in the same type of program, such as a word processor.

However, programs are becoming more capable of sharing not only data but also programming code. As you have seen earlier in this book, you can insert a graphic image created in Windows Paint into a typed document in WordPad and then edit that image right inside WordPad by double-clicking the image. This displays Paint's menu bar and toolbars inside the WordPad window. As programs become more capable of sharing code, you will spend less time worrying about compatible file formats.

27. I wiped out a whole section of my document. Is there any way to recover it?

It's easy to delete a large section of a document. If you highlight the entire document or a section of it to format or copy it and you press a key by mistake while it's selected, the selection is replaced by the keystroke you typed. It happens to everyone. To recover the selection, try the following:

- Most programs have an Undo command. Open the **Edit** menu and choose **Undo**. You'll get the best results by using Undo right after the accident. If you've made several edits since the deletion, you may have to use the Undo drop-down list to undo all the edits from the accidental deletion up to the previous edit. (The Undo list is automatically cleared when you close the document.)

- If you deleted the selection right after saving the document, do not save the document again. Simply close the document window or exit the program *without* saving your changes. If you're worried that you will lose some of your work, use the **File**, **Save As** command to save the file under another name. You can then copy and paste between the two documents to get everything back in order.

- If you accidentally cut the selection by using Edit, Cut or Ctrl+X, simply move the insertion point to where you want the selection reinserted and press **Ctrl+V**.

Installation and Startup Issues

Problem	Quick Fix Number	Page
Installation aborted	28	528
Power failure during installation	28	528
Windows won't start	29	529
ScanDisk runs on startup	30	529
Invalid system disk message on startup	18	525
Started in Safe mode	31	529
Can't uninstall program	32	530

28. While I was installing Windows 98, my computer locked up [or there was a power outage]. What do I do now?

If Windows setup simply stopped responding, wait 10 minutes or more. Hardware detection and other installation procedures can sometimes take a long time. If the installation seems to stall, waiting usually corrects the problem. If nothing happens after 10 minutes, take the following steps:

1. Turn off the computer, wait 20 seconds, and turn it back on. Your previous version of Windows should start.

2. Run the Windows 98 setup program again.

3. When the setup program starts, it asks if you want to start a new installation or use Smart Recovery. Choose **Smart Recovery**. In Smart Recovery mode, the setup program skips the section that caused the problem.

29. Windows won't start. When I start my computer, the screen is blank.

Nothing is more disconcerting than finding a blank screen when you turn on your computer. In most cases, you can easily correct the problem:

- Check the monitor first. Make sure that it is turned on and that the cable from the monitor to the system unit is securely connected.

- The Windows power-saving feature automatically shuts down the monitor and hard disk drive after a certain period of inactivity. If you did not shut down the computer, move the mouse and press a key (the Shift key is a safe key to press), and then wait to see if the computer comes out of Standby mode.

- If the monitor is still blank, press **Ctrl+Alt+Delete** to see if you can restart Windows.

- If your system is locked up, press the **Reset** button on the system unit.

30. At startup, a message appears, indicating that my hard disk may have problems and telling me to run ScanDisk.

It's normal for your computer to run ScanDisk occasionally on startup, especially if you had to shut down Windows by pressing Ctrl+Alt+Delete or using the Reset or power button on the system unit. Let ScanDisk run its full test of your hard disk drive and automatically fix any problems. The next time you start your computer, it should start automatically.

> Do *not* stop ScanDisk when it is in the middle of checking for and repairing problems. If you interrupt ScanDisk, it may run *every time* you start your computer.

31. Windows started in Safe mode, and now the Windows desktop looks different.

Windows typically starts in Safe mode if you install a wrong device driver (especially a wrong video or mouse driver). If Windows cannot start, it automatically restarts and loads standard drivers so that you can use Windows to help correct the problem.

In many cases, Windows automatically corrects the problem itself. If you restart Windows from Safe mode, Windows usually starts normally. However, if Windows continues to start in Safe mode, take the following steps:

1. Open the Windows Control Panel and click the **System** icon.

2. Click the **Device Manager** tab.

3. Click the plus sign (+) next to each device type (such as **CD-ROM** and **Display**). Make sure no devices are conflicting (they would have a caution symbol or a red X next to them).

4. If a device is conflicting, double-click its name and check its settings.

5. In most cases, the properties dialog box for the device has a Driver tab. Click the **Driver** tab, and then click the **Upgrade Driver** button to reinstall or upgrade the driver for the selected device.

> You can force Windows to start in Safe mode by pressing **F8** when you see the `Starting Windows 98` message. This displays a menu that allows you to start in Safe mode or at the DOS prompt.

32. I'm trying to remove a program that I no longer use, but it's not listed in the Add/Remove Programs Properties dialog box.

Not all programs add their names to the list of programs you can safely remove from Windows. If the program is not listed, check the folder in which you installed the program for a Setup or Install file. In many cases, you can run the program's installation or uninstallation utility to remove the program or one or more of its components from your hard disk. (Sometimes, the program displays an Uninstall or Remove option on its Start, Programs submenu.)

Avoid removing a Windows program simply by deleting the folder in which its files are stored. Because Windows programs typically install files in the Windows and Windows\System folder, deleting the program's folder rarely removes all of its files. In addition, the program might have added commands to the Windows startup files, in which case removing the program's files might cause error messages to appear each time you start Windows.

Insufficient Memory

Problem	Quick Fix Number	Page
Check system memory	33	530
Check for free system resources	34	531
Insufficient user resources	34	531
Insufficient GDI resources	34	531
Memory troubleshooter	35	531
Windows locks up	36	532
`Insufficient memory` message	37	532
Low system resources	37	532
Windows won't run program	37	532
System is slow	38	532
`Parity error` on blue screen	39	533

33. How much memory does my computer have?

Before you even start worrying about your computer's lack of memory, you should make sure you know how much memory your computer has. Take the following steps to find out:

1. **Alt+***click* the My Computer icon. The amount of physical memory (in the form of RAM chips) appears near the bottom of the dialog box. Your computer should have 16 megabytes or more installed. If your computer has less, consider installing additional memory in the form of memory modules. ▶See "Install New Hardware" on page 364.◀

2. Click the **Performance** tab. This tab also displays the amount of physical memory installed. The amount of memory (RAM, or random access memory) is displayed near the top of the dialog box.

3. Click the **Virtual Memory** button. The value in the Hard Disk text box, although gray, indicates the amount of free space available for Windows to use as virtual memory.

4. Add the two numbers to determine the total amount of available memory. (Even if your system has plenty of disk space to use as virtual memory, some programs may have trouble running with less than 16 megabytes of bona fide RAM.)

34. My computer has plenty of memory, so why are my programs not running properly?

Windows has some built-in limitations. Although Windows can create its own (virtual) memory by using free disk space, it sets aside limited blocks of memory (called *resources*) for tasks such as displaying data and dialog boxes.

Windows reserves memory for the following three resources: System (to keep track of running programs), User (to manage dialog boxes), and the GDI (to handle graphics). You can have plenty of free memory available, but if these reserved areas start to fill up, you might encounter the same problems as if your system were low on memory.

To check the amounts of available system resources, take the following steps:

1. Click the **Start** button, point to **Programs**, **Accessories**, and then to **System Tools**, and click **Resource Meter**. (If Resource Meter is not on this menu, you must install it using Windows Setup.)

2. The Resource Meter dialog box indicates that it, too, will consume system resources. Click **OK**.

3. The Resource Meter icon appears in the system tray on the right end of the taskbar. Right-click it and choose **Details**. The Resource meter displays bar graphs showing the available System, User, and GDI resources.

If you see that your system resources are running low in any category, close all of your programs and exit Windows. This clears any wayward data and program instructions from memory so Windows can start fresh. To determine how well this fix works, run Resource Meter again after you restart to check the amount of resources you reclaimed in Windows.

35. Can Windows help me troubleshoot memory problems?

Yes, the Windows Memory Troubleshooter can help you determine the cause of many problems related to insufficient memory. To start the Memory Troubleshooter, take the following steps:

1. Click the **Start** menu and choose **Help**.

2. In the Help window, click the **Index** tab and type **trouble** in the text box. Windows highlights `troubleshooting` in the list of topics.

3. Scroll down the list and double-click **memory problems**.

4. Click the **Click Here** link in the right pane to start the Memory Troubleshooter.

5. Click the option that best describes the problem you are having, and then click **Next**.

6. Follow the onscreen instructions to track down and correct the problem.

36. My computer locks up frequently. Is this a memory problem?

The total amount of memory installed on your computer (RAM and virtual memory combined) is no indication of the amount of memory *available* for running a particular program. If you are running several programs or have several documents open, Windows might not have enough memory available to run another program. You can try closing other programs to free up memory, but even after you close some programs, they still take up some of the system resources available for other programs. Try the following fixes to free up memory:

- Close all other programs and run only the program that is causing problems.

- Restart Windows to completely remove any programs from memory. Then try running the program that is causing problems.

> If that program continues to cause problems but other programs do not lock up your system, the problem is probably with that program. Check with the manufacturer to determine if a software fix is available. You might have to upgrade to the latest version of the program. An overburdened power supply can also cause a system to lock up. If you have installed more internal devices (hard disk drives, expansion cards, and so on) than the power supply can handle, the lack of voltage/amperage can sometimes result in the system's locking up. This applies only to components that you have installed inside the system unit. External devices typically have their own power supplies.

37. Windows displays a message indicating that it is running low on memory, or Windows just won't run a program.

Some programs, especially Web browsers, have bugs that cause *memory leaks*. When you exit a program, the program is supposed to turn control of resources back over to Windows. If a program has a bug, it might retain control of the resources, or it might continue to use more and more resources as it runs—until your system completely locks up.

If a program consistently locks up your computer or causes Windows to display a warning that your computer is running low on system resources, use the Resource Meter while the program is running to determine how the program is using resources and whether it returns those resources to Windows on exit. For instructions on how to run the Resource Meter, see Quick Fix number 34.

38. My programs ran faster before I installed Windows 98.

Your programs should run faster in Windows 98. If they run more slowly, the Windows 98 installation probably took up so much disk space that the amount of disk space available for Windows to use as virtual memory has been decreased. Run the Windows Maintenance Wizard, ▶as explained in "Use the Windows Maintenance Wizard" on page 494.◀ The Maintenance Wizard removes unneeded files from your hard disk, including the files that the Windows setup program saved to allow you to uninstall Windows. It also runs Disk Defragmenter, which reorganizes the files on your hard disk. This should improve the overall system performance.

Another way to reclaim disk space is to convert your hard disk drive to FAT32, ▶as explained in "Convert a Hard Disk Drive to FAT32," on page 499.◀ If Windows cannot convert your drive to FAT32, you can use DriveSpace to compress files on the disk; however, a compressed drive is a little slower than an uncompressed drive.

39. Sometimes Windows stops, and I see a blue screen with a message indicating that there has been a parity error.

Parity and fatal exception errors are most commonly caused by faulty memory chips or the wrong memory chips being installed in your computer. Tracking down bad memory chips is a complicated procedure that's best left to qualified technicians.

Keyboard Troubles

Problem	Quick Fix Number	Page
Keyboard not found	40	533
No keys work	41	534
Beeping when typing	41	534
Keyboard locks up	42	534
New text replaces old text	43	534
ALL UPPERCASE OR mIXED cASE	44	534

40. When I start my computer, the message Keyboard Not Found appears on my screen.

In most cases, the Keyboard Not Found message indicates that the keyboard cable has become disconnected or is plugged into the wrong port. First, make sure the keyboard is plugged in to the keyboard port, *not* the mouse port. A PS/2 style mouse port is very similar to a standard keyboard port, so it's easy to get them mixed up.

Check both ends of the cable: the end that connects to the system unit and the end that connects to the keyboard itself. Also, check the entire length of the cable for cracks or exposed wires. Check the plugs, too, to make sure that no pins are bent (these pins bend easily if they're not aligned properly with the socket).

If the cable is in good shape and is connected securely, turn off your computer and open the system unit. Look for a fuse on the motherboard next to the keyboard connection. It is likely that the fuse has blown. Replace it, and the keyboard should work. On a related note, don't plug the keyboard (or anything else, for that matter) into the system unit when the power is on. If you plug in the keyboard while the power is on, you just might blow the fuse.

41. Keys do not work, or the computer beeps when I press a key.

Although Windows is billed as a multitasking environment, sometimes one program needs complete control of Windows in order to perform a particular task. If you press a key and nothing happens or your computer beeps, you have probably opened a program that is performing a complex task or in which a dialog box is displayed that requires your immediate attention.

You can usually determine if a program is demanding your attention by looking at the taskbar. The button for the program typically flashes blue to prompt you to respond. Change to that program and reply to the dialog box, and you should be able to reclaim control of your keyboard. If the button is not flashing, change to each running program and check for open dialog boxes.

42. The keyboard does not work in DOS or Windows.

If your keyboard is functional and properly connected to the system unit, your computer will not display the `Keyboard Not Found` message at startup. However, that doesn't mean that the keyboard will work.

If your computer has a lock on it, make sure it is not locked. The lock on the front of the system unit typically disables the keyboard, making it impossible to type anything or enter commands.

If the keyboard stopped working after you installed another device, the new device might be conflicting with your keyboard. Don't change any settings for the keyboard. Instead, change the DIP switches or jumpers on the new device to prevent it from conflicting with your keyboard.

> Occasionally, a corrupted keyboard driver can cause keyboard problems. You can update the keyboard driver. In Windows Control Panel, click the **System** icon, click the plus sign (+) next to **Keyboard**, and double-click the icon for your keyboard. Click the **Driver** tab and click the **Update Driver** button. Then follow the onscreen instructions.

43. I'm trying to insert text in a document, but when I type, the new text replaces existing text.

Most word processing programs allow you to select the desired typing mode: Insert or Overtype. In Insert mode, existing characters are moved automatically to make room for the text you type. In Overtype mode, anything you type replaces existing text.

In most cases, you can change from Insert to Overtype mode and vice versa by pressing the Insert key or by double-clicking a special icon in the program's status bar. Some programs make it more difficult to switch to Overtype mode to prevent people from turning it on by mistake and replacing huge sections of the documents simply by typing.

44. When I type, characters appear in ALL UPPERCASE OR mIXED cASE.

You must have pressed the Caps Lock key by mistake. Simply press the key again to turn off Caps Lock. Your keyboard should have an indicator light that glows when Caps Lock is on.

Mouse Malfunction

Problem	Quick Fix Number	Page
No mouse pointer	45	535
When I move the mouse, Windows locks up	45	535
Jumpy mouse pointer	46	536
No mouse after hardware installation	47	536
No mouse in DOS programs	48	537
Mouse and touchpad use on a notebook PC	49	537
Mouse pointer too fast or too slow	50	538

45. My mouse pointer disappears, or when I move the mouse, it locks up Windows.

If you are using a mouse or other pointing device on a notebook computer, it is normal for the mouse pointer to disappear when it is on the move. The display simply can't keep up with the quick movement of a mouse. To make it easier to keep track of, you can turn on mouse trails, ▶as explained in "Configure a Mouse or Joystick" on page 373.◀

If you can't bring the mouse pointer into view (on a notebook or desktop computer), turn off your computer and check the mouse cable and plug. Make sure the cable is in good condition (no cracks or exposed wires) and that it is plugged in to the mouse port (not the keyboard port). Check the plug to make sure that the pins are not bent or pushed in. You can repair pins in a plug by using a pair of tweezers and a gentle touch. Reconnect the mouse and restart your computer.

If the mouse cable and plug are in good condition, but you still cannot see the mouse pointer or the mouse locks up Windows when you move it, make sure you have the correct mouse driver installed. This check is tricky when you don't have a mouse to navigate Windows. Take the following steps:

1. Press **Ctrl+Esc** to open the Start menu.

2. Press the down arrow key to highlight **Settings**, and then press the right arrow key to open the Settings menu and highlight **Control Panel**. Press **Enter**.

3. In the Control Panel, use the arrow keys to highlight the **System** icon, and then press **Enter**.

4. In the System Properties dialog box, press the right arrow key to change to the **Device Manager** tab.

5. Press the **Tab** key twice to move to the list of devices, press the down arrow key to highlight **Mouse**, and then press the right arrow key to display the icon for your mouse.

6. Press the down arrow key to highlight the icon for your mouse and press **Alt+R**. This displays the Properties dialog box for your mouse.

7. Press the **Tab** key three times to highlight the **General** tab, and then press the right arrow key to change to the **Driver** tab.

8. Tab to the **Upgrade Driver** button and press **Enter**. This starts the Upgrade Device Driver Wizard.

9. Press **Enter**.

10. Press the down arrow key to highlight the **Display a List of All the Drivers** option, and then press **Enter**.

11. Press the **Tab** key to highlight **Show Compatible Hardware**, and then press the down arrow key to select **Show All Hardware**.

12. Tab to the **Manufacturers** list and use the down arrow key to select the manufacturer of your mouse. If you are unsure, choose **(Standard Mouse Types)** at the top of the list.

13. Tab to the **Models** list and use the down arrow key to select the model name of your mouse. Press **Enter**.

14. Follow the onscreen instructions to complete the installation of the mouse driver.

If this does not work, restart your computer, press **F8** when you see the `Starting Windows 98` message, and choose the option to start in Safe mode. Windows will load a standard mouse driver, and then you can at least use the mouse to select a different mouse driver.

46. My mouse pointer moves erratically across the screen.

Your mouse is dirty. Turn it over and check to see if there's a piece of paper, a dustball, or a hair restricting the movement of the mouse ball. Remove the obstruction.

If you still have problems, shut down Windows and turn off your computer. Turn the mouse upside down, remove the cover from the mouse ball, and wipe the mouse ball thoroughly with a damp paper towel (don't use an alcohol-based cleaner, because it can dry out the rubber). Inside the mouse are tiny rollers that collect a lot of dust. Use a toothpick to gently pick the dust from around the rollers and from the center of each roller. (The dust on the center of the rollers is usually packed on them; gently scrape it off.) Reassemble the mouse, turn on your computer, and you should be ready to roll.

47. I installed a modem [or other device], and now the mouse doesn't work!

Mice and modems both use COM ports. Normally the mouse uses COM1 and the modem uses COM2. If your mouse and modem don't seem to get along, they're probably trying to use the same COM port. Leave the mouse port setting as is, and try changing the setting for the modem (try COM2 or COM4). For internal modems, you have to flip some switches on the modem itself and change the COM port setting in the communications program. For external modems, you simply select the COM port setting in the telecommunications program.

After changing the COM port setting on the modem, you must change it in Windows. Take the following steps:

1. In the Windows Control Panel, click the **Modems** icon. The Modems Properties dialog box appears.

2. Make sure your modem is selected, and then click the **Properties** button.

3. Open the **Port** drop-down list and choose the COM port that matches the new setting on your modem.

The modem might also be using IRQ settings that conflict with the mouse. To track down device conflicts, run the the Windows Hardware Troubleshooter, as explained in Quick Fix number 98.

48. The mouse works fine in Windows, but I can't use it in my old DOS programs.

The Windows mouse driver does not control the mouse in DOS programs. To use a mouse in a DOS program, you must run the DOS mouse driver at startup.

First, install the DOS mouse driver. It should have been included on a disk with your mouse. You might have to copy it manually from the disk to a folder on your hard disk. The file's name is typically mouse.com, mouse.exe, or mouse.sys.

After you copy the DOS mouse driver to your hard disk, you must modify the properties of the shortcut you use to run your DOS program so that it loads the mouse driver. Take the following steps:

1. Right-click the icon you use to run the DOS program and choose **Properties**.

2. Click the **Programs** tab and click the **Advanced** button.

3. Make sure **MS-DOS Mode** is on.

4. Click **Specify a New MS-DOS Configuration**.

5. *If the mouse driver is a .sys file,* move the insertion point to the end of an existing line in the **CONFIG.SYS for MS-DOS Mode** text area and press **Enter**. Type the command for running the mouse driver in the form **DEVICE=C:\MOUSE\MOUSE.SYS** (C:\MOUSE is the location of the driver file, and MOUSE.SYS is its name).

   If the mouse driver is an .exe or .com file, move the insertion point to the end of an existing line in the **AUTOEXEC.BAT for MS-DOS Mode** text area and press **Enter**. Type the command for running the mouse driver in the form **C:\MOUSE\MOUSE.EXE** (C:\MOUSE is the location of the driver file, and MOUSE.EXE is its name).

6. Click the **OK** button. When you return to the Properties dialog box, click **OK** to save your changes.

Now when you click the icon for running your DOS program, Windows will shut itself down, run the mouse driver command lines to enable the mouse, and run the DOS program. You should be able to use your mouse in this DOS program.

49. I have a touchpad on my notebook computer, but I would rather use a mouse. Can I?

Touchpads are nifty tools. You slide your finger over the touchpad to move the mouse pointer, and you click a button to select objects. With some touchpads, you can even tap the touchpad instead of clicking a button to select an object. However, if you are accustomed to using a mouse, you might find the touchpad frustrating to use.

Fortunately, most notebook computers have a separate mouse port or at least a serial port into which you can plug another pointing device. You can usually use a mouse right alongside the touchpad. Turn off the computer, plug the mouse into the mouse port or serial port, restart your computer, and run the Add New Hardware Wizard, ▶as explained in "Install New Hardware" on page 364.◀

If you find the touchpad difficult to use, try changing its settings. Your computer should have come with a utility for adjusting the touchpad settings.

If you installed a mouse in addition to the touchpad, and the touchpad causes erratic behavior as you type, you can disable the touchpad. **Alt**+*click* My Computer, click the **Device Manager** tab, and click the plus sign next to **Mouse**. The touchpad may be listed as a mouse, because it typically uses a mouse driver. Click the driver for your touchpad, and click the **Properties** button. Click **Disable in This Hardware Profile** to place a check in the box, and then click **OK**. Save your settings and restart Windows if prompted to do so.

50. The mouse pointer moves way too fast [or too slow] across the screen. Can I adjust the speed?

You can easily adjust the speed at which the mouse pointer travels across the screen and the speed at which you must click twice to execute a double-click. ▶See "Configure a Mouse or Joystick" on page 373 for details.◀

Modems and Connections

Problem	Quick Fix Number	Page
Modem doesn't work at all	51	538
No dial tone detected	52	539
Modem dials wrong number	53	539
Call is cancelled before it's completed	54	539
Can't connect to online service	55	540
Can't connect to Internet	56	540
Connection broken	57	541
Internet connection slow	58	541
Modem makes too much noise	59	542

51. Windows doesn't even seem to know that I have a modem.

If you have a Plug and Play modem or a PCMCIA modem (on a notebook computer), you can plug in the modem, and when you start Windows, Windows will detect the modem, configure it, and install it automatically without a problem.

With modems that are not Plug and Play-compatible, installation can be quite difficult, especially if you have several other devices installed in your computer—additional serial ports, pointing devices, sound cards, and so on. It is not uncommon for a modem installation to fail or for the modem to work but disable one of your other devices. To track down device conflicts, run the Windows Hardware Troubleshooter, as explained in Quick Fix number 98.

52. Windows displays a message indicating that it could not detect a dial tone.

You can turn dial tone detection off, but before you do that, check your phone line. If you use the same phone line for voice calls from your home or office, make sure the phone is not currently being used. Also check the phone line from your modem to the phone jack to make sure it has not been disconnected. If you have an external modem, turn it off, wait a few seconds, and turn it back on.

If the modem still doesn't work, try turning off dial tone detection by following these steps:

1. Open the Windows Control Panel and click the **Modems** icon.

2. Make sure your modem is selected and click the **Properties** button.

3. Click the **Connection** tab and remove the check mark from the **Wait for Dial Tone Before Dialing** check box. Click **OK**.

4. Click **OK** to save your settings.

> If Wait for Dial Tone Before Dialing is grayed out, it is not an option for your modem.

53. The modem keeps dialing the wrong number.

If you need to dial a 9 to get an outside line or dial a 1 and another number to place a long distance call, check your modem's dialing properties:

1. Open the Windows Control Panel and click the **Modems** icon.

2. In the Modems Properties dialog box, click the **Dialing Properties** button.

3. In the **Area Code** text box, make sure the area code for your current location is correct.

4. If you need to dial the area code to reach a particular number within the same area code, click the **Area Code Rules** button, choose **Always Dial the Area Code**, and click **OK**.

5. If you need to dial an extra number to access an outside line, type that number in the **For Local Calls** text box.

6. In most cases, the **For Long Distance Calls** text box should be blank. If you typed a 1 in this text box, thinking that you have to dial 1 before a long distance number, clear the 1 from this box. Type a number only if your phone system requires you to dial one number for outside local calls and a different number for outside long distance calls. Click **OK**.

7. When you return to the Modems Properties dialog box, click **OK** to save your changes.

54. Windows hangs up before completing the call.

If the line you are calling is busy, Windows might immediately hang up without informing you that the line is busy. If your modem's speaker is turned on, you should hear the busy signal. Try the call again later.

If Windows keeps aborting the call, check to make sure that the phone number you entered is correct. Windows may be trying to dial a number that doesn't exist.

55. I signed up with a commercial online service, but I can't connect to it to use it.

Check the obvious first. Have you entered your username and password correctly? Is the phone number for the service entered correctly? Do you need to dial another number such as 9 or 1 to access an outside line or to dial long distance?

Online services provide their own programs. When you run the online service program, look for a configuration or setup option and use it to check these settings. If the settings are correct, check your modem settings as explained in Quick Fix number 58. If you need to use Dial-Up Networking to establish your connection, see the next Quick Fix.

56. I have an Internet service provider, but Dial-Up Networking cannot establish the connection.

Click the icon for your Dial-Up Networking connection, enter your username and password, and click **Connect**. Watch the Connecting To dialog box for clues. If your modem dials the correct number for your service provider and tries to establish a connection, and the service provider accepts your username and password but then disconnects you, Dial-Up Networking might be set up to use a server type that does not match your service provider's server. Take the following steps to check and change your Dial-Up Networking settings:

1. Open My Computer and click the **Dial-Up Networking** icon.

2. Right-click the icon for your service provider and choose **Properties**.

3. Click the **Server Types** tab.

4. Open the **Type of Dial-Up Server** drop-down list and choose the server type specified by your Internet service provider (usually PPP, SLIP, or CSLIP).

5. Under **Allowed Network Protocols**, make sure **TCP/IP** is selected, and then click the **TCP/IP Settings** button.

6. Most service providers assign you an IP address that identifies your computer on the Internet. Make sure **Server Assigned IP Address** is selected, unless your service provider assigned you a permanent IP address.

7. Most service providers specify a Domain Name Server address. If your service provider specified an address, choose **Specify Name Server Addresses** and type the address in the **Primary DNS** text box.

8. While you're at it, make sure **Log On to Network** is turned off. If this option is selected, Windows looks for a Windows network before logging on, which can cause delays or aborted calls. Click **OK**.

9. When you return to the Dial-Up Networking Properties dialog box for this connection, click **OK** to save the new settings.

If this does not fix the problem, open the Windows Control Panel again and click the **Network** icon. In the list of network components, double-click the TCP/IP entry that is linked to your modem. Click the **DNS Configuration** tab, make sure **Enable DNS** is on, and enter the address of the **Domain Name Server**. Then save your changes and try the call again. If you still have problems, contact your ISP's technical support department.

57. I connect to the Internet or my online service okay, but the connection is broken as I use the service.

Several factors might be at work here. If you use the same phone line for voice calls and you or someone else picks up a phone that's on the same line, you might be automatically disconnected. In addition, if you have a weak phone line connection, an old phone line, or a connection with a lot of noise, the connection might not be clear enough to transfer data.

In addition, if you have call waiting, any incoming calls will automatically disconnect the modem. You should disable call waiting whenever you dial into your online service or Internet service provider. Take the following steps to disable call waiting:

1. Open the Windows Control Panel and click the **Modems** icon.

2. Make sure your modem is selected and click the **Properties** button.

3. Click the **Dialing Properties** button.

4. Choose **To Disable Call Waiting, Dial** and choose or type the number you must dial to disable the call waiting feature. This number is usually ***70**. Click **OK**.

5. When you return to the Modems Properties dialog box, click **OK** to save your changes.

If the problem persists, contact your Internet service provider for help.

58. My Internet or online service connection seems slow.

When you are pulling up Web pages that contain large graphics and audio and video clips, expect your Internet connection to slow to a crawl. These files are large and take a long time to travel over the phone lines. You should also expect your connection to your service provider to be slower than the maximum speed of your modem. And remember that because of phone line noise and other hardware limitations, data transfers via modem are not perfect.

To check the speed of your connection, establish your connection, and then right-click the **Dial-Up Networking** icon (in the system tray on the right end of the taskbar) and choose **Status**. Take a look at the Connected To dialog box. It displays the speed of the connection (in bytes per second) between your computer and the service provider. If you have a 28.8Kbps modem, a perfect connection would list 28,800bps. If you are connected at 24,000bps or higher, consider this a good connection. If it's any slower, you should disconnect, reconnect, and check the speed again. Sometimes you'll get lucky and end up with a cleaner connection simply by reconnecting.

However, having a clean connection does not ensure that you will cruise the Internet at warp speed. Several factors determine the speed at which you can download files, including the speed of the server you are connected to, how busy the server is, how busy the Internet is, and the size of the files you are downloading. If you want speed, try connecting during off-hours, such as late at night and early in the morning.

If the connection itself is slow (you have a 28.8Kbps modem that's connecting at 16,000bps), you can often increase the speed of your connection by specifying a speed that is greater than your modem's maximum speed. To do so, take the following steps:

1. Open the Windows Control Panel and click the **Modems** icon.

2. Make sure your modem is selected and click the **Properties** button.

3. Open the **Maximum Speed** drop-down list and choose a speed that is above the maximum speed of your modem. For example, if you have a 14.4Kbps modem, choose 19200; for a 28.8Kbps modem, choose 38400. Click **OK**.

4. When you return to the Modems Properties dialog box, click **OK** to save your changes.

> If you have trouble connecting with the higher-speed setting, repeat the steps and choose a slower setting. Repeat the steps as necessary until you no longer have a problem connecting.

Here are some other factors that can slow down your Internet connection:

- **Slow Internet service provider.** Not all Internet service providers can provide high-quality service. If the service provider is new and has many new users, the service you receive may suffer.

- **Defective phone lines.** Check not only the phone line from your modem to the phone jack but also the phone line from the jack to your connection box (typically on the outside of the house). A loose wire can result in a weak connection.

59. My modem makes a lot of noise when it's dialing. Is there any way to mute it?

If you are having problems with your modem, you should keep the speaker on to provide audio clues as to what is causing a particular problem. With the speaker on, you can determine if the modem is dialing and whether the line is busy. If you dial the wrong number, you'll even hear voices saying "Hello? Hello? HELLO?!"

However, if your modem is working properly, these audio clues can be more annoying than useful, especially if you are dialing in to the Internet when the rest of your family is sleeping. To mute the speaker, take the following steps:

1. Open the Windows Control Panel and click the **Modems** icon.

2. Make sure your modem is selected and click the **Properties** button.

3. On the **General** tab, drag the **Speaker Volume** slider all the way to the left to mute the speaker, and then skip to step 6. If the Speaker Volume slider is grayed out, proceed with step 4.

4. Click the **Connection** tab and click the **Advanced** button.

5. In the **Extra Settings** text box, type **ATM0**, **ATM1**, **ATM2**, or **ATM3** to set the speaker volume. ATM0 mutes the speaker. Click **OK**.

6. When you return to the Modems Properties dialog box, click the **OK** button to save your settings.

Network Issues

Problem	Quick Fix Number	Page
Network card not working	60	543
Direct cable connection failure	61	543
No computers in Network Neighborhood	62	544
My computer is not in Network Neighborhood	62	544
Can't connect to network computer	63	544
A network computer can't connect to my computer	62	544
Can't share files or printers	64	545

60. I installed the network card and cables, but Windows does not recognize the connection.

Make sure you have installed the cables properly. Focus on the following cable issues:

- If you are using a twisted-pair cable (similar to a phone cable) to connect only two computers, make sure that the cable is a crossover cable. If it is a standard twisted-pair cable, it will not work.

- If you are using standard twisted-pair cables to connect more than two computers, you must use a cable to connect each computer to a central hub.

- If you are using coaxial cables, each network card must have a T-connector. If the computer is connected to only one other computer, the open end of the T-connector must be capped with a terminator.

If the cabling is okay, check the network card on your computer to make sure it is not conflicting with other devices. To track down device conflicts, run the Windows Hardware Troubleshooter, as explained in Quick Fix number 98. If the network card is okay, click the **Network** icon in the Windows Control Panel and check the list of components to determine if the proper network protocols are installed. All computers on the network must be set up to use the same protocols. Remove any unnecessary network protocols from the list.

61. I tried connecting the serial or parallel ports on two computers, but I can't get Direct Cable Connection to work.

Assuming that you are using the correct type of cable, that the cables are connected to the proper ports, and that you installed and configured Direct Cable Connection properly (➤see "Link Your Notebook and Desktop Computers" on page 394◄), three common problems can prevent a successful connection:

- If you are currently connected to the Internet, disconnect. Dial-Up Networking commonly causes problems with Direct Cable Connection.

- The port on one or both of your computers is conflicting with another device connected to your computer.

- One of the installed network components is causing a problem.

First, check your ports. Use the Windows Hardware Conflict Troubleshooter to check for conflicts under **Ports (COM & LPT)** in the System Properties dialog box on the Device Manager tab. See Quick Fix number 98 to learn how to start the Troubleshooter. Do this on both computers.

If your ports have no conflicts, the problem may be caused by the IPX/SPX network protocol. Take the following steps to remove it:

1. Open the Windows Control Panel and click the **Network** icon.

2. Click the **IPX/SPX-Compatible Protocol** entry and click the **Remove** button. Repeat this step for all IPX/SPX-Compatible Protocol entries.

3. Make sure NetBEUI is in the list of network protocols. If it is not listed, click the **Add** button to add it. Then click **OK**.

If you still have a problem establishing the connection, try the following corrections:

- Network Neighborhood must be on the Windows desktop. If it is not present, use the options on the Windows Setup tab in the Add/Remove Programs dialog box to install it.

- Open the Windows Control Panel, click the **Network** icon, click the **Identification** tab, and make sure the Workgroup name is the same on both computers.

- If you are connecting the two computers with a parallel cable, check your computer's setup program to make sure that the parallel port is set up as EPP (Enhanced Parallel Port) or ECP (Extended Capabilities Port). You typically run a computer's startup program by pressing a special key (usually F1 or F2) right after you turn on the computer's power and before Windows starts. Check the parallel port settings on both computers and try to match them.

62. The network connection seems okay, but I don't see any other computers in the Network Neighborhood.

Network Neighborhood displays only those computers that are in the same workgroup. To see other computers, your computer and the other computers you want to access must all use the same workgroup name. In addition, each computer on the network must have a different computer name. To check the computer and workgroup names, open the Windows Control Panel, click the **Network** icon, and click the **Identification** tab.

63. I see the computer in the Network Neighborhood, but I can't connect to it.

If a network computer is turned off or crashes, you will not be able to access it on the network. To determine if the computer is available, choose **Start**, **Find**, **Computer** and search for the computer by name. Then check the following:

- If you cannot find the computer on the network, make sure the computer is running and that it is physically connected to the network. If you are on a large network, inform the network administrator of the problem.

- If you can connect to the computer but cannot access its folders, files, or printer, make sure the computer is set up to share those resources. The person in charge of that computer must mark disks, folders, files, printers, and other resources as shared in order for them to be accessible on the network. (To share a resource, right-click its icon, choose **Sharing**, and enter your preferences.)

- If you can view shared resources on the other computer but not use them, check to make sure you have the proper authorization to use the resources. The resources might be password-protected, and you might not be on the list of authorized users.

64. I can't share disks, folders, files, or printers on my computer with other computers on the network.

Before you can share disks, folders, files, or printers on your computer with other computers on the network, you must install File and Printer Sharing. Take the following steps:

1. Open the Windows Control Panel and click the **Network** icon.

2. On the **Configuration** tab, click **Add**.

3. Click **Service** and click **Add**.

4. Click **Microsoft** in the Manufacturers list.

5. In the Network Services list, choose **File and Printer Sharing for Microsoft Networks** or **File and Printer Sharing for NetWare Networks**, depending on the type of network you use. Click **OK**.

6. Return to the Network dialog box and click the **File and Printer** button.

7. Make sure both sharing options are selected and click **OK**. Then click **OK** to save your changes.

After you install File and Printer Sharing, you must mark each resource you want to share. Right-click the resource in My Computer or Windows Explorer and choose **Sharing**. Then enter the desired sharing preferences.

Printers and Printing

Problem	Quick Fix Number	Page
Bi-directional printing	65	546
Document did not print	66	546
Only part of the document printed	66	546
Missing fonts	68	548
Graphics look bad	69	548
Paper is not feeding properly	70	549
Printout is streaked	71	549
Error printing to LPT1	72	549
Printing takes forever	73	550
Blank page is printing	74	551

65. I keep receiving error messages when I try to print with my new bi-directional printer.

You might not even know that you have a bi-directional printer unless you read the documentation that came with it or the manufacturer made a big deal of it in an advertisement. However, many newer computers are bi-directional, meaning that the print head can print as it passes over the paper in both directions. This speeds up printing, but it can cause all sorts of problems if your computer's parallel printer port does not support bi-directional printing. You'll keep receiving error messages that do not even mention the word "bi-directional."

First, check your printer's documentation to determine if the printer is bi-directional. If it is, the next step is to check your computer's setup program to determine if the parallel port has a bi-directional mode. Follow these steps:

1. Shut down Windows and restart your computer.

2. When you see a message telling you which key to press to run your computer's startup program, press the specified key. (You might have to perform some other step to run the setup program.)

3. When the Setup menu appears, look for the Parallel Port option and select it. (You might have to select an option for configuring peripheral devices in order to find the Parallel Port option.)

4. There should be two Parallel Port settings: one for the port's I/O address and IRQ and another for the mode. Choose the mode option.

5. Scroll through the available modes (usually by pressing **Enter** to view a menu or by using the right arrow key). If there is a **Bi-Directional** or **ECP** (Enhanced Capabilities Port) option, select it.

6. Save your settings and exit the setup program.

> Even if you don't have a bi-directional printer, you should check the Parallel Port setting, as just explained. Many relatively new computers are set to a parallel port mode to accommodate older printers. If you don't have a bi-directional printer, change the mode to ECP.

If the printer did not come with its own cable (most don't), you should make sure you are using a bi-directional cable, too.

If you continue to receive the same error messages when you try to print a document, disable bi-directional printing for the printer. Check the printer documentation or call technical support to determine if you need a special utility to disable bi-directional printing. You might be able to disable bi-directional printing in Windows. Right-click your printer's icon in the Printers folder and choose **Properties**. Click the **Details** tab and then the **Spool Settings** button. Turn on the option for disabling bi-directional printing.

66. I entered the Print command, but the printer didn't print the document [or printed only a portion of it].

Make sure the printer is plugged in and turned on and that the On Line light is lit (not blinking). You can usually make this light come on by filling the printer with paper and then pressing the **On Line**, **Reset**, or **Load** button on the printer. If your printer has panels or doors, make sure they are all closed.

If you're printing to a shared network printer, check to see whether your document did indeed print and was accidentally picked up by somebody else. If not, consult the network administrator.

If everything checks out, but the printer still refuses to print, check the following:

- Check the paper rack on the printer to make sure it is seated properly and that the paper-feed levers are in the proper position for the type of paper that's loaded.

- Turn the printer off, wait a minute, and turn it back on. This clears the printer's memory and can return it to normal. (If your printer doesn't have an on/off switch, unplug it and then plug it back in.)

- In My Computer, right-click drive **C** and click **Properties**. Make sure your hard disk has at least 10 megabytes of free space. If you have less than that, run Cleanup Disk or the Windows Maintenance Wizard to free some space.

- Check to see if printing has been paused. Choose **Start**, **Settings**, **Printers**, and then right-click the printer icon. If Pause Printing has a check mark next to it, choose **Pause Printing** to remove the check mark.

- Check the printer setup in Windows. Choose **Start**, **Settings**, **Printers**, and then right-click the printer icon and choose **Properties**. Make sure the printer is set to the correct port (usually LPT1).

- Check the printer timeout settings. Choose **Start**, **Settings**, **Printers**, and then right-click the printer icon and choose **Properties**. Click the **Details** tab and increase the Timeout Settings by 15 seconds each. The timeout settings tell Windows how long to wait before giving up.

- Check to see if your printer is set up as the default printer. Choose **Start**, **Settings**, **Printers**, and then right-click the printer icon and choose **Set As Default**.

- Make sure the correct printer is selected. Choose **Start**, **Settings**, **Printers**, and then right-click the printer icon and choose **Properties**. Make sure the correct printer driver is being used. If the wrong printer or driver is listed, click the **New Driver** button and choose the correct manufacturer and model.

> When you run into problems printing, it is tempting to keep trying to print the document. That keeps sending the document to the print queue; when you finally do coax your printer into printing, you will get several copies of the document. If you do try to print the document several times, you can use Print Manager to clear the print queue. ►See "Manage Print Jobs" on page 167 for details.◄

If several pages of a document printed, but not the whole thing, check the print settings in the program from which you are trying to print. Open the **File** menu and choose **Print**. Under **Page Range**, make sure you selected the setting for printing all pages (the entire document).

If a portion of a page printed and it is a page with complex graphics and several fonts, it's possible that your printer has insufficient memory to print the document. You should install additional memory in your printer. For the time being, try to use smaller, less-complex graphics and fewer fonts. You might also try printing at a lower resolution. When printing the document, click the **Properties** or **Options** button in the Print dialog box and choose **Draft Output** or a lower resolution.

67. The font I used in the document looks a lot different on the printout than it did on-screen.

Some fonts require two versions of the font: one for the printer and one for the display. If you choose a printer font—one that has a printer icon next to its name in the font list—Windows takes the initiative of assigning a display font for the onscreen text. These fonts might not match exactly.

The easiest way to avoid this problem is to use only TrueType fonts—fonts whose names are preceded by TT in the fonts list. With TrueType fonts, the same font is used for displaying and printing the document. ▶For more information on installing, previewing, and managing fonts, see "Add and Remove Fonts" on page 427.◀

68. When I print a document with images, the images look fuzzy, and the lines are jagged.

If you just installed a new print cartridge in an inkjet printer, use the utility that came with the printer to align the cartridge. There is a little play in the cartridge holder that might cause the color and black ink cartridges to move out of alignment when you change cartridges.

The graphics resolution setting in Windows can also cause graphics to print poorly. To check and change this setting, take the following steps:

1. Click the **Start** button, point to **Settings**, and click **Printers**.

2. Right-click the icon for your printer and choose **Properties**.

3. Check the options in the Properties dialog box for a graphics or resolution setting. If you are using a Windows printer driver instead of the driver that came with your printer, the setting is on the **Graphics** tab. Choose the setting for the highest quality.

4. Click **OK** to save your settings.

The Windows Printers folder is not the only place you can change printer settings. Most programs offer their own print options to control the way they print documents. In Microsoft Word, for instance, you can click the **Options** button in the Print dialog box to make the printer print in draft mode, reverse the order of the pages, and print additional information on each page.

69. The printer feeds the paper improperly or not at all.

Check the paper feed tray. Make sure the tray is seated properly; it's easy to knock it loose when you're loading or unloading paper. Make sure the feed levers are in the correct position. If you have a lever pushed in to print envelopes and you are trying to print on standard paper, the paper won't feed properly.

In some cases, the rollers on the paper-feed mechanism collect paper dust that makes the rollers slippery. Wipe the rollers off as best you can with a clean cloth (use water, not cleaning solution). (You might find it nearly impossible to get to the entire surface of the rollers. Don't force them; just clean what you can.)

> One printer manufacturer used a type of rubber for its print rollers that was especially prone to collecting dust, and later the company had to supply its customers with an abrasive cleaning unit designed to roughen up the rollers.

70. The ink on the printout is streaky. Some areas of the page look very light or blank.

Your ink cartridge might be on its way out, or it might be dirty. If your printer has been sitting for some time, ink might have dried on the print head. Many printers come with a special utility designed to purge dried ink. Check the printer documentation to determine how to use this utility.

Do not try to clean the cartridge with a paper towel or any kind of solution unless the manufacturer recommends it. Touching any of the contacts that connect the print cartridge to the printer could ruin the cartridge.

On a related note, it is tempting to refill cartridges to save money. If you have ever tried to refill an inkjet cartridge, you probably already realize that refilling cartridges is more mess than it's worth. If the mess is not enough to dissuade you, keep in mind that any damage to the printer caused by refilled cartridges usually voids the printer's warranty.

71. Windows displays an error message indicating that it could not print to LPT1. What does that mean?

Assuming you installed the printer correctly (➤see "Set Up a New Printer" on page 369◄), this message is usually harmless. Click **OK** to close the dialog box, and then purge any print jobs that are currently in the print queue (➤see "Manage Print Jobs" on page 167◄) and try printing again. If you receive the error message again, turn off your printer and turn it back on. If you still have problems, refer to Quick Fixes 65 and 66.

If you still receive the error message, your computer might have a problem printing in Enhanced Metafile (EMF) format. Follow these steps to disable EMF:

1. Click the **Start** button, point to **Settings**, and click **Printers**.

2. Right-click your printer's icon and choose **Properties**.

3. Click the **Details** tab and click the **Spool Settings** button.

4. Open the **Spool Data Format** drop-down list and choose **RAW**. Click **OK**.

5. When you return to the printer's properties dialog box, click **OK** to save your change.

72. The printer takes forever to print a document. Is there any way to speed it up?

Printing is one of the slowest operations a computer performs, especially if you are printing high-resolution color graphics. However, there are a few things you can try to speed up printing. First, make sure print spooling is on. Then follow these steps:

1. Click the **Start** button, point to **Settings**, and click **Printers**.

2. Right-click the icon for your printer and choose **Properties**.

3. Click the **Details** tab and click the **Spool Settings** button.

4. If **Spool Print Jobs So Program Finishes Printing Faster** is off, turn it on. Click **OK**.

5. When you return to the printer's properties dialog box, click **OK**.

> Spooling prints the document to a file on your hard disk, which then feeds the printing instructions to your printer. This frees up the program faster so that you can continue working in it. If you print directly to the printer, the program must continually feed printing instructions to the printer.

If print spooling is on and printing still takes a long time, check the free space on your hard disk drive (right-click the drive's icon and choose **Properties**). Make sure your hard disk has at least 10 megabytes of free space. If you have less than that, run Cleanup Disk or the Windows Maintenance Wizard to free some space.

You can try a few other techniques to speed up printing:

- Close or don't use other programs while you are printing.
- Add memory to your printer to allow it to store larger chunks of printing instructions.
- Install an updated printer driver.
- Use only printer fonts and TrueType fonts in your documents. Printer fonts are fastest, because they are built into the printer. TrueType fonts are the fastest soft fonts.
- Lower the graphics resolution or print in draft mode when you do not need high-quality printouts.

73. The printer prints the document fine, but then it spits out a blank sheet of paper.

Check the end or your document to determine if it ends with a page break mark (typically a dotted horizontal line). If you have several blank paragraphs at the end of the document, they might have caused the program to insert a page break. Delete the extraneous paragraph marks.

If the problem persists no matter which document you print, you might have Windows set up to print a separator page between documents. Separator pages are commonly used on network printers to prevent multiple users' documents from becoming mixed up. When you choose to print a document in one of your programs, check the printer options to determine if the program is set up to print a separator page.

Sound Cards and Microphones

Problem	Quick Fix Number	Page
Sound card installation	74	551
No sound from speakers	75	551
Recorded sound does not play	76	552
Microphone does not record	76	552
No sound after installing another device	77	552
No sound in DOS program	12	521
No stereo	78	553
No sound from CD-ROM	14	522

74. I just installed a sound card, and I can't get it to work.

This is a tough one, because the solution can range from as something simple as cranking up the volume to something as complex as fooling around with switches on the card. First, look for simple solutions:

- Are your speakers plugged into the right jack—the output jack? (It's easy to plug the speakers into the microphone jack or the input jack by mistake.)

- If you have amplified speakers, are they plugged into the power supply and turned on?

- Is the volume cranked up? (Most sound cards have a volume control like on a radio.)

- Is the sound cranked up in Windows? Right-click the **Volume** icon in the system tray (on the right end of the taskbar) and choose **Open Volume Controls**. Make sure the **Speaker** and **Wave** volume controls are at their maximum settings and that the Mute options are not selected.

- Are you running a program that plays sounds and that is compatible with your sound card? Is sound turned on (and turned up) in the program?

- Did you install the drivers? The sound card should come with one or more disks containing the sound card drivers. You must run the installation program to set up your computer to use the sound card.

Is the sound card in conflict with another device? Each device has its own Input/Output address and interrupt settings. If two devices try to use the same settings, one or both devices won't work. Use the Hardware Conflict Troubleshooter, as explained in Quick Fix number 98, to identify the conflict.

75. The sound card installation seemed to work, but I still don't hear any sounds.

First, check for obvious problems, as explained in Quick Fix number 74. The solution might be as simple as turning up the volume. Next, check your sound card's properties in Windows. Take the following steps:

1. Open the Windows Control Panel and click the **Multimedia** icon.

2. On the **Audio** tab, under **Playback**, open the **Preferred Device** drop-down list and choose your sound card.

3. Click the **Advanced** tab.

4. Click the plus sign (+) next to **Audio Devices**, and then right-click your sound card and choose **Properties**.

5. Make sure **Use Audio Features on This Device** is selected. Click **OK**.

6. When you return to the Multimedia Properties dialog box, click **OK** to save your changes.

If the problem persists, the WAV or CD audio device might not be installed. Click the **Multimedia** icon in the Control Panel, click the **Advanced** tab, and click the plus sign (+) next to **Media Control Devices**. CD Audio Device and WAV Audio Device should be listed there. If they are in the list, right-click each device, choose **Properties**, and make sure **Use This Media Control Device** is selected. If these devices are not in the list, take the following steps to install them:

1. Click the **Start** button, point to **Settings**, and click **Control Panel**.

2. In the Control Panel, click the **Add New Hardware** icon.

3. When you're asked if you want Windows to search for new hardware, click **No**, and then click the **Next** button.

4. Under **Hardware Types**, click **Sound, Video, and Game Controllers**. Click the **Next** button.

5. Under **Manufacturers**, choose **Microsoft MCI**.

6. Under **Models**, click **Wave Audio Device (Multimedia Control)**. Click **Next**.

7. Click the **Finish** button, and then follow the onscreen instructions. You might be prompted to insert the Windows 98 CD and restart your computer.

8. Repeat these steps, but choose **CD Audio Device (Multimedia Control)** in step 6 to install the CD audio device.

76. I recorded a sound using my microphone, but when I try to play it, I don't hear anything.

Make sure that your microphone is plugged in to the MIC jack on the sound card and that the microphone switch is turned on (if there is one). Then check the recording volume in Windows by following these steps:

1. Right-click the **Volume** icon in the system tray (on the right end of the taskbar) and choose **Open Volume Controls**.

2. Drag the **Microphone** slider all the way up. (If the Microphone volume control is not displayed, open the **Options** menu, choose **Properties**, place a check mark in the **Microphone** check box, and click **OK**.)

3. Click the Speaker window's **Close** (X) button.

If the Microphone volume was already cranked up, take the following steps to make sure your sound card is selected as the preferred device for recording:

1. Open the Windows Control Panel and click the **Multimedia** icon.

2. On the **Audio** tab, under **Recording**, open the **Preferred Device** drop-down list and choose your sound card.

3. Click **OK** to save your changes.

The tough part of tracking down recording problems is determining whether the cause is related to recording or playback. If you still have problems playing back recorded sounds, use the program you are trying to record in to open a WAV file in the Windows\Media folder and play it. If the sound does not play, the problem is probably related to sound output, not sound input. Check Quick Fixes 74 and 75 to correct the problem.

77. I just installed another device on my computer, and now the sound card doesn't work.

If your sound card was working before you installed a new device, the new device is conflicting with your sound card. Use the Hardware Conflict Troubleshooter, as explained in Quick Fix number 98, to identify the conflict. Then change the settings on the new device to settings that do not conflict with your sound card. After changing the settings, run the Add New Hardware Wizard and let Windows search for new hardware.

78. I have a stereo sound card, but I hear only mono output.

Check your speakers. With many desktop speakers, one speaker is connected to the other by a plug-in cable. The cable might have become disconnected. Also, if each speaker has a separate volume control, make sure both controls are turned up. Likewise, if the speakers have a balance control, make sure it is in the center position.

You should also check your output and speaker settings in Windows. To do so, take the following steps:

1. Open the Windows Control Panel and click the **Multimedia** icon.

2. On the **Audio** tab, under **Playback**, click the **Advanced Properties** button.

3. On the **Speakers** tab, open the drop-down list and choose the type of speakers you are using (for example, Desktop Stereo Speakers). Click **OK**.

4. When you return to the Multimedia Properties dialog box, click the button with the speaker icon on it under **Playback**. This displays the volume controls.

5. Under **Speaker**, drag the **Balance** slider to the center position. Click the Speaker window's **Close** (X) button.

6. When you return to the Multimedia Properties dialog box, click **OK** to save your settings.

Video and Display Issues

Problem	Quick Fix Number	Page
Black (blank) monitor	29, 79	529, 553
Fuzzy graphics	80	554
Garbled text	81	554
Flickering screen	82	554
Direct Draw support	83	555
`Display Problems` error message	84	555
`Mciavi` error message	85	555
`Invalid Page Fault in Kernel32.dll` error message	86	556

79. My monitor doesn't display anything; it's just black.

Before you do anything, work through Quick Fix number 29 to check for simple solutions. If the screen is blank, restart the computer using the emergency floppy disk you created. After you restart, take the following steps to check your monitor and display adapter settings:

1. Right-click a blank area of the desktop and choose **Properties**.

2. In the Display Properties dialog box, click the **Settings** tab.

number nine pepper M 32 (English)

3. Click the **Advanced** button.

4. Click the **Adapter** tab and make sure Windows is set up to use the correct display adapter. If the display adapter is incorrect or missing, click the **Change** button and use the Upgrade Device Driver Wizard to choose the correct adapter.

5. When you return to the Properties dialog box, click the **Monitor** tab and make sure Windows is set up to use the correct monitor driver. If the wrong monitor is displayed, click the **Change** button and use the Upgrade Device Driver Wizard to choose the correct driver.

6. Click **OK**, and then restart your computer.

80. Graphics and video clips look fuzzy or blocky.

Your display resolution or colors are set too low. Take the following steps to increase the resolution and color settings:

1. Right-click a blank area of the Windows desktop and choose **Properties**.

2. Click the **Settings** tab.

3. Open the **Colors** drop-down list and choose a setting of **256 Colors** or higher.

4. Under **Screen Area**, drag the slider to the right to set the screen area to **800-by-600** or higher.

5. Click **OK** and restart Windows if required.

81. The onscreen text is garbled.

First, perform Quick Fix number 79 to make sure Windows is using the correct display driver. You might have to obtain a new video driver from the monitor or video card manufacturer or from the computer manufacturer. If Windows is using the correct display driver, try decreasing hardware acceleration. Take the following steps:

1. Open the Windows Control Panel and click the **Display** icon.

2. Click the **Settings** tab and click the **Advanced** button.

3. Click the **Performance** tab.

4. Drag the **Hardware Acceleration** slider to the left one notch to decrease the setting.

5. Click **OK** to return to the Display Properties dialog box, and then click **OK** to save your settings. You might have to restart Windows.

If you still have the same problem, repeat the steps to decrease the Hardware Acceleration setting another notch.

82. My screen is flickering.

Turn off your computer and check your monitor cables. If the power cable or the cable that connects the monitor to the system unit is loose, it might cause the screen to flicker. You should also check the display adapter card inside the system unit to make sure it has not jiggled loose from the expansion slot.

If you continue to have problems, try decreasing the Hardware Acceleration setting for the monitor, as explained in Quick Fix number 81.

83. I have a game that requires DirectDraw, and I can't get the game to play.

Many newer programs, especially Windows games, require DirectDraw. Windows 98 comes with DirectDraw, so it is installed on your computer. However, you must make sure that your video driver supports DirectDraw. To check this, take the following steps:

1. Open the Windows Control Panel and click the **Display** icon.

2. Click the **Settings** tab and click the **Advanced** button.

3. Click the **Adapter** tab.

4. Next to Features, DirectDraw should be listed. If DirectDraw is not listed, obtain an updated video driver from the manufacturer and install it in Windows. To install a new driver, click the **Change** button on the **Adapter** tab, and then follow the wizard's instructions.

You should also make sure you have the most recent version of DirectX. An older version may not support the latest games. Use the Start, Windows Update feature to check for updated software at Microsoft's Web site.

84. My program displays an error message indicating that there are display problems and that it cannot continue.

By not specifying the nature of the display problem, the program doesn't provide much help in tracking down the cause of the problem. Try the following corrections:

- Make sure Windows is set up to use the correct monitor and display adapter. In the Display Properties dialog box, click the **Settings** tab, click **Advanced**, and check the Adapter and Monitor tabs for this information. See Quick Fix number 79 for more information.

- Try changing the **Colors** setting for your monitor to **256 Colors**. See Quick Fix number 80 for details.

- Make sure your display adapter supports DirectDraw, and install an updated video driver if necessary. See Quick Fix number 83 for details.

- Try decreasing the **Hardware Acceleration** setting, as explained in Quick Fix number 81.

85. Windows displays the `Mciavi requires a newer version of Msvideo.dll` error message.

Try reinstalling the Mciavi.drv file from the Windows 98 CD. Take the following steps:

1. Insert the Windows 98 CD into your CD-ROM drive.

2. Click the **Start** button, point to **Programs**, **Accessories**, and then **System Tools**, and click **System Information**.

3. Open the System Information **Tools** menu and choose **System File Checker**.

4. Choose **Extract One File from Installation Disk**.

5. In the **File to Extract** text box, type **mciavi.drv**. Click the **Start** button.

6. Next to the **Restore From** option, click the **Browse** button.

7. Click the plus sign (+) next to the letter of your CD-ROM drive, click the **Win98** folder, and click **OK**.

8. In the **Save File In** text box, type **c:\windows\system**.

9. Click **OK** as many times as necessary to return to the Control Panel, and then restart Windows.

86. Windows displays the `Invalid Page Fault in Kernel32.dll` error message.

First, try decreasing the Hardware Acceleration setting, as explained in Quick Fix number 81. If the error message keeps popping up, work through Quick Fixes 79, 80, and 83 to correct problems with video drivers, display settings, and DirectDraw.

If the problem persists only when you are using a particular program, check the program's documentation or help system to determine if it addresses the issue. If you don't find the answer there, contact the manufacturer's technical support department, either with a phone call or via its Web site.

World Wide Web Error Messages

Problem	Quick Fix Number	Page
Internet Explorer cannot find document	87	556
`Document Contains No Data` error message	88	557
`403 Forbidden` error message	89	557
Other `400` messages	89	557
DNS server problem	90	557
Traffic jams	91	558
Operation timed out	91	558
Can't play selected file	92	558

87. Internet Explorer displays a message saying that it cannot find the specified document or Web page.

Usually, this means that somebody moved or deleted the Web page you're trying to pull up. Try chopping the end off the right side of the page address and entering the shortened URL into the **Address** text box. For instance, if you initially typed **www.yahoo.com/Entertainment/Movies/**, try typing **www.yahoo.com/Entertainment** or just **www.yahoo.com**. You can then use links to move to the specific page you want.

If you still have trouble connecting to the page, and you have been entering abbreviated Web server addresses (for example, **yahoo** instead of **www.yahoo.com**), try typing the entire address.

88. Internet Explorer displays a message saying that the document I tried to open does not contain data.

This error message usually means that the end is chopped off the URL. URLs typically end with a filename, telling Internet Explorer which page, graphic, video, or sound file to open. For example, **http://www.microsoft.com/ie/index.html** opens a Web page document file called index.html. Sometimes, if the filename is chopped off (as in **http://www.microsoft.com/ie**), Internet Explorer might tell you that the document contains no data.

Because you do not know the name of the file, you can't just type it into the Address text box and press Enter. Instead, try chopping more off the right side of the URL. Then type the chopped URL into the **Address** text box and press **Enter**. Most Web servers display their home page whenever you connect to the server. You can then click the links on that page to find a specific page.

89. When I try to open a page, Internet Explorer displays a 403 Forbidden code or some other 400 message.

The 400 messages typically mean that you tried to connect to a Web server where you're not welcome or one that does not recognize your request. Perhaps the server does not allow public access, or maybe you are trying to connect to a site that requires you to pay a subscription price. Whatever the case, you can't do anything to sidestep this message, so just back up and try another page.

90. Internet Explorer says that it cannot find the DNS server.

DNS (short for Domain Name Server) is a system that matches the domain name you type (for example, www.yahoo.com) with its IP (Internet Protocol) number (for example, 129.98.170.98). In plain English, this means that the Domain Name Server finds Web pages.

If you type a page address and the DNS can't find a matching number for the address, Internet Explorer 4 displays a dialog box telling you so. Check the following:

- Did you type the address correctly? One tiny typo (an uppercase letter that should be lower-case, a backslash instead of a forward slash, or even a misplaced period) can give you the DNS error message. Retype the address and press **Enter**.

- Are you connected to the Internet? If your connection was terminated (or you didn't connect in the first place), Internet Explorer can't find the page, because Internet Explorer isn't even connected to the Internet. Establish your Internet connection and try again.

- If you received the error after clicking on a link, the URL behind the link may have a typo. Rest the mouse pointer on the problem link and look at the address in the status bar. If you see an obvious typo, retype the address in the **Address** text box, and press **Enter**.

- If you're connected to the Internet, but you keep getting this error message no matter which Web page you try to load, maybe your service provider's DNS server is down or you have the wrong address for it. Try disconnecting and then reconnecting. If the problem persists, contact your service provider to find out the correct address for the DNS server. Then run the Internet Connection Wizard (▶see "Set Up Your Internet Connection" on page 220◀) and type in the correct number.

91. The Web page doesn't load, or it takes so long to load that Internet Explorer displays a message saying that the operation "timed out."

If a page takes an inordinate amount of time to download, the Web site might be too busy to handle your request. In such a case, after about one minute, Internet Explorer will give up trying to connect to the site and will display an error message indicating that the site is too busy. These traffic jams are not uncommon. Simply wait about five minutes, and then try connecting to the site again.

92. Internet Explorer displays a message indicating that it cannot play the file I selected.

If you click on a link to play a multimedia file (such as a sound file or video clip) that Internet Explorer cannot play itself, you'll get an error message indicating that you don't have the application needed to play files of this type. Internet Explorer will usually let you download the required application or save the selected file to your hard drive so you can play it later.

For now, either skip the file or save it to your hard drive. ▶See "Play Audio, Video, and Other Active Content" on page 265 for details.◀

Email and Newsgroup Problems

Problem	Quick Fix Number	Page
No connection to email server	93	558
No connection to news server	93	558
Cannot send or receive email	93	558
Server times out	94	559
Cannot view newsgroups	95	559
Cannot play attached file	96	560
Outgoing messages are garbled	97	560

93. Outlook Express does not connect to my email or news server.

First, make sure you have established an Internet connection. You cannot connect to the email server unless you are connected to the Internet or an intranet. See Quick Fix number 56 if you are having problems establishing an Internet connection.

If you normally run Outlook Express and let it dial the Internet service provider, try establishing the connection first. To do so, click the **Dial-Up Networking** icon you created to dial into the service provider, enter your username and password, and click **Connect**. Run Outlook Express after the connection has been established, and then click the **Send and Receive** button.

If you are still having problems, check the mail server settings in Outlook Express by taking the following steps:

1. In Outlook Express, open the **Tools** menu and choose **Accounts**.

2. Click the **Mail** tab.

3. Select the email account you are having trouble with and click the **Properties** button.

4. On the **General** tab, make sure your email address is correct. Don't worry about any of the other entries on this tab.

5. Click the **Servers** tab.

6. Make sure you have entered the proper address for both the incoming and outgoing mail servers. Check with your Internet service provider to verify these addresses.

7. If your Internet service provider requires you to log on to the server, make sure **Log on Using** is selected and that you have entered the correct username and password.

8. Click **OK**.

94. When I click Send and Receive, it takes a long time for the messages to be sent or retrieved, and then Outlook Express displays the `Operation timed out` message.

If the mail server you are trying to connect to is down or busy, Outlook Express gives up after trying for a set amount of time. You can try sending and receiving messages later.

If you continue to receive this error message, take the following steps to change the timeout settings:

1. In Outlook Express, open the **Tools** menu and choose **Accounts**.

2. Click the **Mail** tab.

3. Select the email account you are having trouble with and click the **Properties** button.

4. Click the **Advanced** tab.

5. Drag the **Server Timeouts** slider to the right to make Outlook Express wait longer before giving up.

6. Click **OK**.

95. I can connect to the news server, but I cannot view any newsgroups.

If you can establish a connection to the Internet and to your news server, take the following steps to check and change your news server account information:

1. In Outlook Express, open the **Tools** menu and choose **Accounts**.

2. Click the **News** tab.

3. Select the newsgroup account you are having trouble with and click the **Properties** button.

4. Click the **Server** tab.

5. Make sure you have entered the proper address for the news server. Check with your Internet service provider to verify the address.

6. If your Internet service provider requires you to log on to the server, click **This Server Requires Me to Log On**, and then enter your username (account name) and password in the appropriate text boxes.

7. Click the **Advanced** tab and drag the **Server Timeouts** slider to the right to increase the amount of time Outlook Express waits for a response from the server before giving up.

8. If your Internet service provider specified a port number for connecting to the news server, enter it in the **News (NNTP)** text box.

9. Click **OK**.

96. Outlook Express indicates that it cannot play a file that is attached to a message.

If you click the icon for a file that's attached to a newsgroup or email message, Outlook Express will try to play the file using its associated program. If you have not installed a program that can play the selected file type, or if you have not associated the program with this file type, Outlook Express cannot play the file. ▶See "Play Audio, Video, and Other Active Content" on page 265 to learn how to download and install programs for playing various file types.◀ ▶See "Create and Edit File Associations" on page 125 to associate programs with particular file types.◀

97. After I sent a message, the recipient informed me that the message was garbled.

If you sent the message using HTML (Web page) formatting and the recipient's email program does not support HTML, the message she received might have a bunch of HTML tags that she has not encountered before. Before sending a message to that person, open the **Format** menu in the Compose Message window and choose **Plain Text**.

You can change the default format for outgoing messages. Open the Outlook Express **Tools** menu, choose **Options**, and click the **Send** tab. Under **Mail Sending Format**, choose **Plain Text**, and then click **OK**.

If the message is still garbled as plain text, you might have turned on the encryption feature by mistake. Take the following steps to turn message encryption off:

1. Open the **Tools** menu and choose **Options**.

2. Click the **Security** tab.

3. Make sure **Encrypt Contents and Attachments for All Outgoing Messages** does not have a check mark next to it.

4. Click **OK**.

Troubleshooting Aids

Troubleshooting Aid	Aid Number	Page
Windows troubleshooters	98	561
MSConfig	99	561
Dr. Watson	100	562
System File Checker	101	563

98. Can Windows 98 help me track down the cause of a problem?

Yes, Windows 98 comes with several troubleshooters that can help you determine the causes of common problems, including problems not covered in this Quick Fix section. The following is a list of those troubleshooters:

Dial-Up Networking Troubleshooter

Direct Cable Connection Troubleshooter

DirectX Troubleshooter

Display Troubleshooter

DriveSpace 3 Troubleshooter

Hardware Conflict Troubleshooter

Memory Troubleshooter

The Microsoft Network Troubleshooter

Modem Troubleshooter

MS-DOS Programs Troubleshooter

Networking Troubleshooter

PC Card Troubleshooter (for notebook PCMCIA cards)

Print Troubleshooter

Sound Troubleshooter

Startup and Shutdown Troubleshooter

Troubleshooters help by displaying a series of questions that lead you through checks and corrections. To run a troubleshooter, take the following steps:

1. Click the **Start** button and choose **Help**. The Windows Help window appears with the Contents tab in front.

2. In the **Contents** list, click **Troubleshooting**.

3. Click **Troubleshooting**, and then click **Windows 98 Troubleshooters**. This displays a list of available troubleshooters.

4. Click the troubleshooter you want to use. The troubleshooter starts, or a button or link for running the troubleshooter appears in the right pane. If necessary, click the button or link for running the troubleshooter. The right pane displays a list of problems and questions.

5. Click the desired problem or question, and then follow the troubleshooter's instructions.

99. Can I quickly and safely disable commands and devices in order to determine if they are causing problems?

When you are trying to track down the cause of a problem, it often helps to disable commands and devices that you suspect are causing the problem. However, disabling devices and commands can cause further problems, especially if you don't keep track of the changes you make or don't remember how to reinstall the device.

Windows offers a nifty utility called the System Configuration Utility that can help you disable commands and devices without completely removing them from your system. You should still be careful to keep a record of any changes you make, but the System Configuration Utility makes it much easier to return your system to the way it was before you changed its settings.

Before using the System Configuration Utility, you should have some idea of what you want to do. Read the documentation that came with the problem device, or contact the manufacturer's technical support department. If the person tells you to disable one or more commands in Config.sys or Autoexec.bat, use the System Configuration Utility to disable the commands safely. You shouldn't play around with the utility just to see what will happen.

Although I can't give you steps on how to use the System Configuration Utility to correct specific problems, the following steps tell you how to run it and explain the various tabs:

1. Choose **Start, Programs, Accessories, System Tools, System Information**.

2. Open the System Information **Tools** menu and choose **System Configuration Utility**.

   - The General tab lets you choose whether to start Windows using a normal startup, diagnostic startup (to step through the startup commands and ask for your confirmation), or selective startup (for preventing the commands in certain startup files from running).

   - The Config.sys, Autoexec.bat, Win.ini, and System.ini tabs list the commands in your startup file. You can quickly disable a command by removing the check mark from its box.

   - The Startup tab lists the programs that run automatically when you start Windows. Note that the list contains many more programs than are listed on the Windows Start, Programs, StartUp menu. You can prevent a program from running by removing the check mark from its box.

100. Windows keeps displaying a cryptic error message, and I don't even know what to tell the technical support person.

Windows comes with a utility called Dr. Watson that won't help you much but can help a technical support person track down the cause of a particular problem. Dr. Watson keeps track of all computer activity and logs all error messages and system problems. If necessary, you can send Dr. Watson's log to the technical support department to give them specific information about the problem you are having.

If you keep receiving the same error message when working in a Windows program, you should run Dr. Watson at startup and keep it running as you work. Take the following steps to add Dr. Watson to the StartUp menu:

1. Choose **Start, Programs, Accessories, System Tools, System Information**.

2. Open the System Information **Tools** menu and choose **Dr. Watson**. This runs Dr. Watson, but no program window appears. You will see an icon for Dr. Watson in the taskbar's system tray (on the right end of the taskbar).

When the problem you want to solve occurs, right-click the Dr. Watson icon and choose **Dr. Watson**. Type a description of what you were doing (or trying to do) when the problem occurred. Open the **File** menu and choose **Save**. Type a name for the log file, and then click the **Save** button. This gives you a file with a WLG extension, which you can then forward to technical support.

101. How can I tell if one of my Windows system files has become damaged?

Windows 98 has a new utility called System File Checker, which scans essential Windows 98 system files for errors. It can help you reinstall the file from the Windows 98 CD. To scan for bad files, take the following steps:

1. Click the **Start** button, point to **Programs**, **Accessories**, **System Tools**, and click **System Information**.

2. Open the System Information **Tools** menu and choose **System File Checker**.

3. Click the **Start** button.

4. The System File Checker scans the files on your hard disk and informs you of any files that might be corrupted. If the Checker encounters any files that might be corrupted, it allows you to respond by verifying the file so the Checker won't question it again, restoring the file, or ignoring the file for now.

5. When the System File Checker is done, click **OK** or click **Details** for more information, and then click the **Close** button.

PART 4

Handy References

At this point, you should know everything you need to know about Windows 98. You can navigate and even configure the Windows desktop, run your programs, manage files and folders, and even complete a few practical projects.

In this part, you'll find a basket full of useful information that will help you master Windows 98 and become even more productive. Here, you will find keyboard shortcuts, a handy list of DOS commands (assuming you have to go out to the DOS prompt, and even a list of productivity tips to help you make the most of Windows 98.

What You Will Find in This Part

Handy References

Keyboard Shortcuts

Windows 98 Keyboard Shortcuts

Press	To
In My Computer and Windows Explorer	
Alt+←	Move back to the previous view or folder.
Alt+→	Move ahead to the next view if you backed up.
Backspace	Move up one level in the folder list.
In My Computer, Windows Explorer, and the Desktop	
Ctrl+Esc	Open the Start menu. You can then press ↓ to highlight options on the menu and → to open the submenu for the current selection.
Alt+Tab	Change to the desired program when you have more than one program running. Pressing Alt+Tab once changes to the previous program. Holding down Alt and pressing Tab repeatedly lets you choose from a list of running programs.
Ctrl+*drag*	Copy a file.
Ctrl+Shift+*drag*	Create a shortcut to a file or program.
Shift+Delete	Delete selected file(s) or folder(s) without using the Recycle Bin.
F3	Search for a file or folder.
F5	Refresh window contents.
Ctrl+A	Select all items on the desktop or in the current folder.
Alt+Enter	Display the properties of a selected object.
Shift	Bypass AutoPlay while inserting an AutoPlay CD-ROM.

Windows 98 Keyboard Shortcuts *Continued*

Press	To

In Windows Explorer

←	Collapse an expanded folder or select the parent folder.
→	Expand a folder that has subfolders or select the next subfolder.
NumLock+–	Collapse the selected, expanded folder.
NumLock++	Expand the selected folder.
NumLock+*	Expand all folders that are below the selected subfolder.
F6	Toggle between left and right panes.

In Windows Dialog Boxes

Ctrl+Tab	Flip forward through tabs.
Ctrl+Shift+Tab	Flip back through tabs.
Tab	Move from one option to another.
Shift+Tab	Move back from one option to another.
Spacebar	Press the highlighted button, set or clear the highlighted check box, or select the highlighted option button.
Esc	Cancel and close the current dialog box.
Alt+Underlined Letter	Select or deselect the option with the underlined letter.
Enter	Press the highlighted button.
Backspace	Move up one level in the folder tree in the Save As or Open dialog box.
F1	Display help for the currently selected option.
F4	Open the Save In or Look In list in the Save As or Open dialog box.
F5	Refresh the file and folder list in the Save As or Open dialog box.

In Windows Programs

F10	Activate the menu bar. You can then press ↓ to open the selected menu and press ← or → to change from one menu to another.
Alt+Underlined Letter	Open the menu with the corresponding underlined letter.
Underlined Letter	Choose the option with the corresponding underlined letter on the open menu.
Shift+F10	Display the context menu for the selected text or object.
Esc	Close the open menu.
Alt+Spacebar	Open the current program window's system menu (to maximize, minimize, move, or resize the window).

Press	To
Alt+−	Open the current document window's system menu (to maximize, minimize, move, or resize the window).
Ctrl+F4	Close the current document window.
Alt+F4	Close or exit the current program.
Ctrl+C	Copy the highlighted text or object and place it on the Windows Clipboard.
Ctrl+X	Remove the highlighted text or object and place it on the Windows Clipboard.
Ctrl+V	Insert (Paste) the contents of the Windows Clipboard into the current document at the insertion point.
Ctrl+Z	Undo the previous action.
Delete	Delete the selected text or object.
F1	Display help for the program.

Shortcuts with the Windows Logo Key

Windows	Open the Start menu.
Windows+Tab	Open the Task Manager dialog box.
Windows+F	Search for a file.
Ctrl+Windows+F	Search for a computer on your network.
Windows+F1	Display help.
Windows+R	Enter the Start, Run command.
Windows+Break	Display the System Properties dialog box.
Windows+E	Open the My Computer window.
Windows+D	Minimize all windows.
Shift+Windows+M	Restore windows that you minimized.

DOS Commands

With Windows 98, you don't need to know much about DOS. You can run programs (even DOS programs) more easily by clicking icons than by typing commands at the C:> prompt. Managing files and folders (directories) is also easier with My Computer and Windows Explorer. However, if you find yourself at the DOS prompt and you're not sure what to do, you can run Windows from the DOS prompt. To do so, take the following steps:

1. At the C:> prompt, type **cd\windows** and press **Enter**. (cd stands for "change directory," and \windows specifies the directory (folder) you want to change to.) You should now see the C:\Windows> prompt.

2. Type **windows** and press **Enter**.

You can perform similar steps to run your DOS programs and games from the DOS prompt. Take the following steps:

1. To run a DOS program from a floppy disk or CD, first insert the disk or CD into the drive.

2. At the DOS prompt, type the letter of the drive that contains the program disk followed by a colon (for example, **d:**) and press **Enter**. The DOS prompt changes to show the drive's letter.

3. If necessary, type **cd\directory** (where *directory* is the name of the directory in which the program's executable file is stored). In most cases, you can skip this step.

4. Type the name of the program file that runs the program (you can omit the filename extension: .exe, .com, or .bat). Press **Enter**, and the program runs.

If you are accustomed to working in DOS, you probably know the standard DOS commands. If not, use the following table to learn about common DOS commands. You can enter most of these commands at the C:> prompt, but you might have to change to the \DOS directory to run some of the commands. You can type the commands in uppercase or lowercase letters.

For a more comprehensive list of DOS commands and for detailed instructions on how to enter these commands, go to DOS (**Start, Programs, MS-DOS Prompt**), type **help**, and press **Enter**. For information about a specific command in the table, type **help commandname** (where *commandname* is the name of the command) and press **Enter**.

Common DOS Commands

Enter This Command	To
C:	Activate the specified drive. For example, entering **A:** changes to drive A.
CD	Change to the specified directory (folder). You must follow the command with a space, backslash, and directory name: for example, **cd \windows**.
CLS	Clear all text from the screen.
COPY	Copy the specified file. First change to the disk drive and directory where the file is stored, and then enter something like **copy filename.ext c:\data**.
DATE	Change the date on your computer.
DEL	Delete the specified file. First change to the disk drive and directory where the file is stored, and then type **del filename.ext** and press **Enter**.
DELTREE	Delete the specified folder and all of its subfolders. (Be careful with this command.)
DIR	Display a list of the directories and files in the current directory.

Enter This Command	To
DISKCOPY	Create an exact duplicate of a floppy disk. For example, enter **diskcopy a: a:** and follow the onscreen instructions.
EDIT	Edit the DOS startup files or any text-only file.
EXIT	Quit DOS and return to Windows 98.
FORMAT A:	Format the floppy disk in drive A.
FORMAT B:	Format the floppy disk in drive B.
HELP	Display a comprehensive list of DOS commands for which you can obtain online help.
LABEL	Rename a disk.
MD	Make a directory on the current disk or a subdirectory in the current directory.
MEM	Display the amount and types of memory installed on your system. (This is very useful information.)
MOVE	Move files or rename directories.
PROMPT	Change the appearance of the DOS prompt.
RD	Remove the specified directory after deleting all the files it contains.
REN	Change the name of a file.
SCANDISK	Check and repair hard or floppy disks.
TIME	Change the time setting on your computer.
TREE	Displays the directory tree on the current disk drive.
TYPE	Displays the contents of a text file.
VOL	Displays the electronic name of the selected disk.

Productivity Tips

Windows 98 has several features that can help you become more productive. The StartUp menu automatically starts the programs you use the most whenever you turn on your computer. The Windows Tune-Up Wizard optimizes your computer when you're not using it. The Quick Launch toolbar allows you to quickly run your favorite programs. Site subscriptions automatically download updated Web pages from the Internet. And several other features can help you automate the tasks you frequently perform. The following section provides 20 tips to help you take advantage of these Windows productivity features.

1. Run programs you always use automatically on StartUp.

If you use a particular program every time you're on the computer, add it to the StartUp menu so it will run automatically when Windows starts. ▶See "Run Programs Automatically on Startup" on page 460.◀ You can start the program in a minimized window by taking the following steps:

1. Click the **Start** button, point to **Programs** and then **StartUp**, and right-click the program's name. This opens a context menu for the program.

2. Choose **Properties**. The program's Properties dialog box appears.

3. On the **Shortcut** tab, open the **Run** drop-down list and choose **Minimized**. Click **OK**.

If Windows takes a long time to start because it is automatically loading several programs, you can prevent StartUp programs from running. To bypass the StartUp menu, hold down the **Shift** key when Windows is starting.

2. Place shortcuts for the documents you commonly open or edit on the Windows desktop.

Shortcuts represent the greatest timesaving feature in Windows. You can place shortcuts on the Windows desktop, on menus, or wherever you need to in order to quickly access a program or document. Consider placing shortcuts for the documents you most frequently access on the Windows desktop. To create a shortcut, simply right-drag the icon from My Computer or Windows Explorer to a blank area of the desktop and choose **Create Shortcut(s) Here**.

If you commonly access a disk drive, folder, or program, place a shortcut for it on the desktop. You might also want to place shortcuts on the desktop for your printer and for the Windows Control Panel. Don't get *too* carried away adding shortcuts, though. Each shortcut takes some memory to display, and shortcuts are worthless if you can't find them in the clutter on your desktop.

> To quickly create a shortcut on the Windows desktop, right-click the file in My Computer or Windows Explorer, point to **Send To**, and choose **Desktop as Shortcut**.

3. Create a shortcut that returns you to a specific place in a document.

Although creating shortcuts to documents can save you a lot of time, you can save additional time by creating a shortcut that points to a particular place within the document. In other words, the shortcut acts as a bookmark. To create the shortcut, open the document and highlight the portion you want to mark. This can be a sentence in a typed document, a cell in a spreadsheet, or some other selection. Right-drag the selection to the Windows desktop, release the mouse button and choose **Create Document Shortcut(s) Here**.

4. Place your favorite programs on the Quick Launch toolbar.

You can quickly open a program by clicking its icon in the Quick Launch toolbar. Drag the program icon for any program you frequently use to the Quick Launch toolbar to create a shortcut for it.

5. Make a new toolbar for the programs and documents you frequently access.

Create a new folder in My Computer or Windows Explorer and place shortcuts for all your favorite programs and documents in this new folder. You can then quickly transform the folder into a toolbar by dragging it to the top of the desktop or to the left or right side of the desktop.

6. Switch to a program by using a shortcut key.

If your desktop is cluttered with shortcuts, assign shortcut keys to your favorite programs so you won't have to search for and click the program's shortcut icon. Take the following steps to assign a shortcut key to a shortcut icon:

1. Right-click the shortcut icon and choose **Properties**.

2. Click in the **Shortcut Key** text box and press the keystroke you want to use to run the program or open the document. Do not use a shortcut key that Windows uses for some other task (such as Ctrl+C for copying). For example, press **Ctrl+Alt+C**.

3. Click **OK**. You can now run the program by pressing its shortcut key combination.

7. Use the right mouse button for context menus.

Right-clicking an object, selection, option, or anything else in Windows typically calls up a context menu that offers the most common commands available for it. Try right-clicking everywhere: in your documents or on shortcuts, the taskbar, the Quick Launch toolbar, title bars, the Start button, Start menu items, and so on. The right mouse button can help you discover options you did not know about. Try right-dragging, too.

8. Let the Windows Maintenance Wizard optimize your system daily.

The only way to keep Windows from slowing down your system and cluttering your drive is to run the Windows system tools, including ScanDisk and Disk Defragmenter, daily. And the best way to do this is to set up the Windows Maintenance Wizard to automatically run the system tools at a scheduled time (preferably when you are not using your computer). ▶See "Use the Windows Maintenance Wizard" on page 494.◀

9. Open and print documents with drag and drop.

You can use drag and drop in Windows programs to copy and move selected text and other objects within a document or from one document to another. However, you can also use drag and drop to open documents and print them.

To open a document with drag and drop, drag the document's icon from Windows Explorer, My Computer, or the Find: Files and Folders dialog box over the program's icon or shortcut and release the mouse button. Windows runs the program, which then opens the document. If the program is already open, drag the icon over the program's button in the taskbar, hold it there until the program's window jumps to the front, and then drag and drop the file onto the window's title bar.

> You can insert the contents of one document into another by dragging the document file into the window that displays the contents of the destination document.

To quickly print a file, drag its icon over your printer icon (in the Printers folder) and release the mouse button. Windows runs the program, which then opens the document and starts printing it. Another way to quickly print a document is to right-click its icon and choose **Print**.

10. Make Windows print documents later, when you are not using your computer.

Printing is one of the most system-intensive tasks. If you are printing large documents or graphics, you will find that you can't continue working at your normal pace. The solution is to print while you're taking a break or at the end of the day. Take the following steps to defer printing:

1. Click the **Start** button, point to **Settings**, and click **Printers**.

2. Right-click your printer icon and choose **Pause Printing**.

3. Print the documents as you normally would. This places the documents in the print queue, but because you paused the printing process, Windows does not send the documents to the printer.

4. When you are ready to print, make sure your printer is on and has enough paper. Then right-click your printer icon and choose **Pause Printing**.

11. Have Windows notify you when CapsLock or NumLock is on.

If you press CapsLock by mistake when pressing the Shift key, you could end up typing your entire document in uppercase characters. To prevent this from happening, you can have Windows sound a tone whenever you press CapsLock. In the Windows Control Panel, click the **Accessibility** icon and then turn on **ToggleKeys**. When you press any of the locking keys (CapsLock, NúmLock, or ScrollLock), Windows sounds a tone.

12. Schedule Windows updates.

In "Update Windows" ▶on page 420◀, you learned how to download and install files from Microsoft's Web site to update Windows 98 to the latest version. However, you have to remember to do this every month or so. To automate the process, use Task Scheduler to run Windows 98 Update regularly. ▶See "Run Programs Automatically with Task Scheduler" on page 65.◀

13. Set up subscriptions for your favorite Web pages.

The Web is admittedly very slow, even if you have a fast connection. To speed it up on your end, set up subscriptions for your favorite Web pages and have Internet Explorer download the pages when you are not using your computer. ▶To set up Web site subscriptions, see "Subscribe to Sites" on page 250.◀

14. Alt+*click* to display an object's properties.

Instead of right-clicking an icon, you can hold down the **Alt** key and click the icon to display the object's Properties dialog box.

15. Save your CD-ROM drive's Eject button.

The Eject button on most CD-ROM drives is right below the tray in which you load the CD. The tray typically hits your fingers on the way out, and then you have to reach under the tray to press the button and load the next CD. To save some wear-and-tear on the drive (and on your fingers), let Windows eject and load the CD. Simply right-click the icon for your CD-ROM drive in My Computer and click **Eject**. Depending on the CD-ROM drive, this trick might not work for loading the CD.

16. Restart Windows without restarting your computer.

Whenever you choose to restart Windows, it completely restarts your computer, reloading all the startup commands. To have Windows restart more quickly, click the **Start** button, choose **Shutdown**, click **Restart**, and then hold down the **Shift** key and click the **OK** button.

17. Create multiple desktops for different occasions.

If you use your computer for work and play, consider creating two desktops: one for work and one for recreation. You can then quickly log on to Windows using a different name and change from one desktop to another. ▶See "Password-Protect Your Computer" on page 465 to learn how to set up Windows for multiple users.◀

Set up your Windows desktop as desired for work or recreation. When you finish, enter the **Start**, **Log Off** command, and then log back on using a different name. For this to work, you must have Windows Logon selected as your primary network logon option. Open the Windows **Control Panel**, click the **Network** icon, and then open the **Primary Network Logon** drop-down list and choose **Windows Logon**. Click **OK**.

18. Bypass the Windows 98 startup logo.

To speed up the Windows 98 startup, hold down the **Esc** key when Windows 98 starts or right when the startup logo appears. This doesn't cut much time off the Windows startup, but every little bit helps.

19. Automate email.

If you send and receive a lot of email, consider automating Outlook Express to have it send and receive mail at a scheduled time. First, set up Outlook Express by performing the following steps:

1. Run Outlook Express, and then open the **Tools** menu and choose **Options**.
2. On the **General** tab, choose **Make Outlook Express My Default E-Mail Program**.
3. Click the **Dial Up** tab.
4. Make sure **Dial This Connection** is on, and then open the drop-down list and choose the Dial-Up Connection you want to use.
5. Choose **Hang Up When Finished Sending, Receiving, or Downloading** to turn it on.
6. Click **OK**.

After setting up Outlook Express to automatically dial your Internet connection and then hang up when it's done, add Outlook Express to the Task Scheduler. Set up Outlook Express to run at a time just before you usually check your email. ▶See "Run Programs Automatically with Task Scheduler" on page 65.◀

20. On a network, map network drives to make them easier to access.

If your computer is part of a network, you should map the folders and disks you commonly access on the network to your computer. This saves time, especially when you need to save files on a network drive. Instead of having to change to the drive and folder in which you want to save your file, you simply select the drive letter that is mapped to the folder.

Index

X-Z

napster : User name - ~~Lori~~ 16364
Password ~~for~~ Buth

napster : User name - ~~Lori~~ 16364
Password ~~for~~ Buth